We Write for Our Own Time

EDITED BY

# Alexander Burnham

University Press of Virginia

CHARLOTTESVILLE
AND LONDON

# We Write for Our Own Time

SELECTED ESSAYS FROM
SEVENTY-FIVE YEARS
OF THE
*Virginia Quarterly Review*

Acknowledgments for previously published material appear on page xvii.

The University Press of Virginia
© 2000 by the Rector and Visitors of the University of Virginia
All rights reserved
Printed in the United States of America
*First published in 2000*

The title-page sketch is the colophon of the *Virginia Quarterly Review*, a drawing of the journal's editorial office on the West Range of Thomas Jefferson's Academical Village at the University of Virginia. Used by permission of the *Virginia Quarterly Review*.

∞ The paper used in this publication meets the minimum requirements of the American National Standard for Information Sciences—Permanence of Paper for Printed Library Materials, ANSI Z39.48-1984.

Library of Congress Cataloging-in-Publication Data

We write for our own time : selected essays from seventy-five years of the Virginia quarterly review / edited by Alexander Burnham.
    p. cm.
    ISBN 0-8139-1914-2 (cl. : alk. paper)
    I. Burnham, Alexander, 1926– . II. Virginia quarterly review.
AC5.W35 2000
081—dc21                                                             99-36026
                                                                                    CIP

DESIGNED BY LAURY A. EGAN

*For Jeffersonians everywhere*

# Contents

STAIGE D. BLACKFORD
Foreword — xiii

Acknowledgments — xvii

ALEXANDER BURNHAM
Introduction — xix

## *The Nineteen Twenties*

EDWIN A. ALDERMAN
Edgar Allan Poe and the University of Virginia — 3

ROBERT P. TRISTRAM COFFIN
Codfish Chowder and Sun — 8

ANDRÉ GIDE
Classicism — 12

D. H. LAWRENCE
The Bogey between the Generations — 15

## *The Nineteen Thirties*

ALDOUS HUXLEY
Tragedy and the Whole Truth — 21

ANDRÉ MAUROIS
The Myth of Myth — 28

EVELYN WAUGH
The Rough Life — 32

T. S. ELIOT
Personality and Demonic Possession — 38

CONTENTS

THOMAS WOLFE
Old Catawba — 45

ELEANOR ROOSEVELT
Keepers of Democracy — 52

## *The Nineteen Forties*

THOMAS MANN
Thinking and Living — 59

NIKA STANDEN
A Meal in Anacapri — 63

JEAN-PAUL SARTRE
We Write for Our Own Time — 67

MARCHETTE CHUTE
The Bubble Reputation — 73

## *The Nineteen Fifties*

JOSEPH WOOD KRUTCH
Mice: A Dispassionate View — 83

BERTRAND RUSSELL
George Bernard Shaw — 90

VIRGINIUS DABNEY
The Human Side of Woodrow Wilson — 95

LOUIS B. WRIGHT
The Anti-Shakespeare Industry and the Growth of Cults — 105

## *The Nineteen Sixties*

GEORGE F. KENNAN
The Experience of Writing History — 119

CONTENTS

ARTHUR C. CLARKE
Shaw and the Sound Barrier                                124

HENRY STEELE COMMAGER
Do We Have a Class Society?                               131

LOUIS J. HALLE
Space-Travel on the Lake of Geneva                        138

KONRAD KELLEN
Einstein: Personal Reminiscences                          141

ROBERT GRAVES
How to Hold the Reader's Attention                        145


*The Nineteen Seventies*

JOHN H. SCHAAR
... And the Pursuit of Happiness                          153

J. GLENN GRAY
Hegel's Logic: The Philosophy of the Concrete             172

KENNETH CLARK
Thomas Jefferson and the Italian Renaissance              183

CLIFTON WALLER BARRETT
The Struggle to Create a University                       192

CARLOS BAKER
Pound in Venice, 1965                                     201

DUMAS MALONE
The Scholar's Way: Then and Now                           207

EDMUND S. MORGAN
George Washington: The Aloof American                     217

CLOVIS
Attitudes toward Sex                                      234

CONTENTS

EDGAR F. SHANNON JR.
Alfred Tennyson as a Poet for Our Time — 241

## The Nineteen Eighties

MOLLY INGLE MICHIE
A Splendid Day — 257

MILDRED RAYNOLDS TRIVERS
The Berlin Wall: A Memoir — 267

WALTER HARDING
Walden's Man of Science — 275

CHRISTOPHER CLAUSEN
Did You Once See Willy Plain? — 288

ROBERT COLES
Charles Dickens and the Law — 292

WENDY W. FAIREY
In My Mother's House: Images of a Hollywood Childhood — 308

SPENCE W. PERRY
Vietnam: Mirage and Fitful Dream — 319

MARY LEE SETTLE
London—1944 — 331

PATRICIA MEYER SPACKS
The Necessity of Boredom — 347

SCOTT DONALDSON
The Jilting of Ernest Hemingway — 359

FRANCES MAYES
10,369 Rules to Live By — 369

PAUL BAROLSKY
Joyce's Distant Music — 379

CONTENTS

## *The Nineteen Nineties*

GEORGE WATSON
Shakespeare and the Norman Conquest: English in
the Elizabethan Theatre ... 387

LOUIS D. RUBIN JR.
The Passionate Poet and the Use of Criticism ... 399

SIMONE POIRIER-BURES
Return ... 415

BOOTON HERNDON
Corpses Thawing in Springtime: The Bulge Revisited ... 422

ALEXANDER BURNHAM
Okinawa, Harry Truman, and the Atomic Bomb ... 433

DAVID WYATT
The Last Spring at Yale ... 444

The Green Room ... 459

# Foreword

STAIGE D. BLACKFORD

Editor, *The Virginia Quarterly Review*

The *Virginia Quarterly Review*, whose seventy-fifth anniversary this anthology commemorates, first appeared in April 1925. The establishment of such a journal had long been a dream of Edwin A. Alderman, the first president of the University of Virginia. (A faculty chairman had formerly held the top post.) Indeed, Mr. Alderman enunciated this dream in a speech given a decade before the *VQR* came into being. Speaking at the Finals ceremony of 1915, Mr. Alderman described the periodical he envisioned for Mr. Jefferson's University in these terms:

> A magazine solidly based, thoughtfully and wisely managed and controlled ... a great serious publication wherein it shall be focused and set down the very best thought ... of men everywhere in the nation and the world on vital questions in the fields of Economics, Politics, Ethics, Literary Interpretation and Historical Analysis ... I believe this is the academic spot out of which should issue a publication reflecting the calm thought in all these fields of the best men and that if this end can be achieved, nothing could add more to our usefulness and fame.

It took ten years for the industrious Mr. Alderman to make the publication a reality. To give it a firm financial backing, he wrote prominent business and professional men around the country such as Robert Bingham, publisher of the *Louisville Courier Journal*, asking them to pledge fifty dollars per year for a five-year period. From the outset Mr. Alderman also made clear that what he had in mind was not just a regional journal. As he put it in a letter of March 27, 1925, to Dr. Wickcliffe Ross, chairman of the General Education Board of New York City, "Our new magazine is national, not sectional." Two years later, in a letter of April 25, 1927, to Marcelus Green, a lawyer in Jackson, Mississippi, Mr. Alderman wrote, "*The Virginia Quarterly Review* is a journal of national discussion.... The idea is to discuss fundamental matters from every point of view."

Thus, from its inception, the *VQR* was meant to be what its masthead has declared for more than seven decades—"a national journal of literature and discussion." It quickly won a reputation for being just that, as the *New*

*York World* observed in an editorial appearing after the magazine's first issue in the spring of 1925:

> *VQR* is a new departure in Southern publications. The average reader when he picks up a magazine somewhere south of the Potomac is likely to throw it down in a few minutes on account of the hopelessly sentimental flavor of it, but the new review is different stuff: it is no sleepy symposium on the virtues of the late Confederacy, but rather is in line with the tradition of culture at the University under whose auspices it is published. . . . When the South gives us a publication like this, it is a pleasure to welcome it, and, what is even more important, it is a pleasure to read it.

The first editor to provide such pleasure was James Southall Wilson, an eminent scholar of literature and the Edgar Allan Poe Professor of English at the university. Mr. Wilson served as editor for five years and in those years attracted such writers as Thomas Mann, André Gide, Dumas Malone, Gerald W. Johnson, D. H. Lawrence, and Allen Tate. By the time Wilson handed over the reins of editorship to Stringfellow Barr, then a member of the university's history department, in 1930, the *Richmond Times-Dispatch* was calling the *VQR* (in a January 14 editorial) "one of the most substantial magazines in the country." The newspaper discerned "several reasons for its excellence, the chief being that it has sought its contributors from the ranks of writers with international reputation. . . . It has become a member of no school of style or thought, it has refrained from entering and encouraging cheap and gawdy controversy, and it has, to all appearances, founded its methods and progress on tradition."

Barr was to serve as editor for only three years. He resigned to write a book on the Italian statesman Manzini, and later in the 1930s he became president of St. John's College in Annapolis, Maryland, where he established the now renowned "great books program." He was succeeded in 1933 by Lambert Davis, who would later serve for many years as the distinguished director of the University of North Carolina Press. The country was in the depths of the Great Depression, but the quarterly survived. Indeed, when it celebrated its tenth anniversary in 1935, it did so by presenting what the later editor Charlotte Kohler called "the core of the Southern renaissance, including almost every prominent Southern writer except William Faulkner." Among them were Thomas Wolfe, Katherine Anne Porter, Andrew Lytle, John Peale Bishop, Stark Young, Robert Penn Warren, Cleanth Brooks, John Crowe Ransom, and Allen Tate.

Lambert Davis resigned the editorship in 1939 to become an editor at the book publishing firm Bobbs-Merrill. He noted in a letter to the then university president, John L. Newcomb, the free editorial latitude granted by the president. His successor was Lawrence Lee, a poet and English professor. Lee's dubious contribution to the magazine was concocting a blood-red cover. This was quickly replaced by the *VQR*'s traditional orange when Archibald B. Shepperson, also an English professor, replaced Lee after a year in 1940. But Shepperson's stint as editor was also short-lived, with the outbreak of World War II. Although he held the title until 1946, he joined the navy and went off to naval intelligence in Washington in 1942.

There now appeared at One West Range—the original Jeffersonian building (so original it lacks a bathroom to this day) that has been the *VQR*'s home since 1929—the Richmond native whose editorship would extend over four decades, namely Charlotte Kohler. A Vassar graduate, Miss Kohler came to the university as one of the few English graduate students in the 1930s and earned her Ph.D. degree under James Southall Wilson. With the men going off to war, Mr. Wilson turned to his former student, then teaching at a women's college in Greensboro, North Carolina, and she joined the quarterly as managing editor in 1942, assuming the title of editor in 1946.

It was under Miss Kohler's direction that the *VQR* published its Thomas Jefferson bicentennial issue in the spring of 1943, the first time an entire number was given over to an individual. This was repeated at Woodrow Wilson's centennial in 1956, with an introduction written by President Dwight D. Eisenhower.

Miss Kohler also put together the twenty-fifth-anniversary issue in 1950, which laid stress as did the tenth on southern themes and southern writers and included works by Donald Davidson, Gerald W. Johnson, Randall Jarrell, and Stark Young. Another contributor was the Tennessee senator Estes Kefauver. Earlier, in 1947, Miss Kohler wrote the philosopher Bertrand Russell, asking if he would compose an article on George Bernard Shaw. Russell replied that he was amenable to doing such a piece but preferred that the article not run until after Shaw's death. Shaw died in 1950, and Russell's article about him appeared as the lead article in the winter 1951 issue, titled simply "George Bernard Shaw."

Miss Kohler was further responsible for establishing in the 1950s the Emily Clark Balch prizes in poetry and fiction. Named for a Richmond patron of literature who later married a wealthy Philadelphian and left a bequest to the *VQR* upon her death, the Balch prizes of $500 are given annually to the best published poem and short story to appear in a given year, the selection being made by members of the journal's advisory board.

Charlotte Kohler's tenure as editor extended from 1942 to 1975; from President Franklin D. Roosevelt to President Gerald Ford; through World War II, Korea, and Vietnam; from the birth of the atomic age to the landing of men on the moon—a period of thirty-three years. Two months before she retired in June 1975, Miss Kohler brought out her final issue, which marked the journal's fiftieth anniversary. Among the contributors were two who had contributed to the first issue in April 1925, the historian Dumas Malone and the American-born French novelist Julian Green. Other contributors to the fiftieth-anniversary number included Harry S. Ashmore, C. Vann Woodward, Peter Taylor, Reynolds Price, Robert Penn Warren, Allen Tate, and Cleanth Brooks—a true galaxy of southern literature at that time.

In longevity, Charlotte Kohler's reign was like unto that of Queen Victoria. Thus, when I took over in 1975, I told a newspaper columnist, who duly noted it in his column, that I felt as if I was succeeding the noble queen. Two days after the column appeared, Miss Kohler stormed into my office, saying her neighbor was calling her "Queen Victoria, which is bad enough, but you don't look like Edward VII." Now, however, my reign as editor has lasted considerably longer than that of Edward VII. As it nears an end, I can make these observations:

Throughout the *VQR*'s seventy-five years, the university has given the editor absolute editorial freedom to select and publish whatever he or she chooses.

For three-quarters of a century, the *Quarterly* has sought, in Miss Kohler's words, "to get the best of the best" in poetry, fiction, and nonfiction.

Since 1927, the *VQR* has never shirked from publishing articles on the American dilemma of race. It was in 1927 that Ashby Jones, a southern clergyman and chairman of the Interracial Commission of the National Council of the YMCA, published a *VQR* essay entitled "The Negro in the South." Among the more notable essays on this subject was Leslie W. Dunbar's "The Annealing of the South," which appeared in the autumn 1961 issue. In it Dunbar, then executive director of the Southern Regional Council, the south's oldest biracial organization, predicted the South was going to lose again in its opposition to racial equality and ultimately be gratified that it had done so. And at the time of the writing of this foreword, the *VQR* is carrying two articles under the common rubric, "The American Dilemma Revisited."

Since its inception, the *Virginia Quarterly Review* has tried to offer its readers a variety of essays on a variety of topics ranging from foreign affairs to domestic politics, from literature to travel, from sports to sex, from music to medicine. As it now enters a new millennium and a new era, the *VQR* will continue to be what it always has been—"a national journal of literature and discussion."

# Acknowledgments

The editor and publishers are grateful for permission to include the following copyright material in this anthology:

T. S. Eliot, "Personality and Demonic Possession," © Valerie Eliot, from *After Strange Gods,* by permission of Faber and Faber.
André Gide, "Classicism," © Editions Gallimard 1999, an excerpt from *Billets à Angèle* in *Incidences,* by permission.
Robert Graves, "How to Hold the Reader's Attention," by permission of A. P. Watt Ltd. on behalf of The Executors of The Robert Graves Copyright Trust.
Aldous Huxley, "Tragedy and the Whole Truth," from *Music at Night,* by permission of Dorris Haley for the ALH Literary Estate and Random House UK Ltd. UK rights by permission of Mrs. Laura Huxley and Chatto and Windus.
D. H. Lawrence, "The Bogey between the Generations," by permission of the estate of Frieda Lawrence Ravagli and Laurence Pollinger Ltd.
André Maurois, "The Myth of Myth," © Héritiers André Maurois, Paris, by permission of Madame Marie-Ange Masson-Mosca, 1999.
Jean-Paul Sartre, "We Write for Our Own Time (*Ecrire pour son époque*)" © Gallimard 1970 as a chapter in *Les Écrits de Sartre:* also published by Northwestern University Press in *Sartre's Writings,* by permission of the publishers.
Evelyn Waugh, "The Rough Life" © The Estate of Laura Waugh, reprinted by permission of The Peters Fraser & Dunlop Group Ltd.

The editor has made every effort to trace and contact all the authors included in this book, as well as copyright holders, prior to publication. In some instances, however, this has proved impossible. If notified, the editor and publisher would be pleased to rectify any omissions at the earliest opportunity.

# Introduction

I first encountered the *Virginia Quarterly Review* in 1970 in a literary bookstore on New York's Madison Avenue, and my delight was such that I have been a constant reader ever since. Indeed, I was so charmed by the magazine's sanity, its no-nonsense appearance, its enthusiasm for scholarship devoid of ambiguity and ostentation, and for its high regard for the rank and file as well as for those who have reached some distinction that I soon began reading previous issues collected by university libraries since 1925, the year the *VQR* was founded.

It has been a fascinating and rewarding experience. I've been entertained by a grand collection of writers and seven astute editors. When I reached the year 1929 in my reading, I became intrigued by the thought that the *Virginia Quarterly Review,* one of the world's preeminent magazines of intelligent discussion and literature, had been brought to life by a distinguished scholar, Edwin A. Alderman, even as two other publications of note were also being introduced to the public, the *New Yorker* by Harold Ross and *Time* by Briton Hadden and Henry Luce.

Twenty years or so after my acquaintance with the *VQR,* I intrepidly decided to submit one or two essays of my own, and to my further delight the magazine's editor, Staige Blackford, accepted them. My pleasure was enhanced by the belief that I had entered an aristocratic club whose membership rolls over the years included such illustrious names as Evelyn Waugh, Dumas Malone, T. S. Eliot, Eleanor Roosevelt, Louis J. Halle, D. H. Lawrence, Thomas Wolfe, Robert Graves, and Henry Steele Commager as well as writers whose names may be obscure to the general public but whose talents were of equal merit.

Yes, an aristocratic club, but not, I should quickly emphasize, an exclusive one restricted to what passes for aristocracy in this age of pretentious editorial hyperbole, because the *VQR,* unlike most contemporary publications with their slavish attention to the notorious, is unimpressed by mere celebrity. This is in the spirit of Thomas Jefferson, the founder of the University of Virginia, which is the publisher of the *Virginia Quarterly Review.*

Mr. Jefferson (as he is known at the university) once said that a *natural aristocracy* is to be found in virtue and talents. And that has been the object of the *VQR* since its first issue—a presentation of excellence and skill by natural aristocrats wherever they may be found; or, as the magazine put it right from the start, a place where talented men and women may exercise their thoughts "in appealing and arresting fashion" and even (heaven preserve us) where "a fellowship of uncongenial minds" might come together.

In reading over seventy-five years of the *VQR*, I have been astonished by how prescient its editors and writers have been as they alerted readers to events and foretokens that were to shape the violence of the twentieth century. For example, in 1936, even as isolationism held sway over the United States, the journalist Louis Fisher was writing in the *VQR*'s pages that Japan, Germany, and Italy were poised to begin a war "which will be bloodier and costlier" than World War I. Another journalist, Helen Hill, revealed in 1934 how Adolf Hitler could humbug Germany by speaking "to the receptive ability of the least intellectual" of its citizens. "After ten years of accumulated emotion," she wrote, "the German masses are on the move."

Then we have the example of Owen Lattimore, an Asian scholar from Johns Hopkins University. In the early 1950s he was brutally attacked by Senator Joseph McCarthy and charged by a Senate subcommittee (eager to pin the "loss" of China to the Communists on the Truman administration) with promoting Communism. *VQR* readers (as well as a federal court, which threw out the charges) knew that the accusations were absurd. In 1940 Lattimore was issuing warnings in the magazine that the United States was helping to shatter China's "old society" by "supplying the raw materials of war" to the Japanese (then in the process of killing hundreds of thousands of Chinese) in the 1920s and 1930s. This, he said, is "doing more to spread communism than the teaching of the Chinese Communists themselves or the influence of Russia."

And one last illustration of the magazine's mettle: thirty years before heralded newspaper editors of the South were winning Pulitzer Prizes for their courageous stands on civil rights for blacks, the *Virginia Quarterly Review* was publishing in its very first year of publication an essay demanding equal rights for the region's black citizens. The essay was written by Gerald W. Johnson, a journalist and a professor of journalism at the University of North Carolina at Chapel Hill. In 1925 Johnson wrote:

> Every case of denial of a negro's rights under the civil law, every gratuitous insult flung at the race by the lower element among the whites, every needless brutality practiced ostensibly to enforce segregation, every repression of the negro's legitimate aspirations to education, to mental and spiritual self-development and to the right to a peaceable existence under decent standards of living—in short, every unnecessary hardship inflicted on the black South postpones the day when the white South can resume its full membership, political, moral, and intellectual, in this Union.

INTRODUCTION

Impressive though the *VQR* has been in its pluck and determination to publish essays on important issues of the day, I felt that this anthology should be essentially agreeable rather than declamatory. In furthering this mission and confronting such a large number of superior writers over three-quarters of a century, I have not found it easy going to select the required essays for this book. They range from the scholarly, the somber, and the weighty to the lighthearted, the informative, and the merry, which is what a proper anthology of essays should be.

In reviewing my notes on authors (called "The Green Room" at the *VQR*), I am deeply grieved at the number of brilliant essays by incandescent writers (including some literary and professorial VIPs) that I was forced to eliminate. My original manuscript was so large that it filled five large boxes and caused much consternation at the University Press of Virginia, particularly for editor Richard Holway, who undoubtedly foresaw a tome of five or six hundred thousand words or a massive three-volume work.

As a result of my purging, denizens of the publishing business will be shocked to learn in this age of ballyhoo that I set aside numerous distinguished bylines such as George Santayana and H. L. Mencken, personages who have appeared in past anthologies. But I desired to preserve in this book writers less well celebrated but whose work I believed exceeded the essays of the famous in interest, amusement, or relevance.

This said, I must admit that I turned down with much reluctance some truly outstanding essays by prominent authorities, including a former secretary of state, Dean Acheson, and a former candidate for the American presidency, Adlai Stevenson. But their essays were of the moment and ephemeral. An exception I made was the essay by Eleanor Roosevelt, which is, I think, of historical interest and which she wrote at a time of dreadful national tension, when the country and her husband were facing the challenge of a rapidly approaching great war.

Another essay of historical importance was the 1941 contribution by Thomas Mann expressing his acute distress with Germany. He wrote it as Hitler and his Nazi troops solidified their domination of Europe and prior to the United States entering the war. As far as I can ascertain, the essay has never been disseminated beyond the pages of the *VQR*. Apparently this was because the essay was published in Mann's original German and never translated. Therefore, I am most grateful to Hans Schmidt, professor emeritus at the University of Virginia, for his initial reading of the essay that alerted me to its significance, and to Deborah Lucas Schneider, who translates for the Harvard University Press, for her expert translation.

Some essays were impossible to resist and were immediate candidates for inclusion in the anthology. I'm certain that I startled nearby readers at the college library where I was working when I laughed out loud at Waugh's essay on roughing it. (Some readers may find this essay, which appeared in the *VQR* in 1934, objectionable as society enters a new century. But as the *Oxford Companion to English Literature* notes, Waugh's "works of high comedy and social satire" in the 1930s captured "the brittle, cynical, determined frivolity" of the generation that followed World War I. The essay perhaps does the same.) I'm sure I was visibly moved as I read Molly Michie's "A Splendid Day." And I had to strongly resist approaching my library neighbors to insist that they immediately share my enthusiasm for Louis Halle's reflections while sitting in a boat on a Swiss lake and Louis Wright's rebuttal to snobs who can't believe that a man without an Oxford education could have written Shakespeare's plays. I should note that I decided to republish my own essay only after reading the lecture that Arthur Schlesinger Jr. delivered in 1996 before the Society of American Historians. He said he regarded the decision by President Truman to drop the atomic bombs on Japan "as the most tragic decision in our history," but he added: "Yet I have problems in seeing how a responsible President could have done otherwise."

I should also note that I have been obliged to do what I hope may be considered some reasonable trimming on a *few* essays in order to include in the anthology as many as possible. Writers such as Lawrence, Sartre, and Roosevelt were, of course, untouched.

I am most grateful to Shirley Maul, head of Readers Services and Reference of the Vassar College libraries, for allowing me to use the college's elegant Thompson Library for months on end. I read Vassar's complete collection of the *Virginia Quarterly Review* and wrote hundreds of notes in splendid comfort even as winter's snows roared outside or summer's heat made the most luxurious shade tree unsuitable for reading.

I should also like to thank my wife, Joan. Month after month she was the personification of patience as I put together essay by essay a very large manuscript. She made the task a smooth one from start to finish by pitching in without complaint as my aide-de-camp.

In particular I would like to express my high regard for Staige Blackford, the discerning and scholarly editor of the *Virginia Quarterly Reveiw*. He was resolute from the beginning in support of the book, never lost faith, and wrote me many letters of encouragement from the anthology's conception to its completion.

In addition to Staige, I and readers of this book who find it useful and entertaining should thank the six chief editors of the quarterly who preceded him: James Southall Wilson, Stringfellow Barr, Lambert Davis, Lawrence Lee, Archibald B. Shepperson, and Charlotte Kohler. All seven editors in addition to the *VQR*'s founder, University of Virginia president Edwin Alderman, have served their readers well, giving them a magazine

INTRODUCTION

that for the greater part of the century has striven to be "intelligently entertaining on all sorts of subjects, old and new," while endeavoring to provide "more than a modicum of old-fashioned courtesy and good taste" in essays, short stories, poems, and book reviews. Not many "media outlets" can make those admirable claims, I think, as we and the *Virginia Quarterly Review* plunge dauntlessly from the violence and turmoil of the twentieth century into the expectations of the twenty-first.

A.B.

*The Nineteen Twenties*

EDWIN A. ALDERMAN

# Edgar Allan Poe and the University of Virginia

[ SPRING 1925 ]

"CRIPPLED wrists and fingers make writing slow and laborious, but while writing to you I lose the sense of these in the recollections of ancient times, when youth made health and happiness out of everything. I forget for a while this hoary winter of age, when we can think of nothing but how to keep ourselves warm by the fire and how to get rid of our heavy penalties until the friendly hand of death shall rid us of it all at once. Against this *tedium vitæ*, however, my dear friend, I am now fortunately mounted on a hobby, which, indeed, I mounted some thirty or forty years ago, but whose amble is still sufficient to give exercise and amusement to an octagenarian writer. This is the establishment of a university for the education of all succeeding generations of youth in this Republic." Thus wrote Thomas Jefferson to his old friend, John Adams, on October 12, 1823.

On Monday, March 7, 1825, this dream hobby, which Jefferson had ridden for some forty years, became a reality, and the University of Virginia, without ceremony or celebration, opened its doors for the instruction of youth. There were fifty students present on that opening day, and one hundred and sixteen enrolled during that first session, which ended on December 15th, having lasted nine months and eight days.

The second session began February 1, 1826. Thirty-four students matriculated on that day. By February 14, one hundred and thirty-one students had matriculated. On that day—St. Valentine's Day—a century ago, a group of five students enrolled their names, and among them was a slender lad of seventeen, named Edgar Allan Poe, who thus became No. 136 out of a total enrollment of one hundred and seventy-seven for the entire session, which ended at Christmas, 1826.

Poe at first roomed on the Lawn, in a room the location of which is not known, but later he moved to No. 13 West Range, now set apart as a Poe Shrine.

It is interesting to have knowledge that Poe was not without athletic prowess. He swam across the James River, at a point where the distance was six miles. He was an excellent boxer, and once jumped twenty-one feet and six inches on a level with a running start of twenty yards.

Poe elected to take the "tickets" or classes in Greek, Latin, French, Spanish, and Italian, and there is no evidence that he failed to do his work well. He ranked fourth in Senior Latin in a class of ten, and sixth in the final report in Senior French. He was publicly commended for a verse translation from Tasso. Poe's classes came between 7:30 and 9:30 each day, including Saturday. In the long hours at his disposal, he probably spent much time in the Library, situated for the first part of his life at the University in the upper front room of what is now the Colonnade Club, and the latter months of his stay, in the circular room, then just completed, of the old Rotunda. It is recorded that he borrowed from the Library, during the session, the following books:

> Rollin's Histoire Ancienne
> Robertson's America
> Marshall's Washington
> Voltaire's Historie Particulière
> Dulief's Nature Displayed.

But I think it may be taken for granted that he read in the Library room itself many other and very different books from this rather dull and stuffy list. It is not difficult to fancy him poring over Byron, and especially over Coleridge. One can almost recapture the gleam in his eye and the illumination of his face as he scans that flesh-creeping menacing stanza in the "Ancient Mariner:"

> "Like one that on a lonesome road
> Doth walk in fear and dread,
> And having once turned round
>     walks on,
> And turns no more his head;
> Because he knows a frightful fiend
> Doth close behind him tread."

Neither is it difficult to imagine Jefferson himself, who was much about the Library and the University, taking note of the sad-faced youngster who probably wrote, or conceived, "Tamerlane and Other Poems" during his residence there, as he published them the midsummer following.

It is certain that Poe gambled and drank at the University. It was a gaming and bibulous age, and a similar charge might be truthfully laid against some contemporaries of his, later distinguished as scholars, ecclesiastics, and statesmen; but it should be understood that he was not expelled, dismissed, or disciplined in any fashion whatever. During his academic life, six students withdrew, three were suspended, and three expelled. Poe was not included in any of these categories. He was a lonely figure among the high-spirited groups then in attendance at the University, rambling much about the hills and valleys encircling Charlottesville, and giving much time to the activities of the Jefferson Literary Society.

There is something mystical and unrevealed about the brief stay at this University of this imaginative, emotional, creative boy. Thomas Jefferson died on July 4, 1826, in the midst of the second session of the University. This must have made a great stir about the institution to which he was so intimately attached, as it did throughout the young republic. Yet, though Poe must have had knowledge of the world fame of the Father of the University, only once, so far as I can find, in all his writings, and that casually, the name of Jefferson appears. His failure to be impressed in any way by the great philosopher and statesman is a testimony to his carelessness of political honors and his complete absorption in the purely artistic aspects of man and nature. Napoleon once said "My estate is comprised of glory." Poe's estate was comprised of imagination, and on that glamorous ground he lived and died. On this centennial anniversary of his matriculation, I have the desire to speak of him in no critical or technical fashion. That task belongs to those who make of his supreme artistry the study of their lives. I would care to utter, in this first issue of the VIRGINIA QUARTERLY REVIEW, dedicated to literature and the humanities, some intimate words expressing for him the tenderness and affection which his University has always borne for him, as well in the days of his waywardness and eclipse as in this time when the star of his fame has climbed to the zenith and is shining there with intense and settled glory. There is nothing finer in the world than the love that men bear for institutions, unless it be the solemn pride which institutions display in men who have partaken of their benefits. Seven cities claimed the birth of Homer dead through which the living Homer begged his bread. That experience of the elder world is repeated today, save the number of cities is four instead of seven through which the living Poe suffered and struggled. It is the same old story, too, of outward defeat and apparent oblivion, and yet of inward victory and a sure grasping of enduring fame.

I may be frank and say that there was a time when Poe did not greatly appeal to me. I felt the sheer, clear beauty of his song, indeed, as one might feel the beauty of the lark's song, but his detachment from the world of men, where my interests most centred, left me unresponsive and simply curious. The great name of poet had held place in my thinking as signifying a prophet, or as a maker of divine music for men to march by towards serener heights. My notion of the poet came down to me out of the Hebraic training that all of our consciences receive; and Poe did not fit into this conception. I have come, however, to see the limitations of that view, and to behold something admirable and strange and wonderful in this proud, gifted man, who loved beauty and mystery, who had such genius for feeling the pain of life and the wonder of it, who grasped so vainly at its peace and calm, and who suffered, one feels, a thousand deaths under its disciplines and conventions. To me the glory of Poe as a man is that though whipped and scourged by human frailties he was able to keep his heart and vision unstained and to hold true to the finest thing in him, so that out of this fidelity to his very best there issued immortal work.

World poets like world conquerors are very rare. Not many universities have had the fortune to shelter a world poet, and to offer him any nourishment. [. . .] I have often wondered just what the University of Virginia did for Poe in that short year of his life there. He makes no mention of the University in his writings, but that is like him and his detachment from time and place. He saw the University when it was young. He must have heard much talk about him, of the dreams and hopes for the new institution founded on the western borders by the statesman whose renown then filled the world. The great philosopher of democracy and the great classic artist must have often passed each other on the Lawn and doubtless often held speech with each other. [. . .] It is probably true that "Annabel Lee" and the poem to Helen would have sung themselves out of Poe's heart and throat if he had never seen the University of Virginia; but there was inspiration in the place in that time of its dim beginnings. There were noble books there, few in number but great in quality. Byron, Shelley, Coleridge, and Keats and the great Greeks were all there; sincere scholars had set up their homes there. There were unbeaten young with young hearts and passions; there, hopes gleamed and ambitions burned. And then, as now, beauty dwelt upon the venerable hills encircling the horizon, and the University itself lay new and chaste in its simple lines upon the young Lawn. I venture to think sometimes that when he wrote those stateliest lines of his—

> To the glory that was Greece
> And the grandeur that was Rome—

perhaps there flashed into his mind's eye a vision of the Rotunda, with its soaring columns whitened by the starlight and vying with the beauty and witchery of the white winter about it.

It is perhaps easier to answer the question, What has Poe done for his University? We hear much of endowments in connection with universities. The words donor and endowment are the technical phrases of college administration, baffling and alluring the builders of universities. Poe has endowed his alma mater with immortal distinction, and left it a legacy which will increase with the years. It is not the endowment of money, for there was no scrip left in his purse, but simply the endowment of a few songs and a fund of unconquerable idealism. I am not of those who believe that Poe has been to our young men a kind of star that has lighted them to their destruction, as some good Presbyterians believe Burns to have been to the youth of Scotland. The vast tragedy of his life, its essential purity, its hard work, the unspeakable pity of it, have kept his name a name of dignity and the suggestions of his career are suggestions of beauty and of labor. True he is no exemplar to whom we can point our youth, but the fact that there is a little room on West Range in which dwelt a world poet, who never wrote an unclean word and who sought after beauty in form as passionately as a coarse man might seek after gain, has contributed an irreducible total of good to the spirit which men breathe as well as a wide fame to his alma mater that will outlive all disaster, or change, or ill-fortune. May I call it a clear tradition of beauty and poetic understanding, a feeling for the gold and not the dross in life, a genius for reverence, an instinct for honor, and an eye to see burning brightly the great realities that are wont to pale and disappear before the light of common day?

ROBERT P. TRISTRAM COFFIN

# Codfish Chowder and Sun

[ SUMMER 1928 ]

THERE are many kinds of picnics; but my kind is the only kind that satisfies so well that it lasts me through a whole year.

To begin with you must have the Maine coast. But more than that—a particular part of the Maine coast, Casco Bay with its islands, a new one for every day in the year, ranging in size from Great Chebeague and Great Island, each capable of supporting far-flung villages, to the Chunk O' Pork and the Pound o' Tea and Jello with its bushel of soil. And you must have my kind of a family—one in which there are enough babies sprinkled in among the grown-ups to keep a panoramic camera busy. A picnic without a dozen yards of grandchildren would be only half a picnic for my mother. Not any children at all will do, either; they must be babies who take life as a sunrise or a circus or both together even when they still go on all fours.

Then you must have islands with fir trees packed so closely together that you might walk along their tops, if you were spry, and you must have the myrrh of the balsams in your nose along with the smell of the sea all a summer's day. It must be a day in August and one of the kind that you will find nowhere else on this round earth save Maine; northwest wind blowing the sky as clean and clear as a bell, a blue sky that you can fairly hear ring, and white galleons of clouds with flat keels which sail over by thousands and yet never get in the way of the sun. The sunshine turns everything to amber and crystal and pours over the world like a tide. You can hear it lapping the granite coasts. The whole world is very hot yet airy; you can smell the tar in the calking of the boats. Your face turns into a russet banner. Your brain turns into sunlight. The ocean grows darker and deeper blue between the white crests that are coming in from far Spain. The sea and the sun get in under your soul.

I cannot begin to tell you all the ingredients you mix together to make this day of bliss. Somewhere at the beginning you stir in a motor boat of the sort that is wide in the beam, good to hold a small army. You add spray all over everybody, especially the children; for my picnic would lack spice if all of us were not well drenched down with brine and salted down till our eyes were a fast blue. To have the best spray you need a flooding tide to kick up a chop against the wind. Throw into the picnic all the sandwiches, ginger ale, coffee, salads, fruit, cakes, and doughnuts you please, for nothing can spoil the mess. You have the safe *sine qua non* in the baskets at the bottom of the boat. Nothing could kill the flavor of the clams and lobsters you are carrying with you alive. The codfish are alive and waiting, too, out in the ocean you are heading into.

It is well to add an aunt who makes it a point to be prepared. She will have the salt and the pepper all done up in separate packages and marked against mistake; and she will have castor oil and all sorts of unguents and ointments for the aches and the burns the children are bound to collect. A dash of uncles who are landlubbers and who are finding their annual sea a moving and epic affair is always in order. And don't forget the lady who will bring all sorts of cups and spoons and knives and forks that no one will possibly have time to use when you are all into the feast up to the eyes. A demijohn of cold spring water you surely must have. If it is the old-fashioned kind of crock with blue flowers painted on it by hand, so much the better. Add a pinch or two of song. For one should approach this picnic singing, or trying to sing.

After the many islands, all white with granite and dark green with spruces and cedars, all looking as bright and new as they looked on the morning of Creation, you must have the island where you are to land. I am the last person to be finicky, but this island should be absolutely like Pond Island. [. . .] For Pond Island is the last place between Maine and Spain. There isn't a tree on it; the twelve winds from the twelve corners of the sky use it for their playground. The spray of a sou'easter salts the springs that bubble up in its very center. The sheep that bite its grass have to be thickset and low to the earth; they carry their heads raked like the stacks and masts of ocean craft. They are adopted cousins of the gales and the surf. The island can be smelt miles to the lee, since it is one mass of bayberry and juniper.

Pond Island has its name from the many ponds which pit its slopes. [. . .] But one place, open to the open ocean and the White Bull, the reef which bellows and whitens forever with surf on the rim of the horizon, is the holy of holies of all the island's windy beauty. It is Shell Cove, and it is heaped with the petals of flowers that blossom in the sea, white with shells of living things that flourished æons ago and that will go on flourishing for æons to come, God being willing and God being the lover of sheer, delicate, pearly things that He was of old. [. . .] Bones of ships are bleaching among the shells to be your firewood. It is here the feast must be spread. No, no other island will ever do.

The first thing to do is to put most of the babies, with suitable chaperones equipped to feed them, ashore on Pond Island. Those that can run can chase the butterflies which grow bigger out here and fly over like flakes of the clouds and the sky, and those that can only creep can wallow in the sand. The landlubber uncles are best dropped along with the infants and women. But the hardier picnickers are off for the heaving ridges of Lumbo Ledges and the cod which graze there. I shall not dwell on the angling for the savory ladings of the kettles. Deep-sea fishing is a means to an end; it has no beauty or sufficiency in itself. [. . .] The line you fish with here is a hawser, the hook is a grappling iron. This is business, not sport. The fish you catch, though, are satisfactory things. They flop over the boat bottom with belated surprise, bulge-eyed, and plump with their toothsomeness. They have bronze spots on their sleek sides, and deep in their eyes shines the winter moon. They are ripe for the picnic.

The cod taken, you are for the shore and a fire. It is easy to get a cradle of coals as big as a bed with so much old timber frosty with salt lying all about. You fetch the big iron kettle that was cast to feed a family of the pioneer age. Sling it on a green fir-bole and put it over the blaze. Now begins the ritual of your chowder. First you cut salt pork into ribbons and throw it in. When it begins to seethe, throw in halved onions and fry them till they squirm like hissing adders. Dowse in half a jugful of water on the blue fumes. Cut up the codfish and throw them in heads and fins and all. Throw in salt by the fistful, pepper by the pound. Slice potatoes, and in with them. Keep the mess stirred up. Give everybody a stick. Let everybody stir. Too many cooks are the making of this broth. The more cinders and bark you get into the kettle the tastier the pottage. You stir in everything you can find. The spray from the sea, the iodine of kelp, the smell of bayberry bushes scorching in the sun. Even the wind and the blue day get into the chowder sooner or later. It is a wedding of sun and sea.

When the thing begins to smell like Kingdom Come and boils over for the third time, heave it off the fire and set it where everybody can ladle in. Here is molten manhood, liquid thews and sinews. Throw away the cups and spoons the innocency of the thoughtful aunt has prepared. Split sticks and clamp them on clamshells. There you have the only proper spoons for this chowder of the sun. Let everybody squat down on haunches like squaws, fall to, and dip in. By the time the fish are caught and cooked, everybody will be on the far slope of famine anyway, and boiled dogfish would taste like Esau's pottage. But when the chowder before you is the very marrow of the sea and the milk and honey of paradise, you can see how thin the veneer we call civilization is. Aunts who would eat a Boston cracker so modestly that you would never be aware that eating was going on become gorging gluttons. Uncles with dyspepsia devour bones and all. The children wallow in savoriness to their eyes. Of course everybody burns his mouth. But burnt mouths are as much a part of picnics as soiled clothes. [. . .]

When the sharpest edges of hunger are dulled by the chowder, then it is time to fall upon the lobsters. They have been broiling in the coals, and you rake them out now, split them down the back, and pour in butter, salt, and pepper. [. . .]

After the lobsters come the clams. I don't mean those fat, hard-shelled imitations that pass for clams below Cape Cod; those things are quahaugs; we have them in Maine, but no one dreams of eating them. I mean the thin oval vases that have to be mined in the mud. These are really the crown of the feast. So one should leave some corner vacant in his frame for them. Now the kinds of clambakes are legion. But my way of baking clams is the only proper one. You build a series of fires and let them burn down to coals. Then you throw on a layer of rockweed fresh pulled from the water on each. You dump on a peck of clams on top of this and cover all with more rockweed. Then you let nature attend to the rest. And nature is the mother of miracles! I know there are those who roast clams in the open on iron grates and the sides of defunct cookstoves. I know there are those who play the mason and build elaborate fireplaces of bricks or stones. But all this artistry is sheer nonsense. When I am in the open, I cook as the open decrees. I want none of stoves. And when my clams are uncovered, they are wide open yet all have their juice within them, and they have the taste of the rockweed smoked into their every tissue. The best parts of the sea, the sky, and the earth meet in them. They melt away in the mouth and leave one thinking of what a splendid, round, and sufficient thing this old ball of an earth is. I have eaten the best feast the Old Dominion can spread; I have tasted the burnt honey which is the November sweetpotato taken ripe from the ground and roasted on the coals in a Virginian twilight; and [. . .] oysters still dripping with the Chesapeake to give their flavor to the bake. [. . .] But that banquet does not hold a candle to my native clams martyred in rockweed. [. . .]

After the clams are stowed away, if any one has a place for cake or sandwiches or such Monday and Tuesday things, let him fill it. But at the last pile of clams the numbers of us are few. Only the hardiest meet there. And by that time the day is well down.

We go home through the sunset on waters that spread benediction around. We do not notice the departure of the sun, for we have the sun under our belts; and sunshine will be ours for another whole year.

# ANDRÉ GIDE

# Classicism

[ SUMMER 1929 ]

## I

THE TRIUMPH of individualism and the triumph of classicism melt into each other. Now I maintain that the triumph of individualism consists in renouncing one's individuality. Not one of the qualities of the classic style but is purchased by the sacrifice of some satisfaction. The painters and writers whom today we praise the most, have a manner; the great classic artist strives to have no manner; his effort is towards the commonplace. If he gets the commonplace without great effort, he is not a great artist, and that's that! A classic work is strong and beautiful only in so far as its romanticism is repressed. "A great artist"—as I wrote some twenty years ago—"has but one care: to become as human as possible; or better, to become commonplace. And the wonderful thing is that it is in this way that he becomes most individual. On the other hand, the writer who misses this human quality turns out to be bizarre, peculiar, defective. Shall I recall the words of the Gospel? Why not, since I do not intend to twist their meaning: He who would save his life (his individual life) shall lose it; but he who is willing to lose it, shall save it (or, to translate the Greek text more exactly—shall make it truly alive)."

I believe that a work of consummate art probably passes unobserved at first. It is a work in which the most apparently contradictory qualities—strength and sweetness, precision and poetry, logic and freedom, restraint and grace—breathe so easily that they appear natural and not at all surprising. And this is why the first of those pleasures the writer must give up, is the satisfaction of astonishing his contemporaries. Baudelaire, Keats, Browning, Stendhal wrote for the generations that were to be.

However, I do not believe a classic is necessarily unrecognized at once. Boileau, Racine, Le Fontaine, even Molière, were appreciated right off; and although in their writings we now see virtues less esteemed by their contemporaries, yet the authors who seem to us the greatest are at the same time the ones most praised in their own time. In spite of Gautier's rather silly effort to insist on finding unappreciated geniuses among the seventeenth century "grotesques," these last, compared with our great classic writers, cut by no means the figure that a Baudelaire does by the side of a Ponsard or a Baour-Lormian. The public itself was classic, had a taste for the thing which was classic; the qualities it liked and demanded of a work of art were those very ones which make us call it classic today.

## II

Today the word "classic" is in such honour, is so charged with significance, that for a little you might call classic any big beautiful work. This is absurd. There are great works which are in no sense classic—nor are they on that account any the more romantic. This classification holds good only for France, and even in France what could be less classic than Pascal often is, than Rabelais, than Villon? Not Shakespeare, nor Michelangelo, not Beethoven nor Dostoievski, nor Rembrandt, nor even Dante (I cite only the greatest) are classic. Don Quixote is not classic, and neither are Calderòn's plays—nor are they romantic either, but simply Spanish. To tell the truth, I know no other classics, since antiquity, but the French ones (save only Goethe—and there again, he became classic only through imitation of the ancients). Classicism seems to me so peculiarly a French invention, that for a little I would consider the two words, classic and French, synonymous, if the former term could claim to exhaust the genius of France, and had not Romanticism likewise managed to turn French. Anyhow, it is in its classic art that the French genius has most fully realized itself, whilst every effort towards classicism on the part of any other people will forever be artificial, as happens with Pope, for example. Another reason for this is that in France, and in France alone, intellect has a tendency to predominate over sentiment and instinct. This by no means implies, as certain foreigners are disposed to think, that sentiment and instinct are wanting. One need only go through the newly re-opened galleries of the Louvre, both of painting and of sculpture, to realize how profoundly *reasonable* all these works are. What reserve, what moderation! They must be looked at a long time before they consent to deliver up their hidden meanings—so secret is the thrill of them. But is the appeal to the senses—so overflowing in Rubens' pictures—less powerful in Poussin's for being restrained?

Classicism—and by that I mean French classicism—tends wholly towards litotes. It is the art of expressing most, by saying least. It is an art of modesty and restraint. All our classic writers are more emotional than they appear at first blush. The romantic authors, through the exuberance of their expression, always tend to seem more moved than they really are, so that with them the word keeps preceding and overflowing the emotion and the thought. This was due to a sort of fizzling out of taste (the result of a lesser degree of culture) which made them doubt the genuineness of what our classics uttered so modestly. For lack of knowing how to get into them, and read between the lines, they thought our classics cold, and considered a defect what is actually their most exquisite beauty—their reserve.

The romantic author is forever between us and his words, the classic must be sought on the other side of them. A certain faculty for passing too quickly, too easily, from the emotion to the word, is the mark of all the French romantics—and therefore they fail to seize the emotion otherwise than by the word; they fail to master it. The important thing for them is not to be moved, but to seem so. In all Greek literature, in the best of English poetry, in Racine, in Pascal, in Baudelaire, you feel that the word, though it reveals the emotion, yet does not hold it all, and that after the word has been said, the emotion which preceded it, goes on. With Ronsard, Corneille, Hugo (to cite only great names) it seems that the emotion leads to the word and stops there; the emotion is wordy and the word exhausts it; the sole reverberation is the reverberation of the voice.

# D. H. LAWRENCE

## The Bogey between the Generations

[ WINTER 1929 ]

IF YOU ARE a writer, nothing is more confusing than the difference between the things you have to say and the things you are allowed to print. Talking to an intelligent girl, the famous *"jeune fille"* who is the excuse for the great Hush! Hush! in print, you find, not that you have to winnow your words and leave out all the essentials, but that she, the innocent girl in question, is flinging all sorts of fierce questions at your head, in all sorts of shameless language, demanding all sorts of impossible answers. You think to yourself: My heaven, this is the innocent young thing on whose behalf books are suppressed! And you wonder: How on earth am I to answer her?

You decide the only way to answer her is straightforward. She smells an evasion in an instant and despises you for it. She is no fool, this innocent maiden. Far from it. And she loathes an evasion. Talking to her father in the sanctum of his study, you have to winnow your words and watch your step, the old boy is so nervous, so tremulous lest anything be said that should hurt his feelings. But once away in the drawing-room or the garden, the innocent maiden looks at you anxiously, and it is all you can do to prevent her saying crudely: "Please don't be annoyed with Daddy. You see he *is* like that, and we have to put up with him." Or else from blurting out: "Daddy's an old fool, but he *is* a dear, isn't he?"

It is a queer reversal of the Victorian order. Father winces and bridles and trembles in his study or his library, and the innocent maiden knocks you flat with her outspokenness in the conservatory. And you have to admit that she is the man of the two: of the three, maybe. Especially when she says, rather sternly: "I hope you didn't let Daddy see what you thought of him!" "But what *do* I think of him?" I gasp. "Oh, it's fairly obvious!" she replies coolly, and dismisses the point.

I admit the young are a little younger than I am; or a little older, which is it? I really haven't spent my years cultivating prunes and prisms; yet, confronted with a young thing of twenty-two, I often find myself with a prune-stone in my mouth, and I don't know what to do with it.

[ 15 ]

"Why *is* Daddy like that?" she says, and there is genuine pain in the question. "Like what?" you ask.—"Oh, you know what I mean! Like a baby ostrich with his head in the sand! It only makes his rear so much the more conspicuous. And it's a pity, because he's awfully intelligent in other ways."

Now what is a man to answer?—"*Why* are they like that?" she insists. "Who?" say I. "Men!" she says. "Men like Daddy!" "I suppose it's a sort of funk," say I. "*Exactly!*" she pounces on me like a panther. "But what is there to be in a funk about?"

I have to confess I don't know. "Of course not!" she says. "There's nothing at all to be in a funk about. So why can't we make him see it?"

When the younger generation, usually the feminine half of it, in her early twenties, starts firing off "Whys?" at me, I give in. Anything crosses her in the least and she takes aim at it with the deadly little pistol of her enquiring spirit and says: "*Why?*" She is a deadly shot: Billy the Kid is nothing to her; she hits the nail on the head every time. "Now why can't I talk like a sensible human being to Daddy?" "I suppose he thinks it is a little early for you to be quite so sensible," say I mildly. "Cheek! What *cheek* of him to think he can measure out the amount of sense I ought to have!" she cries. "Why does he think it?"

Why indeed? But once you start whying, there's no end to it. A hundred years ago, a few reformers piped up timorously: Why is man so infinitely superior to woman? And on the slow years came the whisper: He isn't! Then the poor padded young of those days roused up: Why are fathers *always* in the right? And the end of the century confessed that they weren't. Since then, the innocent maiden has ceased to be anaemic—all maidens were more or less anaemic, thirty years ago—and though she is no less innocent, but probably more so, than her stuffy grandmother or mother before her, there isn't a thing she hasn't shot her "Why?" at, or her "Wherefore?"—the innocent maiden of today. And digging implements are called by their bare, their barest names. "Why should Daddy put his foot down about love? He's been a prize muff at it himself, judging from Mother."

It's terrible, if all the sanctifications have to sit there like celluloid Aunt Sallies while the young take pot shots at them. A real straight "Why?" aimed by sweet and twenty, goes clean through them. Nothing but celluloid and looking so important: really, *why*—?

The answer seems to be, Bogey! The elderly, today, seem to be ridden by a bogey, they grovel before the fetish of human wickedness. Every young man is out to "ruin" every young maiden. Bogey! The young maiden knows a thing or two about that. She's not quite the raw egg she's supposed to be in the first place. And as for most young men, they're only too nice, and it would grieve them bitterly to "ruin" any young maid, even if they knew exactly how to set about it. Of which the young maiden is perfectly aware, and: "Why can't Daddy see it?"—He can, really. But he is so wedded to his Bogey, that once the young man's back is turned, the old boy can see in the young boy nothing but a danger, a danger to my daughter! Wickedness in other people is an *idée fixe* of the elderly.—Ah, my boy, you will find that in life every man's hand is against you!—As a matter of fact, my boy finds nothing of the sort. Every man has to struggle for himself, true. But most people are willing to give a bit of help where they can. The world may really be a bogey. But that isn't because individuals are wicked villains. At least ninety-nine per cent of individuals in this country, and in any other country, as far as we have ever seen, are perfectly decent people who have a certain amount of struggle to get along, but who don't want to do anybody any harm if they can help it.

This seems to be the general experience of the young, and so they can't appreciate the bogey of human wickedness which seems to dominate the minds of the old in their relation to the succeeding generation. The young ask: "What, exactly, is this Bogey, this wickedness we are to be shielded from?"—And the old only reply: "Of course, there is no danger to *us*. But to you, who are young and inexperienced—!"

And the young, naturally, see nothing but pure hypocrisy. They have no desire to be shielded. If the Bogey exists, they would like to set eyes on him, to take the measure of this famous "wickedness." But since they never come across it; since they find meanness and emptiness the worst crimes; they decide that the Bogey doesn't and never did exist, that he is an invention of the elderly spirit, the last stupid stick with which the old can beat the young and feel self-justified.—Of course it's perfectly hopeless with Mother and Daddy; one has to treat them like mental infants, say the young. But the mother sententiously reiterates: "I don't mind, as far as I am concerned. But I have to protect my children."

Protect, that is, some artificial children that only exist in parental imagination, from a Bogey that likewise has no existence outside that imagination, and thereby derive a great sense of parental authority, importance, and justification.

# The Nineteen Thirties

ALDOUS HUXLEY

# Tragedy and the Whole Truth

[ SPRING 1931 ]

I

THERE were six of them, the best and bravest of the hero's companions. Turning back from his post in the bows, Odysseus was in time to see them lifted, struggling, into the air, to hear their screams, the desperate repetition of his own name. The survivors could only look on helplessly, while Scylla "at the mouth of her cave devoured them, still screaming, still stretching out their hands to me in the frightful struggle." And Odysseus adds that it was the most dreadful and lamentable sight he ever saw in all his "explorings of the passes of the sea." We can believe it; Homer's brief description (the too poetical simile is a later interpolation) convinces us.

Later, the danger passed, Odysseus and his men went ashore for the night and, on the Sicilian beach, prepared their supper—prepared it, says Homer, 'expertly.' The Twelfth Book of the Odyssey concludes with these words. "When they had satisfied their thirst and hunger, they thought of their dear companions and wept, and in the midst of their tears sleep came gently upon them."

The truth, the whole truth, and nothing but the truth—how rarely the older literatures ever told it! Bits of the truth, yes; every good book gives us bits of the truth, would not be a good book if it did not. But the whole truth, no. Of the great writers of the past incredibly few have given us that. Homer—the Homer of the Odyssey—is one of those few.

"Truth?" you question. "For example, 2 + 2 = 4? Or Queen Victoria came to the throne in 1837? Or light travels at the rate of 187,000 miles a second?" No, obviously, you won't find much of that sort of thing in literature. The 'truth' of which I was speaking just now is in fact no more than an acceptable verisimilitude. When the experiences recorded in a piece of literature correspond fairly closely with our own actual experiences, or with what I may call our potential experiences—experiences, that is to say, which we feel (as the result of a more or less explicit process of inference from known facts) that we might have had—we say, inaccurately no doubt: "This piece of writing is true." But this, of course, is not the whole story.

The record of a case in a text-book of psychology is scientifically true, insofar as it is an accurate account of particular events. But it might also strike the reader as being 'true' with regard to himself—that is to say, acceptable, probable, having a correspondence with his own actual or potential experiences. But a text-book of psychology is not a work of art—or only secondarily and incidentally a work of art. Mere verisimilitude, mere correspondence of experience recorded by the writer with experience remembered or imaginable by the reader, is not enough to make a work of art seem 'true.' Good art possesses a kind of super-truth—is more probable, more acceptable, more convincing than fact itself. Naturally; for the artist is endowed with a sensibility and a power of communication, a capacity to 'put things across,' which events and the majority of people to whom events happen, do not possess. Experience teaches only the teachable, who are by no means as numerous as Mrs. Micawber's papa's favourite proverb would lead us to suppose. Artists are eminently teachable and also eminently teachers. They receive from events much more than most men receive and they can transmit what they have received with a peculiar penetrative force, which drives their communication deep into the reader's mind. One of our most ordinary reactions to a good piece of literary art is expressed in the formula: "This is what I have always felt and thought, but have never able to put clearly into words, even for myself."

## II

We are now in a position to explain what we mean when we say that Homer is a writer who tells the Whole Truth. We mean that the experiences he records correspond fairly closely with our own actual or potential experiences—and correspond with our experiences not on a single limited sector, but all along the line of our physical and spiritual being. And we also mean that Homer records these experiences with a penetrative artistic force that makes them seem peculiarly acceptable and convincing.

So much, then, for truth in literature. Homer's, I repeat, is the Whole Truth. Consider how almost any other of the great poets would have concluded the story of Scylla's attack on the passing ship. Six men, remember, have been taken and devoured before the eyes of their friends. In any other poem but the Odyssey, what would the survivors have done? They would, of course, have wept, even as Homer made them weep. But would they previously have cooked their supper and cooked it, what's more, in a masterly fashion? Would they previously have drunk and eaten to satiety? And after weeping, or actually while weeping, would they have dropped quietly off to sleep? No, they most certainly would not have done any of these things. They would simply have wept, lamenting their own misfortune and the horrible fate of their companions, and the Canto would have ended tragically on their tears.

Homer, however, preferred to tell the Whole Truth. He knew that even the most cruelly bereaved must eat; that hunger is stronger than sorrow and that its satisfaction takes precedence even of tears. He knew that experts continue to act expertly and to find satisfaction in their accomplishment, even when friends have just been eaten, even when the accomplishment is only cooking the supper. He knew that when the belly is full (and only when the belly is full) men can afford to grieve and that sorrow after supper is almost a luxury. And finally he knew that, even as hunger takes precedence of grief, so fatigue, supervening, cuts short its career and drowns it in a sleep all the sweeter for bringing forgetfulness of bereavement. In a word, Homer refused to treat the theme tragically. He preferred to tell the Whole Truth.

Another author who preferred to tell the Whole Truth was Fielding. "Tom Jones" is one of the very few Odyssean books written in Europe between the time of Aeschylus and the present age; Odyssean, because never tragical; never—even when painful and disastrous, even when pathetic and beautiful things are happening. For they do happen; Fielding, like Homer, admits all the facts, shirks nothing. Indeed, it is precisely because these authors shirk nothing that their books are not tragical. For among the things they don't shirk are the irrelevancies which, in actual life, always temper the situations and characters that writers of tragedy insist on keeping chemically pure. Consider, for example, the case of Sophy Western, that most charming, most nearly perfect of young women. Fielding, it is obvious, adored her; (she is said to have been created in the image of his first, much-loved wife). But in spite of his adoration, he refused to turn her into one of those chemically pure and, as it were, focussed beings who do and suffer in the world of tragedy. That innkeeper who lifted the weary Sophia from her horse—what need had he to fall? In no tragedy would he (nay, *could* he) have collapsed beneath her weight. For, to begin with, in the tragical context weight is an irrelevance; heroines should be above the law of gravitation. But that is not all; let the reader now remember what were the results of his fall. Tumbling flat on his back, he pulled Sophia down on top of him—his belly was a cushion, so that happily she came to no bodily harm—pulled her down head first. But head first is necessarily legs last; there was a momentary display of the most ravishing charms; the bumpkins at the inn door grinned or guffawed; poor Sophia, when they picked her up, was blushing in an agony of embarrassment and wounded modesty. There is nothing intrinsically improbable about this incident, which is stamped, indeed, with all the marks of literary truth. But however true, it is an incident which could never, never have happened to a heroine of tragedy. It would never have been allowed to happen. But Fielding refused to impose the tragedian's veto; he shirked nothing—neither the intrusion of irrelevant absurdities into the midst of romance or disaster, nor any of life's no less irrelevantly painful interruptions of the course of happiness. He did not want to be a tragedian. And, sure enough, that brief and pearly gleam of Sophia's charming posterior was sufficient to scare the Muse of Tragedy out of "Tom Jones," just as, more than five and twenty centuries before, the sight of stricken men first eating, then remembering to weep, then forgetting their tears in slumber had scared her out of the Odyssey.

## III

In his "Principles of Literary Criticism" Mr. I. A. Richards affirms that good tragedy is proof against irony and relevance—that it can absorb anything into itself and still remain tragedy. Indeed, he seems to make of this capacity to absorb the un-tragical and the anti-tragical a touchstone of tragic merit. Thus tried, practically all Greek, all French, and most Elizabethan tragedies are found wanting. Only the best of Shakespeare can stand the test. So, at least, says Mr. Richards. Is he right? I have often had my doubts. The tragedies of Shakespeare are veined, it is true, with irony and an often terrifying cynicism; but the cynicism is always heroic idealism turned neatly inside out, the irony is a kind of photographic negative of heroic romance. Turn Troilus's white into black and all his blacks into white and you have Thersites. Reversed, Othello and Desdemona become Iago. White Ophelia's negative is the irony of Hamlet, is the ingenuous bawdry of her own mad songs; just as the cynicism of mad King Lear is the black shadow-replica of Cordelia. Now, the shadow, the photographic negative of a thing is in no sense irrelevant to it. Shakespeare's ironies and cynicisms serve to deepen his tragic world, but not to widen it. If they had widened it, as the Homeric irrelevancies widened out the universe of the Odyssey—why, then, the world of Shakespearean tragedy would automatically have ceased to exist. For example, a scene showing the bereaved Macduff eating his supper, growing melancholy, over the whisky, with thoughts of his murdered wife and children, and then, with lashes still wet, dropping off to sleep, would be true enough to life; but it would not be true to tragic art. The introduction of such a scene would change the whole quality of the play; treated in this Odyssean style, "Macbeth" would cease to be a tragedy. Or take the case of Desdemona. Iago's bestially cynical remarks about her character are in no sense, as we have seen, irrelevant to the tragedy. They present us with negative images of her real nature and of the feelings she has for Othello. These negative images are always *hers*, are always recognizably the property of the heroine-victim of a tragedy.

Whereas, if, springing ashore at Cyprus, she had tumbled, as the no less exquisite Sophia was to tumble, and revealed the inadequacies of sixteenth-century underclothing, the play would no longer be the "Othello" we know. Iago might breed a family of little cynics and the existing dose of bitterness and savage negation be doubled and trebled; "Othello" would still remain fundamentally "Othello." But a few Fieldingesque irrelevancies would destroy it—destroy it, that is to say, as a tragedy; for there would be nothing to prevent it from becoming a magnificent drama of some other kind. For the fact is that tragedy and what I have called the Whole Truth are not compatible; where one is, the other is not. There are certain things which even the best, even Shakespearean tragedy cannot absorb into itself.

To make a tragedy, the artist must isolate a single element out of the totality of human experience and use that exclusively as his material. Tragedy is something that is separated out from the Whole Truth, distilled from it, so to speak, as an essence is distilled from the living flower. Tragedy is chemically pure. Hence its power to act quickly and intensely on our feelings. All chemically pure art has this power to act upon us quickly and intensely. Thus, chemically pure pornography (on the rare occasions when it happens to be written convincingly, by someone who has the gift of 'putting things across') is a quick-acting emotional drug of incomparably greater power than the Whole Truth about sensuality, or even (for many people) than the tangible and carnal reality itself. It is because of its chemical purity that tragedy so effectively performs its function of catharsis. It refines and corrects and gives a style to our emotional life, and does so swiftly, with power. Brought into contact with tragedy, the elements of our being fall, for the moment at any rate, into an ordered and beautiful pattern, as the iron filings arrange themselves under the influence of the magnet. Through all its individual variations, this pattern is always fundamentally of the same kind. From the reading or the hearing of a tragedy we rise with the feeling that

> Our friends are exultations, agonies,
> And love, and man's unconquerable mind;

with the heroic conviction that we too would be unconquerable if subjected to the agonies, that in the midst of the agonies we too should continue to love, might even learn to exult. It is because it does these things to us that tragedy is felt to be so valuable. What are the values of Wholly-Truthful art? What does it do to us that seems worth doing? Let us try to discover.

Wholly-Truthful art overflows the limits of tragedy and shows us, if only by hints and implications, what happened before the tragic story began, what will happen after it is over, what is happening simultaneously elsewhere (and "elsewhere" includes all those parts of the minds and bodies of the protagonists not immediately engaged in the tragic struggle). Tragedy is an arbitrarily isolated eddy on the surface of a vast river that flows on majestically, irresistibly, around, beneath, and to either side of it. Wholly-Truthful art contrives to imply the existence of the entire river as well as of the eddy. It is quite different from tragedy, even though it may contain, among other constituents, all the elements from which tragedy is made. (The 'same thing' placed in different contexts, loses its identity and becomes, for the perceiving mind, a succession of different things.) In Wholly-Truthful art the agonies may be just as real, love and the unconquerable mind just as admirable, just as important, as in tragedy. Thus, Scylla's victims suffer as painfully as the monster-devoured Hippolytus in "Phèdre"; the mental anguish of Tom Jones when he thinks he has lost his Sophia, and lost her by his own fault, is hardly less than that of Othello after Desdemona's murder. (The fact that Fielding's power of "putting things across" is by no means equal to Shakespeare's, is, of course, merely an accident.) But the agonies and indomitabilities are placed by the Wholly-Truthful writer in another, wider context, with the result that they cease to be the same as the intrinsically identical agonies and indomitabilities of tragedy. Consequently, Wholly-Truthful art produces in us an effect quite different from that produced by tragedy. Our mood, when we have read a Wholly-Truthful book is never one of heroic exultation; it is one of resignation, of acceptance. (Acceptance can also be heroic.) Being chemically impure, Wholly-Truthful literature cannot move us as quickly and intensely as tragedy or any other kind of chemically pure art. But I believe that its effects are more lasting. The exultations that follow the reading or hearing of a tragedy are in the nature of temporary inebriations. Our being cannot long hold the pattern imposed by tragedy. Remove the magnet and the filings tend to fall back into confusion. But the pattern of acceptance and resignation imposed upon us by Wholly-Truthful literature, though perhaps less unexpectedly beautiful in design, is (for that very reason perhaps) more stable. The catharsis of tragedy is violent and apocalyptic; but the milder catharsis of Wholly-Truthful literature is lasting.

## IV

In recent times literature has become more and more acutely conscious of the Whole Truth—of the great oceans of irrelevant things, events, and thoughts stretching endlessly away in every direction from whatever island point (a character, a story) the author may choose to contemplate. To impose the kind of arbitrary limitations which must imposed by anyone who wants to write a tragedy has become more and more difficult—is now indeed, for those who are at all sensitive to contemporaneity, almost impossible. This does not mean, of course, that the modern writer must confine himself to a merely naturalistic manner. One can imply the existence of the Whole Truth without laboriously cataloguing every object within sight. A book can be written in terms of pure phantasy and yet, by implication, tell the Whole Truth. Of all the important works of contemporary literature not one is a tragedy. There is no contemporary writer of significance who does not prefer to state or imply the Whole Truth. However different one from another in style, in ethical, philosophical, and artistic intentions, in the scales of values accepted, contemporary writers have this in common, that they are interested in the Whole Truth. Proust, D. H. Lawrence, André Gide, Kafka, Hemingway—here are five obviously significant and important contemporary writers. Five authors as remarkably unlike one another as they could well be. They are as one only in this: that none of them has written a pure tragedy, that all are concerned with the Whole Truth.

I have sometimes wondered whether tragedy, as a form of art, may not be doomed. But the fact that we are still profoundly moved by the tragic masterpieces of the past—that we can be moved, against our better judgment, even by the bad tragedies of the contemporary stage and film—makes me think that the day of chemically pure art is not over. Tragedy happens to be passing through a period of eclipse, because all the significant writers of our age are too busy exploring the newly discovered, or rediscovered, world of the Whole Truth to be able to pay any attention to it. But there is no good reason to believe that this state of things will last for ever. Tragedy is too valuable to be allowed to die. And there is no reason, after all, why the two kinds of literature—the Chemically Impure and the Chemically Pure, the literature of the Whole Truth and the literature of Partial Truth—should not exist simultaneously, each in its separate sphere. The human spirit has need of both.

# ANDRÉ MAUROIS

# The Myth of Myth

[ WINTER 1932 ]

I

VALERY, in his preface to the "Persian Letters," showed that periods of order depend on the reign of fictions. Human societies are rendered possible by the acceptance of useful myths. It is not true that incest is forbidden by the gods. It is not true that justice always strikes the guilty. It is not true that Jupiter protects those who sacrifice victims to him. But only let a great number of men sustain such "magic edifices" by their belief, and the edifices will offer shelter to these same men.

Pagan images are followed by Christian images, by social images; but always abstract fictions support civilization. Law is strong not because the police are really omniscient (there is still nothing easier than to commit a crime and go unpunished), but because the myth of Law has its temple in our mind. Kings, ministers, parliaments govern, not because they represent a real power (their armies are made up only of their subjects), but because a convention admitted by everybody incarnates in their persons fictitious might.

Then "during a period of order men grow bolder." Conventions and myths are examined without respect; their true nature and their transparent weaknesses are discovered; men are indignant at having obeyed them. The individual, whose desires have been held in for so long by this imaginary rampart, reproaches himself for his scruples and his cowardice. This is the day of free and "enlightened" spirits. Sincerity and revolution become myths in their turn. The convention of anti-convention, the most exacting of all, replaces the other. "Disorder, and rule by physical violence, return at the expense of order." Before long men must once more "long for the police or for death."

II

Such, during the ten or twelve thousand years that there have been men and that men have been governed, has been the ebb and flow of human societies. The Roman Empire did not survive the myths it had deified; the disorder that followed it was a windfall to the theologies of Asia. The eighteenth-century philosophers believed they recognized the mythical nature of royal power, cut off the head of a King to reassure themselves that he was but a man, then put a crown on the head of a man that they might adore the myth of an Emperor.

Are men condemned then to alternate order and disorder? Must civilizations crumble one after the other? Can nothing but the sufferings of anarchy force us again to respect conventions without which no society can live? It would seem that a wiser race could escape this vicious circle. But the conventions that were formerly accepted are not necessarily the best. They sometimes need to be transformed. How should they be transformed if not by those who deny them?

## III

The reality of history seems to be more complex than the cycle: Order—Disorder—Desire for Order; Conventions—Contempt for Conventions—New Conventions. Myth begins by being myth, that is to say, word, logos; then it is made flesh. Myth engraves itself on the human heart. After ten thousand years of life in society, thinking and feeling man is not the same as a savage of the primitive forest. The appetites of the individual remain strong. He still suffers from repressions, from prohibitions imposed upon him by laws. But upon individual instincts there has been superimposed a social instinct.

The complete individual, who rejects conventions in order to become master of himself (Gide's Prodigal Son, Byron's Corsair), achieves neither equilibrium nor happiness. The tribe is present in him in spite of himself. It is not "society" which condemns him. Society is a myth from which it is possible to escape. But the image of society, in each of us, is not a myth. It is an indestructible reality. The tribal instinct is as strong as hunger, thirst, or desire. Should a man who, lost in the desert and sure of never seeing men again, kill a child or violate a young girl, that man would never again be at peace with himself. The courthouse is a "magic edifice," but "the moral law in our hearts" is not. The sin against society, or against God, may be imaginary, but not the sin against man. Social man was a fiction, but from this fiction he has been born.

## IV

One must therefore distinguish between those conventions which, being new and quite formal anyhow, have remained image or word for us, and those which on the contrary have been assimilated by hundreds of generations and have therefore become instinct and reality. The former may be the object of criticism and of revolution; revolt against the latter is revolt against oneself, from which the individual will perish. "Modesty is no longer Victorian, or Christian, it is human." The laws of marriage will change; marriage itself will perhaps disappear to make place for new forms of union; but a certain sexual discipline will keep its value, as courage will.

That myths thus transformed into instinct are more powerful than any convention, social or divine, intimate experience shows us. I do not believe that Jupiter will strike me with his thunderbolt if I betray an oath, I do not believe I shall be damned if I break an oath, but I know I shall despise myself if I do not keep a promise made to a child. Justice was once a myth, but man has ended by creating gods.

## V

Can social myths, even when they have become instincts, resist analysis that will bare their secret nature? We see, at the end of the Roman Empire, atheistic philosophers who would have liked, through political prudence, to maintain the images of the gods on their pedestals. But Jupiter ceased to be a useful convention from the day he was recognized as a convention. If Gide's Prodigal Son, having observed in his mind and flesh these social inhibitions, could have named them and recalled their origins, would he not have exorcised them?

It seems to me that the human spirit can escape this form of destruction and that the whole spiritual movement of our time, even, is toward respect for certain fictions accepted as fictions.

Science is renouncing the knowledge of the absolute. It no longer claims to construct a true system of the universe. It is proposing hypotheses which permit it to explain known facts and which seem to permit foreknowledge of unknown facts as well. It is ready to change these hypotheses if they cease to tally with phenomena. The scientist knows very well that the electron is a fiction. But as far as our means of observation permit us to judge, everything takes place as if this fiction were a reality. The ether, formerly a convenient concept, is being thrown aside by all modern systems. Doubtless some day the electron will be condemned. This acceptance of relativity does not render science impossible. It insures its solidity and its future. Jupiter died from being recognized as fiction because his priests had presented him as absolute. But hypotheses do not die; they are transformed.

It would be well if politics, following the example of science, renounced knowledge of the absolute and agreed to respect conventions (recognized as such) as long as they were useful. Anger against political myth is as insane as a revolution against ether would be, or a riot against Hertzian waves.

The King of England is a myth, but he is a convenient myth, and therefore deserves to be venerated. The right of property is a fiction; we may believe this fiction is out of date, as we may believe it is indestructible, but it is comic to hate it and puerile to adore it. Science cannot live without hypotheses, nor can human societies without idols. A people destroys one system of conventions only to adore another.

## VI

Myths, condemned by relativity in so far as they are dogmas, find it a support in so far as they are myths. The human spirit recognizes at the same time both its impotence and its strength. Impotence, if it wishes to attain to the absolute. Strength, if it contents itself with pursuing purely human ends. A great many political and moral conflicts have come, in the past, from the refusal to recognize that conventions are but conventions, or from the refusal to comprehend that, though mere conventions, they are nevertheless necessary. Our era seems ready at last to accept fictions as fictions. We know justice is a myth, but we know also that no society, no human life worthy of being lived, can subsist without it. "This generation believes in nothing?" Say rather that it wishes to be free to treat fictions as fictions. But what matter, if it believes in the myth of myth, that is to say in the necessity of maintaining human society through respect for contracts? "Periods of order depend on the reign of fictions."

# EVELYN WAUGH

## The Rough Life

[ WINTER 1934 ]

### I

AS FAR back as my memory extends, the rough life has existed for me as something real and vivid but utterly remote. When I say that I have lived until now in circumstances of practically unvaried comfort, I am not making the pretence of having been cradled in gilded luxury; on the contrary, I am merely stating a commonplace of normal English adolescence. There is very little connection nowadays between wealth and softness of living (indeed, the average footman leads a far softer life than his master). No normally educated Englishman is too hot or too cold, or hungry or thirsty or dirty or tired, for any appreciable length of time. Hot and cold water, thermometers and iodine, blankets and the appearance at regular times of unlimited quantities of food, are the ordinary circumstances of adolescence; they are sound enough foundations on which, with a little ingenuity, one can erect a fair edifice of personal comfort. From the first it was my hobby to develop the opportunities of comfort. At school, when malingering failed, it was always possible to turn to good account the few asperities of routine by making them the contacts against which to impose greater indulgence; scalding baths and vast orgies of crumpet eating succeeded cross-country runs and O. T. C. field days, expunging their memory and no doubt their benefits. With ampler means and greater freedom of choice in later years it has been possible to elaborate and improve this architecture of comfort, sometimes demolishing, sometimes restoring, now polishing some decorative detail, now throwing out whole new wings and terraces, reconciling and adjusting harmony and contrast and slowly bringing into existence a solid product of the art of making one's life tolerable; an inglorious occupation perhaps, but unambitious and, I hope, inoffensive.

But throughout all the years of soft living I have been aware, more keenly at some times than at others, of this second, opposed life which inevitably with the universal growth of comfort, has become a cult: the cult of "roughing it." At first this other life was something which existed only in literature, glamorous and intangible as Arthurian chivalry. Sometimes the voice of authority would break in on my contemplation saying, "It would do you good to rough it for a bit. Make a man of you." But for the most part it remained a poetic fiction quite unrelated to my own leisured existence. Prone on the hearth rug on winter evenings with a bound volume of "Chums" propped between my elbows, I would read of forest life; and as the coals glowed behind the nursery fireguard, picture, at what great distance, camp fires under the open sky where wood sparks volleyed up to join the stars. Or in the summer, dragging a desk chair into a shady corner of the garden, I would read, while bees buzzed among the Canterbury bells, of sledges and wolves and avalanches. I became familiar with the "crack" of the "Winchester" and with numberless italicized phrases—*pampas, bolas, gaucho, kraal, veldt, assegai*—which had for me the same magic and the same remoteness as the palfreys and damozels of Mallory.

The Boy Scout movement was then in its first flower. Every Saturday afternoon Hampstead Heath, where most of my childhood was spent, became overrun with boys of my own age from more densely populated districts who, in decorations curiously hybrid of heraldry and totemism, crept on their stomachs or plunged through the gorse uttering the scalping cries of American Indians, and doing little harm to anyone except the couples of lovers who habitually bestrew the district. I watched them with an interest that was cordial but aloof.

Later, for four years, the entire world adopted the standard of the Wild West, living in disastrous intimacy with firearms; the shops glutted their windows with camping equipment and insecticides.

Later still, various of my acquaintances were continually disappearing into distant parts of the globe to excavate ruins or shoot big game. They returned, some with handfuls of broken pottery, some with tiger skins, most with recurrent malaria, and all with vividly exciting anecdotes.

## II

Thus the conception of the rough life was never absent from my mind, and as my own habits became softer and more circumspect I became aware of a doubt growing up that could only be satisfied by personal investigation. For there must have been a time in everyone's experience—more than one in mine—when a conversation about some amenity of life—cookery for example—has been rudely interrupted by a stern voice from another world. "Well *I* can tell you the best meal *I* ever had. Arrowroot biscuits, rather mouldy at that, and cocoa made in an old cigarette tin. We'd done twenty-six miles safari that day, on foot, through elephant grass—two of my bearers down with dengue, etc. . . . That meal tasted better than anything I ever hope to eat in Europe." Crash! The whole structure of polite living lies in ruins. The little restaurant your informant discovered while motoring in the Dordogne is swept away, and dark doubt mounts in the mind. Has all the building been in vain? Do these men from the Equator and the Arctic Circle really know secrets of luxury that are denied to the inhabitants of more temperate regions? And in books of travel how invariably does one meet the purple passage in which the author—or more commonly the authoress—after fearful dangers and hardships has found in a bush camp comfort which he or she would not exchange for all the luxuries of civilization? So insistent is the witness that every sybarite must at one time or another have been haunted by the fear that he is on the wrong track and that his real goal lies among deserts and glaciers.

It was partly to examine this heresy that I undertook the phase of the journey I am now engaged on—from the River Berbice in British Guiana to the Rio Branco in Brazil. And now I know. I can return in confidence to the decencies and refinements of Europe. I have discovered numerous excellent reasons for such a journey, but luxury was not one of them.

I think I chose a very fair sample of the rough life, offering certainly little apparent danger but about every other negation of physical and mental comfort as it is understood in Europe. It was in fact as rough a route as one can take and still keep within the limits of legitimate travelling. Beyond that, one's journey becomes a feat of athletics. For the essence of athleticism is the overcoming of self-imposed obstacles; one first erects a series of hurdles between two points and then sees how rapidly one can travel between them, or one invents a code of rules to hinder one in propelling a ball across country, or one attempts to reach the summit of a mountain by the *most* circuitous and laborious means. The art of travelling, on the other hand, consists in the avoiding or overcoming of natural difficulties; in choosing a place difficult of access and getting there as expeditiously as possible, with the single æsthetic principle that as far as possible one should employ the materials peculiar to the place: e. g., that in a place where the normal means of communication is by canal, one should go in that way rather than by an aeroplane—and that is because the whole course of the journey is its object, not merely its terminal point. Within these qualifications, then, I can claim that the trip from the Berbice to the Rio Branco gives me authority to expose some of the heresies current about the rough life, again insisting that this essay treats the subject purely from the point of view of the epicure. There are a hundred excellent reasons that made the journey worth while. It is only when they claim to have all the tricks that the men from "the back of beyond" are bluffing.

## III

First there is the heresy about Freedom, which is perhaps the most widespread and mischievous of all. It crops up again and again in one form or another, and takes its origin, I believe, from the praise devoted to the simple life by the classical poets. But nothing could be more repugnant to Horace than "roughing it." When he eulogized the simple life he meant the life of the private citizen as distinct from courtier and politician. It is typical of the rough-life cult that it should have taken over this loyalty with it. For how often almost in paraphrase of Horace's praise of his farm, does one read praise of the camp. The authoress sits by her camp fire, with only her faithful native bearers as companions, crooning their songs in the darkness, and reflects on her independence of all the constraints of convention and civilization. . . . It is needless to quote. Everyone must be familiar with countless examples of this sort of ecstasy.

Well, it is all my eye. I have never encountered any manner of life more restricted in every way and more weighted with responsibility than life in the bush. I would sooner take charge of a troop of preparatory-school boys — I speak who have done so — than of those faithful native bearers, who combine the idleness and dishonesty of children, the blank stupidity of office girls, and the spite and jealousy of a theatrical company. One is completely responsible for and dependent on these people for the whole of one's journey; one has to make every decision in the ordering of their lives, elaborate every detail of their duties and repeat the detail on each occasion that the duty has to be performed. One has to dose them with medicine, arbitrate in their quarrels, instruct them exactly how everything must be done, each time it is done; one has to set them in motion and maintain them in motion by one's own effort, and one is completely dependent on them at every stage, for they are the link which connects you with your stores.

Here one is confronted by another of the fetters which make life in the bush the least free form of existence. Most people who study their own comfort realize soon enough that possessions are a thing to be approached with caution. The moment one becomes attached to any object one's freedom is curtailed. I have for some time adopted the austere policy of denying myself the ownership of anything I cannot put in a suitcase. I undoubtedly lose a great deal of pleasure, but I think I gain more. In the bush one has to possess whatever one wishes to use. Loss or damage to any single thing may render your whole progress impossible; a single man or animal incapacitated and your whole expedition halts with him. I was travelling extremely light, in fact with almost less than an adequate minimum; but I required besides my own horse a pack animal and three men for four weeks' journey. Consider the difference in freedom between a day in London and a day in the bush. In London you wake up, dress, and stand on your doorstep with complete liberty of choice; a vast variety of company at the other end of the telephone, a vast variety of food to eat, of books or entertainment; if the mood is on you you can step into an aeroplane and lunch in Paris or take a train to the country; a vast variety of scenery is at your disposal. In the bush duty besets you at once. Your pack-animal has to be loaded, and though it has been done in exactly the same fashion for twenty mornings, you have to supervise every detail and detect the same mistakes, a rope across the withers which will cause a gall, an unequally balanced pack that will swing loose during the morning; you have to apportion the loads to each man and see he does not surreptitiously add his to the ox's. When everything is ready, and the best, cool hour of the day wasted, you set off without possibility of deviation down the little green tunnel that is your unvarying route.

And what is this freedom from convention I read so much about? What are these prohibitions that beset female travellers in civilized life? I live among normally mannered people, and for the life of me I cannot say I am aware of any of these restrictions. On the whole, it seems to me less onerous to remember one's collar and tie, than perform the cumbrous toilet of the tropics—to shake one's shirt free of ants and search one's boots for scorpions, to rub one's body with bitter oil to keep away ticks. It seems to me more trouble to scramble down the mud bank of a forest stream for one's bath and keep a boy near you kicking up the water to warn off stinging eels and carnivorous fish, than to put on dressing-gown and slippers and go next door to the bathroom. And is it really much more oppressive to wear a bowler hat than a cork helmet? Or if it is the conventions of social intercourse that these authoresses mean, is it not easier to observe the rudimentary rules in which one has been brought up, than to adapt oneself to the extraordinary politeness of savages, to drink bowls of utterly nauseous intoxicants, exchanging compliments by means of an interpreter, to squat in dark huts in absolute silence under the scrutiny of the entire village, to shake hands with some dozens of semi-civilized mission products and pretend to understand the curious jargon of English they have acquired? I do not say that all these things are not of absorbing interest—but where does the sense of Freedom come in?

With this goes the heresy that one sleeps and eats better in the wilds. Do not believe it. Have you read with envy descriptions of the savoury stew pot full of newly shot game? There is nothing nastier. After six hours in the saddle in an atmosphere of moist heat, with two or three hours to wait for one's men to turn up with the stores, when one finds that the last occupants of the rest house have torn up the floor for firewood, have demolished the little bench that was the only furniture, and left the place scattered with rotten fish, one could find in Europe more complete rest than standing up or sitting on a tree trunk alive with ants. And lying on a hammock in the shelter of a Brazilian ranch, I have been kept awake two thirds of the night, after a day of strenuous exercise, by the smell of an ox which happened to have died a week previously some yards away, and which no one had had the trouble to remove.

Gentle reader, the object of this essay is not, Othello-like, to excite your compassion with a chronicle of the hardships and tedium of my journey. It is rather to reassure you of your own standard of living. The remedy for all these troubles—and I could mention a dozen others—is perfectly simple. If you value comfort and physical pleasure, stay at home; don't let the literary globe-trotters shake your faith in the valuable things of our civilization. We have little enough to offer, but at least in Europe we can enjoy bodily ease in a degree which has been impossible in any other age. There are plenty of reasons for travelling in obscure and inaccessible regions, but the sybarite need not concern himself with them. He is on the right track where he is.

T. S. ELIOT

# Personality and Demonic Possession

[ WINTER 1934 ]

I THINK that there is an interesting subject of investigation, for the student of traditions, in the history of Blasphemy, and the anomalous position of that term in the modern world. It is a curious survival in a society which has for the most part ceased to be capable of exercising that activity or of recognising it. I am persuaded that pretty generally, when that term is used at all, it is used in a sense which is only the shadow of the original. For modern blasphemy is merely a department of bad form: and just as, in countries which still possess a Crown, people are usually (and quite rightly) shocked by any public impertinence concerning any member of their Royal Family, they are still shocked by any public impertinence towards a Deity for whom they feel privately no respect at all; and both feelings are supported by the conservatism of those who have anything to lose by social changes. Yet people nowadays are inclined to tolerate and respect any violation which is presented to them as inspired by "serious" purposes; whereas the only disinfectant which makes either blasphemy or obscenity sufferable is the sense of humour: the indecent that is funny may be the legitimate source of innocent merriment, while the absence of humour reveals it as purely disgusting.

I do not wish to be understood as undertaking a defence of blasphemy in the abstract. I am only pointing out that it is a very different thing in the modern world than it would be in an "age of faith"; just as a magistrate's conception of blasphemy will probably be very different from that of a good Catholic, and his objections to it will be for very different reasons. The whole question of censorship is now of course reduced to ludicrous inconsistency, and is likely to remain so as long as the morals of the State are not those of the Church. But my point is that blasphemy is not a matter of good form but of right belief; no one can possibly blaspheme in any sense except that in which a parrot may be said to curse, unless he profoundly believes in that which he profanes; and when anyone who is not a believer is shocked by blasphemy he is shocked merely by a breach of good form; and it is a nice question whether, being in a state of intellectual error, he is or is not committing a sin in being shocked for the wrong reasons. It is certainly my opinion that first-rate blasphemy is one of the rarest things in literature, for it requires both literary genius and profound faith, joined in a mind in a peculiar and unusual state of spiritual sickness. I repeat that I am not defending blasphemy; I am reproaching a world in which blasphemy is impossible.

My next point is a more delicate one to handle. One can conceive of blasphemy as doing moral harm to feeble or perverse souls; at the same time one must recognize that the modern environment is so unfavourable to faith that it produces fewer and fewer individuals capable of being injured by blasphemy. One would expect, therefore, that (whatever it may have been at other times) blasphemy would be less employed by the Forces of Evil than at any other time in the last two thousand years. Where blasphemy might once have been a sign of spiritual corruption, it might now be taken rather as a symptom that the soul was still alive, or even that it was recovering animation: for the perception of Good and Evil—whatever choice we may make—is the first requisite of spiritual life. We should do well, therefore, to look elsewhere than to the blasphemer, in the traditional sense, for the most fruitful operations of the Evil Spirit today.

I regret, for my present purposes, that I have not a more intimate, extensive and accurate knowledge of the English novelists of the last hundred years, and therefore that I feel a little insecure of my generalisations. But it seems to me that the eminent novelists who are more nearly contemporary to us, have been more concerned than their predecessors—consciously or not—to impose upon their readers their own *personal view of life,* and that this is merely part of the whole movement of several centuries towards the aggrandisement and exploitation of *personality.* I do not suggest that "personality" is an illicit intruder; I imagine that the admirers of Jane Austen are all fascinated by something that may be called her personality. But personality, with Jane Austen, with Dickens, and with Thackeray, was more nearly in its proper place. The standards by which they criticised their world, if not very lofty ones, were at least not of their own making. In Dickens's novels, for instance, the religion is still of the good old torpid eighteenth-century kind, dressed up with a profusion of holly and turkey, and supplemented by strong humanitarian zeal. These novelists were still observers, however superficial—in contrast, for instance, to Flaubert—we find their observations to be. They are orthodox enough according to the light of their day: the first suspicion of heresy creeps in with a writer who, at her best, had much profounder moral insight and passion than these, but who unfortunately combined it with the dreary rationalism of the epoch of which she is one of the most colossal monuments: George Eliot. George Eliot seems to me of the same tribe as all the serious and eccentric moralists we have had since: we must respect her for being a serious moralist, but deplore her individualistic morals. What I have been leading up to is the following assertion: that when morals cease to be a matter of tradition and orthodoxy—that is, of the habits of the community, formulated, corrected, and elevated by the continuous thought and direction of the Church—and when each man is to elaborate his own, then *personality* becomes a thing of alarming importance.

The work of the late Thomas Hardy represents an interesting example of a powerful personality uncurbed by any institutional attachment or by submission to any objective beliefs; unhampered by any ideas, or even by what sometimes acts as a partial restraint upon inferior writers, the desire to please a large public. He seems to me to have written as nearly for the sake of "self-expression" as a man well can; and the self which he had to express does not strike me as a particularly wholesome or edifying communication. He was indifferent even to the prescripts of good writing: he wrote sometimes overpoweringly well, but always very carelessly; at times his style touches sublimity without ever having passed through the stage of being good. In consequence of his self-absorption, he makes a great deal of landscape; for romantic landscape is a passive creature which lends itself to an author's mood. It is fitted too for the purposes of an author who is interested not at all in men's minds, but only in their emotions; and perhaps only in men as vehicles for emotions. It is only, indeed, in their emotional paroxysms that most of his characters come alive. This extreme emotionalism seems to me a symptom of decadence; it is a cardinal point of faith in a romantic age, to believe that there is something admirable for its own sake in violent emotion, whatever the emotion or whatever its object. But it is by no means self-evident that human beings are most real when most violently excited; violent passions do not in themselves differentiate men from each other, but rather tend to reduce them to the same state; and the passion has significance only in relation to the character and behaviour of the man at other moments of his life and in other contexts. Furthermore, strong passion is only interesting or significant in strong men; those who abandon themselves without resistance to excitements which tend to deprive them of reason, become merely instruments of feeling and lose their humanity; and unless there is moral resistance and conflict there is no meaning. But as the majority is capable neither of strong emotion nor of strong resistance, it always inclines, unless instructed to the contrary, to admire passion for its own sake; and if somewhat deficient in vitality, people imagine passion to be the surest evidence of vitality. This in itself may go towards accounting for Hardy's popularity.

What again and again introduces a note of falsity into Hardy's novels is that he will leave nothing to nature, but will always be giving one last turn of the screw himself, and of his motives for so doing I have the gravest suspicion. In "The Mayor of Casterbridge"—which has always seemed to me his finest novel as a whole—he comes the nearest to producing an air of inevitability, and of making the crises seem the consequences of the character of Henchard; the arrangement by which the hero, leaning over a bridge, finds himself staring at his effigy in the stream below is a masterly tour de force. This scene is, however, as much by arrangement as less successful ones in which the motive intrudes itself more visibly; as, for instance, the scene in "Far from the Madding Crowd" in which Bathsheba unscrews Fanny Robin's coffin, which seems to me deliberately faked. And by this I mean that the author seems to me to be deliberately relieving some emotion of his own at the expense of the reader. It is a refined form of torture on the part of the writer, and a refined form of self-torture on the part of the reader. And this brings me for the first time to the point of this essay.

I have concerned myself elsewhere with illustrating the limiting and crippling effect of a separation from tradition and orthodoxy upon certain writers whom I nevertheless hold up for admiration for what they have attempted against great obstacles. Here I am concerned with the intrusion of the *diabolic* into modern literature in consequence of the same lamentable state of affairs; and it was for this reason that I took the pains at the beginning to point out that blasphemy is not a matter with which we are concerned. I am afraid that even if one can entertain the notion of a positive power for evil working through human agency, one may still have a very inaccurate notion of what Evil is, and will find it difficult to believe that it might operate through men of genius of the most excellent character. I doubt whether what I am saying can convey very much to anyone for whom the doctrine of Original Sin is not a very real and tremendous thing. I can only ask the reader to examine the texts, and then reconsider my remarks. And one of the most significant of the Hardy texts is a volume of short stories, indeed of masterly short stories, which has never received enough examination from that point of view: I mean "A Group of Noble Dames." Here, for one thing, you get essential Hardy without the Wessex staging; without the scenery dear to the Anglo-Saxon heart or the period peasants pleasing to the metropolitan imagination. Not all of these stories, of course, illustrate my point equally well; the best for my purpose, to which I refer the reader, rather than take up his time to less purpose by summarising the plot, is "Barbara of the House of Grebe." This is not realism; it is, as Hardy catalogues it, "romance and fantasy," with which Hardy can do exactly what he wants to do. I do not object to horror: "Œdipus Rex" is a most horrible plot, from which the last drop of horror is extracted by the dramatist; and among Hardy's contemporaries, Conrad's "Heart of Darkness" and James's "Turn of the Screw" are tales of horror. But there is horror in the real world; and in these works of Sophocles, Conrad, and James we are still in a world of Good and Evil. In

"Barbara of the House of Grebe" we seem to be introduced into a world of pure Evil. It would seem to have been written solely to provide a satisfaction for some morbid emotion.

I find this same strain of morbidity in the work of a man whom I regard as a very much greater genius, if not a greater artist, than Hardy: D. H. Lawrence. Lawrence has three aspects, and it is very difficult to do justice to all. I do not expect to be able to do so. The first is the ridiculous: his lack of sense of humour, a certain snobbery, a lack not so much of information as of the critical faculties which education should give, and an incapacity for what we ordinarily call thinking. Of this side of Lawrence, the brilliant exposure by Mr. Wyndham Lewis in "Paleface" is by far the most conclusive criticism that has been made. Second, there is the extraordinarily keen sensibility and capacity for profound intuition—intuition from which he commonly drew the wrong conclusions. Third, there is a distinct morbidity and hypertrophy of personality. Unfortunately, it is necessary to keep all of these aspects in mind in order to criticise the writer fairly; and this, in such close perspective, is almost impossible. I shall no doubt appear to give excessive prominence to the third; but that, after all, is what has been least successfully considered.

I have touched elsewhere upon the deplorable religious upbringing which gave Lawrence his lust for intellectual independence: like most people who do not know what orthodoxy is, he hated it. With the more intimate reasons, of heredity and environment, for eccentricity of thought and feeling I am not concerned: too many people have made them their business already. And I have already mentioned the insensibility to ordinary social morality, which is so alien to my mind that I am completely baffled by it as a monstrosity. The point is that Lawrence started life so free from any restriction of tradition or institution that he had no guidance except the Inner Light, the most untrustworthy and deceitful guide that ever offered itself to wandering humanity. It was peculiarly so for Lawrence, who does not appear to have been gifted with the faculty of self-criticism, except in flashes, even to the extent of ordinary worldly shrewdness. Of divine illumination, it may be said that probably every man knows when he has it, but that any man is likely to think that he has it when he has it not; and even when he has had it, the daily man that he is may draw the wrong conclusions from the enlightenment which the momentary man has received: no one, in short, can be the sole judge of whence his inspiration comes or what it means. A man like Lawrence, therefore, with his acute sensibility, violent prejudices and passions, and lack of intellectual and social training, is admirably fitted to be an instrument for forces of good or for forces of evil; or as we might expect, partly for one and partly for the other. A trained mind like that of Mr. Joyce is always aware what master it is serving; an untrained mind, a soul destitute of humility and filled with self-righteousness, is a blind servant and a fatal leader. It would seem that for Lawrence any spiritual force was good, and that evil resided only in the absence of spirituality. Most people, no doubt, need to be aroused to the perception of the simple difference between the spiritual and the material; and Lawrence never forgot, and never mistook, this distinction. But most people are only very little alive; and to awaken them to the spiritual is a very great responsibility: it is only when they are so awakened that they are capable of real Good, but at the same time they become first capable of Evil. Lawrence lived all his life, I should imagine, on the spiritual level; no man was less a sensualist. Against the living death of modern material civilisation he spoke again and again, and, even if these dead could speak, what he said is unanswerable. As a criticism of the modern world, "Fantasia of the Unconscious" is a book to keep at hand and reread. In contrast to Nottingham, London, or industrial America, the capering redskins of his "Mornings in Mexico" seem to represent Life. So they do; but that is not the last word, but only the first.

The intensity of the man's vision is spiritual, but spiritually sick. The dæmonic powers found an instrument of far greater range, delicacy, and power in the author of "The Prussian Officer" than in the author of "A Group of Noble Dames"; and the tale which I should use as an example, "The Shadow in the Rose Garden," can be matched by several others. I have not read all of Lawrence's late and posthumous works, which are numerous. In some respects, he may have progressed: as Mr. E. F. W. Tomlin has suggested, his early belief in Life may have passed over, as a really serious belief in Life must, into a belief in Death. But I cannot see much development in "Lady Chatterley's Lover." Our old acquaintance, the gamekeeper, turns up again: the social obsession which makes his well-born—or almost well-born—ladies offer themselves to—or make use of—plebeians, springs from the same morbidity which makes his other female characters bestow their favours upon savages. The author of that book seems to me to have been a very sick man indeed.

There is, I believe, a very great deal to be learned from Lawrence; though those who are most capable of exercising the judgement necessary to extract the lesson, may not be those who are most in need of it. That we can and ought to reconcile ourselves to Liberalism, Progress, and Modern Civilisation is a proposition which we need not have waited for Lawrence to condemn; and it matters a good deal in what name we condemn them. I fear that Lawrence's work may appeal, not to those who are well and able to discriminate, but to the sick and debile and confused; and will appeal not to what remains of health in them, but to their sickness. Nor will many even accept his doctrine as he would give it, but will be busy after their own inventions. The number of people in possession of any criteria for discriminating between good and evil is very small; the number of the half-alive, hungry for any form of spiritual experience, or what offers itself as experience, high or low, good or bad, is considerable. My own generation has not served them very well. Never has the printing-press been so busy, and never have such varieties of buncombe and false doctrine come from it. *Woe unto the foolish prophets, that follow their own spirit, and have seen nothing! O Israel, thy prophets have been like foxes in the waste places. . . . And the word of the LORD came unto me, saying, Son of man, these men have taken their idols into their heart, and put the stumblingblock of their iniquity before their face: should I be inquired of at all by them?*

I would add a few words of retrospect and summary, partly as a reminder of how little, in so short a space, one can undertake to say about such a serious subject as this. In an age of unsettled beliefs and enfeebled tradition the man of letters, the poet, and the novelist, are in a situation dangerous for themselves and for their readers. I have tried to safeguard myself from being taken to be merely a sentimental admirer of some actual or imaginary past, and from being taken as a faker of traditions. Tradition by itself is not enough; it must be perpetually criticised and brought up to date under the supervision of what I call orthodoxy; and for the lack of this supervision it is now the sentimental tenuity that we find it. Most "defenders of tradition" are mere conservatives, unable to distinguish between the permanent and the temporary, the essential and the accidental. Where there is no external test of the validity of a writer's work, we fail to distinguish between the truth of his view of life and the personality which makes it plausible; so that in our reading, we are simply yielding ourselves to one seductive personality after another. The first requisite usually held up by the promoters of personality is that a man should "be himself"; and this "sincerity" is considered more important than that the self in question should, socially and spiritually, be a good or a bad one.

This view of personality is merely an assumption on the part of the modern world, and is no more tenable than several other views which have been held at various times and in several places. The personality thus expressed, the personality which fascinates us in the work of philosophy or art, tends naturally to be the *unregenerate* personality, partly self-deceived and partly irresponsible, and because of its freedom, terribly *limited* by prejudice and self-conceit, capable of much good or great mischief according to the natural goodness or impurity of the man: and we are all, naturally, impure. All that I have been able to do here is to suggest that there are standards of criticism, not ordinarily in use, which we may apply to whatever is offered to us as works of philosophy or of art, which might help to render them safer and more profitable for us.

THOMAS WOLFE

# Old Catawba

[ SPRING 1935 ]

ON THE middle-Atlantic seaboard of the North American continent, and at about a day's journey from New York, is situated the American state of Old Catawba [North Carolina]. In area and population the state might almost strike a median among the states of the union: its territory, which is slightly more than fifty thousand square miles, is somewhat larger than the territories of most of the Atlantic coastal states, and, of course, much smaller than the great areas of the immense but sparsely populated states of the Far West. Upon this area, which is a little smaller than the combined areas of England and Wales, there live about three million people, of whom about the third part are black. Catawba, therefore, is about as big as England, and has about as many people as Norway.

The state possesses, however, a racial type and character that is probably much more strongly marked and unified than that of any European country. In fact, although America is supposed by many of her critics to be a confusion of races, tongues, and peoples, as yet unwelded, there is perhaps nowhere in the world a more homogeneous population than that of Old Catawba. Certainly, there are far greater differences in stature, temperament, speech, and habit, between a North German and a South German, a North Frenchman and a Southern Frenchman, a North of England man and a Devon man, a North Italian and a South Italian, than between a Catawban from the East and one from the West.

The name "Catawba" is, of course, an Indian name: it is the name of a tribe that is now almost extinct but which at one time flourished in considerable strength and number. The chief seat of the tribe was in South Carolina, and there is at the present time a reservation in York County of that state where the remnant is gathered together.

The way in which the State of Catawba got its name rests entirely upon misconception: the tribes that the early explorers encountered were not Catawbas, they belonged probably to a tribe that is now wholly extinct. Yet, so strong is the power of usage and association that any other name would now seem unthinkable to a native of that state. People outside the state have often said that the name has a somewhat tropical laziness in its sound, particularly when prefixed with the word "old," but there is very little that is tropical or exotic either in the appearance and character of Catawba itself, or of the people who inhabit it. To them, the name Catawba perfectly describes the state: it has the strong, rugged, and homely quality that the earth has.

In the state documents during the period of the royal proprietors, the territory is invariably referred to as "Catawba," or "His Majesty's Colony in the Catawbas": the name "Old Catawba" does not begin to appear in state papers until twenty or thirty years before the Revolution, and for what reason no one knows. The typical American method in naming places has been to prefix the word "new" to the name—*New* England, *New* York, *New* Mexico—to distinguish these places from their older namesakes. But if *New* York indicates the existence somewhere of an *old* York, *old* Catawba does not indicate the existence of a new one. The name undoubtedly grew out of the spirit of the people who had dwelt there over a century, and the name did not come from a sentimental affection, it grew imperatively from a conviction of the spirit. It is one of those names that all men begin to use at about the same time, a perfect and inevitable name that has flowered secretly within them, and that now must be spoken.

Anyone who has ever lived in the state for any length of time is bound to feel this: the word "old" is not a term of maudlin affection, it describes exactly the feeling that the earth of that state inspires—the land has a brooding presence that is immensely old and masculine, its spirit is rugged and rather desolate, yet it broods over its people with stern benevolence. The earth is a woman, but Old Catawba is a man. The earth is our mother and our nurse, and we can know her, but Old Catawba is our father, and although we know that he is there, we shall never find him. He is there in the wilderness, and his brows are bowed with granite: he sees our lives and deaths and his stern compassion broods above us. Women love him, but only men can know him: only men who have cried out in their agony and their loneliness to their father, only men who have sought throughout the world to find him, can know Catawba: but this is all the men who ever lived.

The Catawba people are great people for all manner of debate and reasoned argument. Where the more fiery South Carolinian or Mississippian will fly into a rage and want to fight the man who doubts his word or questions his opinion, the eye of the Catawban begins to glow with a fire of another sort—the lust for debate, a Scotch love of argument. Nothing pleases a Catawban better than this kind of dispute. He will say persuasively, "Now let's see if we can't see through this thing. Let's see if we can't git to the bottom of this." A long, earnest, and even passionate discussion will ensue in which the parties on both sides usually maintain the utmost good temper, kindliness, and tolerance, but in which they nevertheless pursue their arguments with great warmth and stubbornness. In these discussions several interesting traits of the Catawban quickly become manifest: the man is naturally a philosopher—he loves nothing better than to discuss abstract and difficult questions such as the nature of truth, goodness, and beauty, the essence of property, the problem of God. Moreover, in the development of his arguments the man loves the use of homely phrases and illustration, he is full of pungent metaphors drawn from his experience and environment; and in discussing an ethical question—say, the "moral right" of a man to his property, and to what extent he may profit by it—the Catawban may express himself somewhat in this manner:

"Well, now, Joe, take a case of this sort: suppose I buy a mule from a feller over there on the place next to mine, an' suppose I pay a hundred and fifty dollars fer that mule."

"Is this a one-eyed mule or a two-eyed mule you're buyin'?" Joe demands with a broad wink around at his listening audience.

"It's a two-eyed mule," the first man says good-humoredly, "but if you've got any objections to a two-eyed mule, we'll make it a one-eyed mule."

"Why, hell, no! Jim," the other man now says, "I ain't got no objections, but it seems to me if you're goin' to have a two-eyed mule you ought to have something better than a one-eyed argyment."

There is a roar of immense male laughter at this retort, punctuated with hearty slappings of thigh and knee, and high whoops in the throat.

"By d-*damn!*" one of the appreciative listeners cries, when he can get his breath, "I reckon that'll hold 'im fer a while."

The story or the "two-eyed mule and the one-eyed argyment" is indeed an immense success, it is the kind of phrase and yarn these people love, and it is destined for an immediate and wide circulation all over the community, accompanied by roars and whoops of laughter. It may even be raised to the dignity of proverbial usage so that one will hear men saying, "Well, that's a two-eyed mule an' a one-eyed argyment if I ever saw one," and certainly the unfortunate Jim may expect to be greeted for some time to come in this way:

"Howdy, Jim. I hear you've gone into the mule business," or, "Hey, Jim, you ain't bought no two-eyed mules lately, have you?" or, "Say, Jim: you ain't seen a feller with a one-eyed argyment lookin' fer a two-eyed mule, have you?"

Jim knows very well that he is "in" for this kind of treatment, but he joins in the laughter good-humoredly, although his clay-red face burns with a deeper hue and he awaits the resumption of debate with a more dogged and determined air.

"Well, that's all right about that," he says, when he can make himself heard. "Whether he's a one-eyed mule or a two-eyed mule is neither here nor there."

"Maybe one eye is here, an' t'other there," someone suggests, and this sets them off again at Jim's expense. But Jim has the determination of the debater and the philosopher, and although his face is pretty red by now, he sticks to his job.

"All right," he says at length, "say I got a mule, anyway, an' he's a good mule, an' I paid one hundred and fifty dollars fer him. Now!" he says, pausing, and lifting one finger impressively. "I take that mule an' work him on my farm fer *four* years. He's a *good* mule an' a *good* worker an' durin' that time he pays fer himself *twice* over! Now!" he declares again, pausing and looking triumphantly at his opponent, Joe, before resuming his argument.

"All right! All right!" Joe says patiently with an air of resignation. "I heard you. I'm still waitin'. You ain't *said* nothin' yet. You ain't *proved* nothin' yet."

"Now!" Jim continues slowly and triumphantly. "I gave one hundred and fifty dollars fer him but he's earned his keep an' paid fer himself *twice* over."

"I heard you! I heard you!" says Joe patiently.

"In other words," someone says, "you got back what you paid fer that mule with one hundred and fifty dollars to boot."

"Egs-actly!" Jim says with decision, to the group that is now listening intently. "I got back what I put into him an' I got one hundred fifty dollars to boot. Now here comes another feller," he continues, pointing indefinitely towards the western horizon, "who *needs* a good mule, an' he sees *my* mule, an' he *offers to buy it!*" Here Jim pauses again, and he turns and surveys his audience with triumph written on his face.

"*I* heard you. *I'm* listenin'," says Joe in a patient and monotonous voice.

"How much does *he* offer you?" someone asks.

"Now, wait a minute! I'm comin' to that," says Jim with a silencing gesture. "This here feller says, 'That's a perty good mule you got there!' 'I reckon he'll do!' I say. 'I ain't got no complaint to make!' 'I'm thinkin' of buyin' a mule myse'f,' he says. 'That so?' I say. 'Yes,' he says, 'I could use another mule on my farm. You ain't thinkin' of sellin' that mule there, are you?' 'No,' I say, 'I ain't *thinkin'* of it.' 'Well,' he says, 'would you consider an offer fer him?' 'Well,' I say, 'I might an' I might not. It all depends.' 'How much will you take fer him?' he says. 'Well,' I say, 'I ain't never thought of sellin' him before. I'd rather you'd make an offer. How much will you give?' 'Well,' he says, 'how about three hundred dollars?'"

There is a pause of living silence now while Jim turns finally and triumphantly upon his audience.

"*Now!*" he cries again, powerfully, and decisively, leaning forward with one big hand gripped upon his knee and his great index finger pointed toward them.

"I'm *listenin'*," Joe says in a calm but foreboding tone.

"I *got* my money back out o' that mule," Jim says, beginning a final recapitulation.

"Yes, an' you got another hundred an' fifty to boot," someone helpfully suggests.

"That makes *one* hundred per cent clear profit on my 'riginal investment," Jim says. "Now here comes a feller who's willin' to pay me three hundred dollars on top of that. That makes *three* hundred per cent."

He pauses now with a conclusive air.

"Well?" says Joe heavily. "Go on. I'm still waitin'. What's the argyment?"

"Why," says Jim, "the argyment is this: I *got* my money back—"

"We all *know* that," says Joe. "You got your money back an' hundred per cent to boot."

"Well," says Jim, "the argyment is this: Have I any *right* to take the three hundred dollars that feller offers me?"

"Right?" says Joe, staring at him. "Why, what are you talkin' about? Of course, you got the right. The mule's yours, ain't he?"

"Ah!" says Jim with a knowing look, "that's just the point. *Is* he?"

"You *said* you bought an' *paid* fer him, didn't you?" someone said.

"Yes," said Jim, "I did that, all right."

"Why hell, Jim," someone else says, "you just ain't talkin' sense. A man's got the right to sell his own property."

"The *legal* right," Jim says, "The *legal* right! Yes! But I ain't talkin' about the *legal* right. I'm talkin' about the *mawral* right."

They gaze at Jim for a moment with an expression of slack-jawed stupefaction mixed with awe. Then he continues:

"A man's got a right to buy a piece of property an' to sell it an' to git a fair profit on his investment. I ain't denyin' that. But has *any* man," he continues, "a right—a mawral right—to a profit of three hundred per cent?"

Now Jim has made his point, he is content to rest for a moment and await the attack that comes, and comes immediately: after a moment's silence there is a tumult of protest, derisive laughter, strong cries of denial, a confusion of many voices all shouting disagreement, above which Joe's heavy baritone finally makes itself heard.

"Why, Jim!" he roars. "That's the damnedest logic I ever did hear. I did give you credit fer havin' at least a *one*-eyed argyment, but I'm damned if this argyment you're givin' us has any eyes a-tall!"

Laughter here, and shouts of agreement.

"Why, Jim!" another one says with solemn humor, with an air of deep concern, "you want to go to see a doctor, son: you've begun to talk funny. Don't you know that?"

"*All* right. *All* right!" says Jim doggedly. "You can laugh all you please, but there's two sides to this here question, no matter what you think."

"Why, Jim!" another one says, with a loose grin playing around his mouth. "What you goin' to do with that two-eyed mule? You goin' to *give* him away to that feller simply because you got your money out of him?"

"I ain't sayin'!" says Jim stubbornly, looking very red in the face of their laughter. "I ain't sayin' what I'd do. Mebbe I would and mebbe I wouldn't."

There is a roar of laughter this time, and the chorus of derisive voices is more emphatic than ever. But for some moments now, while this clamor has been going on, one of the company has fallen silent, he has fallen into a deep study, into an attitude of earnest meditation. But now he rouses himself and looks around with an expression of commanding seriousness.

"Hold on a moment there, boys," he says. "I'm not so sure about all this. I don't know that Jim's such a fool as you think he is. 'Pears to me there may be something in what he says."

"Now!" says Joe, with an air of finality. "What did I tell you! The woods are full of 'em. Here's another 'un that ain't all there."

But the contest is now just beginning in earnest: it goes on furiously, but very seriously, from now on, with these two Horatiuses holding their bridge valiantly and gaining in strength and conviction at each assault. It is a remarkable circumstance that at almost every gathering of Catawbans there is one or more of these minority warriors who become more thoughtful and dubious as their companions grow more vociferous in their agreement and derision, and who, finally, from a first mild expression of doubt, become hotly embattled on the weaker side, and grow in courage and conviction at every breath, every word they utter, every attack they make or repel.

And it has always been the same with the Catawba people. Their character has strong Scotch markings: they are cautious and deliberate, slow to make a radical decision. They are great talkers, and believe in prayer and argument. They want to "reason a thing out," they want to "git to the bottom of a thing" through discussion, they want to settle a thing peaceably by the use of diplomacy and compromise. They are perhaps the most immensely conservative people on earth, they reverence authority, tradition, and leadership, but when committed to any decision, they stick to it implacably, and if the decision is war, they will fight to the end with the fury of maniacs. [. . .]

The Catawban's [. . .] heart is a lonely and secret heart, his spirit is immensely brave and humble, he has lived alone in the wilderness, he has heard the silence of the earth, he knows what he knows, and he has not spoken yet. We see him, silent and unheralded, in the brief glare of recorded event—he is there in the ranks of the American Revolution, and eighty years later he is there, gloriously but silently, in the ranks of the Civil War. But his real history is much longer and much more extraordinary than could be indicated by these flares of war: it is a history that goes back three centuries into primitive America, a strange and unfathomable history that is touched by something dark and supernatural, and that goes back through poverty, and hardship, through solitude and loneliness and death and unspeakable courage, into the wilderness. For it is the wilderness that is the mother of that nation, it was in the wilderness that the strange and lonely people who have not yet spoken, but who inhabit that immense and terrible land from East to West, first knew themselves, it was in the living wilderness that they faced one another at ten paces and shot one another down, and it is in the wilderness that they still live, waiting until the unspeakable thing in them shall be spoken, until they can unlock their hearts and wreak out the dark burden of their spirit—the legend of loneliness, of exile, and eternal wandering that is in them.

The real history of Old Catawba is not essentially a history of wars or rebellions; it is not a history of politics or corrupt officials; it is not a history of democracy or plutocracy or any form of government; it is not a history of business men, puritans, knaves, fools, saints, or heroes; it is not a history of culture or barbarism.

The real history of Old Catawba is a history of solitude, of the wilderness, and of the immense and eternal earth, it is the history of millions of men living and dying alone in the wilderness, it is the history of the billion unrecorded and forgotten acts and moments of their lives; it is a history of the sun and the moon and the earth, of the sea that with lapse and reluctation of its breath, feathers eternally against the desolate coasts, and of great trees that smash down in lone solitudes of the wilderness; it is a history of time, dark time, strange secret time, forever flowing like a river.

The history of Old Catawba is the history of millions of men living alone in the wilderness, it is the history of millions of men who have lived their brief lives in silence upon the everlasting earth, who have listened to the earth and known her million tongues, whose lives were given to the earth, whose bones and flesh are recompacted with the earth, the immense and terrible American earth that makes no answer.

# ELEANOR ROOSEVELT

## Keepers of Democracy

[ WINTER 1939 ]

RECENTLY a radio broadcast was given, based on a story written by H. G. Wells some years ago, called "War of the Worlds." For the purpose of dramatization it was placed in the United States with the names of regions and people who would naturally be involved if such a thing were to happen today. The basic idea was not changed; these invaders were supernatural beings from another planet who straddled the skyway and dealt in death rays, but it was dramatically done with many realistic touches.

I do not wish to enter into a discussion here as to whether the broadcasting company should do dramatizations of this type, nor do I wish to cast aspersions on people who may not have read the original book. But the results of this broadcast were the best illustration of the state of mind in which we as a nation find ourselves today. A sane people, living in an atmosphere of fearlessness, does not suddenly become hysterical at the threat of invasion, even from more credible sources, let alone by the Martians from another planet, but we have allowed ourselves to be fed on propaganda which has created a fear complex. For the past few years, nearly all of our organizations and many individuals have said something about the necessity for fighting dangerous and subversive elements in our midst.

If you are in the South someone tells you solemnly that all the members of the Committee for Industrial Organization are Communists, or that the Negroes are all Communists. This last statement derives from the fact that, being for the most part unskilled labor, Negroes are more apt to be organized by the Committee for Industrial Organization. In another part of the country someone tells you solemnly that the schools of the country are menaced because they are all under the influence of Jewish teachers and that the Jews, forsooth, are all Communists. And so it goes, until finally you realize that people have reached a point where anything which will save them from Communism is a godsend; and if Fascism or Nazi-ism promises more security than our own democracy we may even turn to them.

It is all as bewildering as our growing hysterical over the invasion of the Martians! Somehow or other I have a feeling that our forefathers, who left their women and children in the wildernesses while they traveled weary miles to buy supplies, and who knew they were leaving them to meet

Indians if need be, and to defend themselves as best they could, would expect us to meet present-day dangers with more courage than we seem to have. It is not only physical courage which we need, the kind of physical courage which in the face of danger can at least control the outward evidences of fear. It is moral courage as well, the courage which can make up its mind whether it thinks something is right or wrong, make a material or personal sacrifice if necessary, and take the consequences which may come.

I shall always remember someone, it may have been Theodore Roosevelt, saying in my hearing when I was young that when you were afraid to do a thing, that was the time to go and do it. Every time we shirk making up our minds or standing up for a cause in which we believe, we weaken our character and our ability to be fearless. There is a growing wave in this country of fear, and of intolerance which springs from fear. Sometimes it is a religious intolerance, sometimes it is a racial intolerance, but all intolerance grows from the same roots. I can best illustrate this fear by telling you that a short time ago someone told me in all seriousness that the American Youth Congress was a Communist organization and that the World Youth Congress was Communist controlled. This person really believed that the young people who were members of these organizations were attempting to overthrow by force the governments of the countries in which they belonged.

Undoubtedly, in the World Youth Congress there were young Communists, just as there are a group of young Communists and a group of young Socialists in the American Youth Congress, but this does not mean that either of these bodies is Communist controlled. It simply means that they conform to the pattern of society, which at all times has groups thinking over a wide range, from what we call extreme left to extreme right. The general movement of civilization, however, goes on in accordance with the thinking of the majority of the people, and that was exactly what happened in both the American Youth Congress and the World Youth Congress.

The resolutions finally passed by both bodies were rather sane and calm, perhaps a trifle idealistic and certainly very optimistic. There were amendments offered for discussion, and voted down, which many people might have considered radical; but since there is radical thinking among both young and old, it seems to me wiser to discuss and vote down an idea than to ignore it. By so doing we know in which direction the real trend of thought is growing. If we take the attitude that youth, even youth when it belongs to the Communist party, cannot be met on the basis of equal consideration and a willingness to listen, then we are again beginning to allow our fears of this particular group to overwhelm us and we are losing the opportunity to make our experience available and useful to the next generation.

I do not believe that oppression anywhere or injustice which is tolerated by the people of any country toward any group in that country is a healthy influence. I feel that unless we learn to live together as individuals and as groups, and to find ways of settling our difficulties without showing fear of each other and resorting to force, we cannot hope to see our democracy successful. It is an indisputable fact that democracy cannot survive where force and not law is the ultimate court of appeal. Every time we permit force to enter into a situation between employer and employee we have weakened the power of democracy and the confidence which a democratic people must have in their ability to make laws to meet the conditions under which they live, and, when necessary, to change those laws with due political process according to the will of the majority of the people.

When we permit religious prejudice to gain headway in our midst, when we allow one group of people to look down upon another, then we may for a short time bring hardship on some particular group of people, but the real hardship and the real wrong is done to democracy and to our nation as a whole. We are then breeding people who cannot live under a democratic form of government but must be controlled by force. We have but to look out into the world to see how easy it is to become stultified, to accept without protest wrongs done to others, and to shift the burden of decision and of responsibility for any action onto some vague thing called a government or some individual called a leader.

It is true today that democracies are in danger because there are forces opposed to their way of thinking abroad in the world; but more than democracies are at stake. When force becomes so necessary that practically all nations decide that they must engage in a race which will make them able to back up what they have to say with arms and will thus oblige the rest of the world to listen to them, then we face an ultimate Armageddon, unless at the same time an effort to find some other solution is never abandoned.

We in this country may look at it more calmly than the rest of the world, for we can pay for force over a longer period of time; and for a while at least our people will not suffer as much as some of the other nations of the world, but the building up of physical forces is an interminable race. Do you see where it will end unless some strong movement for an ultimate change is afoot?

Someone may say: "But we need only go on until the men who at present have power in the world and who believe in force are gone." But when in the past has there been a time when such men did not exist? If our civilization is to survive and democracies are to live, then the people of the world as a whole must be stronger than such leaders. That is the way of democracy, that is the only way to a rule of law and order as opposed to a rule of force.

We can read the history of civilization, its ups and its downs as they have occurred under the rule of force. Underlying that history is the story of each individual's fears. It seems to me a challenge to women in this period of our civilization to foster democracy and to refuse to fall a prey to fear. Only our young people still seem to have some strength and hope, and apparently we are afraid to give them a helping hand.

Someone said to me the other day that, acknowledging all the weaknesses of human nature, one must still believe in the basic good of humanity or fall into cynicism and the philosophy of old Omar Khayyam. I do still believe that there is within most of us a basic desire to live uprightly and kindly with our neighbors, but I also feel that we are at present in the grip of a wave of fear which threatens to overcome us. I think we need a rude awakening, to make us exert all the strength we have to face facts as they are in our country and in the world, and to make us willing to sacrifice all that we have from the material standpoint in order that freedom and democracy may not perish from this earth.

# The Nineteen Forties

THOMAS MANN

## Thinking and Living

[ SUMMER 1941 ]

LYING before me on a piece of velvet is a memento from my travels, a small ornamental object I was awarded as an honor. It is a little gold key with rings attached to it, engraved on one side with three stars forming a triangle, a pointing hand, and between them the Greek letters ΦBK. The other side bears the name of the owner, the date 1941, and also the year when the society of American scholars that uses this key as its emblem was founded: It has been in existence for 165 years, and last March I was admitted to the chapter in Berkeley.

It was a kind gesture for which I am most appreciative—how could I not be? A capacity for appreciating life and all that life brings with it is the chief and most fundamental capacity of a writer; for being a writer does not involve inventing things, it involves taking things that occur and making something out of them. And that, in turn, involves thinking about what they mean. But "think" and "thank" are related words; thinking has a great deal to do with thanking. We show thankfulness for life by writing about it thoughtfully. *Viel zu denken, viel zu sinnen gibt's beim zarten Lebensfaden*—"There is much ground for thought, much for reflection in the fragile thread of life"—says one of the Fates in *Faust,* the work of a writer who could not conceive otherwise than that thoughts are gifts of gratitude offered to life by the mind, and the only life that can truly be called living is the life of the mind.

To my sense of gratitude it appears as if many thoughts could be attached to the small gold emblem on my desk. Phi Beta Kappa stands for "Philosophia biou kubernetes," "philosophy, the guide of life." A fine, meaningful maxim, it seems to me, and one enormously relevant today, even though it is the legacy of a bygone century.\* It strikes me as relevant, however, because it makes the connection between philosophy and *life,* emphasizing the responsibility that philosophy bears for life as its leader and mistress. I would call it a democratic maxim, for the high form of pragmatism that makes philosophical reflection—*thinking*—responsible for human

\* In the original German text Mann translates the Greek word *kubernetes* as *Führer* (in the feminine form because philosophy is a feminine noun). In 1941 a reader of the German text would have been reminded of another *Führer:* Adolf Hitler. *Trans.*

[ 59 ]

life, and for the consequences in life and reality, is something fundamentally democratic. The most profound cause for the weakness of democracy in Germany and for the country's present catastrophic state lies not in the political sphere, but rather in the psychological and intellectual sphere. It lies in the lack, perhaps on the most basic and essential level, of a kind of pragmatism that boils down to respect for real life, a sense of intellectual responsibility for life and for the effects that ideas have on reality, on the social and political lives of real people.

Recently I read an essay containing reflections on culture and freedom by an Englishman who was openly critical of the nature of the German intellectual tradition and its ultimate destiny. It is fair-minded, respectful criticism, and that makes his accuracy in hitting the exact sore spot I have in mind only more devastating. "I feel for German culture a sympathy which is deep and genuine," says the author. "But at the same time this feeling of sympathy has always been accompanied by a feeling of despair. It is as though every road taken by German poets and philosophers led to the edge of an abyss—an abyss from which they could not withdraw, but must fall into headlong,—an abyss of intellect no longer controlled by any awareness of the sensuous realities of life."

That is excellently put, and it is unnecessary to tell this critic that the "despair" and pain that the foreign admirer of German culture feels on regarding it is all too familiar to those of us who belong to this culture and stand in its traditions. Every nation has its own peculiar characteristics, and no matter how blithely and complacently its people may accept and embody them, these qualities will be a source of pain to its intellectuals. But Germans feel this pain most acutely and radically, and the British writer I have quoted does not stint with examples of the "orgies of national self-flagellation" in which great representatives of the German philosophical tradition have indulged—to the great detriment of their popularity, of course. One of the most "despairing" is Nietzsche—and he had good cause, for where did the catastrophic fate that guides the paths of German philosophy appear more clearly than in him: namely, the tendency to teeter on the brink of the intellectual abyss where all sense of responsibility for the consequences of an idea in the sphere of human reality vanishes.

Nietzsche, creator of the most fascinating and colorful philosophy—or poetic intellectual criticism—of our time, was himself of a delicate and artistic nature, capable of deep suffering; a man to whom all brutality and primitive robust health were foreign; a *Christian* nature, if not in the religious sense of the word, then at least in the sense of his constitutional makeup. But in heroic opposition to his own self, he developed an intemperate, antihumane doctrine, having as its favorite concepts power, instinct, dynamism, the "superman," unreflecting cruelty, the "blond beast," and amorally triumphant vitality. At times, in his private correspondence, an utterly different Nietzsche from the author is revealed. When Friedrich III, the liberal, pro-English kaiser died of cancer,* the man who glorified Cesare Borgia wrote from Italy to a friend that this death was a great and decisive misfortune for Germany; the last "hope for German freedom" had died with him. This is the simple, natural, and unaffected statement of an intellectual who as such loved freedom and was dependent upon it. It is the instinctive and—compared with the hectic boldness of his philosophy—even banal expression of Nietzsche's relationship to real life. His philosophical doctrine, by contrast, was an intoxicated romantic poem, which he composed without giving a thought to how his ideas might look in the context of political reality, and his great and tragic work contributed disastrously to the very death of "German freedom" he mentions in his letter.

"But that's not what I meant!" Such is the lament heard everywhere time and again when an idea is actually put into practice. But the obscuring and corrupting effect real human life has on ideas is not the same as the reckless arrogance of an intellect that boldly—and culpably—dismisses reality, refusing to take it into account in the least. Who can doubt that Nietzsche would turn over in his grave if news ever reached him there about what has been done with his philosophy of power? If he were alive, his personal fate would match the simple, intellectually unpretentious passage from the letter I quoted; it would have nothing to do with his doctrine. The man who lived as an emigrant already in the kaiser's day—where would he be today? He would be here with us in America, and American forbearance might even see to it that he was elected an honorary member of Phi Beta Kappa . . .

I am not joking, although of course hypothetically transporting the dead to the present day can only be a form of intellectual jest. The scholarly society on whose mysterious, Masonic-sounding name I have been musing is as old as the nation and its freedom, but if this name could ever lose its relevance, today it remains contemporary to an astonishing degree. The present era has impressed on the conscience of all of us that thought has a duty to life, and the notion of philosophy as *l'art pour l'art*, as an intellectual game and adventure separate from the rest of life, strikes us today as catastrophically lacking in good sense and a foolish sacrilege.

Unmistakably, the intellectual trend of the present day is leading to a *moral* epoch, an epoch of new religious and moral distinctions and a new recognition of good and evil. That means a certain simplification and rejuvenation of intellectual life, as opposed to all weary and skeptical sophistication. It is the intellect's way of "rebarbarizing" itself. We have become aware of evil in a form so utterly degraded and repellent that we have decided to take the side of good, straightforwardly and without a trace of

---

* After reigning for three months in 1888. *Trans.*

irony, in a way that would have been regarded as insufficiently "intellectual" only a short while ago. Freedom, truth, justice, humanity—intellectuals dare to defend them again, showing more daring thereby than in attacking and mocking them. We are no longer embarrassed by them, as we thought we had to be when it seemed they could be taken for granted. Now, when they are in the gravest danger of being destroyed, the scholar or intellectual has become aware that they are his daily bread, the air he breathes, life itself; and he grasps the fact that he must fight for them or be destroyed himself.

Philosophy shares the fate of democracy. It is forced to be militant from the simple motive of self-preservation. In the world that Hitler's victory would bring about, in a gestapo world of universal enslavement, there would be no philosophy at all any more, just as there would be no democracy. There would also be no religion and no morality. Very few people realize, even today, what a moral catastrophe such a victory would mean for the human race. Very few can imagine the psychological devastation, moral chaos, and hopelessness that would result if humanity were forced to accept the final triumph of evil in the world, the triumph of lies and brute force, as a *fait accompli*. The impression that the great Lisbon earthquake made on people in the eighteenth century has not been forgotten, and that was only a phenomenon of nature. That natural catastrophe cost the Lord many thousands of believers, for people said to themselves, understandably, that a world in which something so horrible could happen could not possibly be ruled by an all-benevolent, all-wise God. I venture to say that the anti-religious effect of the Lisbon earthquake would be child's play compared to the morally ruinous and devastating effect of a final victory by Hitler.

Does this mean that philosophy must subordinate itself to politics and itself become political? That is not what I am saying. What I mean to say is that the problem of humanity forms a unity whose various spheres and forms of expression cannot be separated from one another. The fatal error of the educated German upper class was to draw a sharp dividing line between the intellect and life, between philosophy and political reality, and to look down disdainfully on the sphere of society and politics from the heights of an absolute culture. That is why this class in Germany is now so humiliated and powerless.

Philosophy as the guiding force of life means something else as well: It means that philosophy must take life as its point of orientation and polestar. The glorification of "life" at the expense of intellect, so fashionable only a short while ago, was folly, and it is no less a folly for the intellect to indulge itself in sterile, uncaring games at the expense of life. Totalitarian politics is foul, diabolical evil. The true totality we oppose to it is that of human nature.

NIKA STANDEN

# A Meal in Anacapri

[ SPRING 1944 ]

O NE GREAT HELP in getting off to a good start in Anacapri—this was about eight years ago—was the very fact that I had come to Anacapri, instead of staying in Capri, the fashionable resort down the side of the mountain, where most of the visiting foreigners stay. It was out of season, and the Anacapresi were pleased at an interruption of the dullness of their lives.

Not that my arrival was any great event, but a new person always gives something to talk about. The island of Capri had been recommended to me for a rest cure for a serious illness, and I took lodgings with a comfortable balcony, where I reclined all day on a chaise longue. I had nothing to do but listen to conversation, which floated up to me from the street below, and the Anacapresi always seemed to have time for plenty of conversation. A new arrival who is never seen provides ample talking material, for there is no limit to speculation, and I soon knew, not only about the village, but all about myself.

I am sufficiently Italian to know that the important thing—the paramount thing—is to be known as a *signora seria*. I must have got off to a good start in this also, for it was not long before I heard myself praised for the steadiness of my life, and my habit of not smoking.

Several ladies called, and were vary sympathetic about the illness, recommending different climates, different positions on the chaise longue, and different vegetable tonics. The only thing which could cause even the minutest flutter was a visit from the local priest—that is, from the priest for that particular division of Anacapri—a dignified old cleric, who talked to me very charmingly about the antiquities of the village, which are quiet and modest, making no comparison at all with those of the other end of the island, where the odor of Tiberius still lingers.

The climate was delightful, and very effective, for soon I was able to get up, and a little later I could walk about the village in a modest way. I was even invited to a dinner, given by the priests of Anacapri for well-to-do and respectable citizens, so that my social progress must have been really splendid. The priests looked formidable, all together in black. They explained that they wished to beautify the church with a new statute of the Virgin, and the party was to discuss ways and means of raising money for this. It was decided to hold a lottery, and of course I took a large block of tickets. I was introduced to the *Arciprete,* but for the rest of the evening he was out of conversational range, although within earshot, for I heard him, talking to a Lady who obviously had known neither Sin nor Temptation, saying that Modern Woman was a scandal, for she painted her lips and dressed without seemliness. I had prudently worn a most decent black garment, with long sleeves and high neck, so I felt that my *serietá* would remain undimmed.

When the lottery day arrived, I could stay up all the time and walk about quite a lot, though I was still to avoid excitement. I took my seat in the piazza, among all the villagers, waiting to hear who were the fortunate ones. The *Arciprete* came onto the platform, where the priests and the local dignitaries were, and began a little speech about the new statue. Then a little seven-year-old girl, in an angelic white dress, but with flashing black eyes, was blindfolded and began drawing the numbers from a bowl, and the *Arciprete* announced the winners, beginning with the lowest prizes.

Tension mounted high for the last to be announced, the first prize. I remembered the doctors' orders, and began to relax. The *Arciprete* read out the number "Cento Settant' Otto."

"Who has Cento Settant' Otto?" Everything began to swim around me; there was no doubt about it, the number on one of the tickets in my hand was 178.

"Will the owner of 178 please step forward to receive the prize?" Still swimming in my dream, I moved out into the aisle, and began to step forward. I had suddenly become the owner of the first prize, and this was, by the munificence of one of the rich citizens, a beautiful little grey donkey.

As I stumbled along the aisle, I had to do some quick thinking. To receive the donkey was simple, but what to do with it was a problem. Was I to take it back with me to London, to become the Costers' Pearly Queen? By the time I reached the platform, I had the solution. Directly after the *Arciprete,* with a little bow, had delivered the halter of the donkey into my hands, I asked him who was the villager the most unfortunate, the most poverty stricken, and the most industrious, who would benefit most from the gift of a donkey. For I intended to bestow my prize in the village, upon the person most worthy to receive it. At this the *Arciprete* literally radiated.

"Ah! What fortune," he said, "what fortune that we should have among us such a fine and beautiful and distinguished *signora,* who will become a benefactress to the village. For after winning this fine and handsome prize, what does she do but offer to give it away to the most needful citizen. If it would please the *signora,* I suggest that she might give it to Gennaro Squagliuzzi, who is a poor fisherman, and has eleven children, and is pious and diligent, and it is hard for him to fill all the mouths that cry to him for bread."

How things got started, from then on, I was not able to remember clearly. The meeting, that is to say the whole village, resolved itself into a procession, which went slowly from the piazza to the hut of the Squagliuzzi family.

When we reached Gennaro's hut, the *Arciprete* had his speech all ready, and it was very fine indeed. The gist of it was that I was a public benefactress, and worthy of heaven knows what honors in the village. Also, I was a very fine *signora seria,* with every virtue and every grace. Gennaro Squagliuzzi, who looked just as a fisherman from Capri should look, was embarrassed, and sincerely grateful. His worn-looking wife called all the blessings of the saints upon me, and kept on kissing the medal of the Virgin that hung on her black dress. We were not invited into the house, but Gennaro made a little impromptu speech that was dignified and most moving. He enumerated his eleven difficulties, with a short eulogy of me between each. Peppino was a fine strong lad, but lazy; Nunziatina was a good girl, and the donkey, the munificent gift of the *signora,* would be wonderfully useful when she bought things in the village; and so on down to Cecchina, who had just been weaned; and finally Nicolino, who had been baptized only last week, and was already quieter because his original sin had been driven out. The whole family would be eternally grateful to the fine and beautiful *signora,* who had made them such a rich gift, and they would all pray for her.

The very next morning the brass band of the village assembled right under my balcony to play tunes for me, especially "The Last Round Up," which had taken the island by storm. I invited them all to come up to the balcony, to drink what in Italian is called a Vermouth of Honor. They declared themselves to be honored by this, perhaps just as honored as I truly felt myself to be.

The same evening I went out to dine with the priests again. I sat next to the *Arciprete,* who told me what an admiration he had for the best type of Nordic womanhood, especially when it was tempered with Italian blood, as in my case.

A few days later I had a delightfully worded, formal dinner invitation from Gennaro Squagliuzzi. His house had been cleaned spick and span. Since it was a two-room affair, we were to eat in the kitchen, and to make the occasion more festive, the big bed in which half of the family slept had been pushed into the other room, and a new coat of whitewash applied to the walls. All the Squagliuzzi offspring were present, so dreadfully scrubbed that I felt sorry for them. At first, we grown-ups, including the children down to number eight, drank our respective healths in marsala. Conservation proceeded on stately lines: we enquired into each other's families and in-laws, and Signora Squagliuzzi asked me how many children I had. So urgent was her tone of voice, that I felt ashamed to own to less than four, whom I invented and named on the spot.

The dinner was ready. The table was laid with a shining and obviously new white cloth, and a big bunch of red paper carnations adorned the center. Gennaro explained that we were to have a typically Caprese meal, with typical Caprese *allegria,* pointing to the jugs of wine on the table. He had been fortunate, he said, and was able to offer me a very special dish. It was a naked cuttlefish, boiled and dark brown in color, as large as Nicolino's head, with heaven knows how many tentacles. It tasted to me like very strong-flavored India rubber, and its looks were worse than its taste. I must have been successful in eating it all down with a poker face, but my virtue served me ill, for another and larger helping was heaped on my plate. However, it was socially a successful meal, and we parted with thanks for each other's exquisite kindness, as they say in Italy.

For the rest of my stay in Anacapri, my reputation remained on the same high level. I retired again to my chaise longue, and made few public appearances; thus the legend about me was not dulled by familiarity. What did happen, I had known was going to happen, for I had tried cuttlefish once before, and found out not only that I do not like it, but also that I am violently allergic to it. I came out in boils, many of them, in inconvenient places. The whole village said: "*Povera signora,* she is so ill, and has come to Anacapri to get better. The good food and good climate here will soon make her well." The scars of the boils have always remained with me.

As for the original ailment, which brought me to Anacapri, the rest cure was complete.

# JEAN-PAUL SARTRE

# We Write for Our Own Time

[ SPRING 1947 ]

WE TAKE our stand against certain critics and authors. We declare that salvation must be won upon this earth, that it must be won for the whole man by the whole man, and that art is a meditation on life, not on death. It is true that for history, only talent is important. But I have not yet entered history, and I do not know how I will enter it: perhaps alone, perhaps in an anonymous crowd, perhaps as one of those names that one finds in the notes of textbooks on literature. In any case, I shall not worry about the judgments that the future may pronounce upon my work, because there is nothing I can do about them. Art cannot be reduced to a dialogue with dead men and men as yet unborn: that would be both too hard and too easy. In my opinion, this idea constitutes the last trace of the Christian belief in immortality: just as the sojourn of man upon this earth is represented as a brief testing time between Limbo and Hell or Heaven, so a book is supposed to enjoy a transitory period that is approximately the same as that of its effectiveness; after that, disincarnated and free as a soul, it enters eternity. But at least for Christians our sojourn upon earth is the decisive factor and eternal beatitude is only a reward. Yet people seem to believe that the career our books have after we are no more should be justified by the life we once led. This is true from an objective point of view. Objectively, we are classified according to our talent. But the perspective our grandchildren will have upon us is not infallible, since others will come after them and judge them in their turn. It goes without saying that we all write out of need for the absolute; and a work of the spirit is, indeed, an absolute. However, people make a double mistake on this score. First, it is not true that a writer raises his sufferings or his errors to the level of the absolute by writing about them; and it is not true that he redeems them. People say of the unhappily married man who writes well about marriage that he has made a good book *out of* his conjugal misery. That would be too easy. The bee makes honey *out of* the flower by causing *real* transformations in the substance of the flower; the sculptor makes a statue *out of* marble. But the writer makes books out of words, not out of his sorrows. If he wants to stop his wife from behaving badly, he should not write about her; he should beat her. One cannot *put* one's misfortunes into a book, any more than one can put a model on a canvas; one draws inspiration from one's misfortunes—and they remain as they are. Perhaps one gets temporary consolation from placing oneself above them in order to describe them, but once the book is finished, one finds them again. Bad faith begins when the artist tries to give meaning, a sort of immanent finality, to his troubles and persuades himself that they are there *so that* he can talk about them. When he justifies his own sufferings by this deception, he makes himself ridiculous; but he is despicable if he tries to justify the sufferings of others in the same fashion. The most beautiful book in the world will not redeem the sufferings of a child. We cannot redeem evil, we must combat it. The most beautiful book in the world redeems itself and redeems the artist, but not the man; no more than the man can redeem the artist. We want the man and the artist to win salvation together; we want the work of art to be an act as well; we want it to be expressly conceived as an arm in man's struggle against evil.

The other mistake is equally serious: there is in every human heart such a hunger for the absolute, that people have often confused eternity, which would be a timeless absolute, with immortality which is only a perpetual delay of execution and a long series of vicissitudes. I understand this desire for the absolute very well. I desire it also. But need we go so far afield to look for it? It is there all around us, under our feet and in all our gestures. We make absolutes, just as M. Jourdain made prose. You light your pipe and that is an absolute; you don't like oysters and that is an absolute; you join the Communist Party and that is an absolute. Whether the world is matter or spirit, whether God exists or does not exist, whether the judgment of future centuries is favorable or hostile to you, nothing will ever be able to negate the fact that you passionately loved such and such a picture, such and such a cause, and such and such a woman; that you lived that love from day to day: lived it, willed it, and undertook it; and that you engaged your whole being in it. Our grandfathers were perfectly right when they used to say as they drank their glass of wine: "One more that the Prussians won't have." Neither the Prussians nor anyone else. People may kill you or deprive you of wine for the rest of your life; but that last drop of Bordeaux that slipped over your palate, no God and no man can take away from you. No relativity; nor the "eternal course of history"; nor the dialectic of perception; nor the dissociations of psychoanalysis. That drop of wine is a pure event and we, too, in the very depths of historical relativity and our own insignificance are absolutes, inimitable and incomparable, and our choice of ourselves is an absolute. All the vital and passionate choices that we are and that we are perpetually making with or against other people, all the common undertakings into which we throw ourselves from birth until death, all the bonds of love and hate that unite us with each other and that exist only in so far as we feel them, the enormous complexes of movements that supplement or negate each other and that are lived, this whole discordant and harmonious life combines to create a new absolute which I like to call the *time*. The time is intersubjectivity, the living absolute, the dialectical wrong side of history. It is born in the pangs of events that historians will later stick labels on. Blindly, in fury, in fear, and in enthusiasm, it lives the meanings that they will later define by rational methods. In its own time, each word, before it is an historical slogan or the recognizable origin of a social process, is first an insult or a call or a confession. Economic phenomena themselves, before they are the theoretical causes of social upheavals, are suffered in humiliation or despair. Ideas are tools or flights; facts are born of intersubjectivity and unsettle it as emotions unsettle the individual soul. Men make history out of dead times, because each time, upon its death, enters into relativity and takes its place in the line of the centuries with the other dead. Then people try to throw new light upon it, dispute its meaning with their new knowledge, resolve its problems, prove that its most ardent searchings were doomed to failure, that the great undertakings of which it was most proud had opposite results to those it hoped for; suddenly its limitations appear and its ignorance. But all this is *because that time is dead;* those limits and that ignorance did not exist "at the time": men do not live a lack; or rather, that time was a perpetual overstepping of its own limits toward a future which was *its* future and which is dead with it. It was *that* boldness, *that* imprudence, *that* ignorance of its own ignorance: to live means to make short-term provisions and to manage on one's margin. Perhaps our fathers, had they had a little more knowledge, would have understood that such and such a problem was insoluble and that such and such a question should not have been raised in those terms. But the human condition requires that we make our choice in ignorance; it is ignorance that makes morality possible. If we knew all the factors that condition events, if we could play our hand without uncertainty, risk would disappear; and with risk courage, fear, waiting, the final joy and effort; we would be languid gods, but certainly not men. The bitter quarrels of the Babylonians over the meaning of omens, the bloody and passionate heresies of the Albigensians and the Anabaptists today seem to us errors. At the time man engaged his whole being in them and in expressing them at the risk of his life let truth live through them, for truth never yields itself directly; it only appears through errors. The fate of human Reason was at stake in the quarrel of the Universals and in that of the Immaculate Conception or Transubstantiation. And at the time of the great lawsuits of certain American states against the professors who taught the theory of evolution, it was again the fate of Reason that was at stake. It is absolutely at stake in every period in connection with doctrines that the next period will condemn as false. It is possible that some day the belief in evolution will seem the greatest folly of our century: yet, in supporting it against the churchmen, the American professors *lived* the truth, they lived it passionately and absolutely at great risk to themselves. Tomorrow they will be wrong, today they are absolutely right: the time is always wrong when it is dead, always right when it is alive. Let people condemn it after the fact, if they wish; nevertheless, it had its own passionate way of loving itself and tearing itself apart, against which future judgments will be of no avail; it had its own taste which it alone tasted and which was as incomparable, as irremediable as the taste of wine in our mouth.

A book has its absolute truth in its own time. It is lived like a riot or a famine, with much less intensity, of course, and by fewer people, but in the same way. It is an emanation of intersubjectivity, a living bond of rage, hatred, or love between those who have produced it and those who receive it. If it gains ground, thousands of people reject it and deny it: we all know very well that to read a book is to rewrite it. *At the time* it is first a panic, an escape, or a courageous affirmation; at the time it is a good or a bad *action*. Later, when the time has died, it will become relative; it will become a message. But the judgment of posterity will not invalidate the opinions men had of it during its lifetime. People have often said to me about dates and bananas: "You can't judge them: to know what they are really like, you have to eat them on the spot, just after they have been picked." And I have always considered bananas a dead fruit whose real taste escaped me. The books which pass from one period to another are dead fruits, too. In another time they had a different taste, sharp and tangy. We should have read "Emile" or the "Persian Letters" just after they were picked.

Thus we must write for our own time, as the great writers did. But this does not imply that we must shut ourselves up in it. To write for our time does not mean to reflect it passively. It means that we must will to maintain it or change it; therefore, go beyond it toward the future; and it is this effort to change it which establishes us most deeply in it, for it can never be reduced to a dead mass of tools and customs. It is in flux, it perpetually goes beyond itself; in it the concrete present and the living future of all the men who compose it exactly coincide. If, among other characteristics, Newtonian physics and the theory of the noble savage help to define the first half of the eighteenth century, we must not forget that the former represented a consistent effort to wrest fragments of the truth from the fog of ignorance in order to reach, beyond the contemporary state of knowledge, an ideal science in which phenomena could be deduced mathematically from the principle of gravitation, and that the latter was an attempt to go beyond the vices of civilization and restore a state of nature. Both theories outlined a future; and if it is true that this future never became a present, that men later renounced the Golden Age and the idea of making science a strictly logical chain of reasons, it is nonetheless true that these profound and vital hopes sketched a future beyond men's daily cares and that in order to penetrate the meaning of our day-to-day existence we must approach it with the future as our point of departure. One cannot be a man or make oneself a writer without drawing a line on the horizon beyond oneself, but this going beyond oneself is in each case finite and unique. One does not go beyond *in general* and for the simple pride and pleasure of going beyond; Baudelairian dissatisfaction represents only the abstract scheme of transcendence and, since it is a dissatisfaction with everything, ends by being a dissatisfaction with nothing. Real transcendence requires that one wish to change certain definite aspects of the world and any going beyond is colored by and characterized by the concrete situation it seeks to modify. A man throws himself completely into his plan for freeing the Negroes or restoring the Hebrew language to the Jews of Palestine; he throws himself into it completely and at the same time expresses man's fate in all its universality, but it must always be through a unique and dated undertaking. And if people say to me, as does M. Schlumberger [a critic], that one also goes beyond one's time when one strives for immortality, I shall answer that this is a false going beyond: instead of wishing to change an intolerable situation, one attempts to escape from it and seeks refuge in a future that is entirely strange to us, since it is not the future that we *make,* but the concrete present of our grandchildren. We have no way of affecting that present; they will live it for themselves and as they wish, situated in their own time as we in ours. If they make any use of our writings it will be for their own ends, ends which we did not foresee, just as one picks up stones on the road and hurls them in the face of an aggressor. It would be quite vain on our part to throw off on them our effort to prolong our own existence: they have neither the duty nor the desire to do so. And since we have no means of acting upon these strangers, we shall present ourselves to them like beggars and beg them to lend us the appearance of life by using us for any purpose whatsoever. If we are Christians, we shall accept our lot humbly, provided only that they still speak of us, even though they use us to show that faith is ineffectual; if we are atheists, we shall be very happy if they still concern themselves with our anguish and our errors, were it even to prove that man is miserable without God. Would you be satisfied, M. Schlumberger, if after the Revolution our grandsons saw in your writings the most obvious example of the conditioning of art by the economic structure? And if you do not have that literary destiny, you will have another that will be hardly any better: if you escape from dialectical materialism, it will only be to serve the ends of some psychoanalysis. In any case, our grandchildren will be impudent orphans, so why should we concern ourselves with them? Perhaps of all of us, only Céline will endure; it is theoretically possible, although highly improbable, that the twenty-first century will remember Drieu's name and forget Malraux'; in any case it will not espouse our quarrels, it will not mention what today we call the betrayal of certain writers; or if it mentions this, it will do so without anger or contempt.* And what difference does it make to us? What Malraux and Drieu are for us is an absolute. In certain hearts there is an absolute of contempt for Drieu and an absolute of friendship for Malraux that one hundred posthumous judgments will not be able to shake. There is a living Malraux, a lump of warm blood in the very heart of our time, and there will be a dead Malraux at the mercy of history. Why should the living man try to fix the image of the dead man he will one day be? Certainly he lives beyond himself; his gaze and his concerns go beyond the death of his flesh; the presence of a man and his weight are measured not by the fifty or sixty years of his organic life, nor by the borrowed life he will lead in future centuries in the minds of strangers: they are measured by his own choice of the temporal cause that goes beyond him. The story is told that the runner of Marathon was dead an hour before he reached Athens. He was dead, yet he still ran; he ran dead and as a dead man announced the victory of the Greeks. It is a beautiful myth and shows that the dead act for a little while as if they were still alive. A little while—one year, ten years, fifty years perhaps, in any case, a finite period; and then they are buried for the second time. This is the measure that we propose to the writer: as long as his books provoke anger, embarrassment, shame, hatred, love, he will live, even if he is only a shadow. After that, the deluge. We are for a finite morality and a finite art.

* Louis-Ferdinand Céline (1894–1961), pseudonym of L.-F. Destouches, French novelist; Pierre-Eugené Drieu la Rochelle (1893–1945), essayist, poet, and novelist; André Malraux (1901–1976), French novelist, essayist, and art critic. *Ed.*

MARCHETTE CHUTE

# The Bubble Reputation

[ AUTUMN 1949 ]

EACH GENERATION passes judgment on its own writers and is convinced that posterity will agree. This state of confidence is not necessarily shared by all the population, but the average literary critic has it in full measure. It is his trade to make calm, considered judgments, and it is the duty of the common people to respect these judgments. Art is art, and a man of true intelligence can always recognize it.

According to this theory, art is not that vigorous, untidy growth which amuses the common people. Anyone can amuse the common people and they will not lack for entertainers in any age. Art is something which can be apprehended only by a trained mind of delicate perceptions and which belongs, in that sense, only to a few. The literary critic perceives a work of art from afar. He hails it, and gradually he attracts a small group of readers who have equally delicate perceptions. In time a coterie is formed, hushed and apart, and the fortunate writer is thus assured of immortality through the vigilance of the wisest of his contemporaries.

What actually happens in real life, which is unfortunately so far removed from ideal conditions, is rather different. The artistic writer who is hailed by his contemporaries usually ends as a footnote in college textbooks, and the vigorous writer who pleased ordinary people shines out as a major star in the firmament. This does not always happen, but it happens often enough to be discouraging to men of judgment. It happened, for instance, in the case of a writer named William Shakespeare.

If you had asked a well-read Elizabethan what contemporary poet had the best chance of immortality he would have answered without hesitation: Sir Philip Sidney. His second choice would probably have been Edmund Spenser and after that either Samuel Daniel or William Warner, both of whom were famous poets in their own day although no one reads them now.

If the well-read Elizabethan put Shakespeare on his list he would not have been thinking of his plays; cheap reprints of popular playhouse productions did not entitle a man to the honored name of poet. Shakespeare was a candidate for poetic honors only because of his two narrative poems, "Venus and Adonis" and "The Rape of Lucrece." Shakespeare had written these in his late twenties, modeling them on the best rules, and as a reward for his obedience he had won the approval of his artistic contemporaries. There was a real chorus of praise for these two poems, summed up in Richard Barnfield's exuberant apostrophe to the author four years later:

> And Shakespeare thou, whose honey-flowing vein,
> Pleasing the world, thy praises doth obtain;
> Whose Venus, and whose Lucrece, sweet and chaste,
> Thy name in fame's immortal book have placed.

Shakespeare paid no attention to the critics who had so thoughtfully placed him in fame's immortal book, and he wrote no more of his correct and pleasing narrative poems. Instead he concentrated on supplying his fellow actors with plays. Shakespeare was a professional actor as well as a playwright, and he was content to follow the actor's trade of pleasing the mass of ordinary people instead of the chosen few.

In the course of pleasing the theatre public during the 1590's, Shakespeare gave them Falstaff and Shylock and King Richard and Puck and Juliet, lavishing his gifts as a poet upon them for love, not for reputation. It was just as well he did not care for a reputation as a playwright, since he certainly did not get one. The critics went on praising "Venus and Adonis" and "Lucrece," and only two men mentioned his plays at all.

One of these men was a minor writer named John Weever who wrote, or rather burbled, a sonnet to Shakespeare at the end of the nineties. Weever chiefly praised Adonis and Lucrece, but he had heard of the existence of characters named Romeo and Richard and declared that they must be saints since Shakespeare begot them. It is to be hoped that "honey-tongued Shakespeare" did not read this offering, with its lush emotionalism. There are few things more irritating to a writer than to be given lavish praise for the wrong reasons.

The one other writer to notice Shakespeare as a playwright was Francis Meres, who had been commissioned by a London publisher to write a popular handbook on culture. There were a great many of these books, since the middle-class London public was eager for short-cuts to an education, but Meres went farther than most and brought his survey down to the contemporary London literary scene. Meres was patriotically convinced that English poets were as good as any in the world, and he did not hesitate to call William Warner "our English Homer" or compare Matthew Roydon to Dante. Shakespeare was compared to Ovid, since Ovid was the greatest writer of love poems in antiquity; but Meres also knew that Shakespeare had written a great many plays and he went on firmly to compare him with Plautus in his comedies and Seneca in his tragedies. This was meant as a compliment, since every Elizabethan schoolboy knew that the two Romans were the most important playwrights of antiquity, but again this was one of those irritating compliments that praise a man for the wrong reasons. Shakespeare had once tried to write like these two models of classicism, imitating Plautus in "The Comedy of Errors" and Seneca in "Titus Andronicus." But he had long since outgrown this period of youthful imitation and no longer attempted to write by the classical rules that his literary contemporaries worshipped. He had more difficult, inward rules of his own.

The praise of a man like Francis Meres carried small weight in literary circles. He was very little more than a popular hack, and his praise of Shakespeare was directed at middle-class Londoners, who already knew that they liked Shakespeare and did not need to be told. No serious critic mentioned his plays, with a single exception. A well-known literary man of the period, Gabriel Harvey, jotted down some random notes on contemporary writers and remarked among other things: "The younger sort take much delight in Shakespeare's 'Venus and Adonis'; but his 'Lucrece,' and his tragedy of 'Hamlet, Prince of Denmark,' have it in them to please the wiser sort." To link "Hamlet" with a youthful, ornamental poem like "The Rape of Lucrece" seems almost shocking to a modern reader, but from the contemporary point of view it was very liberal-minded of Harvey to single out a common playhouse production and give it the dignity of literature.

By the time Shakespeare wrote "Hamlet" his reputation as a poet had receded somewhat in the more advanced literary circles. He was still being doggedly praised for the "sweetness" of his two narrative poems, but this kind of sweetness and ornamentation was no longer popular with younger literary men. A new school of writing had emerged at the end of the century—bravely disillusioned, bitter, and satiric—and like any new school of writing it disapproved of its elders. Shakespeare was one of the elder writers and to the young moderns he was beginning to seem a little old-fashioned.

His reputation at Cambridge University is shown in a two-part play, called "The Return from Parnassus," which some bright young undergraduates wrote for Christmas production around the turn of the century. The chief butt of the play is a simpering, would-be aesthete named Gullio from Oxford (no Oxford man could ever be very intelligent in the eyes of Cambridge), and one proof among many of Gullio's stupidity is the fact that he considers Mr. Shakespeare the best poet England ever produced. "Let this duncified world esteem of Spenser and Chaucer. I'll worship sweet Mr. Shakespeare and to honor him will lay his 'Venus and Adonis' under my pillow."

The name of Shakespeare reappears in the play when the cast discusses a poetry anthology that had just been published. Shakespeare was lavishly represented in this particular anthology, for the compiler was John Bodenham, an experienced editor who knew exactly what the public wanted to read. The boys at Cambridge were not interested in merely popular work and they gave Shakespeare a kindly but rather patronizing pat on the back. They admit the sweetness of his verse is attractive, but he spends too much time writing about love when he should deal with graver matters.

Later on in the play Shakespeare's name appears again, but this time the tone is definitely hostile. The theme of the play as a whole is the difficulty experienced by men of culture when they try to make a living in an unfeeling world, and the two heroes of the play are eventually so desperate that they decide to become actors. The most prosperous acting company at that time was the Chamberlain's company, headed by Burbage, Shakespeare, and Kempe, and so Burbage and Kempe are shown on-stage giving the two scholars an audition. (Kempe had left the company before the play was written, but Cambridge did not always know the latest theatre news from London and in any case his name was useful for its comedy effect.) Kempe, like Gullio, is a butt, but while Gullio was an educated fool Kempe is shown as a complete illiterate. The boy who played Kempe could be sure of a shout of derisive laughter from his Cambridge audience when he reached the line that called Shakespeare a better writer than any university-trained scholar. "Few of the university pen plays well; they smell too much of that writer Ovid, and that writer Metamorphosis, and talk too much of Proserpina and Jupiter. Why, here's our fellow Shakespeare puts them all down." The heroes of the play do well at the audition and are offered acting positions with Shakespeare's company, but they realize that this would be a degradation and turn the offer down.

> But is't not strange these mimic apes should prize
> Unhappy scholars at a hireling rate?
> Vile world, that lifts them up in high degree,
> And treads us down in grovelling misery.

Burbage and Shakespeare and their fellow "apes" were making a good deal of money, and therefore no man of true culture could permit himself to associate with them.

"The Return from Parnassus" is a youthful piece of high spirits, written by youngsters who were exaggerating freely for comedy effect. Nevertheless, the point of view that is expressed here was seriously held by most of the educated men of the period. A piece of writing was almost automatically disqualified for consideration as a serious work of art, if it made money and was enjoyed by ordinary people. Art was for the few, preferably the few that had been educated at Oxford or Cambridge. If the common people liked it, something was clearly wrong with it.

Ben Jonson spoke for the average literary man of the period when he characterized the mass London audience as "the beast, the multitude. They love nothing that is right and proper. The farther it runs from reason and possibility with them the better it is." When one of Jonson's ambitious tragedies was a failure, his fellow playwright, Francis Beaumont, assured him it was because he had not "itched after the wild applause of common people." When John Fletcher's new play, "The Faithful Shepherdess," expired, Beaumont and Jonson and Chapman and other playwrights announced that it was because the vulgar public had been unable to appreciate its "elegant propriety," and they protested the fact that an artist was expected to present his work to ignorant throngs,

> Scarce two of which can understand the laws
> Which they should judge by.

It seemed to the dramatists of the period that the more carefully they wrote their plays the less the London public appreciated them. After "The White Devil" was a commercial failure, its author, John Webster, noted bitterly, "Should a man present . . . the most sententious tragedy that was ever written, observing all the critical laws, as height of style and gravity of person . . . yet, after all this divine rapture . . . the breath that comes from the uncapable multitude is able to poison it."

Webster went on to give a list of the most prominent living playwrights. He singled out for special mention the most learned ones—Chapman, Jonson, Beaumont and Fletcher—but he also added a kind word for "the right happy and copious industry of Mr. Shakespeare, Mr. Dekker, and Mr. Heywood." From the contemporary point of view there was nothing odd or unsuitable in linking Shakespeare with two popular playwrights of the period like Heywood and Dekker. All three had been writing for the stage a long time, none of them paid much attention to the "laws" of writing, and all of them consistently pleased the "incapable multitude." The fact that Shakespeare was a genius quite escaped Webster's attention. He was judging by the fashions of his own day, and Shakespeare was not fashionable.

Ben Jonson found it more difficult to make up his mind about Shakespeare. Six years after Shakespeare's death, Jonson was asked to contribute some verses to a folio edition of Shakespeare's plays that his fellow actors were preparing, and Jonson wrote a poem praising his friend as no one ever had before. Meres had once compared Shakespeare to Plautus and Seneca, but Jonson compared him to Euripides and the rest of the mighty Greeks.

> He was not of an age, but for all time.

It is a wonderful tribute and the only contemporary judgment on Shakespeare that a modern reader can look at without cringing.

How far this represents Jonson's considered opinion it is hard to say, since Shakespeare's work went directly contrary to everything that Jonson, with his classical training, believed. Jonson had the highest admiration for

Shakespeare as a human being, but he felt that his plays lacked the control that a classical background would have given. "I loved the man, and do honor his memory, on this side idolatry, as much as any. He was, indeed, honest, and of an open and free nature; had an excellent fantasy; brave notions and gentle expressions; wherein he flowed with that facility that sometimes it was necessary he should be stopped." Jonson went on to say that Shakespeare had often written lines that "were ridiculous. But he redeemed his vices with his virtues. There was ever more in him to be praised than to be pardoned."

The publication of an expensive posthumous edition of his plays put Shakespeare's reputation on a much firmer footing with literary men. Jonson's praise was a great help, since Jonson had just been given honorary degrees by both Oxford and Cambridge, and throughout the rest of the century Shakespeare took a place alongside Jonson and Fletcher in what Milton's nephew called "the happy triumvirate." The more Shakespeare's plays were read the more they were liked, but the critical fraternity could not help feeling that there was still something wrong with the man who lacked "the polishments of art." As John Evelyn, the diarist, said in 1661, "I saw 'Hamlet, prince of Denmark,' played, but now the old plays begin to disgust this refined age."

The battle of might be called "art *versus* Shakespeare" came to its climax at the end of the seventeenth century. The point of view of the century as a whole was that Shakespeare was an untutored genius who somehow managed to achieve wonderful results, but at the end of the century a prominent critic rose in his majesty to deny that the results could be called wonderful. The critic was Thomas Rymer, a clever, learned, and vigorous writer whose only fault was his conviction that everyone should obey the classical rules and adhere to what he called "good sense."

Rymer chose "Othello" for his victim and waded into the slaughter with the gusto of a man convinced of the rightness of his cause: "Shakespeare's genius lay for comedy and humour. In tragedy he appears quite out of his element; his brains are turned, he raves and rambles, without any coherence, any spark of reason, or any rules to control him." Shakespeare's reason for mixing comedy with his tragedy was that it "brought in the rabble. . . . Carpenters and cobblers were the guides he followed. And it is then no wonder that we find so much farce . . . in his tragedies. Thereby unhallowing the theatre, profaning the name of tragedy; and instead of representing men and manners, turning all morality, good sense and humanity into mockery and derision."

It was the duty of a true poet to show the members of the upper classes as ladies and gentlemen, but Shakespeare, "running after his masters the cobblers," is incapable of this kind of writing. The language he assigns to Othello is clearly ridiculous. "Some drayman or drunken tinker might possibly treat his drab at this sort of rate, and mean no harm by it; but for His Excellency, a my lord General, to serenade a Senator's daughter with such a volley of scoundrel filthy language is sure the most absurd maggot that ever bred from any poet's addle brain." Desdemona is almost as bad—a disgracefully vulgar girl. "The Italian painters are noted for drawing the Madonnas by their own wives or mistresses; one might wonder what sort of Betty Mackerel, Shakespeare found in his days, to sit for his . . . Desdemona."

What Shakespeare should have written, according to Rymer, was a different kind of play altogether. He should have left out most of the words, since "words are a sort of heavy baggage, that were better out of the way, at the push of action." He should not have made Iago a soldier, since a stage soldier should be "open-hearted, frank, plain-dealing . . . a character constantly worn by them for some thousands of years." He should have made the characters speak in a consistently refined fashion, and avoided the "villainous, unnatural images" of which this playwright's head was unfortunately full. And above all, as every literary critic had agreed since the dawn of literary criticism, he should have brought the story to a moral conclusion. A better ending would have been for Desdemona to faint with fear in the last act and Othello, thinking he had killed her, to cut his throat. Then Desdemona could have recovered, virtue would have been rewarded, and the audience "might thereupon have gone home with a quiet mind, admiring the beauty of Providence."

A modern reader likes to feel that unfortunate critical mistakes of this kind belong only to the past. Surely the present age has a different yardstick, and a better one. But when a modern critic feels he will be able to fit each writer in his proper niche, an echo drifts back from the equally confident critics of the Elizabethan, the Jacobean, and the Caroline age. And this melancholy echo murmurs, quoting a phrase from Ben Jonson, "The hell thou wilt."

# The Nineteen Fifties

JOSEPH WOOD KRUTCH

## Mice: A Dispassionate View

[ SUMMER 1950 ]

I

MR. JAMES THURBER once complained that in his household they seemed "to have cats the way other people have mice"; but with me it was once the other way around. We had mice the way other people have cats.

In the beginning it was the war and the refugee problem which was responsible. One of the laboratories in Cambridge University had maintained for a long time a family of noble rodents which, like many other noble families, was perfectly ordinary in every respect except the fact that the family tree was a matter of careful record. Students of heredity did not want the line broken if Cambridge should be bombed out or meet other wartime disasters.

Accordingly the heads of the family were shipped over to a geneticist at Columbia University where they proceeded immediately to the chief business of a mouse's life—prompt, immoderate, and continuous reproduction. In a few weeks the descendants had become ancestors and two of the original refugees were presented to me. They were no longer of any Importance to Science because a geneticist, though he sounds very much like a genealogist, is really the opposite. The one is interested only in ancestors and the other only in descendants.

My two were white—albinos, that is—and were supposed both to be females—which indeed they were, though I had momentarily what looked like good reason for doubting the fact. I soon discovered that both, though very tame and charming, were, perhaps just because they represented a well-known family, rather unenterprising. Settled on top of a card-table, provided with sleeping quarters and several tunnels constructed of Christmas cards, they were apparently quite content and made no move to climb down.

After they had been settled there for some weeks, I left them in charge of the maid while I went away for a visit. A few days later a long-distance telephone call informed me that one had given birth to a litter of nine. Since I was at that time shamefully ignorant, I had to go to an encyclopedia to confirm my guess that the mother had been with me too long already to have been in an interesting condition when I received her. Obviously her companion must be the father. "This," I said to myself, "reveals a nice state of affairs. The Professor of Genetics at Columbia can't tell a male from a female and that is carrying delicacy too far, at least for a scientist." But my indignation was short-lived. Two days later came another long-distance call. The other mouse had just given birth to a numerous litter.

Now, parthenogenesis, or virgin birth, is common enough among certain insects but it would be almost as surprising in a mouse as it would be in a human being. Even the proudest families which find themselves threatened with extinction cannot do it that way. Some proletarian, living unsuspected in my wainscoting, had obviously exhibited the enterprise which the aristocrats lacked. This humble Romeo had climbed the balcony instead of waiting for his Juliet to come down.

Now, I exclaimed jubilantly, I shall have an opportunity to check up on Mendel for myself. The babies, still pink and naked, gave no clue. But if they had really been fathered as I suspected, then when the fur appeared it would be in every case plain mouse-grey. Albinism is a recessive characteristic and therefore would not appear in any issue of this first cross, though, of course, if inbreeding continued, approximately one-fourth of the second generation would be white, the other three-fourths grey.

Before long it was evident that Mendel and I were both right so far as this first generation was concerned, and, before very much longer, so far as the next was concerned also. Within a year I knew mice very well indeed, not only scientifically but personally. We were having mice the way other people have kittens. And very much like kittens they are too, except that one has them even more frequently and more abundantly than kittens can be supplied by the most assiduous mother-cat.

## II

The unauthorized love-match between the aristocratic lady and the man of the people turned out fine. The succeeding generations inherited the tameness and gentleness of the mother with the enterprise of the father. Soon a sort of family village had to be founded—a large, screened cage two stories high with separate boxes for the families set up by the grandchildren, a community dining-hall, and a community playground, complete with a miniature version of the old-fashioned squirrel-wheel in which young and old delighted to ride. Mice are among the most playful of all creatures and they devised endless games in the wheel—sometimes a tug-of-war in which contending parties tried to turn it in opposite directions, sometimes a co-operative enterprise with one clinging to the wire while the other rode him round and round. When the apparatus was full, would-be risers often queued up to wait their turn.

Besides being extraordinarily playful, mice are also extraordinarily devoted parents. Father will curl up with the babies when the mother leaves them for a few minutes; other females will do the same if they happen to have no babies of their own at the moment, and in fact are not always able to resist the temptation to kidnap the young, whom they take to their own nest. When it seems for any reason desirable to move a family, the mouslings are carried by the skin of the neck exactly as a cat carries kittens, though I once saw a baby, grown too large to be transported that way, led firmly back into the nest by the ear when his mother disagreed with him in thinking that he was not yet old enough to be allowed out. Mice are also fanatically clean, washing themselves and their young with exactly the same gestures a cat uses.

The sign that a new family is about to be born is a sudden frenzy of activity on the part of the mother who begins frantically to tear paper into bits and to carry it, piece by piece, into the nest, where it is arranged into a ball with a small hole open in the side. Tame as my mice were, they wanted privacy at this moment and if I tried to peer in at the opening, the mother would seize a bit of paper and deftly close the hole in my face with all the decisiveness of a ticket-seller in a French railway station when, suiting the action to the word, he announces joyously: "Le guichet est fermé" and goes out to lunch.

## III

In even the largest and happiest families one individual is likely to stand out, and so it was here. In this case the "personality" was a certain female, plain mouse-grey but carrying, as I knew from her families, the recessive albinism inherited along with, perhaps, some of the tameness of an English, laboratory-bred mother. Her name, for reasons totally inadequate and not necessary to go into, was Sabrina—generally shortened to Sabe.

Sabe was unusually charming—even for a mouse. What I can have looked like to her when she was on the floor and I standing over her, I cannot imagine, but she knew me, or at least knew a human being. She would come halfway across a room to join me, hoping that I would extend my hand on the floor so that she could crawl onto it and be carried about. Especially she liked to be taken to investigate strange places—a bookshelf for instance. When I brought her close, she would climb onto the books, disappear behind them for perhaps three minutes, then reappear in the space left by some missing volume and wait expectantly at the very edge of the shelf until I extended a palm which would transfer her to some other spot. This would go on until one of us tired—and it was usually I. Once when I forgot to put her back in the cage and she was outside all night, she came running from a corner when I came in next morning and waited at my feet to be taken up.

Her end, like the end of nearly all mice, was sad. I noticed a lump on her back which I described to the geneticist and asked for a diagnosis. "How old is she?" he asked. "About two years," I replied. "Ah, then it is senility," he said. "That is very old indeed for a mouse. Few ever reach that age. You had better practice euthanasia, for if you don't the tumor will turn cancerous and she will die soon." "Is that common?" I asked. "It is universal," he said. "All mice that reach that age die of cancer."

The situation seems to be simply this. Mice, being completely inoffensive creatures, can play only one rôle in the general economy of nature—that of supplying food to other creatures. They are eaten by almost every carnivorous animal not too large to find them less than a mouthful—by, to name a few, cats, skunks, weasels, snakes, owls, hawks, crows, and even foxes, who can sometimes be seen in an open field, pouncing like a cat. No mouse, therefore, is likely to live long, and so thrifty nature does not bother to endow them with a capacity for a long life which they would so seldom have any opportunity to use. To keep the species going, she gives them, not the longevity which would be useless, but the astounding and precocious fertility which is, from nature's standpoint, just as good. But I, not sharing nature's detachment, think it a pity that a creature which so usually meets a violent death should be so afraid of it. The terror of a cornered mouse is unmistakable, and its eyes far too vividly suggest those of the hunted man which seem to say: "I knew this was bound to come. But has it really come so soon?"

## IV

None of Sabe's children or grandchildren ever quite took her place but one of them, while still young, foolish, and not quite housebroken, was the occasion of the greatest furor ever created in my household by a mouse, and was ultimately responsible for increasing prodigiously the respect in which I hold the feminine head of that household.

I had left him, one morning, investigating my desk, and had forgetfully gone away for an hour or two, only to discover when I returned that he had disappeared, obviously through a crack in the wainscoting. He was a very promising mouse whom I did not want to lose, and, besides, I was not sure that he was capable of looking after himself. Presumably he would come out after dark to look for food but I did not want to sit up all night either. To my conventional mind, the obvious solution seemed to be a live-trap, but though I was in New York at the time, the city did not seem to yield one. There were, of course, mechanisms for strangling victims. There were also traps for woodchucks and other large animals, which obviously would not do for a baby mouse. The situation seemed hopeless until my companion suggested, rather timidly, that she saw no reason why I should assume that a trap was necessary. What that tenderly brought-up mouse would want was comfort. If I left him some food and a good bed, he would probably accept both.

It seemed almost too simple, but I prepared a small cardboard box about three inches square, lined with cotton and provided with a mouse-size entrance way. I put it on the floor and went to bed. Next morning I hurried not too hopefully into the room. There was no sign of the mouse—but just to make sure, I put my hand over the hole and lifted the box. There was still no stir and I almost threw it aside without taking off the cover. But I did take it off and there, curled up in the cotton, was the mouse, too comfortable and too snug even to open an eye when the box was lifted and the cover removed.

Now this incident, as I said then and have often repeated, revealed the workings of genius, which consists in the ability to see a solution which the ordinary mind—represented in this case by my own—would not see. The solution was bold and simple, thus exhibiting two characteristics of most genius-solutions. And it was possible only because the mind which conceived it refused to be led to the impasse created when the habitual statement of the problem is accepted. "Catch" suggests "trap" and a trap is something you can't get out of. But here a bold mind broke this link in a train of usual associations. It saw that the unique aspect of this situation was that the thing trapped would not want to get out. And from that unique aspect came the solution.

Sometimes my companion thinks that I lay too exclusive a stress on this particular demonstration of her genius. She thinks, though she does not put it this way, that she has been at least as brilliant on other occasions, and when I enlarge upon this one, she may ask if some other incident, which she recalls to my attention, did not do her as much credit. But I am always compelled to say "Not quite." And if she seems distressed, I insist that the reason is simply that so favorable an opportunity to exhibit genius has never again presented itself. As Samuel Johnson once said in explaining why brilliant writers often seem quite unremarkable in ordinary society: "Unusual talents require unusual opportunities for their exercise."

A change in my living habits which made it necessary for me to be away from home for considerable periods put an end to my living on intimate terms with mice. But not until I had learned a great deal. I was a subscriber to two magazines, one edited in the interests of the laboratory-breeder and the other for hobbyists like myself. I had even some idea of founding a new one myself but I never got further than the selection of a name. It was to be called, with a slight bow in the direction of another well-known publication, Good Mousekeeping.

## V

I have read that even a hungry kitten will not kill a mouse unless it has been taught to do so, and from my own experience I learned the obverse of this fact—namely, that mice are not "naturally" afraid of cats. When one of my cats approached the mouse-cage—and he was of course quite fascinated by it—the mice were not terrified but tremendously curious. Often the cat mounted to the top, sometimes curled up there to sleep; and the mice, instead of running to hide, were very anxious to get close to him. More than once when he put his face down to sniff, a mouse would climb up on a box, stand on his hind legs to bridge the remaining distance, and rub noses through the screen.

Here was something very much like the lion and the lamb lying down together. At least the lamb was willing and the lion somewhat uncertain at worst—only because, I assume, he had been conditioned by past experience to regard mice as food. Why then is not Utopia just around the corner? Why do the people so furiously rage? How beautiful are the feet of those who preach the ways of peace!

The answer, it seems to me, does not lie in "human nature" *per se* any more than it does in cat nature or mouse nature. It is the world we never made rather than the world we do make which insists that we live as we do in bloodshed and hate. We have in ourselves no natural impulse to do that, any more than a kitten has a natural impulse to kill a mouse. We too have to be taught. But the thing which teaches us is something from which we cannot but choose to learn—the ineluctable contingencies of that part of the natural world which is beyond the reach of change by mice or men. If we do not live as it insists, then it is difficult to see how, as a race, we can live at all.

Perhaps it is some consolation to know that the fault is older than we are, but it makes the hope of any completely fundamental reform extremely remote. Even if human nature can be changed, the evil does not have its ultimate roots in the psyche. They reach down into physiology and, indeed, into that whole pre-human, even pre-animal scheme, which does not ask the cat if it must "hate" mice but which leaves him only one alternative if he should refuse to eat them. No feet walk more persistently in the paths of peace than the feet of the mouse. And yet what does it profit him—in this world which is, presumably, the only one a mouse will ever know? Merely the rôle of He Who Gets Eaten rather than that of He Who Eats.

Throughout most of nature, at least, there is so seldom a tertium quid. And that makes one wonder whether, at best, ultimate goodness can be practiced by any except individuals willing to take for themselves the consequences of it. Perhaps it is best to lose the whole world in order to save one's own soul. But perhaps, also, if ultimate goodness really is required, there is no other way of doing it.

BERTRAND RUSSELL

## George Bernard Shaw

[ WINTER 1951 ]

SHAW, considered psychologically, was an almost perfect example of the shy man with an inferiority complex. When I first knew him his shyness was still obvious. He came to my flat on one occasion to read a new play of his, then still unpublished and unproduced, to about twenty friends. He was pale and trembling with stage fright, in spite of the audience being so small and well-disposed. I think his wit was developed entirely as a sensitive man's armour against an intrusive world. The stories that he used to relate about his family rather bear out this view. I do not vouch, in any way, for the truth of the stories, only for the fact that he related them. He used to aver that nearly all his family had been drunkards who, as a result of drink, had ultimately become insane and retired to a private lunatic asylum which, according to him, existed mainly for the benefit of the Shaw family. The most remarkable of these relatives was the uncle who committed suicide by putting his head into a carpet bag and then shutting it. This uncle almost invariably made his appearance at Shaw's excellent luncheons.

For the first forty years or so of Shaw's life he was poor and struggling, admired by a small élite, but regarded as a mountebank by the larger public. His admirable novels were read by hardly anybody and such success as came his way was as a music critic. His friendship with Webb,* which was very deep and sincere, gave him a more articulate and rational gospel than he would otherwise have had and an intellectual outlet for his sympathy with the underdog. After he became a dramatist, the activities of the Fabian Society took up a smaller amount of his attention than they had done earlier, but he still remained active in connection with this work. The Webbs used to divide mankind into the A's and the B's. The A's were artists, anarchists, and aristocrats; the B's were bourgeois, bureaucrat, and benevolent. They always used to add that Shaw was an A and they were B's. Shaw, however, was only temperamentally an anarchist. Intellectually, he had a belief in strong government—too much belief, I should say, since it inclined him to sympathy with dictators.

* Sidney and Beatrice Webb, leaders of the Fabian society, an organization advocating socialism. They also helped to found the London School of Economics. *Ed.*

I think the greatest service Shaw did was in dispelling humbug by laughter. We all talk in a different way from that in which people talked before Shaw, and even our emotions hardly allow themselves such delicious exhibitions of concealed egoism as were customary in Victorian times. No one nowadays tells a boy: "It hurts me more than it hurts you," and few people have the face to speak of "a fate worse than death." It is no longer necessary to assume that all parents love their children and all children love their parents. We can admit to feelings of vanity, which, though just as common formerly as they are now, were for some reason thought to belong only to all the rest of the world and not to oneself. There is certainly much less insincerity in family relations and in people's estimate of themselves than there used to be. The later stages of the change perhaps owe most to Freud, but the earlier stages, so far as England is concerned, were brought about by Shaw. This was a great work, and one for which we should all be grateful.

I am afraid, however, that, since humbug changes its character from time to time, attacks on humbug must also be dated. There is in one of Shaw's plays an advanced lady who comes back from Madeira, after living there for thirty years, with the same advanced opinions with which she went there, and is astonished to find that they are no longer advanced. Something of the same fate is liable to befall Shaw. His themes are of their time, not eternal. Like Restoration Comedy, they will be to future historians a valuable historic record, but they are not, like Shakespeare's tragedies, capable of remaining appropriate through all changes of manners and social systems. Shakespeare says:

> "As flies to wanton boys, are we to the gods,
> They kill us for their sport."

Although all the mad kings have been dethroned, these lines from "Lear" have not ceased to be appropriate. I do not think that anything as perennial will be found in the writings of Shaw. He was, in fact, though incredibly clever, not wise. However, we cannot expect any man to possess all the virtues and we are very grateful to Shaw for his wit, without demanding anything more profound; and it must be said that his wit does sometimes light up absurdities in a manner which is quite astonishing. For example, in "Arms and the Man," the Bulgarian boasts of the number of his horses and his houses and the Swiss hotel-keeper starts on a catalogue: "I have ten thousand knives and forks and the same quantity of dessert spoons" and so on. I do not myself enjoy Shaw so much when he is wholly serious, as in "Saint Joan." I become worried by wrong history and by the reading of a Shavian manner of thought and feeling into an earlier age.

Shaw had developed to a very fine point the art of making his opponent in controversy look silly. Sometimes, as is apt to happen to adepts in this art, knowledge of his own virtuosity made him careless. During the First World War it appeared in something that he published that he believed Alaska still belonged to Russia. Naturally, somebody wrote to correct this, but Shaw managed to reply in such a manner as to make it seem that the corrector was a fool. The same characteristic showed in more serious ways. He thought himself entitled to positive opinions on scientific matters about which he knew very little. He ardently endorsed Samuel Butler's criticism of Darwin, and, from this starting point, came to agree with everything that Samuel Butler* had said. I was once present at an "Erewhon Dinner," at which about a dozen admirers of Samuel Butler's were gathered. Shaw was among them and made a speech, giving his support to all that was most disputable in Butler's many opinions. The same belief in vitalism which led Shaw to agree with Butler against Darwin led him later to admire Bergson,† whose *clan vital* he popularized in "Back to Methuselah." His whole attitude in biological matters was antiscientific and led him to a profound scepticism about medicine. There is reason to believe, however, that he could not have attained his great age without the help of medicine at certain crucial times. It is interesting to observe that the "inheritance of acquired characters," which was preached by Butler and Bergson and adopted by Shaw, is now the official doctrine of the Soviet Union, of which Shaw in his later years was a passionate admirer. In all these various supporters of the inheritance of acquired characters the psychological source is the same; namely, a belief in the omnipotence of will and the unwillingness to admit any boundaries set by nature to what man can achieve. This doctrine is wholesome in so far as it is true, since it encourages hopefulness and effort, but when it is pushed to extremes it becomes an encouragement to futile schemes and authoritarian arrogance.

Shaw's plays are, in one respect, a reversion to a much earlier type, for his characters do not aim at being complete, rounded human beings, but are each an embodied point of view in an argument. His plays, in fact, are dialogues in dramatic form. They make one laugh, because one is accustomed to the absurdities they show up; but I am afraid that, in proportion, as they are successful in causing people to abandon the various kinds of humbug displayed by all the characters except the hero, their mirth-provoking quality will diminish. The final judgment upon Shaw will be, I think, that he was enormously useful as a reformer, but that his effectiveness as an artist was, to a large extent, temporary.

So far I have been speaking of Shaw as a public character; I will add a few words as regards my personal contacts with him.

* Samuel Butler (1835–1902), author of *The Way of All Flesh*.
† Henri Bergson (1859–1941), French philosopher, 1927 winner of the Nobel Prize in literature for his philosophical works.

I first heard of Shaw in 1890, when I was a freshman at Cambridge. I heard of him from another freshman, who became my lifelong friend and who had been reading him on "The Quintessence of Ibsenism." Ibsen, in those days, was still more or less of a novelty in England. I did not meet Shaw, however, until the International Socialist Congress in 1896, where the German delegates, no doubt much to his satisfaction, concluded that he was a reincarnation of Satan. I later came to know him well owing to my friendship with the Sidney Webbs. He and I stayed with them in Monmouthshire at a time when he was just learning the technique of playwriting. He used to have a sort of chess board, with the names of the characters instead of pieces, and when writing a scene he would have the characters who were present in position on the chess board. He showed already some of the toughness which secured him such a long life. He had just been learning to ride a bicycle, and had not yet thoroughly mastered the art. Coming to a fork in the road at the bottom of a hill, I dismounted, and he ran full tilt into my bicycle. He was precipitated twenty feet through the air and landed on his back on the hard road. He jumped up at once and went on with his ride, whereas my bicycle was buckled and unusable, and I had to go home by train. At every station where the train stopped, he on his bicycle had already arrived, and put his head into the window and jeered.

Like the man in "The Hunting of the Snark," I will now skip forty years, to a time when the Shaws and the Webbs together came to visit me at my house on the South Downs. The house had a tower, from which there was a fine view, and we induced them all to climb the stairs. Shaw was in the van, Mrs. Shaw in the rear. During the whole of the ascent, Shaw talked without ceasing and Mrs. Shaw, from behind, ineffectually called up: "Don't talk while you're going up stairs, G.B.S."

When I was young, it was considered clever to suggest that the vanity which he displayed was a pose. This, however, was to do injustice to his wit. It was, in fact, just as great as he pretended, but he knew how to exhibit it in such a manner that it would seem shrewd to suppose he was putting it on. I was present on two occasions which I think will prove my point. On one of these occasions, Bergson, who was in London, had been invited to a luncheon to meet a number of philosophers and Shaw. Before Bergson's professional colleagues, Shaw began expounding the visitor's philosophy and, as was to be expected, gave an exposition which by no means recommended it to his professorial auditors. Bergson mildly intervened to say: "Ah no, it is not qvite zat," but Shaw swept aside his intervention, saying: "My dear fellow, I understand your philosophy much better than you do." Bergson clenched his fists and became white with anger, but just succeeded in not making a scene.

The second occasion was when the elder [Czechoslovak statesman Thomas] Masaryk was on an official visit to England. He invited Shaw, [novelist

H.G.] Wells, [novelist Frank Arthur] Swinnerton, and myself to come see him unofficially at 10 o'clock in the morning. With the exception of Shaw, we all arrived punctually, but Shaw marched in late, began at once: "Masaryk, the foreign policy of Czechoslovakia is all wrong," held forth on this theme for ten minutes, and then marched out of the room, without waiting for Masaryk's reply.

On one occasion Wells allowed himself to say in print that if in a shipwreck he had to choose between saving Shaw and saving [Ivan] Pavlov, he would let Shaw drown. After this, there was no limit to the abuse that Shaw would heap on Pavlov.

Shaw could be very cruel when his vanity was involved, but on other occasions, his kindness and generosity were equally remarkable, especially when he was still young. His kindness and his cruelty were equally essential parts of his incredibly vigorous personality.

VIRGINIUS DABNEY

# The Human Side of Woodrow Wilson

[ AUTUMN 1956 ]

A MAN who danced hornpipes on station platforms while campaigning for the presidency and jigs in the White House after his election; who was fervently addicted to Gilbert and Sullivan, loved limericks, wrote some good ones himself, and recited nonsense verse on many occasions; was one of the best story-tellers of his time and a mimic of rare talent; who doubled as a successful football coach at two universities while serving as professor; and who, although slanderously assailed in whispering campaigns from coast to coast as a rake and libertine, was, in fact, a notably affectionate husband and father.

That man was Woodrow Wilson. Admittedly the prevailing picture in the public mind is far different. Wilson is commonly regarded as having been an austere, humorless, stern, even arrogant individual who could brook no disagreement from anyone, whose obstinacy in refusing to accept reasonable reservations to the Covenant of the League of Nations led to its defeat in the Senate, and who broke with most of his friends before he died. Then, too, many people believed the gossip and calumny involving his relations with women.

Woodrow Wilson undoubtedly was in some respects a bundle of contradictions. It would be ridiculous to picture him as behaving most of the time like an end man in a minstrel show, but it would be equally so to regard him as a ruthless, opinionated person with ice water in his veins, or as an unfaithful husband.

True, Wilson was intolerant of stupidity; he did not "suffer foods gladly." A man of great intellectual power himself, he found it difficult, at times, to restrain his scorn for his mental inferiors. Furthermore, his tragic illness and paralysis, brought on by his fight for the League of Nations against the advice of his doctors, affected his attitudes, and was the chief cause of his "breaks" with several long-time friends.

My own acquaintance with Mr. Wilson began when he was Governor of New Jersey. He visited in the home of my parents at the University of Virginia, and I, a boy at the time, was entranced by his buoyant and witty personality. I hung around my father's study door listening to the screamingly funny anecdotes which the Governor of New Jersey was reeling off to his onetime college chum. My father, Richard Heath Dabney, a Heidelberg Ph.D. who served on the University of Virginia faculty for nearly half a century, had a sense of the ridiculous as keen as Wilson's, and their antics were something to behold.

A story he told father serves to illustrate the lighter side of his nature. While president of Princeton University he was guest of honor at a dinner in the West. The host and hostess were enormously impressed by the great Dr. Wilson, and they concluded that the dinner would have to be extremely formal. And so it was, until Wilson got so bored that he inquired if the assembled company liked limericks. The hostess answered primly in the affirmative, whereupon Wilson recited the following, which was far less well known then than it is today:

> There was a young monk of Siberia
> Whose existence grew drearier and drearier,
> Till he burst from his cell
> With a hell of a yell
> And eloped with the Mother Superior.

A great roar went up around the table and the ice was broken. Wilson entertained the company with stories and verse for the rest of the evening.

This side of Wilson's personality had come forcibly to the attention of his fellow-students on numerous occasions at the University of Virginia. For example, when he was chosen to award the prizes for foot-races and similar athletic contests, he decided, egged on by his friend, Dabney, to recite some bits of doggerel which had nothing whatever to do with the occasion. Somewhere in the program he awarded the prizes, but he also included such items as the following:

> 'Twas in the gloaming by the fair Wyoming
> That I left my darling many years ago.
> But memory tender brings her back in splendor
> With her cheeks of roses and her brow of snow.
>
> But where in thunder is she now, I wonder?
> Oh my soul, be quiet, and my sad heart hush!
> Under the umbrella of another fellow,
> Ah! I think I see her paddling through the slush!

Several years after leaving the university, he wrote Miss Ellen Axson, soon to become the first Mrs. Wilson: "It may shock you—it ought to—but I'm afraid it will not, to learn that I have a reputation (?) amongst most of my kin and certain of my friends for being irrepressible, in select circles, as a maker of grotesque addresses from the precarious elevation of chair seats, as a wearer of all varieties of comic grimaces, as a simulator of sundry unnatural, burlesque styles of voice and speech, as a lover of farces—even as a dancer of the *can-can!*"

Wilson began his professorial career at Bryn Mawr in 1885, and went thence to Wesleyan University at Middletown, Connecticut. At Wesleyan, his fame as a lecturer and public speaker was beginning to spread, and so was his fame as a football coach.

As a member of the coaching staff there (although he himself had never played football) he helped devise winning plays which gave Wesleyan a championship team. He was specifically credited, furthermore, by the college Alumnus Magazine with inspiring the eleven to tie Lehigh, after it had fallen two touchdowns behind. When the outlook was blackest, Professor Wilson rushed out in front of the bleachers, gave the students a going over for not cheering as they should, beat time to the college yell with his umbrella, and "continued this violently" until the players caught fire and tied the score. The Lehigh team credited him with saving the game for Wesleyan.

When he joined the Princeton faculty in 1890, he again took on the job of helping to coach the gridiron warriors. "It was a particularly welcome sight one afternoon in October to see Woodrow Wilson come striding out upon the field, take his place behind the eleven with Captain Poe, and proceed to whip the team up and down the sward, a function which Wilson continued daily to discharge through the long grind of ten weeks," said Professor Winthrop M. Daniels.

Wilson was greatly liked by the students at Princeton. During his twelve years as a teacher there, he was elected four times by the senior class as the most popular member of the faculty. The principal reason seems to have lain in the brilliance of his witty and stimulating lectures on political science. More than two-thirds of the students who had the right of choice elected to take one or more of his courses. [...]

When the "cloistered" Dr. Wilson was elected Governor of New Jersey, there was much shaking of heads by the practical politicians. They wondered whether anybody with only a theoretical knowledge of public affairs could possibly do well in the job. They were aware, however, that this "schoolmaster" was a person of great force.

He soon showed that he meant business, by breaking with New Jersey's Democratic bosses. In his final interview with Boss Jim Nugent, the latter shouted at Governor Wilson, "You're no gentleman!" Wilson's retort, as he showed Nugent the door was, "You're no judge!"

Wilson used a different tactic on the eve of the meeting of the State legislature. Invited to eat fried chicken and waffles with the members of the Republican-dominated Senate at a country club, he sang songs and danced "in every comical combination anybody could think of." As he described the occasion in a letter to a friend, "the evening was one unbroken romp," and he led one Senator "several times around the big dining room in a cakewalk in which we pranced together to the perfect content of the whole company." A few weeks later he wrote the same friend that all four of his major reform bills had passed the Senate *unanimously*, and that the hijinks at the club had undoubtedly played and important part in the result.

"I am on easy and delightful terms with all the Senators," he wrote. "They know me for something else than an 'ambitious dictator.'" He added that the newspapermen were "dazed" by his almost incredible success with the legislature.

He impressed the rank and file in New Jersey, as well as the lawmakers. One of his favorite stories concerned the comment of two laboring men who were leaving a big meeting in Newark, where the Governor had spoken.

"That's a smart guy," said one of them.

"He's smart as hell," said the other. "What I don't see is what a fellow as smart as that was doing hanging around a college so long."

Edward E. Davis, a prominent Philadelphia newspaperman who covered the New Jersey Legislature during this period, said he couldn't understand "the notion that got abroad that Woodrow Wilson was cold," and he added:

"There never was a man in the Governor's chair at Trenton who had such a human way of expressing himself. . . . He seemed to be one of the happiest men I ever met. . . . No one could be in his presence for five minutes without being charmed. . . . In moments of leisure he was in the habit of joking with the newspapermen and laughingly reciting limericks."

All this contributed to his tremendous success as Governor of New Jersey and his nomination to the presidency in 1912.

Soon after his nomination, a whispering campaign began. It involved his friendship with attractive Mrs. Mary Hulbert Peck, whom Wilson had met in Bermuda in 1907, and with whom he had carried on an animated correspondence during the intervening years. The fact that Mrs. Peck divorced her husband in 1912 added fuel to the flames. The further fact that Mrs. Peck (or Mrs. Hulbert, as she called herself after her divorce) was a devoted friend of the whole Wilson family, that she visited them and they visited her, was largely ignored.

There is general agreement among those who have read the more than two hundred letters which Wilson wrote Mary Hulbert that they are almost entirely impersonal and concerned with public affairs. Wilson undoubtedly found Mrs. Hulbert a stimulating personality, and enjoyed exchanging views with her. The substance of many of his letters to her has been published.

Wilson wrote similar letters to other able and charming women who, like Mary Hulbert, were friends of Mrs. Wilson—such as Edith Gittings Reid, wife of a Johns Hopkins professor, and Nancy Toy, who was married to a member of the Harvard faculty. There is every reason to believe that his relations with each of these talented women were completely correct. True, it was unwise for him, a public man, to carry on so extensive a correspondence with any woman other than his wife, even though—as in all these cases—Mrs. Wilson approved his doing so. She approved because she felt that she herself was "too grave," and that "since he married a wife who is not gay, I must provide for him friends who are."

William Allen White, like Wilson's other biographers, made an earnest effort to get the facts concerning Wilson and Mary Hulbert. The noted Republican editor concluded that the scandalous stories told were "slanders as foul and unfounded as were ever peddled in any campaign." Gamaliel Bradford, the historian, termed them "utterly baseless." Such has been the unanimous verdict of all serious students.

Professor Stockton Axson, of the Princeton faculty and Wilson's brother-in-law, would have been the first to denounce Wilson as a faithless husband, had he been one, yet Wilson had no more staunch defender throughout it all than Dr. Axson, who often spoke and wrote of Wilson's deep devotion to his sister.

That devotion was beautiful and profound, and was expressed in countless ways. It was strikingly set forth in a moving letter Wilson wrote from Bryn Mawr in 1888 to his friend Dabney, who had just informed him of his own approaching wedding. "Marriage has been the *making* of me both intellectually and morally," Wilson declared. He felt the same adoration for his wife more than a quarter of a century later, when she died in the White House. On that occasion he wrote Mary Hulbert: "God has stricken me almost beyond what I can bear." Later he said of Ellen Axson: "She was the most radiant creature I have ever known. Something like an aura of light always surrounded her."

The first Mrs. Wilson was not only a lovely and talented person, but at crucial points in his career she had given her husband excellent advice. She was credited, for example, with tipping the scales in favor of his running for Governor of New Jersey, and with keeping him in the race for the Democratic nomination for the presidency in 1912, when he was on the verge of dropping out. [. . .] The human qualities which contributed so largely to his success as Governor of New Jersey stood him in good stead in the presidential campaign of 1912. Wilson realized that many persons contrasted his scholarly approach with the riproaring, virile personality of "Teddy" Roosevelt, against whom he was running. Consequently he sought to overcome this impression by getting as close to his audiences as he could. Salting his speeches with punchy anecdotes, he set out deliberately to see if he could make the newspapermen laugh louder than Teddy had been able to make them do. When the veteran correspondent, Charles Willis Thompson, dropped his pencil and guffawed uproariously at a story Wilson told, the latter looked down at him from the platform with a satisfied smile. And when, on another occasion, someone in the audience yelled "That was a good one, Woody," the candidate mentioned it later to newspapermen with obvious relish. "They called me Woody!" he said, his eyes dancing. He was clearly pleased that he was thus hailed.

Later in the campaign, he made a whirlwind trip through New Jersey. One evening he returned to his hotel at Cape May, after delivering a dozen or more speeches. He looked haggard and exhausted, and his friend, Judge John W. Wescott, told him he ought to go to bed at once.

"Judge, I haven't the slightest intention of going to bed," said Wilson. "I'm going to recuperate by having some fun with you boys."

Judge Wescott then gave the following account:

> The "fun" consisted of an animated conversation that lasted until nearly 2 o'clock in the morning. I am not exaggerating in the least when I say that Mr. Wilson told us twenty or more funny stories. They came from every age and every clime.... In turn he told his stories with an Irish accent, a Negro dialect, a German, Italian, and French tone of voice. There was a clever point connected with each story. He had us laughing during all the time he was talking. If you had been in an adjoining room, when he was telling his Irish story you would have sworn it was an Irishman talking, and so on with the different nationalities.
>
> Not one of the stories he told was shady or off-color. Indeed, this was characteristic of the man.... He was the cleanest-minded man I ever came in contact with.

This somewhat strenuous evening with "the boys," piled on top of twelve or fifteen speeches, would seem to have been enough to put Wilson in bed for a week. Yet very much to the contrary, when the party broke up, he looked "as if he had just come out of a refreshing sleep"!

Some time afterward, Judge Wescott asked Dr. Cary Grayson, the White House physician, how Wilson managed to stand the strain of the presidency. Dr. Grayson replied:

"The answer is the medical power of fun. The President lightens his labors by his wit and his enjoyment of storytelling."

Wilson's first years in the White House were, in the main, happy and successful. During those years, the fun-loving side of his personality was more obvious than it later became, when Mrs. Wilson's death and the simultaneous outbreak of the first World War left him desperately depressed. [...]

The coming of war in Europe was, of course, a great trial to him, and he felt that he had to devote himself unreservedly to his governmental duties. George Creel, head of the Committee on Public Information, wrote that "Mr. Wilson's regard for his time became an actual obsession; everything and everybody were excluded that did not bear upon the task." Contrary to the practice he had followed in New Jersey, he made no particular effort to become friendly with the leaders in Congress, and this lack of personal contact became more obvious as his responsibilities grew.

Nor were his relations with the Washington press as cordial as they had been with the correspondents in Trenton. Mr. Wilson felt that after he became President, many of the papers were entirely too concerned with trivialities. "Sob sisters" enraged him by speculating as to the love affairs of his three daughters.

Not long after his election, Wilson had received a large group of correspondents at Sea Girt, New Jersey. Asked about the mail he was getting, he replied that it was quite heavy, and that he felt somewhat like the frog in the well: "Every time he jumped up one foot he fell back two." Next morning one of the New York papers headed the story "Wilson Feels Like Frog." [. . .]

The death of Mrs. Wilson and the outbreak of the war in Europe had subjected President Wilson to an almost constant emotional ordeal. His wife's passing left him horribly depressed, and the world crisis added greatly to his burdens.

Mrs. Wilson died on August 6, 1914. For some eight months, the President lived in "tomb-like seclusion." Then, in the spring of 1915, the gloom which enveloped his spirit was gradually lifted through the companionship of a beautiful and attractive widow, Virginia-born Edith Bolling Galt. Mrs. Galt had met the President through the latter's cousin, Miss Helen Bones. Within a few months, if not weeks, he had fallen deeply in love with her, and had characteristically consulted his daughters as to how they would feel if he married again. They gave their approval.

Although various members of the Cabinet and other leaders of the Democratic party felt that the President's remarriage so soon after his first wife's death probably would wreck his chances for a second term, he married Mrs. Galt in December, 1915. She brought cheer and warmth into his life, and they were inseparable thenceforth. So inseparable, in fact, that President Wilson saw few other people during the succeeding years, except the minimum required by his official duties. He talked over many of his problems with his wife, whose practical cast of mind was no less useful to him than her great social charm, but otherwise retired within himself to a much greater degree than formerly. "I rarely consult anybody," he told Ida Tarbell in the autumn of 1916, when America was drawing closer and closer to involvement in the war. [. . .]

During the strenuous days when America was on the verge of entering the war, or had actually gone in, President Wilson found time for relaxation with few persons, except Mrs. Wilson. She writes: "When he left his desk or office, he apparently closed that door in his mind, and was ready to play; then he would play with the abandon of a boy. Frequently, at night, we would go to the Oval Room upstairs after dinner and he would put a record on the Victrola and say: 'Now I'll show you how to do a jig step.' He was light on his feet, and often said he envied Primrose, the minstrel dancer, and he wished he could exchange jobs."

President and Mrs. Wilson made it a practice for years to attend Keith's Vaudeville every Saturday night. Wilson preferred vaudeville to any other type of theatrical performance. Another means of diverting his mind from his super-human task was, he said, to "get a rattling good detective story, get after some imaginary offender, and chase him all over."

There is general agreement that the strain of the prewar and war years aged Mr. Wilson greatly. His hair was much grayer, the lines in his face much deeper. Yet when the Armistice terms were finally accepted, he was still capable of having his little joke. As the war ended, he remarked to [his Private] Secretary Tumulty: "I feel like the Confederate soldier General John B. Gordon used to tell of, soliloquizing on a long, hard march during the Civil War: 'I love my country and I am fightin' for my country, but if this war ever ends, I'll be dad-burned if I ever love another country.'"

By the time of the armistice, President Wilson apparently was suffering from arteriosclerosis or some similar trouble. More than one physician remarked that the signs of this disability seemed clear to any practiced eye, and that it would explain some of the otherwise unaccountable things that Mr. Wilson did at the Paris Peace Conference and thereafter.

So deep was his dedication to the cause of world peace that he refused to spare himself. He contracted a violent case of the then-deadly influenza in Paris, and Dr. Grayson was much alarmed. Before the President could get his strength back, he had to plunge into wearisome haggling with the Big Three—Clemenceau of France, Lloyd George of Great Britain, and Orlando of Italy.

While Wilson was under this almost unparalleled strain, Tumulty wrote to warn him that he might wreck his constitution. Wilson's reply was, "Constitution? Why man, I'm already living on my by-laws!"

Partly as a result of such rare humorous interludes, he managed to keep going. On his return to the United States he plunged into the fight for ratification of the League of Nations.

Unfortunately he made it clear that he would accept no amendments or reservations to the Covenant of the League. This was generally regarded by his friends as a bad mistake, since they felt that reasonable reservations ought to be accepted. They accordingly advised him that unless he swung across the country arousing the people on behalf of the League, ratification would fail in the Senate.

President Wilson was in a state of virtual exhaustion, and was told by his physicians that the trip would be dangerous, if not fatal. He had been under such pressure that he had had no time to prepare a single speech for his tour, and he expected to make something like a hundred. It was before the day of presidential ghost-writers. Weary and worn, plagued by raging headaches, he threw himself into the campaign with what little strength he had left, and refused to listen to Dr. Grayson's urgent plea that his itinerary allow for a week's rest at the Grand Canyon. He said he could not justify taking any time whatever for relaxation on so vital a mission.

His breakdown near Pueblo, Colorado, in September, 1919, was the almost inevitable result. A crippling stroke, which paralyzed his left side, followed soon after his return to Washington. He was an invalid until his death in 1924.

It was during this period of invalidism that he broke with his long-time friend and confidant, Colonel Edward M. House, and with Private Secretary Tumulty and Secretary of State Robert Lansing. Had he been in normal health, it is altogether possible that these breaks would not have occurred. Yet it is understandable that under the circumstances, the public should have considered the rupturing of these long-standing friendships as climactic evidence of "Wilsonian arrogance."

The tragic paralytic in the White House, who was not seen at all by the public for many months, and then was glimpsed only on rare occasions when out for an automobile drive with his devoted wife, was far from being the vigorous, alert figure who had taken over the presidency only a few years before. The closing years of his life strengthened the popular feeling that his was a cold and remote personality.

Yet even during his serious illness, when the Senate sent a delegation to confer with him, a spark of the old wit crackled to the surface. One of the group was Republican Senator Albert B. Fall, who said, "Mr. President, we have all been praying for you." "Which way, Senator?" Wilson inquired with a chuckle.

Later, when the patient was more fully recovered, Secretary of State Bainbridge Colby arranged for an acquaintance to see him about a matter which the party in question deemed important. Colby asked Wilson after the interview what impression the man made on him. "That of a bungalow," said Wilson. "How is that?" asked Colby. "No upper story," was the reply.

Despite the strain of inauguration day in 1921, when the broken man turned over the presidential office to his successor Warren G. Harding, Wilson came through "smilingly and with a whimsical, humorous twist to his comments," said the correspondent of the Detroit Free Press.

Until only a couple of months before his death, Mr. Wilson attended Keith's Vaudeville every Saturday night. The street outside was usually filled with people who wanted to see the former President as he hobbled in, and the audience always gave him and Mrs. Wilson a standing ovation as they entered and departed. Mr. Wilson's love of light comedy and slapstick humor never left him.

It was, he liked to say, the "Irish" in him that accounted for this. His "Irish" was Scotch-Irish, and he was fond of attributing his frivolous qualities to his forebears, the Wilsons, who came to this country from Northern Ireland. The Woodrows, on the other hand, were blown-in-the-bottle Scots for many generations—serious, dour, crusading preachers and other intellectuals. Woodrow Wilson often referred to these two elements as battling for supremacy inside him.

The "Irish" in him deserves far more emphasis than it has received. Few, if any, Presidents in our history have been so adept as story-tellers, so prankish in their lighter moods, quicker in repartee, more affectionate in their intimate friendships, or tenderer in the family circle than Woodrow Wilson. The myths of coldness, hardness, humorlessness, and ruthlessness that have grown up around his name should be dispelled in this centennial year.

LOUIS B. WRIGHT

# The Anti-Shakespeare Industry and the Growth of Cults

[ SPRING 1959 ]

ONE of the fastest-growing industries in the country is the anti-Shakespeare business, a vigorous offshoot of the Shakespeare industry itself. For better than three hundred and fifty years, Shakespeare has been a name to conjure with in the theater and the printing house. A few good shots of Shakespeare have often been enough to bring back to health an ailing stock company. A popular edition of Shakespeare has been the iron-and-oyster tonic needed to restore the vigor of more than one impotent publishing house. Beginning in the late eighteenth and continuing through the nineteenth century, worshippers of Shakespeare became a cult, and the very word took on a mystic influence as idolaters did obeisance to the Bard of Avon.

Shakespeare idolatry induced a natural reaction. Certain intransigent souls refused to bow to Baal and went in search of another god. The undiscriminating worship of Shakespeare and the absurd legends of his perfection and omniscience fostered by professional literary critics and amateurs alike undoubtedly account for the effort to dethrone the deity.

The activities of the iconoclasts have produced some of the oddest and funniest books in print. Readers in search of unconscious humor should turn to this body of literature which has been accumulating with almost arithmetical progression ever since Delia Bacon in 1857 published "The Philosophy of the Plays of Shakespeare Unfolded" to advance the authorship of her namesake, Sir Francis Bacon. Today almost anybody with a typewriter and a willingness to abandon his mind to nonsense can find a publisher for a book asserting that somebody else wrote Shakespeare. Some of these books are marvelous beyond belief in their imaginative concepts, in their zealous accumulation of irrelevant detail, in their plausible "proof" of the author's particular candidate. Most of them are entertaining for people with a taste for "whodunits" or science fiction. If one can suppress the intrusion of facts of social and literary history, many of them sound convincing. At any rate, there is a growing audience for these books which a canny publisher may not wish to overlook.

Various cults have arisen to advocate the authorship of this or that candidate. These cults have all the fervor of religion, and indeed, the whole movement is permeated with emotion that sweeps aside the intellectual appraisal of facts, chronology, and the laws of evidence. The disciples of the cults, like certain other fanatic sectarians, rail on disbelievers and condemn other cultists as fools and knaves. One of the curious phenomena of the cults is the bad manners and arrogance displayed at times by their members. Some of them write abusive letters to disbelievers, heckle speakers of the opposite persuasion, threaten libel suits against those who disagree in print, try to suppress unfavorable reviews of their books, and occasionally threaten bodily violence. One gets the impression that they would gladly restore the faggot and the stake for infidels from their particular orthodoxy. They have discovered "truth" according to their lights, and they are angry and unhappy when the world refuses to embrace it.

The variety of candidates advocated by these dedicated souls is beyond belief. They begin with Francis Bacon, select a noble roster from Burke's Peerage, and include even Queen Elizabeth I herself, who seems to have spent her time plying a goose quill instead of attending to the business of state, as historians have hitherto believed.

Bacon has had the longest history and has accumulated the most terrifying bibliography on the subject, but there are runners-up panting for his claim. These include Sir Walter Raleigh; Roger Manners, fifth Earl of Rutland; William Stanley, sixth Earl of Derby; Edward De Vere, seventeenth Earl of Oxford; Sir Edward Dyer, and almost any other knight or nobleman, literate or illiterate, whom someone has dreamed of nominating. In addition there are a few less exalted candidates, including a whole syndicate of writers headed by Ben Jonson, and, lately, Christopher Marlowe, who died before most of Shakespeare's plays were written. There is not much to choose from among the candidates. All have an equal claim to the laurels and all have equally persuasive and plausible advocates.

If a reader cannot endure to have Shakespeare of Stratford as the author of plays that he admires, let him choose any of these candidates. They all have devoted followers who will welcome a new convert to their beliefs with the enthusiasm accorded a repentant sinner at a Holy Rollers' revival. If the convert is to be happy in his new faith, however, he must mind his own behavior. He must not question the received dogma; he must be infinitely solemn about it all.

If there is any one quality more lacking than all others in the anti-Shakespeareans, it is a sense of humor. A fog of gloom envelops them. When a busy scholar will not argue with them, their pride is hurt. Yet serious Elizabethan historians say that one might as well expect a professor at the Harvard Medical School to debate with a chiropractor about the treatment of spinal disease. The anti-Shakespeareans talk darkly about a

## THE ANTI-SHAKESPEARE INDUSTRY AND THE GROWTH OF CULTS

conspiracy of orthodox college professors to maintain the authenticity of "that yokel" or the "butcher boy of Stratford." The refusal of scholars to waste time over the controversy, they reason, is part of a plot to keep enthroned an impostor named William Shakespeare of Stratford. The preoccupation with this plot theory has developed a neurosis among the anti-Shakespeareans that may account for an unhappy truculence that sometimes makes them unwelcome in polite company.

The plot or conspiracy theory is hard to understand, for if any professor thought that the smallest mote of information could be found to prove another authorship of the plays, he and all his graduate students would be scrambling to find that morsel of truth. The professor brilliant enough to find another author for Shakespeare's plays would assure himself of an undying reputation; he would be certain of translation to an Ivy League job; and his book would pour in royalties. Not even professors are so unworldly as to put behind them a prospect for fame and prosperity because of a morbid loyalty to a dramatist dead these three and a half centuries.

Scarcely a week goes by that some devoted soul does not write to the Folger Shakespeare Library protesting its alleged orthodox advocacy of William Shakespeare's authorship. Here is an institution, they imply, that is a part of the dark "conspiracy" to suppress the truth! When the newspapers were full of reports that Marlowe was really Shakespeare, an alarmed friend called to ask if the Folger's materials were about to be "devalued." The Folger Shakespeare Library—which is concerned only in part with Shakespeare, for its primary concern is with the history of Western civilization in the sixteenth and seventeenth centuries—has not the slightest interest in maintaining the authorship of William Shakespeare of Stratford or any other candidate. It is merely interested in the quality of evidence produced. Its materials would have the same value to learning if someone proved that General Ulysses S. Grant wrote the plays—a thesis as convincing as some being advocated.

The identity of the individual who wrote the plays is relatively unimportant. The important thing to be remembered is that truth does matter, and that the integrity of scholars trained in the history and literature of the Elizabethan period will not let them substitute fanciful theories and hypotheses for documentary evidence that has stood the test of centuries.

For all the dust stirred up by the anti-Shakespeareans, they have not adduced a single shred of objective evidence to prove that William Shakespeare of Stratford did not write the plays in the accepted canon or that anyone else is the author. Their so-called "case" rests on conjecture, surmise, and self-induced hypothesis. They simply get a vision that someone other than Shakespeare wrote the plays, and they take off in pursuit of circumstantial evidence to prove their contentions. Nothing stops them. Their candidate may have died before Shakespeare wrote his plays. If so, they evolve an ingenious theory to prove him still alive and able to push a pen. The greater the absurdity, the greater their zest.

Lawyers have shown a special tendency to plead cases against William Shakespeare. The game probably appeals to their sporting instinct to see what they can do with a doubtful case. Lawyers are trained to do the best they can for their clients regardless of the weight of evidence against them. When a lawyer takes the case of the Earl of Oxford, for example, he is not deterred because there is no scrap of credible evidence to prove that Oxford ever wrote a single play attributed to Shakespeare. As a good lawyer he feels compelled to magnify the most tenuous suppositions into evidence which he hopes the jury will accept as gilt-edged truth.

The techniques of the trial lawyer, which are those used by the anti-Shakespeareans, are quite different from those practiced by professional historical scholars. The lawyer is out to win the case by his skill of persuasion regardless of the evidence. The historical scholar, on the contrary, is trained to analyze evidence, not to win cases. He must get at the truth by weighing the pros and cons of each piece of testimony regardless of whether it favors his particular thesis.

By parading a host of friendly witnesses before the jury, even if they have nothing relevant to say, by suppressing evidence damaging to their clients, and by abusing the opposition, lawyerlike advocates sometimes manage to present a persuasive case for Oxford, Derby, or some other contender. All of this is legitimate in a court of law if the attorney for the plaintiff can get away with it. But it is not sound scholarship.

Although the anti-Shakespeareans usually begin by impugning the testimony of accepted scholarship and by anticipating rebuttal by calling it prejudice, they are the first to scream over adverse criticism. They invariably claim to be the victims of the prejudice of orthodox scholars who are in a conspiracy to protect their vested interests in "that Stratford fellow."

Why they think anyone has a vested interest in William Shakespeare is a mystery that passeth understanding. Aside from a few curio vendors at Stratford-upon-Avon who might have to alter their stock a bit, nobody has any vested interest in maintaining Shakespeare's superiority simply out of deference to William. He hasn't even any lineal descendants to worry, out of filial piety, about his claim. If Delia Bacon's ghost proves that Francis wrote the plays, Stratford-upon-Avon will continue to be crowded with tourists and business will be as brisk as usual. Swarms of visitors will come to do reverence to one of the shrewdest operators in history. The emphasis might shift just a trifle but the Birthplace will continue to be worth visiting by Britons and Americans, who both appreciate a skillful hoax. Stratford's business might even improve with notoriety. William Henry Ireland's Shakespeare forgeries, for example, are prized collector's items fetching a high price at auction, and Thomas J. Wise's literary forgeries are much sought after. One American library that bought Wise's forgeries thinking they were genuine was much distressed when the hoax was revealed, not at being hoodwinked originally, but at failing to acquire two of the forged books, which it hurried to buy before the price went up.

The Shakespeare industry is safe, even if the anti-Shakespeare business is also booming. Instead of being grumpy about the world's lack of appreciation of their endeavors, the anti-Shakespeareans ought to be happy. So long as they can keep up the smoke a few people are going to believe that some fire must be there. They profit from Barnum's biological observation that a sucker is born every minute.

To a trained historian of the period, it is a nine days' wonder that anyone takes the anti-Shakespeareans seriously because their whole case is built upon a few simple premises, all of which are erroneous. Their initial errors are these: (1) that Shakespeare was an ignorant country boy without any education; (2) that nothing is known about William Shakespeare, which argues that he was not an author of repute; (3) that only a nobleman or someone of exalted station could have written plays dealing with kings and courts; (4) that the author of the plays was so learned as to be almost omniscient, and hence he could not have been a boy who had only a grammar school education.

Not one of these statements is accurate, but upon them a great tissue of supposition is built, and lengthy books solemnly propose candidates with the qualifications of the ideal author of the plays.

The truth is that a great deal of carefully-documented evidence about which there can be no dispute certifies to the reality of Shakespeare. This is printed with precision and accuracy in Sir Edmund Chambers' two-volume work, "William Shakespeare: A Study of Facts and Problems" published at Oxford by the Clarendon Press in 1930. Though some further details have come to light since 1930, Chambers' work presents enough indisputable evidence to settle the problem for reasonable men who do not let their emotions govern their minds. About the identity of Shakespeare as the author of the canonical plays there is no "mystery" whatever except in vivid imaginations.

Though nineteenth-century idolaters attributed omniscience to the author of Shakespeare's plays, a careful reading shows that he was often exceedingly careless and demonstrated no profound book learning. Shakespeare not only could give a seacoast to Bohemia, but he could garble history, mix up facts, muddle his classical allusions, use sloppy grammar and syntax, and make as many gaffes as any other thirsty writer trying to finish a scene in time to get to the tavern for a drink with the boys. The plays contain no more book learning than any bright boy could have acquired in grammar school or picked up in his later reading. Other dramatists of the period are more learned—and less read—notably Ben Jonson.

The anti-Shakespeareans clearly are worried because Shakespeare never went to college. That is one of the roots of their trouble. They think that the author of these great plays should have had a diploma to hang on his wall, a diploma just like their dentist's. This view, much emphasized, is a touching illustration of the faith that Americans have in a college education. They forget that some of the writers of the world's greatest literature, from Homer to Hemingway, never darkened the doors of a college, and some of them had much less schooling than Shakespeare. Even learned Ben Jonson, who could spout Latin and Greek at the drop of his pint pot, got all his schooling at Westminster, supplemented by a spell of bricklaying, his stepfather's trade. The grammar school in Shakespeare's age was an educational institution that grounded its students in Latin and some Greek and provided the fundamentals of literary learning. And at Stratford, almost in sight of his father's house, Shakespeare had available one of the best grammar schools in all England. University education in the Elizabethan period was chiefly designed to turn out theologians, and the curriculum would have provided little to stimulate a dramatist like Shakespeare to anything except satire. Neither Oxford nor Cambridge offered a course in English literature or English history until long generations after Shakespeare was sleeping under his monument in Trinity Church. Some of Shakespeare's contemporaries went to the universities, but not many of them stayed to finish and none learned much that was useful in the theater.

The notion that one learns to be a great writer in a college or university class is a delusion that few students and no successful writers harbor. An experience of life is a much better school, as the literary geniuses of the world demonstrate. Cervantes, son of a poor apothecary and barber-surgeon, had little schooling but his writings are as immortal as Shakespeare's. Molière, the son of an upholsterer, lacked even a grammar school education and at fourteen could only read, write, and figure a little. Yet he was bright enough to cut a tolerable figure in French literature. Dickens was innocent of formal education and Mark Twain picked his up as a printer setting type. Yet both Dickens and Mark Twain wrote about a variety of subjects without benefit of diploma. Mark Twain even described knights and kings—in "A Connecticut Yankee at King Arthur's Court"—which would surely suggest that the work must have been the creation of some highborn author familiar with royal courts.

If the anti-Shakespeareans who argue the "ignorant country boy thesis" don't want to stand in the corner wearing a dunce cap themselves, they ought to learn a little about the curriculum of the Latin grammar schools of Shakespeare's time—and about the sterility of much university education. If Shakespeare had gone to either Oxford or Cambridge, he might have turned out to be a parson. He certainly would not have learned about the manifold aspects of life reflected in his plays by listening to the logic-chopping theological discussions that occupied so much of university teaching.

The notion that Shakespeare was not highborn also troubles some skeptics, especially Americans, who have a naïve and uninformed concept of the education and cultivation of the nobility in Shakespeare's lifetime. The author of these plays, they insist, must have been at least a lord, for did he not show an intimate acquaintance with kings and courts, and did he not write about many great nobles? And the skeptics cite passages from the history plays to prove this intimate knowledge. If they took the trouble to investigate the sources of the history plays, they would find that the author took his material from popular works of history, took it wholesale, in huge chunks. Literary etiquette in Shakespeare's time was not squeamish. When an author needed a good passage and found one lying around loose, it merely showed enterprise to appropriate it. When Shakespeare needed historical background, he turned to such works as Raphael Holinshed's "Chronicles of England, Scotland and Ireland," and since the narrative and even conversations were already written down in good prose, all he had to do was to alter the prose to blank verse.

Many of the passages that the anti-Shakespeareans solemnly exhibit as proof of the author's high birth are originally from Holinshed. And who was Holinshed? We know less about him than about Shakespeare, but it is believed that he was the son of a country squire and that he may have gone to Cambridge and become, as Anthony Wood reported, a poor "minister of God's word." He was no courtier. Indeed, he acquired much of his education in the print shop of Reginald Wolfe, where he served as a translator. We are certain that no member of the House of Lords wrote the "Chronicles of England, Scotland and Ireland."

The "noble lord" theory of the authorship of Shakespeare's plays is promoted nowadays chiefly by Americans. It represents a kind of snobbery and is of a piece with the effort of many plain citizens to find a lord in their genealogies. Most of these genealogies themselves are complete myths. Very few Americans can produce clear proof of their descent from any titled Englishman of Shakespeare's time or later. Yet a surprising number of the anti-Shakespeareans have De Vere, Stanley, or some other nobleman's name in their backgrounds and fancy themselves descended from the Earl of Oxford, the Earl of Derby, or someone else of their choice.

An analysis of the writings of the nobility in the reign of Elizabeth I does not suggest that literary genius flourished exceedingly among them. But it was fashionable to appear literary, and a few, including the Earl of Oxford, received a certain amount of adulation as men of letters. Many noblemen kept a stable of authors as modern politicians employ speech-writers. When sonneteering was in fashion, a nobleman might get one of his tame poets to dash off a cycle of sonnets for him to use in wooing the object of his next seduction. Most of the nobility around Elizabeth were too busy trying to retain a foothold on the slippery ladder of politics to devote themselves wholeheartedly to letters. Even when a nobleman signed a poem, it is now impossible to tell whether it is his own work or the effort of a ghost-writer. It would be much easier to believe that the Earl of Oxford or the Earl of Derby hired Shakespeare to write for them than to think that they foisted their compositions on the playwright.

Some of the anti-Shakespeareans make much of the fact that Shakespeare's manuscripts have not survived and that a deep mystery enshrouds their loss. Very few Elizabethan dramatic manuscripts have survived anywhere, and those only by chance. Nobody kept plays because they were the work of great literary masters. In fact, plays were not regarded as "literature" at all, and men laughed scornfully at Ben Jonson when he had the consummate egotism in 1616 to publish his plays and call them "The Works of Benjamin Jonson." Plays were not considered of any greater literary value than the scripts of television shows today. Once a printer had used a manuscript play, he threw out the dead copy and was glad to get rid of the rubbish. When the Puritans came into power, they closed the theaters in 1642 and kept them shut for eighteen years. In that time, playhouse copies of manuscripts were lost, thrown out, eaten by rats, used for various inelegant purposes, or they simply moldered away. They were not objects of a collector's veneration. They were the reverse and were hated by the Puritans as textbooks from the devil's schoolhouse. It takes no vivid imagination to understand what a Puritan would do with the manuscript of "Romeo and Juliet."

Some anti-Shakespeareans even talk about Shakespeare's signatures as "hen scratches" and evidence of illiteracy! In their innocence they do not know that Shakespeare wrote a characteristic hand of his day, and that many a learned pedant from the university wrote much more crabbedly.

The notion that nothing is known about the man Shakespeare is another evidence of innocence. Much more is on the record about Shakespeare than about many other Elizabethan men of letters. He was the son of a prosperous Stratford businessman; he engaged in business and bought land and property; he was involved in litigation; and he was a popular actor, theatrical manager, and playwright. His activities resulted in definite written records. Furthermore, contemporary references to Shakespeare the playwright and author are fairly common and he was held in high esteem throughout the seventeenth and eighteenth centuries. So great was his fame that the editors of the Third Folio tried to assign a number of non-canonical plays to Shakespeare. Not until late in the eighteenth century did anyone dream of another author for Shakespeare's plays. In 1769 Herbert Lawrence published "The Life and Adventures of Common Sense," in which he suggested that some unidentified person wrote the plays. That was the first and only time the question ever touched common sense. In 1785 another Englishman decided that Bacon must have written the plays but it was not until 1857 that the Bacon boom really started. In that year Delia Bacon, a spinster from Hartford, Connecticut, published her book in which she asserted that the plays were the work of a group headed by Bacon, Raleigh, and Edmund Spenser. In the very same year William Henry Smith by coincidence published "Bacon and Shakespeare" attributing authorship to Bacon. Since that time the Baconians have multiplied until their published works would fill a trash wagon. Delia Bacon, grandmother of the cult, contemplated opening Shakespeare's tomb, and Nathaniel Hawthorne tells how she spent an all-night vigil in Trinity Church trying to make up her mind to lift the stone if "her single strength would suffice." She desisted and presently the Mayor of Stratford wrote Hawthorne, then American consul at Liverpool, that she was lunatic.

The Baconians have grown into a vigorous cult, but many other cults have risen to challenge their views. Each cult thinks ill of other cultists. The Oxfordians, for example, think the Baconians are crackpots, and the advocates of the Earl of Derby think all the others are benighted.

The Bible of the advocates of the Earl of Oxford is "'Shakespeare' Identified in Edward De Vere, the Seventeenth Earl of Oxford" published in London in 1920 by J. Thomas Looney. In the second edition of this work, published in New York in 1948, one of the American admirers of the author included a tribute in which he complained at the tendency of reviewers to make "a labored quip on the author's name." Looney does not produce any objective evidence to show that Oxford wrote Shakespeare's plays. He surmises that since Oxford did write unidentified plays he must have written Shakespeare's. His method is to read Shakespeare and find references that he thinks parallel situations in Oxford's career. By the same method one could prove that the Song of Solomon was written by Marilyn Monroe. Since Looney, others have written about the Earl of Oxford but they merely amplify Looney's exegesis.

The Bible of the advocates of the Earl of Derby is a two-volume work by a Frenchman, Abel Lefranc, "Sous le masque de William Shakespeare," published in Paris in 1919. Unlike many authors of such books, Lefranc was a literary scholar, in another field. His work contains a fair amount of information about William Stanley, the sixth Earl of Derby, and some useful footnotes on this and that, but after two volumes he produces no single shred of evidence that Derby wrote Shakespeare's plays. So long as Lefranc stuck to studies of Rabelais, or Clement Marot, in his own familiar bailiwick, he was a creditable scholar, but when he strayed across the English Channel into a period that he did not know, he was a babe in the British woods. It is an advantage not to know much about the subject when launching a venture of this type.

One ingenious book "proves" that the poet Edmund Spenser was not Edmund Spenser at all but Edward Seymour, Earl of Hertford, and that by Catherine Grey he had three sons who are known to us as the writers Robert Greene, Thomas Nash, and William Shakespeare. Shakespeare in this book's thesis is still the author of the plays but he is not really Shakespeare but the son of Edmund Spenser who is not really Spenser but the Earl of Hertford.

Another new twist to the Bacon thesis cropped up in a series of articles published in January, 1956, in the Indianapolis Star, which reported the astonishing views of a local cryptographer who claimed in all seriousness to have discovered that Bacon not only wrote the works attributed to Shakespeare but also edited the King James Version of the Bible and was the author of the works of Montaigne and John Milton, John Bunyan's "Pilgrim's Progress," Izaak Walton's "Compleat Angler," Thomas Gray's "Elegy in a Country Churchyard," Edgar Allan Poe's "Raven," William Cullen Bryant's "Thanatopsis," and Rose Hartwick Thorpe's "Curfew Shall Not Ring Tonight." Presumably Bacon also wrote his own books in his spare time. That would certainly make him the most industrious penman known to history.

Problems of chronology never stand in the way of a candidate for the authorship of Shakespeare's plays. When a dedicated advocate of Christopher Marlowe arose a few years ago, he resurrected the dead and put a pen in his hand. From then on authorship was easy. The latest resurrectionist is the author of a book to prove that the plays were written by no less a personage than Queen Elizabeth I herself. Acceptance of this author's thesis requires one to believe that all of Shakespeare's plays were written before 1602 when the Queen gave up ghost-writing for Shakespeare, presumably because of the frailties of age. The fact that the later plays are filled with allusions to events after the Queen's death apparently can be dismissed as a matter of no moment.

Those who read Shakespeare's plays for hidden meanings and secret cryptograms find an outlet for their energies which they believe rewarding. Although two of the greatest living cryptographers, Colonel William Friedman and Elizabeth Friedman, in "The Shakespearean Ciphers Examined," have shown with extraordinary patience and objectivity that not one of the cryptographic "discoveries" concerning Shakespeare has a shadow of validity, these dedicated believers will never be convinced. They work in a realm of faith not of fact.

The multitude of books disputing the authorship of Shakespeare's plays must provoke our thoughtful contemplation. They all represent a triumph of inspiration and industry over conventional scholarship and dull logic. They throw a great deal of light on the ways of erring men to literature. As for concrete proof, they are pretty much on a par. They are all convincing to their authors and to the cults that gather around them. They all contain much of wonder and mystery. They probably serve a good purpose. If these writers were not proving that somebody else wrote the plays, they might be swamping the presses with books about Shakespeare. There are already too many books and too many articles about Shakespeare—at least twice too many. God in his mercy has sent the anti-Shakespeareans to drain off some of this potential writing into other and more distant bibliographies.

How does one acquire the skill to write anti-Shakespearean books? First one must develop the habit of willing suspension of disbelief. Then one must break the hampering bondage to accepted facts and recorded knowledge. After that the way is clear. All one then needs is the capacity to climb into a soap bubble and soar away into Cuckoo-Land.

# The Nineteen Sixties

ARTHUR C. CLARKE

# Shaw and the Sound Barrier

[ WINTER 1960 ]

THERE seem very few subjects in which Shaw was not interested, and fewer still on which he was not prepared to express his opinion. Nevertheless, it may surprise most people to learn that towards the end of his life the ubiquitous playwright concerned himself with such advanced ideas as space-travel and supersonic flight. It happened in this manner.

During the summer of 1946 I wrote a paper entitled "The Challenge of the Spaceship"—yes, I had been reading Toynbee—, which was an attempt to evaluate the effects of interplanetary travel upon human thought and society. After I had presented it as a lecture to the British Interplanetary Society in London, it was published in that organisation's Journal, and later in a number of books and periodicals all over the world (such as, for example, the UNESCO magazine Impact). Most of the basic ideas in this paper have now reached a considerably larger audience by being incorporated in the closing chapters of "The Exploration of Space" and I shall not attempt to repeat them here. My main thesis was that the crossing of space would not merely be an exciting scientific stunt, but would have profound cultural repercussions affecting philosophy, art, religion, and indeed every aspect of our society. I drew a parallel—which has now become something of a cliché—between the Renaissance and the coming age of space exploration, suggesting that the moon and planets might play a rôle during the next century not unlike that of the Americas in the fifteenth and sixteenth centuries.

In the paper I made a passing reference to Shaw, and soon afterwards I came across the magnificent speech with which Lilith closes the play "Back to Methuselah": "Of life only there is no end; and though of its million starry mansions many are empty and many still unbuilt, and though its vast domain is as yet unbearably desert, my seed shall one day fill it and master its matter to its uttermost confines. . . ." This, I thought, showed a considerable sympathy with the ideals of astronautics, so I sent Shaw a copy of the British Interplanetary Society's Journal containing my lecture—not in the least expecting a reply.

Much was my surprise when one of the famous pink postcards arrived, completely covered with shaky but perfectly legible handwriting:

Ayot Saint Lawrence, Welwyn, Herts.
25 Jan 1947
FROM BERNARD SHAW

Many thanks for the very interesting lecture to the B.I.S. How does one become a member, or at least subscribe to the Journal?

When de Haviland [sic] perished here the other day it seemed clear to me that he must have reached the speed at which the air resistance balanced the engine power and brought him to a standstill.

Then he accelerated, and found out what happens when an irresistible force encounters an immovable obstacle.

Nobody has as yet dealt with this obvious limit to aeronautic speed as far as I have read.

G.B.S.

The reference is to a tragic event of a few months earlier. On 27 September 1946, Geoffrey de Havilland had been testing the experimental DH 108 jet plane over the Thames, making the last run before a forthcoming attack on the world speed record. He put the plane into a dive, reached the highest speed then attained by man—and was killed instantly when the tremendous forces encountered in going through the sonic barrier tore the aircraft to pieces.

What I did not realise at the time—and indeed have discovered only recently—was that Shaw was a close neighbour of de Havilland's and knew the young test pilot quite well. This helps to explain one of the points in his second letter.

The receipt of this card filled me with mixed feelings. I was naturally flattered by the response, and was also surprised to discover that at the age of 91 Shaw was willing to join an organisation with aims as advanced as ours. (Back in 1947, anyone who talked about such things as artificial satellites and long-range rockets was still regarded as a little touched. VANGUARD, ATLAS and TITAN were still hidden in the mists of the future.) At the same time, I did not know exactly how to reply—for the main point of his letter was complete nonsense. It did not require any knowledge of aeronautics to appreciate this; it was a matter of common sense. *If* de Havilland's plane had reached the speed at which the engine power balanced the air resistance, it would continue at that speed like a motor car that is flat out. It would certainly not be "brought to a standstill," and the last thing the pilot could do would be to accelerate, since by definition he had no excess power with which to increase his speed any further.

After some thought, I sent Shaw the following tactful reply, hoping to put him right without hurting his feelings:

King's College,
London.
27 Jan 1947

Dear Mr Shaw,

I am very gratified by your interest in my article and in this Society, and have great pleasure in enclosing further details, as well as our latest publication. I hope that "Astronautics and Poetry" amuses you.

Although the precise cause of de Havilland's death is still unknown, it seems likely that the accident was due to some structural failure. As you say, the limit of speed is set when air resistance equals engine thrust. But the latter can always be increased with more powerful motors, so there is no absolute limit—only a limit for any particular type of machine. V.2, for example, had more than a dozen times the thrust of de Havilland's machine, and a number of rocket-propelled aircraft are nearing completion which will have speeds in the 1,000 m.p.h. range.

In the vacuum of space, of course, where the rocket works at maximum efficiency, there is no resistance and no speed limit at all. A motor of any power could build up any speed as long as its fuel supply could be maintained.

Purists may object to my oversimplification; there is, in fact, a natural limit of speed—that of the velocity of light. However, as light travels almost a million times as fast as sound, I felt justified in ignoring this complication in the (vain) hope that Shaw would do likewise.

We know now that it was supersonic flutter, produced when the DH 108 traveled too fast at too low an altitude, which broke up the plane. And there is a sinister little story about the aircraft's wreckage which, as far as I am aware, has never been told elsewhere. After the crash, all the pieces that could be found were dredged out of the Thames and brought back to the factory for examination. It was here, late one night, that the engineers working on the cause of the accident were startled—to say the least—by the sound of something moving inside the mass of twisted metal. It was a loud scratching noise, travelling with some determination from place to place. The engineers were perhaps more relieved than they would care to admit when, a few minutes later, one of the broken combustion chambers disgorged a small crab.

Shaw wasted no time in answering my letter. Back by return of post came his cheque, application for membership to the B.I.S.—and this time not a card but a two-page letter. I have since read it a good many times, and it remains one of the most baffling communications I have ever received:

31 Jan 1947

I am not convinced about de Haviland. It is necessary mathematically to have a zero to count from to infinity, positive or negative, Fahrenheit or Centigrade; but the zero is not a physical fact: it is only a convention: and infinity means only the limit to human counting. I approach the subject, being a dramatist, first from my knowledge of the man, and my conviction that he would accelerate to the utmost of his machine if air resistance stopped him. And this would smash his machine as it actually did smash, in spite of all assumptions that speed cannot exceed the velocity of light and that above the stratosphere is sheer vacuum, both of them mathematical conventions and not scientific facts.

Besides, what proof is there that he was above the stratosphere when his machine broke up?

However, this may be only my ignorant crudity; so do not bother to reply.

G.B.S.

Despite the polite brush-off in the last paragraph, I felt that it was impossible to let such hopeless confusion go quite unchallenged, so after some thought I replied as follows:

8 Feb 1947

Dear Mr Shaw,

Thank you for your letter. I am so glad that you have decided to join our Society.

I am afraid that my comments on de Havilland may not have been quite clear. He was actually at a relatively low altitude when the accident occurred, and my point is that whatever limit may exist to speeds *in* the atmosphere there can be none to speeds outside it. This has been proved experimentally by V.2 which traveled six times as fast as de Havilland's plane (reaching England from Germany [sic] in five minutes and attaining a maximum speed of 3,600 m.p.h.) At heights of more than thirty miles the German scientists were unable to detect any appreciable air resistance, even at this extremely high speed.

This concluded, perhaps none too soon, the Clarke-Shaw correspondence. But Shaw continued to be a member of the British Interplanetary Society until his death three years later; he still holds the record as the oldest member we ever had.

Today, when men have flown at two thousand miles an hour and are preparing to travel twice as fast, this echo from the early days of supersonic flight (all of ten years ago!) seems somewhat quaint and old-fashioned. It may even be a little unkind to preserve what some might consider the words of genius in its dotage. Though it is true that Shaw never hesitated to lay down the law on any subject, even one about which he knew nothing whatsoever, the younger G.B.S. would surely have produced a less eccentric letter than that of 31 Jan 1947.

Yet whatever one may think of the old man's aeronautical confusion, it is hard not to admire his efforts to keep abreast of the times. How many of us will do as well at the age of 91?

# GEORGE F. KENNAN

## The Experience of Writing History

[ SPRING 1960 ]

I JUST WANT to make a few very informal observations about the nature of history as a subject and about the condition of the historian. My excuse for doing so is simply that I came to this work unusually late in life, after a quarter of a century, in fact, in a wholly different sort of occupation. The impressions I have gained of these matters have something of the quality of the naïve. And since the naïve is occasionally amusing, whether or not it is instructive, I thought you might just possibly like to hear what these impressions are.

One of the first things that dismayed me, as I tried to put pen to paper with a view to relating historical events, was to discover the hopeless open-endedness of the subject of history itself: its multi-dimensional quality, its lack of tidy beginnings and endings, its stubborn refusal to be packaged in any neat and satisfying manner. I was soon brought to realize that every beginning and ending of every historical work is always in some degree artificial and contrived. No matter what you told, there was always something that had gone before, or came afterward, which you didn't have time to tell about, or which you didn't know about, and which was nevertheless essential to the completeness of the tale.

This open-endedness of the historical subject applied, I was brought to realize, not just to the longitudinal dimension of chronology, but also to the latitudinal dimension of related subjects and related happenings. No matter what field of human activity you selected for treatment, there were always a dozen other fields that had something to do with it, which you couldn't treat. And wherever you tried to draw the boundary between what you could write about and what you couldn't, it was always an artificial boundary, doing violence in some degree to the integrity of the presentation itself.

The perfect historical work, in other words, could not be written. If you were a great enough historian, if you were sufficiently learned in the environment of your subject as well as in its central core, then you might be able to do a good job of concealing from all but the most perceptive of your readers the untidiness of the outer limits of your presentation. But the untidiness would be there, nevertheless. There would always be a border, however well concealed, beyond which the firmness of your knowledge trailed off into the obscurity of your ignorance, or where the obvious limits on the patience of publishers and readers made it impossible for you to tell all you knew.

In addition to this diffuse quality of the subject, I was startled to discover how rigorous, when you stopped to think of it, were the limitations of perspective. History, it seemed, besides being open-ended, partook also of the nature of a sphere. You couldn't see it from all directions at once. You could see it only from some tiny, fixed point in its ample stratosphere. This point was always arbitrary in relation to the subject. An infinite number of other points could conceivably have been selected. Each would have revealed something which you, from the perspective of your particular point, were unable to reveal. Every point was, therefore, severely limited in its possibilities. Not only that, but there was a real question as to what latitude you really had in selecting the point you were going to use—whether, in fact, it was not already substantially selected for you.

This brought up, as you will readily see, the whole perplexing question of subjectivity. I had naïvely supposed, before I tackled this work, that there was a body of unrevealed or unappraised historical fact lying scattered around, like so many archeological fragments, in the archival and bibliographical sediment of the ages, and that the historian's task was only to unearth these fragments, to order them, to catalogue them, and to arrange them in a manner that would permit them to tell their own tale. I was soon to learn that it was not this simple. These fragments were there, all right; but they had, it seemed, no single, definitive tale to tell. They could be arranged in an infinite number of ways, and each had its specific implications. Much was left to the powers of insight of the arranger. He had to do this arranging on the strength of his own good conscience, and to take personal responsibility for the product. This was the task of analysis and interpretation. And this meant that the fixed point from which one viewed history was actually none other than one's own self—one's self in the most intimate personal sense.

The describing of historical events, in other words, was partly an act of the creative imagination of the writer. You might know the bare skeleton of circumstance: that such and such occurred on such and such a day. The fact remains: you weren't there; you didn't see it. To arrive at its true significance—to understand its atmosphere, its meaning for those who experienced it, its relation to other events—you had to put yourself in the place of the people who were there; you had to apply to the historical record something which, however you tried to make it informed and dispassionate, was still an act of the imagination.

But then the question arose: was your imagination not the product of what you yourself had known in life? Of the things you had seen and experienced, as the inhabitant of a specific historical age? And if so, could you really visualize the happenings of another age? Could you conceive of things outside the range of your own experience? If not, then were you not really imposing a distorting lens upon the stuff of history by the very act of attempting to describe it? Was it not history which was serving as a framework for the product of your own imagination, rather than your imagination which was serving to illumine the facts of history?

I recall once seeing a performance of Gogol's Revisor (The Inspector) in one of the leading theatres in Stockholm. It was Gogol's old classic, all right. The words were correctly translated. The script was faithfully followed. Yet what was represented was not Russia but Sweden. Gogol's profound and despairing caricature of bureaucratic life in a Russian provincial administrative center of the early nineteenth century, with all its sad and despairing humor, had been somehow transformed into a jolly, colorful, little Swedish fairy tale, with characters who were like painted dolls—a very creditable performance, a very enjoyable and creative one, in its way; but it was Sweden, not Russia.

One was obliged to wonder whether this was not substantially what one did to any historical subject one touched, no matter how objective one tried to be. I wrote two volumes about certain phases of international life in 1917 and 1918. I did my best to describe things as I thought they looked to the actors in that drama. Sometimes I thought I had succeeded in tolerable degree. But I also had panicky moments of wonder as to whether I had done anything closer to reality than a sort of historical novel. In any case, I was forced to realize, when I looked at the volumes in retrospect, that however revealing they were as a record of the time to which they pertained, they were probably more revealing as a record of our own time—of the outlook and manner of thought of a citizen of the 1950's. I realized then why someone was once caused to remark that all history was contemporary history.

On the other hand, I did see that it was possible to do better or worse in this respect. It was possible to enhance one's capacity for visualizing history by means of the very effort of studying it. One thing supported another. The more you steeped yourself in the environment of your subject—the more, let us say, you supported a study of political events with a parallel study of the art, the religious beliefs, the folklore, the economics, and the manners of the times—the more your imagination could rise to the task. You could, in other words, lift yourself, to a degree, by your own intellectual bootstraps. But this meant that if you really wanted to get near to your subject, it was yourself you had to change. The mere amassing of more data would not do it. To understand a past episode, you had to make yourself to some extent a citizen of the epoch in question. You had to make its spirit, its outlook, its discipline of thought, a part of your own nature.

But this was something which you did only at a certain personal price; and the nature of this price was again one of the things that struck me very strongly about the writing of history. It was something which I can only describe—and I hope the term will not sound too bizarre to you—as its loneliness.

I do not mean to use this term in any self-pitying way. I have enjoyed no less than anyone else the company of my colleagues in the academic life—their company, that is, in the sense of the association one has with them in the odd moments of relaxation: over luncheon tables, and that sort of thing. I even discovered that scholars, so long as they have not constituted themselves a committee to deal with academic-administrative affairs (in which case something very strange indeed happens to them), are the most amusing and companionable of men. I should also like to stress that what I am about to say applies only to the studying and writing of history, not to the teaching of it. But it does appear to me that the studying and writing of history is a relatively lonely occupation.

The historian is lonely, first of all, vis-à-vis the historical personages who are the objects of his study. He lives for long periods among these people. They absorb his attention, his thoughts, sometimes even his sympathies and antipathies. Yet generally speaking, they are not really his companions. They surround him, silently and inscrutably, like figures in a wax museum. He can see them to one extent or another, in the literal sense, depending upon the stage of pictorial or photographic representation in the period when they lived. But they are inanimate. He sees them only frozen in poses—in a series of *tableaux morts.* Sometimes, to be sure, words are to be seen issuing from their mouths, hovering above their heads, to so speak, like the bubbles of utterance that emerge from characters in a comic strip. But one does not actually hear the voices; and one is often not sure whether the words were really theirs or those of the author of the comic strip. In any case, the human context of the utterance: the elusive nuances of circumstances, of feeling, of environment, of intuition and telepathy—the things that made that particular moment unlike any other moment that ever was or will be—all this is seldom to be recaptured. Only, perhaps, in cases of the most profound and selfless and erudite identification of the historian with the period of his study does there occur that intimacy of acquaintance which permits historical personages really to become alive again in their own right—not as products of the arbitrary imagination of the writer, but in reasonable resemblance to what they really were.

But even where such people become real for the historian, he, let us remember, does not become real for them. Their mutual relationship is a one-way street. *He* takes an interest in *them.* He supports them. He becomes their posthumous conscience. He tries to see that justice is done them. He follows their trials and experiences, in many instances, with greater sympathy and detachment than any of their egocentric and jealous contemporaries ever did.

But do *they* support *him*? Not in the least. They couldn't care less. Most of them would snort with contempt if they were to be made aware of the identity of those who would later undertake the effort to interpret their lives and strivings to future generations. Statesmen often conceive themselves to be working for posterity in the abstract, but they have little real respect for individual members of it, in a world where youth is never what age was and where the good old times will never be recaptured. Historical characters would have little solicitude for the brash member of a future generation who takes upon himself so presumptuously the burden of interpreting *their* doings and *their* difficulties.

The historian assists then, like a disembodied spirit, at the activities of his characters. To them, he has a duty, a responsibility, of understanding and of sympathy. But he himself remains unseen, unknown, unaided. This, for my money, is loneliness.

And it is not only vis-à-vis the inhabitants of the past that the historian is lonely. The study of history is something that cuts one off from the age in which one lives. It represents—let us face it—a certain turning of one's back on the interests and preoccupations of one's own age, in favor of those of another. This association with the past cannot occur, if only for reasons of time, otherwise than at the expense of the association with the present.

This is something which one's contemporaries, polite as they may be, rarely really understand or forgive. Every age is egocentric—and fiercely so. Every age thinks itself to be the most important age that ever occurred. Is not the present generation, after all, the occupant of that incomparably most important place in human history—the area between the past and the future? The very idea that one of the members of this generation should turn away from its absorbing and unprecedented concerns to give his attention, professionally and at length, to the affairs of people who suffer from the obvious inferiority of not being alive at all: this, to any normal and full-blooded contemporary, is little short of insulting. It implies that there were people long ago whose lives were so much more important and interesting than our own that the mere contemplation of them from a distance is held preferable to a direct participation in the affairs of our own age, despite all its obvious glories and mysteries. What body of the living, intoxicated by the illusion of progress and the belief in the uniqueness of its own experience, would ever forgive *that*?

The historian too often finds himself, I fear, in the position of the man who has left the noisy and convivial party, to wander alone on cold and lonely paths. The other guests, whom he has left behind, murmur discontentedly among themselves: "Why should he have left? Who does he think he is? Obviously, he doesn't like our company. He thinks us, plainly, a band of frivolous fools. But we are many; he is one of very few. We therefore are clearly right, and he is wrong. The devil take him. Let him sulk." So they say. And so he does.

So much for the historian's loneliness. Let me just mention one more thing that has grown upon me in the course of this work. It is the realization of how deeply one has to dig to find the justification for what one is doing. There are, after all, so many discouragements.

A librarian friend of mine told me the other day that it was most doubtful, in view of the inferior quality of present-day American paper, that anything I, or any of my colleagues, had recently written would still be legible fifty years hence. Since one of the few real consolations of writing history is the faint hope that perhaps one has accomplished something for the ages, this was a shattering thought.

Then, too, there is the atom, with all its grisly implications. I find it hard to forget that we live in an age when all sorts of people who haven't got the faintest concern for history—who don't even know, in fact, what it is—have it already in their power to put an end not only to great portions of the historical record (this, various military characters have done very successfully at frequent intervals in the past), but to both the writers and the readers. It is an uncomfortable reflection that this entire work of the study of the past—its subject, its rationale, its practitioners, its customers, its meaning—that all this is vulnerable, or soon will be, to the whims of brother Khrushchev or brother Mao or even certain of our American brethren that I could name, not to mention others who may, with time, come into the power of disposition over these apocalyptic weapons.

Even if men manage to avoid, by some unaccountable good fortune, the plunge over this particular abyss, one sees that humanity is now living, anyway, in the midst of some sort of a biological and technological explosion, by which the terms of life are being altered at an ever-increasing pace. A part of this explosive process is the multiplication of the historical record, particularly the recent one. Even the major events of the present century—events which appeared to people at the moment to be of major, headline significance—have accumulated in such volume as to place them quite beyond the apprehension of the layman. It is the rarest of persons who today has any comprehension of the series of events which, just in his own time and that of his father, has brought him where he is today. Even the historian feels increasingly inadequate to this task. He can only wander around, like a man with a tiny flashlight amid vast dark caverns, shining his little beam here and there for a moment on a tiny portion of the whole, but with the darkness always closing up behind him as it recedes ahead. More history is probably written today than at any time in the past; and with respect to distant ages, once largely lost to historical knowledge, we are no doubt making progress. But with respect to the doings of our fathers and grandfathers, or even our elder brothers, we are, I fear, fighting a losing battle. The dizzy pace of change is carrying us into the future faster than we can pay out the delicate thread of historical scholarship that is our only link to the past.

What, then, is the use? Has this pursuit of history become no more than a superfluous habit—something that people assume their children ought to study in school simply because this has always been done within their memory? Are the conditions of our lives being altered with such rapidity that the record of the past would have little to tell us even if we could keep up with the explosive expansion of its volume?

Each of us, I suppose, has to answer these questions for himself. I am personally convinced that they must be answered in the negative. It may be true that it is becoming increasingly difficult to reconstruct an adequate record of the past. It may be true that there never was a time when history was less susceptible of apprehension, in its entirety, by the layman. It may be true that we are condemned to explore only tiny and seemingly unrelated bits of a pattern already too vast for any of us to encompass, and rapidly becoming more so. All these things, to my mind, merely make the effort of historical scholarship not less urgent but more so.

It is clear that the spectacular mechanical and scientific creations of modern man tend to conceal from him the nature of his own humanity and to encourage him in all sorts of Promethean ambitions and illusions. It is precisely this person who, as he gets carried along on the dizzy pace of technological change, needs most to be reminded of the nature of the species he belongs to, of the limitations that rest on him, of the essential elements, both tragic and helpful, of his own condition. It is these reminders that history, and history alone, can give; for only history can expose the nature of man as revealed in simpler and more natural conditions, where that which was elemental was less concealed by artificialities. And to the supplying of these reminders, which is the historian's task, it is not necessary that one should know or understand the whole unconscionable and spreading panorama of history. A little bit, looked at hard and honestly, will do. In this little bit will be found, in the measure of the devotion applied to it, the compensation for all the essential imperfection of the historical art, for all the struggle with subjectivity, for all the loneliness, for all the questioning as to whether anyone will ever read what you wrote or whether it would do them any good if they did.

HENRY STEELE COMMAGER

# Do We Have a Class Society?

[ AUTUMN 1961 ]

I

WHEN in the 1830's Alexis de Tocqueville prepared to write that magisterial study of America which is still the most penetrating of all interpretations of our country, he hit upon one basic and pervasive theme that gave meaning to the whole: equality. And he entitled his great work "De la Démocratie en Amérique," which, accurately translated, means "Concerning Equality in America." Equality was the key that unlocked the meaning of America in history and that explained all that was most significant about the strange new nation. Equality made manhood suffrage inevitable; equality demanded universal public education; equality did away with social differences and class distinction; equality banished idiom and imposed uniformity of speech, equality invaded the domestic circle, the law courts, the legislative chamber, the churches, the universities, the literary salons and the ateliers.

Nor was Tocqueville alone in seizing upon equality as the master-theme of American history and the master-principle of the American character. Even before independence Benjamin Franklin had observed that in America we never ask of newcomers, Who are you? but only, What can you do? And in his "Letters of an American Farmer" the remarkable St. Jean de Crèvecoeur noted the same thing—that in America men threw off the burdens of generations and centuries and stood on their own feet. Thereafter a thousand travelers, a thousand commentators, a thousand interpreters composed variations on this same theme: the American was a classless society. Family didn't count: inheritance didn't count: position didn't count: the only thing that counted was ability and character. In America every man was on his own.

This was what every newcomer learned, too, some with consternation, some with delight. In America officers were expected to sit down at table with privates, British prisoners complained; worse yet, they were expected to associate with the help! In America nobody had to take his hat off to the Parson, Norwegian peasants wrote home to their incredulous families: here the parson was just like everybody else! In America everybody took his turn—even the Secretary of State had to wait his turn at table, wrote an astonished English visitor. In America there are no officers swaggering down the streets, expecting everyone to get out of their way; in fact, there are no officers at all. In America everyone can speak his mind—you don't need to stand silent while the squire lays down the law, or vote the way you are told! In America everyone goes to school, wrote a Polish girl, the poor and the ragged sit with the rich and the well clothed. So it went, in a thousand letters, nay a hundred thousand, all with the same theme: there are no classes in America!

But now a whole host of sociologists have discovered that we do so have a class society. American society, they tell us, like the Danish society of the eighteenth century, is divided into nine categories, and if it cannot be said, as was said of the Danish, that the upper three may not speak to the lower six on pain of death, the differences are nevertheless pervasive and ostentatious. We have long been familiar with the divisions of Upper, Middle, and Lower class; now each of these is divided into three sub-categories, and there is no school child so obtuse that he cannot tell you the stigmata that distinguish middle-middle from upper or lower-middle. Furthermore, the sociologists have traced in relentless detail the manifestations of class membership. Those manifestations, we are assured, pervade the whole body of our social activities. They regulate child training, fix living conditions, determine the schools we attend and the subjects we study, the associations we join, the newspapers and magazines we read, the way we vote, the way we court and make love, our preferences in literature and in art, our speech and our manners, and a hundred other things as well.

What is more, the sociologists add, we are all class conscious and we are all status seekers. The most important things we do, the most vital decisions we make, are influenced by our yearning for status. We marry above us, if we can: we mortgage our future for a ranch house in the right neighborhood: we stint ourselves to send our children to an "Ivy League" college: we work overtime to join the country club: we conduct ourselves circumspectly so that we will be acceptable to the Right People: we select our friends—or they select us—to provide some kind of social security or to help us climb the social ladder: we choose our religion not to please God but to please Man.

II

Is this an authentic picture of American society?

In one sense what the sociologists have discovered, and the opinion pollsters have recorded, is all true enough.

Americans are conscious of class, and of status, and differences in class and in status are commonly associated with differences in habits and attitudes of mind. But the interpretation which so many sociologists put upon all this is misguided. For concern with status and awareness of class are in fact characteristic of a society where class and status are so fluid and so malleable that they can be changed by almost any one, at almost any time, in almost any circumstances.

The whole concept of class is an Old World concept, and when Henry James wanted to dramatize most sharply the differences between the New World and the Old he did it—in his wonderful essay on Hawthorne—in class terms:

> No State . . . no sovereign, no court, no personal loyalty, no aristocracy, no Church, no clergy, no army, no diplomatic service, no country gentlemen, no palaces, no castles, nor manors, nor old country houses . . . no cathedrals, nor abbeys, nor little Norman churches; no great Universities, nor public schools, no Oxford, nor Eton, nor Harrow. . . .

The more closely we look at class in the Old World, the more we are impressed with the abiding character of those distinctions that James conjured up. The essential characteristic of class in the Old World is that it is commonly a legal condition and carries with it legal properties. It is a condition associated with Kings and Queens, Lords and Ladies, the Army and the Navy, Palaces, Cathedrals, privileges, titles, and ceremonies. It is therefore a condition not normally subject to the vagaries of politics or of the economy, or even of individual eccentricity. It is a condition which the individual does not control and which cannot ordinarily be changed. But the term class in the United States has none of these attributes or connotations. It is not legally fixed. It is not inherited. In so far as it exists it is something that is earned. In all this the difference between Old World class and New is one not of degree but of kind.

But equally important, class in the Old World has not only legal character, it has other fixed and almost ineradicable characteristics as well. It is—as Henry James makes clear—institutionalized. In England it is connected with and dependent on great institutions like the Monarchy, the Church, the Army, the Public School, the University. These are the properties—one might almost say the monopolies—of the upper classes, and they are not the property of the other classes. Until recently it was almost impossible for a member of the middle or lower orders to enter Eton or Harrow, Oxford or Cambridge, Dartmouth or Sandhurst. That is no longer true, but it is still true that these are the institutions that assure consideration at the Foreign Office, the Army, and the Navy, that give you a box at Lord's and entry to the leading clubs, and that without them such consideration is hard to obtain.

Class in Europe, and in England, is institutionalized in many other ways as well. Its most overt characteristic is perhaps accent. Every Englishman, wrote George Orwell bitterly, is branded on the tongue at birth, and the observation is valid not only for the English but for most Europeans as well. But who, in America, has ever been able to relate class to accent? As early as the 1790's Noah Webster was able to assert that Americans generally spoke the best English in the world, and that America presented a pleasant uniformity of speech instead of the Babel of tongues that betrayed class or region with every syllable in most of the Old World. With exceptions—the exceptions imposed upon us chiefly by large-scale immigration—what was true in the 1790's is still true: that no one in America confesses his class by his accent, that none in America are branded on the tongues with their class mark.

### III

What still persists in the Old World, and what America has almost wholly escaped, is the psychology of class. Almost everyone in America—at least among the whites—thinks of himself as "middle class," which is to say no particular class at all. A few, and among Negroes and Puerto Ricans more than a few, will somewhat bitterly confess that they belong to the "lower" class, but practically none, not even millionaires or Ivy Leaguers, are so brazen as to claim membership in an "upper" class. Yet even in so democratic a country as England substantially half the population cheerfully proclaims that it is "working" class or "upper" class, and in most Continental countries—the Scandinavian are an exception—the majority of the people know just where they belong on the social scale, and accept their position with equanimity.

And, whatever the sociologists may conclude, class membership has in fact fewer overt manifestations in America than in Britain or on the European continent. Thus, English newspapers are directed to class audiences: The Times and the Guardian are read by the élite, and are content with a modest circulation: the Herald, the Express, and the News of the World are read by the "working" classes (and by university dons) and boast a circulation of five million or more: and few papers occupy a middle ground. But in the United States papers like the Post-Dispatch or the Washington Post or the Courier-Journal have the same circulation as their less highbrow rivals. American newspapers are not, on the whole, directed to one class, but to all classes alike. Much the same can be said too of the mass circulation magazines, that they are read by people of all interests and groups and classes.

So, too, with education, at almost every level. What is most distinctive about English schools in how greatly they differ from one another; what is most distinctive about the American is how much they are alike. Manchester Grammar School is as good academically as Eton or Winchester, but the children whose names are in Burke's peerage rarely go there; and whatever the relative intellectual status of Oxbridge and Redbrick Universities, no one is in doubt about their relative social status. But—outside parts of the eastern seaboard—nobody in America thinks private schools important socially, while the notion that the Ivy League carries with it some kind of social éclat, is one assiduously nourished by writers for Esquire or Playboy but regarded as absurd west of the Hudson.

In England religion, too, has class connotations. Those who went to Eton or Winchester, Oxford or Cambridge, were automatically Church of England; indeed, if they were not they could not even enter these institutions as recently as the 1870's. Because in England the Church is established, and its clergy have political as well as social privileges, the terms Church and Chapel are social as well as religious terms. This is less true on the Continent, where there is less religious diversity and where "dissenters" are not sufficiently numerous to constitute either a social class or a problem; but even on the Continent some kinds of dissent are better socially than others. But in the United States any connection between religion and social or class position is fortuitous, fluctuating, and local. If it was, at one time, true that a Virginia gentleman would take only the Anglican path to Heaven, it was equally true that in Boston it was the Unitarian church that had social prestige, in Philadelphia the Quaker, and in Baltimore the Catholic. Today the socio-religious picture can only be described as kaleidoscopic.

The simple fact is that while it is relatively easy to place a man or a woman in his or her proper social class in England or France, Germany or Italy, it is almost impossible to do so in the United States, except where color or some foreign accent is added. Any English shopkeeper can tell instantly—by accent, dress, and manner—whether his customer is a Gentleman or a Lady, but no American shopkeeper can, and few would if they could. Again, in most countries of Europe, the pattern of class characteristics is logical and coherent and the ingredients harmonious: given any one of them, the others can be assumed. Thus, in England, if you hear a "public school" accent you are safe in assuming an Oxbridge education, the Church of England, a preference for cricket and rugger football, a habit of reading the Guardian and of listening to the Third Program, a profession, a country estate and a London club—all of it familiar to us from that best of all social historians, P. G. Wodehouse. Thus, even in democratic Denmark, an "old boy" from Herlufsholm School will ordinarily have a "family" name—not Jensen or Larsen or Andersen but something double-barreled and probably German or French; a manor house on one of the islands with a farm attached; he will take his Lutheranism lightly, speak with an upper-class accent, and read the conservative Berlingske Tidene in preference to the equally good but radical Politiken.

What explains the absence of clear or abiding class distinctions in the United States? Even the question is a bit misleading. For might we not say that in America it is the classless society that is the norm, and that what needs explanation is even the hint of class divisions or class psychology? Those who settled America, and those who came to it for three centuries, were in a sense refugees from the class system: with few exceptions (and those rooted in religion which had its own leveling logic) members of the upper classes did not leave Old-World security for the insecurity of the New. Nor, when Americans revolted from the Mother Country and set up on their own, did they propose to duplicate the Old-World class system. Not only was there no legal basis for class in the first American Constitutions, but these Constitutions swept away even the vestigial remnants of the class system: primogeniture, entail, and the Established Church. And how prophetic that when officers of the Revolutionary army tried to organize a Society of the Cincinnati on an hereditary basis, public opinion reacted as if they had proposed to re-establish the Divine Right of Kings.

## IV

The United States, then, did not inherit the formal institutions of a class society and did not recreate them: the Monarchy, the Aristocracy, the Church, the Army, the Navy, and so forth. It started with a clean slate. But how has it escaped the development of class divisions for the past century and three-quarters?

Let us admit, first, that it did not wholly escape them. Slavery and the plantation system furnished the basis for the creation of a planter class in the ante-bellum South, and that class displayed many of the stigmata of the Old-World class system. Members of that class were clearly "ladies" and "gentlemen"; they were very conscious of race and boasted their "Norman blood." They had a distinctive accent; they belonged, most of them, to the Church of England; they combined membership in the professions (including the military) with "planting" which was more elegant then plain "farming"; they thought of themselves as Cavaliers, and accepted the Code of Honor; they professed contempt for democracy and for majority rule; they indulged in that romanticism which glorified the Past rather than the Future. All of this—or all but the nostalgia for this—was swept away by the Civil War and Reconstruction.

Outside the South the circumstances of American life were not favorable to the development of a class society.

First, there was the open frontier, and cheap land, which made for a mobility within the American society unparalleled elsewhere in the Western world. Second, there was the continuous impact of immigration—hundreds of thousands, and then millions of newcomers from every country of Europe, all bringing with them an instinct and a passion for the classless society. Third, there was an open society which invited the young—and not the young alone—to strike out on their own, to try their luck with a new job, a new career, a new profession, a new life: after all, everything was possible in the new world! Fourth, the rise of a business economy, which has always been leveling, promised new and glittering economic rewards as a substitute for the old-fashioned rewards of social rank. Fifth, there was religious freedom, and denominationalism, which broke the crust of religious status as physical mobility broke the crust of social status. And finally there was popular education, more nearly universal then elsewhere in the world, and reaching up into the university, which by ending upper-class monopoly on learning ended its monopoly on power as well. This is a process going on even now in Britain and France and Germany.

All these influences still operate, some of them—like education—more powerfully than ever before. They discourage hardening of the social arteries, they disrupt fixed social patterns, they introduce a new ferment into social conduct. One manifestation of their operation is an increased awareness of the claims of class, an increased concern for class distinctions. After all a true class society—the French of the eighteenth century or the English of the nineteenth—takes its position and its characteristics for granted; it is only where social relationships are fluid, where not only the prerogatives but even the overt manifestations of class can be quickly and easily acquired, that these things are not taken for granted. If there is a power élite in the United States, perhaps the most interesting thing about it is that anyone with sufficient talent can join. If the Ivy League does have social advantages, the most interesting thing about it is that any bright student can enter. If church affiliations or cultural interests are connected with social position, the most relevant observation to be made about them is that they can be changed at will and achieved at will. Even color is no longer a certain index of class, and the rise of the Negro to middle-class status is as inevitable as was the rise of the Irish and Italians of earlier generations. Sociologists will doubtless continue to divide us all into categories, but the categories are not like separate levels in a building; they are like currents in a flowing stream.

# LOUIS J. HALLE

## Space-Travel on the Lake of Geneva

[ SUMMER 1965 ]

THE SENSE of detachment from the world that comes to one who finds himself alone in a small boat on a wide expanse of water is like what a lone astronaut in space must experience. Far from shore, floating on the unruffled surface of the Lake of Geneva, I feel myself in a state of levitation. There is space below me as above. I hang in the void. My skiff, the *Lark*, is sustained on a mere film that divides the nothingness below from the nothingness above. Its suspension is so sensitive that it trembles or rocks at my slightest motion. In this spatial environment, governed by the pure laws of physics and mathematics, every motion produces compensating motions. I move delicately, knowing my dangerous dependence on the principle of equilibrium.

The lowest of the three segments into which the Lake of Geneva may be divided—below which it empties into the Rhône and so flows away under Geneva's successive bridges—is called "le petit lac." Living on one shore and having my place of work on the opposite, I go back and forth by boat rather than drive around to get caught in the traffic-jam at the Pont du Mont-Blanc. The distance as the lark flies is some four kilometers. In my own *Lark* this takes me forty minutes, but I have a motor boat, the *Snark II*, which makes it in six minutes at top speed. The *Snark II* serves me for an automobile. I use it even within the city, for I can park it closer to the shopping and business centers than I could a car.

Managing a boat is altogether different from managing a car, simply because the medium that supports it lacks the stability of solid earth. The consequent sense of uncertainty and danger, a sense which is never absent, keeps the intellect alert and stimulates forethought. One has to anticipate possible contingencies and be prepared for them in advance, because it is generally too late when they are upon one. A boat, unlike a car, cannot be equipped with brakes, and this in itself poses problems. One throws the motor into reverse to counteract the forward motion that otherwise continues in accordance with the inexorable law of inertia—but always having in mind that if the motor should stall at that moment one's momentum would remain unchecked, whatever lay ahead. Bringing a small boat up to a pier in a high sea is an adventure. One must figure out one's approach in advance. When one parks a boat one has to lash it with ropes or chains as if it were a wild beast. Often it does seem like a wild beast, with a will of its own. It may plunge and buck and tug at its moorings, apparently frantic—keeping this up day and night, perhaps, until one wonders how much longer it can be held captive. A car has nothing like such spirit.

I cross the Lake in bad weather as in good. I cross it even when that massive north wind, the *bise*, roars down upon the huddled city of Geneva, driving the combers before it like wild horses. These horses with their foaming manes are my allies when I am going from my home to my place of work, for then I ride with them, carried on their backs. Returning against them is an altogether different matter.

The *Lark*, despite her fragility, is a willing craft in any weather. One would hardly believe that such a dainty mahogany shell could survive such a pounding environment as that of the Lake in a *bise;* but she does so precisely by virtue of her daintiness. Anyone who has watched a sleeping duck in a crashing sea knows what I mean: a monstrous comber advances upon it, seeming ready to overwhelm it—but at the critical instant the duck, still sleeping, rises up to the comber's shoulder and slides down off its back as it sweeps on. This happens because, contrary to appearance, the water on which the duck is suspended does not itself advance as the wave advances. It is merely lifted by the passing wave as bed-clothing is lifted by passing a stick horizontally under it. The water lifts and falls *in situ,* the duck (or the *Lark*) lifting and falling with it.

Coming back against the weather, however, the *Lark* and I have been defeated twice in the eight years of our association. Unlike the water, the air does advance, and the wind may be too much for such a featherweight as the *Lark*. In one case I spent the best part of two hours fighting my way against it with mighty tugs at the oars, but had to take refuge at last in a small harbor a couple of kilometers below my home. Another time, by my Odyssean effort I broke an oarlock. Someone on shore saw me and telephoned the Gardes-Port, one of whom came out in the police-launch to rescue me. ("Ah, Monsieur le professeur!" he cried when he saw who it was, and I felt like Odysseus returning to his native shores.)

My first *Snark* was an open boat with an outboard-motor. In heavy weather there was nothing for it but to drive over the waves at top speed so that the shower of spray from each fell where the boat no longer was. To go fast in such a sea, however, one had to take every wave at just the right angle. Colliding with a wave head-on would be like colliding with a stone wall, and if one took a wave broadside one might be overturned. In *Snark II,* however, I have a sliding hard-top to form a cabin about me and in heavy weather I proceed slowly, letting the successive showers of spray spill from the roof. Even so, the way that each wave must be met has to be quickly calculated.

There is less regularity in the parade of the waves than one would like. They are extraordinarily individual, varying in their height, their spacing, their steepness, and even in the angle of their approach. Some are lovely and some utterly mean. The navigator has to improvise a different tactic for each one, and this keeps him busy. During the period of a rough crossing he lives with the intensity that a matador must feel as he fights the repeatedly charging bull.

The dangerous wave is the one that, increasing in steepness as it advances, breaks at last just as one is caught and lifted upon it. Its foaming top may then break right into an open boat, and if it catches any small boat broadside may roll it over. I have, on occasion, turned about and fled from such a wave, coming up into the weather again only after it has broken and passed.

Once or twice a winter, in still weather, we have something like an English fog on the Lake, only whiter. I venture into it at half throttle, one eye on my compass and the other on the wreathed prow beyond which is only whiteout. After about fifteen minutes of this blind navigation I drop to dead-slow. My landfall on the opposite shore may be the faint silhouette of a tree that shows suddenly some ten meters ahead. There is just time to reverse gears (my heart in my mouth). Then I have to figure out where I am and the direction of the place I had intended to be, whether up or down shore. A deviation of only one degree from a true compass-course means that my landfall may be hundreds of meters above or below my intended destination. Once, on my way home, having done some circling in the fog and so got off course, I nevertheless made my landfall, at last, by almost colliding with the dinghy that I had left fastened to the *Snark's* mooring-buoy to bring me ashore. Although this was pure coincidence, it provided a moment in which I still take satisfaction. It was like achieving the perfect solution of a mathematical problem on which one thought one had gone astray.

Crossing the Lake by night, on my way home after a day of worldly activity, I find myself suddenly detached from the world, out in the darkness and solitude of interstellar space. Bounding the void far away are two horizons of beaded lights that represent either shore, meeting together for a special display at what one identifies as the center of Geneva. Geneva is simply another galaxy that happens to be closer than, say, the Great Spiral Nebula in Andromeda (which one may discern more faintly above).

Who would ever have thought that such a perfect solitude could be found within the encircling arms of so crowded a city?

KONRAD KELLEN

# Einstein: Personal Reminiscences

[ WINTER 1966 ]

EINSTEIN rarely wore socks, avoided the telephone, and felt that the zipper was one of the most ingenious mechanisms ever invented by man. He drank no liquor and served none to his guests, who were offered tea or ginger ale instead. He was interested in almost everything, and gave every topic and visitor his undivided attention. But sometimes he would rise abruptly—even in the middle of a sentence—and state apologetically yet firmly, "I have to work now." He would then retire to his study without any further ceremony, leaving it to his wife and faithful secretary to entertain the guests a little longer. There was nothing in the least offensive about this; it was obvious that on such occasions Einstein's brain had suddenly begun to spin, and that thereupon, without further delay, he "had to work," whether he or anybody else liked it or not. It seemed as though he had received orders from elsewhere, and he followed them good-naturedly, expecting the same from those around him.

He had very definite likes and dislikes, and his personal judgment about individuals or groups was by no means of Olympian detachment. In particular, he disliked and distrusted politicians and professors. He sometimes would declare some dignitary to be a "great crook" on no more evidence than a newspaper photo. He had particular disdain for public-opinion surveys, but felt that they were part and parcel of modern democracy. A moderately talented young man in search of a profession was advised by him as follows: "Become a public-opinion pollster. There you will never be unemployed. We know, after all, that people are ruled by being told tall stories—so the rulers must constantly test and see what they can get away with."

Einstein was no great admirer of the American university system. He told a visitor that he preferred the European system, where the students were not "treated like school boys," but left free either to work or waste their time in pubs. "Naturally," he added, "most of them waste their time in pubs. But those few who don't receive a better education than those in the United States. The European system of education is aristocratic, and, at least as far as education is concerned, I'm in favor of an aristocratic system."

In most other respects, however, Einstein preferred American institutions. He liked the political freedom, the democratic equality, and the social mobility of this country. He took his citizenship very seriously and was very indignant when his wife suggested during the 1952 presidential elections that he should stay home because he had caught a cold. He insisted that he would go to the polls and vote for Stevenson, whom he called "an intelligent man, and not a demagogue."

At the same time his attachment to any country, even the United States, which he preferred to any other country he had ever lived in, had definite limits. When he was queried by an FBI agent about a man who had applied for a government job, he replied that the applicant was a good and honorable man.

"But is he patriotic?" asked the agent. "Well," said Einstein, "he is as patriotic as an intelligent man can be." The agent, reported Einstein, had seemed a little taken aback, and Einstein was worried lest he had done the applicant some harm. But he insisted that his reply had been reasonable, and that it would be wrong to chalk it up against the man.

The fact that he was a Jew, and that the Jews in the entire world were so terribly proud of "their" Einstein pleased him and sometimes amused him, sometimes embarrassed him. He was able to forget his exposed position at times, and almost agreed to be godfather to the newborn son of a friend, until he was reminded by his wife that the Jews from Tel Aviv to Los Angeles would be petrified if he did anything so wicked. In this connection, the following word of his comes to mind. When he was once asked whether he thought that his theories might ever be proved wrong, he said: "I cannot tell. But should they stand, the Germans will say that I was a German, while the French will say that I was a European. Should they prove wrong, the French will say that I was a German, and the Germans will say that I was a Jew."

His personal relations were uncomplicated and unsentimental and it seemed that he never tried to impress anyone in any way whatever. Even if his behavior seemed at times unusual, he never played the eccentric. He merely did as he pleased, and was therefore almost always pleased. He did not enjoy going to barbershops, for example, and therefore never went; whatever haircutting was administered to him was done by his wife. He never hurried and never permitted anyone to hurry him. Once, at a time when transcontinental telephone calls were still a romantic rarity, an excited fellow astronomer called him from India, to tell him about a breathtaking discovery. Einstein told his secretary to advise the impatient Indian to sit down and write him a letter instead. "If he really has made an important discovery," Einstein then said to his visitor, "it certainly should keep for a week or two." He never carried money on his person and he refused to wear a hat. A straw hat presented to him in Panama, which was made of the finest straw and could be folded like a handkerchief, was worth several thousand dollars. Would it not have been more eccentric if he had worn it, or gone shopping or to the barber like an ordinary citizen?

His use of language, even outside his chosen field, was as carefully weighed and scientifically accurate as that of few people. To a friend who had sent him an article on some political question, he wrote: "I think it [the article] comes closer to the truth than anything I have read on the subject." He did not say, as others might have: "Very true!" He would not presume to know the truth. Nor would he think that it might be *the* truth; that it came "closer to the truth" was his way of putting it, and characteristic for his attitude. Finally, he did not say, as most others would out of thoughtlessness or even presumption, "than anything else"; he would say "than anything I have read on the subject," leaving open the possibility that someone else might have written something still closer to the truth. And, of course, to introduce his judgment with the words "I think," instead of saying, as most people, that such and such *is* so and so, speaks for itself.

Every person who talked to Einstein was taken completely seriously by him. He once carried on a lengthy conversation with a twelve-year-old boy on the subject of whether the earth was turning or not. The boy took the position that it just did not seem as though the earth were turning, and that he therefore did not believe it. Einstein told the boy that he was merely stuck in the pre-Galilean view; that astronomical observations indicated that either the entire universe with all constellations was turning around the earth in the most convoluted, complicated, and improbable fashion, or that the earth, too, was moving in certain ways; and that of the two explanations for the constantly changing situation in the heavens the second was by far the more probable. When the boy replied that there might be a third as yet undiscovered answer to the observed phenomenon, Einstein said: "Of course. But have you found it? If so we shall discuss it."

Einstein did not feel that his fame or accomplishments entitled him to any particular privileges. He lived in his simple house in Princeton and permitted himself no luxuries except to sail occasionally in his small boat. (Once, when he was already seventy-one, he capsized and had to be pulled out of the water. But this did not dampen his enthusiasm for the sport.) In fact, he did not even feel comfortable about the ordinary amenities of life. He always worried lest he use up too much of another person's labor. The fact that a cook, a tailor, an architect, or even the combined crew of a public utility were, after all, paid for their labor, did not assuage his misgivings on this point; he insisted that it was parasitic to use up the labor of others.

This attitude toward human labor was somehow connected with his political views and these were often misinterpreted. Many considered him a Communist or at least a fellow-traveler. This was wrong, even if he refused to preface a highly critical book on the Soviet Union with these words to the author, in a friendly letter: "One must not forget that Communism has provided an acceptable minimum living standard to the Soviet masses." But he hated every form of dictatorship, and was an outspoken individualist.

Everybody knows that Einstein played the violin; but he also played the piano. The difference was that on the violin he played a considerable range of standard compositions, while he used the piano mostly to play his own creations, as they came to him while he played. An over-enthusiastic visitor once suggested to him that these effusions, or at least some of them, should be recorded for posterity, but Einstein rejected this. He laughed and said: "There is already much too much material about me that those poor researchers will have to wade through after my death. Why add to their burdens?"

Einstein was married twice; the first time to a Swiss citizen to whom he used to refer as a "wild woman," the second time to a distant cousin who became something of a general manager for him. He once told a friend that the sight of a pretty young woman tended to make him sad, as it reminded him of the short span allotted to people on earth. But this was not in conflict with his generally positive views of life, even if he complained from time to time that there were so many "crooks" who always "got away with it." His optimism was in fact of a different and grander type than that of most people. When he once told a visitor that he felt an atomic chain reaction, poisoning the entire atmosphere, was a definite possibility, and the visitor thereupon sadly concluded that "that would be the end of everything," Einstein laughed: "But, my dear friend, you forget the fish in the oceans! They would come to the shores, and in a few million years everything would be just as before!"

Before Einstein died on April 18, 1955, in Princeton, he regained consciousness during his first night at the hospital, after having lost it in the afternoon. He talked for quite a while. But he talked in his German mother tongue, and it was one of those tragic, or perhaps not so tragic, turns of fate that there was nobody around who knew German. Nurses and doctors, more concerned about the patient's physical situation than the parting words of the genius, did not know German and merely recorded the fact that he spoke. In this way his last words were forever lost. Whether this is a misfortune for humanity or not, it seems a form of higher justice. For in his later years, indeed during all his life, Einstein did not seem to be a man who expressed every thought that came to his mind. Thus, what he said on his deathbed, he might not have said to friends and posterity, anyway.

ROBERT GRAVES

## How to Hold the Reader's Attention

[ WINTER 1968 ]

I HAVE never been a schoolmaster, although my father tried to steer me that way. He was a poet, famous as the author of Irish songs, including "Father O'Flynn," "Trotting to the Fair," and the "Jug of Punch," now often mistaken for folksongs. He was also a school inspector under the then English Board of Education with the poet Matthew Arnold among his elder colleagues. Both earned their bread and butter from education, both made it their lifework to improve conditions of Government-supported schools—especially for the teachers. My father's main triumph was to win Government permission for laying out school playgrounds where children could learn football and other organized games instead of fighting and throwing stones at one another in the street. Since National education in England was then controlled only at the elementary level, it was on the reading and writing of English that Matthew Arnold and his colleagues concentrated.

Naturally my brothers and sisters and I got the backwash of our father's grammatic exactitude. He used to wince dramatically at our lapses. "So me and Clarissa picked strawberries like you said we could." (Wince.) "You mean, my dear Robert: 'So Clarissa and I picked strawberries as you said we might.' *Like you said we could,* my boy—I agree that Shakespeare used 'like you said' at least once, and of course any grammatical absurdity is permissible in popular drama, but 'like you said' has always been regarded as slovenly among the educated. No, I didn't doubt that you *could* pick strawberries; which is why I told you that you *might.*"

I've grown up like my father, I admit. My children speak well enough, but recently I had to discipline a grand-daughter for saying "different than"—a usage which now seems to have gained an unshakable hold on the States and which has a long if discreditable semi-literary history in England, beginning about the time of the Cromwellian Wars. I told my grand-daughter "*Compared than* any of your friends, Antonia, you speak pretty fair English." Alas, "compared than" will soon be as firmly rooted as "different than," having already reared its ugly head in Australia. Now, tell me, am I a snob? And what is good English?

The writing of good English is too often regarded as an intellectual attainment, won by a short course of intense study. This is to mistake Good English for Success English, a language everywhere sold by correspondence courses to underpaid business executives who hope with its help to become overpaid business directors. Success English is directly descended from Success Latin, otherwise called Rhetoric, the avowed aim of which was to make a bad cause seem better by a skilful hypnotic arrangement of words. Yes, of course: Success English has its uses. All leading nations this side of the Iron Curtain offer as many goods as possible for sale to all their citizens as a means of stimulating them to produce more goods for sale abroad; and of course expendability is an important sales asset, in so far as it staves off market saturation. Thus Success English in the English-speaking world has become an instrument of such outstanding economic importance that its varying degrees of psychological impact are studied with minute care at the high-research level. A century ago Success English closely resembled Success Latin in being a well-woven sonorous Ciceronian-type oratory, a famous example of which has long stuck in my memory:

> If you want a really fine, unsophisticated family pill, try Dr. Rumboldt's liver-encouraging, kidney persuading, silent perambulator: twenty-seven to the box. This pill is as mild as a pet lamb and as searching as a small tooth-comb. It don't go fooling about but attends strictly to business, and is as certain for the middle of the night as a twenty-dollar alarum clock.

Modern Success English can be deceptively unrhetorical in tone: as it were quiet, familiar bed-time persuasion by an uncle or elder sister to some perplexed junior, but always with a memorable last line telling him what he should buy, sell, or be.

Yet for innocent teachers of English, most of whom have had no direct contact with trade, commerce, or industry, and some of whom, like myself, could never sell a sack of grain in time of famine, Success English seems crooked English: the use of language to distract a reader's attention from factual discrepancies, not to say falsehoods. Their task, especially at the more elementary levels, is to teach straight English, both as a moral discipline and as a help to honest communication between friends. The crooked can be no business of theirs.

Now, our language, though the richest in the world, is the least disciplined and therefore the easiest to write badly; there is perhaps no such thing as *talking* bad English, at any rate among those who claim it as their mother-tongue. I am all in favour of dialects: the greater the diversity of dialect the less danger there will be of over-centralization and loss of independent local vagaries and obsessions.

Ideally we should be encouraged to speak our own dialects, though *taught* to write straight English. I hesitate to say "literary" English because "literary" has now come to mean affected, lifeless, far-fetched, snobbish. And I don't want to call it Oxford English if only because there's an Oxford in Mississippi which can't compare in semantic correctness with Cambridge, Massachusetts. And because, although Oxford, England, is the home of the authoritative thirteen-volume Oxford English Dialect Dictionary and its companion, the six-volume Oxford English Dictionary (each volume weighing some seven or eight pounds), yet both works are collections of *precedents*—not, like the dictionary sponsored by the French Academy, Tables of the Law laying down which verbal forms are correct and which are not.

So let us settle for "Mandarin English." As you all know, despite the immense diversity of dialects under the old Chinese Empire, the Imperial Court imposed on all outlying provinces the acceptance of a common written sign-language, in which their officials could report and correspond without misunderstanding. And this became possible because, though spoken Mandarin was a purely Court Language, the signs had the same *sense,* if nothing like the same *sounds,* in every dialect throughout China. There is already a Mandarin-English convention shared by the London Times and the New York Times, the main news columns of which, apart from occasional spelling differences, are bound by the same rules of grammar and show little vocabularistic variations. This should be made the basis of elementary education. And, of course, teachers of English (like my father) find themselves losing their original dialects and talking Mandarin English as an example to their pupils and families.

English is a vernacular language. "Vernacular" originally meant a sort of Latin spoken by slaves, *vernae,* of foreign parentage born in Roman households: a pidgin Latin with most of its case-endings and conjugational forms ironed out. English is indeed doubly a vernacular, because Norman-French began as a pidgin Latin, spoken by Gallic provincials conquered by Caesar's uneducated and mainly non-Roman legionaries; and English was a pidgin Norman-French spoken by William the Conqueror's Anglo-Saxon serfs. Nevertheless, for centuries, Latin remained the sole language of culture and Government in England and France, Italy and Spain, so that when a national vernacular reached the dignity of acquiring a literature it was subjected to whatever Latin grammatic rules, taught in the monkish schools, were still relevant to it.

Thus even now the grammatic test of written English, written French, and the rest, is much the same: "does it offend the basic rules of Latin?" Which is why I quarrel with, say, *different than.* One can be *better than, worse than, other than*—*melior quam, pejor quam, alius quam,* but one can't be *differens quam,* "different than," because "different" means in Latin "separating from" and one can't be *separating than.* My father's objections to "Me and Clarissa picked strawberries like you said we could" were also based on Latin rules. The polite convention is for the "I" or "me" to come second, not first; and though it is possible in English to say "It's me" or "that's him"—by analogy with the French "c'est moi" or "c'est lui"—the Latin-conscious French insist that active verbs are governed by a nominative noun or pronoun. "Like you said" is not Latin: either it is *Ut dixisti* meaning "as you said" or *Sicut dixisti* meaning "like as you said."

Of course in love letters, or family letters, we write as we talk because our correspondents imagine our voice speaking to them and know its inflections so well that they seldom miss the sense. It is quite different when we write to strangers, whom we can't expect to understand our individual usage of words, or even to be glad of a letter from us; so we take great trouble to make our sentences formal and Mandarin-like.

It is not generally realised how far vocal inflexions clarify sense. In speech we need no punctuation at all. If I say: "Everyone in the audience shakes his head and thinks I'm a fool," that's one thing; but if I say "Everyone in the audience shakes his head and thinks 'I'm a fool,'" that's something very different. Or take: "The room smelt of onions. I simply had to force open the window and at once felt better." Which when written down might mean, not that I took the simple easy measure which presented itself for my comfort, but that violence was forced on me by sheer necessity: "I *simply had* to take forceful action." Or take the proverb "Stuff a cold and starve a fever." When it is written down, the sense of the normal vocal inflexions is lost. Like "Give a dog a bad name—and hang him," it really means if you overfeed a man with a cold you're liable to make him so sick that you'll have a fever case on your hands.

Again, "only" in written prose governs the sense of the word which it immediately precedes: "I only saw Absalom" should mean "I only *saw* Absalom, I didn't speak to him or hear what he said." So teachers ought to emphasise the importance, for instance, of writing "I saw only Absalom" or "I alone saw Absalom" if what one means is not: "I only *saw* Absalom." And they should explain punctuation as the means of helping the eye to understand what the ear understands easily enough: giving it an exact musical score to translate into sound.

In medieval times the few people capable of reading books spelt out each word aloud, and recognised the meaning by the sound. Not until two centuries ago did the movement of the reader's lips become unusual. And only in the last century have educated people acquired the art of reading up to four hundred words a minute. This rate amounts to about twenty-four thousand an hour. In conversation the voice goes at about one fourth the speed. And the reading eye is, as a rule, far shrewder than the ear. Are we not all more easily deceived by a telephone message than by a letter?

The craft of writing good English is based on a single principle: never to lose the reader's attention. Since the most obvious ways of losing it are to offend, confuse, or bore him, good writing can be reduced simply to the principle of active care for his sensibilities.

I am told that in the United States the English teachers entrusted with educating younger and relatively underprivileged students and therefore— I deeply deplore this "therefore"—therefore drawing smaller salaries and living in more difficult circumstances, are those who appear to be the most conservative in their views of what is good English. Clever young university professors now tend to be liberal and to give the language full rein. But although I have defined a born gentleman or lady as one who knows by instinct when to wear the wrong clothes, and the born writer as one who knows exactly when to take grammatic liberties with the language, yet I expect universities to be seats of learning rather than workshops of creative writing. They should concentrate on teaching Good English, Straight English, Plain English, Mandarin English, not (to borrow a metaphor from non-figurative art) how to paint with a spray gun or sculpturally harmonise the random *objets trouvés* of the junk heap. Yet when students are called upon to analyse and discuss the English classics, these same liberal professors do not oblige them to write in Classical English themselves but encourage the use of slipshod, if vivid, colloquial English.

This is a healthy sign only if it means making a breakaway from the academic English hitherto obligatory for Ph.D. theses. The 1776 Revolution, which was a protest against the imposition of English political theory on English colonists with their own way of life, had this unfortunate result: it led ambitious early-nineteenth century Americans to look elsewhere in Europe for their re-education—to France, Italy, and especially Germany. Germany was enjoying a famous period of enlightenment and producing remarkable scientists, historians, and philosophers. Their bellicose madness had not yet begun; they were not even anti-Semites, but the good boys of Western culture. Unfortunately, they were saddled with the German language, which had always been a monolithic one, not an omnium-gatherum vernacular. Although simple in grammar and accidence, it lacked the fluidity of English; also it denied its writers the licence that every Briton and every American claims: to borrow whatever phraseology he pleases from anywhere he likes and pass it as current coin. The strong party in the Revolutionary Congress that wanted to cut the main taproot with England had voted to make German the official language of the United States; and this would have become law had not a splinter vote in favour of Hebrew saved English for the country.

German is a curiously cumbersome language, and, as all delegates to the United Nations become aware, linguistically out of step with English, French, Italian, Spanish, and Russian. A German delegate in the old League of Nations days at Geneva once barked at the official interpreter: "Sir, why do you rudely wait until I have finished my sentences instead of translating them phrase by phrase as you do for my fellow-delegates?" "Pardon, your Excellency," the interpreter answered, "but you give me no option. I patiently and soberly for the triumphant main verb, which on putting at the end of your excessively long rhetorical periods you with much severity insist, to wait am obliged." American Academic writers, even though they might not, as it were, reserve the final thunder of the German main verb, have learned from German scholars to load their writings with the longest and least necessary words in or out of the dictionary; which produces a mental fatigue encouraging readers to suppose that the theme and its handling are too awe-inspiring for dispute. The Germanic prose style lingers on in psychological and sociological university studies. The avowed object is to be scholarly, which implies writing in a language that only dedicated scholars can understand, one purged of all colloquialism, levity, or emotion; and this style has long dominated highbrow literary journalism and even musical and artistic criticism, though any creative work with life in it should obviously be discussed in correspondingly live English.

The fact is that honest writers try to give their readers as little mental fatigue as possible. The most frequent cause of badly written English is a confusion of mind due, if not to ignorance, either to emotional stress or to dishonesty. [. . .]

# The Nineteen Seventies

JOHN H. SCHAAR

# ... And the Pursuit of Happiness

[ WINTER 1970 ]

"Our object, like that of all sentient beings, is happiness."
—Constitution of the New Harmony Community of Equality, 1825

"I fear we are not born to be happy."
—Nietzsche

I

NEW HARMONY, unhappily, lasted but two years; and that may be all there is to say finally about happiness. Perhaps the last word on every fundamental human subject is a platitude, something everybody knew all along. Even so, that is no argument against discussing the basic matters, but only against pushing the discussion too far. There may be useful things to say right up to the final point.

The premise that superficiality is wisdom may seem unpromising, but the realities of the case demand it. Happiness is a peculiarly difficult subject to frame and to analyze. Certainly I am not qualified to discuss it by virtue of deep personal knowledge. Lack of personal experience, however, never stopped an academic man from writing. He consults other writers, more learned than himself, and grows professionally wise on his reading. So I searched the authorities, hoping to find an end to my own ignorance. A little reading produced two disappointing conclusions.

When writers turn to the subject of happiness, their tone becomes grave, even mournful. It seems that happy men do not write about happiness; or, at least, writing about happiness makes men sad. Happiness, as [English] Archbishop [Richard] Whately said, is no laughing matter.

As if that were not puzzling enough, the search also uncovered a great variety of conceptions of happiness, no one of which has ever held indisputable sovereignty over the rest. Webster's big dictionary defines the term as "a state of well-being characterized by relative permanence, by dominantly agreeable emotion ranging in value from mere content to positive felicity, and by natural desire for its continuation." One's first response to such a string of serious words on such a common topic is the suspicion that their author was unsure of himself. That suspicion grows with reflection, for the phrase "relative permanence" reminds one that the root of the word happy is hap, which also lies at the root of happening and happenstance, and branches into accident, fortune, and fate. Happiness originates in a thing of the moment and reaches to the lot that befalls one in life—a sardonic etymology, suggesting that our happiness owes less to our deliberate efforts than to accident and fortune.

That reflection gains strength from another feature of the case. Happiness as a goal of action is unlike the other goals that men pursue in one important way. Ordinarily, if you want to reach a goal you must take steps deliberately directed toward it. If you want to become an eminent scholar or an excellent billiard player, you will have to give many years to your books or your billiards. Happiness is different. It is a target which can be hit only by aiming at something else. The thought must have struck Hawthorne, who likened happiness to a butterfly, which flits away when chased, but which may come and light on your hand if you will only sit quietly, occupied with something else. Enough Webster.

A ponderous encyclopedia of law defines happiness as "that enjoyment of life which attends upon, and is almost identical with, welfare." That definition is a triumph of professional ignorance over nature, for daily observation teaches that welfare and happiness are often not synonymous. Your child is not made happy when you deny him that extra cookie for his own good. Men still usually prefer the moment's happiness to the long future's welfare, despite four hundred years of Protestantism and two hundred years of Utilitarianism, despite even old age.

Moving from the law to the poets and the sages, one meets only variety. Aristotle thought the happiest life to be the life of study and contemplative activity, a view similar to that of Augustine, who held that of all the goods, only wisdom and knowledge of God could make a man happy. But when the great scholar Max Weber was asked why he studied and thought so much, he replied that he wanted to see how much he could bear—not the words of a happy man. Leaving the few aside, perhaps John Adams was right when he said that the happiness of the common man consists first in his dinner and then in his girl. Hume thought it impossible to establish qualitative distinctions among kinds of happiness—as did Bentham, with his notorious "pushpin is as good as poetry"—and held that all who are happy are equally happy, regardless of the ground or content of their happiness. Boswell reports that when this argument was mentioned to Johnson, that gentleman gravely made a distinction: "Sir, that all who are happy are equally happy is not true. A peasant and a philosopher may be equally *satisfied* but not equally happy." For centuries the philosophers agreed that happiness is the highest good, though they disagreed about what constitutes happiness. Kant ended the agreement even on the formal proposition when he argued that "nothing can possibly be conceived in the world, or even out of it, which can be called good without qualification, except a Good Will." In effect, Kant argued that being worthy of happiness is higher than happiness.

Many men have supposed that man is made for happiness, or that the search for happiness is the prime force of human action, but others have doubted this. Some men have believed that our greatest happiness lies in giving happiness to others, but Shakespeare knew "how bitter a thing it is to look into happiness through another man's eyes." La Rochefoucauld made the same thought sting when he said you can always endure the unhappiness of your friends. Some men have thought that happiness consists in the possession of a solid estate, while as many others have said that it is granted only to those who have no anchors in the things of this world. Power, virtue, love, solitude, friendship, the pleasures of the senses—each has been recommended by some, and rejected by others, as constituting true happiness.

I mention these endless and irritable arguments among the authorities in order to make a few basic points. First of all, it is clear that logic and learning are impotent in this matter, incapable of adjudicating among the many claimants. Furthermore, this babel teaches that there are as many conceptions of happiness as there are powerful human desires. Finally, one ought to have sense enough not to presume that he can unsnarl the tangle by advancing his own conception as correct and definitive. Dr. Johnson's pronouncement was the wisest ever made on the meaning of happiness: if you look up the word in his "Dictionary" you will find it defined as felicity; look up felicity and you will find it defined as happiness. So I shall not field a personal conception of happiness and advance it against all opponents. Rather, I shall discuss some of the notions and theories of happiness proposed by some influential American writers. My intention is modest: to make clear what a dazzling and motley thing the "right to pursue happiness" is.

## II

It is proper to begin with Jefferson, for it was he who taught us that the pursuit of happiness was our birthright. But it is helpful to remember that the notion was not original with him. Jefferson himself said, in reply to a rather ungracious charge by John Adams, that when he composed the "Declaration" he aimed not for originality but for vigorous expression of the common opinion. As applied to the term that matters here, Jefferson's appraisal is accurate. The notion that men had a right to pursue happiness was well on its way toward becoming a major premise of libertarian political argument by the middle of the eighteenth century. By the Republican period, the idea had become a rallying cry for the most varied political groups. Indeed, a phrase very like Jefferson's was used by George Mason in the Virginia Declaration of Rights of May, 1776. Mason there wrote that men had certain inherent, natural rights, "among which are the enjoyment of life and liberty, . . . and pursuing and obtaining happiness and safety." Furthermore, Jefferson's affirmation that the people had the right to lay the foundations of government on such principles "as to them shall seem most likely to effect their Safety and Happiness" was much older in America than either his or Mason's expression of happiness as a natural right. In his "Vindication of the Government of New-England Churches," written in 1717, John Wise held that the main business of the state is to attend to "the happiness of the people." James Otis, in his "Rights of the British Colonies," of 1764, said that the end of government is to "provide for the happy enjoyment of life, liberty, and property," and ten years later, in his treatise on "The Legislative Authority of the British Parliament," James Wilson argued that the whole purpose of the political compact was "to ensure and to increase the happiness of the governed. . . . The consequence is, that the happiness of the society is the *first* law of every government." In the same year, Josiah Quincy, Jr., stated that the purpose of government was to advance "the greatest happiness of the greatest number." So these ideas were in the air, and Jefferson was in fact voicing the common view of the matter. Whatever happiness itself might be, men in America had the right to pursue it.

The question that matters, then, is, in what does happiness consist? In early America, four main answers were given to this question. I shall first briefly state these answers, and then offer some fuller comments on two of the more interesting writers on the subject.

1. The notion of happiness, strictly speaking, does not enter Puritan writing to any extent until early in the eighteenth century. John Cotton employs the word in his discourse on "Christian Calling," and it appears in the title, though not in the text, of a sermon delivered by William Hubbard in 1676. Even though the word was not used, however, the things for which it stood were sought. There were two such things, and the progress by which the one came to crowd out the other epitomizes the course by which Massachusetts-Israel became Massachusetts-U.S.A.

The first is suggested in John Smith's "Description of New England," a pamphlet written in 1616 to encourage settlers to come to the New World. Smith straightforwardly appealed to material motives, to the promise of prosperity.

> Who can desire more content, that hath small meanes; or but only his merit to advance his fortune, than to tread and plant that ground hee hath purchased by the hazard of his life?

> For I am not so simple to thinke, that ever any other motive than wealth will ever errect there a commonweale, or draw companie from their ease and humours at home to stay in *New England* to effect my purposes.

The other was expounded in John Winthrop's masterly address on "Christian Charity," delivered while the colonists were still on board ship. His elevated sentiments express a different conception of the purpose of the settlement, and open New England's dialogue between piety and prosperity.

> The end is to improve our lives to do more service to the Lord, the comfort and increase of the body of Christ whereof we are members, that ourselves and posterity may be the better preserved from the common corruptions of this evil world, to serve the Lord and work out our salvation under the power and purity of His holy ordinances.

Winthrop's view was the official one. The felicity of a Christian consisted partly in doing good works in this world, though still moving through daily life as a pilgrim, living amidst the comforts and pleasures of the world with "weaned affection," as John Cotton put it, and partly in enjoying the "happy state of reconciliation to God." In doctrine, at least, happiness had nothing to do with the pleasures of prosperity. It was an austere sort of happiness, the sort found through righteous service and obedience here, and through concentration on the hoped-for bliss to follow hereafter.

H. L. Mencken's caustic remark, that Puritanism was the gnawing worry that someone somewhere might be happy, was about as right and as wrong as such deft comments usually are. The early years were a time of severe trials in which the very life of the Puritans was under peril. The pursuit of happiness is irrelevant when the pursuit of mere life is the pressing business. Very soon, however, perhaps around the third quarter of the seventeenth century, life itself became secure, and there was energy to spare for other things. The Puritans then did not respond simply with the fear that the pursuit of happiness would corrupt their kingdom. They sanctioned the pursuit, provided that the goals sought were of a certain kind: the happiness of grace, and the happiness of humble and righteous service to others in one's daily occupation.

But the two ends soon became confused, and then the second consumed the first. The Puritans could never quite disabuse themselves of the notion that godliness, which was to be pursued for its own sake as the only true good, brought prosperity to all it touched. It was easy, given the full theory of general and special providences, to slide from the notion that prosperity is a sign of divine favor to the notion that prosperity itself should be pursued as part of a godly way of life. With that easy step, the fall from gratitude for grace received to self-congratulation for virtue achieved was inevitable. By the time of Cotton Mather the cycle was complete. In one sentence he admonishes the faithful to serve loyally and do good for the pure sake of good, even to "monsters of ingratitude," while in the very next sentence he gleefully assures do-gooders that they shall receive "bountiful and seasonable recompences." The seed was there from the beginning, planted by Calvin, who had written that "riches should be the portion of the godly rather than the wicked, for godliness hath the promise in this life as well as the life to come."

At any rate, the fall from Puritanism to Yankeeism was rapid and complete. The Puritan stood erect, his backbone stiffened by virtue and piety, head high and eyes fixed on heaven, only so long as his feet were planted in the thin and grudging earth. When the wilderness was transformed into firm and comfortable estates, his spine softened, and his vision lowered from the higher realm to this one, with the necessary result that he could no longer enjoy the goodness of either without guilt. The real difficulty was there from the beginning in that too-sharp contrast between eternal felicity or horror on the one side and worldly joy or gain on the other. To choose either exclusively is to lose the best of both. A noble culture and religion must find a view of life profound enough to understand both the joys and the burdens which attend a regard for our responsibilities, and to achieve a repose in the face of both joy and sorrow. That repose is simultaneously less and more than what most men have meant by happiness.

2. The second answer given to the question of happiness in early America was a straightforward materialism, often phrased in a Lockean vocabulary. In this view, happiness consists in the satisfaction of material desires, especially the security of substantial property and a comfortable station in society. A great number of solid Americans expressed this view, and a few must speak for the rest.

John Dickinson, in his "Letters from a Farmer in Pennsylvania," 1767, forged a chain out of happiness, freedom, and property, with property as the anchor, and used the chain thus made to bind the British Parliament. "Let these truths be indelibly impressed on our minds—that we cannot be Happy without being Free—that we cannot be free without being secure in our property—that we cannot be secure in our property, if, without our consent, others . . . may take it away—that taxes imposed on us by Parliament, thus do take it away." Noah Webster's "Examination into the Leading Principles of the Federal Constitution," 1788, announced the fundamental Whig proposition that happiness for the individual lay in property securely held, and that happiness for society lay in property widely distributed.

> Virtue, patriotism, or love of country, never was and never will be . . . a fixed, permanent principle and support of government.

> But . . . a general possession of land in fee simple . . . is the very *soul of a republic*. While this continues, the people will inevitably possess both *power* and *freedom;* when this is lost, power departs, liberty expires, and a commonwealth will inevitably assume some other form.

Chancellor Kent, speaking in the New York Constitutional Convention of 1821, provides the last example. Throughout that memorable debate, Kent spoke in defense of sound Whig principles. He saw abundance already all about him, and he held that those who did not yet enjoy it need only work for it. Instead, the rabble seemed bent on improving their own lot by action aimed not at advancing themselves through honest industry, but at plundering their betters. The results could only be disastrous all around, for it was evident to Kent that American prosperity was the mark of divine favor, and sufficient for the achievement of happiness.

> Discontent in the midst of so much prosperity, and with such abundant means of happiness, looks like ingratitude, and as if we were disposed to arraign the goodness of Providence. Do we not expose ourselves to the danger of being deprived of the blessings we have enjoyed? When the husbandman . . . has filled his barns and his graneries . . . if he should then become discontented and unthankful, would he not have reason to apprehend that the Lord of the harvest might come in his wrath, and with his lightning destroy them?

The idea that property is the foundation and means of happiness is a very old one, and it gained new impetus from many English and American publicists of the seventeenth and eighteenth centuries. In the thought of Locke, for example, a man's property was regarded as the objectification or extension of his personality, so that the condition of the latter could be appraised by examination of the former. In time, the possession of a decent competence came to be regarded by the middle classes as the very substance of goodness and happiness. The property had to be solid and tangible, something a man could set his foot upon and survey with proprietary eye. It is an idea still widely held in our own day, but with a shift of accent that makes all the difference. In the earlier periods, no writer stressed the joys of property as the means of pleasant consumption. The emphasis was always on possession. Today material goods are seen as the means to happiness only if the goods can be used up. Happiness lies not in acquisition but in consumption.

3. An answer which had some advocates in early America was that which saw happiness as consisting in the fulfillment of man's communal and fraternal needs. This was perhaps the happiness that Tom Paine had in mind. It was surely what was meant by Paine's friend Joel Barlow, and by Walt Whitman, who often wrote as though the whole American destiny lay in

"amativeness," and for whom democracy was a synonym for "adhesive love." But the strongest and most lyrical affirmation of the fraternal conception of happiness came from Thoreau, whose essay on friendship in "A Week on the Concord and Merrimack Rivers," is the noblest ever written by an American, and among the noblest written by any man.

This view of happiness was very much in the minority: as Thoreau put it, "You may tread the town, you may wander the country, and none shall ever speak of it...." Most Americans were convinced that happiness was prosperity, and for this what was needed was individual enterprise, not friendship: getting ahead required leaving others behind. Tocqueville detected a strange melancholy and sense of loss pervading American life despite its energy and comfort, and surely the missing element was the element identified by Thoreau. Tocqueville thought the root lay in the inherent tendency of democracy to set each man apart from his fellows, causing him to forget both ancestors and successors, and leading him to believe that he alone was responsible for his destiny.

Driven out of American life by the pursuit of prosperity, and purged from political discourse by the language of contract and natural rights, the conception of friendship as the substance of a happy life found a fugitive haven in the classic literature of the nineteenth century. Innocently loving male pairs occupy the ethical and thematic centers of our greatest early novels: the chaste affection of Natty Bumppo and Chingachgook; the "cosy, loving pair" of Ishmael and Queequeg; the dream journey of Huck and Nigger Jim; Dana's discovery of the comradeship of sailors. These pairs must always meet and move in nature, the forest and the river, for they sense that society would misinterpret and corrupt their natural union. It is as though the novelists had reached by a different route the liberal conclusion that interest and antagonism, not affection and harmony, are the motive forces behind society and state. Friendship has no need for institutions, builds none, and is jeopardized by those that others build.

One member of each pair is white, the other dark. This is an oblique way of saying that these unions are natural in another meaning of the term, that is, illegitimate. Banished from society, fraternity can survive only in the shaded regions, and among the children of those regions. The American sense of loneliness in the midst of crowds and hunger in the midst of abundance reaches mythical expression in the fraternal pairs of these great books. Driven out of our conscious lives, the conception of happiness as the fulfillment of the fraternal sentiment haunts us ever more insistently in the dreamwork of our literature.

4. The last main answer to the question was that which equated happiness with the living of a socially virtuous and useful life. This was probably the dominant view among the men of the founding. The author of the "Declaration" thought along these lines, and so did Benjamin Franklin—

in his later years. Since those men and that moment hold authority in American political life, the views of Franklin and Jefferson merit careful attention.

## III

The young Franklin, he who was to become the characteristic American, gave an answer to the question of happiness which was so radically un-American that both he and America agreed to forget it. The answer was presented in what Franklin called "a little metaphysical piece" entitled "A Dissertation on Liberty and Necessity, Pleasure and Pain," published in 1725 when he was nineteen. The piece was provoked by Franklin's reading of Wollaston's "Religion of Nature." Franklin thought some of Wollaston's reasonings were murky, and in the "Dissertation" he set out to shed a truer light on the subject.

Section II of the essay opens with the proposition that to suffer is to live. Creatures do nothing until they are excited by some uneasiness or pain: men do not pursue happiness; they flee pain. "We are first mov'd by *Pain*, and the whole succeeding Course of our Lives is but one continu'd Seriès of Actions with a View to be freed from it."

Pain produces a desire for relief, and this desire will be exactly as strong as the pain which produced it. The satisfaction of this desire is what men call happiness, or pleasure, and no happiness can be greater than the pain which gave rise to the desire to escape. "*Pleasure* is wholly caus'd by *Pain*," and "the Sensation of Pleasure is equal, or in exact proportion to the Sensation of Pain."

These axioms established, Franklin's argument marches toward its conclusion with geometrical rigor. Every living creature has as much pain in its life as it has pleasure, and "no Condition of Life or Being is in itself better or preferrable to another: the Monarch is not more happy than the Slave, nor the *Beggar* more miserable than *Croesus*." Since "the *highest Pleasure* is only Consciousness of Freedom from the deepest *Pain*," all attempts to show that some kinds of pleasure are qualitatively superior to others are idle. Furthermore, just as no given condition or station of life is preferable to any other, life itself is not preferable to death. Pleasure and pain cancel out, so that if some living being has enjoyed during its life ten units of pleasure, it must also have suffered ten units of pain. The overall result is zero, which is exactly what it would have been had the creature never lived at all. Finally, Franklin concludes, since pleasure and pain are equal and inseparable, "*No state of Life can be happier than the present*...." So much for the prospects of progress in this world, and for the joys of paradise in the next.

It is hard to know what construction to put on this "little metaphysical piece." Read seriously and straightforwardly, it emerges as a mocking repudiation of the American dream almost at the moment of its conception. But that may be too heavy; perhaps it is enough to see Ben's prank as just another young man's slaying of his Sunday school teacher. Franklin himself thought of the essay as a youthful "erratum" in a generally sound and upstanding life. At first he considered it quite a clever piece, but as time went on he began to suspect that although the argument might be true the conclusions were not useful. Later still he began to suspect that it might not even be true. Discussing the essay in his "Autobiography," he "doubted whether some error had not insinuated itself unperceived into my argument so as to infect all that followed, as is common with metaphysical reasonings." Prudence dictated retreat: "There were only an hundred copies printed, of which I gave a few to friends, and afterwards disliking the piece, as conceiving it might have an ill tendency, I burnt the rest, except one copy. . . ." It is worth adding that Franklin does not specify the insidious error.

We do not really know if Franklin still held in 1776 the views he had declared in 1725. Prudence censored them from his expression, but vanity and reason may have kept for them a place in his private mind. If he did retain any part of them, he must have enjoyed a deliciously subversive chuckle when he read his friend Jefferson's "Declaration," for if "no state of life can be happier than the present," what could be more futile than a revolution fought for the right to pursue happiness? There is a work for Sisyphus.

As if this political heresy were not enough, Franklin moved on to strike at the utilitarian theory of the relations between virtue and happiness. He summarized the argument of the first part of the "Dissertation" in the statement that "nothing could possibly be wrong in the world and that vice and virtue were empty distinctions, no such things existing. . . ." This implies that anything called virtuous action, resting as it does on "empty distinctions," cannot be justified or supported on the ground that it produces happiness, because happiness is produced specifically by the successful flight from pain.

This is a keen comment, one that goes to the heart of the American inability to escape utility—the belief that virtuous action is useful action and that the virtuous man is the happy man. Yet Franklin respected it so little, or feared it so much, that he burned it. If we ask why he did that, the answer is, perhaps, that he simply could not take his subversive idea in any hopeful direction. So, he first strode resolutely up to the edge, looked over, and then drew back. To see where he retreated after his view over the edge, one need only read the section of his "Autobiography" where he describes his earlier intention to publish a small book on "The Art of Virtue."

> In this piece it was my design to explain and enforce this doctrine: That vicious actions are not hurtful because they are forbidden, but forbidden because they are hurtful . . .; that it was therefore everyone's interest to be virtuous who wished to be happy even in this world.

In the manuscript of the "Autobiography" there appears at this point a marginal note which perfectly summarizes Franklin's chastened vision after the view over the edge: "Nothing so likely to make a man's fortune as virtue."

## IV

Thomas Jefferson called himself an Epicurean, and that seems to me an accurate self-appraisal. Most of his many scattered comments on the nature of happiness and virtue, and on the relation between the two, do have an Epicurean ring.

In his "Syllabus of the Doctrines of Epicurus," Jefferson summarized his theory in one definition and three short propositions: Happiness is the aim of life; Virtue is the foundation of happiness; Utility is the test of virtue. He defined happiness as "to be not pained in body, nor troubled in mind. i.e., In-do-lence of body, tranquility of mind." Virtue consisted in prudence, temperance, fortitude, and justice. Utility meant for Jefferson what it means commonly: that which is useful or beneficial to oneself or others. What is considered useful varies from society to society. In summary, as he wrote to John Adams in October of 1816, if an act "effect[s] the happiness of him to whom it is directed, it is virtuous. . . . The essence of virtue is in doing good to others, while what is good may be one thing in one society, and its contrary in another."

There, briefly, is the theory, and it immediately raises a question. What is the connection between this theory of happiness and political action? For Epicurus, happiness was found in the garden, not in the assembly. It required withdrawal from politics. (Montesquieu thought that Epicurean doctrines had contributed much toward the corruption of Roman political virtue.) For Jefferson, too, happiness was to be found at Monticello, not Washington. The pursuit of happiness in this Epicurean sense, then, is obviously not even a political pursuit, let alone a revolutionary one. Yet Jefferson used the phrase in a political and revolutionary document. There seems to be an incompatibility between the action and the theory.

The problem can be solved in a certain way. For Epicurus in particular, and for Epicureans as a type, withdrawal from political life was necessary for the achievement of happiness. But for Jefferson that withdrawal was not possible: there were just too many political problems and possibilities.

Hence, the pursuit of happiness had to be postponed until the political world was set aright. Jefferson nowhere indicates that happiness is to be sought or found in political action. The whole thrust of his thought leads, not to the conclusion that men pursue happiness in the political realm, but that political action is unfortunately necessary from time to time in order to arrange the public affairs so that it will be possible for individuals to pursue happiness in the private realm. It is possible to justify political involvement in Epicurean terms, as Jefferson did, but only at the expense of making public life entirely secondary and instrumental to private life.

If this is accepted as a solution to the political problem raised by Jefferson's theory of happiness, then the way is cleared for an approach to a different order of problems. What are the prospects of success in the quest? Granted the right to pursue private happiness, what hope have we of overtaking it? Is nature so constituted that the pursuit can succeed, or is there something in the constitution of things that dooms the quest to failure? Jefferson apparently feared that there were two such factors, one in the general constitution of nature, the other specifically in human nature.

The factor in nature is pain, or grief. In effect, Jefferson was faced here with his own form of the problem of theodicy. Although he wanted to see nature as perfect in every part, and a model for all human actions, he had to confess that he detected a flaw in nature's beneficent design. In wondering about this, Jefferson risked blasphemy against the only god that really mattered to him. How deeply this troubled him can be measured in a passage from a letter to Adams of April 8, 1816:

> My temperament is sanguine. I steer my bark with Hope in the head. My hopes, indeed, sometimes fail ... There are, ... even in the happiest life, some terrible convulsions, heavy set-offs against the opposite page of the account. I have often wondered for what good end the sensations of grief could be intended. All our other passions, within proper bounds, have an useful object ... I wish the pathologists then would tell us what is the use of grief in the economy, and of what good it is the cause, proximate or remote.

The element in human nature which stood as an obstacle—perhaps an immovable one—to the achievement of happiness is self-love, or selfishness. As he wrote to Thomas Law in June of 1814, Jefferson wished it could be abolished:

> To ourselves ... we can owe no duties, obligation requiring ... two parties. Self-love, therefore, is no part of morality. Indeed it is exactly its counterpart. It is the sole antagonist of virtue, leading us constantly by our propensities to self-gratification in violation of our moral duties to others ... Take from man his selfish propensities, and he can have

nothing to seduce him from the practice of virtue. Or subdue those propensities by education, instruction or restraint, and virtue remains without a competitor.

In one sense Jefferson should not have wondered about the "use of grief in the economy," for in his own thought it was only through the opposition of pleasure and pain, or grief, that one could distinguish what was virtuous from what was vicious. Yet in another sense he had a very real problem. Having defined happiness as "not to be pained in body nor troubled in mind," he obviously had to be concerned about the value of pain and suffering. One way to solve this problem is to hold that pain is a necessary condition for the very possibility of leading a virtuous life. One could argue that it is our egoism, our propensity to self-gratification even at the expense of giving pain to others, which makes the struggle toward virtue or nobility meaningful. If the noble or virtuous life is easy, then it is lacking in that very thing which makes it noble, namely, the effort to rise above self-gratification and impose a law on the self in obedience to a higher imperative.

But Jefferson did not follow this path. He believed, on the contrary, that life could be virtuous without pain and without the existence of selfishness, temptation, and shortage. As he put it, virtue can exist "without a competitor." Indeed, it would be best if all its competitors were simply eradicated from the human heart.

The conclusion of the matter, it seems to me, is that the Jeffersonian pursuit of happiness guided men in an endless circle: to be happy, be virtuous; to be virtuous, be useful; to be useful, make men happy; to make men happy, be virtuous; and around again and again. Furthermore, the whole process seems thoroughly subjective—each man rolling around his own circle—until we remember the final element of the theory, the element that specifies utility as the test of virtue. If we ask who is to judge whether happiness (virtue) is happiness, the answer is, the other men around you. What they regard as useful is what you shall regard as virtuous, as that which produces happiness.

Jefferson in effect first assimilated private to social virtue, and then reduced both to utility. Virtue in this usage is mainly negative and conservative. It means remaining innocent, not paining oneself or others. It also means that one should do what others deem useful. Bringers of new values thus become immoralists, in Nietzsche's sense; and Jefferson's doctrine logically condemns both Jesus and Socrates. The reward of happiness naturally follows such "virtuous" behavior because that behavior is shaped precisely to please others, the givers of all rewards.

With this, the theory completes its circle. When actions must be deemed useful in the eyes of others before they can he deemed virtuous in one's own eyes, then there is laid the ethical foundation for what Tocqueville called the tyranny of the majority, and the psychological foundation for what Riesman has called the other-directed personality. The theory escapes both subjectivism and the confrontation with pain—with the possibility that individual virtue may not bring happiness—but it does so only through a total flight to society. The pursuit of happiness, a phrase which Jefferson used to justify a revolution for freedom, and by which he sought to license the individual for a private quest, turns out to be a race which one can enter only by giving up private judgment and individual freedom.

It is but a step from this to the bleak paradox of our own day. Today we tell ourselves, in an endless stream of books and essays and addresses, that true happiness consists in self-expression. And yet, when one tries to realize this happiness, he discovers, to his despair, either that he has no self to express, or, to his embarrassment, that he seems to express himself about the same way everyone else does. I have tried to suggest that the seed of this sad discovery was already there in Jefferson's theory. The seed is the enduring American inability to escape utility as the test of virtue and to insist that virtue must have a social reward.

V

Very little of this seems relevant today. We have come far from the Puritan conception of happiness as piety or the Jeffersonian conception of happiness as virtue. Even Franklin's notion that happiness consists in doing useful things for others—with the understanding that such action will also bring prosperity to oneself—is not widely shared today. The Whiggish theory of happiness as possession of property has undergone a shift of emphasis toward consumption which amounts to a virtual recasting of the original idea. Even the notion of happiness as the fulfillment of fraternal affections has been recast into something like social acceptance. We have produced a three-sided conception of happiness of our own, with little help from history or philosophy.

1. Happiness consists in bountiful consumption. It is impossible to document this idea with precision because we are dealing here, not with a specific concept or theory, but with an atmospheric condition. The mass media daily bombard and entice us with jazzy visions of the delights of consumption: the Bower of Bliss plus the hygienic conveniences of technology. One has to assume that these visions, to a significant extent, describe our folkways and articulate our dreamways. If you could open the head of the typical American and dump his thought patterns out on a table for examination, what you would see there would be, not deep grooves cut by religion, ritual, and custom, through which all the forces of life flow,

but snatches of advertising jingles and a network of S-R arcs leaping from forces in the Id to objects in the world of consumption. We perhaps forget how telling an indicator of our outlook is provided by the fact that we accept a statistic called the Gross National Product as the main official measure of the public wellbeing. No politician today would dare suggest that the nation is swollen with luxury, even though a long and powerful tradition teaches that luxury is the death of republics.

2. Happiness consists in having fun. Happiness is thrill and novelty, romance, speed, and games. And it is all very expensive and very energetic. We have made happiness hum.

And yet, if you watch the members of the lonely crowd busy having fun, you will see a curious thing. The bright laugh darkens suddenly to doubt and puzzlement, even sadness, as though the person was not sure he was enjoying himself. There are certain features of the situation which might well produce doubt.

The fun culture is highly commercialized and lacking in spontaneity, powered by an engine outside the person rather than within. The fun morality is very vulnerable to peer group judgment, not self-directed and sure of itself, but needing confirmation in the noisy approval of others. It has none of the attributes of the serious play of children. At its margin, it shades off into the search for oblivion, whether in alcohol, sex, gadgets, or drugs. All this suggests that much of our fun activity is not undertaken in and for itself, but as a means to other purposes.

Perhaps one of those purposes is the achievement of status and social approval. In large and growing sectors of our society—not alone in youth culture—a person who does not have much fun is looked upon as some sort of unfortunate fellow, a little disagreeable, and not a very desirable "friend." On the other hand, a person who has lots of fun thereby raises both his own prestige and the prestige of those around him. He has a high "Happiness Quotient," which a contemporary psychologist of some notoriety is able to measure on a useful instrument of his own devising called a Euphorimeter. It is advantageous to know such a person because the acquaintance enhances your social standing. Besides, with any luck at all, some of his happiness will rub off on you.

There might be still another purpose, drearier than the first. Perhaps a large part of our feverish pursuit of fun has as its real function that of filling the empty hours which technology has brought to millions of people who lack both the inherited culture and the personal resources to know what to do with their time. We seek fun in order to kill time—as though we were not thereby killing eternity too. Ours is an age which, although it has achieved great physical successes, has lost psychological and moral meaning for the individual. Men are adrift, their customs hollowed, their religions desiccated, their futures threatened by the very technological powers that once promised happiness. In such a time, men must keep frantically busy in order to fill the emptiness, and having fun is increasingly the recommended way of keeping busy.

The fun theory of happiness nearly excludes the very dimensions of life which make genuine delight and joy possible: activity which is undertaken not for self-gratification, but out of disinterested care and appreciation for the activity itself; admiration for esthetic elaboration of impulse, which requires discipline and knowledge; belief in the reality of intangible and unmeasurable values. For these the fun theory substitutes the criteria of display, motion, and instant reward.

3. Happiness as self-actualization or self-realization. On one level, this conception is mainly ludicrous, and a trifle pathetic. On another level, it appears as the most important contemporary theory of the good life.

We are flooded with books and articles telling us that happiness consists in being liked by others so that they can be manipulated to one's own ends. There is an equally large how-to-do-it literature telling one how he can, at home, in just a few minutes a day, overcome shyness, guilt, and pessimism, thereby retooling his personality from a negative, drab, unpopular model, into a positive, bouncy, popular model. In this view, happiness is an internal state, a psychological condition. Still, we are assured that the psychological bounce resulting from faithful performance of the happiness exercises will provide the energy needed for success in the external world. Adler, slightly vulgarized, has replaced Franklin, greatly vulgarized, as the true prophet of happiness.

On another level, the conception of happiness as self-realization or self-actualization has more intellectual merit. It is, in fact, the chief contribution of our time to the perennial discussion.

The new conception is mainly the contribution of psychologists: Kurt Goldstein, Erich Fromm, Carl Rogers, Gordon Allport, and Abraham Maslow are among the more important. There are of course differences among these writers concerning both the nature of the forces or potentials in the self that are to be actualized, and the process by which these potentials become actualized, but all of them agree on the main point, which, in Maslow's phrasing, is "the necessity for the postulation of some sort of positive growth or self-actualization tendency within the organism, which is different from its conserving, equilibrating, or homeostatic tendency, as well as from the tendency to respond to impulses from the outside world" ("Motivation and Personality," p. 341). In this view, then, there is a natural tendency, an entelechy, for the organism to become whole, for one to become oneself. And to become oneself is to be happy, for happiness is the feeling-tone which accompanies self-actualization. It is a by-product of successful self-realization. "Happiness is an achievement brought about by man's inner productiveness . . . the accompaniment of all productive activity, in thought, feeling, and action" (Fromm, "Man for Himself," p. 189).

There is much to be said about this theory, but space permits only a few comments.

John Dewey has persuasively argued that the notion that men aim at self-actualization or happiness rests on a confusion between ends-in-view and standards of judgment. Men's aims or ends are objects of desire, and are always concrete and specific: the love of this woman, the defeat of that rival. Desires are specific, but self-actualization as an object of desire is so vague as to offer the actor no counsel. Not all desires, however, are approved, whether by the individual's own moral sense, or by the moral sentiments of his community. Hence, there must be a standard for adjudicating between desires, and the self-actualization-happiness principle offers one such possible standard. Happiness, then, really seems to be not an end men can aim for, but a possible standard by which to judge the worth of the ends they do aim for.

It follows that we must forget self-actualization in order to get it. Furthermore, observation suggests that the man who does aim consciously at self-actualization runs the risk of becoming a psychological athlete, forever flexing his psychological muscles. He easily becomes very self-centered, even priggish in a curious sort of way, and, given the vagueness of the goal, a waffler in the intellectual and moral life.

Even when the concept is taken to be a standard of judgment rather than an end-in-view, it easily leads to an extreme subjectivity of doctrine and expression, if not always of action. For most men, most objects of desire are culturally set. One accepts the group's valuations as his own, even while pretending that he has chosen. Self-actualization is today operationally translated as "do your own thing"—something that has never happened on a large scale among any populace outside the nursery and Bedlam, where it can be permitted because there is a keeper who holds ultimate power over all the inmates. These new doctrines, then, given the climate of opinion of our day, are peculiarly likely to lead their believers into delusions of autonomy, while delivering real power to the custodians—the Hobbesian sovereign who bases his claim to obedience on the need for order in the best interests of the subjects themselves.

Another aspect of the self-actualization theory stresses, as Lawrence Kubie has written, "freedom and flexibility to learn through experience, to change and to adapt to changing circumstance." This is rapidly becoming one of the leitmotif notions of our day. In a large body of literature, the ability to adapt becomes the measure of health and happiness.

Modern life surely does demand that ability, but what if modern life is mad? The very malleability of human nature can be the ruin of man. We can adapt to almost any circumstances, can become almost anything. But the notion of man, the idea of what it means to be a man, is a work of art, a highly artificial and restrictive set of distinctions valuing some things and scorning others. In short, given the malleability of our species, our ability to become almost anything, the question of what is worth becoming remains basic and inescapable. The canon of adaptability, while it might enhance happiness under modern conditions, offers no counsel on that question.

These are the ideas which now have us in their grip, and it is a melancholy thing to see how few resources they leave us when the pursuit of the theory does not achieve the promised reality. Perhaps we have lost sight of, or have lost the courage to confront, the knowledge that it is man's lot to be always a beggar at the gates of the kingdom of happiness, and that he is in the greatest danger when he thinks he has found the key to the gate. Perhaps the counsel of sanity here is that the attainment of limited goals, and the achievement of a temporary and qualified unhappiness, is the highest felicity which men and nations can realize in an indifferent universe. We cannot take the "hap" out of happiness, and much of our present unease may lie in the attempt to do exactly that.

I have only one other suggestion to make, surely an imprudent one, perhaps even an un-American one. It may be that the pursuit of happiness is a goal unworthy of a great nation or a great man. Certainly the men and nations we admire the most have not been the happiest ones. Admirable men have sought nobility, or beauty, or magnanimity, or purity of heart—all treasures of the spirit, and not conditions of the external world. The pursuit of happiness, as defined in America, may be a pursuit peculiarly congenial to the genius of democracy in that it does, in the end, mean the sovereignty of desire. Desires are something we all have, and if we take desire as the norm, there is no way to establish the superiority of any one of them over any of the others. But while this is an orientation congenial to a mass democracy, it is not one which points the way toward excellence.

It may even be that in announcing our goal as happiness we are selling ourselves short, and denying something that runs very deep in human life. The history of so many human ideals, institutions, customs, and beliefs makes sense only on the supposition that men do many of the things they do in order to make their lives, not happy, but worthwhile, demanding, difficult, challenging, even painful. Willingness to sacrifice happiness and pleasure for other things seems at least as basic to human life as does the pursuit of happiness. And if that willingness is the source of much that is terrible and cruel in the human record, it is also the source of nearly everything that is beautiful and noble.

Does that mean we must give up all talk and hope of happiness, manfully consigning it to the trashbin of youthful dreams? Of course not. In "The First Circle," Solzhenitsyn tells a fable which states the whole matter. Two prisoners are having a conversation about happiness. One of them, a professor, tells how, building on Goethe's line from "Faust," ("Oh, moment, stay! You are so fair!") he had once demolished the notion of happiness:

"At one of my prewar lectures . . . on the basis of that quotation from *Faust* I developed the melancholy notion that there is no such thing as happiness, that it is either unattainable or illusory. And then a student handed up a note written on a piece of graph paper torn from a tiny notebook: 'But I am in love—and I am *happy!* How do you answer that?'"

"What did you answer?"

"What can you answer?"

J. GLENN GRAY

# Hegel's Logic: The Philosophy of the Concrete

[ SPRING 1971 ]

I

ANYONE with the temerity to read his way through George Friedrich Wilhelm Hegel's "The Science of Logic" will conclude nowadays that it is truly a monstrous book. First, it is monstrous in length, some 850 solid pages in a recent and excellent English translation by A. V. Miller. Second, it is monstrously difficult to understand. One of the hoariest of German academic jokes is that only Hegel and God knew what Hegel was talking about and after Hegel's death . . . , well, the joke can be completed in a dozen different ways! Third, it can be exquisitely boring, as any student can discover for himself by sampling a few paragraphs, selected at random. Even the Table of Contents repels. The three major subdivisions are: The Doctrine of Being, The Doctrine of Essence, The Doctrine of the Notion. Everything goes by threes in Hegel, as nearly everyone knows, except in this case for the two superdivisions of the work: Objective Logic and Subjective Logic.

Yet to call a book monstrous should not imply a disparagement in the moral sense. As a phenomenon the monstrous in thought is anything that does not fit customary and familiar patterns. Some of the greatest works of Western literature are equally monstrous: Aristotle's "Metaphysics," Dante's "The Divine Comedy," Goethe's "Faust" (especially Part II), and several others. Such creations require a supreme effort of the reader. They command him to slow his pace of comprehension, even to delay full understanding until he has penetrated farther and perhaps reread several times. They summon him to enter into unfamiliar complexities, to dare new ways of grasping himself and his world—in Biblical language, to wrestle with the angel of the Lord. If the books are monstrously great, they will loosen his intellectual moorings and provide him with an experience that can be salutary, though perilous.

Though I have long been a student of Hegel, I had always managed to avoid "The Science of Logic" in favor of his more accessible writings.

When I was recently asked to lecture on it, I accepted the invitation because it would force me to do what I had long believed I should do. Realizing that one of the two or three most helpful ideas of my life derived from Hegel, I now felt a kind of duty to trace the idea to its fount and origin in Hegel's "Logic." However difficult it would be to mediate Hegel to a heterogeneous group of college students, it was clear that I should make the attempt.

As I struggled through the book, I sought to picture in my mind the manner of man this was who wrote it and his situation at the time. One must always assume that a philosopher is a human being like the rest of us. Hegel's external situation while composing it was unlikely enough. He was not giving it as a lecture series to university students, chapter by chapter, as is the case with many other large tomes of his. Instead, he was at the time the principal or headmaster of a boy's secondary school at Nuremberg, and it is clear that he couldn't have first tried it out on those boys! It follows that he must have written it on weekends and in the evenings after work and on summer vacations. Moreover, he was newly married at the time, a man of forty-one to a girl of twenty and they were having children during the years of its composition, 1812–1816. I find it hard to imagine a work less suited to this romantic and tempestuous phase of a man's life. Yet Hegel's marriage from the outset seems to have been a happy, harmonious one—contrary to Nietzsche's dictum that Socrates' marriage proved once and for all that a philosopher should never marry!

Perhaps a few words about Hegel's biography are in order. He was born in 1770, just two hundred years ago last August, which explains all the Hegel Congresses that were held last year in America, Europe, Russia, and probably every continent on the globe, with the possible exception of Australia. Hegel was the perfect example of a late bloomer as a student in seminary and university; his professors had no high opinion of his talents, especially in philosophy. His close friends as a youth, Hölderlin the poet and Schelling the philosopher, were, on the other hand, morning glories, boy wonders, what the Germans call *Wunderkinder*. At the tender age of twenty-three Schelling was a full professor at the University of Jena and rescued his stodgy friend Hegel from an obscure job as house tutor to rich men's children, a kind of higher servant position, common in those days. Schelling got him appointed to an unpaid lectureship at Jena. Hegel seemed to be launched on a university career, but alas! Napoleon interfered and at the Battle of Jena in 1807 defeated the Prussians and closed the university. Hegel was forced to take a job as editor of a miserable little newspaper in the small town of Bamberg. He did manage to publish at this time his first major book, "The Phenomenology of Spirit," now one of the great classics, in an edition of a few hundred copies, most of which remained unsold for years. Again his friends rescued him and got him the position of principal at the Nuremberg Gymnasium, where he wrote the "Logic," as I have said, and where he also found his mate. But it was not until 1816 that his reputation grew sufficiently for him to get an offer of a university job at the University of Heidelberg and his first professorship at the age of forty-six. It was also the first decent salary he earned and marked the end of a long period of struggling with poverty.

Then came a dramatic reversal of fortune. The Germans seemed to realize at last they had another great philosopher in their midst. In two years he was called to the University of Berlin and there for the next thirteen years he was a kind of philosopher-king, attracting students from all over, even from the remote and obscure province of the United States of America. For a time his philosophy threatened to sweep every other into oblivion, including that of Schelling, whose later years were as ignored and disappointing as Hegel's early ones had been. At the very zenith of Hegel's powers and fame, a cholera epidemic in Berlin claimed his life unexpectedly; he was given a state funeral despite the laws that cholera victims had to be burned.

Intellectually the world has never been the same since then. Hegelianism always comes in two wings, the Right and the Left. Marx and Engels seized on the dialectical method in his "Logic" to produce the Communist ideology that has revolutionized our modern world. The right wing used the historical and political content of his philosophy, much less radical in nature, in which Hegel tried to synthesize Greek and Roman humanistic philosophy with Christianity to develop a conservative doctrine of state and society. To this day the tug-of-war goes on. If we didn't know that truth is stranger than fiction—since reality ever beggars imagination—it would be hard to believe that this monstrous book could conceal within it such explosive force.

## II

The reason for this explosive force is largely due to two pervasive ideas in his "Logic." If one succeeds in freeing them from their obscure Teutonic form, they are—*mirabile dictu*—not very difficult to grasp. Moreover, in good Hegelian fashion, when adumbrated they tend to merge into a single comprehensive idea. To be sure, the word idea, as we normally use it in English, is inadequate for what Hegel has in mind. These thoughts of his are much rather concepts, even Platonic Forms, which is to say they are not restricted to one man's head but purport to describe the way the world is. Indeed, these ideas are not pictorial representations at all, but have their objective being in history and culture. The task of the solitary thinker,

Hegel, is simply to bring them to consciousness, thus rendering subjective and intelligible for us an objective state of affairs.

The first idea, of course, is that of dialectic, which Hegel calls the *movement* of reflection, a favorite and basic word of his. In Hegel's vision of the world and of thought everything is in motion, including the one who is possessed by the intellectual vision. Reflection is dynamic to the core, even as the world process itself is—with things ceaselessly coming into being and passing out of being. In so many respects Hegel is an Aristotelian, that predecessor whom he respected most of all. Like Aristotle he possessed the passion to know everything that is, and has the same encyclopedic range of factual knowledge. It is indeed frightening to realize how much Hegel knew and reading him is an exercise in humility. Again like Aristotle, Hegel combined this enormous learning with a bold, even arrogant, speculative daring. With Aristotle he is convinced that everything is potentially knowable, including God and the cosmos. After Immanuel Kant had just persuaded his fellow Germans that man's mind could not advance a step beyond sense phenomena without falling into irresolvable contradictions and therefore that things-in-themselves are intrinsically unknowable, Hegel advanced the opposite doctrine that reality or things-in-themselves are precisely what the awakened intellect can and does know.

In his inaugural address at the University of Heidelberg in 1816 he told the assembled students and professors that:

> Man, because he is mind, should and must deem himself worthy of the highest; he cannot think too highly of the power and greatness of his mind, and, with this belief, nothing will be so difficult and hard that it will not reveal itself to him. The being of the universe, at first hidden and concealed, has no power which can offer resistance to the search for knowledge; it has to lay itself open before the seeker—to set before his eyes and give for his enjoyment, its riches and its depths.

Such doctrine must have astounded the assembled throng. It and other similar dicta of Hegel's prompted the contemporary philosopher Martin Heidegger to remark once that "Hegel's rationalism cannot be praised or blamed enough!"

Like Aristotle, too, he was convinced that everything in this dynamic universe is goal-directed or teleological. Things don't simply come into being and disappear from being, but acorns are always becoming oak trees, boys becoming men, wandering tribes becoming organized states, states becoming cultures which create imperishable works of art, religion, philosophy before they cease to be, their imperishable works being reworked and transformed by other cultures and civilizations. History and everything in it is a gigantic process moving from a state of potentiality toward actuality, from the implicit to the explicit, from the natural to the intellectual or spiritual, from the abstract to the concrete.

But the driving force behind this ceaseless movement is not, as it was with Aristotle, a biological unfolding of the forces of life itself. Instead, Hegel went behind Aristotle to Heraclitus, to those thought-provoking fragments which proclaim that "Strife (Polemos) is father of all and king of all." "Men do not understand how that which draws apart agrees with itself; harmony lies in the bending back, as for instance of the bow and the lyre." "Opposition unites. From what draws apart results the most beautiful harmony. All things take place by strife."

The underlying cause of the movement of thought as of all other things is for Hegel contradiction. As he puts it again and again in his "Science of Logic": "Everything is inherently contradictory . . . it is only in so far as something has a contradiction within it that it moves, has an urge and an activity." This great law of contradiction is for him the principle of all self-movement and vitality. Everything alive is, as he writes, "In one and the same respect, *self-contained and deficient, the negative of itself.*"

Accordingly, for Hegel movement and not rest is primary, becoming and not being. Indeed, he opens this monstrous book with the assertion that being and non-being or Nothing are pure abstractions and are in reality the same thing. Only in becoming do we get something that is determinate, concrete, and subsistent. *"There is nothing which is not an intermediate state between being and nothing."* That which we call the being of any thing is merely a *moment*—Hegel's term for phase or stage—of its reality or truth. Non-being is likewise contained within it, also a moment or stage. Becoming is the unseparatedness of both moments, that more concrete and explicit stage in which both are swallowed up. In all finite things, as Hegel puts it, the germ of decease is already inherent: "The hour of their birth is the hour of their death."

What does all this mean? For one thing, it means that the contradiction in everything drives it irresistibly toward greater completeness. Hegel calls this driving force "The portentous power of the negative": *die ungeheure Macht des Negativen.* This is another of his favorite phrases. The negative, the No, is portentous or monstrous because it stubbornly refuses to let anything be what it is, to rest in its attained state or stage. Instead, the No in us is forever driving us toward the opposite of what we are. Despite ourselves we are forced into more complex relations with the world of our fellow human beings, and into the web of culture.

Secondly, contradiction means more precisely that the opposite of what we are at any given moment does not signify simply annulling what we were before, but its preservation at a higher level. Hegel discovered to his great delight a German verb that contained even in popular use the two opposite meanings that lie at the core of his dialectic. The verb is *aufheben* and unfortunately we have no proper English equivalent. British translators nowadays usually render it: to sublate. Earlier it was translated frequently: to sublimate. But Freud spoiled that rendering, since for him sublimation refers to what happens to the sexual drive, the libido, which when partially suppressed gives rise to the arts and all other manifestations of culture. *Aufheben* means in German, on the one hand, to preserve something, to maintain it, or store it. "I'll save this dress or suit or quotation, or what not, for possible later use," a German might say and use the verb *aufheben*. On the other hand, it means to cause to cease, to put an end to, to annul or cancel, as when a judge annuls a marriage or a law suit or a teacher cancels a lecture or an appointment. Hegel appropriated these opposite meanings of a single word and, naturally for him, fused them into a third in developing his dialectical method. Something, anything, everything is, in the relentless movement of thought, negated in its isolated individuality (*negare*), yet preserved in its essential nature (*conservare*) and at the same time elevated to its place and rôle as a *moment* in the whole of reality (*elevare*).

It is important to remember that these three stages in the movement of thinking are not evolutionary in nature nor even temporal in the usual sense. I did not find once in his "Science of Logic" their description as thesis-antithesis-synthesis, by which is predecessor Fichte was fond of denoting these stages. Rather they co-exist in each other at one and the same time. Nevertheless, it aids our understanding to think of such stages or moments as a movement from the unreflective, immediate state of being an isolated particular thing or person to a state of otherness or alienation brought about by reflection, the negative stage, to a third state in which both previous ones are brought into a reconciliation at a higher level. This reconciliation is temporary, however, and soon gives way to a new spiral development. At the risk of oversimplification, one could liken the first stage to the child, at one with himself; the second stage to adolescence, where the youth is alienated from himself, his parents, and nearly everything else (at least nowadays!); the third stage to adulthood, where childhood and adolescence are momentarily reconciled and one learns to accept his past in some sense.

In the third place, contradiction as the portentous power of the negative which drives all things toward greater completeness is an "inwardizing" process, that is, a making internal of what had been merely external. It represents a penetration by mind of the natural, the potential, the merely implicit and unformed. Reflection is a recollecting of what has been and a preserving in the present of the past, not as such but in a thoroughly spiritualized, subtly transformed way. Hegel plays with the German word for recollecting—*erinnern*—to make inner. Mind or *Geist* uses the external, natural, abstract, unrelated and transforms it into the internal, intellectual, concrete, and complexly related. Yet that which is truly "inwardized" is not held as a private possession of the individual, but flows outward into the institutions of society and the state and world culture. Hegel opposed harshly his Romantic contemporaries in their insistence on a private inner world that was immensely superior to, and alienated from, the public social and political one. For him mind truly developed was objective mind, revealed in institutions of every kind, economic, political, religious, cultural. The highest manifestations of mind or spirit flow into imperishable works of art, religion, and philosophy and create a kind of absolute mind.

Characteristically Hegel carries his principle of the interpenetration of the negative and positive into every sphere. In his discussions of truth and error, of virtue and vice, good and evil and every other polarity of common sense, he never tires of reminding us that "Their truth consists only in their relation to one another, that therefore each in its very notion contains the other; without this knowledge, not a single step can really be taken in philosophy."

It is clear then that for him the only complete truth is the whole story. "The true is the whole" is his most famous dictum in "The Phenomenology of Spirit," a dictum taken for granted in all his later writings including the "Science of Logic." Anything short of the whole is bound to be one-sided, partial, abstract to a degree, infected with negativity, finitude, and incompleteness, hence partly false.

Can any individual hope to know the truth, the whole story? Or is Hegel's so-called absolute idealism a kind of relativism, after all? It is often taken in this way. One of the ironies of the Hegelian heritage is that it frequently issues in a species of historicism which makes all philosophies simply a plaything of the particular *Zeitgeist* reigning at the moment.

Yet I would have to answer the question of whether any individual can know the whole story with a yes and a no. No, in the sense that history has no end and the truth is ever a becoming. All viewpoints of mortals are inevitably partial, hence partly false; ever and again the future reveals their one-sidedness. Yes, in a sense, too, for Hegel teaches that the individual as thinking reason contains in some fashion the whole in himself. The universal is in him, the individual, when he is fully developed and completely rational in the form of a concrete universal. Mind, even the individual mind as a union and a unity of the particular and the universal, is able to envision and encompass total reality. History is both never-ending and yet completed in that individual mind which has attained a knowledge of the structure of the whole.

Toward the end of his "Logic," Hegel envisions in a speculative *tour de force* the absolute Idea—with a capital I, Plato's use of Idea—which is a unity of thought and reality or of thinking and being, and declares it to be alone "imperishable *life, self-knowing truth,* and is *all truth.*" He goes on to assert that this absolute Idea, the whole of nature and spirit, can be grasped and apprehended in different modes by art, religion, and philosophy, and to do just this is precisely their true function and goal.

## III

One can easily get intoxicated with this elaborate vision of Hegel's, as did many of his Berlin students, insisting that their master's system had to be accepted or rejected in its entirety. After a hundred and fifty years most readers of Hegel are more inclined to sobriety, even though at present another wave of Hegelian fervor is upon us. Nevertheless, within this vision of the unity and lawfulness of historical existence, there is an idea which I for one fully accept and which I have long found helpful in illuminating the experiences of this baffling and terrible age of ours. It is the idea of the concrete to which I now want to turn, by first explaining what Hegel meant by it and then by illustrating it with examples drawn from my own experience.

Normally we mean by anything concrete that which is particular and perceivable by the senses, and by abstract we mean what is non-sensible, without time-space existence. This table is concrete and that student to whom I am responding. If I were to speak about the form of all tables, tableness, or about man rather than to that student over there, I would be talking abstractly.

In the realm of thinking, however, particularly philosophical thought, Hegel teaches us that the situation is different. There the concrete is the many-sided, the complex, and contextual—anything seen in all its relationships together with its origins and ends. Hegel takes the word concrete in its etymological sense of *concrescere*—to grow together. The abstract, on the other hand, from *abstrahere*—to draw out from—, is anything seen apart from its relations and context in a living whole. For example, a history of art, studied without reference to a people's religion, economic system, political institutions, et cetera, would be abstract. It might be desirable, of course, to study art history in this way, but one would not understand the whole truth of art unless one understands it as an organic expression of a people's entire way of grasping their world. The same can be said of any other single discipline. The true is the whole and the whole truth is the concrete.

Hegel illustrates vividly what he means by concrete and abstract in a curious little essay, titled "Who Thinks Abstractly?," found among his posthumous papers, apparently written for a newspaper at some point in his career. He begins by remarking that the uneducated think abstractly, not the educated. So the translation runs. But his term for the educated is *die Gebildeten*—the informed, one might say, except that would mean almost anything else than having lots of information. *Die Gebildeten* are those who are *in form*, whose minds through the discipline of learning and reflection are able to see the many-sidedness of the real.

Then he instances the case of a young man who has murdered someone being led to the gallows in the presence of the populace. (Hegel's time was almost as terrible as our own!) Perhaps some ladies remark on how strong, handsome, and interesting he looks and meet with indignation on the part of the uninformed multitude. How could a murderer be handsome or interesting? "This is abstract thinking," Hegel writes, "to see nothing in the murderer except the abstract fact that he is a murderer, and to annul all other human essence in him with this simple quality." Then he describes an opposite kind of abstraction among refined classes of people in Leipzig, where they bound flowers around the guillotine and on the criminal about to be executed, indulging in all manner of sentimentality on such gruesome occasions.

What does he contrast with this abstract kind of thinking? The cross on which Jesus was executed. But the cross "has lost its one-sided significance of being the instrument of dishonorable punishment and, on the contrary, suggests the notion of the highest pain and the deepest rejection together with the most joyous rapture and divine honor."

Let me cite one other example from this little essay. Hegel observes that for a servant nothing can be worse than to work for a man of low class, and nothing better than to have a nobleman for a master. Why? The low-class man thinks of the servant as nothing but a servant and treats him accordingly. He gives himself airs vis-à-vis the servant and relates himself to the servant merely in terms of this single predicate. And Hegel remarks, a bit humorously, it is best for a servant to work for a Frenchman of rank. There the servant will be treated as a friend, who can tell his master the latest news, instruct him about the newest girls in town, and freely talk back to his employer and contradict him when he, the servant, is in the right. In short, the French master thinks of the employer-employee relation concretely, recognizing this relation as only one quality of the servant, never forgetting his more important human qualities.

I want to turn now to some illustrations of my own. Years ago I wrote my doctoral dissertation on Hegel and promptly thereafter got drafted into the army just in time for the Second World War. It is not an exaggeration to say that I had plenty of opportunities in the next four and a half years to witness abstract thinking in the mentality of that abstract institution, the American military organization. Indeed, Hegel's idea served as a kind of revelation when I got close to the front in Italy, France, and Germany.

Despite the danger and discomfort of frontal areas—and I had no heroic instincts whatever—I found myself spiritually more comfortable there than in rear areas. One day it came to me suddenly why this was so. At the front men behaved toward each other like human beings. The colonels looked like privates and all "the spit and polish" of barracks life disappeared, the endless saluting and standing at attention. There was a pragmatic reason for this, of course: for German snipers, colonels were more desirable targets than simple GI's! But the real reason went deeper. Everybody was dependent on everybody else at the front, and the imminence of danger and death forced men to think and act towards their fellows concretely.

So far as I know Hegel never wrote about abstract hatred which springs from abstract thinking. I learned to know it in the war and to dread it. Near the front there was plenty of hatred, but it was concrete, directed toward the German soldiers near at hand who had destroyed a friend of yours perhaps or scared you half to death by their shells the night before. The Germans were mean so-and-so's, but they were men, not unlike yourself, and probably hating the kind of discomforts and danger they were exposed to as much as you did. In rear areas and at Army, or Army Group, Headquarters the Germans were, on the contrary, that dreadful abstraction, "the enemy," no longer human at all, fanatical Nazis to be destroyed like wild beasts. I remember a mild mannered comrade of mine, whom we used as a clerk in our little unit, once reading me a letter from his sweet wife in which she begged him to kill five Germans as a personal favor for her. She was thousands of miles distant, had never been harmed by any Germans, but nevertheless burned with abstract hatred.

I have already described this abstract hatred in my book, "The Warriors," and won't develop it any further. I wish I could say that my observation of abstract thinking and hatred was confined to the war years. In fact it seems to me, in moments of discouragement, to become ever more pervasive in our society.

Once or twice in my life I have been in places abroad where I was cordially disliked and despised simply because I am an American. One must himself experience such a thing to grasp adequately the sense of outrage I felt then. Being an American, I told myself, is only one aspect of me and hardly the crucial one. If they were to dislike me after acquaintance for my ideas, or personality, or habits, it would be unpleasant but bearable. After all, one knows enough against oneself to understand another person's dislike. Yet the experience was strangely salutary. For I realized then, for the first time deeply, what it must be like to be a black man in our society and to be hated by so many simply because of the color of your skin.

Abstract thinking and its offspring, abstract hatred, are surely at the root of many of our most intractable problems today. One notices them everywhere, in the slogans (the term originally meant battle-cry) of politics and advertising, the rhetoric of our radicals on the right and the left, in the propagandistic war of the sexes, now renewed once again, in the exploitation of the generation gap. When I listen to young dissidents describe their image of "the establishment" in our college, I feel alternately amused and very sad. They seem to imagine a group of wealthy trustees dictating policy to our President who in turn passes their dictates to us at faculty meetings. And we impose these policies on them. Those of us on the inside, so to speak, who know many trustees and harassed presidents as well as our individualistic colleagues, are unable to tell these young radicals how absurd their image of the institution really is. Of course, it is not only the young who are guilty of this sort of abstract thinking. All of us indulge in it in those many areas of life where we are not truly "in form."

One should always resist the temptation to be edifying. Hegel himself insisted that philosophy's function could never be to edify, but rather to describe things as they are. Nevertheless, it is to be hoped that those who ponder the implications of this thought about the truly concrete will receive some practical guidance for the movement of their own thinking.

KENNETH CLARK

# Thomas Jefferson and the Italian Renaissance

[ AUTUMN 1972 ]

THOMAS Jefferson has been my hero ever since my schooldays, when an intelligent schoolteacher gave us a term off from Tudors and Plantagenets and introduced us to the study of American history. At almost the same time—I suppose it was in about 1918—I read for the first time that masterpiece of compressed and imaginative learning, Jacob Burckhardt's "Civilization of the Renaissance in Italy," a book which in some ways has influenced my life more than any other; and it set working in my mind the concept of the universal man, the man for whom all branches of knowledge and experience could be related and used for the advancement of human happiness. It is from this point of view I shall venture to speak about Thomas Jefferson.

Jefferson was a man of insatiable curiosity. He wanted to master every branch of knowledge so that he himself could use it for the good of others. First of all agriculture, for that was the basis of life: he never tired of studying new methods and discovering new seeds and plants. But his interest was not solely material, because he was also a resourceful botanist, introducing many new species of flowers. Closely connected with agriculture, the weather. For years Mr. Jefferson noted the weather each day, and one of his first instructions given to any traveler or emissary was to do the same. Then irrigation, and, from that, the study of canals, not only for irrigation but for transport. What else? Philology: he made a vast comparative study of Indian dialects, which was lost or stolen in a packing case. Paleontology: he reconstructed the first mammoth. Archeology: I am told that his unearthing of mounds in Virginia was amongst the first pieces of scientific excavation ever achieved. He was, however, not interested in geology, not foreseeing how it could be made of use to man. What else? Meteorology, astronomy, chemistry, anatomy, mechanics, civil engineering. And, of course, architecture, of which I shall have more to say.

Such achievements were made possible by a rare combination of will power, industry, and intelligence. He can seldom have spent an idle moment. But he had two sources of pleasure which can, in a sense, be called relaxations, music and horsemanship, in both of which he excelled.

This character of the universal man was hardly known in antiquity, perhaps because the disciplines of rhetoric and philosophy were too demanding; and it was certainly not admitted in the middle ages, with the possible exception of Roger Bacon, because all intellectual activities were directed towards the love and knowledge of God. The idea that one man should master all knowledge and put his knowledge into practice was an invention—if you like, a fantasy—of the early Italian Renaissance. It was part of what Burckhardt called The Discovery of Man. It grew out of a state of society that existed above all in the Florentine republic from about 1400 onwards, and was recommended by several thinkers of the time: but only one man achieved it, Leon Battista Alberti.

It is possible to know a lot about Alberti, because, although his papers do not fill eighteen volumes (and more to come), he left over a dozen dialogues on morals and society in which he and his family are the chief speakers; he left a book on the theory of painting (the first ever written), a book on sculpture, a book on the moving of weights, a book on mathematics, a book on excavating a Roman galley, an immense book on the art of architecture, the first since Vitruvius, and an autobiography, the first since St. Augustine. In this autobiography he tells us how he questioned everyone he met about the mysteries of his craft, scholars and artisans, down to the very cobblers, and in this way acquired every sort of accomplishment, the knowledge of which he imparted freely to others. His only two relaxations were music and horsemanship.

I do not think one can fail to be struck with the resemblance to Thomas Jefferson, and it is confirmed when we look at their portraits: Alberti's bronze relief of his own profile, which he executed himself, and Houdon's bust of Jefferson. We see the same proud, wilful heads—taut, determined, self-confident. The poet Blake wrote a famous aphorism: "Damn braces; bless relaxes." It sometimes comes to our minds when we study these two extraordinary men.

Since Alberti's life is not very familiar, and his writings are relatively inaccessible, I want to speak about him in a little more detail, because I believe that his character and achievements may throw a little more light on the already brilliantly illuminated figure of Jefferson.

Alberti was born in the year 1404. He learned Greek and Latin at the University of Padua, and throughout his life had a remarkable facility in languages. He then moved to Bologna, where he studied law. Evidently he overworked, and suffered some kind of breakdown. Letters, he tells us, which had once seemed to him like vigorous and sweet-smelling buds, now swarmed beneath his eyes like scorpions. But he conquered this breakdown, as he conquered all physical weakness; for, as he said, "A man can do all things with himself if he will." And he developed an almost morbid industry. "Although at no hour of the day could you see him idle, yet that he might win for himself still more of the fruits of life and time, every evening before going to bed he would set beside himself a wax candle of a certain measure and, sitting half undressed, he would read history or poetry until the candle was burnt up. The followers of Pythagoras used, before they slept, to compose their minds with some harmonious music. Now our friend finds his reading no less soothing than was the sound of music to them; but it is more useful. They fall into a profound sleep in which the mind is motionless; but he, even when asleep, has noble and life-giving thoughts revolving in his mind; and often things of great worth become clear to him, which, when awake, he had sought with unavailing effort." He had only two recreations, riding and music. He was an outstanding performer on the viol, and so great was the power of music on his spirits that when he underwent an operation music allayed his pain.

After the law he turned to mathematics, and received instruction from the leading mathematician of his day. But as a typical humanist, Alberti did not practice mathematics for its own sake, but in order to secure control over the forces of nature, in particular how to use the powers of wind and water. He invented a means of measuring the depths of the sea, a hygrometer for measuring damp, and various devices for raising weights. He was interested only in the practical application of his studies, for, as he said, "Man is born to be of use to man. What is the point of all human arts? Simply to benefit humanity. So the wise will blame those who studiously devote themselves to complicated and unimportant subjects."

With his outstanding abilities as a writer and a classical scholar it was almost certain, in humanist Italy, that Alberti should enter the public service. He became a civil servant in the Roman curia. But here my parallel with Thomas Jefferson must be suspended because Alberti had no gift for politics. His love of action was subordinate to his love of order. What can a supremely intelligent man do who is distressed by the imperfections of society, whose sense of human needs prevents him from retiring into pure science and mathematics, but enjoins him to put his technical knowledge to human use? There is really only one answer. Become an architect. And what is an architect? Alberti put his definition into the first chapter of his book: "Him I call an architect who by sure and admirable method is able with mind to advise and in execution to complete all those works which, by the movement of weights and the conjunction of bodies can, with the greatest beauty, be adapted to the uses of mankind: to which end he must understand all noble and excellent sciences." Here the parallel may be resumed. Alberti, like Jefferson—and for that matter Christopher Wren—, began as an amateur architect; that is to say he did not learn his art in a stonemason's yard, but in a library. This charge of amateurishness was leveled against him by nineteenth-century critics, although anything less amateurish than his two churches in Mantua it would be hard to imagine. But his efforts to recreate the architecture of antiquity were largely dependent on literary sources. He never executed an exact copy, as the Virginia Capitol in Richmond is a copy of the Maison Carrée in Nîmes, but he did use out of context certain Greco-Roman motifs derived from the triumphal arch. To the creation of architecture he brought all his knowledge of forces, weights, and materials, and all his experience of human needs.

Alberti did not build very much—three churches, one palace, one renovated façade. But he did write the first book on architecture since antiquity. It is a great book. Several times in the text Alberti admits to feeling that he has bitten off more than he can chew; and in consequence there are a certain number of digressions, and, as in all humanist writing, down to Montaigne, the number of classical examples quoted is exasperating. But it is all there. Amongst other things he describes pieces of architecture that he did not build: a country villa and a small ideal city. Let me quote from the description of the country house: "It must be near the city upon an open, airy road; it must make a cheerful appearance to those who go a little way out of town to take the air, and for this reason I would have it stand pretty high, but upon so easy ascent that it should be hardly perceptible to those that go to it till they find themselves at the top and a large prospect opens itself to their views. Nor should there be any want of pleasant landscapes, flowery meads, open champains, shady groves and clear streams. . . . I would have the whole body of the house perfectly well lighted that it be open to receive a great deal of light and sun. Let all things smile and seem to welcome the arrival of your guests. Let those who enter be led from square rooms into round ones and again from round into square, and so into others of mixed lines, neither all round, nor all square. And let the passage to the bedroom be, if possible, all on one floor," Well, that was written in 1444—in what we call the late middle ages. It was realized in the United States of America in the 1770's, in Monticello, Jefferson's beautiful and lovable house.

I will not take up time with Alberti's descriptions of an ideal city, which are scattered throughout his ten books of architecture. It consists of a series of straight streets leading to piazzas. He gives the width of the streets and the sizes of the piazzas, and by a curious coincidence both plan and proportions are practically the same as Thomas Jefferson's first plan for Washington. As is well known, this was superseded by the radial plan of l'Enfant. But one Albertian idea was actually realized in the State of Virginia. I mean the piazza with colonnaded buildings on two sides, and a domed temple at the end. Nothing, I am sure, would have given Alberti greater pleasure than that the colonnaded buildings should present in succession the orders of architecture, and that the temple should be a perfect sphere, and in fact be used as a library. I doubt if there is a more Albertian concept in existence than what Mr. Jefferson called his "academical village."

The correspondence between Jefferson's architectural ideas and those of Alberti can be explained in concrete terms. Jefferson's architectural mentor, Palladio, had drawn very freely on Alberti's "Ten Books," sometimes using the same phrases, and this is particularly true of the passages on the planning of ideal cities. But why should there be so many other points of resemblance between the *Uomo universale* of early fifteenth-century Florence and the Universal Man of late eighteenth-century Virginia? Thomas Jefferson had spent five years in France, and one would have supposed that a parallel with the French Enlightenment would have been more apropos. The answer is twofold: first that the Encyclopedists of the eighteenth century were themselves heirs to the humanists of the fifteenth century, and secondly that the eighteenth-century Enlightenment came at the end of a period of sophistication. In fact, by the time Jefferson reached Paris the great age of the Encyclopedists was over. From 1784 to 1789 French society was on the brink of collapse—and knew it. The Florentine republic, on the other hand, was on the way up. Its founders, Salutati, Traversi, and Bruni, were confidently reconstructing a political system and a society that had broken down in the aftermath of the Black Death and the wars of rival factions. Just as the republic seemed to be reaching a point of stability it was attacked by a tyrant, Giangaleazzo Visconti of Milan. Bruni writes of him in words that Jefferson might have applied to George III: "I would not think this serious if our struggle was with other people, for then conditions would be the same on both sides. But now our struggle is not with another people, but with a tyrant who watches continually over his own affairs, who has no fear of cavillers, who is not hampered by petty laws, who does not wait for the desires of the masses or the deliberation of the people." I might add that Giangaleazzo was also a great deal more intelligent than George III.

These early humanist chancellors, at the turn of the fourteenth century, ascribed the success of their cause to the republican inheritance and constitution of their city. They believed earnestly that free men could achieve anything. But they were not pure idealists. They had no patience with elaborate philosophical theories. They subscribed to a philosophy of common sense.

This was the climate of opinion which survived in Florence up to about 1440. There was about it an earnestness and a certain naïvety, very different from the society of Diderot and d'Alembert. It must be admitted that the humanists had a Voltairean side. Alberti himself wrote a satire called "Momus," which in its destructive impudence is remarkably similar to "Candide," and Lorenzo Valla's "de Voluptate" has been justly compared to the "Dictionnaire philosophique." What a subject to appear in the late middle ages! I don't suppose that Jefferson had ever heard of Valla, but without "de Voluptate" the pursuit of happiness might never have appeared among the "self-evident truths."

On the other hand, one discovers in the early Florentine republic a kind of democratic puritanism and a distrust of pomp and rank that are entirely Jeffersonian. "A man's a man for a' that" appears in many variations in the speeches and dialogues of the time; for example, in Poggio's dialogue (On Nobility), where it is put rather incongruously into the mouth of that exquisite scholar and arbiter of taste, Niccolo Niccoli. "Eminence," he says, "conferred on individuals by social and political distinctions is a hollow sham and people are distinguished only by their personal virtues that they activate in private." This legend of the unassuming frugality of early humanists was still alive a hundred years later, when Vasari wrote his "Lives of the Painters." He records how Donatello, the greatest artist of the early humanist group, had refused to accept the scarlet cloak that Cosimo dé Medici had sent him as a present.

Another point of likeness, which has a direct bearing on the concept of the universal man: the Florentine humanists and the founding fathers of the American republic were both working in an untilled field. Things had to be worked out afresh. Constitutions and political morality had to be deduced from Plutarch and Cicero. In both his book on the Art of Painting and in his Ten Books of Architecture Alberti claims emphatically that he is the first to write on these subjects and has nothing to support him except the texts and ruins of antiquity. One must remember (although it is always difficult to do so) that these books were written before the invention of printing. The oppressive sequence of classical examples that they contain were all drawn from manuscripts which had to be sought for in the uncatalogued libraries of Rome and Florence. A manuscript of Vitruvius had existed in the twelfth century in the library of Cluny; no doubt several were available to Alberti. But they had not acquired those elaborate commentaries on the obscure text that became available almost a hundred years later in the edition printed in Como in 1521. Alberti had to work it out for himself.

Do it yourself. That could have been the motto of the Founding Fathers, from Benjamin Franklin downwards, and it was certainly the motto of Thomas Jefferson when he built Monticello with (as we are told, but I am not sure if it is correct) the help of the only copies of Vitruvius and Palladio in America. Of course, this independence led to what I may call, with respect, a kind of experimental crankiness. Alberti may have had to work out the laws of classical architecture for himself, but behind him lay a great tradition of fine building, so that he could give plans, elevations, and measurements, without those curious adjustments and displays of ingenuity which one finds in Monticello and even in the University of Virginia.

I hope I have persuaded you that the resemblance between Thomas Jefferson and the Florentine Humanists of the early fifteenth century, Alberti in particular, is not a matter of fancy or coincidence but the result of similar personalities, placed in similar circumstances. I must now consider the great differences that lie between them. To take first the circumstances. Fifteenth-century Florence was an urban culture, based on a long tradition of commerce and banking. Jefferson believed passionately and almost exclusively in an agrarian community. "The people," in whom he so often said that he placed his trust, were in fact the yeoman farmers and agricultural laborers of Virginia, together with a few craftsmen necessary to maintain the life of a small town. This is a type of citizen not represented at all in the dialogues of Poggio and Alberti.

It is true that Gianozzo, the representative of the plain but honest man in Alberti's most famous dialogue, "della Famiglia," recommends the pleasures of living in a villa surrounded by one's own farms. But he also advises his young hearers to avoid public life, and he makes a speech on making money which has been quoted as the first apologia of bourgeois capitalism: "A man cannot set his mind to greater or more liberal work than making money. Business consists of buying and selling and no one of any sense can consider this a base occupation, because when you sell it is not only a mercenary affair; you have been of use to the buyer, and what he pays you for is your labour." It might be any enlightened manufacturer of the mid-nineteenth century, but not Thomas Jefferson. In fairness to Alberti one must remember that this was a semi-fictional character being used for dramatic effect. In another dialogue, speaking for himself, Alberti says: "I would have been certain to make money if I had turned from literature to commerce. I lived subordinate to others when, with my talents, I could have had important transactions under my control. But I have always preferred to wealth and comfort the understanding of things, good discipline and the mysteries of art." This Jefferson might have said, although his interpretation of art would have inclined towards the useful rather than the ornamental arts.

The truth is that Jefferson, in spite of the time and intellectual energy he spent on architecture, was not an artist. His very honesty of mind, which (in addition to his weak voice) prevented him from being an orator, stopped him from paying too much attention to the actual way in which things are presented. The Ciceronian arts of persuasion, so carefully cultivated by the humanists, would have been distasteful to him. All art has in it an element of artifice which was foreign to the constitution of his mind. We may even question how much he allowed himself to be moved by works of art. Everyone knows his famous letter about the Maison Carrée at Nîmes—"Here I am, Madam, gazing whole hours at the Maison Carrée like a lover at his mistress. The stocking weavers and silk spinners around it consider me a hypochondriac Englishman." Strong words from Mr. Jefferson. There are other enthusiastic descriptions of architecture. On the other hand, when he was in Milan not only did he describe the Cathedral as "a worthy object of philosophical contemplation, to be placed among the rarest instances of the misuse of money," but he never noticed the architecture of Bramante or visited the masterpiece of the greatest of all universal men, Leonardo da Vinci's Last Supper. More surprising still, he does not seem to have tried to get on to Vicenza. That the devoted student of Palladio's writings should have made no attempt to see his original buildings is rather disappointing. But Jefferson's whole attention was concentrated on the cultivation of rice and raisins, and the amount of Italian rice that he could smuggle out in his pockets. Nor can we truly say that his interest in architecture was a later development, because he had begun work on Monticello ten years earlier. As Secretary of State he submitted a design for the President's residence based on the Villa Rotonda in Vicenza. Considering how notoriously difficult that famous building is to imitate, and still more to adapt, he would have been well advised to go and look at it. Perhaps it is just as well that to the eighteen recorded copies of the Villa Rotonda there was not added a nineteenth, and that we have Hoban's White House instead.

Finally, I see a considerable difference in what might be called the religious philosophy of Thomas Jefferson and that of the early Florentines. They were, it is true, united by a religion of work. The idea of a *Vita Contemplativa* would have been equally contemptible to both of them. But this religion of work was held with different ends in mind. Jefferson, although in his lifetime he was attacked as an atheist, was in fact a religiously minded man with an entirely Christian approach. His composite Gospel, in four languages, from which miracles and revelations have been excluded, could have been compiled only by one for whom the moral teachings of Christ had supreme authority; and, as you know, Jefferson frequently spoke of himself as "a real Christian."

The humanists, on the other hand, had no Christian beliefs at all. Priests and theologians have always been fair game for satirists, but there is a difference in tone between the religious indignation of Erasmus' satires and the mere contempt of Valla. So what beliefs kept the early humanists on the path of duty? What induced Alberti to work so hard and recommend so earnestly a moral life? The answer is Platonism: or rather that form of stoic philosophy which derived its ideals from Plato, and was transmitted by Cicero. It was the Platonic conception of harmony that inspired Alberti's most interesting thoughts about architecture, and aroused that outburst of emotion at the spectacle of nature which Jacob Burckhardt interpreted in a romantic vein, and which I will therefore quote in a more literal translation: "In summer the yellowing cornfields and fruit laden trees brought tears to his eyes. 'Look,' he would exclaim, 'how we are surrounded by witnesses accusing us of idleness. There is nothing in nature but brings, in the course of a year, some great gain to mankind. And what can I show well made according to the strength that is in me?'"

Alberti worked because he felt that in doing so he was at one with the forces of nature. He believed in the Platonic concept of the universe as one great harmony. Thomas Jefferson, as you know, had a particular dislike of Plato; in fact the only man I have ever known who disliked Plato more was one of the great Americans of our own time, Judge Learned Hand. Jefferson would certainly not have shed tears at the sight of yellowing cornfields, but would have taken infinite pains to find out how to get a second crop. He believed, and it is revealed in all his writings, that the solution of moral problems was implicit in the successful life of action. Perhaps, after all, this is not so far from the beliefs of civic humanism up to about 1450. But the shadow of Plato was never far away, and in the second half of the century Platonism, in the writings of Pico della Mirandola and Marsilio Ficino, took control of Italian thought for over a century. Even the aging Alberti dutifully sat at the feet of the brilliant young teachers. My parallel between Thomas Jefferson and the founders of the humanist renaissance is over. Of course it was always incomplete, because Jefferson was President of the United States, and the humanists were (relatively) small-town men. He had to deal with a huge, formless country, chaotic, divided, unsure of its aims and its future; a country that was dangerously poor (whereas Florence was dangerously rich) and perpetually seeking the foreign aid which it has since so generously dispensed. Half the continent was still French or Spanish. There were vast problems to be settled, to all of which he applied his remarkable intelligence and a diplomacy that is unexpected in so stubborn a character. There is really no comparison with the problems of Chancellors Salutati and Bruni. But we may remember that the wilful inscription on his tombstone—"and not one word more"—does not mention either the Presidency or the Louisiana Purchase. The three achievements for which Jefferson wished to be remembered—the Declaration of Independence, Religious Liberty in Virginia and the University of Virginia—are all aspirations that go back to the first age of humanism.

CLIFTON WALLER BARRETT

# The Struggle to Create a University

[ AUTUMN 1973 ]

## I

THE VISITOR to the University of Virginia is almost invariably enthralled by the grace and beauty of its architecture. For him it breathes an atmosphere of peace and harmony, an invitation to the pursuit of learning in an idyllic setting. His thoughts, not unnaturally, turn to the nearby "little mountain" and he has a vision of the Sage of Monticello in his peaceful old age engaged in the delightful occupation of designing a university and watching it grow steadily and harmoniously until it emerges an authentic masterpiece, the product of his genius. What a delightful scenario and how far from the actual facts! It would be difficult for our visitor to comprehend the years of struggle and turmoil that attended the gestation of the University. It did indeed make steady progress but only by the exercise of the utmost dedication and fortitude in surmounting a multitude of obstacles and surviving a series of crises. Our observer would be edified to learn that the rhythm of the University's creation was underscored throughout by the counterpoint of the founder's personal woes, his desperate financial problems, physical disabilities, and heartbreaking family circumstances. Only then could he fully appreciate the indomitable character of the creator.

## II

In 1809, Thomas Jefferson returned from Washington to Monticello. He was now approaching sixty-six and his rugged constitution had suffered during eight strenuous years of the Presidency. The mansion at Monticello had been finished but the estate was sadly run-down and was producing a diminishing income, a situation that would not improve during ensuing years of embargo, war, and depression. Jefferson was compelled to embark on a syndrome of mortgages and loans, a practice that continued during the seventeen years that remained to him.

## THE STRUGGLE TO CREATE A UNIVERSITY

Jefferson had declared that all his wishes ended where he hoped his days would end, at Monticello. How eagerly he looked forward to a life of repose in the bosom of his family, with ample time for reading and study. These hopes were realized, as he did indeed find himself welcomed by his beloved daughter, Martha, her husband, and their eleven children. Jefferson had hoped, too, for a stimulating intercourse with cultivated individuals. Here his hopes were fulfilled to overflowing as visitors poured into Monticello in a never-ending stream. In truth, the cost of entertaining these distinguished characters imposed a further burden on his already strained resources.

Politically, Jefferson welcomed retirement from the arena in which he had figured so prominently for thirty-five years. He had suffered enough from the bruising partisan battles and he was tired of the venomous assaults on his mind, his character, and his religious beliefs. In this respect, his hopes were vain. As long-time leader of the Republican party, his advice and support were constantly sought. His devotion to the young nation forbade his remaining silent on measures he deemed essential to its well-being, many of which he had himself initiated.

It was indeed an extraordinary man who, in the face of his manifold personal problems and commitments, could summon up the energy and the enthusiasm, the mental and physical strength to carry out the infinitude of measures necessary to create a new university, to purchase the land, to plan the grounds and buildings, to supervise the construction, to direct the engagement of professors, to devise the curriculum, and, finally, to act as chief executive officer and also as Secretary, taking notes, writing the minutes, and compiling voluminous reports for the authorities in Richmond. To quote an early historian of the University, "The thousand and one matters that college presidents and boards of trustees usually leave to professional architects and skilled labor, were thought out and carefully specified on paper by the 'Father of the University of Virginia.'" It should be remembered that all of this was done in the face of the opposition, at times exceedingly bitter, of competing localities, institutions, and, significantly, of religious bodies.

Jefferson's first idea of a university for the Commonwealth stems from his proposal in 1779 to develop and improve his alma mater, William and Mary. Later, he abandoned these efforts and pursued the idea of a new, centrally located institution.

In 1784 Congress appointed Jefferson Minister Plenipotentiary with headquarters in France. During his sojourn of five years in Europe, he became acquainted with some of the best authorities on education. He visited schools and colleges, interviewed professors, and read the available treatises. He returned to America determined to utilize what he had learned from the best minds of the old world in the improvement of education at home.

After Jefferson's return, we hear no more about the transformation of William and Mary. On January 18, 1800, he wrote the eminent British savant, Joseph Priestley: "We wish to establish in the upper country, and more centrally for the State, an university on a plan so broad and liberal and *modern,* as to be worth patronizing with the public support, and be a temptation to the youth of other states to come and drink of the cup of knowledge."

In 1806, a young Virginian of twenty-eight, Joseph Carrington Cabell, arrived in Washington with letters of introduction to Jefferson. He was a graduate of William and Mary. Cabell, like Jefferson, had enjoyed exposure to European culture. He had gone to Europe in 1803, had studied in Paris and the Italian universities, and had visited Cambridge and Oxford. Cabell shared with Jefferson the hope of benefiting their native state by means of progressive ideas imbibed during their European experience.

The young man attracted Jefferson so strongly that he attempted to lure him into service in Washington, but Cabell longed to return to Virginia and to identify himself with the interests of his own people. As had Jefferson, Cabell hoped to remodel their alma mater, William and Mary, into a premier university. Jefferson discouraged this and instigated his private secretary to write Cabell: "If the amelioration of education and the diffusion of knowledge be the favorite objects of your life, avail yourself of the favorable dispositions of your countrymen, and consent to go into our legislative body. Instead of wasting your time attempting to patch up a decaying institution, direct your thoughts to a higher and more valuable object. *Found a new one that will be worthy of the first State in the Union.*"

Cabell followed this advice and became a member of the Legislature in 1809. His complete dedication to Jefferson's great vision and his unwearying partisanship during crucial sessions in Richmond were in large measure responsible for the establishment and funding of the University. Later Cabell was to be joined by John Hartwell Cocke and Francis Walker Gilmer to form that invincible trinity that enabled Jefferson to gain the victory.

In 1810, with Cabell's support, the Legislature established the Literary Fund to be devoted to the encouragement of learning. This fund became the fountainhead, the main source of funds for the future University.

Jefferson was deeply depressed by the war with England in 1812 but strangely enough this war provided an opportunity for the amelioration of his financial problems. When the British burned Washington in 1814, the Congressional Library went up in flames. In response to this tragic event, Jefferson offered his own library to Congress as a replacement. It was probably the finest in the country and had been collected over fifty years. Jefferson, by act of Congress, was paid a grudging $23,950, a tremendous bargain for the nation. These funds provided the means for the payment of pressing debts. Characteristically, Jefferson used a part of the money for the purchase of books for himself and thus began the gathering of his third library which eventually reached 1,000 volumes destined for the future University of Virginia. Unhappily, after his death, the books were sold for the benefit of his creditors.

## III

1814 was a year of decision and the beginning of twelve years of unceasing struggle. By now, the shadowy outline in Jefferson's mind had assumed definite form in the shape of a carefully delineated plan for an academical village with its separate buildings for professors, single-story dormitories, and the powerfully motivating idea of humanistic and scientific disciplines carried on in the liberating atmosphere of freedom of inquiry. In this year Jefferson was elected a member of the Board of Trustees of Albemarle Academy. He promptly suggested the idea of expanding the Academy into a higher institution to be called Central College, a symbol of his thoughts about location. He moved to accomplish this by an act of the Legislature.

1815 was devoted to preparing the Legislature for the adoption of Jefferson's plan and Cabell introduced a bill to carry out his intent. By now a formidable opposition had become established. It naturally included the Federalists who, on principle, were opposed to anything Jefferson might suggest. There were, in addition, the powerful lobby of William and Mary which feared its extinction, the rivalry of Washington College at Lexington [now Washington and Lee University], the municipal pride of Staunton and other localities. The bill finally passed the lower house but failed in the Senate.

1816 was the memorable year in which an act was passed changing the name of Albemarle Academy to Central College. A Board of Visitors was appointed, consisting of Jefferson, Monroe, Madison, Joseph Cabell, David Watson, and J. H. Cocke.

1817 was the year in which construction of the first building of the University was begun. At the first official meeting of the Board, Jefferson recommended the purchase of a field of forty-seven acres one mile distant from the town at a price of $1,421.25. This transaction was approved and the University thus acquired its first land. On this occasion a subscription list was initiated, Jefferson, Cabell, and Cocke each pledging $1,000. The proceeds of this list made it possible to begin building and authorization was granted for the construction of the first pavilion. Jefferson's plan called for buildings of architectural grace and beauty. He had previously asserted that it was not more costly to build a beautiful home than to build an ugly one and he stoutly refused to adopt a more economical version.

On October 6, the cornerstone was laid for the first pavilion, Number VII, now the Colonnade Club. The day became an unofficial holiday in Charlottesville and almost the entire citizenry turned out to witness a solemn ceremony made particularly impressive by the attendance of three Presidents of the United States.

1818 was a year of notable progress. By now, the Legislature had become convinced of the desirability of establishing a superior centrally located State University and it was so resolved. Provision was made for an annuity of $15,000 from the Literary Fund. The act also provided for a Board of Commissioners to meet in Rockfish Gap in August. This Board was to render a report recommending a site for the new university, a building plan, the branches of learning to be taught, the number and the character of the professorships, and the general organization of the institution. No agenda could have suited Jefferson better and we can conjure up a glimpse of him, now seventy-five, meeting with his fellow commissioners. He was chosen to preside and almost immediately established an atmosphere of harmony which lasted throughout the entire deliberations. Never did his talents show to better advantage. As we would say today, he had done his home work. As against the vague pretensions of Williamsburg, Lexington, and Staunton, he offered a precise architectural design and a detailed plan of organization. He had the further advantage of being able to offer land already purchased, buildings under construction and funds in excess of $40,000. As a final clincher, he produced charts demonstrating that Charlottesville was the true center of the State geographically and with respect to population.

The result might have been foreseen; a large majority voted in favor of Jefferson's plan, a vote almost immediately made unanimous. It only remained to appoint a committee, which included Jefferson and Madison, to draft the report for the General Assembly. A cynical observer remarked that most of the clauses had been drafted at Monticello long before the Rockfish Gap meeting.

Now there began the struggle to secure approval of the report in Richmond. Cabell led the fight. The Christmas season was at hand and many legislators were anxious to go home. Despite doctor's orders, Cabell stuck to his post and persuaded many to do likewise. "Even if danger to my life existed which my friends apprehend," he declared, "I could not risk it in a better cause." Opponents of Jefferson and Albemarle united in solid ranks and Cabell marshaled his supporters. "I consider the establishment of the University," wrote Delegate John Taliaferro of Fredericksburg, "of more vital consequence to the State than the sum of all legislation since the founding of government."

Unhappily, during this period, Jefferson's health began to show signs of deterioration. After the Rockfish conference, he rode to Warm Springs to seek relief from his afflictions, but he returned to Monticello worse off than before.

By January, 1819, Cabell's efforts had produced a more favorable atmosphere in Richmond. Unfortunately, his intensive efforts caused him to suffer hemorrhages of the lungs which at times endured for seven or eight hours. On January 28, a signal victory was won when an act was passed which designated Albemarle as the site of the University of Virginia. The long battle was over and the University had received its official baptism.

A new board convened on March 29 and elected Jefferson Rector. Jefferson and General Cocke were appointed a Committee of Superintendence. There now began a period of seven years during which Cocke's unwearying supervision of all of the details of construction earned for him a secure place in the history of the founding of the University.

During this fateful year Jefferson suffered a paralyzing blow. In the previous year he had endorsed notes of his friend, former Governor Wilson Cary Nicholas, in the amount of $20,000. During the panic of 1819 these notes fell due. Nicholas was now bankrupt and helpless. The entire burden fell on Jefferson and he was forced to execute a general mortgage on his property and to find money to pay interest of $1200 a year, a burden he bore until his death. He rallied from this disaster but only after an illness of such severity that for several days his family feared for his life.

The years 1820 to 1824 were devoted to the completion of the buildings on the Lawn and the Ranges. This was made possible by loans of $180,000 from the Literary Fund. This had required a major effort on the part of Jefferson and Cabell. Jefferson warned in a letter to Cabell in January, 1821, that without sufficient funds the University could not be completed for thirteen years, that is, 1834, or long after his death. He stated that "even with the whole funds we shall be reduced to 6 professors, while Harvard will prime it over us with 20 professors. How many of your youths she has now, . . . I know not; but a gentleman, lately from Princeton told me he saw there the list of students . . . and that more than half were Virginians." Although discouraged by the slowness of legislative action, with a touch of that steel so engrained in his character, Jefferson declared, "I have neither vigor of body or mind left to keep the field. But I will die in the last ditch." It had been hoped to finish all of the buildings by the autumn of 1821 so as to permit the opening in 1822. This hope proved a delusion. The annual report for 1821 stated that 6 pavilions, 2 hotels and 104 dormitories had been completed at a cost of $114,000 and it was estimated that the remaining buildings called for in the plan would bring the grand total for constructing the University to some $200,000. In the meantime the project of building a library had been introduced. Jefferson had consulted the architect, Benjamin Latrobe, who had recommended a building of impressive proportions as a capstone on the north side of the Lawn. Inspired by this suggestion, Jefferson had designed the building called the Rotunda to be used for a library and for other purposes. It was estimated to cost $46,000 and Jefferson was determined to postpone opening until this library as well as the other buildings had been finished and were ready to receive professors and students.

To ward off possible criticism of the elevated style and decoration of the buildings, Jefferson wrote: "We have no supplementary guide but our own judgements, which we have exercised conscientiously, in adopting a scale and style of building believed to be proportionate to the respectability, the means and the wants of our country, . . . not what was to perish with ourselves, but what would remain, be respected and preserved thro' other ages."

During the year 1822, Jefferson, now seventy-nine, fell on the terrace steps at Monticello and broke his left arm. He wrote Cabell on December 28, "You do not know, my dear sir, how great is my physical inability to write. The joints of [my] right wrist and fingers, in consequence of an ancient dislocation, are become so stiffened that I can write at but the pace of a snail. The copying of our report, and my letter lately sent to the Governor, being seven pages only, employed me laboriously a whole week."

In 1824 the Legislature forgave the loans of $180,000. There was also an appropriation of $50,000 for the purchase of a library and apparatus. In view of this grant, Jefferson opened a credit of $18,000 with Boston booksellers to supply "desirable volumes covering every field of learning" to the new University. Jefferson himself compiled a list which covered 7,000 volumes. Four years later, a survey credits the University of Virginia with 8,000 volumes compared to 30,000 to Harvard, 8,500 to Yale, and 8,000 to Princeton, a relative position which, unhappily, it has not occupied since.

With the financial situation clarified, the Board attempted to draw up what might be considered the first budget for the University. The annuity of $15,000 was now free of encumbrance and with rent anticipated from the hotels and dormitories, the income gave promise of reaching $35,000, a far cry from the present budgets of $100,000,000. In any event, this income was not deemed adequate to permit ten professorships and the number was reduced to eight. At this point a decision was made to send an agent to Europe to recruit qualified professors and the choice fell on Jefferson's young friend, Francis Walker Gilmer, a most fortunate circumstance, as Gilmer was to perform an invaluable service for the University. The attempts to engage suitable men in the United States has been unsuccessful and Jefferson was not to be satisfied with individuals of inferior talents and attainments. On February 23 he had written Cabell: "You know that we all, from the beginning considered the high qualifications of our professors as the only means by which we could give to our institution splendor and preeminence over all its sister seminaries." And in a letter to Richard Rush introducing Gilmer, he said: "We do not expect to obtain (in Great Britain) men of the first eminence . . . but we do know that there is another race treading on their heels, preparing to take their places, and as well, and sometimes better, qualified to fill them."

Gilmer sailed for England in early May. He promptly began his visits to the academic centers of Cambridge, Oxford, and Edinburgh. Before doing so he secured his first recruit, the German George Blaetterman. Gilmer received a warm welcome in Cambridge, but his efforts were fruitless, and it was only after his arrival in Edinburgh that he succeeded in engaging his first English professor, Thomas Hewlett Key. In the meantime he had become quite discouraged and shared this feeling with Jefferson, who himself had become fearful of the failure of the mission. Gilmer wrote: "I will, if it be possible in Europe, procure fit men; but I will rather return home, mortifying as it would be, without a single professor, than with mere impostors." With the engagement of Key, things looked up, and soon George Long, a friend of Key, was secured. Charles Bonnycastle and Robley Dunglison completed the roster of five professors. Shortly after his arrival in New York, he secured John Patton Emmet as the sixth.

That Gilmer could have accomplished such an important objective in so short a time is striking testimony of his magnetic personality. To persuade five professors to cross the ocean in the winter to become identified with a new and untried institution located in what many in England regarded as a wilderness was a rare feat of salesmanship. He had performed a service without which the University could not have opened.

Gilmer's return voyage to America was a harrowing experience of thirty-five days of unspeakable weather and his health never recovered from its effects. After some weeks of recuperation in New York, he was back in Virginia. His state of mind was not improved by the savage assaults on the engaging of English professors. The Boston Gazette published biting references to "His Grace That" and "My Lord This." In July he came to Farmington in Charlottesville. By this time all efforts to improve his failing health were unavailing. He died on February 25, 1826, in his bedroom at Farmington. Among his last sayings was "Such is the martyrdom I have endured for the Old Dominion—she will never thank for it—but I will love and cherish her as if she did."

## IV

1825 should have been a year of celebration. The University at long last was opening its doors. The great day was set for February 1. A postponement became necessary as three English professors were not to arrive until March. The weather was abominable. Albemarle was a sea of mud. The delay had caused some applicants to go to other colleges. By March 7, some forty students had straggled in and classes had begun. During the year the roll increased to 116. There now arose a serious problem of discipline. Jefferson had long cherished a plan of student self-government. It was an idea whose time had not come. The young men, some under sixteen, were, in general, poorly prepared. They were, for the most part, scions of prominent and wealthy families; the roll-call reads like a register of F.F.V.'s. Many were undisciplined and given to drinking and gambling. Some carried firearms. The result was a series of disturbances, virtually riots, carried on by masked students. Jefferson, then eighty-two, was obliged to take stern measures and, although a proponent of self-government, he proved a good disciplinarian. Three students were expelled, the rules of conduct were drastically revised, and enforcement was placed in the hands of the faculty.

The year of celebration thus became for Jefferson a period of anxiety and frustration. The situation was exacerbated by heartbreaking family problems. His son-in-law, Thomas Mann Randolph, had become estranged from his family. Randolph's financial affairs had forced him into virtual bankruptcy. He publicly accused his own son, Thomas Jefferson Randolph, of being the cause of his misfortunes. This was a bitter blow for Jefferson, who had the greatest affection for and trust in his grandson and had previously made him caretaker of his own properties. What affected him most, however, was the galling knowledge that he was powerless to help his beloved daughter, Martha. Within the year Jefferson's own affairs had reached such a critical stage that he was moved to the extreme measure of petitioning the Legislature for authorization to conduct a lottery of his properties. He wrote Madison on February 17, 1826: "The practice occurred to me of selling on fair valuation and by way of lottery, . . . If it is permitted in my case, my lands here alone, with the mills, etc., will pay everything and leave me Monticello and a farm free. If refused, I must sell everything here, perhaps considerably in Bedford, move thither with my family, where I have not even a log hut to put my head into. . . ." The Legislature reluctantly enacted the lottery scheme and the machinery was set in motion. The response was so poor that friends attempted to raise money by public appeal. Subscriptions came in and it is believed that Jefferson died on July 4, 1826, in the happy but mistaken hope that Monticello would be saved. In any event he left his beloved University firmly established and with a noble future ahead.

CARLOS BAKER

## Pound in Venice, 1965

[ AUTUMN 1974 ]

HE WAS OLD when we met him first, the grizzled veteran of a thousand wars, literary and other, and standing then on the brink of his eightieth birthday. They said that he would celebrate the occasion quietly in Paris, taking the train from Mestre in a day or two. This was thought to be fitting for several reasons, not least that Paris was the place where he had established himself forty years earlier as both catalyst and contributor to modern literature—a bearded Caliban, in his own words, fiercely intent upon casting out the Ariel of pretentious rhetoric.

The idea of meeting him had come up casually enough the night before. We were dining on scampi and grilled tournedos in Harry's Bar, enriched by small glasses of champagne in a seemingly endless procession. Young Cipriani, the manager's son, hovered attentively. He was an old friend of our host, Gianfranco Ivancich—handsome, brown-haired, brown-eyed, forty-five, kindly, generous, brilliant, and articulate, a Venetian by ancient lineage. Some said his family could have belonged to the Italian nobility, though they had long ago declined the honor.

"Do you know Pound, Ezra Pound?" Gianfranco said.

"No. Is he here?"

"In Venice, yes. Across the Canal." Gianfranco pointed over his shoulder. "Have you met him?"

"No. Only an exchange of letters, not very satisfactory."

"Recently?"

"Six or seven years ago."

"You did not quarrel?"

"Not exactly."

"I am giving him lunch tomorrow. He will soon be eighty. He is leaving Paris the day after. Will you come?"

"Yes," we said, and it was arranged.

Next morning Gianfranco appeared promptly at our hotel, still merry and bright and full of talk. We crossed a corner of the Piazza San Marco and boarded the traghetto. The day was bright and cool, with a brisk breeze. "Ideal October," said Gianfranco, gazing back at the Palace of the Doges. Waves were slapping the docks of the line of hotels. The far side was sunnier and warmer. Our feet echoed on the pavements and made small thunder-sounds over the arches of the lesser bridges. Deep in the warren of dwellings and shops we crossed a final canal. Gianfranco pointed out the house of Cipriani. "It is where he stores the wines for Harry's Bar," he said, "and here is Mr. Pound's."

It was a narrow house fronting the sidewalk. The handsome white-haired lady who answered our knock was Olga Rudge, an Ohioan by birth, a former concert violinist, the mother of Pound's daughter Mary. She embraced Gianfranco, shook our hands. The ground-floor room was square and rather barely furnished, with an open fireplace and a narrow stairway leading to the room above, the twin of this one. An American girl was there also, very pleasant and quick, with a short neat haircut. Last year she had done a portrait head of Pound, cast now in bronze. Neither the head nor the poet was yet visible.

He came deliberately down the stairs, a tall old man with square shoulders and thinning hair abundantly long and swept back from his forehead. Both beard and hair were gray, not white. His eyes were blue and he had a way of opening them wide and fixing his visitors with an intense stare, all the more disconcerting because the stare was not accompanied by speech. He was meticulously clean—hair, skin, the knobbly hands, the nails—and as gracious as one can be without words. The suit he wore was of gray flannel, with a blue shirt and a dark blue Italian tie. He shook his head vigorously when Miss Rudge insisted that he wear a topcoat but in the end, as we walked out, he made a compromise, draping the camel's hair coat like a cloak around his shoulders, and carrying a cane of yellow wood. "He must always have his stick," said Olga Rudge, smiling.

We had heard of his decrepitude, but it did not show. His carriage was erect, his gait deliberate and easy, there was neither hesitation nor shuffling as he picked up his black shoes rhythmically and set them firmly down. When I walked ahead to snap his picture as he crossed a couple of bridges, he turned profile at the moment the shutter clicked. He was very slender, probably weighing no more than a hundred and twenty-five, and in profile rather hawk-like. His head was thrown back, he was enjoying the sun and the light breeze. A few Venetians greeted him as he passed and he bowed back politely, with never a break in his stride. He might have been a lord.

This meeting, I thought, was like coming into a strange theater towards the end of the final act. We knew in a general way the drift the play had taken: the birth-scene far off in Hailey, Idaho, in 1885; the bachelor and master of arts in 1905–1906; the expatriate on the grand tour in 1907. We had read the early books, "A Lume Spento," and then those others that came in quick succession after he had settled in England, "Personae," "Exultations," "Canzoni," "Ripostes." The learned and multilingual young man established a reputation so rapidly that Robert Frost, meeting him in London in 1913, could write home to a friend, "I don't mind his calling me raw. He is reckoned raw himself and at the same time perhaps the most prominent of the younger poets here." W. B. Yeats praised his "vigorous creative mind," adding that he was "certainly a creative personality of some sort," even though it was still too early to predict his future line of development. "His experiments are perhaps errors," wrote Yeats, "but I would always sooner give the laurel to vigorous errors than to any orthodoxy not inspired." And then later at Stone Cottage, Coleman's Hatch, in Sussex, while the war raged across the Channel: "Ezra Pound and his wife are staying with me, we have four rooms of a cottage on the edge of a heath and our back is to the woods."

It was Yeats who had told Pound that Frost's "North of Boston" was the best thing that had come out of America for some time. Frost, rather bemusedly, called Pound "the stormy petrel" who had sent a "fierce article" to Harriet Monroe's Poetry magazine in Chicago, "denouncing a country that neglects fellows like me." Yet Frost, though glad enough of the public acclaim, could not help feeling that Pound was concerned with personal power. "All I asked," he wrote, in a free-verse poem addressed to Pound but wisely never sent, "was that you should hold to one thing: that you considered me a poet. That was why I clung to you as one clings to a group of insincere friends for fear they shall turn their thoughts against him the moment he is out of hearing. The truth is I was afraid of you."

Others feared him, too, but turned to him for aid. Helping to launch and publicize the Imagist movement, guiding such little magazines as The Egoist, Blast, and The Little Review, he had hurled himself with restless energy into a program for the rehabilitation of modern poetry, backed by what Harriet Monroe called his "love of stirring up and leading forth other minds." T. S. Eliot soon acknowledged his priceless editorial assistance with "The Waste Land" by dedicating the poem to him and lauding him in Dante's phrase as "il miglior fabbro," as, in a manner of speaking, he had turned out to be. Ernest Hemingway, on first meeting him in Paris in 1922, had written, like Frost before him, an attack on Pound that was never sent, though presently, as he told a friend, he discovered that Pound was really "a great guy and a wonderful editor," and volunteered to teach Ezra to box in return for lessons in how to write.

Some years later, when Hemingway gashed his forehead in a domestic accident, Pound sent him from Rapallo a typical message: "Haow the hellsufferin tomcats did you git drunk enough to fall upwards thru the blithering skylight!!!!" And Hemingway, four years after that, stated forthrightly that "any poet born in this century or in the last ten years of the preceding century who can honestly say that he has not been influenced by or learned greatly from the work of Ezra Pound deserves to be pitied rather than rebuked."

So we came that noonday in Venice by tortuous route to the door of the small ristorante where Gianfranco was known and received with obvious affection, and where Pound was treated with the deference due his age and reputation. He sat down at one end of the table and Gianfranco, flanked by Olga Rudge and the girl sculptress, at the other. Pound listened intently to all that was said, nodded and smiled in response to observations, widened his eyes once or twice in that special gesture of his, and said absolutely nothing. Gianfranco had warned us of this "vow of silence," and thought that it was an act of contrition for having said too much over Rome Radio in the time of Mussolini. At home, of course, he talked with those closest to him, to his beautiful daughter Mary at Schloss Brunnenburg, to his adoring grandchildren. The taciturnity was reserved for public gatherings, and this counted as one. As befitted his years, he ate sparely, declining soup and only lightly sampling the *malfatta,* a delicious kind of ravioli cut on the bias. After two mouthfuls he pushed his plate away, astonishing my wife by saying to her the only two words he had yet uttered: "too heavy." At the next course he delicately made way with two small scallopini washed down with half a glass of dry white wine.

I mentioned the letter he had sent me from Rapallo in the spring of 1959, less than a year after his release from twelve years' imprisonment in St. Elizabeths Hospital in Washington, D. C. It was a typically aggressive and humorous-serious document poorly typed with blue ribbon on stationery of the Albergo Grande Italia & Lido, and dated April seventh.

> Carlos Baker, Princeton, where Woodrow slopped.
> Yr/ bk/ on Hem, serious re/ literature and Paris, but you are ham ignorant of history. Whether any servant of Princeton dares combat the age-old falsification and READ any history, let alone adjusting his ideas to the 17 facts that the sons of hell and brain-washed adorers of F. D. R. spend billions to hide I do not know. There are faint signs that soon truth will trickle into the margins, but not into the main stream of u.s. university sewage. I see Chris Gauss [Dean of the College at Princeton who had died in November, 1951] has passed on, but suppose Dex. White still rates above Andrew in Neibuhrian rhomboids.
> frankly yrs. Ez Pound.

At this date I could not recall enough of the letter to quote back at its author, but I did speak of Christian Gauss, at which Pound nodded and smiled, and I wondered aloud at what he had meant by the phrase "Niebuhrian rhomboids." But Pound only grinned, folding his thin clean hands on the table before him.

The voluble conversation at the other end of the table now drew us in. We knew only vaguely of Pound's happy liaison of many years with Olga Rudge, and of their child, Mary de Rachewiltz, now a beautiful woman of forty who lived with her half-Russian, half-Italian husband in a castle in the Tyrol. It was not in fact until six years later, with the publication of Mary's charming autobiography, that we learned the whole romantic story. The book was called "Discretions" as a kind of echo of her father's "Indiscretions," published in 1923 only a couple of years before Mary was born at Bressanone. At the time of her birth another woman in the maternity ward had lost her baby and it was arranged that she should nurse the skinny little girl to blooming health, which she achieved in the farming community of Gais in the Tyrol as fosterchild to Johanna Marcher. The Marchers she called Mamme and Tatte. Pound and Olga Rudge were known to her as Mammile and Tattile, although later she began to call Pound by the name of Babbo, and went often to Venice so that her real parents could smooth away the rough edges of her peasant upbringing; here she learned Italian and English as supplementary to the Tyrolese patois that she spoke the rest of the year, swam at the Lido under Babbo's admiring supervision, and was hopefully given a violin by her gifted mother. Educated at a convent school in Florence with the musical name of Regio Istituto delle Nobili Signore Montalva alla Quiete, she first went to Rapallo just before the war, and fell in love with Casa 60, Sant' Ambrogio, a tall house of orange stucco with painted Ionic columns and a green front door overgrown with honeysuckle. She was back in Gais when the news filtered through that Italy had surrendered, and she worked steadily through the rest of the war in hospitals in the north of Italy while Babbo kept quietly at his translations.

Then in 1945 a pair of partisans, ex-fascist convicts eager for reward money, knocked with the butt of a gun on the door at Sant' Ambrogio. Babbo was working on Confucius. "Seguici, traditore," they said, and took him away. Olga Rudge and Mary saw him later at the Disciplinary Training Center near Pisa. He had aged noticeably; the army fatigues he was wearing did not fit his slender frame; he was writing the first batch of Pisan Cantos on a borrowed typewriter. When Mary saw him in 1953, he had already languished for eight years in the Washington madhouse under indictment for treason. She must not bring her children there, he told her. "St. Elizabeths is no fit place for the children to see their grandfather in. And there are rumors: granpaw might get sprung." Then one evening she heard the Italian newscast: il poeta Americano had been released, the indictment dismissed. After twelve years in limbo he could return to Italy on board the *Cristoforo Colombo,* a voyage of discovery in reverse. In Sirmione in 1957 Mary had said to Archibald MacLeish, who had labored so long to set Pound free, "He has a right to do whatever he likes, anything that makes him happy. . . ." After his release MacLeish sent a generous check to be used to keep Pound warm and there was another from Hemingway that he framed as a memento of an old friendship.

If his remorse still held, it did not show as he sat happily in this small left-bank ristorante. Except for the silences in the intervals of the conversation. Afterwards we ambled back to the narrow little house beside the small canal where a green bottle, some bits of straw, and a hemisphere of orange peel floated somnolently. Pound climbed the steps slowly to the skylighted room at the top of the house. He was not puffing and his color was good, though in that severe light his face looked drawn and the skin almost transparent. He drank a demitasse and took a sip or two of brandy. When a tape recording of a recent canto was put on and played, he listened attentively to his own voice, reading the lines with a kind of gruff eloquence and pronouncing the frequent foreign phrases with the easy skill of an old European hand. When we left he stayed in his chair, watching the patterns of afternoon sunlight on the floor.

Two afternoons later in Paris, Pound and Miss Rudge were met by Dominique de Roux, who was then on the point of publishing the first French translation of the "Cantos." "He is in a state of profound remorse," M. de Roux told reporters. The vow of silence was still in effect, though he relented occasionally. "I regret my past errors," he told de Roux, "but I hope to have done a little something for some artists."

On Friday the 29th, the day before his birthday, he sat on a sofa beside Miss Natalie Barney in the drawing room of her house where she had entertained the Parisian intellectuals of the 1920's and wordlessly received old friends and new admirers. He wore horn-rimmed glasses, a checked brown sports jacket, brown pants, and crepe-soled shoes. The long wings of his shirt collar were spread as of old over his lapels, and his hands rested on the grip of his yellow cane. Asked who were his favorite modern poets, he named Cummings and Auden, and permitted himself a two-word judgment of the work of Allen Ginsberg. "He's vigorous," said Pound. It was the word Yeats had used for Pound's own talent long ago in England.

By this date we were far away among the Austrian Alps, staying at the Hotel Taube in the market village of Schruns in the Vorarlberg. While Babbo sat beside Miss Barney on the Parisian sofa, we were walking out to the neighboring village of St. Gallenkirch. Some of the men of the town were laying sewer-pipe along the bank of the stream, and others were raking leaves. Bedding was being aired at the windows of the houses, and some of the women were sweeping their porches with rough brooms made of twigs. The lunch at the Taube was typical—four small trout apiece, cooked whole, with a home-made champignon soup, parsleyed potatoes, and a salad of lettuce, red peppers, white beans, string beans, and cole slaw. For dessert there were rolled pancakes with a custard filling.

After one bite, my wife pushed her dessert-plate towards me across the table.

"Don't you like them?"

"Yes, but after all the rest, they're too heavy."

"You're echoing Ezra Pound."

"Yes," she said. "Poor old man."

DUMAS MALONE

## The Scholar's Way:
## Then and Now

[ SPRING 1975 ]

I

SEVERAL years ago, at a meeting of scholars, I heard one of them address a disconcerting question to his fellows. They were predominantly academic and in varying degree humanistic, and, in discussing grants and other aids to research, they had been comparing their situation unfavorably to that of scientists. The questioner went a good deal further. "How long," he asked, "will they put up with people like us?" For the purposes of this article I am interpreting the word "they" to mean, not the distributors of research funds, but the people of the country by whom persons like us have been tolerated and, in the last analysis, supported. Neither at the time nor thereafter was I greatly disturbed by the question on my own account. Being of a sanguine temperament, I expect society to put up with me a while longer, after doing so these many years. But I have been impelled to reflect on the scholar's life, as I have experienced and observed it for upwards of half a century of time and change, and to ponder over his prospects. As the present informal report will show, I have been engaged to a very considerable extent in reminiscence. This can be very boring to everybody else, but in point of time my life as a scholar has virtually coincided with that of the Virginia Quarterly Review as a journal, and some indulgence may perhaps be claimed for a contributor to its first number.

Before saying anything else I should issue a modest disclaimer about that contribution. It was a book review, dealing with a topic I knew little about. I must have found that it had not been assigned and have asked the editor, James Southall Wilson, to let me write it. I often did that in those early days, and, through his generosity and tolerance, gained my first experience as a reviewer.

At that stage I hesitated to call myself a scholar. I remembered that when I was a little boy and signed myself "your scholar" in a letter to my teacher, I was told that my attainments did not warrant my use of that term as yet. Half a century ago, still somewhat incredulous that I was now entitled to be called "Doctor," I thought of myself primarily as a teacher. (In fact, I still do, though now banished from the classroom on grounds of excessive seniority.) In Mr. Jefferson's University, to which I came shortly after I acquired a union card in the form of a Ph.D. degree, I first practiced the teacher's trade in a wing of the Rotunda that had been used for storing rifles during the First World War and had not been redecorated. I called the dismal place the Black Hole of Calcutta. This was during the presidency of Edwin A. Alderman, a majestic potentate of whom I stood in some awe, though he did a lot for me. For example, he came strolling by the Black Hole of Calcutta one day, tapping his cane on the concrete walk as he was wont to do. He took one look at the room and ordered it painted—as it was soon thereafter in glaring white.

If I may indulge further in local reminiscences, I afterwards taught on the top floor of an ancient building across the road from the present office of the Virginia Quarterly Review. This was not without architectural merit, but it reminded me of a caboose in a day when people were more familiar with trains than they are now. It has long since disappeared, as has also the building where I had formerly taught at Yale at the corner of the Old Campus—a Romanesque structure called Osborn Hall, which always seemed to me rather like a dinosaur.

Looking back through the years, I cannot remember ever having a really good classroom anywhere. Nor can I remember that I ever minded very much. Good light, maps, and a blackboard were all I felt the need of. While ugliness and positive discomfort should certainly be avoided, it has seemed to me that, in the sort of educational process I was engaged in, the importance of physical facilities can be easily exaggerated. There is certainly no call for luxury. The prime factors were and are and ever will be the teacher and the students—the persons, not the fittings. Distaste for teaching has been more fashionable among academic scholars in recent years than it was when I started out, but it has never infected me, and I cannot help wondering why anybody who really dislikes teaching and does not want to be bothered with students should join the faculty of a university. Pure research can be pursued elsewhere.

I have no disposition whatever to minimize the appeal of research. About a dozen years after I made my modest contribution to the first number of this Quarterly I read a delightful book by Bliss Perry, then a retired Harvard professor of English. I seized upon its title, "And Gladly Teach," as applicable to myself, being all the more eager no doubt because at the time I was not only in exile from Mr. Jefferson's academical village but also confined to an office and engaged in publishing other people's books. I knew that Chaucer was being quoted, but I never was as familiar with that author as I should have been and I was slow in finding out that he spoke not only of the joy of communicating knowledge, but also of the pleasure of acquiring it. In fuller form the quotation reads: "And gladly wolde he lerne, and gladly teche." I perceive no conflict except for time.

In the strict academic sense, Mr. Jefferson, father of a university, was not a teacher, but he was unquestionably an enthusiastic learner. "Nature intended me for the tranquil pursuits of science," he said, "by rendering them my supreme delight." It should be noted that by "science" he meant knowledge, all knowledge. In his vocabulary what we call science would have been rendered as natural history or natural philosophy, and to him a conflict between science and the humanities would have been inconceivable. He found supreme delight in the pursuit of both. Humanists and scientists today might not express themselves in superlatives, but they may be assumed to have made a like discovery. Speaking from my own experience in my particular field, I do not hesitate to say that I have found historical investigation to be a most fascinating activity. Topics vary in interest, to be sure, and some seem hardly worth pursuing, but in general it can be said that almost anything becomes more interesting as more knowledge of it is gained, and many an investigator has launched on a voyage of exploration and discovery that turned out to be thrilling. Among the most enjoyable hours of my own life have been those spent in repositories of historical sources and in my own study, living through great events with great men. And I must confess that, after years of association with Thomas Jefferson, George Washington, John Adams, and other giants of our early history, I am relatively indifferent to contemporary celebrities.

The quotation from Mr. Jefferson suggests that his delight derived from the pursuit rather than the attainment of knowledge—from the chase rather than the quarry. Thus his self-revealing statement stands in marked contrast to the widely quoted assertion of a noted football coach that the only point in playing the game is to win it. The gladiators who contend before huge crowds for pay, at the risk of limb if not of life, may get some pleasure from the exercise of their strength and skill, but in the professionalized and commercialized sport of our day there is little place for fun. I hope fun will never disappear from the playing fields of learning. Perhaps no one who has turned professional in any field can have quite the enjoyment he had as an amateur. To recapture that first fine careless rapture may be as impossible as for age to recover youth. But there are some advantages that accrue with the passage of slow time. While curiosity is one of the things that come naturally, concentration is not. Yet, although never easy, it does become easier as habits of study are formed. In this respect, therefore, the "old pro" may have a better time than the tyro. He is rather like a tennis player who no longer has to be watchful of his strokes, or a golfer who does not need to think about his form. At any rate, as an "old pro" I can testify that the pleasures of the chase have not declined, although energy undoubtedly has and the quarry has often been disappointing.

Almost a century after Mr. Jefferson expressed his delight in the pursuit of knowledge, William James bemoaned the worship of the "bitch-goddess success" and the "squalid cash interpretation" of the word success, saying that these constituted our national disease. It seems to me that this national disease (which may, indeed, be described as international) has become more prevalent and more virulent during my lifetime. In our glorification of financial success we have come close to making a virtue out of greed, once regarded as a cardinal sin, and by equating happiness with material success we have disregarded the experience and wisdom of the ages.

Worship of the bitch goddess and the golden calf was certainly prevalent half a century ago. That was the era of Calvin Coolidge in which the stock market kept going up. But as I look backward it seems to me that the dollar mark was not on as many things and activities as it is today. It was not so evident in the world of sport for instance. And, as I remember, it was less conspicuous in the world of learning. Scholars have made a much better living in the last decade or so than most of them used to make. I am well aware that the doctors of philosophy are still far behind the doctors of medicine in worldly goods, as I am that their prospects have worsened of late. There is little likelihood that they will ever become affluent, and I am not suggesting that, as mortals go, they are avaricious. I have gained the general impression, however, that the scholars of my generation as a group had more modest financial ambitions than their present-day successors.

So slight was my own financial wisdom when I entered the guild of scholars that I may have been somewhat less than typical, and by rights I can speak only for myself, but I am sure I was far from alone in hopes and anticipations. At the outset I expected, and in fact I have received, rich compensation from the good life I led—from doing what I liked to do. In those optimistic days I probably took a decent livelihood for granted, but I rightly assumed that the scale of values in the Academy differed from that of the market place. President Calvin Coolidge was saying that the business of America was business, but it did not occur to me that this was true of a scholar or a university. To my young mind they were eternally dedicated not only to the pursuit and transmission of knowledge, but, beyond that, to the increase of understanding. That is, they were to seek and proclaim the truth.

To me as a young scholar this was a wondrous thought, and through the years until this day it has seemed to me that the quest for truth is akin to the search for God. In an era of declining faith I have found it a veritable religion. But lest I seem pompous and pretentious, let me hasten to say that the rôle I conceived for myself as a budding historian was a modest one. I did not expect to penetrate to the heart of things and ascertain their deepest meaning. That rôle I resigned to the philosophers. I did not expect to arrive at a philosophy of history and in fact have never done so. My hope was to come as near the truth as possible with respect to the particular events or movements I was working on—to find out as nearly as I could what really happened and what it meant. I could not hope to rid myself wholly of presumptions, prejudices, and inhibitions, but I never doubted that I must try to do so. Accuracy and fair-mindedness were the main desiderata; carelessness and special pleading were to be sedulously avoided. In the realm of human affairs the attainment of absolute truth is hardly to be expected, but the principle that truth is better than falsehood is fully attested by the experience of the human race. Accordingly, it would seem that the historian is warranted in believing that a fair and accurate account of what happened in the past is intrinsically desirable.

In the aftermath of the First World War, when my professional life as an historian may be said to have begun, there were difficulties in the way of any observer of human affairs who sought to be fair-minded. It was the period of the Red Scare, the Palmer raids, and other manifestations of fear that bordered on hysteria. (Similar psychology, after the Second World War, was exploited by Senator Joseph McCarthy.) It was a relatively easy time, however, to do justice to our ancient foes and recent allies, the British; and, as a teacher, I could try to do so when dealing with the American Revolution. The effort to understand their point of view as well as ours did not cause me to become a Tory, but in my novitiate it was to me a memorable experience. This was in an academic setting, and, as I now realize, it was not until I was engaged in advanced study in a university that I really became aware that there is such a thing as intellectual freedom.

Since truth is often unpleasant and may be very upsetting, entire freedom to pursue and proclaim it does not appear ever to have been granted by any society. But my personal experience has confirmed my original impression that in our society the scholar enjoys more of it than almost anybody else. The scientist enjoys most, and historians may owe their freedom in considerable part to the relative indifference of the public to them. In recent years historians have attacked time-honored interpretations of our past, but generally they have been less controversial than economists. Some restrictions are self-imposed by scholars on pedagogical grounds, or in deference to public opinion, or for some other prudential reason, but I doubt if members of any other group express themselves in public and private with comparable candor. Politicians and businessmen certainly do not. Free-lance writers may be more daring, but they have to please some sort of audience. A scholar does also if he wants his books to sell widely, but otherwise his chief concern is to gain the approval of his peers and to satisfy himself.

During my apprenticeship and for some years thereafter few academic scholars that I knew had much expectation of reaching the general public directly and most of them held popularizers in low esteem. Though I did not have much hope that any publication of mine would be reviewed anywhere except a professional journal, I never thought that scholars should write just for one another and I was unwilling to agree that their writing had to be dull. On the other hand, I thought then as I do now that every true scholar must abhor any manipulation of facts and exploitation of sex or sensation in order to gain popularity and make money. If he enters the marketplace he should be as scrupulous as a judge.

Having outlived most of the scholars of my generation, I use the past tense in speaking of them. They may be regarded as old-fashioned by their present-day successors, but to me, on looking back, they seem considerably more deserving of envy than commiseration. On the whole, in fact, they appear to have enjoyed a very good life. Rarely did they make what would now be regarded as a good living, but within modest limits they had security after they had proved themselves. As a rule the world was not too much with them—not enough, some may now say. Of relatively few of them could it have been truly said that getting and spending they laid waste their powers. They were more fortunate than many of their more prosperous and powerful contemporaries in that they were doing what they really liked to do. Their life, though generally less littered with paper and less eroded by committee meetings than that of professors today, was not devoid of drudgery and even in the best places it was not idyllic. Nevertheless, one may doubt if ever in human history men of learning in relative number have enjoyed greater privileges and opportunities. Yet, during the last decade or two, as the "old pros" have been passing from the scene, there have been inescapable signs of impatience with the sorts of things they and others like myself have spent a lifetime doing. It is not surprising therefore that someone should ask, "How long?"

## II

At this point I am reminded of what some wag called the battle hymn of Phi Beta Kappa. That was very early in my professional life, when Robert Browning was more in vogue than now, and the reference is to his poem on the funeral of a grammarian of the Renaissance. That dedicated man of learning was thus described in part:

> So, with the throttling hands of death at strife
>   Ground he at grammar;
> Still, thro' the rattle, parts of speech were rife:
>   While he could stammer. . . .

Also, I am reminded of my old professor of Greek. who could always be distracted by a reference to patronymic terminations or the iota subscript, with the result that we rarely got through half the assignment in Plato. To me it seemed in later years that, by his excessive concentration on linguistic minutiae and grammatical precision, he inadvertently devitalized the language he loved, thus exemplifying the failure of the humanists to be humanistic. While in his classes, however, I clearly perceived his great love for that language and that civilization. Therefore, I cannot bring myself to call him a pedant. I am well aware that our age suffers from lack rather than excess of strict grammarians, and I distinctly prefer him to certain purveyors of pretentious nonsense who have appeared more recently among professed humanists. Though there may now be more pedants in governmental bureaus, they can still be found in academic circles. They may be hard to identify, since the line between pedantry and scholarship is often faint. Yet there are those who, in their concern for technical perfection, sacrifice substance to form and the spirit to the letter. Unwittingly, no doubt, but unfortunately, they squeeze the juice out of learning and leave it a pallid thing. Also to be deplored are those who, consciously or unconsciously, employ jargon to obscure thought or conceal the lack of it. Like the bureaucrats who use gobbledygook they are contributing to the debasement of the English language.

The list of doctoral dissertations on any commencement program amply attests the absurdities no less than the diversity of present-day scholarly endeavor. Some of these titles suggest that academicians are running short both of humor and of significant things to do. Very properly they hold that what seems trivial may turn out to be important, and that what is unimportant to one may be important to another. Very properly they hesitate to tell their colleagues what not to investigate. De gustibus non est disputandum. They are convinced that limitations imposed by uninformed outsiders would be disastrous to the course of free learning. All the more reason, therefore, for self-regulation and the exercise of such common sense as may be available. Since there seems to be too much of everything in the world at present, except for food and energy, it would appear that in scholarship as elsewhere there is need for birth control.

I do not remember hearing as much about irrelevance lately as I did during the great student uprising, but, in our materialistic civilization, irrelevance has long been a charge against academic learning, and no doubt it has been a characteristic complaint of the young against their formal education from the time that this began. If by relevance is meant usefulness in meeting the bread-and-butter needs of struggling individuals day by day, or in providing immediate solutions for current political, economic, and social problems, it obviously involves and requires more than art, music, or literature can offer. The application of such a test to the whole world of learning would be manifestly unjust and almost if not quite as absurd as its application to the arts. Speaking of the field I am most familiar with, that of history, let me repeat what I have said many times before, namely, that we cannot expect to learn from the record of the past just how to solve specific present problems. "The earth belongs always to the living generation," according to Mr. Jefferson, and that generation must work out its problems in the light of its particular circumstances. George Washington cannot tell us how to attain peace in the Middle East, nor can Alexander Hamilton show us how to check inflation.

To a degree that is unexampled in recorded history, the present generation is on its own. The revolutionary changes that have occurred in my own lifetime can be matched by those of no previous millennium, and, as our knowledge goes, the future of the human race may never have been so bleak. Under these circumstances the sort of investigation of the past that I have been engaged in may appear to be an exercise in futility. The same can be said of many other activities, to be sure, and no doubt the race will escape disaster in my time, but I have often wondered if in the last analysis such work as mine can be socially justified. Generally I convince myself that it can be, and I always realize how much it means to me, but of course the world could have done without it. No generation can escape the past, however, and this one is not so different from the others that it can learn nothing from them.

Since present-mindedness is the natural state of man as well as animals, there would appear to be no likelihood of its being in short supply in a university or elsewhere in our society. To urge its cultivation by scholars seems quite unnecessary. They are not conspicuously other-worldly. It is difficult, indeed, to tell them from everybody else. Many of them nowadays are students of the contemporary world, and some view with professional interest the fads and fashions of the moment. As an historian I take a more lordly position and devote myself to things less fleeting. No one person can explore in depth more than a small segment of the vast field of history, but one can at least be aware of the stupendous record of the past and remind oneself and others that it comprises the accumulated experience and wisdom of mankind. Without it the present would be an orphan wholly devoid of inheritance—a player on a large and empty stage—a lone figure on a boundless plain that offers no perspective. The past is more than prologue. It is full of intrinsic interest, as anybody who explores it can easily find out. And one may doubt if any generation ever needed the past more than does the present one, to keep it from being swept from its moorings by the flooding tides and tempestuous winds of change. Human nature seems to have changed little if at all, and out of the depths of experience, through countless generations, human beings have drawn their most enduring principles and their priceless values.

The past is not the private property of the historian. In fact, he has to spend so much time on events that he does not always attend sufficiently to values, and these may be best set forth by others. There is life to be perceived beyond the documents and other formal records, and, in Matthew Arnold's phrase, the scholar should see this steadily and try to see it whole. Considering how much there is of it, that is a large order, and some scholars of our day seem to think there is no real need to fill it. Their concern, instead, is to view history and life from a fresh angle. That is a laudable ambition and fresh light is always welcome, but what about the old angles? There are a number of vantage points from which the members of my particular group, the historians of my generation, tried to look and these I would not abandon.

I suppose I was first aware of political and military history, but there was special emphasis on the economic when I began. In the works of Charles A. Beard, then much in vogue, this was connected with constitutional history, which I always liked though my knowledge of constitutional law is still very limited. Somewhat by accident I got into biography, which I liked best of all, though I never regarded it as sufficient in itself and always insisted on calling myself an historian and not a biographer. Social history came to the fore at an early stage of my professional life, and on my return to academic circles after some years in administration, I found to my dismay that all my colleagues seemed to know more about intellectual history than I did. I had to work very hard to catch up and am not sure that I ever really did. Because of the accelerated expansion of knowledge in all fields in the last decade or two and the inescapable requirement of specialization, the scholar of today faces a dilemma. The attempt to arrive at the wholeness of things has become increasingly difficult and not even in the limited area of his own inquiries can one be confident that he has attained it. But no more than the pursuit of truth should that attempt ever be abandoned.

I have had no particular occasion to view the past from the angle of quanto-history or psycho-history, which have come into vogue more recently. In their efforts to attain truth these relative newcomers seem to be moving in opposite directions. The quantifiers want to measure everything, while the psycho-historians, seeking to get behind the facts and to read between the lines, speculate about everything. It seems to me that the former should be encouraged to measure everything that can be measured, but should be reminded that in human affairs many things cannot be. Members of the latter group may be warned against excessive recourse to imagination. Having had no training in psychoanalysis I have never presumed to apply it to either the living or the dead. Any biographer must be in some sense a psychologist, but I have sedulously avoided the lingo of the professional and have claimed no peculiar insight into the minds of historic characters. In seeking to understand them I have drawn on my personal experience and observation and have exercised such common sense as I may be possessed of. It seems to me that historic characters, like one's contemporaries, should be judged in the light of their circumstances as honestly and fairly as the limitations of the judge's personality will permit. Fortunately, the persons with whom I have had most to do as a biographer have not seemed to require the services of a psychiatrist.

Ideally, the scholar should welcome light from any quarter, and I myself have benefited enormously from the co-operation as well as the labors of my fellows. I gain the impression, however, that in my time the competitive spirit has grown among scholars as it has in our society generally. Increased competitiveness would seem to be a natural consequence of the increased commercialization of our life. The professionalization of sport has emphasized the importance of winning, and in recent years there has been much talk of the adversary system. I may have been unaware of what was going on, but I do not remember ever having heard the expression in connection with scholarship before the great student uprising, when confrontation was the order of the day. At that time much was said about the need for commitment; professors were exhorted to descend from their ivory towers and take a stand. But blindness and intolerance are frequent accompaniments of commitment, and important though this may be in current controversy it has obvious dangers when carried into the field of learning. The analogy of the courtroom should not be pressed too far and the distinction between history and propaganda should be maintained. Complete objectivity is impossible to attain, as full justice seems to be, but the scholar is not obligated as a lawyer is to make a case for the defense or the prosecution. An easy way to attract attention is to take a strong position on some controversial question, and in a noisy age there is a great temptation to shout. On occasion, perhaps, some degree of exaggeration may be justified for pedagogical reasons, and at times unpleasant news may be tempered to the mood of the audience, but the supreme obligation of the scholar is to present that which, after scrupulous inquiry and careful reflection, he believes to be the truth. Fidelity to this must ever be his hallmark, whether he be an old pro or a new one, whether his voice be loud or low. And it is to be hoped that society will put up with him a great deal longer.

EDMUND S. MORGAN

# George Washington: The Aloof American

[ SUMMER 1976 ]

## I

THE KING of England, George III, was fond of farming. His favorite diversion was to ride about his lands, chatting with the tenants about the crops. "Farmer George," he called himself. His arch-opponent, George Washington, had the same fondness for farming. He too enjoyed riding about his lands and talking about the crops. Indeed there was nothing else he enjoyed quite so much. But there the likeness ceased. And among the many other matters that differentiated George Washington from George III none was more striking than his greater dignity and reserve. George Washington would never have taken the liberty of calling himself "Farmer George," nor would he have allowed anyone else to do so. Even his close friends took care to keep their distance; and those who forgot to were apt to be brought up sharp.

A familiar anecdote, though perhaps apocryphal, well illustrates Washington's customary posture toward himself and toward others. During the meeting of the Constitutional Convention in Philadelphia in 1787 a group of Washington's friends were remarking on his extraordinarily reserved and remote manner, even among his most intimate acquaintances. Gouverneur Morris, who was always full of boldness and wit, had the nerve to disagree. He could be as familiar with Washington, he said, as with any of his other friends. Alexander Hamilton called his bluff by offering to provide a supper and wine for a dozen of them if Morris would, at the next reception Washington gave, simply walk up to him, gently slap him on the shoulder, and say, "My dear General, how happy I am to see you look so well." On the appointed evening a substantial number were already present when Morris arrived, walked up to Washington, bowed, shook hands, and then placed his left hand on Washington's shoulder, and said, "My dear General, I am very happy to see you look so well." The response was immediate and icy. Washington reached up and removed the hand, stepped back, and fixed his eye in silence on Morris, until Morris retreated abashed into the crowd. The company looked on in embarrassment, and no one ever tried it again.

It seems a most un-American reaction, not the sort of thing that Americans like to see in the men they honor, certainly not the sort of thing one would look for in the leader of a popular revolution today. Yet Americans then and since have honored George Washington far beyond any other man in their history. Moreover he earned the honor, and his dignity and reserve, the aloofness that still separates him from us, helped him to earn it.

## II

How is part of the larger story of American independence, the story of how the American Revolution transformed some of the least lovable traits of a seemingly ordinary man into national assets. For besides his aloofness, Washington had other characteristics which at this distance appear less than admirable, but which served him and the nation well in the struggle for independence.

Perhaps the most conspicuous of these traits, conspicuous at least in his surviving correspondence, was an unabashed concern for his own economic interest. Although Washington was fair in his dealings and did not ask favor of any man, he kept a constant, wary, and often cold eye on making a profit, ever suspicious (and not always without reason) that other men were trying to take advantage of him. Like most Virginia planters, he complained that London merchants were giving him too little for his tobacco or charging him too much for the goods he bought from them. When he rented to tenants, he demanded to be paid punctually and dismissed men's inability to meet their obligations as irresponsibility or knavery. If a man was so foolish as to try cheating him, he was capable of a fury that comes through vividly in his letters, as when he wrote to one associate that "all my concern is that I ever engag'd myself in behalf of so ungrateful and dirty a fellow as you are."

In operating his plantation at Mount Vernon he inveighed endlessly against waste of time, waste of supplies, waste of money. "A penny saved is a penny got," he would say, or "Many mickles make a muckle," by which he apparently meant that many small savings would add up to a large one. Even in dealings with his mother he was watchful, for he thought she had extravagant tastes. He was ready to supply her real wants, he said, but found her "*imaginary* wants . . . indefinite and oftentimes insatiable."

Even after he left Mount Vernon in order to win a war and found a nation, his intense absorption with his estate persisted, somehow curiously out of place now, and out of proportion to the historic events that he was grappling with. In the darkest hours of the war and later during some of the tensest national crises he took time to write to the managers of his plantation about making it show a profit. In early December 1776, for example, after fleeing across the Delaware with the remnants of his army, he sent home instructions to make do without buying linen for the slaves "as the price is too heavy to be borne with." And while he was president, his weekly directives to his managers far exceeded in length the documents he prepared for his subordinates in government. [. . .]

Washington was continually alert against theft, embezzlement, and shirking by his slaves. Slaves would not work, he warned his managers and overseers again and again, unless they were continually watched. And they would take every opportunity to steal. They would feign sickness to avoid work. They would stay up all night enjoying themselves and be too tired the next day to get anything done. They would use every pretext to take advantage of him, like Peter, who was charged with riding about the plantation to look after the stock, but, Washington suspected, was usually "in pursuit of other objects; either of traffic or amusement, more advancive of his own pleasures than my benefit."

Washington's opinion of his managers and overseers was hardly better. He hired a succession of them who never seemed able to satisfy him. In 1793, after a bad year, he got off a series of blistering letters to the overseers of the five farms into which Mount Vernon was divided. Hyland Crow, for example, was guilty of "insufferable neglect" in failing to get fields plowed before frost. "And look ye, Mr. Crow," wrote the President, "I have too good reasons to believe that your running about, and entertaining company at home . . . is the cause of this, now, irremediable evil in the progress of my business." And Thomas Green, in charge of the plantation's carpenters, got a similar tongue lashing. "I know full well," said Washington, "that to speak to you is of no more avail, than to speak to a bird that is flying over one's head; first, because you are lost to all sense of shame, and to every feeling that ought to govern an honest man, who sets any store by his character; and secondly, because you have no more command of the people over whom you are placed, than I have over the beasts of the forists: for if they chuse to work they may; if they do not you have not influence enough to make them . . ." [. . .]

### III

A cipher Washington would not be and could not be. He would run his own affairs in his own interest. And he was very good at it. But if that was all he had done, we should never have heard of him, except perhaps as one of many prosperous Virginia planters. Fortunately it was not merely interest that moved him. Dearer by far to him was honor. Honor required a man to be assiduous and responsible in looking after his interests. But honor also required a man to look beyond his own profit, though where he looked and how far might be a question that different men would answer differently.

At the simplest, most superficial level Washington's love of honor showed itself in a concern with outward appearances. His attachment to Mount Vernon, for example, did not stop at the desire to make a profit from it. He wanted the place and its surroundings to look right, to honor the owner by the way they looked; and this meant giving up the slovenly, though often profitable, agricultural practices of his neighbors. He stopped growing tobacco and turned to the rotation of cereal crops that were approved by the English agricultural reformers of the time. He tried, mostly in vain, to substitute handsome English hedgerows for the crude rail fences of Virginia. And he insisted that all weeds and brush be grubbed out of his plowed fields, not simply for the sake of productivity, but because the fields looked better that way. He would rather, he said, have one acre properly cleansed than five prepared in the usual way.

Similarly, as commander-in-chief, he wanted his soldiers to look well. Their uniforms must be kept in order and "well put on." Otherwise, he said, there would be "little difference in *appearance* between a soldier in rags and a soldier in uniform." Appearance mattered especially to him when French troops were coming: his army must not be dishonored by looking shabby or careless. Even the huts for winter quarters must be built of an identical size: "any hut not exactly conformable to the plan, or the least out of line, shall be pulled down and built again agreeable to the model and in it's proper place." And when Washington became president, he showed the same concern for appearances in furnishing his house and decorating his coach in a plain but elegant style that he thought was appropriate for the head of a republican government.

But a man who craved honor could not gain it simply by putting up a good appearance. This was only a shade removed from vanity, and Washington from the beginning betrayed none of the vanity of a John Adams. Indeed his concern with appearances included a horror of appearing vain. He would not assist would-be biographers for fear, he confessed to a friend, of having "vanity or ostentation imputed to me." He would not even allow Arthur Young, the great English agricultural reformer with whom he corresponded, to publish extracts from the letters, for fear of seeming ostentatious or of giving occasion for some "officious tongue to use my name with indelicacy."

But if Washington was not vain, his very fear of appearing so argues that he did care deeply about what people thought of him. Although honor was in part a private matter, a matter of maintaining one's self-respect by doing right regardless of what the world demanded, it was also a matter of gaining the respect of others. Washington wanted respect, and he sought it first where men have often sought it, in arms.

The story of his youth is familiar, how his older brother Lawrence returned from the siege of Cartagena to fill young George with dreams of military glory. We see him at the age of 21 leading an expedition to the Ohio country and the next year another one, in which he fired the opening shots in the final struggle between France and Britain for the American continent. From the outset he made it plain that he was in search of honor: a letter penned at his camp in the Ohio country informed the governor of Virginia in words that Washington would later have eschewed as ostentatious, "the motives that lead me here were pure and noble. I had no view of acquisition, but that of Honour, by serving faithfully my King and Country." Military honor seemed to Washington to be worth any sacrifice. "Who is there," he asked, "that does not rather Envy, than regret a Death that gives birth to Honour and Glorious memory?"

But it was not necessary to die in order to win military honor. Armies were organized to express honor and respect every hour of the day, through the ascending scale of rank, from the lowliest private soldier up to the commander-in-chief. Officers often worried more about their rank than they did about the enemy. On his expedition against the French in 1754 Washington, along with other officers of the Virginia militia, was mortally offended by a captain in the British army who appeared on the scene and claimed to outrank all provincials, even those of a higher nominal grade. Washington later resigned his commission rather than submit to this kind of dishonor. Thereafter he sought in vain for a royal commission in the regular British army in order to avoid such embarrassment. Failing to obtain one, he served again with the provincial troops when the Virginia frontier needed protection and provincial command was urged upon him, because he thought "it wou'd reflect eternal dishonour upon me to refuse it."

Washington continued to regard rank as a matter of high importance. Throughout the Revolutionary War he had to press upon Congress the need for the utmost care and regularity in promotions in order to avoid offending officers who felt they had been given the grade they deserved. And the last years of his life were complicated by a dispute with John Adams over the order of rank in the general staff of the army that Congress created to prepare for war with France. But Washington recognized that an officer had to earn the respect that his rank entitled him to. And one of his ways of earning it was by cultivating the aloofness which became so marked a characteristic of his later years.

He may have begun with a large measure of native reserve, but he nourished it deliberately, for he recognized that reserve was an asset when you were in command of others. Mount Vernon, like other large plantations, was a school where the owner learned that giving orders and having them carried out were two different things. Slaves were in theory completely subject to the will of their master or overseer; but they were men, and like other men they gave obedience to those who could command their respect. And respect, in Washington's view, could not be won by familiarity. Familiarity bred contempt, whether in slaves or soldiers. Washington described the posture that he himself strove for in a letter of advice to a newly fledged Colonel in the Continental Army. "Be easy and condescending in your deportment to your officers, but not too familiar, lest you subject yourself to a want of that respect, which is necessary to support a proper command." With regard to enlisted men it was necessary to keep a still greater distance. Officers were supposed to be gentlemen, and they were expected to enhance the respect due them as officers by the respect due them as gentlemen. To make an officer of a man who was not a gentleman, a man who was not considered socially superior by his men, would mean, Washington said, that they would "regard him no more than a broomstick, being mixed together as one common herd." Fraternizing with private soldiers was "unofficer and ungentlemanlike behaviour," cause for court martial in Washington's army. The commander-in-chief, then, must be all the more a figure apart, a figure to be respected rather than loved, a figure like the George Washington on whom so much honor was to be heaped and who, though without ostentation, dearly cherished the accolades.

Interest and honor, in Washington's view, were the springs that moved all men, including himself. And although the two might come in conflict and pull men in different directions, they need not do so. Often they were bound up together in curious ways. When Washington declared that he was seeking only honor in the Ohio country, he demonstrated that this was his motive by offering to serve without pay. But in making the offer he was trying to shame the Virginia assembly into giving provincial officers *more* pay. British officers got 22 shillings a day; Virginia was paying only 12 shillings 6 pence, and Virginia officers were accordingly resentful. But their resentment was not directed so much toward the pecuniary disadvantage as it was toward the implication that they were not as worthy as their British counterparts. It seemed so dishonorable not to be paid on the same scale that Washington would have preferred no pay at all. Interest and honor were intertwined.

Interest and honor were likely to be linked in all public service. In seeking honor a man sought the respect of others, of his family, of his social class, of his friends, his town, neighborhood, province, country. And people, however grouped, generally accorded respect to someone who served their interests. A man seldom looked for honor in promoting the interests of a group to which he did not belong. Consequently in serving the interests of others he might well be serving his own, especially if he took a large enough, long-range view.

How large a view Washington took before 1774 is not easy to assess. It certainly extended to the boundaries of Virginia, for he had served both in the colony's military and in the House of Burgesses. But his quest for a royal military commission looks like a yearning for rank, not for a larger sphere of action. It seems unlikely that Washington, any more than John Adams, would have expanded his horizons beyond his own province, had the colonies' quarrel with England not reached the boiling point. During the tumultuous decade before weapons replaced words Washington imbibed the ideas of republican liberty that animated the spokesmen for American independence. He cannot properly be counted as one of those spokesmen. But he was convinced, long before the fighting began, that the English government was lost in corruption and was determined "by every piece of Art and despotism to fix the shackles of slavery upon us." When Virginians sent him to the Continental Congress to join other Americans in resisting that threat, his horizons, like those of John Adams, expanded in the vision of a national republic. For the rest of his life, instead of serving only a county or province, he would serve a whole new nation. Honor and interest would remain the springs that moved him. But the honor and interest of George Washington somehow became the honor and interest of America.

## IV

To announce to the world the independence of Americans required daring, perhaps more so for Washington than for any of the other founding fathers, and perhaps more than he or they could have realized at the time. In accepting command of the yet non-existent Continental Army in June 1775, Washington staked his honor on defeating in battle the world's greatest military and naval power. And he staked it on behalf of a nation that was also as yet non-existent. For a year he commanded a rebel army, high in spirit and low on ammunition. By the time the great Declaration turned the rebellion into a war for independence, the nation was materializing, and it would have been reasonable to expect that those who had embraced independence would rush to defend it with their lives and fortunes. But few Americans were yet as ready as Washington to face the meaning of independence. Washington found that he was in command of an army continually in the process of dissolution and that he was under the direction of a Congress that grew increasingly short-sighted and timid, unwilling to take any steps that the fickle public might momentarily disapprove.

What was worse, the very cause in which he was embarked forbade him to take effective measures to remedy the situation. The republican liberty that Americans espoused required that the military be subject to the civil power, and Washington accepted the condition, even when the civil power became incompetent, irresponsible, and corrupt, even when he was obliged to share the blame for the errors of his Congressional masters. He aimed at honor in the eyes of the people, but as a republican he could not attain his goal by appealing to the people over the heads of their elected representatives.

The most he could do, while he tried to keep his army in being, was to point out to his masters, with unwearying patience, what experience had taught him but not them, namely that while men can be moved by honor, they could not be moved by it for long unless it marched hand-in-hand with interest. Washington had so fully identified his own interest and honor with the interest and honor of the new nation that he served without pay. But he knew that an entire army of men could not be sustained by honor alone. Enthusiasm for republican government would not alter human nature. Nor would it support a man's wife and children. If Congress could not make it in the interest of men to join the army and stay in the army, whether as enlisted men or as officers, the army could not last. Men had to be paid and paid enough to make it worth their while to face the hardships of military life while their neighbors stayed home. Washington acknowledged that men would fly readily to arms to protect their rights—for a short time, as they turned out to drive the British from Concord and Lexington. "But after the first emotions are over," Washington explained, "to expect, among such People, as compose the bulk of an Army, that they are influenced by any other principles than those of Interest, is to look for what never did, and I fear never will happen." And he went on to give the results of his own appeals to men to remain in the army for the honor of it. "A soldier reasoned with upon the goodness of the cause he is engaged in, and the inestimable rights he is contending for, hears you with patience, and acknowledges the truth of your observations, but adds that it is of no more Importance to him than others. The Officer makes you the same reply, with this further remark, that his pay will not support him, and he cannot ruin himself and Family to serve his Country, when every member of the community is equally Interested and benefitted by his labours."

Washington was never able to persuade Congress to pay his officers what he thought they should get, nor was he able to persuade them to enlist men for long enough terms to give him the disciplined striking force that he needed to meet the British on equal terms. The result, as he continually lamented, was "that we have protracted the War, expended Millions, and tens of Millions of pounds which might have been saved, and have a new Army to raise and discipline once or twice a year and with which we can undertake nothing because we have nothing to build upon, as the men are slipping from us every day by means of their expiring enlistments." For a man in search of honor it was difficult to bear. The public blamed him for not taking action against the enemy, and he was unable even to explain to them why he did not. To have done so would have been to explain to the enemy how weak he was and thus invite an attack he was not equipped to repel.

It hurt his sense of honor, too, to have to rely so heavily on the French. At the beginning of the war Washington had not expected much help from France. He thought that they would supply him with arms and ammunition in return for the trade they would gain, and in order to annoy the British. But he had not counted on military assistance and would have been happier to win without it. In the end French troops and the French navy were essential to his victory for the simple reason that the states would not field a large enough force themselves, even though he was persuaded that they could have done so.

The victory, nevertheless, was his. For eight years he presided over an army that would have dissolved without him. He put up with militia who came and went like the wind. He put up with officers, commissioned by Congress, who scarcely knew one end of a gun from the other. He put up with a horde of French volunteer geniuses who all expected to be generals. He led men who had no food, no shoes, no coats, and sometimes no weapons. He silenced one mutiny after another. He prevented his unpaid officers from seeking to overturn the delinquent government. And he did it all with the aloof dignity which earned the awesome respect of those he commanded, and earned him in victory the honor of the nation that had come into existence almost in spite of itself.

V

Washington valued his laurels. When he retired to private life at Mount Vernon, it was with a full consciousness that any further ventures in public life might only diminish the honor that was now his. Far better, after so many years' service, to keep out of the political hurly burly, and this he longed to do. There remained, however, a threat that could not merely diminish but perhaps destroy both the honor he had won for himself and the independence he had won for Americans. That could be the consequence if the republic which he had fought to bring into being should itself dissolve.

The threat stemmed from the weakness of the central government. Washington had worried about it all through the war. By 1778 it had become evident to him that the states were sending lightweight men to Congress while the heavyweights stayed at home. The result was that "party disputes and personal quarrels are the great business of the day whilst the momentous concerns of an empire . . . are but secondary considerations . . . ," that "business of a trifling nature and personal concernment withdraws their attention from matters of great national moment." He could not complain to the public, but he could to his friends in Virginia. "Where are our Men of abilities?" he asked George Mason. "Why do they not come forth to save their Country? let this voice my dear Sir call upon you, Jefferson and others." "Where?" he demanded of Benjamin Harrison, "is Mason, Wythe, Jefferson, Nicholas, Pendleton, Nelson, and another I could name [meaning Harrison himself]?" They had all, it seemed, deserted Congress for Virginia.

Nor did the situation improve as the war dragged to a close, supported by French arms and French credit. While the state governments grew stronger, Congress seemed to hobble on crutches. All business, so far as Washington could see, was merely "*attempted,* for it is not done, by a timid kind of recommendation from Congress to the States." By the time peace came he was convinced that a new constitution creating a more effective national government was necessary to replace the Articles of Confederation. But he was still a republican and knew that this would not be possible until the people of the United States felt, as he did, "that the honor, power and true Interest of this Country must be measured by a Continental scale; and that every departure therefrom weakens the Union, and may ultimately break the band, which holds us together." To work for a more effective national government was, he believed, the duty of "every Man who wishes well to his Country, and will meet with my aid as far as it can be rendered in the private walks of life."

To go beyond the private walks of life was more than his intention, and even there he was wary of becoming associated with any enterprise that might endanger his standing in the public mind. He was uneasy about his connection with the Society of the Cincinnati, the organization formed by the retired officers of his army. To his surprise it had drawn heavy public criticism as the entering wedge of aristocracy. Washington was so baffled by the criticism that he asked his friend Jefferson to explain it to him, which Jefferson did with his usual grace and tact. The principal trouble was that membership was to be hereditary; Washington therefore insisted that this aspect of the Society be abandoned. When some branches of the society declined to give it up, Washington determined not to serve as its president or attend its meetings, even though he thought the public jealousy wholly unwarranted.

Washington believed that as a private citizen pursuing his own interests he could still be working for the good of the nation. He engaged without a qualm in a scheme that would benefit him financially, while it bolstered

American independence in a way that he thought was crucial. Before the Revolution he had begun investing heavily in lands in the Ohio country, where as a young man he had made his military debut. While war lasted, the country lay empty of white inhabitants save for a few hardy souls who dared brave the Indian raids organized by the English. With the coming of peace began a great folk exodus from the established regions of the East (mainly from Virginia) over the mountains into the empty West. Washington expected the stream to swell steadily with immigrants, who would leave the monarchical tyrannies of the Old World for the republican freedom of the New. "The bosom of America is open," he declared, to "the oppressed and persecuted of all Nations and Religions. Let the poor, the needy and oppressed of the Earth, and those who want Land, resort to the fertile plains of our western country, . . ."

It was an axiom of the 18th century that the strength of a country lay in its people, and Washington like other Americans wanted the country to grow as rapidly as possible. His only reservation about immigrants from Europe was that they not settle in a group and thus "retain the Language, habits and principles (good or bad) which they bring with them." It was important that they become Americans. It was even more important that all who trekked over the mountains, whether immigrants or natives, remain Americans either by inclination or by force and not slip under the dominion of England or Spain. Both countries had retained footholds in the West, and the rivers flowed relentlessly into the Mississippi toward Spanish territory. The easiest, cheapest mode of exporting whatever the people of the West produced would thus be to ship it downriver to New Orleans. Fortunately, as Washington saw it, the Spanish forbade such shipments, and the Continental Congress was in no position to secure the privilege for Americans, though settlers had no sooner arrived in the western country than they began to demand it.

Washington was persuaded that the West would gravitate to Spain and Britain unless the people there were bound to the East by the only ties that could bind men over the long run, ties of interest. The way to hold them in the nation was by building canals that would give settlers on the Ohio River a shorter water route to the East than the long float down the Mississippi. Washington accordingly devoted his energies to promoting two companies that would build canals from the Ohio and the Great Kanawha to the heads of navigation on the Potomac and the James. "The consequences to the Union," he wrote to his friend James Warren, "in my judgment are immense . . . for unless we can connect the new States which are rising to our view in those regions, with those on the Atlantic by *interest,* (the only binding cement, and not otherwise to be effected but by opening such communications as will make it easier and cheaper for them to bring the product of their labour to our markets, instead of going to the

Spaniards southerly, or the British northerly), they will be quite a distinct people; and ultimately may be very troublesome neighbors to us."

It did not bother Washington that in pressing for these canals he was furthering his own speculative interests as well as those of the nation. But he was embarrassed when the Virginia legislature, in chartering the companies to carry out his project, awarded him 150 shares in them. How would this be viewed by the world, he asked himself. Would it not "deprive me of the principal thing which is laudable in my conduct?" Honor and interest could apparently run together if the only benefit he received from the project was an increase in the value of his western lands, but honor would depart if he profited directly from the enterprise he had advocated. On the other hand, if he declined to accept the gift, would it not appear to be an act of ostentatious righteousness? He escaped the dilemma by accepting the shares but donating them to the support of a school in Virginia and to the foundation of a national university, another project designed to foster national feeling. The future leaders of the nation assembled there as students from all parts of the country would learn to shake off their local prejudices.

The canals were not completed in Washington's lifetime and could not fulfill the political function he envisaged for them. Moreover, the union was threatened more by the impotence of Congress than by the disaffection of western settlers. By the terms of the peace treaty, the British outposts in the Northwest should have been given over to the United States, but the British continued to hold them. They were also doing their best to hasten the expected collapse of the republic by refusing to allow American ships in the ports they controlled in the West Indies and elsewhere in the world. Congress, with no authority to regulate American trade, was unable to retaliate.

The debility of Congress seems to have bothered Washington as much for its damage to the nation's reputation abroad as for its depressing effects at home. To be unable to retaliate against the economic warfare of the country he had defeated in battle must render the nation "contemptable in the eyes of Europe." Because he had identified his own honor so completely with that of the nation, the contempt of Europe touched him personally and deeply; and he felt the shame redoubled when the people of western Massachusetts broke out in rebellion and neither the state government nor the national government seemed able to cope with them. "For God's sake," he wrote to David Humphreys, "tell me what is the cause of all these commotions; do they proceed from licentiousness, British-influence disseminated by the tories, or real grievances which admit of redress? If the latter, why were they delayed till the public mind had become so much agitated? If the former why are not the powers of Government tried at once?" Europeans had said right along that a republican government was incapable of the energy needed to support itself in an area as large as the United States. Now the Americans seemed bent on exemplifying the criticism. "I am mortified beyond expression," said Washington, "that in the moment of our acknowledged independence we should by our conduct verify the predictions of our transatlantic foe, and render ourselves ridiculous and contemptible in the eyes of all Europe."

As the situation worsened, Washington argued among his friends for an extension of Congressional power, but at the same time he despaired of its doing much good, for "the members [of Congress] seem to be so much afraid of exerting those [powers] which they already have, that no opportunity is slipped of surrendering them, or referring the exercise of them, to the States individually." By 1786 he was convinced, rightly or wrongly, that the country was fast verging toward anarchy and confusion, to a total dissolution of the union. He thought that the convention called to meet at Philadelphia to recommend changes in the national government offered the only hope of rescue, but it seemed so forlorn a hope that he was wary of attending it. When elected as a delegate, he delayed his acceptance to the last minute.

Washington was ready to do everything possible, he said, "to avert the humiliating and contemptible figure we are about to make in the annals of mankind." He was alarmed to hear that otherwise respectable people were talking of a need for monarchical government, and he feared that his refusal to attend the convention might be interpreted "as dereliction to republicanism." But on the other hand if the effort to save the republican union failed, the persons who made the effort "would return home chagrined at their ill success and disappointment." "This would be a disagreeable circumstance for any one of them to be in," he said, "but more particularly so for a person in my situation." His situation was unique. It was he, after all, more than any other man, who had won independence for the nation. If the nation proved unworthy of it and incapable of sustaining it, the fault would not be his. He would still retain something of the honor he had gained in the struggle, even though it would be sadly diminished. But if he associated himself with a losing effort to save what he had won, he would reduce still further the significance of his achievement.

In the end, of course, he went and inevitably was elected to preside over the convention. The document it produced, whatever its defects, seemed to him the best that could be obtained and its acceptance the only alternative to anarchy. He would not plead in public for its adoption, but to his friends he made plain his total support of it and his opposition to proposals for amending it before it was put in operation. His friends in turn made plain that if it were adopted he would be called upon to serve as the first president.

Again in terms of honor and interest Washington weighed the risks of accepting office. His inclination was to stay at Mount Vernon, to make the place more profitable and keep it looking the way he wanted it to. To preside over the new government "would be to forego repose and domestic enjoyment, for trouble, perhaps for public obloquy." There would be no honor in presiding over a fiasco, and he suspected that there was a sinister combination afoot among the Antifederalists to defeat the effective operation of the new government if they should be unsuccessful in preventing its adoption. But if he should be convinced, he told his friend Henry Lee, that "the good of my Country requires my reputation to be put in risque, regard for my own fame will not come in competition with an object of so much magnitude." The good of the country did require Washington to take the risk.

## VI

The good of the country, perhaps its very survival, required above all that its citizens should respect its government, that they should not regard it with the contempt that the state legislatures had shown for the Continental Congress. And no one else but Washington could have given the presidency and the new government the stature they attained by his mere presence. His own honor was already so great that some of it could flow from him to the office he occupied.

Not least of the assets he brought to the task was the commanding dignity that he had won by his deliberately cultivated aloofness, the posture that demanded respect and honor from those below him, magnified now by men's memories of his previous triumphs. There was no need for fancy titles. John Adams and the new Senate worried about how to address him, and to Washington's annoyance Adams made himself ridiculous by arguing for the exalted forms of address employed for the kings of European countries. Washington carried so much dignity in his manner that he required no title to convey it. Though he would not have consented to "Farmer George," he did not need "Your Highness." He nevertheless took his usual pains to avoid familiarity. In Washington's view, the president of the Continental Congress during the 1780's, by opening his doors to all comers, had diminished what little authority the Articles of Confederation allowed him and thus brought the office into contempt. Washington would be less available to every Tom, Dick, and Harry who wished to gawk at him.

He would also keep his distance from the other branches of government. The absence of a strong executive branch had been one of the great weaknesses of the old government that the Constitution tried to remedy. But it was up to the new president to strengthen the new government by maintaining in full vigor all the powers that the Constitution assigned to his office. It was up to him to establish the separation of executive and legislative branches that the Constitution stipulated. That Washington succeeded is a matter of record.

While magnifying the role of the president in government was important to Washington, it seems to have come easily, one might say naturally, to him, and he actually concerned himself more with the international standing of the nation. Improving the strength and reputation of the United States in relation to other nations became his main focus. In this area his special view of human motives proved to be a special asset. His own concern with private interest and his conviction that this was the principal spring of human action had grown with time. And he saw, in the nations of the world, collections of men who had combined in their own interests and pledged their honor, as he had pledged his, to serve those interests. It was in vain, then, to appeal to the honor of any country against the interests of that country and of its people. Honor for a Frenchman lay in serving the interests of the French, as for an American it lay in serving the interests of Americans. Although Washington was convinced, like many men of his time, that the interests of different countries need not conflict, he was certain that no country would or ought to act against its own perceived interests. To expect any country to do so was folly; and it was criminal folly for any man charged with his country's interests to trust another country with them, as for example Congress had done in instructing its envoys to be directed by the French court in the peace negotiations with England. [...]

Distrust of foreign attachments took firm root beside Washington's other political instincts, and during his years in command of the army and in retirement at Mount Vernon he had advocated a stronger national government, not merely to prevent internal dissolution but to keep the country from falling under the influence of one of the more energetic monarchies of the Old World. Early in 1788, when war clouds were gathering over Europe and the Constitution had not yet been ratified, he had written to Jefferson of his fear that the several states, uninhibited by any effective central direction, might be drawn into the European quarrels.

As president, Washington was at last able to exercise control over foreign relations, and in doing so he never swerved from the maxim of national interest that he had sought to impress upon Henry Laurens. That maxim, as he interpreted it, dictated that, apart from commercial transactions, the United States should have as little to do as possible with any other nation. The true interest of the United States consisted in staying clear of foreign alignments and supplying all sides with the products which its fertile lands could produce in abundance. If the United States could maintain a policy of strict neutrality, the endless wars of the European monarchs would serve both to advance the price of American products and to swell the stream of immigrants needed to fill the empty American West. Accordingly, as the threatened European war became reality, it was Washington's consistent policy to build the power of the United States by asking no favors of foreign countries and giving none. The aloofness which he associated with command was the proper posture to give power and respectability to a nation as well as an individual.

Although Washington anticipated commercial benefits from this policy of neutrality, he did not think it wise in negotiating treaties to take undue advantage of the bargaining position offered to the United States by the distresses of other countries. In his view, since he believed nations acted always according to their interest, a treaty was useful only so long as its provisions coincided with the interests of both countries. [. . .]

The important thing, Washington believed, was for Americans to discern their own interest as a nation and to pursue it without trying to take advantage of other countries and without allowing other countries to take advantage of the United States. This was the message of his Farewell Address, both in the version drafted by James Madison in 1792 and in the much different final version drafted by Alexander Hamilton in 1796. He put it more succinctly himself in a letter to William Heath in 1797:

> No policy, in my opinion, can be more clearly demonstrated, than that we should do justice to *all* but have no political connexions with *any* of the European Powers, beyond those which result from and serve to regulate our Commerce with them. Our own experience (if it has not already had this effect) will soon convince us that *disinterested* favours, or friendship from any Nation whatever, is too novel to be calculated on; and there will always be found a wide difference between the words and actions of any of them.

In staking his own honor on the pursuit of national interest, Washington did not come off unscathed. He had committed himself so closely to the nation and its government that every attack on government policies seemed to be an attack on *him*. And by the time he left office the attacks were coming thick and fast, including some that were openly directed at him, charging that he had deserted the republican faith and was squinting at monarchy. Although he professed to be unmoved by these diatribes, his friend Jefferson testified that "he feels these things more than any person I ever yet met with." And because Jefferson himself was a critic of national policies, Washington could not dissociate Jefferson from the assaults.

Washington's last years were saddened by this seeming repudiation of him, but his republican trust in the ordinary man remained unshaken. Less than a year before his death in 1799 he was still affirming that "the great mass of our Citizens require only to understand matters rightly, to form right decisions." And so far as his own honor was concerned his faith was justified. The mass of citizens did not deny him in the end the full measure of honor that was due him. Nor did Jefferson, even though Jefferson thought it was the president rather than the people who needed to understand matters rightly. Fourteen years after Washington's death Jefferson recalled how the president had often declared to him "that he considered our new Constitution as an experiment on the practicability of republican government, and with what dose of liberty man could be trusted for his own good; that he was determined the experiment should have a fair trial, and would lose the last drop of his blood in support of it."

Although Jefferson feared that Washington's emphatic assertion may have hidden a waning confidence in the experiment, there is no evidence that this was the case. To the end Washington cherished his honor, and to the end his honor demanded the preservation of the American republic, free of every foreign connection. That was the meaning of independence for Washington. He was even ready, perhaps a little too ready, to don his old uniform and command a new army in the war with France that seemed so imminent in 1798. When he died the next year, he could not have been sure that his republic would in fact sustain its independence. And had he lived another year he would have found little to cheer him in the election that elevated Jefferson to the presidency. But he need not have feared. The republic did survive and long preserved the aloofness from foreign quarrels that he had prescribed for it. His honor survived with it, and posterity has preserved his image in all the aloofness that he prescribed for himself. Although the mass of citizens have learned to look upon most of their other historical heroes with an affectionate familiarity, they have not presumed to do so with Washington. The good judgment that he was sure they possessed has prevented a posthumous repetition of the folly perpetrated by Gouverneur Morris. Americans honor the father of their country from a respectful distance. And that is surely the way Washington would have wanted it.

CLOVIS

## Attitudes toward Sex

[ AUTUMN 1976 ]

I

IN ONE of those aphoristic statements that sum up human experience, Pascal observed that man is at once the glory and the disgrace of the universe. This paradox of the extremes, taking various forms, is basic to life as we know it. An impartial summation of all human experience would have to report that it comprehended an ineffable beauty together with such horror as sanity cannot contemplate. Here the paradox resides in the fact that, knowing both exaltation and suffering, man may know them not separately but as aspects of a single experience. This, surely, is the secret of Greek and Shakespearian tragedy. The suffering that is the theme of *The Trojan Women* is redeemed by the beauty that alone remains when the suffering is over. The sordidness of the life presented in *Hamlet* is transfigured by the exaltation that alone remains when, having ended, the tragedy is seen as a completed whole.

This polarity, whatever the form it takes, is fundamental. But how do we define the poles? Jeremy Bentham's conception of "pleasure" and "pain" is grossly inadequate; for it implies hedonistic pleasure, taking little or no account of the exaltation that may, on occasion, come as religious experience even to us unbelievers.

These remarks are preliminary to noting that an important part of mankind, if polled on the question of what is the most intense pleasure life affords, would cite the physical intimacy between the sexes that culminates in intercourse; and, if polled on the separate question of what was life's most exalting experience (at least potentially), might well give the same answer. What we sum up in the short word "sex" is the satisfaction of an appetite, a satisfaction that affords the most intense physical pleasure known, and that may involve, at the same time, a beauty so exalting as to intimate the existence of another and higher realm of being. But the experience of sex is also polar. The larger experience of sacred love, so to speak, may include within it the experience of profane love.

Today, for the first time, sex has become a subject to be taught by public means—to the public at large and, if only as a matter of their preparation for the future, to children in elementary and secondary schools. Such teaching is necessarily twofold, for it is not possible to teach the physical facts of sex without, at the same time, teaching a normative attitude toward it, implicitly if not explicitly.

Teaching the physical facts poses no problem, now that sexual activities of every imaginable sort may be demonstrated by hired actors on movie screens or on the stage, in theaters that invite the public to come in and see. The problem is, rather, what attitude of mind should accompany the teaching of the physical facts. One attitude conceives the object of sexual relations to be simply that of providing physical thrills. Another may conceive it to be something greater. In one attitude, sex may be a casual indulgence, a pastime, or sport. In another it may be a rite, even a sacrament. The sexual intercourse of Dostoyevsky's Fyodor Karamazov with the imbecile beggar-girl, "Stinking Lizavetta," which he undertakes in response to a dare by his drinking companions, is merely a bestial act. At the other extreme, intercourse between two persons who are enduringly attached to each other by the bonds of a mutual and exclusive private affinity may bring with it the highest experience of which man is capable. The point is that it is easier to teach what is represented by the bestial extreme than by the other. The problem to which this article addresses itself arises out of this point.

An extraordinary situation has now been created by the sudden lifting of virtually all the traditional limits to the public display of what has hitherto been private. There has been no time for custom to develop public taste with respect to such display, for it to establish a new canon of publicly accepted values and social tolerance. Consequently, a cultural foundation for distinguishing the various possible attitudes toward sex in terms of better and worse is missing. This means that, with the field of teaching and the field of commercial exploitation suddenly opened wide, they have been pre-empted, and fashion is being set, by minds that do not represent the best in our paradoxically polar humanity. Those who produce books or movies revealing everything we should know about sex are none of them Shakespeares. At the worst, they represent all the sordidness and cynicism of which our kind is capable.

There are, undoubtedly, some books and some movies that, explicit as they may be, represent valid teaching; but, for the most part, what is ostensibly teaching cannot be clearly distinguished from what is merely commercial exploitation. The lifting of the bars against sex in public has presented opportunities to exploit a voracious curiosity on the part of us all, thereby tempting commercial interests to compete with one another in the inventiveness and variety of sexual activities they present and the explicitness with which they present them. In an effort, generally disingenuous if not cynical, to save the self-respect of the public who pay for their wares, and to assume the trappings of respectability for themselves, they have commonly done this under the guise of a high purpose, invoking the auspices of individuals who, as professors of a science called "sexology," claim to be engaged in the noble mission of education, which is to promote knowledge and disseminate truth.

Certainly this hypocrisy is not the whole of the matter. There are also the honest educators who are genuinely concerned to avert the confusion, the unhappiness, the psychological shocks, and the failures that may be the lot of those who grow up in ignorance, gaining their notions of what sex is only by mysterious reports or haphazard and embarrassing experiences. But these educators, too, are likely in their practice to exemplify the fact that it is easier to teach the mechanics of sex than to teach what lifts it above the mechanics.

The dimensions of the problem become evident when we note that what lifts sex above its mechanics remains, still, a matter of private and unarticulated experience rather than public knowledge, and that one cannot assume the private experience even in educators with normal-school degrees and the best of intentions. (The communication of such experience is what poets are for, but in our day they have come to conceive their vocation otherwise.) The educators, too, present the sexual intercourse of human beings as not essentially different from the graceless intercourse of dogs in the street. This is what our children are widely taught, through lectures, books, and movies—with such additions as that people masturbate exactly like the chimpanzees in the zoo.

Let us recognize the fact that this teaching is all quite true. It is true as zoology, true as general behavior common to the vertebrates of the class Mammalia, man included. There is nothing false, in itself, in teaching that men and women, when aroused to it, rub against each other just like dogs and chimpanzees. However, while this is not false in itself, how grossly inadequate it is!—and therefore how misleading! Although man is an animal in the fullest sense of the word, he is unique in the possession of certain qualities altogether unassociated with any other animals, and in a way of life that represents those qualities. Without escaping his animal heritage, which remains, he has in some respects risen above it. If he is capable of performing the sexual act just like any dog, he is also capable of a higher vision, which has manifested itself in the creation, over the centuries, of his cultural monuments. This particular animal has built the Parthenon, has composed the B-minor Mass, and has given a large meaning to the word "love." To describe him as a chimpanzee may not be untrue as far as it goes, but it stops short of describing him adequately. Therefore it is not enough to stop at the point where one has taught the child only what he has in common with the chimpanzee.

Today, however, tradition is broken, the line of our cultural development has parted, and all the customary answers of the past to the questions of what the relations between men and women should be are suddenly of doubtful relevance. For the moment, then, we are reduced to the elemental, represented by the dogs in the street. For the moment, this is about all we are able to teach our children.

## II

I return to the fact that, in teaching the physical procedures of sex, we necessarily teach a normative attitude toward it, even though we teach it only by default. If the physical procedures are all that we teach explicitly and ostensibly, giving them no particular social context and no cultural meaning, then our teaching is bound to imply that those procedures represent nothing more than animal acts like eating or excreting, acts that are performed for the physical pleasure and relief they provide. Even in teaching the mating behavior of birds, however, an ornithologist will point out those aspects of it that strengthen the psychological bond between a mated pair. He will thus give their mating behavior a social context and an associated emotional significance.

Today, however, we are at a loss to know what social context, and what associated significance, to give human sexual relations. If only by default, then, we invest those relations with less dignity than we attribute to the equivalent relations among birds. Indeed, we invest them with no dignity at all.

The overriding role of the normative attitude, its primacy, may be exemplified by differing contexts for the public display of nudity. The nudity of young men and women in ancient Greece, as represented in statues and vase-paintings, is altogether different from that displayed in the latest theatrical review that shows men and women cavorting naked on the stage—not because the physical bodies are different but because the attitudes are different. The question we ought to be debating, therefore, is not so much that of whether young men and women should show themselves naked in public as that of the normative attitude in terms of which they might do so. Nakedness can be dignified, as in the Parthenon frieze, or it can make men and women appear as undignified as pigs in a wallow.

We are faced, today, with the need to answer the normative question: What is proper to us? Our dilemma is that, at this stage of our evolution, we can answer it with respect to a wide range of human behavior and human attitudes only in terms of varying cultures, each of which is artificial. Whether people greet each other by shaking hands or by rubbing noses depends entirely on the artificial customs of particular societies. Such customs have no extrinsic authority, no authority of God or nature. There are other cases, however, in which a norm of human behavior does have the authority of nature. If, for example, the question were raised whether the proper way for men to walk was on two legs or on "all fours," it could be answered by reference to the human anatomy, which is clearly adapted to walking on two legs, and not at all adapted to "all fours." This, then, is not a matter of cultural relativism but of what nature, so to speak, intended.

The example I have given is not as remote from the theme of this article as one might think. A conspicuous feature of the current sexual revolution is the campaign to have homosexual relations accorded the same normative standing as heterosexual, even to the extent of instituting homosexual "marriages," which would be given the same legal status as heterosexual marriages. This is quite different from a demand for tolerance of what would still be recognized as deviation from the norm, for it is a claim that homosexual relations represent the norm no less than heterosexual. Is it not obvious, however, that the differing anatomies of the two sexes are complementary, that they are quite specifically designed for each other, that nature has fitted them to each other, not in some loose way but as specifically as the sword and the scabbard are fitted to each other? This fitness, moreover, applies to more than the principal sexual organs alone, for it includes the mutual destinies of egg and sperm. Here, in the choice between heterosexual and homosexual relations, we can see what is natural and what is not.

I do not propose the persecution of those who feel attracted to members of their own rather than the other sex. Some of the most admirable persons who have ever lived have, after all, been among their numbers. I daresay there are grounds for compassion toward them, since they are driven to seek a satisfaction for which the human anatomy is not designed. In any case, I would consider that what consenting adults do in private is no one else's business. But I would feel there were solid grounds for opposing the teaching and public demonstration of homosexual relations as being entirely normal, because it is just as clear that we are designed for heterosexual rather than homosexual relations as that we are designed to walk on two limbs rather than four.

I return, now, to the conceptual element, to the larger understanding, the vision, the awareness of the beautiful, the capacity for self-transcendence, which may be realized by man but not by the chimpanzee. Just as the symmetrical form and fitness of the more elaborate flowers, or the beauty of the falcon's flight, has been the theme of poets, so the symmetry and fitness to each other of the male and female parts in the human anatomy seem to me an equal object of poetic delight. An orchid, in its elaborate and delicate adaptation to the bee that fertilizes it, and the reciprocal adaptation of the bee—this does not seem to me more beautiful than the way the human organs are made for each other, are made for the completion of what is otherwise partial.

At this point I am aware that what I am saying must have a touch of the ludicrous for the reader. I appear to be reporting what is merely an idiosyncratic attitude, an attitude personal to me. What my own thinking represents cannot be an attitude belonging to our common culture precisely because that culture is suddenly without any attitude toward sex—except, in the absence of anything else, a preoccupation with its mechanics and the changes that may be rung on them. In attempting to say, here, why there is more to sex than that, or why there should be, I take the risk of embarrassment which must attend the revelation of what is private and personal. But the risk must be taken in the hope of contributing to the development of higher values and higher standards than are being publicly associated with sex today.

The fact that sex may be enjoyed at something like a sacramental level does not mean that it may not, the world being what it is, continue to be enjoyed at the lower levels as well. Perhaps such enjoyment, at least among the young, is not inconsistent with richer experience as maturity develops.

Variety contributes to enjoyment at the lower levels, and one element of variety is a variety of partners. A widespread supposition today, in a world bent on minimizing or denying temperamental differences between men and women, is that a variety of partners is as satisfying to women as to men. If it is true, however, as it has generally seemed to be, that in sexual relations the emotional commitment of women tends to be greater than that of men (for sound biological reasons, considering what consequences they may entail for women), the continuing development of mores that promote such variety will mean an increase of emotional and psychological disturbances for the women who live accordingly. As for men, it has been said that they tend to be polygamous in youth but monogamous as they grow older. (These are matters on which I believe that neither I nor my readers can properly be dogmatic.)

If the lower levels of enjoyment, which appeal chiefly to those who are at an early stage of sexual experience, gain from variety, I would hold that the higher levels associated with full maturity gain from the private affinity of two persons bound to each other in a permanent and exclusive association.

Time, measured in years, counts at the higher levels. The bonds of private affinity are fully realized only between a man and woman who have shared the same bed night after night and all night long, over years that grow into decades. In such a relationship, it seems to me, the element of privacy is essential. The relationship, in all the varieties of its expression, is a secret between the two, excluding the rest of the world, and the secret is a part of the bond.

Over the years, men and women slowly change; but in the bond I refer to they change together and in complementarity, so that at the last, in age, they are no less to each other than when, under the different circumstances of their passionate youth, they first came together.

Considering the natural beauty of this relationship, and its difference in age from what it was in youth, should we not view with contempt those books that, to leave no part of the market unexploited, pretend to teach how couples in old age can manage their relations so as to obtain from sex, still, the same physical "kick" as in youth? This is as pitiful and repulsive as it is unnatural. It represents the limitations of those who, separated from cultural tradition and any higher knowledge, can see in the relation between the sexes no possibilities beyond the momentary thrill of the orgasm.

I return, in conclusion, to the plight in which our society finds itself. It has broken with a cultural tradition that had sought to keep secret the physical aspects of human sexual relations, hiding them beneath a vast amount of humbug. It has brought those aspects, all naked, into the open street for display. However, the lack of a traditional context of public values and cultivated taste for such display, the lack of normative conceptions, has left the field open to those who do not hesitate to exploit every possible aberration of human sexuality, generally under the guise of education, and has made it virtually impossible, even for those with the best intentions, to teach the mechanics of sex in terms that give it a greater meaning than what it has for the beasts of the field.

The inadequacy that this represents may be for the present day only. After the destruction entailed in a revolution, one may hope for a rebuilding, in the realm of the spirit as in the realm of material things. Our intellectuals, as a class, have led the way in the destruction of the taboos that have hitherto surrounded sex, calling for the abolition of its censorship and of all restrictions on its public display. Perhaps this has been because they have not really believed in human dignity, in man's possession of special attributes that lift him above the level of the other animals. Now, however, the destruction of taboos has been so far completed as to show that it is not enough in itself. The intellectuals may therefore be expected to see that their achievement has left an emptiness. Under the circumstances, one must ask them to be dissatisfied with it and, being dissatisfied, to concern themselves once more with what it is that, in sex as in other matters, makes man truly man.

EDGAR F. SHANNON JR.

# Alfred Tennyson as a Poet for Our Time

[ AUTUMN 1977 ]

I

During the past year, there has been a program on educational television called "Anyone for Tennyson?" The series began with readings and discussion of Tennyson's poetry, and subsequent installments treated other Victorian and modern poets. The title is catchy and one that says something about Tennyson and about poetry in our time. Both the name of the program and the fact that reading and discussing poetry can attract a significant television audience suggests a new attitude toward Tennyson and toward poetry that emboldens me to pursue the topic of Alfred Tennyson as a poet for our time.

Tennyson's life from 1809 to 1892 spanned much of the reign of Queen Victoria (1837–1901). She made him Poet Laureate, to succeed Wordsworth, in 1850; and, upon the recommendation of Gladstone, raised him to the peerage as a Baron in 1883. The adulation in his own time by people of all classes throughout the English-speaking world is probably unmatched in literary history.

Soon after his death a reaction set in, and until about 25 years ago, it was fashionable to denigrate Tennyson, like all things Victorian, and to think of him as a complacent exponent of a self-satisfied, self-important, and self-righteous age. But historical research and literary criticism have now winnowed fact from prejudice, and "Victorian" is anything but the word of opprobrium that it once was. Indeed, Victorian literature, history, and culture have become the "rage." Beards, hair, and wire-rimmed glasses widely replicate personal styles of 100 years ago. Victorian societies and journals multiply. If Tennyson is the Pre-Eminent Victorian, as Joanna Richardson maintains in a book by that title, then the extent of serious and favorable evaluation to which he is now being treated (more than 60 books and articles listed in last year's Victorian bibliography) is not surprising. Yet he is not merely significant in relation to a historical and cultural milieu. Nor is this purely an indication of tides in artistic taste. Rather, I wish to suggest, the circumstances of his life, the conditions of his era, exceptional creative powers, poetic insight, and the personal predilections of method and subject matter which his poetry displays make him not only an enduring poet, but a poet of singular pertinence for our time.

Matthew Arnold once said "that poetry is at bottom a criticism of life; that the greatness of a poet lies in his powerful and beautiful application of ideas to life,—to the question: 'how to live?'" Tennyson's great strengths are the beauty through the meaning and sound of words and feeling through the evocation of the senses and emotions with which he is able to communicate ideas about life. His poetry is addressed to the central question, "how to live?"; that is, to the values that each of us as an individual must choose. He does not write from a perspective of privilege and ease, as his title, Lord Tennyson, might suggest. He knew the vicissitudes of the ordinary existence that we must bear. In his own life, he experienced the mixed potential and the human predicament for good and ill.

## II

The son of a country parson, Tennyson was one of eleven children. His father, moody and sometimes violent toward his wife and family, was subject to periods of depression and drank to excess. As Tennyson approached manhood, his relationship with his father became so strained that he entered Cambridge University before he was adequately prepared in order to escape from the atmosphere of his home and from his father. For the family, money was always a problem; and when his father died, Tennyson left Trinity College, Cambridge, heavily in debt and without a degree—"a drop-out," as we would say. Two years later, Arthur Hallam, his brilliant best friend at college, who had become engaged to his sister, died suddenly at the age of 22. The brother to whom he was the closest in age and affection for a time became a drug addict. He was deeply attracted to a beautiful young lady who married someone else for money and social position. One of his younger brothers went incurably insane and had to be confined to an asylum for life. He found his true love in Emily Sellwood, but after they had been engaged for three years, her father required them to stop seeing each other and corresponding because Tennyson had no prospect of having enough regular income to support a wife. It was 14 years from the time that he and Emily first met before they were finally married, when Tennyson was 41.

His first two volumes of poetry were harshly received by some of the reviewers and sold slowly. When he was 33, he lost in a business speculation most of what little money he had inherited and had to undergo extended medical treatment for what was virtually a nervous breakdown. Even after he became the leading poet of his time and at last financially secure, all was not serene. His and Emily's first child was stillborn. Lionel, the second of his two sons, able and promising in every way, died in his early thirties; and the poet lived to see most of his closest friends precede him to the grave. All his life he had to combat a brooding tendency toward melancholia. Whatever positive outlook he achieved regarding the lot of individual men and women was hard won. He shared the uncertainty and the anxiety that have become hallmarks of our time.

If Tennyson's life, then, corresponds in many particulars to modern experience, the characteristics of the times in England have remarkable parallels with those of the United States today. To compare mid-20th-century America to Victorian England may seem startling; but, like ours, it was an age of rapid change in the conditions of living, in social, economic, religious, and cultural attitudes and beliefs, and in the nature of authority and the source of political power. The railway (first opened in 1830), the steamboat, and the telegraph symbolized the speed of change and the increased tempo of human existence, just as the automobile, the airplane, the radio, and television have done in our own; and the Victorians experienced the same keen problems of adjustment—what Alvin Toeffler calls "future shock." Science and technology produced unprecedented economic growth and faith in industrial and material progress. By 1870, England was economically and militarily the most powerful country in the world. The population of the United Kingdom more than doubled and concentrated in London and the industrial centers of the Midlands, so that England became a largely urban, instead of rural, nation. Successive extensions of the franchise in elections for Parliament moved the locus of power from the aristocracy to the populace (except for women) and from the land to the cities. The rights of women became a leading cultural and political issue. Money and social prestige based on wealth, often accompanied by greed and dishonesty, became a standard of success. The rich and privileged enjoyed the most affluent society the world had ever known, while millions existed in abject poverty—creating what Disraeli called the "two nations." Advances in scientific knowledge in geology and biology undermined traditional Judeo-Christian beliefs and the Biblical account of creation. An agonizing conflict of faith and doubt became typical of the era and led many people to see man's life as purposeless and merely a physical or animal existence. Others clung even more determinedly than ever to a fundamentalist, evangelical creed. It was a time of crumbling and uncertain values, and of contention between old and new ethical standards. Despite a rigid surface morality, fraud, injustice, and sexual license permeated Victorian society. In the last quarter of the century, materialism and progress began to seem inadequate to assure the future, and pessimism tended to undermine self-confidence.

To reflect such an age is surely to speak to our own. Tennyson was fully aware of the ambiguities, irony, and paradox, and of the psychological complexity, that we find in human life and that modern critics have prized among literary criteria of excellence. He sometimes reflected these attributes of experience through direct statement, but he characteristically achieved his "powerful and beautiful application of ideas to life" indirectly, through the use of myth and legend, of the quest, of dreams, madness, and trance. All these devices are typical of contemporary literature and appeal to our sensibilities as among the most effective for conveying aesthetic pleasure and truth.

Here is an example of Tennyson's castigating his age directly, though the tone is quite ironic and he expresses social criticism dramatically through a *persona*, the protagonist in *Maud*:

> Why do they prate of the blessings of Peace? we
>     have made them a curse,
> Pickpockets, each hand lusting for all that
>     is not its own;
> And lust of gain in the spirit of Cain, . . .
>
> But these are the days of advance, the works
>     of the men of mind,
> When who but a fool would have faith in a
>     tradesman's ware or his word?
> Is it peace or war? Civil war, as I think
>     and that of a kind
> The viler, as underhand, not openly bearing
>     the sword.
>
> Sooner or later I too may passively take the
>     print
> Of the golden age—why not? I have neither
>     hope nor trust;
> May make my heart a millstone, set my heart as
>     flint,
> Cheat, and be cheated, and die: who knows? we
>     are ashes and dust.
>
> Peace, sitting under her olive, and slurring
>     the days gone by,
> When the poor are hovelled and hustled together,
>     each sex, like swine,
> When only the ledger lives, and when only not
>     all men lie;
> Peace in her vineyard—yes!—but a company
>     forges the wine.

> And the vitriol madness flushes up in the ruffian's
> head,
> Till the filthy by-lane rings to the yell of the
> trampled wife,
> And chalk and alum and plaster are sold to the poor
> for bread,
> And the spirit of murder works in the very means of
> life, . . .

Now let us consider an instance in the indirect method of poetic commentary in "Oenone," in which Tennyson depicts Paris, the son of Priam, King of Troy, as judging who is the most beautiful of the three principal goddesses, Hera, Pallas Athene, or Aphrodite. Tennyson employed classical myths extensively as a vehicle for exploring alternative answers to the question, "how to live?" By illuminating, through mythic and legendary material, the tensions among values, he makes us think and arrive at our own judgments independently.

In this poem, Oenone, a mountain nymph who is Paris's beloved, recounts the events; and we hear each goddess advance the arguments for the attribute which she represents: power, wisdom, and beauty. Tennyson as poet does not underline the decision that Paris should have made for wisdom and self-control instead of for beauty. The commentary occurs in the jealous and psychologically valid interior monologue of Oenone. War and the sacking of Troy by the Greeks is, of course, the outcome that the ending of the poem foreshadows but does not state. While the flaw in Paris's decision may seem obvious, we should not overlook the symbolic significance that the myth gives to the necessity of choices in human life and to the fact that such choices always bear consequences which can be fatal to individuals and to society. Ironically, even with the most careful reasoning, in the light of the information available at the time, the consequences often cannot be foreseen.

As presented by Hera, power, properly used, especially for unselfish ends and for the good of humanity, has genuine worth. Kept in perspective, beauty, too, is surely a desirable attribute in life; but in Tennyson's version, Aphrodite promises Paris, if he decides for her, "the fairest and most loving wife in Greece." Since each of the goddesses proffers to Paris a means of his own self-aggrandizement, they are really bribing him and corrupting the ideal of a disinterested judgment turning solely upon reason and merit. Yet among several alternatives in life, a most loving wife could be a wise decision for a man to make and could lead to his greatest happiness. Paris's selecting Aphrodite and a loving wife, however, illustrates the ambiguity of circumstances in which we have to make choices. Helen is not simply a young woman capable of being the most beautiful and the most loving wife that Greece can provide. She is already a wife—somebody else's wife. Thus ideals clash. To fulfill what is an ideal for Paris means destroying that of Menelaus. Also, to gain Helen, Paris must abandon and alienate Oenone, whose love turns to bitterness and hate.

In "Ulysses," through the motif of the quest, the poet once more portrays the relativity of values. For Tennyson's Ulysses, the routine of life in Ithaca after his return from the Trojan War has palled; and he sets off on a final search for adventure. The poem celebrates a zest for action, a longing for knowledge and experience, and the courage and determination of an aging man to persevere against adversity:

> How dull it is to pause, to make an end,
> To rust unburnished, not to shine in use!
> As though to breathe were life. Life piled on life
> Were too little, and of one to me
> Little remains: but every hour is saved
> From that eternal silence, something more,
> A bringer of new things; and vile it were
> For some three suns to store and hoard myself,
> And this gray spirit yearning in desire
> To follow knowledge like a sinking star,
> Beyond the utmost bound of human thought.

And again:

> . . . Come my friends
> 'Tis not too late to seek a newer world.
> Push off, and sitting well in order smite
> The sounding furrows; for my purpose holds
> To sail beyond the sunset, and the baths
> Of all the western stars, until I die.
> . . . . . . . . . . . . . . . . . . . . . . . . . . . . . . . . . . . . .
> Though much is taken, much abides; and though
> We are not now that strength which in old days
> Moved earth and heaven; that which we are, we are;
> One equal temper of heroic hearts,
> Made weak by time and fate, but strong in will
> To strive, to seek, to find, and not to yield.

Yet as admirable and inspiring as Ulysses's courage is, we must recognize that in setting off on his quest, he is truant in his obligations as husband and king. He rejects the faithful Penelope, dismissing her as "an aged wife," and leaves to his son Telemachus the responsibility of improving the lot of the Ithacan people. An escapist, he forsakes duty for excitement. Some readers, in their enthusiasm for Ulysses's heroic posture, fail to see that Tennyson intends us to be aware of the values that are being subverted, as well as of those being celebrated. Furthermore, Ulysses's quest seems to represent nearly as much the enactment of a wish for death as of a love of life.

## III

As E. D. H. Johnson has shown in *The Alien Vision of Victorian Poetry,* madness, dream, and trance are non-rational elements that Tennyson effectively employs to convey both mystery and meaning in his poetry. Tennyson treats the derangement of the protagonist of *Maud,* through whose inner monologue the poem is related, with the greatest psychological subtlety. After killing his loved one's brother in a duel, the protagonist loses his mind for a time; but the spark of Maud's love for him, which persists in his brain during his period of irrationality, eventually restores him to a shattered sanity. In the meantime, Maud has died, and the protagonist believes that he sublimates self by going off to fight for his fellow Englishmen in the Crimean War. In an illuminating essay entitled "Sex, Symbolism, and Psychology in Tennyson's *Maud,*" Roy Basler sees Tennyson as anticipating Freud here, "by recognizing the complex phases of self in his hero, by giving due weight to the unconscious, and by crediting the essentially non-rational causality in psychic phenomena in general. . . . It would be difficult," he concludes, "to find a twentieth century writer who penetrates so deeply or handles so subtly, for all the accumulation of science in the intervening years, the complex problem that is man."

Whereas psychic trauma can be so severe as to cause complete withdrawal from reality into madness, dreams seem to be for Tennyson a means for the sleeping mind, released from its ordinary engagements with the affairs and activities of everyday life, to resolve mental and emotional conflicts. Maud's appearance to the protagonist in a dream as a guiding heavenly spirit begins his return to rationality. The poet's movement in *In Memoriam* from despair over Arthur Hallam's death to affirmation, is advanced significantly by his dream of a journey by water with the spirits of Poetry and Art and other civilizing human attributes to a reunion with Hallam aboard a ship that sails into the cosmos. Yet dreams, like life, are ambiguous and cannot be depended upon as sure guides for action. For example, a dream in *Enoch Arden* leads to a fateful misinterpretation. Annie has a dream of Enoch, her sailor husband who has failed to return from a Pacific voyage, sitting under a palm tree. Taking this to mean that he is dead and in heaven, she marries his rival. Actually, the dream represents a fleeting glimpse of reality. Having been shipwrecked, Enoch is a lone survivor on a Pacific island. He is eventually rescued and returns to England to encounter an ethical dilemma.

The trance, however, is always trustworthy and raises the imagination to a point of visionary poetic perception. Tennyson had a psychic capacity to experience trances, which he described as follows:

> A kind of waking trance I have frequently had, quite up from boyhood, when I have been all alone. This generally has come upon me thro' repeating my own name two or three times to myself silently, till all at once, as it were out of the intensity of consciousness of individuality, the individuality itself seemed to fade away into boundless being, and this not a confused state, but the clearest of the clearest, the surest of the surest, the weirdest of the weirdest, utterly beyond words, where death is almost a laughable impossibility, the loss of personality (if so it were) seeming no extinction but the only true life.

Undoubtedly, Tennyson's finest use of the trance occurs in lyric XCV, the climax of *In Memoriam*. The passage starts with an everyday domestic scene in which Tennyson, his mother, and younger brothers and sisters are having tea on a summer evening on the lawn of the rectory at Somersby as dusk and then darkness fall. There is no hint of a mystical experience to come. As one by one the family leaves him and the lights go out in the house, and as Tennyson remains rereading Hallam's letters by a lamp, he rises to a spiritual reunion with the soul of his friend and to a sense of penetrating into ultimate reality:

> So word by word and line by line
> The dead man touched me from the past,
> And all at once it seemed at last
> The living soul was flashed on mine,
>
> And mine in his was wound, and whirled
> About empyreal heights of thought,
> And came on that which is, and caught
> The deep pulsations of the world,
>
> Aeonian music measuring out
> The steps of Time—the shocks of Chance—
> The blows of Death. At length my trance
> Was cancelled, stricken through with doubt.
>
> Vague words! but ah, how hard to frame
> In matter moulded forms of speech,
> Or even for intellect to reach
> Through memory that which I became:
>
> Till now the doubtful dusk revealed
> The knolls once more where, couched at ease,

> The white kine glimmered, and the trees
> Laid their dark arms about the field:
>
> And sucked from out the distant gloom
> A breeze began to tremble o'er
> The large leaves of the sycamore,
> And fluctuate all the still perfume,
>
> And gathering freshlier overhead,
> Rocked the full-foliaged elms, and swung
> The heavy-folded rose, and flung
> The lilies to and fro, and said
>
> 'The dawn, the dawn,' and died away;
> And East and West, without a breath,
> Mixt their dim lights, like life and death,
> To broaden into boundless day.

Although the vision fades and the poet's consciousness returns to familiar surroundings, the symbols perfect the attitude of harmony. The gentle breeze stirs the perfume of the flowers; the rose of passion unites with the lilies of purity and innocence. Dawn dispels darkness and the paradoxical, yet unifying elements in human experience, east and west, and life and death, merge in the prospect, not merely of a literal new morning but of the limitless life of an eternal day.

## IV

If we turn now from these elements of Tennyson's creative imagination and insight, there are two subjects that engaged Tennyson's attention and that give him a particular interest for our time: they are science and the position of women. *The Princess,* a long poem in seven cantos of blank verse, published in 1847, is the work in which Tennyson addresses himself comprehensively to the nature, education, and rights of women and to women's relationship to men. This was a daring work for its time, for it appeared more than 20 years before John Stuart Mill's famous essay *On the Subjugation of Women* and before any of the women's colleges was established at Oxford or Cambridge. The Princess inaugurates a women's college for the study of the advanced knowledge that men pursue. She is such an extreme advocate of women's liberation that men are barred from the college on pain of death. A medieval joust in a tale-within-a-tale and the mock-heroic tone of the first two-thirds of the poem show the extent to which Tennyson felt it necessary to approach the subject obliquely. Nevertheless, he trenchantly exposes the weaknesses, both for individuals and for society, of traditional male domination and mere domesticity for women. In the end, the Princess makes a hospital of her sexist college, and the Prince and the Princess are united in an idealized marriage. But the Prince is committed to the Princess's goal of full intellectual development for women, to a changed status for them in marriage, and to repeal of discriminatory laws. He sees men and women as complementary to each other:

> Like perfect music unto noble words;
> And so these twain, upon the skirts of Time,
> Sit side by side, full-summed in all their powers,
> Dispensing harvest, sowing the To-be,
> Self-reverent each and reverencing each
> Distinct in individualities,
> But like each other even as those who love.
> Then comes the statelier Eden back to man:
> Then reigns the world's great bridals, chaste
>     and calm:
> There springs the crowning race of humankind.

*The Princess* shows Tennyson addressing himself to a problem that we Americans in the final quarter of the 20th century still have not been fully able to resolve. Confronting Tennyson's views, whether or not we concur with them, helps us to clarify our own.

We may say that Tennyson was the first English poet forthrightly and convincingly to adapt modern science to poetry. Yet the discoveries of modern science constantly raised the possibility of a mechanistic universe, devoid of a loving or purposeful God concerned for man. Hence, the poet's conception of the attributes of Nature and of the relationship of Man, Nature, and God is central to a criticism of life and to answering the question "how to live?" *In Memoriam* reflects Tennyson's willingness to face the implications of geology and developmental biology squarely:

> Are God and Nature then at strife,
> That Nature lends such evil dreams?
> So careful of the type she seems,
> So careless of the single life.
> . . . . . . . . . . . . . . . . . . . . . . . . . . . .
> 'So careful of the type?' but no.
> From scarped cliff and quarried stone
> She cries, 'A thousand types are gone:
> I care for nothing, all shall go.
>
> 'Though makest thine appeal to me:
> I bring to life, I bring to death:

> The spirit does but mean the breath:
> I know no more.' And he, shall he,
>
> Man, her last work, who seemed so fair,
> Such splendid purpose in his eyes,
> Who rolled the psalm to wintry skies,
> Who built him fanes of fruitless prayer,
>
> Who trusted God was love indeed
> And love Creation's final law—
> Though Nature, red in tooth and claw
> With ravine, shrieked against his creed—
>
> Who loved, who suffered countless ills,
> Who battled for the True, the Just,
> Be blown about the desert dust,
> Or sealed within the iron hills?
> . . . . . . . . . . . . . . . . . . . . . . . . . . . .
> O life as futile, then, as frail!
> O for thy voice to soothe and bless!
> What hope for answer, or redress?
> Behind the veil, behind the veil.

For Wordsworth, and for a number of Tennyson's other predecessors, Nature had been a symbol of permanence, soothing man's sense of evanescence. Tennyson accepts the evidence of the fossils, the flux of the earth's surface over eons of time, and the evolution of Nature:

> There rolls the deep where grew the tree.
> O earth, what changes thou hast seen!
> There where the long street roars, hath been
> The stillness of the central sea.
>
> The hills are shadows, and they flow
> From form to form, and nothing stands;
> They melt like mist, the solid lands,
> Like clouds they shape themselves and go.
>
> But in my spirit I will dwell,
> And dream my dream, and hold it true; . . .

Tennyson's dream lay in the enduring spirit. The heart of man, Tennyson asserts, finds God, however we describe the deity—"He, They, One, All, within, without; / The Power in darkness whom we guess,"—not in the observations or facts of science nor in the rational propositions of philosophy, but through intuitive experience and feeling. As a consequence, *In*

*Memoriam* presents God as both transcendent and immanent; God and Nature, properly understood, are not at strife but one; and out of darkness come "the hands / That reach through Nature, molding men."

## V

As Tennyson aged and the century waned, his vision of mankind darkened. This somber view infuses his most ambitious undertaking, the *Idylls of the King*, which, after some 50 years of shaping, he completed in 1885, when he was 76 years old. This *magnum opus* in twelve books, corresponding to the twelve parts of a traditional epic, derives its subject matter from the legends of King Arthur and has sometimes been dismissed as little more than a medieval charade. Actually, it represents Tennyson's most penetrating poetic analysis of the life of his time and depicts the disintegration of an ideal society through materialism, sensuality, hypocrisy, falsehood, and distrust. In the words of Jerome H. Buckley:

> Could Arthur's kingdom remain true to its first principles, could it rise in time of crisis to what Arnold Toynbee would call the moral challenge, it might learn to control its successes, and turn to social good its manifold selfish energies. But increasingly committed as it is to the values of expediency, sensuality, and self-interest, it must face its certain doom.

> In final effect, then, the *Idylls*, which traces the rise of a purposeful order and the gradual catastrophic betrayal of its sustaining idealism, stands as an oblique warning, if not a direct ultimatum, to 19th-century England.

The *Idylls of the King*, if not a direct ultimatum to 20th-century America, is as much a warning to us as it was for Victorian England. It is a fable for our time. Earlier in this century, it was fashionable to deplore the *Idylls*; now the poem is receiving extensive attention as meeting elevated canons of literary and aesthetic criticism and providing a remarkable exegesis of aspects of contemporary life. In the days of Watergate, Lockheed International bribes, Fanne Foxe and Wilbur Mills, Elizabeth Ray and Wayne Hays, even Merlin's fall to the enticements of Vivien has a curiously current ring.

Finally, I conceive of Tennyson as a poet for our time because of the hope that he offers for the future. Few poets have seen so fully the complexity, contradictions, and exacting demands that face us in resolving the question "how to live?" As befits a poet for our time, he can be, to use the words that he applies to Virgil, "majestic" in his "sadness at the doubtful doom of humankind." But, despite uncertainty about the destiny of the human race, he never ceases to remind us, as he says in *In Memoriam,* of the "mighty hopes that make us men." By illuminating the ambiguities, ironies, and paradoxes by which we must exist, Tennyson forces us to examine the opposing and often dehumanizing values of our time. He makes us come to grips with what each one of us ultimately believes about self and the nature of the universe. He insists upon the spiritual as the true reality and upon the validity of the unseen. Yet he would not have us abandon the physical world or the battle of life in an attempt to reach the spiritual by a short-cut. He asserts the necessity of each individual's fulfilling his responsibility for the development of others as well as of himself.

Life for Tennyson is a process, and the human race, as in his late poem, "The Making of Man," has yet to undergo millenia of evolution before the final pronouncement, "It is finished. Man is made." But exercise of will, struggle, and suffering, Tennyson believed, can lead to ethical as well as physical evolution, to an eventual purification of the race, and to what he called that "one far-off divine event to which the whole creation moves." That apotheosis is not inevitable, and it depends upon man's continuing moral effort and heightened ethical consciousness. Tennyson evokes the timeless and modern feeling of inadequacy of the here and now and expresses the persistent desire for something fuller, richer, and more satisfying than life presently affords. Yet his view of human dignity, of spiritual integrity, and of the creative power in the universe, encourages us to say of man, with William Faulkner, "he will prevail."

# The Nineteen Eighties

# MOLLY INGLE MICHIE

# A Splendid Day

[ SUMMER 1980 ]

*One must wait until the sunset to see how splendid
the day has been.*
—Anon.

THE SURGEON did not pussyfoot around about the likelihood of my dying. He said that half the people with my disease were alive one year after diagnosis. Only three out of a hundred were alive five years later. The night I found out the diagnosis, I scribbled down a list of dreaded tasks that I would never have to do again—

(1) give large dinner parties
(2) clean the oven
(3) scrub floors
(4) wash delicate things by hand
(5) remove stains.

The second thing that I did was to get a calendar and try to figure out a convenient time for me to die.

Then I made a list of people who are already dead, people I would enjoy seeing. I drew it up like a list for a cocktail party.

Until my surgeon told me that I was dying, I never cared much for euphemisms. I preferred the word "dying," for instance, to "passing on" or "going to sleep in the Lord." Now, however, I've decided that dying is a word that absolutely requires a euphemism if you're about to do it.

People recoil if I tell them that I'm about to die. They (and I) feel better if I say I'm about to "kick the bucket" or to "check out" or to "bow out." It's not the metaphorical humor of these euphemisms that makes them more acceptable socially. It's rather, I think, that they describe a familiar scene. All of us at some time have kicked a bucket or checked out or bowed out. But none of us has ever died. Moreover, kicking the bucket and checking out and bowing out are positive actions that we have taken cheerfully and vigorously *at a time that suited us.*

Things to be glad about while dying of cancer:

(1) I don't have to worry about getting cancer anymore. (I always expected to get cancer of the foot because of the X-ray machines that we played with in shoe stores when I was a little girl.)
(2) I had a wonderful trip to Jamaica.
(3) I don't have to worry about gray hair. I don't have to worry about rosacea.

There are only two REAL benefits.

(1) I found out that people love me who I would never have guessed loved me. I would have died without knowing.
(2) I won't have to learn the metric system.

Having cancer is, as it happened in my case, a pain in the lung—a particularly unjust location for my cancer since I have never smoked a cigarette in my life. My parents, also nonsmokers, reared me in Winston-Salem, North Carolina, the tobacco capital of the world. Like many people in Winston-Salem, my parents owned some stock in Reynolds Tobacco Company.

When my lung malignancy was first diagnosed, I began to wonder why I had been afflicted with this particular malignancy by Whoever's In Charge of Distributing Cancer, hereinafter referred to as WICODCA. I've never believed that the Lord is in charge of that sort of thing. I decided that WICODCA, having failed to ruin the cigarette industry by giving smokers cancer of the lung, decided to afflict the children of stockholders. I had visions of a surgeon-general's warning, printed on the bottom of tobacco company stock certificates: "The Surgeon General of the United States has determined that owning stock in cigarette companies is a danger to the health of your children."

WICODCA is housed in an inconspicuous brick building near McLean, Virginia, jointly financed by a grant from HEW, NIH, and ACS. No one works there except technicians who keep the computers working properly and secretaries who mail out computer print-out sheets when they are requested. No one knows who feeds the information into the computer—it appears in the night. On the night of Oct. 11, 1978, my name was fed into the computer:

> Molly Ingle Michie 243-54-7152
> October 4, 1932, female, multipara,
> Caucasian, housewife,
> Charlottesville, Virginia
> Broncho-alveolar cell carcinoma
> CAUSE UNKNOWN

(The cause is often speculated upon, with other patients; for examples, "heavy smoker for 18 years" or "worked with asbestos" or "mother took DES while carrying this child," etc.)

HEW, NIH, and ACS obviously are not pleased with having the source of the information a mystery. They have at various times considered canceling funding of the operation because of this peculiarity. But the information is extremely valuable, up-to-date, and accurate. Assembling the data from hospitals around the country would be more time-consuming and expensive. They have conducted studies for accuracy. When information coming directly from WICODCA is compared to information coming from hospitals, it has been found that the hospital information contains many errors. Also the follow-up on WICODCA is immediate and accurate. In the night, death notices and five-year "cures" are fed in. Responses of various patients to various treatments are also available.

A circle of love formed itself around my bed there in the hospital. No one withdrew or said the wrong thing. Their sorrow was obvious; their strength was apparent and available without my asking. Nothing that I would need—emotionally, physically—would be denied to me.

The hospital staff was uncannily tactful. They cared that I hurt, and they were eager to help. A chaplain came in the next morning. She had done her homework. She knew I was a Unitarian and that she couldn't assume that I would welcome her. She did a beautiful job. She asked open-ended questions that really required no responses from me—just sort of puzzlements about tragedies and sorrows. She let me know subtly that she thought there were some comforting answers and that she would share those answers any time I called. Then she left—a perfect job, under very difficult circumstances.

I had read Elisabeth Kubler-Ross's classic *Death and Dying* during the summer—certainly not in anticipation of my own death but because so many of my relatives are 70 and 80 and obviously concerned with the prospect of dying. As I read the book, however, I did think of myself and what my reactions would be if I learned I had a terminal illness. Kubler-Ross describes five phases: denial, anger, bargaining, depression, acceptance. I decided that I would probably skip the first three phases and plunge headlong into a deep depression. The denial and anger and bargaining stages seemed too irrational for a cool-headed lady like me. Facts are facts, malignant cells are malignant. "Why me?" is so obviously answered by "Why *not* me?" Getting mad at God seemed so childish.

But anger came in a strange free floating form. There *must* be someone to blame, someone who robbed me of precious time—the very prime of my life. My anger, free floating, gradually took an animal form. A tiny albino falcon appeared over the door of my hospital room, a vicious fellow with pink eyes and long pink talons. I named him A. F., which stood for Albino Falcon and for Anger, Free Floating. He was ready to attack anyone who abused me in any way—callous nurses, bearers of inedible meals, inconsiderate visitors, or cleaning personnel who might wake me from a nap.

He rode on the back of my wheelchair or stretcher when I was transported for tests or examinations, looking for callousness or carelessness in any form. For four days no one was callous or careless. A. F. was getting frantic and larger. He began flapping wildly around the room. Clearly he would have to attack an innocent, if a proper villain could not be found soon.

Monday morning the nurse announced that at 1:30 that afternoon I had an appointment at radiation oncology where I would discuss a proposed course of radiation therapy. A. F. and I were jubilant—a perfect villain! A. F. and I settled down, he to sharpen his talons and I to ponder my hatred of radiation and all doctors and technicians who practiced it.

When I graduated from Hollins College in June 1954, I was given by my parents a glorious graduation present, summer school at Oxford University. Tom happened to attend that summer session also. We rode up from London on the same train, met briefly in the station, and caught the same ride to our dorm at St. Hilda's College. By the time the session was over, we were fairly sure that we were in love. We decided, however, not to make any long-term commitments until we had seen each other on home turf. The romantic spires of Oxford might have made anybody seem a delightful prospective spouse. But Tom looked even better to me surrounded by friends on the grounds of the University of Virginia, and by his attractive relatives at his father's home in Charlottesville, than he had punting down the Cherwell at Oxford. Tom liked my parents and friends in Winston-Salem, too. We decided definitely to marry.

He was starting his second year at the University of Virginia law school, and I was looking forward to my first job as an assistant librarian at Bowman Gray Medical School in Winston-Salem. One of my duties was to gather articles and books for doctors who were preparing papers for medical journals. Dr. Richard L. Masland, professor of neurology, asked me one day for a stack of articles on the possible causes of Down's syndrome. Because of my impending marriage and my enthusiasm for many healthy babies, I was fascinated in a horrible sort of way by the articles I gathered.

Some of them speculated that the cause was a particular disaster that occurred to the mother during the eighth week of pregnancy—perhaps an operation involving anesthesia or a sudden blood loss or the mother's being somehow deprived of oxygen by smoke inhalation or strangling on a piece of food. One article said that medical x-rays to the abdomen of pregnant women might be the cause of several birth defects—blood disorders and Down's syndrome among them. During slow times in the library, I actually started looking up articles about the detrimental effects of radiation and deciding that neither I nor Tom nor any of our children would ever be x-rayed. I developed a full-blown, somewhat irrational phobia about x-rays.

The Navy hospital where I received prenatal care for our first child, Tommy, required a chest x-ray of each mother. I had mine taken with tears running down my cheeks. After the children were born, the perversity of nature and the Fates manifested itself. I was the only mother on the block with an enormous x-ray phobia, yet I was the only mother on the block whose children constantly needed x-rays.

Our first three boys were born in 1957, 1958, and 1959 (on our fourth anniversary we had three children). I had a hard time coping with them all. They were constantly closing each other's fingers in doors and tripping over toys and having possible concussions. Our second son, John, was born with one foot slightly out of position. Our third son, Ned, had unusual torsion in his thighs (a result of sleeping only on his stomach, as it turned out, but an indication to his pediatrician that there might be a congenital hip dislocation). At two, Ned had a positive T.B. test that required many chest x-rays through the years.

George, our fourth son, born in 1964, had a number of accidents requiring x-rays. When he hurt his elbow in gym class, the technician x-rayed his right elbow from three different angles. The doctors still couldn't tell if there was a break or a peculiarity in his bone structure, so he asked for an x-ray of the *left* elbow in order to compare. I was constantly being presented with a terrible choice—an x-ray or a deformed elbow. I always had to choose the x-ray. My hatred of x-ray machines and personnel grew. The personnel found me terribly amusing or terribly annoying. I became increasingly paranoid. Would the hostile technician leave the machine on just a little longer than necessary to get even with a troublesome parent?

I discovered a way to avoid a few routine x-rays. John, like Tommy, was born while Tom was in the Navy, and the hospital again required a chest x-ray of me. I noticed that the doctors wrote "negative" by "chest x-ray" on my chart. Then he wrote out an order form and handed it to me. I just tore up the form. So, we always did that on job applications and college health forms, too. Most camps and colleges require only T.B. skin tests now, anyway, but Vanderbilt's form required an x-ray. On May 9, 1975, Tommy's doctor examined him and wrote May 9, 1975, as date of most recent negative chest x-ray. He handed Tom the x-ray order form, and Tommy left.

*Rip!*

James Thurber's grandmother always thought that electricity was leaking out of outlets, and I had that same feeling about radiation seeping out of open x-ray room doors. I always hurried past radiation room doors—holding my breath and hugging the far wall of the corridor. Now I was being wheeled into the radiation room itself. A. F. and I were in a state of wild tension.

Unfortunately, the first person we met was NOT a possible target. She was one of the most beautiful women I've ever seen—a Dutch woman, a person of such warmth and sympathy that A. F. immediately flapped off in disgust. Her job, she said, was to make things go smoothly for the patient. She was available for questions or to make contact with the radio-therapist, to adjust medications, to hear complaints—anything I needed I should feel free to ask her. She pushed me into an examining room, chatting, smiling, discovering mutual friends. When I was draped and ready to see the doctor, she left. A. F. returned immediately, perching on a cabinet top.

Into the room came a small, oriental man. A. F. attacked immediately, sinking his pink talons into Dr. Meng L. Lim's yellow neck. World War II lasted from my ninth to my 13th year. Every Saturday afternoon during that time I went with my friends to war movies. We ate popcorn and watched Japs torture heroic American pilots. I developed a hatred and fear of the Japanese. Here was Dr. Lim—Japanese and a radio-therapist. Already he was talking about how many rads he would need to give me to stop the cancer's growth. Already his fingers were looking for evidence of new growth. With his yellow, torturer's mind, I knew he was *hoping* to find new growth.

I began asking him questions to which I probably did not really want to know the answers. I had refrained from asking them of my surgeon, Ivan Crosby, partly because I didn't want to know and partly because I like him so much and because he obviously hated to give me bad news. I asked him once during the weekend if my kind of cancer was possibly—hopefully—finicky, liking to eat only pleura exclusively. He shook his head sadly and said, "It's not very finicky. It likes other things, too." I did not ask Ivan *which* other things.

I did ask Dr. Lim immediately. He would enjoy giving me bad news. "If the cancer spreads," he said, "it will most likely go to your liver or to your brain." He told me to come back in one week to be marked for radiation treatments on the linear accelerator. An orderly came to wheel me back to my room.

A. F. let go of Dr. Lim's neck and settled himself on the back of the wheelchair, licking his talons, obviously calmer than before. I felt calmer, too. Some of my anger had found a target. As we were wheeled down the long hall of the radiation oncology department, I began to notice other defects that could absorb some of my anger. The Dutch therapist waved a cheerful goodbye. She was going to make things difficult for A. F. and me, but we would prevail by ignoring her.

Tom's sister, Emily, is a pretty, vivacious woman seven years younger than he, a talented teacher, mother of three delightful children. She has been married for 20 years to John Gennari. They met while she was at Vassar and he was at Yale and married the year they graduated. She worked in the Yale library while he was in medical school and then began producing a child every two years, while he did his residency and internship here in Charlottesville at U.Va. Medical School. John is handsome, witty, brilliant, and incredibly patient. He's the only doctor in our immediate family, and we call him for advice, confirmation of diagnoses, comfort. He is a nephrologist, now at the University of Vermont in Burlington, but at the time of my operation he was finishing his tenth year of research at Tuft's New England Medical Center. John's willingness to help us enabled us never to seek a second opinion or a fancier medical center. When Dr. Lim prescribed 2000 rads to the full right lung and 2000 to a smaller area where they thought the tumor originated, we called John, who said he would ask the head of his radiotherapy department about the dosage, the machines, and the doctors in that department at the University of Virginia. He called the next night to say that his department head said that she did not know Dr. Lim, but that Dr. William C. Constable, the director of radiation oncology, was internationally known. She said that U.Va. had terrific equipment and that we should do whatever Dr. Constable said.

Tom called Dr. Constable, who agreed to see us that very day. He's a Scot, with a crisp but kind manner. He seemed slightly bemused by our anxiety but was thoroughly courteous and unhurried. He said that all decisions about dosages are discussed by the entire department, that he personally had gone over my x-rays and treatment recommendations with Dr. Lim, and that the recommendation for dosage and treatment would be the same at any major medical center in the world.

I liked him immediately. He could have been a flight surgeon with the RAF in my war movies. Better still, he had on his bulletin board a copy of Murphy's Law. I liked being treated by someone who realized that "anything that can go wrong, will."

I soon found out for myself that the department was impeccably run, that Dr. Lim is not Japanese but Chinese, and that he is a warm, thorough, helpful doctor, with a good sense of humor and a real concern for his patients. A. F. and I, however, retained our hostility toward him while we looked around for other more suitable targets. A. F. always taloned him on sight.

Mark-up on Monday was a nightmare for me. I lay on a hard table, in an incredibly uncomfortable position for someone who had just had a thoracotomy, while pretty, cheerful technicians x-rayed me repeatedly and drew on me with purple magic markers. They would decide that my spine was not exactly straight, move me ever so slightly, and x-ray again. I begged for lead blankets to cover my vulnerable right lung and liver, but they giggled and said there were no lead blankets in radiation oncology. "After all," said one technician, "you are scheduled for 4000 rads. From these little x-rays you get only a few millirads." A. F. clawed her lovely cheeks.

Finally I was marked to their satisfaction, told not to remove the purple marks until the ten treatments were over, and released. By this time, all four of the girls had talon scratches on their cheeks. *Marked*—what a horrible word! How appropriate for such a horrible word to be chosen for use in such a horrible place. A marked man means a doomed man. Why not say I had been decorated with a purple pen—embellished—drawn upon? But *marked*? Marked is a word in need of a euphemism.

Treatments began the next day. The linear accelerator looks like a machine from *Star Wars*. I got on its one outstretched arm, my back resting on an open plastic grid. When I was lying comfortably, the arm would move under the machine itself. Technicians would line up my marks with a pattern on the machine above. Computer lights would flash. The technicians would leave the room. A high pitched sound would begin and last for about 15 seconds. The technicians would return, punch a button, the whole machine would revolve 180 degrees, and I would be zapped through the back for 15 seconds. Then the arm would swing me out again and I would dismount. The technicians were all young and beautiful, cheerful and friendly. They chatted with me and with each other. I was convinced that they chatted and drank coffee while they zapped me, and that whether I was zapped for 15 seconds or 25 depended on the whim of three silly 19-year-olds. A. F. got them all.

The next day Dr. Constable himself came in the treatment room to check the set-up. He waited for me outside. Then he showed me how the machine's timing was locked into a computer—how warning bells would ring if anything started to go wrong. How a computer printout recorded every rad and every second. Murphy's Law could not apply to this machine. Nothing could go wrong. A. F. gave him one good scratch for not telling me that the day before.

## A SPLENDID DAY

The next week I met another lovely chaplain. She, like the first one, did not intrude on my privacy in any way. She let me know that she was available for my spiritual comfort and then she talked amicably about many interesting things and said that she was trying to get the patients' perspective on radiation treatments, so that she could be helpful if they were distressed by some aspect of the procedure. She left me then to talk to another patient.

When later I was in position on the linear accelerator arm, this chaplain appeared. I was somewhat startled, since I was nude to the waist and unaccustomed to being visited by clergy while unattired. When my marks and their pattern were lined up to their satisfaction the technicians left. The chaplain stayed behind a moment, patted me on the arm comfortingly and said, "Remember, we're with you all the way." Then she left.

Tears of anger streamed down my cheeks, "You're not with me," I wanted to scream. "If you've got any sense, you and all those pretty technicians are behind thick lead shields. There's no one in here being sizzled but me." A. F. shredded *her* into bite-sized pieces.

I found one more object to vent my anger on in that department—a squawk box in its reception area. When a patient enters the corridor of the radio oncology department, there is a comfortable-looking waiting room with magazines, pictures, aquariums, etc. on the right. On the left is just a row of chairs lined up against the corridor wall. All of the patients sit in the lined up chairs waiting to hear their names called over the squawk box. The volume is turned very low and there is a lot a of static, so no one talks to anyone else for fear of not hearing his name called. If you do miss your name, a friendly lady at a desk nearby will usually say, "Mrs. Michie, I think they called you back." I never got to know another patient, even though I saw some of them ten or 20 times. We all sat silently, lined up, listening for our names.

Even though I knew that the lovely Dutch therapist was waiting to help, eager to help, I never told her or Dr. Constable or Dr. Lim my complaints. I didn't tell them because I wanted some targets for my free floating anger. I know from experience that the old poem is true:

> "I told my anger to my friend
> And telling made my anger end.
> I held my anger from my foe
> And holding made my anger grow."

A. F. ripped that squawk box off the wall on our last visit to the beautifully run radiotherapy department. It was a department full of talented, dedicated people who had given me months full of happy hours, months that I could not have expected from any other course of treatment.

Ninety-nine percent of the people in the world, including me, want to die when they're very old, and, I imagine, a similar percentage would choose to die suddenly. I've had to search for satisfactions to be found in dying in middle age—in the prime of life. But satisfactions in dying slowly have been obvious and not hard to find:

I've had time, with no demands, to put things in order and to gain perspective.

I've never been much of a nature lover, but now that I'm seeing it for the last time I am appreciating it. I've had time to watch the woods fill up with snow. I watched spring come twice, first here and then again at Bucknell in Pennsylvania during parents weekend. It was gorgeous.

I've had time to savor the good foods of summer—watermelon, cantaloupe, blueberries, peaches, fresh asparagus, corn on the cob.

I've had time to view the boys anxiously but calmly, and to see that they are terrific: mature, confident, and capable. My boys talked to me about interesting philosophical questions. I'm sure we would not have talked like that except for my illness. I might have lived to 90 and never have known them so well.

I've had time to find out that many people love me—people who I would never have guessed love me.

These satisfactions are not available to some who die slowly. Sometimes the disease is too painful, too disfiguring and distressing, too controlling of body functions to give the victim time for the pleasures I've listed. Sometimes the family and friends cannot be supportive because of their own fears and conflicts or because of economic pressures or other circumstances—small children to care for, for example.

I have been fortunate on both counts. I have a relatively painless lung cancer so that my time is not consumed in struggling with discomfort or unpleasant treatments.

My family and friends are incredibly supportive—freeing me from demands and chores, letting me talk and helping me put my thoughts and things in order—an enormous satisfaction—a summing up.

...

*In the nine months between the diagnosis of her disease and her death, Molly Michie was never at a loss for composure, cheer, or courage. And she never went into depression. She died at 2 P.M. on Monday, July 2, 1979, exactly 25 years from the day she first met Tom at the train station in Oxford.*

MILDRED RAYNOLDS TRIVERS

# The Berlin Wall: A Memoir

[ AUTUMN 1981 ]

BERLIN was a divided city when we arrived in 1957. When we left in 1962, Berlin had become two cities side by side with a Wall in the middle.

"This is a city," shortly after arrival I wrote in my journal, "that has to be taken apart and then put back together again. Berlin is not even one city, it is two cities, each with its separate government, separate currency, separate telephone systems, separate transportation systems. And yet the people who ride the big yellow double decker busses in West Berlin are the same people who ride the old broken down busses of the People's Own Transportation Company in East Berlin. They share the same language, the same culture, the same church and, until recently, the same history. They have known together Berlin's greatness when it was the capital of a world empire and they have suffered together the Allied bombing and the destruction and capture of the great city in the final days of Hitler's War. They are Berliners, all, sharing a common pride in the past and sharing, each in its own way, in the suffering of a divided and unhappy present."

Postcards of the Brandenburger Gate used to show the mighty monument, under which the Prussian kings had ridden in triumph, restored after the war, its red sandstone columns rising against a blue sky, a red flag flying from its pediment and, in the foreground, a sign reading in German and in English, "Attention! In 70 meters you will be leaving the American sector of Berlin." Blue uniformed members of the West Berlin police stand on one side, green uniformed and black helmeted members of the People's Police, or Vopos, on the other side.

After Aug. 13, 1961, the scene at the Brandenburger Gate repeats itself: the same red flag, the same police, but where there was once a broad avenue leading through the Gate there is now a thick wall of cement blocks which separates the one half of the city from the other. And the Wall continues to the north and to the south through the central and populated area, with barbed wire thereafter, so that the whole city of East Berlin has been effectively sealed off from West Berlin. This is the Wall of Shame, as it is called in West Berlin, Krushchev's "solution" to the "Berlin Problem." Because he did not dare end, in the final analysis, the Four Power status of

Berlin, as he had threatened in November 1958, he allowed the East Germans in August of '61 to build a Wall around their part of Berlin. By erecting the Wall the East Germans were able to prevent the mounting flood of refugees from East Germany and at the same time help stabilize the East Germany economy.

When we first arrived, it was an easy matter to roll down the broad East-West boulevard through the Brandenburger Gate to Unter den Linden, Berlin's former grand thoroughfare. There were few guards at the sector border, and they waved on our Mercury with its occupation army license plates without any hesitation. But as the political pressure increased, so did the number of guards; and as the East Germans were given more and more ostensible authority by the Russians, whose purpose it suited to stay in the background, the manner of the guards became more and more belligerent. Now they stepped forward as if to challenge your entry and, if they thought they could get away with it, they signaled you to halt. Their favorite target was a small Volkswagen driven by two American school teachers newly arrived from the States and not too sure of their rights as members of the occupation forces. They were waved to a halt peremptorily and made to show their passports, although the guards knew and the school teachers knew that this was forbidden. Not to show your passport was one of the ways of keeping the city open. As long as Berlin was occupied by the Four Powers, the East German Vopos had no authority whatsoever to stop an American car and demand to see the passport. Whenever they did, and it was reported to Army headquarters, a protest was immediately sent to the Russians.

I became an actor in this border drama in the fall of 1960 when friends from Washington, a member of President Eisenhower's staff and his wife, came to visit us in Berlin. We had invited the commanding general, the United States minister, and other officials for lunch at noon. My friend and I decided to spend the morning sightseeing in East Berlin, allowing ourselves enough time to get dressed before our guests arrived. I wanted to show her ruins of the old palaces that had once given Berlin its elegance and the impressive hulk of a ruin that had once been the famed German Cathedral, as well as show her Marx-Engels Square where the castle of the Hohenzollerns for hundreds of years had dominated the city, until the Russians removed it stone by stone. The guards at the Brandenburger Gate, as we drove through, looked for one fleeting moment as if they might signal us to halt, but I thought nothing of it. No matter how often I drove to East Berlin there was always a certain underlying tension: the few people I met walking the streets were not friendly; I would not have wanted to turn to one of those impassive faces for help, and if I did ever ask for directions, they were always given hurriedly, as if the person asked might get into trouble by answering. And since that day when a beardless boy in uniform signaled me to pull over to the side in Alexander Square, where I was the only car to be seen, and bawled me out in German for driving too slowly, I was never sure what traffic regulation I might unwittingly be breaking. Yet I went regularly to East Berlin, because it represented the old historic Berlin and also, I may as well confess it, because I felt my presence in some obscure way was helping keep the city open.

But East Berlin, interesting as it was, was profoundly depressing: poor, neglected, row on row of bombed buildings that had neither been removed nor restored, and everywhere that gray, that sad anonymous look with which socialism manages to cover over what may once have had charm. So after an hour of sight-seeing, my friend and I drove with a sense of relief west down Unter den Linden, glad to be leaving East Berlin behind. At the Brandenburger Gate the guards did not wave us on, not even grudgingly; instead they waved us to a halt. I pretended not to get the signal, but the young Vopo who stepped out in front of the car forced me to stop. He asked for my passport in German. I acted as if I didn't understand. He kept repeating "Pass! Pass!" and I kept shaking my head. He signaled me to get out of the car and follow him into the guard house, and as we walked along he looked down at me, shook his head threateningly, saying "No pass! That's bad, very bad! Did you leave it in the school room?" And he shook his head at the thought of the consequences. But as he was young and blond and the same age as our oldest son back in the States, I felt more sympathy than the fear he was trying to instill. In the guard house I was told to sit down and wait for his superior, a dark-haired young man in his middle twenties. I explained in English, when he came, that I was a member of the occupying forces, as my license plate indicated, and that I did not need to show my pass. He listened carefully, spoke a few words to my blond guard, and motioned me to go. I was accompanied back to the car where my friend still sat, quietly waiting, and we drove through the Brandenburger Gate and back to West Berlin in time to change for lunch.

The end of the story was amusing. When the luncheon guests were told about the incident, it was decided that a protest should be lodged immediately with the Russians and that the political adviser, who also happened to be the host, should drive in an official car to Karlshorst, the Russian headquarters, that afternoon to see his counterpart, Colonel Odintsov. When the blue official car approached the guards at a crossing near Karlshorst, it was halted; the driver was instructed to turn back and approach East Berlin by Friederichstrasse, where Checkpoint Charley is now located; there the car was waved through. Colonel Odintsov received two protests instead of one and assured the American diplomat that the East Germans had exceeded their orders and that such incidents would not be repeated, an assurance that was always given and would continue to be given so long as the Russians chose to honor in word the Four Power agreement.

The transformation of the sector line to a boundary had been a gradual one. In the beginning—or rather at the end, if one is speaking of Nazi Germany—the Russians occupied the whole city by virtue of its capture. Their troops had encircled the city, their artillery had pounded the buildings that the Allied bombing had still left standing, and their fire gutted them; they also took possession of the Reichschancellery and confirmed that Hitler was dead. A colleague who entered Berlin as a member of a U.S. Army liaison group in the early days of its capture described how he had gone under orders to the Reichschancellery to photograph the grave of Hitler and Eva Braun, but how, when he returned on orders the following day barbed wire barred his progress and he had been commanded to leave at once. For purposes of their own the Russians had decided to conceal what evidence they had found, even from their allies. This was the first step, our friend claimed, in the implementation of a policy that shut out the Allies more and more from any cooperation in administering the occupied city. When the armed forces of the Allies arrived and the division of the city into four separate sectors was completed, the Russians set about running their sector according to their ideas. They shipped everything of value back to Russia (that is when the streetcar tracks were removed), they set up their own Communist city government, they printed their own currency, they replaced private businesses and shops with state-owned ones, and they limited communication with the other three occupied sectors so as to be able to control better their own. Streets that connected the Russian sector with the French or British or American sectors were blocked off, not completely as happened later with the Wall, but sufficiently so that only pedestrians could go back and forth. At main thoroughfares which remained open, guards were stationed to check passports. And the telephone cables between East Berlin and West Berlin were cut.

The Allied machinery that had been set up for the Four Power occupation of Berlin still creaked along, the Kommandatura functioning like an old mill where the waters still turn the huge millstones but where no one brings any wheat to be ground into flour. Or seldom. The French and British and Americans still invited Soviet officers to their receptions but only a chosen few came. In return the Allies and the foreign diplomats were invited to East Berlin to see Russian films. Once—it was in February 1961—we had the pleasure of entertaining in our home for lunch my husband's counterpart, the Soviet political adviser and his wife, Mrs. Odintsov. I spent the morning in the kitchen preparing the meal the maid was to serve: soup, because it was unthinkable to begin a meal in that cold climate without soup, chicken from our commissary, corn pudding for old time's sake, and I don't know what else, except that we surely had apple pie a la mode for dessert. My aim was to show off how well we ate in America but at the same time to avoid capitalist ostentation. I never knew whether I succeeded. Since Mrs. Odintsov, a plain round-faced woman, spoke no English nor French nor German and I no Russian, we contented ourselves with smiling at one another while our husbands talked on various non-political subjects. The luncheon had been set up expressly to facilitate communication between the two political advisers; the situation was becoming increasingly hazardous and every effort was being made by our people to avoid a confrontation. The attempt to better relations missed fire, however, as far as the political advisers were concerned; exactly three weeks after the luncheon, Colonel Odintsov was abruptly transferred to Central Asia and left without paying the customary courtesy calls to colleagues.

Why did he leave? No one knew. Perhaps Moscow disapproved of a Red Army officer lunching alone with his American counterpart. The colonel had asked if he should bring his translator with him, a woman presumed to be a KGB informer but had been dissuaded. "You speak German," my husband had said, "my wife and I speak German. You can translate for your wife. Why do we need a translator?" Maybe the Russian translator had complained to the KGB? At any rate, at the time the Wall was erected Colonel Odintsov had not been replaced and a major was serving as acting political adviser.

Some weeks after Colonel Odintsov left, the woman translator left too, but in her case there was no mystery about her departure. Her husband was a captain at the Berlin Air Safety Center, probably the only Four Power agency which still functioned on a regular basis. When, at a spring party where vodka and whiskey flowed freely, it was discovered that the captain and the wife of a British sergeant were missing from the fun, a search party with flashlights was organized up and down the dimly lit corridors and through the empty rooms of the Old Ministry of Justice building. They were found in a loving embrace at one end of the building, and as a result the Russian captain and his translator wife and the British sergeant and his plump wife were returned home at once to their respective countries.

We had our own version of the love that laughs at sector borders among our military, but so effectively was the story hushed up that we only learned of the incident while attending a diplomatic luncheon in the French sector. My husband and I were surprised at the Gallic laughter and the rapid fire witticisms that ran from one end of the table to the other at the mention of the name of a certain Russian diplomat. I, who was always taking French lessons at whatever post we served in order to speak the language better, found that I knew more French than I had suspected when the subject was so interesting. By the second course I had pieced together the romance, and by the time dessert was served I not only knew what had happened but I understood for the first time why a military family, neighbors of ours, had suddenly and for no apparent reason, been ordered back to the States before their tour of duty had been completed.

The French added a gaiety to Berlin that the heavy Hohenzollern city lacked. Unfortunately for us, however, their sector was far from ours, and their wives stayed in Berlin as little as possible. "Monotonous," they called the city, "boring." As for East Berlin, they labeled it a dead city. "No movement, the streets are empty, it's like the plague." We had closer relations with our British colleagues; we played tennis with them at the British Club and drank tea beside the swimming pool, celebrated the queen's birthday as their guests, and entertained one another often at dinner parties.

I could understand the reluctance of the French to remain in Berlin. "I like Berlin but find it very depressing," an entry in my journal for 1959 reads. "What is it that makes me so sad? Is it the gray weather and the rubble-dust sun? Or the gray buildings that have been battered beyond recognition? Or the heavy people, who, like the buildings are no longer intact, each with a story of deprivation and loss?" [. . .]

No matter how firm the Allied policy, no matter how determined they were to maintain the Four Power status of the beleaguered city in the face of every Soviet threat, it was the Berliners themselves who kept the divided city open. They, both East Berliners and West Berliners, refused to accept the reality of the division. In spite of borders and border guards and increasing harassment, in spite of the miles and miles of barbed wire separating West Berlin from the rest of Germany, in spite of the chicanery of the East Germany authorities and the endless regulations designed to keep them apart, they went back and forth as if they were living in one city, not two. Thousands upon thousands came every day to work in the offices and stores of West Berlin and on their day off they thronged the Kudam, Berlin's fashionable center, and we stared at them as we sat in the cafes, their clumsy shoes, their broad Russian trousers, the peasant scarves on the heads of the women and the same shapeless Socialist handbag made of cheap plastic that they all carried. We never realized how many came until they stopped coming. When the Wall was built West Berlin shrank like a woolen sock that has been washed in boiling water. [. . .]

The traffic from West to East was small but constant. The opera in the white and gold Opera House on Unter den Linden was always well attended from West Berlin, including our military who came in full uniform in order to "show the flag"; and the theaters had their regular patrons. The Maria church, Berlin's only remaining 13th-century cathedral, was jammed with visitors from the West whenever the old Bishop Dibelius preached, most of them coming by train in small groups, entering the cathedral as unobtrusively as possible and leaving as quickly as possible when the service was ended. And then there were the countless Berliners, like our cleaning woman, who made it a practice to visit their relatives regularly, smuggling "goodies" past the border guards—oranges, real coffee, a Western newspaper.

The numbers of those who could visit East Berlin without fear of being detained by the authorities was not large, however. Those who had moved from the Russian sector after the War and taken up residence in West Berlin so as to escape the Russian occupation did not dare risk returning, even for a day. Still less did those dare cross the sector line from West to East who had fled for one reason or another from East Germany into West Berlin. They must have lived in perpetual fear that they would be taken back. [. . .]

The Berliners who went back and forth across the sector borders were no threat to the authorities. It was the influx into Berlin of ever increasing numbers from East Germany which brought about the Wall. They came on visits to East Berlin and then carefully masking their intentions took the subway or elevated or perhaps walked across the border to West Berlin, carrying their belongings on their backs. Before Khrushchev's ultimatum to the Allies in November 1957 their number was manageable; those who did not choose to remain in West Berlin were flown to West Germany. But the more Khrushchev threatened to make the Allies leave Berlin, the more East Germans decided the time had come for them to leave East Germany. The more he declared his intention of ending the Four Power occupation of the city, the more they saw their only chance of escape escaping them. And so they came in ever increasing numbers, farmers, teachers, technicians, whole families of them, young boys, elderly couples, all leaving while the leaving was good. Most of the refugees had obtained permission to visit relatives in East Berlin and then, having reached the big city, they slipped into West Berlin. [. . .]

By August 1961 the number of refugees from East Germany had reached the number of a thousand a day. And more were coming. It was clear to everyone that something would have to be done, for the East German economy could never bear such a strain. "The situation has become very dangerous," I wrote in my journal on August 11th. "Grave faces at the MacDougall's dinner party last night. I sat next to the police president and we talked about the refugee problem all through dinner. 'What will the East Germans do?' I asked him. 'They'll shut up East Berlin so tight that not even a mouse will escape' was his answer. But how? No one knew. H. thinks the East Germans will cordon off East Berlin from East Germany so the refugee stream will be cut off at its source. Colonel P. is afraid the Russians themselves will intervene, perhaps move in one of their divisions. I told the police president it reminded me of 1938 in Europe when Hitler so dominated the political scene that we watched him fascinated as a bird by a snake, knowing he was going to strike but not knowing when or where."

Saturday, August 12th, the children and I began the summer vacation we had been looking forward to for months. Old friends from Unteraegeri in Switzerland had been able to rent for us an apartment in a chalet next door to their home. We would take the French military train out of Berlin, make connections in Baden with an express which would take us to Zurich, and from there we would take a Swiss train to Zug where our friends would meet us. All went according to plan, and after we had unpacked and changed our clothes, we went over to our friend's home for dinner. It was Sunday, August 13th. As I was sipping an aperitif before dinner, Hans, the 30-year-old son of the family, turned to me solemnly and asked what I thought about Berlin? I waved aside his question. "But I've come here to Switzerland to get away from Berlin! You've no idea, how wearing it is," turning to our hostess, "this pattern of crisis that we have in Berlin! We're always having crises, and this last one with the refugee build-up has been especially hard." Hans begged my pardon. "I didn't know. I've been listening to the news all day, and I thought with the Wall—perhaps—but I won't talk about it any more." "Wall? What Wall?" And the story was out. During the night when we were on the train, the East Germans had stretched barbed wire across all the border crossings and placed armed soldiers there to prevent anyone from leaving East Berlin. The subway and the elevated had been halted. Armored cars rolled into the squares and Russian forces surrounded the city. Our people had first learned of the East Germans' move at three in the morning. The British, French, and American commandants were meeting, the mayor had made a speech counseling restraint to the West Berliners who were massed at the Wall, and the East Germans were busy strengthening their lines.

When the children and I returned to Berlin a few weeks later, my husband met us at the station and drove us immediately to the Brandenburger Gate. It was unreal. There were soldiers, real live soldiers with guns in their hands, standing in line before the Gate. Over their heads we could see the barbed wire and the tank obstacles that had been erected as a Wall. Crowds of people stood at the Western end of the Gate, not anywhere as many as there had been the Sunday of the Wall, my husband told us, when the square had been full of angry West Berliners and the authorities had been afraid they might storm across the barbed wire and bring out the Russian tanks that encircled the city. We walked up to the soldiers, being careful not to overstep the border line and I saw that they were young and blond and very real. I understood why the Allies had not moved forward from their sectors to take down the barbed wire that had been erected on the far side of the border line. No one wanted war, certainly not the Berliners who kept saying at every crisis previous to the Wall, "Not war! For God's sake, no war! Not for this city!" And how could war have been avoided so long as soldiers barred the way?

WALTER HARDING

# Walden's Man of Science

[ WINTER 1981 ]

I

WHEN Thoreau in 1853 was asked to join the Association for the Advancement of Science (now the "triple A's," or American Association for the Advancement of Science) our country's most prestigious scientific organization, it took him nine months to even answer their letter, then only to turn them down, and comment privately in his journal, "The fact is I am a mystic, a transcendentalist, and a natural philosopher to boot. Now I think of it, I should have told them at once that I was a transcendentalist. That would have been the shortest way of telling them that they would not understand my explanations."

"Mystic" and "transcendentalist" are not words in great favor with most of the scientific community, either in Thoreau's day or in ours, and so scientists have understandably tended to look rather scoffingly at Henry Thoreau. They have delighted in pointing out that he was not always accurate in his natural history observations; that he regularly confused the wood thrush and the hermit thrush, the black-throated blue warbler and the indigo bunting, the red-breasted and the white-breasted nuthatch; and that the mysterious "night warbler" he sought vainly all his life to identify was quite obviously the common oven bird; that he thought he saw a prairie chicken in the woods of Maine a thousand miles outside its range and yet never spotted the common and spectacular rose-breasted grosbeak in his native Concord until he was 36. He mistook the distinctive hole-drilling of the yellow-bellied sapsucker for the work of the downy woodpecker, and he accepted unquestioningly the mistaken folklore that a bittern produced its weird pumping sound by sucking up gallons of water and belching it forth. That seemingly is not a very good record for a man who liked to think of himself as at least an amateur ornithologist, but when we remember that there were no good field guides to American birds in those days—Thoreau at times even had to resort to British ornithologies to try to identify American birds—it is not so surprisingly bad. In a field such as botany (and Thoreau thought of himself as an amateur botanist too), where the excellent field guides of Asa Gray became available just at the time Thoreau needed them (and Thoreau despite his notorious parsimony ended up with three volumes of Gray in his personal library), he made very few mistakes—in fact the only one I know of is a lifelong confusion of the black and white spruces.

But getting back to the scientists and their complaints about Thoreau, they didn't deny that he could write, but his writing, they insisted, was literature, not science. Whenever he sat down to write, *they* thought, he dipped his pen in Transcendental ink (as Poe said of Hawthorne); and while what came out might be beautiful, one could not trust it scientifically. They loved to cite as a perfect example of this one of the most beautiful similes in Thoreau's *Journal:*

> Ever and anon the lightning filled the damp air with light, like some vast glow-worm in the fields of ether opening its wings.

A lovely, a beautiful, a lyrical simile, one difficult to better in the realms of literature until you stop to realize—as the scientists quickly did—that glowworms have no wings.

But the skepticism was not all on one side. Thoreau was equally questioning of the techniques and accomplishments of the scientists as his comment on the Association for the Advancement of Science implies. When an ornithologist friend complained that Thoreau never shot any birds to study them, Thoreau replied aptly, "If I were to study you, should I shoot you?" When another ornithologist friend started to say to him, "Now, if you hold the bird in your hand...." Thoreau interrupted with, "I'd rather hold the bird in my affections." And when Harvard, Thoreau's alma mater, opened its Lawrence Scientific School in the 1840's, the first major breakthrough for modern science into the traditional classical college curriculum, and Emerson (of all people) boasted that Harvard now "teaches all the *branches* of learning," Thoreau scoffed, "Yes, but none of the *roots.*" Thoreau complained in his *Journal,* "How little I know of that *arbor vitae* [and he could have substituted any species of the flora and fauna of Concord] when I have learned only what science can tell me." He lamented the boasted cool objectivity of the scientists, saying, again in his *Journal,* "I cannot help suspecting that the life of these learned professors has been almost as inhuman and wooden as a rain-gauge or self-registering magnetic machine. They communicate no fact which rises to the temperature of blood-heat. It doesn't all amount to one rhyme." If the scientists thought Thoreau too poetic and Transcendental, he in his turn thought them not poetic and Transcendental enough.

The irony of all this, though, is that as Thoreau grew older, he found himself growing more scientific in his methodology. Over and over again, and more frequently with each passing year, he fulminated as he did in 1851 in his *Journal,* "I fear that the character of my knowledge is from year to year becoming more distinct and scientific; that, in exchange for views as wide as heaven's scope, I am being narrowed down to the field of the microscope. I see details, not wholes nor the shadow of the whole. I count some parts, and say, 'I know.'"

If one examines the daily journal that Thoreau kept for 25 years (a journal more than two million words in extent and that printed fills 14 volumes) he finds Thoreau's complaint justified. More and more space is devoted to scientific details—lists of flowers he has found, data on the weather, notations on the arrival and departure of migratory birds, etc. Still later he began to make huge charts of such facts completely outside of his *Journal*. And readers of *Walden* will remember the pages there he devotes to measurement of the length, the width, the depth, and the temperature of the pond. Facts seemed finally to have run wild with him. The methodology of the scientists of his time—and remember that the science of Thoreau's lifetime was primarily taxonomy, "the orderly classification of flora and fauna"—proved contagious, and Thoreau was caught up in the very faults he condemned.

But there is an even greater irony than that. Although Thoreau lamented and bewailed that he was impelled willy-nilly to fill up his pages with trivia at the expense of broader views or, to put it in other words and not exactly to coin a phrase, "to lose sight of the forest for the trees," ironically it is now proving of great value to our present-day scientists that Thoreau recorded all that trivia. You may recall that in *Walden,* after listing all those measurements of the pond, Thoreau suddenly saw them fall into place, and realized that from this welter of details he could predict the deepest spot in the pond. Gather enough trivial facts, he discovered, and grand conclusions could be discovered from them. Just so are a few perceptive scientists of our day discovering the value of all this seemingly useless data Thoreau had gathered together.

One of the earliest scientists to realize the value of Thoreau's collections of facts was the late, great Harvard ornithologist Ludlow Griscom. Griscom had long wondered what had happened and what was happening to the bird populations of this country—how different are the bird populations of today from those of the past? What species are increasing? What species are decreasing? What varieties have disappeared from a locale? What species are new to an area? In order to answer his questions, he had to know what the bird populations had been like some time in the distant past, obviously the more distant the better. Imagine his delight then to discover that probably the oldest extant comprehensive survey of the bird population of a given area was the data given by Thoreau in his journals and charts for Concord, Massachusetts, less than 15 miles from Griscom's own base in Cambridge. In the journals alone Thoreau had made 8433 ornithological entries over 25 years. With that data at hand, along with similar data compiled by William Brewster, a lesser known Concord ornithologist of the turn of the century, Griscom found that by adding his own personal observations of the 1930's and 1940's, he was able to make the first comprehensive study of the changing bird populations of an area over an entire century. His *Birds of Concord* is now an ornithological classic, and it was made possible only because of Thoreau's recording of seeming trivia a century before.

Following Griscom's lead, the Harvard botanist Richard J. Eaton has since then made a similar study of the changing patterns of flora of the Concord area, based on Thoreau's 19th-century botanical notes in his journals and Eaton's own 20th-century findings. His *Flora of Concord from Thoreau's Time to the Present Day* is thus another invaluable scientific tool made possible only because of Thoreau's record-keeping. (I should also add that because Thoreau also botanized on many of his so-called "excursions" to spots such as the tops of Mount Monadnock and Mount Washington in New Hampshire, the northern Maine woods, the sand dunes of Cape Cod, and even the Minnesota prairie, similar historical botanical studies of these areas have recently been made or are now in process.)

Still another example of Thoreau's mania for collecting facts about nature has proven useful to modern scientists. Thoreau rarely made entries in his journal without a comment on the weather. Thus we have in his pages rather full weather records for Concord for more than a century ago. These entries have now turned out to have significant use for us. The National Weather Service has incorporated them onto their computerized weather records for the country, and thus they are now regularly being used to help predict the vagaries of American weather. It is interesting to note that when the National Weather Service described the winter of 1976–77 in the East as the "coldest since the Founding of the Republic," Robert Quayle, its director, specifically cited Thoreau's notes as part of the basic data used in making that statement.

Incidentally, as scientists pore over Thoreau's records they are now often finding his independent and prior discovery of species that did not get into scientific literature until years later when rediscovered by more conventional scientists who reported their findings in scientific journals. Thus Eaton discovered that Thoreau had described the witch's broom, a parasite of spruce trees, in his *Journal* for Feb. 2, 1858, while it was not until 1871 that botanists rediscovered and named it. (Eaton points out that had Thoreau only reported his discovery, what we now know as *Arceuthobium pusillum* might be known as *Arceuthobium Thoreuii*.) And similarly entomologist E. Newton Harvey of Princeton University a few years ago discovered in Thoreau's journal for Aug. 8, 1857, an unmistakable description of a rare glowworm, the Phengodes, predating any known identification of the species by an entomologist. (So Thoreau did know about glowworms after all!) Or to take one last unusual example, in 1970 Physicist C. W. McCutchen announced in *Science* the discovery of what he named McCutchen's D-line which is "an abrupt change in surface curvature near the top of a small ridge raised by viscous shear stress at the edge of the film." It can be observed when a layer of oil spreads across a water surface. Poor Mr. McCutchen had basked in the glory of his discovery only a few weeks when R. S. McDowell of the Los Alamos Scientific Laboratory announced, again in *Science,* that Thoreau had discovered and reported on exactly this same phenomenon in his *Journal* for June 4, 1854, 116 years earlier. And undoubtedly as Thoreau's journals continue to be explored and particularly as the expanded journal volumes of the new Princeton edition of Thoreau's writings start appearing, it will be found that he made other similar discoveries.

## II

I seem to be implying here that all of Thoreau's contributions to science were accidental and due *only* to a compulsion he developed in his later years to record facts for fact's sake alone. If that is the impression I have given, it is a faulty one, for what I have noted so far is only a small part of his contribution to science. Let us turn then to some of his other work.

It is not as widely known as it should be that despite his frequent questioning of the methods and motives of science, Thoreau was not only on friendly terms with a number of the outstanding natural scientists of his day, but he also made direct contributions to their endeavors. Thus he collected specimens of the fauna of the Concord area for Louis Agassiz, eventually supplying him with several hitherto unrecorded species of fresh water fish, a new tortoise, and a new mouse. He corresponded with and visited frequently Thaddeus William Harris, the entomologist, and collected specimens of insects for him. And over the years Thoreau donated so many items to the museum of the Boston Society for Natural History that he was named an honorary member of the society.

It is also comparatively little known that Thoreau wrote one scientific treatise, his "Succession of Forest Trees," which he gave before the Middlesex Agricultural Society at its annual meeting in Concord in 1860, a year and a half before he died, and which was not only published in the *Transactions* of that society, but also reprinted in the Commonwealth of Massachusetts *Agricultural Report* for that year and in the pages of the *New York Tribune,* then the country's leading newspaper. Some years earlier, in his work as a professional surveyor of woodlots, Thoreau had noticed that when a pine woodlot is cut down, it grows up to oak, and vice versa. When he inquired of the local farmers as to the reason, they laid it to "spontaneous generation" of the new seeds. But Thoreau's mind was too logical to accept such a farfetched answer, and he began a study of every such woodlot reversal he came across. Gradually he gathered sufficient evidence to prove that squirrels and birds transmitted both acorns and pine cones long distances in their search for food and often dropped them or stored them and then forgot them, and thus were quite inadvertently their planters. He was able to demonstrate that every pine grove was thus literally an oak nursery and vice versa, and that as soon as the large trees were removed, the baby trees of the other specie, hitherto kept diminutive by the shade, were ready to spring up. (I have here somewhat oversimplified Thoreau's theories.) This was the theory that Thoreau enunciated to the Middlesex Agricultural Society. As one eminent biologist (Deevey) has said, "Though he over-emphasized the reversibility of plant succession . . . his conclusions remain essentially unaltered after . . . [a century] of intensive labor by competent botanists," and his essay on the subject is still the standard work.

Thoreau's work on the succession aroused his interest in the related problems of tree growth, dispersal of seeds, and so on. His fatal illness was brought on, in part at least, because he spent a snowy day in early December of 1860 going over a recently cut woodlot on Fair Haven Bay in Concord studying the tree ring patterns on the new stumps and thereby caught the cold that eventually brought about his death by tuberculosis in the spring of 1862. But to go back to the tree rings, he not only discovered independently the principles of tree-ring growth but also the idea of dating pieces of lumber by their tree-ring growth patterns. He was so excited by his growing discoveries in these fields that in late 1860 he started work on a new book, or actually two new books—one on the varying patterns of the dispersion of seeds and the other on native fruits and berries. Unfortunately, even though he compiled more than 600 pages of manuscript on these topics, he died before he was able to bring them to completion; and the manuscript lies now in the Berg Collection of the New York Public Library, almost completely unpublished. One short portion of it, an essay on "Huckleberries" more nearly completed than the rest, was ingeniously edited by the late Professor Leo Stoller of Wayne State University and published privately a few years ago. It proves to be some of the most charming and rewarding nature writing Thoreau ever did. It and as much of the remainder of the Berg manuscript as can be meaningfully edited will eventually be published in the new Princeton edition of Thoreau's writings. It makes us realize all the more fully how much we lost by Thoreau's early death and how preposterous the old theories were that he had written himself out with the publication of *Walden* in 1854. Let me digress a bit and share with you a few paragraphs from the "Huckleberry" essay I just mentioned:

What sort of a country is that where the huckleberry fields are private property? When I pass such fields on the highway, my heart sinks within me. I see a blight on the land. Nature is under a veil there. I make haste away from the accursed spot. Nothing could deform her fair face more. I cannot think of it ever after but as the place where fair and palatable berries, are converted into money, where the huckleberry is desecrated. It is true, we have as good a right to make berries private property, as to make wild grass and trees such—it is not worse than a thousand other practices which custom has sanctioned—but that is the worst of it, for it suggests how bad the rest are, and to what result our civilization and division of labor naturally tend, to make all things venal.

A., a professional huckleberry picker, has hired B.'s field, and, we will suppose, is now gathering the crop, with a patent huckleberry horse rake.

C., a professed cook, is superintending the boiling of a pudding made of some of the berries.

While Professor D.—for whom the pudding is intended, sits in his library writing a book—a work on the Vaccineae (that is, huckleberries) of course.

And now the result of this downward course will be seen in that work—which should be the ultimate fruit of the huckleberry field. It will be worthless. It will have none of the spirit of the huckleberry in it, and the reading of it will be a weariness of the flesh.

I believe in a different kind of division of labor—that Professor D. should be encouraged to divide himself freely between his library and the huckleberry field.

But, to return to Thoreau as scientist, another remarkable characteristic of his endeavors is his pioneering in fields of science that had not in his own day even been named and/or developed. For example, in the history of science it is usually thought that limnology—"the scientific study of physical, chemical, meteorological and biological conditions in fresh waters" started with the work of Forel in 1868, six years after Thoreau's death. But as Edmund Deevey, the Yale limnologist, has pointed out, Thoreau anticipated many of the findings of limnologists—perhaps most notably the principles of thermal stratification in bodies of water and its effects on the flora and fauna—and reported on it in 1854 in *Walden*. Thoreau gathered his data using such homemade devices as a rope tied to a stone for measuring depths and an ordinary household nonlocking thermometer to measure temperature stratification. Deevey and more recently a group of marine biologists chiefly from the Massachusetts Institute of Technology have rechecked Thoreau's data using the most specialized and highly developed of modern instruments, such as radar, and found to their amazement that Thoreau's findings were virtually as accurate as their own.

Still another comparatively new field is that of phenology, "the study of climate focusing on those events of plant and animal life which are repeated year after year and which taken together make up a calendar of the seasons." The term "phenology" was coined by a German scientist, D. C. Fritsch, in 1853 but, at least according to the *Oxford New English Dictionary*, did not reach our language until 1875. Yet Thoreau was constructing a calendar of the seasons as early as 1852. Aldo Leopold, the well-known Wisconsin naturalist, once termed Thoreau "the father of phenology" in America, but that on investigation proves a not particularly accurate term, for other Americans, Thomas Jefferson among them, were gathering such data long before Thoreau, although, like Thoreau, not of course using the term "phenology" itself. But there is no denying that Thoreau did independently gather and correlate data in a manner which we would now describe as "phenological."

Much more rewarding is a study of Thoreau's contribution to another and far more significant science—ecology. A new edition of *The Correspondence of Henry David Thoreau* was published in 1959, of which I shared the privilege of being co-editor with Carl Bode. We were fortunate enough to be able to include a number of hitherto unpublished Thoreau letters, among them one which he wrote on Jan. 1, 1858 to his cousin George Thatcher in Bangor, Maine, in which speaking of a mutual friend, Edward Hoar, we reported Thoreau said, "Mr. Hoar is still in Concord, attending to Botany, Ecology, etc." Our book had been in print only a few weeks when a note by Paul Oehser, then director of publication for the Smithsonian Institution, appeared in *Science*, the official magazine of the American Association for the Advancement of Science. It pointed out that this letter pushed back the known history of the word "ecology" eight years, for up until our edition was published it had been universally assumed that a German Darwinian by the name of Ernst Haeckel coined the word in 1866. Yet from the fact that Thoreau seemed to be using the word almost in passing one could assume that it had achieved general usage at least eight years before the date Haeckel claimed to have coined it. Thus I thought we had accidentally corrected the history of an important and significant word. I thought that until several years later I received a letter from Richard Eaton of Harvard (the same Richard Eaton whom I have already mentioned as the author of the *Flora of Concord*) asking if by any chance the 1858 letter was a forgery. Not only had he been completely unable to discover any other usage of the word previous to Haeckel's claimed coinage of it in 1866, but he had also learned that Haeckel had spelled it "oecology," a spelling that prevailed until the international Madison Botanical

Congress on Aug. 23, 1893 adopted the simpler "ecology" spelling. So here was Thoreau using a word eight years before it had been invented and a spelling 35 years before it had been developed. While in all the years I have handled Thoreau manuscript letters I have never seen a letter that I even suspected of being forged, I was and am perfectly aware of the fact that Thoreau manuscripts today bring such a fabulous price on the market—the going price at the moment being a thousand dollars or more a page—that it is going to be only a matter of time before some clever and unscrupulous individual is going to start forging them. With the 1858 letter, however, I was able to prove conclusively that it was not a forgery. It is now in the Berg Collection of the New York Public Library, and they have documentary evidence (that is, bills of sale) for every transaction in its journey from George Thatcher, who originally received the letter from Thoreau, to its present resting place at Berg.

How then do we explain the use of the word "ecology" in that letter? In Thoreau's handwriting it had certainly seemed to read "E-c-o-l-o-g-y." But when, in the light of Mr. Eaton's inquiry, I checked other examples of Thoreau's handwriting at that point in his life, I discovered that Thoreau's capital E's looked nothing like that. They were very rounded, and this was angular. What was this mysterious word then? By the process of further examination of his handwriting I finally deduced that the initial letters were not "Ec" but "Ge," and the word was not "Ecology" but "Geology." And I confirmed that fact when I examined Thoreau's *Journal* for the preceding day, Dec. 31, 1857, and discovered he records there Hoar's having visited *quarries* in the area. Thus the word was a product of my imagination rather than of Thoreau's usage. With a decidedly red face, I wrote up an account of the whole incident, and it was published in *Science* in an attempt to correct my error. Imagine then my further embarrassment when the first supplement to the *Oxford English Dictionary* appeared in 1972 to discover that they there listed Thoreau's letter of Jan. 1, 1858 as the earliest known use of the word and the *New York Times*, in reviewing the supplement burbled, "How much of the history of feeling lies in the simple fact that the first citation for ecology derives from Thoreau." I have written again in embarrassment, this time to the editors of the *O.E.D.*, sending all the evidence, and its editor, R. W. Burchfield has kindly replied, "I can quite easily see, from the reproduction of the handwritten work, how the error arose." But I fear I am to go down in history, if at all, as the man who corrupted the O.E.D. And I am sure that stories of Thoreau's supposed use of the word "ecology" will continue to pop up.

Nevertheless, even if he did not actually coin the word, I doubt if anyone will challenge the fact that Thoreau was our first major American ecologist and was so before the word entered our vocabulary. It is interesting to note how he first happened to wander into that branch of science all by himself.

As I have already indicated, one of Thoreau's chief sources of income was surveying. (His writings never provided him with enough to live on, even though he could honestly boast he lived on 27 cents a week.) He was a very careful and accurate surveyor.

Indeed, he could easily have worked full time as a surveyor if he had wished, but he preferred working just enough to pay for his few daily necessities and spending the remainder of his time observing the world of nature, and writing. Now one of the reasons surveying was so popular in Concord in his day was because in 1844 the railroad from Boston first reached Concord, and all at once the woodlots of Concord were a valuable source of fuel for the metropolis. Farmers, who for generations had not cared whether their property lines were here or there, suddenly wanted to know exactly which trees were theirs and which were their neighbors. And so Thoreau found a booming market as a surveyor. But ironically, in acting as a surveyor, he was bringing about the doom of the Concord woods he loved so much. No sooner did he survey woodlots than they were cut down. Realizing the demand for fuel was inevitable, Thoreau began casting about for more efficient use and replacement of the woods. That is why he pondered on "The Succession of Forest Trees," why he studied tree ring growth, and how he even developed theories on the most propitious time for maximum yield to harvest a woodlot. He studied tree growth patterns until he was able to demonstrate that trees (at least those common in the Concord area) grow most swiftly in their first 50 years; but despite their slowing of growth in the second 50 years, they actually produce more wood because of the greater diameter of the tree; while in the third 50-year period the advantage of greater diameter is outweighed by the even slower growth. Thus for efficiency's sake, the trees of Concord, he concluded, should be harvested towards the end of their second 50-year period. He also pointed out that the Concord farmers' constant shifting from woodlot to pasture and back for a piece of land was probably the most inefficient method of tree-growth developed. One ordinarily does not think of Henry Thoreau as an efficiency expert; but when it was a question of preserving his beloved woods of Concord, we find him using the techniques of the profit-makers, though he found his profits in beauty rather than in coins. And as he saw Concord's forests go, he began to realize more and more that we were gradually losing all of our greatest natural resources. In a day when his countrymen thought our resources inexhaustible, he realized, a century ahead of his time, just how exhaustible they were and are. And so he pondered the problem of how to save our resources. Using more efficient methods of harvesting timber was one way. But that was not enough. So he pondered and pondered further and eventually came up with an idea quite amazing for the rugged individualist Yankee that we know Thoreau to have been. He was the first American in this entire country to call for the establishment of public parks and forests—local, state, and national—to preserve our national resources. All this a quarter century before we got around to establishing our first national park at Yellowstone in the 1870's. Let me quote another passage from that "Huckleberry" essay:

> Among the Indians, the earth and its productions generally were common and free to all the tribe, like the air and water—but among us who have supplanted the Indians, the public retain only a small yard or common in the middle of the village, with perhaps a graveyard beside it, and the right of way, by sufferance, by a particular narrow route, which is annually becoming narrower, from one such yard to another....
>
> I am not overflowing with respect and gratitude to the fathers who thus laid out our New England villages.... At the same time that they built meeting-houses why did they not preserve from desecration and destruction far grander temples not made with hands?
>
> What are the natural features which make a township handsome—and worth going far to dwell in? A river with its water-falls—meadows, lakes—hills, cliffs or individual rocks, a forest and single ancient trees—such things are beautiful. They have high use which dollars and cents never represent. If the inhabitants of a town were wise they would seek to preserve these things though at a considerable expense. For such things educate far more than any hired teachers or preachers, or any at present recognized system of school education....
>
> It would be worth the while if in each town there were a committee appointed, to see that the beauty of the town received no detriment. If here is the largest boulder in the country, then it should not belong to an individual nor be made into door-steps. In some countries precious metals belong to the crown—so here more precious objects of great natural beauty should belong to the public.
>
> Let us try to keep the new world new, and while we make a wary use of the city, preserve as far as possible the advantages of living in the country....
>
> Most men, it appears to me, do not care for Nature, and would sell their share in all her beauty, for as long as they may live, for a stated and not very large sum. Thank God they cannot yet fly and lay waste the sky as well as the earth. We are safe on that side for the present. It is for the very reason that some do no care for these things that we need to combine to protect all from the vandalism of a few.

So much for Thoreau and ecology.

Now let me raise one final question—how did Thoreau the writer accomplish so much in the field of science, a field he professed to care little about? I believe it is because great scientists and great writers possess two important characteristics in common—they are unusually observant, seeing what others do not see, and they are able to perceive relationships between their observations that others do not perceive. I do not think I need demonstrate that these are characteristics of all great scientists, but I would like to show briefly that they are characteristics of Thoreau.

Studying the great mass of criticism that has gathered around Thoreau's *literary* works, one finds the critics of his works frequently commenting on his wonderfully observant eye. Yet they should not confine themselves to his observant eye, for Thoreau was wonderfully observant with *all* his senses. And as a result he has written some of the most sensuous prose in our language. We can not only see what he writes about, but we can almost literally smell it, taste it, hear it, and feel it. In a passage from his *Journal* for Aug. 4, 1851, a fairly typical passage, for example, note how he uses every sense:

> As my *eye* rested on the blossom of the meadowsweet in a hedge, I *heard* the note of an autumnal cricket, and was penetrated with the sense of autumn. Was it *sound?* or was it *form?* or was it *scent?* or was it *flavor?* It is now the royal month of August. When I hear this *sound*, I am as dry as the rye which is everywhere cut and housed, though I am drunk with the season's wine.

Because Thoreau did thus use every sense he became one of our most powerful writers. But, as I have said, one cannot simply revel in one's senses. He must make something of his observations. Some years ago when I was working on my biography of Thoreau and was reading his massive journals through for the umpteenth time, it suddenly struck me how often Thoreau had that additional ability of "putting things together." As I have said in my book, *Days of Henry Thoreau:*

> "[Thoreau] could never take anything for granted, and looking at the world about him with a questioning mind, he was constantly discovering things that others had not noticed. When from the top of a mountain he noticed the shadows of clouds in a valley, he quickly figured how to calculate their height accurately. When he noticed the pattern with which star fungi split, he puzzled out the reason. When he observed water squirting through leaks in a dam, he noticed their varying jets and reasoned that it was related to the varying heads of water above the leaks. When he discovered that turtles tended to bury their eggs three inches beneath the soil, he tested with thermometers and proved that the overall day and night temperature was greatest at this depth. And when he noticed that some of the shingles on his neighbor's roof were blacker than others, he figured out that those

were the poorer or sappy shingles which absorbed the most water in a rainstorm. As his friend and first biographer Ellery Channing said of him, "He was alive from top to toe with curiosity."

It is indeed appropriate that the very final entry in that 14-volume, 25-year *Journal* that Thoreau kept, a notation made after what was probably the last walk he ever took, for he soon after relapsed to bed with tuberculosis and died the next spring, reads

> After a violent easterly storm in the night, which clears up at noon (Nov. 3, 1861), I notice that the surface of the railroad causeway, composed of gravel, is singularly marked, as if stratified like some slate rocks, on their edges, so that I can tell within a small fraction of a degree from what quarter the rain came. . . . Behind each little pebble, . . . extends northwest a ridge of sand an inch or more, which it has protected from being washed away. . . .
>
> All this is perfectly distinct to an observant eye, and yet could easily pass unnoticed by most.

Yes, Thoreau had that "observant eye" and saw much that "could easily pass unnoticed by most." It was what would have made him a great scientist "had Emerson not spoiled him," as one of Thoreau's contemporaries put it. But I personally am grateful that Emerson did spoil him, for he made an even greater writer.

# CHRISTOPHER CLAUSEN

## Did You Once See Willy Plain?

[ SPRING 1982 ]

THE TIME I came nearest to meeting W. B. Yeats was late on a summer day in 1969 after I had been up all night on the train from Copenhagen to the Hook of Holland and then all day on the boat to England. I had gone through customs three times in the last 24 hours and been searched for drugs at Harwich, apparently as a punishment for carrying hardly any luggage. Now I was waiting for the bus to take me the last two miles of the journey home, where I could soon and safely collapse. As I stood in the raging British sunshine, bright-colored bubbles floated back and forth on my eyelids, and below my half-awareness of the clank and roar of British traffic I was perhaps one-quarter aware of a whine from somewhere above, rather like a flying lawnmower. I did not look up.

"Biplane," said a voice behind me. It sounded incredibly satisfied. It also sounded old and a trifle un-English, but what made me turn around and attempt to focus was the plain exultation in it. "Converted fighter," it continued.

The man must have been about 75 and had what used to be called a military bearing, though he was thin to the point of fragility and might just as well have been some elegant kind of waltzing poet-soldier, now superannuated, out of an operetta. The disconcerting fact was that he was speaking to me—there was no one else near the bus stop—and flagrantly demanding some sort of answer. I turned my eyes to the sky and tried to focus again. The plane seemed to be an antique crop-duster.

"Sure is," I said, and then, afraid that I sounded too American and might offend this dotty old plane-spotter, added: "Quite right."

"*I* used to be in fighters," he went on, "in the first war." He rolled up the left sleeve of his suit jacket and shirt as far as they would go and held up his wrist. "See that?"

I grunted as neutrally as possible. How could I fail to see his wrist? I began to wonder if the bus would ever come. It was about as old as the biplane, and if it broke down I might have old arm-flasher on my hands for hours. Why did his relatives let him wander around like this?

"All reconstructed," he explained with relish, still holding up his arm. "All the way to the shoulder. The Flying Circus did that to me." His tone of pleasure suggested that a strong man might quail to hear what he had done to the Flying Circus in return, and I did not ask. "Have you heard of Sir Edward Carson?"

It so happened that I had. His eyebrows gave the impression that he did not often meet young people who had the foggiest idea what he was talking about.

"He was the organizer of the Ulster Volunteers. He organized us in 1913 to put down the riffraff. The Irish rebels and all." He did not literally pound on his thin chest, but that was the effect. "I was Ulster Volunteer number one, the first." He peered at me. "What might your name be?"

I told him. "Lamb," he said, and we shook hands. At this moment the bus came heaving and gasping into view. As it pulled up, I stood back to let him get on first—that way he could not sit down next to me. But he moved back to let a middle-aged woman with a laundry basket get off. He lifted his hat energetically, with a flowing motion that brought into play all of his original and reconstructed limbs.

"Afternoon to you, Mrs. Pierce."

"How are you, Mr. Lamb?" the woman replied. "And how's your daughter getting on in this warmer weather?"

"Better, thanks, Mrs. Pierce. I'm just out now fetching her tablets for her." He replaced his hat on his head, and the lady went clunking across the street towards a launderette. "After you, Mr. Clausen."

So I got on the bus and he sat down beside me. By this time I didn't mind particularly; it now seemed unlikely that he was the raving sort of madman, and in spite of being exhausted I was mildly interested in hearing more of his adventures.

"And *did* you fight the rebels?" I asked when the bus was under way and we had paid our fares to the beefy young conductor.

"Ah, no," he answered regretfully, looking out past me at the rolling Essex fields. "Never had a chance to. We fought the Kaiser instead. The day the war started, Carson volunteered us as a regiment." He shook his head, perhaps regretting Carson's choice of the Kaiser as an enemy preferable to other Irishmen. "Something like 85 percent of us got killed. If I hadn't gone into air I'd have been killed. One brother was killed. He was in air."

"Do you know Yeats's poem about the Irish airman?" That had been one of my favorite poems since I was a freshman in college.

"Willy Yeats! That bloody faker." He sneered past me at the window. "Yes, I know that poem."

"Why do you say he was a faker?" I was, I think, merely curious to see where the conversation would get to in the few minutes before the bus got us to the village and we went forever in what I felt confident would be our separate directions.

"Huh. All that pretense of heroic Ireland. He was no more Irish than Harold Wilson. He spent the Troubles in England. Spent half his life here. I had him twice in my house in Hampstead, before the war."

"Really?" At this I perked up. Yeats was, after all, sacred to me at that time. Mr. Lamb had turned out to be a link, though I was not certain what sort of link. He might, of course, be making it all up, but everything he had said had a truthful off-handedness to it. "What was he like?"

He wrinkled up his nose. "Striker of poses. He would recite verse in the front room in a great bardic voice, with that mane of white hair fluttering. Affected through and through."

I waited for more, but the subject of Yeats did not interest him, and there was no more. When the bus reached my stop, I rose to get off and nodded a farewell towards my companion. He got up from his seat.

"Will you have a lager with me at the Half Butt, Mr. Clausen?" he asked courteously.

There was a struggle with my fatigue, but in those days I was inclined to be deferential towards old people. Besides, he obviously had not finished, and my curiosity would be good for another few minutes.

"Thanks, I'd love to. A fairly short one—I've just come from Denmark. From the boat at Harwich."

He looked shrewdly at me. "Ah. And would you be Danish yourself?" There was a note of skepticism.

"No, American. My great-grandfather was Danish."

"Ah. You're all mixed up over there in America, aren't you." I took it that he meant genealogically and nodded.

We went into the saloon bar. There was a young woman behind the bar, and Mr. Lamb again lifted his hat.

"Afternoon, Mr. Lamb," she said cheerfully. "What would you like?"

"Afternoon, Mrs. Richards. A Harp for Mr. Clausen, and a half of bitter for me." He paid and sat us down at a table in a very dark corner, next to the silent juke box. "This Harp is made by the Guinness people. You've had Guinness stout?"

"Yes," I said.

"Liffey mud, they call it. Have you been to Ireland?"

"Yes," I said. "Just to Dublin and Limerick. I liked Dublin."

He nodded. "I haven't been back over but once since the war. Since 1919, that is. What do you think of all this trouble over there?"

I shrugged, which was clearly the only possible answer in this situation.

"They need to shoot more of them." He patted his closely cropped white hair. "That's it. That's the only way to stop it. Don't you think?"

"I don't know."

"Well, perhaps I'm seeing it too simply." He shook his head again. "My great-nephew's in the forces over there. We were always a military family." He pointed to my beer glass. "Do you like that?"

"Yes, indeed."

"Are you over here on holiday, then?"

"More or less." To forestall the usual questions about what it meant to drop out for a year, I asked him how long he had lived in the village. Only four years and some months, he said. He had moved down from London to be with his daughter.

"From Hampstead?"

"Ah, no. That was a long time ago. I was bombed out in Hampstead in 1940."

I nodded. Then I remembered my beer and drank some more of it, even though it was making me sleepier.

"Bloody bomb came right down the chimney. The next day I went back." There was an affectionate lingering on the last word. "They put me in the quartermaster's department because of my age." He made a face that expressed loathing and disgust at the English government's imbecility in coming between a man and his war. "Carson was dead; nobody could do anything for me."

Is it credible that I might have yawned here? It was warm in the saloon bar, and I had not slept in 36 hours. And I had finished my Harp. Mr. Lamb rose to his feet.

"Time I was off," he said. "I've been keeping you."

I protested that he was not, and that it had been most pleasant. I was only sorry to be so tired.

"Go rest yourself." He picked up his hat and made for the door. "Cheerio, Mrs. Richards. A great pleasure, Mr. Clausen."

"Thank you again," I managed lamely, and then he was gone and I finally got to go home.

That was the closest I ever came to meeting Yeats, who after all had died years before I was born. It all happened just as I have told it, and I have not even robbed Mr. Lamb of his true name, since in this case art could never improve on life. For a long time, after I had caught up on my sleep, I thought about going to see him with a notebook and getting his memories of great men and events down in circumstantial form, as befitted the literary scholar I was already on the verge of aspiring to become. I went so far as to look him up in the phone book and get directions from the neighbors, who encouraged the project. But I never went; an unscholarly reluctance to badger an old man for his long-ago names and dates always prevented me. What he had told me, he had told me, and like the Wedding Guest I would have to be satisfied. So that no one else can intrude upon his retirement I have suppressed the name of the village in this account, whose protagonist may after all still be a slim and keen-eyed watcher of the skies in his eighties. I like to think of him patrolling the byways of East Anglia at some pace midway between a march and a gambol, scanning the heavens from time to time, occasionally rewarded by the sight of a craft out of his own season, and spurred by it to find an unlikely hearer for whatever artifacts of memory and experience seem on that day to need passing along.

ROBERT COLES

# Charles Dickens and the Law

[ AUTUMN 1983 ]

I

SOME of the important details of the life of Charles Dickens are as familiar to many of us as the various qualities of mind and heart which we have come to associate with such memorable characters as David Copperfield and Philip Pirrip, otherwise known as Pip; or Esther Summerson and Little Dorrit; or yes, Vohles, Jaggers, and Stryver, three lawyers whose names suggest no strong authorial admiration. As a boy, Dickens knew poverty. His father was a clerk in England's Navy Pay Office; he was, as well, all too relaxed when it came to spending the modest salary he earned. When Dickens was 12 years old (in 1824), his father was sent to prison because he had accumulated debts and lacked the means of paying them. This prison, Marshalsea, figures prominently in *Little Dorrit*, even as it did in the life of the young Dickens, who spent time behind bars in accordance with prevailing custom: a debtor's family often accompanied him when be became locked up. As a child, Dickens also worked for extremely low wages in a shoe-blacking factory: he pasted labels on bottles. In his spare time he wandered the streets of London, a penniless lad curious to understand the teeming confusion of a great port city. It was only the death of his paternal grandmother that enabled his father to be released from prison. She left a small legacy to her son. The lesson would never be forgotten by a novelist who was forever reminding his readers, through the workings of one or another plot, how arbitrary fate can be and how good can come of bad—or, of course, vice versa.

At 15 Dickens was studying law as an attorney's apprentice. He mastered shorthand. He read legal texts long and hard. He also, in a matter of months, became bored. He loved the English language, dreamed of using it in one way or another. In 1829 he became a court reporter for the Court of Chancery, whose majestic inscrutability would, decades later, dominate *Bleak House*. By 1832 he was bored with that job, too. He tried journalism: first the *True Sun*, then *Mirror of Parliament*, then the *Morning Chronicle*. His specialty was parliamentary reportage. He had a keen eye for 19th-century English politics—its moral postures, its moments and longer of theater, both high and low, its possibilities, and its sad limitations. He also had developed a compelling manner of narrative presentation—strong, suggestive prose. He worked quickly. He observed exactly. He rendered accurately. Moreover, he was astonishingly energetic—a quality he'd never stop possessing. He traveled anywhere and everywhere in search of a good political story. All London became his routine beat; all England easily tempted him, if he felt the story demanded that extra effort.

Inside him burned, even then, a writer's desire to expand upon incidents, convey a given atmosphere, give moral shape to a particular factuality. In December 1833, the *Monthly Magazine* published Dickens' first sketch of London street life. In August 1834, he began using the name Boz, and by February of 1836, at the age of 24, he had published *Sketches by Boz*—with the additional explanatory title, *Illustrative of Everyday Life and Everyday People*. Shortly thereafter he began the first of his Pickwick pieces—"The Posthumous Papers of the Pickwick Club." By now he was ready to marry, and to shift course as a writer. He abandoned the writing of conventional journalism, though he worked for a while (two years) as an editor. At the same time he immersed himself in his own world—reported on the workings of his mind's imagination, its exceedingly vigorous life.

Soon enough a substantial segment of the English reading public, rich and poor and many, many in between, became familiar with the antic and sometimes soberly edifying carryings-on of Samuel Pickwick and his fellow clubsmen Nathaniel Winkle, Tracy Tupman, Augustus Snodgrass—and those they met: Alfred Jingle, Dr. Slammer, Mr. Wardle, his daughters Bella and Emily, his spinster sister Rachael, Samuel Weller, Job Trotter, and the landlady Mrs. Bardell, not to mention those two shady lawyers Dodson and Fogg, and that shrewd master of realpolitik, the lawyer Perker. Samuel Pickwick, we all know, survives crooked lawyers and even, it seems, the temptations of love. He retires to the country with his servant Sam Weller for a long and restful life. Dickens, on the other hand, with the publication of Pickwick Papers in book form (1838), had ahead of him more than 30 years of demanding labor.

No matter the success those years brought, there was in this greatest of storytellers an unyielding attachment of sorts to his early social and moral experiences; he worked them over repeatedly in the later novels—*Bleak House, Hard Times, Great Expectations, Tale of Two Cities, Little Dorrit*: down-and-out English life, the exploitation, and, not least, the miscarriages of justice. No acclaim, no money, no amount of achieved influence seemed enough to stop him from looking closely at a nation he both loved and yet found urgently in need of reform. Nor did his success as a writer and an eager public speaker, if not performer, prevent him from going back, time and again, to the memories generated by an earlier life: the child in a debtor's prison, the youth struggling with a harsh and mean life, the young man observing lawmakers at their shilly-shallying or corrupt worst, and, above all, the apprentice writer taking note of lawyers—who, of course, are right there when men and women go to prison, or lose whatever rights or privileges they may have had, or find themselves in severe straits because the laws work this way rather than that way or on behalf of these people rather than those. Charles Dickens in his fifties, the most celebrated writer in Britain, still scanned hungrily London's lowlife, a substantial population, indeed; and, doing so, gave us not only memorable characters (Jo of *Bleak House,* the Dorrits of Marshalsea Prison, the prisoner Magwitch) but also terribly searching moral issues to consider and (he would surely have hoped) to connect in their continuing significance to our own considerably later lives.

Again and again lawyers figure in the penetrating enactments of ethical conflict which Dickens insisted on making a central element of his most important novels. In *Bleak House,* of course, the issue is not just lawyers, but the law itself—its awesome, pervasive, perplexing, unnerving presence. Even in Dickens' lifetime, some of the tedious, if not outrageous aspects of London's Chancery Court had succumbed to reform. And, too, Dickens knew when he wrote *Little Dorrit* that the very Marshalsea Prison he described (and knew as a young inmate) no longer was the giant debtors' world of old, filled with entire families whose crime was an inability to pay their bills. For all his urgent responsiveness to Victorian dilemmas, Dickens was a moral visionary who wrote *sub specie aeternitatis;* hence the continuing provocation and edifying satisfaction of his novels, not to mention the still mighty power of his caricatures. The fog of *Bleak House,* after all, still obtains. The law still offers many of those caught in its exertions any number of frustrations, confusions, delays. Men, women, and children still find themselves irritated, then confounded, then outraged, and finally maddened by cases which affect them deeply, and seem to go on and on and on—maybe not for generations, as happened in *Jarndyce v. Jarndyce,* but long enough for particular children to suffer in extended custodial fights, and for particular workers and families to suffer while the responsibility for, say, dangerous environmental pollution is argued in court for months which become years.

Yet *Bleak House* is much more than a novel that portrays the outcome of a legal impasse. Too much is made, one can argue, about the protracted nature of the celebrated Jarndyce litigation. In one enumeration, made in the well-known first chapter, Dickens does indeed mention "procrastination," but he also mentions "trickery," and he mentions "evasion," and "spoliation." He even makes reference to "botheration," surely of interest to this proudly self-conscious age wherein the social sciences, especially psychology and psychiatry, are thought to explain so much to us. Nor is that list, certainly applicable to our contemporary scene, intended as a précis of a novelist's coming preoccupations. *Bleak House* is, ultimately, about character—even as, occasionally, professions such as the law or medicine come down (or up!) to that: how so-called practitioners skirt various temptations (or fail to do so); and how a certain lawyer or doctor justifies his work, comes to terms with his perceived obligations, responds in mind and heart to the hurt, the vulnerability, the alarm if not panic of his clients, his patients. Even as in *Middlemarch* we see George Eliot trying to comprehend the fate of Dr. Lydgate—the transformation of an avowedly idealistic young doctor into an all too (by his own early and high standards) compromised and self-serving one—the many chapters of *Bleak House* offer their own chronicle of a profession variously practiced, its supposed purposes variously interpreted, and, alas, not always to the good.

## II

Of all Dickens' lawyers, Tulkinghorn of *Bleak House* is surely the highest in rank—that is, the one who has achieved the most professional success. He is a distinguished lawyer and advisor to one of England's most powerful families. True, Dickens tips his hand (as he so often does) with the name of Dedlock: Sir Leicester is indeed a baronet who (with others in England's 19th-century nobility) is headed nowhere. The social foolishness, the moribund paralysis, intellectual and moral, of a particular upper class is more than indicated in the early chapters of *Bleak House*. But Sir Leicester is, nevertheless, rich and influential, and, we eventually learn, more decent than many of his ilk; and to be his lawyer is, well, to be a notable success. Tulkinghorn is no Lawyer Tangle, arguing his way to no apparent purpose in the obscure, dreary, muddy, fog-enshrouded trenches of the law: "'Mr. Tangle,' says the Lord High Chancellor, latterly something restless under the eloquence of that learned gentleman.

"'Mlud,' says Mr. Tangle. Mr. Tangle knows more of Jarndyce and Jarndyce than anybody. He is famous for it—supposed never to have read anything else since he left school.

"'Have you concluded your argument?'

"'Mlud, no—variety of points—feel it my duty tsubmit—ludship,' is the reply that slides out of Mr. Tangle.

"'Several members of the bar are still to be heard, I believe?' says the Chancellor with a slight smile.

"Eighteen of Mr. Tangle's friends, each armed with a little summary of eighteen hundred sheets, bob up like eighteen hammers in a pianoforte, make eighteen bows, and drop into their eighteen places of obscurity."

For Tulkinghorn, such "duty tsubmit," such ingratiating bowing and scraping, such "obscurity," is hardly the point of a legal career. He holds his own with the best; he manages, even, to have the high-and-mighty watch their step with him around—indeed, cower before his acquired legal knowledge: the facts of their personal lives which, inevitably, become his property. Here is a description by no less than the wife of Sir Leicester Dedlock. She has just told her daughter that she dreads a certain person. The daughter asks: "An enemy?" The mother replies: "Not a friend. One who is too passionless to be either. He is Sir Leicester Dedlock's lawyer; mechanically faithful without attachment, and very jealous of the profit, privilege and reputation of being master of the mysteries of great houses." A bit further on the lady expands: "He is indifferent to everything but his calling. His calling is the acquisition of secrets, and the holding possession of such power as they give him, with no sharer or opponent in it." Still further on her husband adds this: "He is, of course, handsomely paid, and he associates almost on a footing of equality with the highest society."

That is about as far as Dickens really wants to go in explicit psychological analysis. He does let Lady Dedlock's apprehensiveness, elsewhere in the novel, turn into an occasion for psychological speculation rather than diagnosis: "Whether he be cold and cruel, whether immovable in what he has made his duty, whether absorbed in love of power, whether determined to have nothing hidden from him in ground where he has burrowed among secrets all his life, whether he in his heart despises the splendour of which he is a distant beam, whether he is always treasuring up slights and offences in the affability of his gorgeous clients—whether he be any of this, or all of this, it may be that my Lady had better have five thousand pairs of fashionable eyes upon her, in distrustful vigilance, than the two eyes of this rusty lawyer, with his wisp of neck cloth and his dull black breeches tied with ribbons at the knees."

Still, a mood of suspicion and fear and guilt is not to be confused with a clear, precise moment of apprehended truth. Tulkinghorn, we know, listens and stalks and prompts respect if not outright alarm. But his exact purposes are not evident—as if Dickens believed that we are, really, what we manage to present of ourselves to the world around us. Put differently, the depiction of a given social and professional reality is for one 19th-century novelist a sufficiently complex psychological evocation. For many of today's readers, however, the more Tulkinghorn's enigmatic but exceptionally significant involvement in this long and darkly suggestive story is chronicled, the more we search for motives, a ruling mode of comprehension for us of the 20th century. And the less satisfactory, I suppose, Dickens' stubborn refusal becomes—as in this tantalizing moment, wherein a chance for "depth analysis," as we call it, is once more forsaken:

"He passes out into the streets, and walks on, with his hands behind him, under the shadow of the lofty houses, many of whose mysteries, difficulties, mortgages, delicate affairs of all kinds, are treasured up within his old black satin waistcoat. He is in the confidence of the very bricks and mortar. The high chimney-stacks telegraph family secrets to him. Yet there is not a voice in a mile of them to whisper 'Don't go home!'"

Here we are granted drama, even melodrama; certainly we note a touch of irony, even poignant irony—though, to be sure, no sympathy. Perhaps at this moment, in frustration if not annoyed condescension, we begin to remind ourselves that Dickens is not George Eliot, after all, or Tolstoy. He was, that is to say, not notably enchanted by the possibilities offered by the novel for the analysis of personality—our moral life as it is prompted by the various emotional reasons each of us finds compelling. Yet, that observation is all too categorical—and unsatisfying. In fact, Dickens was a direct predecessor of Kafka, of Flannery O'Connor. He believed in the literal truth that exaggeration aims to apprehend. He believed in the down-home, concrete reality which inspired his flights of fancy called caricatures. What were they, those caricatures, but emphatic statements with respect to especially salient personal qualities, whose moral import, often enough, the author believed to be well worth a particular literary effort?

Moreover, when Dickens wants to explore rather distinctly a certain character's mind, he does so without hesitation or awkwardness. Here is Bucket presented to us; Bucket the first detective to enter English literature; Bucket whose activities also connected with the legal system Dickens wanted to portray; Bucket who was as much an urban walking man as Tulkinghorn: "Otherwise mildly studious in his observation of human nature, on the whole a benignant philosopher not disposed to be severe upon the follies of mankind, Mr. Bucket pervades a vast number of houses, and strolls about an infinity of streets: to outward appearances rather languishing for want of an object. He is in the friendliest condition towards his species, and will drink with most of them. He is free with his money, affable in his manners, innocent in his conversation—but, through the placid stream of his life, there glides an undercurrent of forefinger."

That last phrase may not be the kind of abstract declaration we have, alas, found so congenial: the superego as a factor in our mental activity. But "forefinger" will do—as a means of reminding us that this fellow Bucket, like others (let us pray!) who hunt down criminals, supposed or actual, is impelled by voices which worry about what is right and what is wrong; voices which, too, urge that such worries not be altogether abstract but, rather, worked into the fabric of a given occupational life. If Bucket is a covert moralist, then what is Tulkinghorn? He is not immoral, one gathers. He seems to be without moral anguish of any kind—a lofty one who prompts alarm, even panic, in others, while he goes about his weighty business. In Tulkinghorn, Dickens may have all too uncannily anticipated our contemporary scene: as in a supposed value-free social science, or the proclaimed worth of professional neutrality, or the dispassionate claims of the adversarial system, not to mention the carefully cultivated, circumspect anonymity of our psychiatrists. Tulkinghorn is contained, cool; oh, so cool—as the saying goes: a real professional! Such a person is best probed, perhaps, by a psychological observer keenly attentive to the powerful influence social and cultural norms exert on human motivation, not to mention behavior. Dickens was such a psychological observer.

As for Bucket, it is not just a latent moralism which attracts our interest in him. He is one of those relatively "minor" characters in a Dickens novel who comes to attract our strongest scrutiny, if not perplexity, because his various activities and attitudes remind us, needless to say, of our own continuing social and ethical dilemmas. Bucket is the one who, initially, goes after such good and decent people as Gridley and George, and, lo and behold, our dear and defenseless Jo, the incarnation in *Bleak House* of all that is vulnerable and innocently injured in this high-powered life we call "civilized." Why such a pursuit? Why, of all people, hound Jo? What Dickens thought about Jo is contained in one of the most memorable passages he ever wrote: "And there he sits munching, and gnawing, and looking up at the great Cross on the summit of St. Paul's Cathedral, glittering above a red and violet-tinted cloud of smoke. From the boy's face one might suppose that sacred emblem to be, in his eyes, the crowning confusion of the great, confused city;—so golden, so high up, so far out of his reach. There he sits, the sun going down, the river running fast, the crows flying by him in two streams—everything moving on to some purpose and to one end—until he is stirred up, and told to 'move on' too."

What kind of "inspector" hunts down such a child? Why, a man who has a job to do! Is Jo guilty of a crime, or is he not? Never mind urban problems and problems of class and caste; never mind a child's hurt life, a city's rampant evil as it bears down on those least able to protect themselves, assert their claim to citizenship. After a while this harsh, moralistic Bucket begins to win us over: he is decent and fair as he does his duty. We know that this is one agent of the law, who will not be gratuitously mean spirited. He has driven Jo out of the city (to his death!) because he believes him (wrongly) to have been a criminal. But Dickens is unwilling to push this matter as far as he might—the personally good worker who obeys his superiors and hurts others, no matter their decency, their merit. Rather quickly we see Bucket befriending all the people we've come to love: he wards off the Smallweeds from Sir Leicester, helps preserve a marriage (that of the Snagsbys), works hard (if in vain) to rescue Lady Dedlock, and discovers who it is (Hortense) who really killed Tulkinghorn. Now, we are pleased: this is a professional man who clearly acts in the service of "good." Again one poses the issue, now in the form of a question: why didn't Dickens push matters in quite another direction—explore the matter of the loyal, efficient, hard working professional man (avowedly well-intentioned and honorable) whose loyalty to a given job, a given social and economic system, persuades him that (for instance) the Jos of this world would have to be put in their place, made to stop loitering and begging, prevented from distracting and disturbing the rest of us?

Perhaps the answer is that Dickens (and indeed, the entire 19th century) had yet to feel as desperate as we have come to feel—hopelessly, so often, caught in the grips of one or another totalitarian system. The utter evil, the everyday evil, worked into the daily lives of millions of law-abiding citizens of this or that state, the evil of the Holocaust and the Gulag, were surely beyond his exuberantly reformist, Christian sensibility. But his moral intuition is as broad and deep as his moral yearning—and so Bucket, for more than a few pages, deeply troubles us: we who have heard one self-proclaimed totalitarian functionary after another (doctors and lawyers among them) assert their loyalty to duty as an excuse for what they ended up doing to others.

In the Victorian legal system—its workings, its possibilities for some, its constraints and worse on others—Dickens keeps managing to embody our century's moral dilemmas; in the novelistic tradition, they have been considered by Conrad and Solzhenitsyn, and in the tradition of the political and philosophical essay, by Camus and Hannah Arendt. "The one great principle of the English law," Dickens tells us, "is to make business for itself." No wonder, then, that one attorney in *Bleak House* gets called Vohles: a "vole" in a card game is a situation in which the dealer gets all the winning cards. Over and over Dickens emphasizes the ordinary in Vohles, the regular and conventional: "Mr. Vohles is a very respectable man. He has not a very large business, but he is a very respectable man. He is allowed by the greater attorneys who have made good fortunes, or are making them, to be a most respectable man. He never misses a chance in his practice, which is a mark of respectability; he is reserved and serious, which is also a mark of respectability; his digestion is impaired, which is *highly* respectable; he is making hay of the grass which is flesh, for his three daughters and his father are dependent on him in the Vale of Taunton."

Therein is, I fear, an account all too contemporary—we earnest, hard working, thoroughly loyal, occasionally (but discreetly) troubled citizens, always at a ready for Alka-Seltzers (maybe, if necessary, a visit to the psychiatrist for our psychosomatic ailments) and, as well, prepared with our psychological or moral justifications: I do it for my wife, my children; I do it for my family, my very well-deserving family; so, hands off, you with the forefinger, you preachy cultural essayists or social critics, you thinly disguised moral rhetoricians masked as lecturers who come to one or another university!

## III

In *Great Expectations* Dickens continues to explore this theme—the relationship between the practice of a profession (the law) and the moral life as it (one hopes) presents its predicaments, if not outright demands, on all of us. The lawyer Jaggers is, surely, one of Dickens' best-known characters. He is a tough, hugely successful (and just plain huge) barrister who strides the legal netherworld of London to the accompaniment of everyone's awe. Dickens knew how hard-pressed life was for thousands of English families in mid-19th-century England, and he knew the legal side of such desperation—a jungle of suspicion and fear and hate. He was especially attentive to the meanness and spitefulness, the crazy outbursts of anger, the trickery and cunning, the resort to lies and more lies which characterize so-called "low life": hungry, jobless men, women, children with few if any prospects become reduced to a fate not only marginal with respect to its "socio-economic" character but also with respect to its very humanity. True, as Dickens reminded us in *Bleak House* with Esther Summerson and in *Little Dorrit* with the character whose name titles the novel, human dignity is not really ever extinguished, only put in severe jeopardy. But there was plenty of that jeopardy for the people Jaggers knew so well, and to this day the problem remains: what can an earnest, competent lawyer do, given the hard facts of a continuous and severe exploitation of men and women by their fellow creatures?

The very name Jaggers, needless to say, suggests the cut-throat quality of a particular existential situation. One is a bit indirect, uneasy, evasive here: Jaggers himself is not so easy to write off as yet another of Dickens' villainous lawyers. He is imperious and gruff; he is as manipulative as . . . well, an attorney of his caliber and practice would naturally be. He trades in secrets, skirts the edges of the law, bullies strangers and associates, keeps all sorts of tricks up his sleeve—and yet is by no means a moral monster. He is oddly compelling, even touching, in his blunt poses of neutrality, aloofness, skepticism. The more we get to know him (and Dickens wants us to do so, thereby rescuing a character from the limitations of the caricature) the more we wonder at his purpose—and at that of Dickens as well in making him so arresting and complex. He is, after all, the instrument of the boy Pip's moral and spiritual journey. He is, also, capable of saving a soul or two amid the hellish life he observed and, within limits, dominated.

And he shows evidence of anguish—the constant handwashing which bespoke a keen recognition of just how sordid a given job was.

In a sense, then, Jaggers is the lawyer who has to work in a world exceptionally flawed by sin and suffering—and, somehow, not himself slip hopelessly into that world. No question, he profits from that world—as a person who wields his influence and receives the urgent entreaties of a bewildered and impoverished population of Londoners and as a lawyer who can pick and choose among would-be clients. His very credibility as a character attests to Dickens' moral seriousness at this point in his literary career: we don't laugh at Jaggers or with him either at the various people with whom he works. Nor do we simply enjoy his brusque power, his moments of mocking arrogance, his clever instincts for survival. He is, we begin to feel, a lonely and driven figure himself. He belongs with those who wait on him: Molly, for instance, his servant woman, whom he defended on a murder charge. She was a tramp, wild and crude. Upon her acquittal she went to work for him. She is, we learn, Estella's mother, the father being the convict Magwitch, Pip's benefactor. Dickens unashamedly wove such a tight-knit plot—a reminder to all of us how intimately we are connected to one another as members of a particular society. Molly is an animal barely under control, we are persuaded; and Jaggers, her keeper, is himself a predator one minute (not hesitating to push aside the law, even violate it, while fighting as someone's courtroom advocate) and the proverbial dumb beast another minute—lost and mute and confused when not at work, hence not able to show his swagger, his cunning, his crude and relentless appetite.

His legal associate Wemmick also tells us something about ourselves, I fear. This lovely, genial, generous, thoughtful and considerate man (at home) becomes a willing agent of greed and brute force at work. Dickens once again wants to emphasize the duality of our natures, the capacity we have to split ourselves in half, live without shame our contradictory lives: acquisitive and coldly impersonal under one set of circumstances, tactful and sensitive and utterly humane in another setting. John Wemmick's Walworth Castle is necessarily just that—a refuge, a bastion, a place which offers protection against the marauding, normally bankrupt demands of the covetous world outside. There is in him, at home, an element of the self-reliant yeoman, once England's proudest claim. He builds. He plants. He fixes things. He dreams of yet further projects to make life in the country more relaxed and enjoyable. But even in the castle, he's always storing things, calculating how much property he's been able to accumulate. He's not a lavish party-giver—someone bent on self-advertising consumption. But he knows the reassuring comfort that accumulated property can bring, and he is willing to be, day after day in a law office, the strong-faced sidekick of a big deal criminal lawyer—do his various errands, collect cash for him, and, one gathers, help work up his cases. In today's (English) terms,

Jaggers was a flamboyant, sly, if not always unkind and sometimes socially discerning and compassionate barrister; whereas Wemmick was his firm's chief solicitor—someone who didn't need to wash his hands after seeing each client, as was Jaggers' wont. Rather, a trip to the outer precincts worked right well—as it does, perhaps, for some of us today.

## IV

Dickens was not, however, beyond imagining redeeming possibilities in the lives of the individuals he created—and, too, in the work they did. Sydney Carton, in *A Tale of Two Cities,* a well-known character, indeed, in the world Dickens created (especially to high school students!) is (we sometimes forget) a lawyer. He drinks too much. He seems aimless, sad, troubled. He helps the lawyer Stryver free Charles Darnay, who has been accused of committing treason—a spy for France. Unlike *Bleak House* or *Great Expectations,* this novel does not directly approach the law as a profession. Sydney Carton's work as a lawyer is shown to be clever, even brilliant; but our interest in him has to do with his human qualities, *per se,* rather than a professional predicament which tests the moral strength of those qualities. His moral strength is, to be sure, tested—but by an international crisis, by a social revolution, and, not insignificantly, by the constraints and turmoil of love. It is as if Dickens were saying to us: I have shown you, in *Bleak House,* how terribly perplexing and crippling the law itself can be; and I have shown you in *Great Expectations* how terribly insinuating the law can be, morally and psychologically, as its practitioners struggle with the hypocrisies and worse of an industrial order (one not totally unlike our own); now let me take a lawyer and put him in the midst of a tumultuous political scene, a time of drastic upheaval, and see not what happens to his profession or what he does with his profession, but what happens to him as a human being. In *Bleak House* the law is fog; in *Great Expectations,* at times, the law is a snake—an aspect of man's post-Eden fate; in *A Tale of Two Cities* the law is a given person's trade—a footnote, as so much we do can end up being, to an ongoing spiritual struggle, one all too commonly masked, as a matter of fact, by the seeming excellence of our professional and even personal adjustment.

Not that such was the case with attorney Carton. He comes to us dissolute, if nothing else. His crony Stryver is not *quite* dissolute—though the difference between the two, Dickens wants us to realize right off, is more apparent than real. They drink together, offer evidence of a mutual cynicism, an essential boredom with life. Stryver is what his name suggests, still pushing for money and influence. But he is in many respects burned out—morally, for sure, and psychologically, as well. Carton is smarter by far, but also less self-protective. He is our professional man who has a good head on his shoulders and might go far but seems curiously paralyzed, hence headed for alcoholism, suicide, or (is it our fate to hope?) a psychiatrist's office where, presumably, he will be enough helped to—what? Resume work with the Stryvers of this world? Abandon one sort of practice for another? Seek another occupation?

No, we are likely to declare: the problem is not Carton's profession; the problem is Carton himself. He needs to see a doctor. But is that the case? Do we find ourselves wanting Stryver to have *his* head examined? Stryver, whom Dickens describes as "a man of little more than thirty, but looking twenty years older than he was, stout, loud, red, bluff, and free from any drawback of delicacy"; Stryver who "had a pushing way of shouldering himself (morally and physically) onto companies and conversations"? Once more Dickens is our late 20th-century social observer, quite ready to confound us with the ongoing riddle of this psychological era: why is it that some who seem quite obnoxious in every way are not usually regarded as candidates for psychiatric scrutiny, while others, in comparison exceedingly refined and decent, are quickly considered in serious difficulty, and quite in need of "help," as we choose to call it?

For Dickens, the law and the prison which awaits those who violate the law were not only recurrent subjects to be explained in novel after novel. Nor was the interest in those subjects a mere consequence of an early personal experience. Like other 19th-century social critics and moralists who had not once been in trouble with the law or inside a prison, Dickens took close stock of an emerging industrial order and was truly aghast. In *Hard Times* he lets us know how much so—how vicious he deemed not only the treatment accorded the poor but also the burden put upon those who were not at all poor. Again and again we are reminded that exploitation cuts both ways—that those who coldly manipulate others, or bring up their children to do so, will pay a stiff price, indeed: the fear, the suspiciousness, the nervous, self-justifying smugness, the isolating arrogance which, in sum, amount to a vision of the blind leading the blind, the meanly powerful worrying over the sadly hurt.

In *A Tale of Two Cities* he dares suggest that all London is a prison of sorts, and Paris, too. The streets are narrow and confusing. Even Tellson's bank, which has offices in both cities, and to which the affluent come to tap their resources, is dark and dingy, has its "own iron bars proper." The Paris bank has a "high wall and a strong gate." Mention is made of "depositors rusted in prison." Jerry Cruncher, the bank's odd-jobber, is an "inmate of a menagerie"; and he has rust on his fingers and is at the beck and call of anyone and everyone. As with France's royalty, and eventually, its murderous revolutionaries, England's rich and powerful know constant apprehension, can take little for granted, keep a wary eye on friends and all too numerous enemies. And, needless to say, in *Little Dorrit,* that theme of pervasive confinement, of jails as the lot of people badly isolated from one another, reaches a climax—Marshalsea Prison, the Circumlocution Office, Bleeding Heart Yard: England's bureaucratic and legal and commercial and moral confusions, duplicities, aberrancies as, in sum, a heavy, collective constraint upon a particular nation's people.

But Dickens not only regarded closely a nation and criticized it with earnest passion (through humor, gentle or biting; through sentiment, gentle or mawkish or extremely touching; through caricatures and heroic portraits and sustained imagery and shrewdly engaging character portrayal and plots which have a way of holding the reader, no matter their lapses into the all too expectable); he was, as mentioned, his own kind of moral visionary. In his essay on Dickens, a fine one, a trenchant one, and maybe an autobiographical one, George Orwell emphasizes this side of Dickens, his strong interest in seeing justice done. Orwell stresses the presence in Dickens of a "native generosity of mind" and reminds us how continually, in those many novels, we are reminded of the twin importance of "freedom and equality." Dickens hated all who lord it over others, as Orwell did. Let any onetime victim rise up far enough, they both knew, and the danger of yet additional wrongdoing immediately arises. Our century, alas, has made such an observation (stressed throughout *A Tale of Two Cities*) a huge and awful banality—and the result, of course, has been the untimely deaths of millions and prisons whose size and nature even a prophetic novelist with the imagination of a Dickens could never possibly foresee.

In a memorable phrase Orwell calls Dickens a Christian out of a "quasi-instinctive siding with the oppressed against the oppressors"; and one can scarcely disagree. Dickens took careful, calculated aim at those oppressors and, like Orwell, knew that they can appear, out of nowhere it seems, in every possible location—among the poor as well as the rich, among people of all races and backgrounds, among professional men and intellectuals as well as men of commerce, and among women as well as men. Madame de Farge in *A Tale of Two Cities* need only be mentioned; and Skimpole, in *Bleak House,* whose clever, self-enhancing egoism bears an astonishing resemblance to what can be found in various centers of literary and artistic activity. Dickens knew well what we have called "the culture of narcissism," the seductive power of the mirror. His prisons have mirrors in them—a double jeopardy! So does the London courtroom where the prisoner Charles Darnay fights for his life with the help of the lawyers Stryver and Carton. Even the members of the crowd watching the trial become "mirrors reflecting the witness." There is, of course, and necessarily so, a last-ditch narcissism at stake in many courtrooms: a life itself will be saved or lost—not to mention the personal reputation (and sense of self-worth) of this or that lawyer. But for Dickens any particular trial is emblematic—

as in Kafka's *The Trial:* our desperate situation as human beings revealed by our inability to recognize just how trapped we are within our own world of eager pretentiousness and by the endless circularities we pursue as if they were a straight road to an absolutely certain destination.

V

Dickens himself, despite the gloom so many of his stories contain (and the gratuitous quality to their happy endings), was not without hope. He found decency in ordinary, unassuming people, the humble of this earth who (we are promised, we were solemnly warned) would inherit the world. He saw plenty of evil—and children, always, as victims, as born prisoners who never seem to get their sentences fully commuted. Yes, Pip marries Estella, one ending of *Great Expectations* tells us. Yes, Esther Summerson marries Dr. Allen Woodcourt, *Bleak House* informs us. Yes, Arthur Clennam finds Little Dorrit, and Sydney Carton finds Lucie Manette, and through those two women each man is affirmed—all the pain and suffering of their early lives somehow caused to recede in personal significance. But in all Dickens' novels the meanness and brutishness of this life is made abundantly clear. Pip's famous moment of searching introspections, his trenchant statement about himself and his life, turns into an authorial comment on justice and its vicissitudes, on our fate as human beings, born into an arbitrary and imperfect world and soon enough to depart: "In the little world in which children have their existence whosoever brings them up, there is nothing so finely perceived and so finely felt, as injustice. It may be only small injustice that the child can be exposed to; but the child is small, and its world is small, and its rocking-horse stands as many hands high, according to scale, as a big-boned Irish hunter. Within myself, I had sustained, from my babyhood, a perpetual conflict with injustice. I had known, from the time when I could speak, that my sister, in her capricious and violent coercion, was unjust to me. I had cherished a profound conviction that her bringing me up by hand, gave her no right to bring me up by jerks. Through all my punishments, disgraces, fasts and vigils, and other penitential performances, I had nursed this assurance; and to my communing so much with it, in a solitary and unprotected way, I in great part refer the fact that I was morally timid and very sensitive."

But there is, the same author knew, a chance to reverse things, to render a kind of fitting if finite justice—a redemption here on earth that must precede any further redemption to be gained elsewhere in the universe. Dickens' interest in practical, everyday charity (of the kind Jesus offered again and again as He walked Galilee nearly two thousand years ago) is well underscored in this extraordinary passage in *Little Dorrit*—another one of his hurt souls looking back and looking ahead. "As the fierce dark teaching of his childhood had never sunk into his heart, so that first article in his code of morals was, that he must begin, in practical humility, with looking well to his feet on Earth, and that he could never mount on wings of words to Heaven. Duty on earth, restitution on earth, action on earth; these first, as the first steep steps upward. Strait was the gate and narrow was the way; far straiter and narrower than the broad high road paved with vain professions and vain repetitions, motes from other men's eyes and liberal delivery of others to the judgement—all cheap materials costing absolutely nothing."

So it goes, or we hope it will go, for ourselves—a chance to do the Lord's will in the way He showed: daily tasks, obligations, possibilities of charity. Sometimes I hear Dickens faulted—he saw wrongs, but he failed to give us an overall scheme to right them. In view of the various all-encompassing ideologies we have seen at work in this century—ones offering personal and social rehabilitation on the grandest scale—we can be grateful, maybe, for Dickens' restrained reformism, his humane egalitarian liberalism, and, one also insists, his down-to-earth Christianity, so beholden to Jesus of Nazareth rather than the various "principalities and powers" which have come to speak so confidently, if not imperiously, in His name. In that last regard, Orwell does well to quote from a letter Dickens wrote to his youngest son in 1868: "You will remember that you have never at home been harassed about religious observances, or mere formalities. I have always been anxious not to weary my children with such things, before they are old enough to form opinions respecting them. You will therefore understand the better that I now most solemnly impress upon you the truth and beauty of the Christian Religion, as it came from Christ Himself, and the impossibility of your going far wrong if you humbly but heartily respect it. . . . Never abandon the wholesome practice of saying your own private prayers, night and morning. I have never abandoned it myself, and I know the comfort of it."

What is the law but a necessarily finite effort on our part to find some earthly vision which at least partakes in a small way of that larger Biblical vision offered us by the Hebrew prophets Jeremiah, Isaiah, Amos, and by the one who followed them, Jesus Christ? A vision of what? A moral vision, surely. A vision, put negatively at first, of what must *not* be done—so that, over time, we will edge nearer to a more honorable and decent world, where "equal justice" will not only be a phrase cut in the marble of a particular Washington, D.C. building, but something known and felt to be a daily given the world over. Meanwhile, we all struggle with this life's hardships, its terrible lack of justice, a curse for so many; and we struggle, also, to figure out how to change that state of affairs—through (among other ways) laws written, through laws challenged, through laws argued and argued, through interventions here and there on behalf of one person, then another.

In the midst of those struggles a moral visionary such as Charles Dickens is no small ally. He takes in his hands the abstract matters of a subject matter, legal ethics, and gives them the complex, provocative life of a story. He gives us character as fate shapes it. He gives us chance and circumstance, good luck and bad luck, humor and melancholy—an opportunity not to figure out the world theoretically, but put oneself in it correctly. As a moral visionary, he left us situations to heed, people to know, a whole range of ethical matters to attend in a very special way—the personal immersion enabled by a novel. One can, he knew (to use the phrase of our contemporary, American novelist, the Southerner Walker Percy) "get all A's and flunk life." One can, he knew, do well in a course called "legal ethics" or "moral reasoning" and go on to be a not so honorable and straightforward and compassionate human being. The novels of Dickens offer reminders enough of people who preach a good tune to others and fail to heed it in the everyday particulars of their lives—the Mrs. Jellybys of this world. The novels of Dickens offer us *ourselves,* plenty of us flawed, all too many of us thoroughly wretched, yet, more than a few of us sometimes graced by moments and longer of honor.

Recently I came across this observation, made by Viktor Frankl, a physician who only barely survived years of Hitler's hell: "We who lived in concentration camps can remember the men who walked through the huts comforting others, giving away their last piece of bread. They may have been few in number, but they offer sufficient proof that everything can be taken from a man but one thing: the last of the human freedoms—to choose one's attitude in any given set of circumstances, to choose one's own way." As one goes over those words again and again, surely it is not inappropriate to think of Charles Dickens and his enormous, hard-earned moral quarry, which he dug and dug, a lifetime's effort. He knew how constrained we all are, how hard it is for us to break free, to achieve a measure of continuing dignity. His exhortation of a particular profession, the law, was meant to honor its possible role in our lives—at its best a bulwark against anarchy and a pointer in the direction of fairness. Still, there are awful lapses, as he knew, and as we in this century have also come to know—to the point that the often isolated and lonely good folk of the world of Charles Dickens seem to reach out to join hands with those Dr. Frankl describes: orphans all amid the terrible human disasters of our history, yet also heroes whom each of us needs to remember with a certain tenacity, perhaps, as we go about our daily lives, our daily business, including that of the law.

WENDY W. FAIREY

## In My Mother's House: Images of a Hollywood Childhood

[ SPRING 1985 ]

THERE is a passage in *Daniel Deronda,* George Eliot's final novel, that urges the benefits of passing one's childhood in a well-loved place. Pitying the heroine whose unrooted early years have left her without inner guidance in a venal, aimless milieu, the author is prompted to reflect:

> A human life, I think, should be well-rooted in some spot of a native land, where it may get the love of tender kinship for the face of the earth, . . . a spot where the definiteness of early memories may be inwrought with affection, and kindly acquaintance with all neighbours, even to the dogs and donkeys, may spread not by sentimental effort and reflection, but as a sweet habit of the blood.

I marked these lines in my copy of the novel with the sense of my own deprivation. My childhood "spot" was a large Spanish-style house in Beverly Hills, California. But how can George Eliot's prescriptions apply to a place like Beverly Hills, a film-world town where not a single family goes back for generations and even the palm trees are arrivistes in an artfully transformed desert? What does such a place offer? What does it determine? I retain my early memories—of our house, friends, a fig tree in the back yard, even as George Eliot would have it, a series of cherished dogs. But do these suffice to anchor a life? More than anything else, Beverly Hills for me is the place that I was happy to get away from. At 15, fortified by notions of culture and opportunity culled largely from 19th-century novels, already my taste in fiction, I went East to a Connecticut boarding school where we all had blue blazers, sports tunics, and riding gear, was grafted onto the East coast, and never again spent any amount of time in California. To have grown up then out West, in Beverly Hills among the film people, became an autobiographical tidbit, obtrusive yet incidental, always potentially embarrassing, to be disclosed with discretion depending on my faith in the listener.

It was at boarding school that I discovered how my background could be a source of interest and oddity for others. Most of the girls were Northeasterners and seemed to me insulated in a privileged enclosure of mutual acquaintances at well-known schools. Boarders from California, of whom there were only four, included a tennis and basketball star—eventually captain of both teams—from a well-to-do San Francisco family, two not at all preppy Santa Barbara sisters, one with a reputation, merited or not, for being rather loose, and finally, myself, small and a little mousy, fingers invariably spotted with ink, the student with the highest average in the school and a home in Beverly Hills where my mother, Sheilah Graham, worked to pay for my acquisition of an Eastern patina through her job as a Hollywood columnist. The word of this connection soon got about, and if my oddity did not diminish, at least my usefulness increased when I was able to obtain autographed photographs of their movie idols for the starstruck girls. These hung on the walls in the cell-like dormitory rooms. "To Anne, Best regards, Paul Newman." "For Lynn, Best wishes for success from Gregory Peck." One friend, home with me over a vacation, actually lunched with Rock Hudson at his studio. We have a photograph of the occasion: a resigned Rock Hudson seated between the two girls, my friend turning toward him, her face sweetly joyous with excitement, myself turned away, a look in my eyes of assiduous blankness, indifference a personal necessity.

I think that I could much more plausibly, more usefully too in terms of a guiding heritage, have come from somewhere else—Connecticut, perhaps, or Pennsylvania. I had an eighth-grade classmate at the California school where every morning as a prelude to the required Pledge of Allegiance, we would face eastward, stretch out our arms, and recite a Hindu Salutation to the Dawn, who did much better than I as a product of Beverly Hills. Already at 13, effusive, beautiful and fast, she was vibrantly consummate in artifice. I remember her entrance at one of the school's well-organized, well-chaperoned semiformal dances. Chestnut hair cascading about her face, she awed the rest of us with the height of her heels and the low cut of her strapless, scarlet gown. My heels on the same occasion were one inch high and my gown, which was pink, had a box neck with tulle ruffles on the straps. The girl's older sister was a starlet who dated Lance Reventlow, Barbara Hutton's playboy son, and whose picture would appear with his in movie magazines. Their father was a movie producer, their mother an alcoholic. Later on in life I would hear intermittently about my classmate: she had married, divorced, remarried, then divorced again a young Los Angeles millionaire, then married someone else much older than herself with whom she had moved to the Caribbean and set up as partners in a liquor-export business. A friend who saw her at 30 reported that she was still beautiful and that she was living, at this point between marriages, in an apartment in Hollywood where the walls were covered with mirrors, the rugs and furniture were white, and where there were also several white cats. Visiting on the same occasion was another classmate whose family yacht had once taken our whole eighth-grade group to Catalina Island. As an adult, this person raised chihuahuas and casually proclaimed her wealth in the clutter of rings on her fingers.

Not everyone of my acquaintance from California has had a bizarre and vulgar destiny. But if they haven't, then what is their connection with the place? Many have led lives with at least the continuity of affluence, having achieved wealth of their own through luck or application, in marriage or in careers which are surprisingly often Hollywood careers—in film, in television, in the music and recording business. Others are the logical failures, dead as suicides or, less dramatically, simply unsuccessful people, drifting, curtailed by famous parents, not up to the steadfast effort of tending their own lives.

As for myself, the intent to do and be something quite different goes way back. At 11 or 12, sitting with my mother before bedtime in my recently redecorated room, I asked a question. Did she think that I would grow up to be an intellectual? The prospect struck me as not beyond my reach, but I did not underestimate the challenge. My mother's answer, perhaps purposely vague but nonetheless reassuring, included her standard encouragement that "my time would come" with the addition in this instance that if I continued to study hard she was sure I could be whatever I wanted.

What I wanted was to be part of a world of subtle grace and thoughtfulness. In one of my private fantasies I imagined having a father—not our own who was divorced from my mother, lived far off in England, and was a fairly crass man of business—but an intellectual father whom I would seat in my scenario at the foot of our oblong mahogany dining table, and there, dignified and subdued, he would lead the family in discussions of politics and culture. Now that I think of it, it is odd that my fantasy never displaced my mother from the head of the table—or at least the end that I considered the head because that is where she sat, the end at which the housekeeper would set the dinner platter and which I associate with my mother's presence and absolute predominance. I cannot remember her role in the imaginary discourse. I think that I had her simply sitting there, listening to my well-modulated patriarch.

We were, in fact, my mother's children, the beneficiaries of her success, the well-cared-for dependents of her household. In 1947, drawing on all her savings, she mustered a down payment on an old but elegant Beverly Hills Spanish-style house, and there we lived for close to 12 years with the assurance in many ways, particularly in the beginning, of utter order and solidarity. It wasn't simply that the white stucco walls had a fortress-like thickness or that we were accommodated with pets and bicycles and a Ping-Pong table on the back veranda. It was the orderly life of the house, the reassuring points of reference for me in the people who worked there: my mother whom I would always seek out briefly after school, never afraid to interrupt her, on my way outside to play in the high, wall-enclosed backyard; the housekeeper in the kitchen, making pastry dough or cooking or ironing laundry; the secretary tapping out my mother's daily column on her typewriter in the bookcase-lined den; the Filipino gardener, working shirtless out of doors, adjusting the sprinkler system or trimming the edges of the manicured front lawn. It was a house full of industry, a self-sustaining enterprise, in which my part, taking it serenely for granted, was to go my own way within its enclosure.

For what we lacked—which was not a great deal, but our house had no tennis court or swimming pool—we had access to the private courts and pools of movie people in the area. My mother arranged for us to swim in the pools of James Mason and Anne Baxter and to go with our tennis teacher to the courts of Dorothy Lamour, Robert Stack, and Kirk Douglas. The stars were never home—or at least not visible—only the servants and the dogs. I was particularly drawn to Anne Baxter's shaggy black Newfoundland, wistfully observing us from behind a wire enclosure, as if he too wouldn't mind a dip to cool off from the California heat, yet with too much dignity to make a fuss, unlike Dorothy Lamour's yapping little poodles. But their barks dissolve in memories of the overriding stillness. The streets of Beverly Hills were tree-lined and hushed. Children played under the supervision of servants in their walled-off back gardens.

It is only when I push beyond these pictorial recollections to the greater stir and tension of the place that my own lack of ease reasserts itself. Not that there wasn't the beguilement of privilege. We took full advantage as a family of Hollywood's wooing and propitiation of my mother, who, given her own start in life in an orphanage, was happy to share all conceivable advantages with her children. And so my brother and I tagged along for film previews and lunches at the studios, weekends in Palm Springs, and even the trips to Europe. Fringe benefits were a family pastime. We exploited them as it suited us, yet still in our minds stood aloof from Hollywood cant and shallowness. It was easy to mark the separation between ourselves and someone like Zsa Zsa Gabor, who sat in our living room advising against animation of the face because it caused wrinkles, yet managing to emit great gushes of insincerity. "Dahling, vat lovely cheeldren!" Such people became items in my mother's column. "My paragraphs," she would call them. For her, the banter was part of work, not cause for worry. For me, it was somehow more threatening, offending my stubbornly held notions of a world of greater taste and truth and also my own sense of self-importance. I did not like standing idly by while silly people talked with my mother. It was a bore and also an indignity to be so unobserved by people I had judged and found wanting. I recall the poor press agent who patiently ignored my scorn as I sat wedged in a corner of the lunch table at the Beverly Hills Brown Derby, eating the steak that had been ordered for me. He was confiding about the stars to my mother in what I considered a grating, officious, ignoble manner. My mother I did not fault since this was simply her part in an expedient masquerade. But the press agent, as far as I was concerned, was irretrievably implicated in the avidity for publicity, the lack of respect for privacy, the self-seeking and insecurity which marked the typical Hollywood conversation.

Often on such occasions the press agent lunching with us would ask celebrities to our table. Tony Curtis, Doris Day, Hitchcock, or Lucille Ball would get up from where they were relaxing or talking business, stride toward my mother with a "Dahling, how are you?" and proceed to promote themselves before retreating with a "So lovely to see you." My revenge for the perfunctory notice taken of me was my own satiric observation of the process: star, press agent, and columnist so seemingly caught up in the effusions of the moment when the sole end in everyone's mind was business—the items in my mother's column which would publicize. Yet when anyone—a star or even a press agent—showed an interest in me that I deemed sincere and intelligent, I suspended my usual suspicion, absolved the person of phoniness, and expanded in my mind the small circle of Hollywood people whom we considered genuine and worthwhile. Ingrid Bergman was nice to me when I met her in Paris. My mother interviewed her in the bar of the Hotel Raphael while her three children by Roberto Rosselini played on the floor of the dark oak room. She asked me questions about my school which her daughter Pia Lindstrom had attended, and I did my best to give informative, clever answers. I also liked Maureen O'Hara, my mother's more intimate friend—they had met on the set of *How Green Was My Valley* and struck up a close bond. Maureen attended our annual Christmas Eve parties at which I would play carols on the piano. I remember her seated in one of our quilt-upholstered arm chairs, beautiful to me with her red hair, pale complexion, and Irish accent. She confided in my mother as a friend, not a columnist, the details of her romance with a Mexican businessman who draped her in jewels and bought her a house, or so she thought, in Mexico while promising to divorce his wife and marry her as soon as his children grew up. When they did, he asked for the jewels back, and she discovered that the house in Mexico was not in her name. She brought a lawsuit against him and they compromised, she keeping most of the jewels and he the house. "I do hope," said my mother in a telling slip of the tongue, "that Wendy will be happy in her marriages."

The fact that the stars led flamboyantly unsettled lives or that the smooth serenity of Beverly Hills had its precarious underside in the movie business—all ostentation, uncertainty, and hustle—would most likely have been forgivable if as a family we had remained immune to these currents. But we didn't. I wonder how many other Hollywood children have experienced my own sense of the disruption of an idyll, the gradual inroad into privileged, smooth-edged young lives of turbulence and insubstantiality. A husband of my mother's came and went. He moved in his possessions, carrying innumerable shoes in cardboard boxes up our curving staircase with its iron-wrought banister and on to my mother's bedroom. I sat on the stairs and watched his intrusion. The wedding reception at our home was so splendid that one Hollywood paper named my mother "Hostess of the Year." Marilyn Monroe put in an appearance, arriving hours late as usual, and had her picture taken kissing my little brother. Three years later the stepfather was evicted—although he had in some ways proved quite helpful to my mother, he was not, in fact, a good man, and I welcomed his departure with a grim kind of glee. He and I had been particular antagonists, covert for the most part, though once when he had kicked the dog, I had openly defied him, and my mother, watching the scene, had feared that he would strike me. But he hadn't. And at last, thank God, he was gone.

Nonetheless after that, things were never the same. I was alarmed to see my mother cry from the strain of the divorce. Also around the same time, I began to perceive the embattled nature of her job—the irascibly asserted demands of her newspaper employers, her brinkmanship with irate stars stung by her items into the threat of lawsuits, her exercises in self-assertion over sycophantic press agents. I was angry at what I considered her failure to sustain a protected world, and I buried myself more determinedly than ever in interests and fantasies which posed an alternative to Hollywood.

And finally, we left. We folded up our tent. With my brother set to follow me back East to boarding school, my mother rather suddenly, in 1959 when I was 17, sold the Beverly Hills house and set up in the East with considerably more modest homes in New York and Connecticut, still continuing to write a column but from a broader base. Our old house was bought by newlywed Warren Cowan of the Rogers and Cowan Agency and Barbara Rush, the actress. They renovated it from top to bottom, changing even its basic shape by the addition of a major wing. They also built a swimming pool in the backyard. And once we left Beverly Hills, it was as if we had never been there, perhaps because we had only been part of the place, tenuously at best, by virtue of our mother's job. The whole enterprise had seemed solid enough, but it was precariously dependent on one woman's effort. As long as that effort was sustained, it was not a fragile construct, but it was, nonetheless, a construct with fragile roots. We were self-created in Hollywood like many other people living there—all the stars with changed names. Our home, for all the life within it, for all the solidarity of its walls, was very much like a stage set. And this particular tour de force was over.

And then for years, that I had grown up in Beverly Hills meant nothing to me, save perhaps a certain standard of living. But even this had left its wry aftertaste. Our perquisites were in great part the spillover of my mother's position in Hollywood—we had no substantial family wealth. When I myself chose a less well-paying occupation, I faced the awkwardness of being left with habits of affluence which I no longer had the means to support.

Of course, one could always try oneself to be rich and famous, and the fact that I suspect I would succeed if I tried is undoubtedly a reflection of my past. But another part of the Hollywood legacy is the loss of faith in this impulse. My brother had a flash of success when at 23 he published a novel about youth, sex, and alienation which was then sold to the movies with my brother himself engaged to write the screenplay. On the crest of his good fortune, he bought a green velvet suit, ate out in expensive restaurants every night, married a movie star's daughter, and set off with her in first-class passage on an Italian ocean liner bound for Naples—I went down to the New York pier to see them off. A year later, his money all spent, he retreated to a cabin in the woods north of San Francisco. And there he has remained ever since, though no longer married to the actor's daughter, herself yet another Hollywood child who currently lives still further to the north in the California mountains and makes her living as a Tarot card fortune teller. My brother has held a job for some years now as the second cook in a rural Czechoslovakian restaurant. I am not saying that he is satisfied with this in many ways marginal life—his most recent passion is jazz piano composition and he would like to sell his songs, but he is unwilling to do what he and I both know to be necessary—to engage in those humiliating efforts of self-promotion. For both of us, dreams of success partake of a fantasy of purity. One writes a brilliant book—the only motive being love of truth and language—and the success, if it comes, is simply one's dessert—it has not been a greedy calculation.

A diffidence about striving for power, a fear of preeminence has been identified as a particular problem for women, a part of their acquiescence in their suppression within the culture. In my case and also that of my brother, this same sort of diffidence is linked with our Hollywood past. We had such great scorn for the people around us who were so avidly, so crassly, sometimes so poignantly scrambling that it is difficult to give ourselves over to any unironic efforts of self-aggrandizement. Our mother was an untrammeled, self-made woman, committed to the notion of her own destiny, a taker of risks with the underlying courage of one utterly responsible for herself. A great reader, her literary models, the characters in whom she recognized herself, were those who plunged into life with sufficient resilience to withstand the consequences. I, on the other hand, respecting her bravado and achievement but in need of a different fiction, have been drawn to books like the novels of George Eliot in which the aspiring individual is always tempered, contained, judged within a moral framework, and the only permissible happiness comes with the subsuming of egoism in the identification with some greater common good. And thus I became a professor and dean at an Eastern college.

Hollywood, I think, has been an important place for me but largely in a negative way—in the cultivation of doubts and antipathies. It showed me, as I went about the task of constructing a self, what I must work hard not to be. Or to put this a bit more concretely, however I might admire a star like Ingrid Bergman, transcendent in dignity and beauty, the admiration was passive; it called for no action; it bore no relation to my own sense of self. On the other hand, I felt it within my power, and I would do everything which that power allowed, to be as different as possible from the likes of Zsa Zsa Gabor. And so spurred by a generalized specter of vulgarity and self-absorption, I strove to turn my own egoism to more civilized and intelligent account, yet at the same time always a bit afraid of what I might want, what I might be if I ever relaxed my diligence and discipline.

Recently, however, I have had a shift in thought concerning the women of Hollywood, the garish women as well as the beautiful transcendent ones, that has helped to make the stubborn fact of a Hollywood past seem both more palatable and more useful. This change is connected with a recent Christmas visit to Palm Beach, Florida, where my mother now maintains an apartment for the winter in a pleasant oceanside condominium. It always startles me to reencounter Palm Beach, a place so much like Beverly Hills in the sparkling stillness of its pastel-colored mansions enclosed by their well-tended lawns and high walls and hedges. But since we don't own one of these mansions and since it annoys my mother that she is poor by Palm Beach standards, she retaliates with the pronouncement that it is an indignity to be, as she puts it, a second-class citizen in a place where the first-class people are so third rate. Palm Beach, she points out, is not a place where people work or necessarily owe their wealth to any personal talent or exertion. The women organize charity balls and dress for parties. And yet my mother lives there, and I visit her at Christmas for a one-week stay of indolence and sunshine.

The contrast, of course, is that Beverly Hills was an industry town. Its residents, including women like my mother, were successful professional people. And if sex was often a blatant issue in their lives, gender at least was not a prohibition. The familiar names that have entered this piece—Anne Baxter, Dorothy Lamour, Marilyn Monroe, Ingrid Bergman, Maureen O'Hara, even Zsa Zsa Gabor—are the names of working women, successful working women with whom as a child growing up in Beverly Hills I came into contact. They may have been helped or hindered by husbands or lovers or studio moguls; they may have appeared in roles on the screen as every man's desire and right. But these nevertheless were women who made their own money and as often as not bought their own mansions. Perhaps a third of the houses on our block were owned by women—not just the stars but women writers, costume designers, agents, and others. It is the significance of this simple perception and proportion that has caused me to think a bit differently about my own connection with Hollywood and the efficacy of a Hollywood childhood in a life that has taken an intentionally different turn but that has always involved both the fact of work and a stress on its importance.

Visiting my mother two Christmases ago in Palm Beach, I found the achievement of Hollywood women crystallized in a peculiar image. My mother invariably has a few biographies and autobiographies of the stars, which publishers send to her, lying about on her coffee table. On the occasion in question, one of these was *Mommie Dearest,* Christina Crawford's best-selling memoir of her relationship with her mother. I picked it up and read it through, though resentful of the encroachment into my vacation of such a vituperative tale. A mother's monstrosity is not a comfortable subject, and I was happy as I read to contrast Joan Crawford with my own mother, who, simply to launch the list of differences, never drank. But there was one image in the book which touched a strange chord of memory. Christina Crawford describes the care which she and her brother took, if they wished to play outside in their back yard in the mornings, not to make noise which might disturb their mother sleeping in her bedroom upstairs. Although my own mother always woke up early, the part of the description which to me was utterly familiar was the focal point of the mother in her bedroom, her presence irradiating from that center and asserting its force over the rest of the household. My own mother's room was spacious and extremely comfortable. Even when she was married, it was furnished to meet her own needs—a dressing-room annex was built for the husband's. Her day would always start with breakfast in bed, not in spoiledness or indolence but in conservation of her energy which would be called upon later in demanding ways. She was enormously productive even before rising from her bed: talking with her children, scribbling ideas on spiral notepads, making phone calls, and generally planning the day's activities. There was one phone extension on the bedside table and a second on the enormous desk which occupied a part of the room more officially given over to work. In another corner of the room was a reclining chair where my mother would often sit, at its full backward tilt, in the late afternoons. She also used to rest by stretching out flat on the floor, and I would come in and lie next to her and chat. This main room was part of a suite which also included a dressing room and a bathroom and, finally, the husband's annex, off to the side.

There is no question in my mind that my mother had a room of her own.

She had, in fact, a whole house of her own, an emblem of her strengths and independence. I speak about my own mother as a particular case but also as an example of a successful woman in Hollywood. It is possible that my viewpoint is naïve, based as it is on the selective memories of childhood—and that a less impressionistic analysis could place the women of Hollywood in a more ambivalent light. However powerful a figure Joan Crawford may have loomed to her children as she slept off her hangovers in her bedroom, it is difficult to avoid the acknowledgment of her perversity and instability. Then, too, one might ask, is it a sign of vulnerability or of an essential autonomy to rival Moll Flanders in the number of one's husbands? I have never forgotten a spread in a late 1950's fan magazine of Lana Turner pictured in succession with each of her five husbands (she has since had two more), each younger looking than the preceding one as she, intersecting with their curve toward youth, starts off young and gets progressively older, in the end much older than the last and youngest husband. The pictures suggest a quest, an appetite, a bizarre reversal of familiar gender roles. They also in a strange way validate Lana Turner. She is the center of interest, the important personage. The figure of the husband is that of an interchangeable appendage. But what does it feel like to marry seven husbands? I know that I myself wouldn't like it. Still, it is possible that the most desperate or aimless experience can always be ordered into a convenient fiction—of glamour, of struggle, of survival. At the end of the career and the marriages comes, if nothing else, the vindication of the autobiography. Lana Turner, I note, has recently published her own "true" story, *Lana: The Lady, the Legend, the Truth*.

My story has been an effort to define a legacy. I realize that a part of this legacy is a perspective about women, an impression of their capacity. It never occurred to me from my experience as a child in Hollywood to think of women as at a disadvantage or as tactically located outside the center of power or interest. As the daughter of a Hollywood columnist, I saw a great deal of activity that I considered wasteful or absurd, and I came to dislike the general assumptions of the Hollywood world. But my childhood was too replete with women of some energy or purpose, women who commanded attention, for me to have escaped an incorrigibly feminocentric vision of reality. I knew the dominance of my mother, who for so long sustained our household and our lives, ably seconded by those subsidiary figures of authority, the cooks and the secretaries. I felt the presence of the stars, living up and down the streets of Beverly Hills in their mansions. I noted other women, too, less famous ones but merged for me in a general impression of female effectiveness: the clever woman who produced my mother's radio show; the woman screenwriter, a family friend, with a house and tennis court at Malibu and a charming, unemployed husband; yet another friend who owned a lingerie shop in Beverly Hills which specialized in silk and satin nightgowns for the celebrities and whose retired husband, nicknamed Pops, took long naps after lunch; and then finally, just a further example, the third ex-wife of J. Paul Getty whose earlier career as an opera singer was in evidence during the carol singing at our Christmas parties and who showed great personal courage when her son went blind and died.

If many households, many cultures, contain strong women, the anomaly of women in Hollywood was the flagrance of their scope and freedom and, in so many cases, the truly picaresque dimension of their lives. Or perhaps the central paradox is that they were picaresque and professional at the same time. I myself was wary of picaresque adventures. I determined to value balance, self-containment, clarity of purpose, continuities, the challenge of marrying one husband. Nonetheless, the self, the female self, looms from my childhood as a bold conception. And since I did indeed want to work and to do well in my chosen terms and, all in all, to lead a life in which my own efficacy mattered, this conception, the residual imprint of Hollywood with its mansions and its palm trees long behind me, has proved, I find, a legacy of substance.

SPENCE W. PERRY

# Vietnam: Mirage and Fitful Dream

[ SPRING 1985 ]

I

THE EXPERIENCE of war can never be fully communicated. War has a broken, furtive character that prevents a full expression of its reality. Beyond the difficulty with reporting its objective manifestations, battles won and lost, planes shot down, towns seized and farms ransacked, ground lost or advanced upon, there is a subjective dimension having to do with the perceptions, emotions, and feelings of those involved that is often totally uncapturable, or if captured, which can only be indicated or given scant notation. Relating the objective and the subjective dimensions to each other is difficult if not impossible at the time the events occur and emotions are felt. For this reason, our understanding of armed conflict usually becomes better over time. As war recedes, its reality comes clearer.

In all the American experience with war, the Vietnam conflict offers the most horrible example of gross misperception, contemporaneous with the event. The blurred vision, the cataracts of various hues from rose to gray, were not monopolized by any one party to the conflict. The American vision was, of course, badly flawed. But the South Vietnamese, the North Vietnamese, and the insurgents all possessed astigmatisms of their own.

The only perceptions for which we are ultimately responsible before the face of history, however, are our own, and at this point, ten years after the fall of Saigon, American misperceptions are the only ones that are relevant for us as we hastily attempt to understand history to avoid its repetition.

Misperceptions in armed conflict lead to what Von Clausewitz termed the "frictions of war." It is these frictions that cause the reality of conflict to deviate from plans and projections. If the frictions become great enough, and the deviation between plan and reality becomes great enough, defeat may result. This is particularly true when military leadership is not flexible and refuses to alter its perceptions to meet new realities.

In large part America lost the war in Vietnam because its senior political and military leadership never knew the reality it faced. This lack of accurate vision was not due to a shortage of signals. There were abundant indicators that the American perception was flawed. Some signals were to be found on the battlefield. Other indicators were not directly related to combat, but they were reflective of the context in which the fighting took place; and they were probably more important in many respects because they were related to people and policies that controlled events on the battlefield.

## II

The colonel was overweight, not seriously but enough that he puffed and grunted as he settled into the back seat of his battered '66 Chevrolet sedan staff car. It was a cloudy, unusually cool April day in Saigon. There was a fine mist in the air, hinting at the spring monsoon. Mr. Kanh, the colonel's driver, nosed the car past the sentry gate and out of the U.S. compound headed for BOQ 1. The colonel took lunch at the BOQ every day, precisely at noon. Although the University of Virginia had made the colonel a lawyer, West Point had made him a soldier, and the first imprint predominated. He had no trouble with the question of whether he was first an officer or a judge advocate. In his mind, he was an officer who also happened to be a lawyer.

A young Army captain sat next to the colonel. He was new in the country and was convinced that every venture forth was a cavalier invitation to assassination.

The colonel turned to the captain. "Gray and chilly today. Reminds me of France in '44. It was on a day just like this I killed my German." The colonel smiled. "It was damp and cool, and my glasses kept getting fogged up so I had trouble lining up my sights. But I got him." Nostalgia.

The colonel was not alone. He was representative of an entire generation of U.S. military leadership that had trained for two decades to fight tank battles with massed infantry on the plains of Northern Europe. Now he and his peers were called upon to lead small unit combat in rice paddies and thatched hamlets. The disillusionment was profound. Expectations, however, cried out to be fulfilled regardless of external realities, and so the U.S. military worked for a decade to apply an irrelevant tactical solution to the problem at hand.

The logistics of the war were reminiscent of earlier, large-scale American conventional wars. The troops carried too much gear; there was too much tail and too little tooth; the units were too large; the command and control systems too inflexible and the staffs overly elaborate. There was a reliance on conventional strategic bombing out of proportion to the enemy being sought.

In hindsight this has been realized and said. At the time, this was not the case. The large-scale approach to combat was the standard wisdom. A wisdom inherited from Grant and the Union Army in the Civil War in which employment of overwhelming material resources over time and slow attrition of the enemy to achieve victory became standard American military doctrine. The military imagination born of necessity by a Stuart or the three-dimensional thinking of a Jackson had proved inadequate to the purposes of the Civil War; they and the approach they represented had been disparaged and rejected for a century.

When, toward the end of the Vietnam adventure, the real nature of the conflict was at last understood by those empowered to influence events, the realization came too late. Having spent their opportunity fighting a mini-World War II for the Vietnamese, the U.S. military leadership found itself without time or residual enthusiasm to make an effective change in tactical approach. Indeed, even the change represented by Vietnamization in the early Seventies retained elements of the earlier vision: while the fighting of the war was at long last turned over to the Vietnamese (from whom it should never have been taken away), they, too, were in turn reequipped in the final hours to fight a European war.

The military sedan pulled under the porte-cochere of the BOQ. In the French days, the building had been a popular restaurant. Now, with its stucco chipped, white paint peeling, and crimson shutters hanging akimbo, it had more the appearance of a dilapidated, Depression-era motel on U.S. 301 than of a former haunt of elegant colons. Still in all, the air conditioning usually worked, and the kitchen was within a tolerable range of approximating basic American fare—hamburgers, cheeseburgers, ham sandwiches, salad bar.

The colonel, the captain following, took a table in the senior officer's section in the BOQ 1 dining room. The colonel brushed aside the mimeographed menu.

The petite Vietnamese waitress hovered attentively.

"Hamburger," he said gruffly, shortly, "French fries," he paused, fixed a beady stare at the girl. "Tell chef fry bun," he said slowly, evenly.

"Yes, sir," she replied. After taking the captain's order, which was a duplicate of the colonel's with no requirement that the bun be fried, she scurried off to the kitchen.

"You see, captain," the colonel began, "the war is a strange mix. On the way here we passed the chopper pad for the Third Field Hospital. They were off-loading casualties, men that had been hit less than an hour ago. And yet, here we are, about to drink beer and eat lunch in air conditioning."

"Saigon," said the captain, "seems crowded, the air has a musty, foul quality to it, except just after the evening rain, the beggars, the poor. . . ."

"It was beautiful once. Just three or four years ago it had a rare elegance," the colonel said. "It's only been recently with the flood of refugees, first from the relocation programs aimed at getting the peasants beyond Viet Cong control and then with the dislocation caused by the Tet offensive, that the city changed. Only after Tet did the sandbags and barbed wire appear."

The waitress placed lunch before the officers. The colonel poked at his bun.

"Bun not fried," he growled. "You take back, tell chef fry bun," he said, an edge in his voice. The waitress took the offending plate and returned through the swinging doors to the kitchen.

"As I said," the colonel continued, "much of the change is relatively recent. But there is still a lot to enjoy. The Mayfair, Le Admiral, both still have good French cooking, although the wine is from Algiers, and don't question too closely about the source of the steak—its either old water buffalo or high-jacked beef from Aussie stores, depending on which day you're there. You can still get a good drink, expensive but good, at the bar at the Majestic hotel. You look out over the river and the city, the place looks like the set for an old Bogart-Greenstreet movie."

The waitress returned with the much-traveled burger. The colonel poked again.

"Bun still not fried," he groused. The waitress flashed a perky smile.

"Chef say no need fry bun, bun fresh!"

The captain had finished his lunch. The colonel began, resignedly, to dine.

## III

Colonel Duc rose in his crisp tan fatigues to greet the junior naval officer in his rumpled whites. The senior Vietnamese Army judge advocate looked out across the dimly lit high-ceilinged room from beneath hooded eyes. He was a young and fit 50, but he moved from behind his heavy desk with the deliberation of an older man. The as yet unheated quiet of the early morning was broken only by the muted ka-whump, ka-whump of ceiling fans and the muffled sound of Saigon rush-hour traffic along the quayside below the shuttered, floor-to-ceiling windows.

"Good day, lieutenant. I was told you would call, that you are the new technical advisor to the directorate of military justice."

"Yes, sir," the lieutenant replied, "the colonel asked me to come over and introduce myself. He was concerned whether there had been any gap in meeting your requirements between the departure of my predecessor and my arrival."

"Ah yes, Captain Koritizinsky, a most esteemed officer. We shall miss him." The colonel motioned to chairs beside the round glass-topped coffee table. "To answer your question, no, things seem to arrive on schedule. Of course, the projections of last year are not adequate to meet our current needs. We must have more concrete, cement block, and roofing tin than we originally projected. The court-martial rate, especially for desertion, is much higher, and our courtroom capacity is not adequate. We need more space to hold court-martials."

The colonel gestured to the tray of drinks and snacks before him, "A drink—cognac or Seigi soda perhaps—a pastry?"

"Brandy will do fine."

The colonel poured generous portions in highball glasses.

"We miss Captain Koritizinsky. He understood our problems, a superb advisor. He went to Paris on R&R. I gave him the names of some old friends at the Sorbonne and the names of some good restaurants run by my countrymen. I think he had a good time."

"He told me his trip was memorable."

A smile crossed the colonel's round and creased features.

"You will have to understand," he said, "that our methods are necessarily more direct than yours, we do not have the luxury of endless appeals. Our determinations must have a swift finality. Of course, we are in a civil war, and the free South is fighting for survival. Our soldiers are less sophisticated than yours. A direct approach, clear answers, satisfy their expectations, and ours for fighting the war. We have not many lawyers, perhaps 200, in all of the Republic."

The colonel and the young American who was his "advisor"-counterpart sat quietly, beneath the fan, the lines between them drawn, the one experienced and intransigent; the other helpless to influence events and hopelessly miscast.

And so it was with American-Vietnamese relationships. They were not without cordiality, often there was real affection on a personal level. But there was also an unspoken agreement to disagree and a denial of roles. The South Vietnamese had fought their war for 30 years, and the prospect of unending conflict lay before them as an endless pilgrimage. If the Americans could end it with a quick fix—money, men, smart bombs—well and good. But they doubted at the gut level such fixes would work, and they knew that in the long term it was their lot to fight the war to victory or what was more likely—and more Vietnamese—an accommodation.

The lieutenant knew this, just as he knew of the allegations that the cement, the concrete block, and the roofing tin would go for Colonel Duc's relatives' houses and his rental properties in Saigon's slums. His chances of offering effective advice to the worldly-wise Duc or of influencing the course of Vietnamese military justice were nil.

The fragility of the veneer the Americans were trying to impose came home to him later in the year when, as part of his nation-building mission, he taught at the University of Saigon Law School. The law faculty had originally functioned as a junior college of public administration, founded under French rule to train low-level civil servants to support the colonial regime. By 1968 the law school, with more than 10,000 students, was a massive draft evasion opportunity for the sons of well-off or well-placed Vietnamese. Teaching at the law school was done on Continental lines, with lectures fed back on true-false exams rather than through the freewheeling class discussions and end-of-term essays that characterize American legal education. The lieutenant taught in the American tradition, and the cultural shock was, at first, considerable. Silence greeted his efforts to stimulate classroom debate. But after a few sessions, the students began to enjoy the chance to participate. Three particularly vocal students who sat together in the front row especially caught the teacher's eye. He looked forward to the challenge they posed.

The course was Constitutional Law. The Republic had a new constitution (provided, wags said, by USAID lawyers, who had drafted the document during a long evening over a bottle of good bourbon), and the lieutenant thought a course in comparative constitutional law, contrasting the French and American approach to national organic law, might prove interesting and useful. For some weeks the class moved forward in a lively fashion, but one morning, the three students were not present. Since many pupils had jobs and other demands on their time, this did not at first seem ominous. But as the absences multiplied and stretched over days, the lieutenant became concerned. At last, he asked a known friend of the students to account for the absence of the three stars.

"Professor," the student nervously replied, "it is very dangerous for law students to be political. They have been arrested."

That afternoon as he sat on the terrace of his billet in the damp chill of a monsoon evening, an item on an inside page of the *Saigon Daily News* caught the lieutenant's eye. Headlined "Law Students Fate," the article stated, "Three law students at the University of Saigon were arrested today on charges of subversion. As the students disappeared into the Ministry of Interior Building under guard, an official when asked the law students' fate replied:

'They go somewhere.'"

The lieutenant never saw them again. The class lapsed back into lectures with docile students writing down every word. The lieutenant's closing lecture on Jefferson, Adams, and constitutional theory sounded hollow in his ears. He was glad to be done, glad another advisor would assume the podium in the fall. The applause at the end of the last hour, followed by the fervent pleas of students for passing grades to fend off the army did nothing to ease the lieutenant's sense of hopelessness. "Let them all pass," he thought. "Due process be hanged."

## IV

The three who disappeared into the dark halls of the Interior Ministry were not so different, in many ways, from the 14 who went home. The members of both groups were young and idealistic and natural leaders. The major difference between the three and the 14 was one of focused purpose.

The 14 were North Vietnamese sailors who had crewed the torpedo boats that allegedly attacked the U.S. destroyers *Maddox* and *C. Turner Joy*. This incident provided the *causas belli* that led to the Gulf of Tonkin Resolution. On their second run at the destroyers, their torpedo boat had been blown out of the water by cannon fire and the 14, rescued from the sea, had fallen into American hands. For more than two years they were held in a special section of the Marine Brig outside Da Nang. (Under the Geneva Convention prisoners of war may not be commingled with ordinary criminal prisoners.)

During their internment, they maintained strict unit discipline and carried out individual programs of self-improvement (calisthenics, reading, endless chess games, and political education). Now, in 1968, they were to become bargaining chips in an effort to establish a dialogue on POW matters between the United States and North Vietnam.

On the level of international politics, the North Vietnamese had made it clear they desired no discussion of prisoner release or exchange at any level. Still, senior U.S. officials decided that perhaps a de facto relationship on POW matters could be made to evolve as a result of events. It was decided to release the 14, hoping that such action on the U.S. side would stimulate similar action by the North Vietnamese.

Under the Geneva Convention and in accordance with longstanding U.S. policy developed during the Korean War, there can be no forced repatriation of prisoners held in U.S. custody (the 14 were among the few POW's under U.S. control. The U.S. had learned in Korea that running POW camps was a losing proposition and ordinarily turned over troops captured by its forces to the South Vietnamese). Before any prisoner release, it was necessary for the 14 to be interviewed at least twice by State Department officials and representatives from the International Committee of the Red Cross to insure that their desire to return was voluntary and genuine.

The young man from the embassy wore a gray cord suit, and his Red

Cross colleague from Switzerland wore the relaxed clothes Europeans wear on holiday—sport shirt (a bit formal) and tan slacks. They sat kneecap-to-kneecap on the small twin engine Piper flying north from Saigon.

At 15,000 feet they were comfortably above the threat of groundfire. But as the evil-seeming green jungle slipped below, running from the inland mountains to the thin, harsh-white sliver of coast, the stunning realization came once again to the young man that somewhere down there were people who would kill him if they could. People who would kill him not because of any personal affront or wrong, but simply because of his round eyes, white face, and the passport he carried. At times such as these, he wanted desperately to believe airplane designers and manufacturers employed effective zero defect systems, that the mechanics had not partied too late or drunk or doped too much the night before, and that the pilot wanted to get down in one piece and at the right place as badly as did he.

The Piper swept in low past Monkey Mountain and made a sharp turn to the left for its approach to Da Nang, then one of the busiest airfields in the world (but so unlike O'Hare). The drive from the airport up into the hills where the brig was located was first through Da Nang's busy streets of urban slum and squalor, then the road passed through a ruined countryside of small farms littered with the refuse of war. Burned-out trucks and armored personnel carriers, discarded ammo boxes, and miscellaneous pieces of metal and wood, ration cans, and items of clothing, all spoke of those who had passed that way and fought, repeatedly and without finality.

The brig consisted of a dozen low, wooden, tin-roofed buildings. It shimmered in the waves of heat. The stillness and pervasive menace of the place combined the qualities of fitful dream and mirage.

The interviews were arranged with each man individually, beginning with the commanding officer, Captain Bau. The captain was in his mid-twenties, dignified, composed, precise in his answers, which were translated by a local Marine-employed Vietnamese interpreter. (The young man always wondered what would become of these Vietnamese employees if the Americans were to leave—no one seemed to have an answer. It was an uncomfortable question that left his seniors at the embassy looking away from him at 15-degree angles, appearing to notice something of sudden and profound interest in a Diffenbachia or a picture or a wall just off his shoulder.)

Captain Bau sat across the camp table and listened intently to the questions put to him by the Swiss representative.

"Do you wish to return to North Vietnam?"

"Yes."

"You do not wish to stay in South Vietnam?"

"No."

"Do you wish us to try to repatriate you to a neutral country?"

"No."

"Do you fear persecution when you go North? After all, your mission was a failure, your boat was destroyed, and you and your men were captured."

"It is possible. But I am willing to go back and see what happens. So are my men. Our families are there."

"It is then, your firm desire to be repatriated to North Vietnam and this choice is freely made by you?"

"Yes."

"Sign this please," said the Swiss observer, pushing a mimeographed statement across the table which committed the individual executing it to return to his own side.

The captain signed with a government-issue black ball-point pen. He rose, bowed slightly to the young man and the Swiss, and turned to go. As he reached the screened door of the hut, he turned and said, "We have been well treated, but I and my men will be glad to be going home. Good-bye."

The other 13 were interviewed one-by-one. These interviews, like that with the captain, revealed a universal desire to return. There was a remarkable freedom from fear. Their ideological grasp appeared limited, they were not long on revolutionary theory or rhetoric, but there was no doubt in their minds about the rightness of what they had attempted to do, nor was the stolid stoicism with which they had borne two years of captivity feigned.

Although their basic endowments were similar, the 14 were also different from their contemporaries in the South. They presented a serious, mature face to the world, with an awareness of what it was to commit oneself to a life of political action with all the risks and dangers that might entail. They had sorted through what was important to them, and they had a capacity for making altruistic decisions on behalf of their cause. The 14 appeared unified in their experience. For them the war was the drama of their generation.

When they were released, the North Vietnamese sailors piloted their small craft to the mouth of a river near the port of Vinh. The admiral commanding the U.S. Navy task force which oversaw their release watched them disappear on his flagship's radar.

"Add one motor whaleboat to the North Vietnamese navy's Order of Battle," he said.

Their contemporaries in the South largely viewed life differently. In the South, the lucky ones lounged about Saigon's cafes and the university, or took some post in the civil government or the military that offered maximum safety with minimum deprivation. The unlucky became soldiers and fought until they were killed or became maimed beggars on Tu Do Street. The luck was largely a matter of money and class, both huge distinguishers of persons.

The dichotomy must have held true for the preceding generation as well. One can only imagine what a contrast there must have been between Captain Bau's father and Colonel Duc.

## V

Every morning in Saigon at 0800 the doors opened to the briefing theater at Military Assistance Command, Vietnam. The senior officers filed in, taking preassigned places in the rising tiers of comfortably upholstered, push-back seats. The briefing officer, collapsible pointer at the ready, stood by to begin. He was a thin, deeply tanned Army lieutenant colonel. At 0805 the lights went down, and the tan curtains parted to reveal a silver screen. For the next half hour the briefer toured the country reporting in his authoritative, unemotional "briefer's voice" on the action in the war of the previous 24 hours. Across the screen flashed maps, figures, and slides of battle action.

"Light resistance was encountered by three MAF Marines . . . an A-4 fighter off the *Constellation* was downed . . . RF-PF forces near Na Trang turned back a night attack . . . Hamlet Evaluation System reports an increase of 223 hamlets classified as 'relatively secure' . . . ."

The Navy commander listened with bemusement, his chin resting on his hand. Last week he had asked colleagues on the staff Long-Range Planning Task Force just what was meant by "relative security." There was a consensus among his colleagues that if the enemy wasn't coming over the wire every night things were relatively secure. He wondered how that standard compared to the situation in the cities back home he had seen aflame on the Armed Forces television evening news after Martin Luther King's death. The States—the World—seemed so far away. From the window of his paneled office he watched the Pan Am "freedom birds" at Tan Son Hut, waiting for takeoff in the late afternoon sun, knowing they would not cross the California coast until the dawn of yesterday—and yet sometimes the news from the States seemed so immediate.

The briefing drew to a close. The commander decided to ask one of his questions. He had become somewhat noted for asking the question no one wanted to hear at the morning briefings.

"Colonel," the commander said, "what is going to happen tomorrow?"

"How do you mean, Commander?"

"The briefing always tells us what has happened. You never get into what is planned, what is going to happen."

"Thank you very much, Commander. This ends the briefing." A quick snap of the collapsible briefing pointer gave finality to the colonel's statement and was the signal for a massive, seemingly unanimous exodus.

The commander pushed his way through the exiting brass to the podium to press his point with the colonel, who seeing the commander approach out of the corner of his eye, was hastily gathering his notes to make good his escape.

"I was serious Colonel, it seems to me you could tell us something."

"This is not an operational briefing, Commander, you have no need to know."

"Perhaps in a strict sense, yes. But I do long-range planning for the staff, and knowing as much as I can about what's going on now would certainly help me plan for the future."

"Well, access is not my department. You'll have to see somebody else about that."

The commander turned away, frustrated and a little angry. He could not know now that his maverick reputation would precede him back to the States and that upon his return, despite his training at the Naval War College and his deep selection for commander at 36, his career would be at an end. He would return to San Diego with his wife and, after a bitter terminal tour in a backwater job at the naval station, pass his middle age in Chula Vista running a convenience food store while drawing his half-pay retirement check.

The commander was not alone. The list of professional casualties Vietnam engendered is hard to measure. The definition of casualty is difficult. Does a cashiered major with tenure on a university faculty, a returned naval captain practicing law in Houston at a $100,000 a year or an Army captain who never made major and took up bartending in Santa Fe constitute a casualty? Perhaps all that can be said is there are literally thousands of men and women who were deemed to have failed or to have behaved unsatisfactorily in what for many was the most dramatic period of their lives because of acting upon intelligently and honestly held views. Others suffered a more subtle form of damage, tailoring their opinions to fit the moment's fashion. There was a company view in Vietnam, and one departed from it at one's peril. The sanctions ranged from transfers to dangerous duty, with possible death or injury, to professional death, to the lowered self-esteem that comes from self-compromise.

## VI

In Vietnam, the nature of the war was misperceived. The people for whom we fought the war and their goals were not understood. We did not understand the nature of our relationship with our allies. We did not know our enemy, his motivation, his strengths as well as weaknesses. When, from time to time, (and far more frequently than one might think), truth tugged at the system's elbow through clear-eyed observers, they were turned away and often punished for their trouble.

The disparity between America's vision of the war and the reality grew, and the frictions of the war increased to the point where it was no longer possible to continue. In the end, at home, there was no longer a sufficiently coherent vision of the war to engender the political support necessary to its continuation.

It even took a long time for the participants to come to terms with what to call the end when it came.

In 1984 the lieutenant, long since home from the war, long since past the trauma of reentry, was broiling a steak on the grill of his suburban terrace. The night was soft, cool, early June, and his eight-year-old nephew played on the lawn, falling down on his belly yelling:

"Here they come, here they come!"

The boy—fresh and appealingly innocent—called to his uncle from where he lay on the ground.

"Is this the way you do when the planes come?" he asked.

"Sometimes—you've got it down pretty well."

"Were you ever in a war?" the boy asked.

"Yes," said the lieutenant.

"Did you win?"

"No, we lost," the chef replied, "it was called Vietnam."

"Oh," said the boy, his tone reflecting disappointment and disgust.

The lieutenant wished he could have given the boy a different answer.

It was somehow demeaning, even after all this time, to have to admit he was not on the winning side. But he called it as he saw it.

MARY LEE SETTLE

# London—1944

[ AUTUMN 1987 ]

I

How do I capture a city and a time? It began in the back of a camouflaged RAF lorry that smelled of oil. I clung to the side as the driver swung the lorry fast around the curved Cotswold road from Bourton-on-the-Water to the railway station. All I had left of the uniform I had worn for ten months as an aircraft woman second class in the Women's Auxiliary Air Force of the RAF was the pair of issue shoes, heavy black masculine clodhoppers. I carried the suitcase I had kept hidden full of civilian clothes to wear on leave, a civilian ration book, some clothing coupons, and my discharge papers (my ticket). I was dressed in the suit I had worn to go into the WAAF at the recruiting station in Kingsway. That was the beginning of the time in London, and it ended, 18 months later, not in London, but at a dinner party in New York the evening after I came home from the war.

Why, after all this time, do I need to recall this? There is an old man, dreaming of Piccadilly in 1944, when he was young and drunk and a bomber pilot. A friend, who brought back a hidden wound of one forever relived day, has shot himself nearly 40 years later. I know that they, in their way, and I in mine, have no hope of ever being civilians completely.

Others, now in their seventies, sat on the floor, loose limbed against a wall, like the Cambridge undergraduates they were before the war, while one of their number read an elegy to a dead leader and aesthetic guide when they were brave and young, and in a naïve intrigue against the worst of the world that bred them. What they were remembering was being young, in love with dedication and one another, and flirting with the dull edges of legality.

The ones who were children in the years of war are still as fascinated as they were when they played at identifying planes, followed battles, in the illusion that they could be followed. They have missed ever since finding in themselves the answer to the most atavistic question in a man's soul. It is the question that makes *The Red Badge of Courage* a great war book whose author never fought in a battle: "Would I fight or would I turn tail?"

They envy the silence of those of us who find it hard to speak; it is our fault. We have left them to the shallow, to a war told by correspondents or seen in old movies. The witnessed events, the quick impassioned romances they imagine, the over-simple pictures of courage and love—all the iron nostalgia, gleaned from romance and from their own demands that the war be as they imagine it, is the hardest of all to wipe clean with recall.

What we found in London then was controlled by where we came from. Did we come on leave, away from the cold and boredom and waiting of being in the forces to the luxury of London, of baths, and pink gin, and some worn remains of graceful living? Or from America to the first glimpse of the danger and deprivation of a city at war? I had done both of these, so that in October 1943 the city I came to was not a surprise.

I had learned its streets on leave when I had wandered there in the anonymity of my air force blue uniform. It was then that I had found the noontime concerts at the National Gallery, the cheap food at the NAAFI, and what was left of the London of Dickens, of Shakespeare, so familiar to me that I hardly had to ask a direction, even though I had never seen it before. I had walked through miles of London streets, all the day and into the blacked-out night.

Osbert Sitwell wrote that the blackout made a medieval city of London. It didn't. There were no pine torches, no wax tapers shining through windows to defeat the darkness. Instead, it was the opposite. London was plunged into the terrible present century and lay exposed under an open, dangerous sky. The pitch darkness was inside of rooms, as if they were caves deep underground before the blackout curtains were drawn and the lamps were lit.

Outside, in the street, London became country again under a changing sky. The buildings were dark monoliths; the streets canyons between cliffs. There were snaggled bombed-out gaps in the townhouse rows that let the moonlight in through high windows that had once been such private rooms, here a fragment of wall paper with faded rain-streaked animals of a nursery, there a drunken toilet, still clinging to the wall. Many of the ancient churches were only ruins that looked like stone lace that etched the night sky. During the blitz they had been low on the priorities of the fire fighters.

To new arrivals in London, it seemed pitch black out of doors, too, but not, by 1943, to Londoners. People had become conscious again of the phases of the moon, the light from stars. They had regained their country eyes. The darkness was full of noises, the echo of footsteps, of people talking, the cries for taxis. Sound itself seemed amplified and dependable in the half-blindness of the street. The smell was of dust, of damp plaster in the air, and of the formaldehyde scent of the smoke from dirty coal that lodged in the yellow fog. The stained sandbags, the rust, the dull, peeling paint, damp that made great dark lines down the walls, made London seem like a long-neglected, leaky attic.

It was fear that was medieval, and largely unadmitted to this day, fear of the full moon, the bomber's moon, as our ancestors had shrunk from its insane light and the cry of the wolf.

## II

I had been sent to London several weeks before to find a job, on orders from the medical officer of my station who had given me sick leave. I was suffering from signals shock, a common aural breakdown after too many hours of enemy jamming on the transmitter/receiver in flying control. Those of us who suffered from it had begun to hear ghost signals from nonexistent aircraft through the electronic repetitive noise of the German jamming that I can rehear, more than 40 years later, as I recall the time. Both the M. O. and I knew that I was not quite sick enough to be invalided out, even though I was of no more use as an R/T operator.

"I wish I had a way to work my ticket, too. I'm bloody cheesed off," he said sadly, sitting on the end of my cot in sick bay, his feet tucked up, his arms around his knees. I see now that he was very young. "Why waste your time issuing repaired shoes when you could do a proper job? You are lucky."

I guess I was. I knew people, unlike the others I had left. So between Herbert Agar and a friend in Parliament I was on my way to the train for London in the back of the RAF lorry two weeks after I came back off sick leave. I left the WAAF an aircraft woman second class, pay 14 shillings a week, on Saturday, and on Monday I reported to the American Office of War Information in Carlos Place, conveniently across from the Connaught Hotel as a "simulated" major in the American Army, a civilian rank for those of us serving in war zones.

London to me that week, at least, was comfort, good food, clean American people after the months of loneliness, a PX card, and a glamour that I had not expected. I was exhausted, my weight thirty pounds below normal, my nerves jangled from signals shock, and still so enmeshed in the discipline, the deprivation, and the language of the forces, that on the first morning I stood to attention beside a colleague's desk and asked to be excused. "Honey," he said, "you're out of the army. You can pee whenever you want to."

Almost everybody was old at the Office of War Information. I had come from a world where nobody was over 22, except some high ranking officers, who seemed, in their thirties and the fact that they were regular Air Force, as far away as tin gods, who could not be forgiven their mistakes, their preoccupations, or their power over us.

The people in the OWI were famous, too, or so they seemed to me, and I, who only now realize that I was exotic to them, found them glittering with reputation. The courage of some of them was to be honored more than those I had left in one way. They brought to the war more intelligence and less physical resilience than being there required. Some of them were too old, too tired, too sedentary for what they had volunteered to do, be in London through the attrition of the days, the "little blitz," the buzz bombs, the V2s, and the debilitating atmosphere of neglect, dirt, and exhaustion that had built up.

There they were, those who had wangled their way into war, at the wrong place, doing, in excesses of patriotism or curiosity or self-proof, work that was the wrong work, at the wrong time. They were valuable in some terms I had not run into as an aircraft woman. There were fine editors, good writers, movie actors, poets, in the halls of the OWI at Carlos Place, and I realize now that I was as glamorous to them as they were to me. Somehow I had touched the war they had come to. I knew things I couldn't tell. Gaunt, and nervous, aesthetically pleasing in the fashion that pleases at a given time, an object of interest, I had had the experience they had come to share. What I had learned to take for granted, service in the forces was, to them, a fascination. It made them seem somehow younger than I was. I had a sense of knowing things—oh, not events—civilians seem always to expect those—but gray expanses and hours, days, months, of damp indifference.

They didn't quite know what to do with me. They were professionals, some of the best of American editors, from prewar publishing when it was an art, from the *Paris Herald Tribune*, the *Saturday Evening Post*, the Viking Press, the *Louisville Courier Journal*, *Harper's Bazaar*, to name only the ones I remember best. I, who had been hired as a "writer," had no experience at all beyond a few poems, a few short stories, all unpublished, all long since lost. I was, to them, an oddity, a rescued fragment. One of my bosses told me that I would never have passed a security check in the States, because I was a "premature anti-fascist," having started trying to join up before we went to war. So I was used at first as a courier to take VIPs to the BBC for interviews. Accidentally I was plunged straight from lorry to limousine, from the barracks to tea at the Savoy with Robert Sherwood, Alfred Lunt, and Lynn Fontanne.

I took Irving Berlin to the BBC, and he, with a capacity for friendship I have seen in few other people, made friends. He was tiny in uniform, too old already to be there; he moved like a cricket, doing everything anyone asked him to do. He treated others with a sense of rare peerage, as if it were the norm for people, and he was the kindest and also the funniest person I met in all the time I was escorting VIPs. He had brought over *This Is the Army* to play for the troops.

One evening we were to meet for a drink at Claridge's, and he was late. He came rushing in, apologizing as he ran, and sat down at the table. He said, "I have just had one of the most embarrassing days of my life. You know, we take "The Army" around to the hospitals. We have a small show, just the leads, designed so that we don't need a stage. Then I go with two or three of the singers around the wards to entertain the men who can't make it to the performance. There are some wards where they are too badly wounded even for that. The commanding officer was taking me around to them, where I always said a few words, hoping to cheer them up a little. I noticed that we kept passing one ward, not going in. I asked why, and he said that the men were too badly off. I bounced in anyway. I told him that if they were conscious I was sure a few words from home would help a little. It was too late to stop me. There they lay, and I started my little speech about how proud we were of them, what brave men, all that. Usually, even from the very sick I got some reaction. From these—none. So I laid it on a bit thicker. I told them how proud their country was of them, how I represented their parents and their sweethearts to tell them we honored them as great Americans. I got no reaction at all. In the hall, I said, what is the matter with those men? They don't react at all. The commanding officer said, 'I tried to tell you, Mr. Berlin. That was the VD ward.'"

## III

The entertainers, the people in the OWI, the film divisions, some of the foreign correspondents existed, I'm sure, without knowing it, within a caul of privilege they took for granted. It was not safety; they had come to a city where they could be killed, and most of them had come, as I had, in convoy. But their London, to me, was unreal, a stage on which a play called "the war" was running. Even the uniforms some of them wore were like costumes—well-cut, no grease marks, not butt-sprung, no inground dirt, no fading, scratching, no ill-fitting crotch crease—in short not the issue I was still used to.

Most of them had no experience of the strictures we lived by, of being caught by raids late at night so that we had to sleep where we could, away from the cars they seemed to be able to call at any time. They did not step over the out-flung arms of families who had slept in the tube stations for nearly four years. Where once, in uniform, I had been caught in Piccadilly Tube Station by a raid, in this new time, I trailed my evening skirts along the narrow track between the sleeping bodies and the trains.

Those who ate in restaurants had no inkling of what it was like to live on rationing, on scrounging unrationed food, fish or carbohydrates that meant standing in queues hour after hour, gray-faced with fatigue. One time I was in a taxi with a woman, made innocent by money rather than fame, and she saw a queue at the horsemeat shop in Paddington. She said, "Isn't it amazing that those people still keep pets?"

Three days after I arrived I was taken to dinner at a black market restaurant by Burgess Meredith and Paul Douglas, who were in the film division, and who had decided I needed feeding. Where we went I still don't know. We were driven through dark unfamiliar streets by one of those London cabbies who seemed to find his way like a night animal, with only the tiny slits of blue light showing from the masked headlights that gave no light to drive by, but only warned pedestrians.

We walked into an overpowering smell of food, a luxury of clean white table clothes and damask napkins from "before the war," which had already become a magic time, dimmed and changed by nostalgia. I remember that the room was dark, with that cave-like atmosphere of London restaurants that used to imitate old libraries or men's clubs, with their dark woodwork and their leather banquettes along the walls. In the corner Mac Kriendler from 21 in New York sat with a foreign correspondent I have forgotten. It was the only black market restaurant I ever saw in London.

People who knew each other had turned it into a home away from home where they had the comfort of being with their own in that network of fame I had hardly known existed. There they sat, correspondents, actors, Hollywood writers who had been trained to write too quickly from first impressions, and would write about the war in the same way, imagining the rest. Many a hungry GI slogged through minds in such meeting places, or the Ritz Bar, while the professionals and the shallow gambled with war, having no idea that they were missing everything about it but the events.

They ordered for me with great care. They treated me gently, but unwisely. I had been living on wartime rations, only two-thirds of that issued to men in the forces, on the theory that women were smaller and needed less food. I can still see the plate of food, and smell it. A lamb chop, two inches thick, a baked potato with two week's ration of butter melting on it, and green beans. The smell of melting fat, of rich meat, made my gorge rise, I prayed to get to the lady's room in time. I was violently sick. The rest of the evening was spent with them taking turns holding my head over the loo while I had the dry heaves. After that I learned to face carefully both the new food and a certain aura of fame.

By the winter of 1943-44, in the first preparations for the invasion, troops from all over the world gathered on leave in the West End of London. Cries for taxis and women in all their languages were plaintive in the blackout. Small, dim, blue lights, the only color allowed, read Bar, Pub, Restaurant. When the blackout curtains, which were hung like labyrinths at the doors, were pushed aside, you were met by a wall of light and noise, and the uniforms, by that year, of all the allies.

Sometimes there were mistakes. The Tivoli Bar at the Ritz had all the elegance and aloofness of a London club. It was another home for a mixture of the kind of Americans who knew about the Ritz, Guards officers, and assorted English ladies with what Hilaire Belloc called "loud and strident voices." Outside, in Piccadilly, it had a faint blue sign like all the rest.

Two American officers, new to the darkness of the streets, had picked up two girls of the hundreds who haunted the West End. They had seen only the faint blue word, "bar," and they pushed aside the blackout curtains and escorted the girls into one of the most exclusive rooms in London.

The two girls had been a long time in the streets. One's teeth were snaggled, the other had dirt scratched down her bare legs. Their clothes were filthy. It was obvious, but only for a second, that the two young men were actually seeing them for the first time. There was hardly a pause. They showed them to the table, pulled back their chairs, and followed the perfect Chesterfieldian advice, "Treat the duchess like a whore and the whore like a duchess." There was not a word said by the waiter, who entered into the scene with all the arrogant politeness he would have shown any other customer. I was never prouder of my countrymen than I was then, when they, far more insouciant than the British around them, soothed the feelings of a pair of embarrassed Piccadilly whores.

We spent the days in make-work and met in bars, in restaurants, and turned them into havens. There was no place else to go. The Petit Club Francaise had more movie actors, ballet girls, and American writers than the Free French it had been opened for. The long front room of the Connaught, which looks comfortably like a large drawing room, gathered the OWI and the foreign correspondents. There were scores of places, all over London, where people found their own.

It took time for me. I seemed flung from group to group at first. I remember Claude Cockburn, who was Frank Pitcairn of the *Daily Worker*, to whom I lent ten pounds when he had run out of money one night in the back bar of the Cafe Royal. He paid me back with ten shares of *The Week*, a Communist broad sheet he published every week with all the low life "capitalist" intrigues he could find in either the British or the American government. It earned me a black dossier as a part owner of a Communist magazine. I was fascinated with all of this, with the paradox of a mixture of secrecy as a flirtation and of naïve hope among most of the intelligent people I met then.

I had lunch, through Cockburn, in one of London's fashionable restaurants with the editor of the *Daily Worker* and a Communist deputy from Belgium who looked like the bust of Beethoven. I asked him when he became a Communist. He smiled and said, "When I was 50. It was not, with me, a youthful error."

Maybe I was being recruited, I don't know. I must have disappointed them if I was; I was too curious, too questioning, and, by then, far too experienced at being a pawn to blind authority to be attracted to dictatorship, proletarian or otherwise. Only a few months before I had had to run along behind a proletarian sergeant who was as mean as a snake, as she rode her bicycle through an RAF station.

I sat on the stairs in a gold satin dress at a ball in one of the grand houses in Grosvenor Street with a pink Guards officer, 19 years old. He looked with some disdain at the people dancing. He said, "I'm frightfully sorry you see us like this. Before the war [that already magic time] half these people would not have been asked here."

I said, "Before the war I would probably not have been asked here." He was killed in the invasion.

## IV

We talked as people have not talked in England since. We talked on trains, in bars, in canteens, in Lyons Corner Houses, on buses, as if our statements had to be made before it was too late. There are glimpses in my memory of walks, of talk—a walk in the park with Archibald McLeish when he tells me that he has spent the rest of his life finding out that what he knew at 18 was true, an officer from an English regiment who tells me he hates the bloody Yanks. One has stolen his girl.

An OSS officer from Hollywood tries to convince me that I must be a Communist. "But you do recognize the historic inevitability, don't you?" He sounds annoyed. The joke was then that the OSS and MI5 spent more time following each other and all of us than on German spies.

I sat on the wall by Hyde Park Gate across from the hospital with a young American fighter pilot who flew P38s. He had just been posted to a station in the south of England. On the way through New York on leave he had seen a wonderful new musical, and he sang to me, "Oh, what a beautiful morning." It was the first song I ever heard from *Oklahoma*. He was killed the next week.

I lived then in Gloucester Terrace, near Gloucester Road Tube Station, in a top floor flat that I had been sent to by the English Speaking Union, one of those nests of threadbare gentility that had survived all over Kensington, with ladies clinging to them, literally, for their dear lives, measured not in coffee spoons, but in patched linen, polished tables, and the eking out of rations in bone china cups.

Doreen Green, who hastened to tell me that she had been brought up in a large Georgian country house outside of Dublin, explained at once that it was not the money, but the duty that made her even consider letting a room, that she did, after all, have an income but it was, you know, in trust. She lived there with her 15-year-old son, and one of those ancient splay-footed nannies left after the children were grown. I had first stayed there when I had come to London on leave, in uniform, but in the fall of 1943, there were evening dresses hanging in my cupboard in the genteel pastel bedroom with its embroidered runners and its pale rugs, and Victorian china knickknacks, all the thin fragility of the genteel poor. She had told me the first time I went there that she was divorced from a husband who had lived too long in France when he was young and had picked up beastly habits, you know, from those people.

If London had become drab and shabby, flats like this one were threadbare instead, for shabby has an air of neglect about it, but threadbare is worn down with care, with meticulous patching, with make do and make do. There was something of this in Doreen's small, pinched face, too, as if she would make do through the war as the others did, because she had to, and because the time was overwhelming except in the safety of the Irish antique furniture she had there, all that was left for her of what had been, at least in memory, a great Anglo-Irish house outside of Dublin. As with all of us, her safety was more psychic than real, since the flat was on the vulnerable top floor.

From time to time, several evenings a week, during the late fall and on into the winter, she gave us tea when I was there, dressed in her Air Raid Precaution uniform, ready to go on duty through the night, a woman too frail, it seemed, to survive an ordinary day. It was women like her, now forgotten in the more dramatic annals of the war, who sat all night, night after night, on watch in the ARP stations, middle-class soldiers, dim with worry that their homes would not be there when they went off duty.

During the nights of the "little blitz" when the air raid warning went, we would gather in the tiny living room of the flat on the ground floor, and pretend not to be afraid. The ancient splay-footed nanny, who seemed as much of a fixture in such homes as the dear antiques, the careworn and beautifully patched linen, would say, as the ack-ack guns in Hyde Park shook the house, "Is that one of theirs or one of ours?"

Dutifully Desmond or his mother would say, "Nanny, it's one of ours."

That Christmas an ice storm turned the trees in Hyde Park into a glittering parody of Christmas trees, and the children picked up silver strips of foil in the street that had been dropped by German aircraft to confuse our radar, and took them home to decorate their houses.

Almost imperceptibly London moved out of winter into a drab spring. The weather was cold, the days were gray, and there was a sense of watching the sky, as a farmer watches it, to read the future in it. At night, once in a while, if the sky was clear, a German plane got through the defenses of the city, and you could see it, a tiny bug pinned in the sky by the searchlights that converged on it. I was told after the war by a Luftwaffe pilot that they were sent over London alone as punishment.

## V

I had been moved, in one of those decisions that seemed to have been made for the sake of decision itself, down to the radio section in Dean Street, Soho, to the broadcasting studios of both "black" and "white" radio—black to the resistance in Europe and white to whoever would risk their lives to listen to Aaron Copland.

For two years there had been rain soaked graffiti all over London saying *Open the Second Front Now*. In early June, the days were so long that we seemed always to be walking in twilight under a solid blanket of American and English bombers across the sky all the way to the horizons. Some of the men I worked with and the correspondents got edgier and edgier, drank more, caroused more, fell into silences. If there had been not a single spy in London, the world would have known from the poised waiting, the draining out of London of troops, that at last what we all called then The Second Front was going to be opened.

Then, for 48 hours, day and night, in early June the loud drone of the planes overhead never ceased. I walked down to the station early one morning. For some reason neither I nor anyone else in the flat had been able to sleep. I walked in to the only other person there, who was sitting in her office watching the wall. I asked what was happening, and she snapped, "None of your business. Shut up." For some reason I still can't fathom she had been let in on the secret, and was sitting there vicariously invading Europe. It was the morning of June 6.

Everything changed in that day. London woke up, the pace was faster. I was assigned to the midnight briefings at the Ministry of Information in the London University building. They seemed futile, since correspondents and troops were already coming back and forth in an open corridor that made London seem like a part of the front itself.

Then, on June 13, in the middle of the night, the first buzz bomb flew over London, the engine cut, and it crashed into a house, killing six people.

## LONDON—1944

It was the first of Hitler's long-rumored secret weapons. They came, self-propelling bombs with little stubby wings. They looked like huge cigars, and they sounded like motorcycles in the air. The more that were shot down coming over the coast, the more came into London. We began to listen; we listened all the time, whether consciously or not, to the cutoff of the engines which meant that the buzz bomb would either crash straight down or glide.

Everyone thought their own part of London received the brunt of them, and there were rumors of targets that had been chosen. Nothing was chosen. They fell completely indiscriminately, ludicrously. I went home to Gloucester Terrace one evening to find Doreen sobbing. I thought after all the time she had forgotten how to cry. One of her best friends a few streets away had been wiped out with her whole family an hour before. She kept saying, "They were only getting ready to go to the theater," as if that had to do with their silly useless deaths.

I walked down with her to watch the digging out of their bodies from the trash heap that smelled of dust and plaster that had been their home, and I made her go back to the flat and put sugar in her tea when I saw that they were about to bring out the first body. Usually she would pretend she didn't like sugar so that Desmond and Nanny could have more of the meager ration. She confided in me that she drank her tea with lots of sugar for energy when she was on duty, since it wasn't rationed at the ARP station. When I brought home the Mars Bars they seemed fond of, a present from the PX, she sliced them and served them for tea on Irish china so thin you could see her hand through it as she passed the plate. Somehow the memory of teatime with her, and the death in the other house seem linked together, as they should be.

On a train coming in from a grand weekend in Wiltshire, I met an unattractive, shy young refugee from Germany, who had been conscripted into the Pioneer Corps. But when he began to talk about music, his face took on a glow. He asked me if I would go with him to a prom concert in the Albert Hall. We climbed up to just below the great round glass roof. Away in the distance, a tiny figure, Myra Hess, played to the kind of silence she commanded from the huge crowd. In the middle of a Mozart cadenza a buzz bomb rode over the Albert Hall. We could see its faint shadow through the dirty glass. The pure, small sound of Mozart was the focus of a dead silence. Her fingers never faltered. We were hypnotized by her concentration, and the bomb exploded a hundred yards away across Kensington High Street in Kensington Gardens. She had kept us from a panic that could have killed many people. It was the last concert there until the war was over.

Late at night, after the last tube, sometimes I had to stay in the bomb shelter at the MOI. There was no way to get home. One evening after the midnight briefing, Gene Solo, who was a Hollywood script writer attached to the film division, said, "Don't sleep here. We all have a room at the Savoy and a car. Come with us." I said I would come if I could have a quart of milk to drink.

When I got there, there was a poker game on a table that had been drawn up between two twin beds. It seemed to have been going on for some days. Dixie Tighe, William Saroyan, Gene Solo, Irwin Shaw, and a man from *Newsweek*, were the people I remember. I lay down behind the safe broad backs of Solo and Saroyan, drank my two weeks ration of milk in a room that reeked of gin and cigarettes, and went to sleep deeply for the first time since the buzz bombs had started and I had had to sleep in the shelter. I was waked in the morning by Saroyan throwing pound notes in the air and yelling, "I've won! I've won."

What made for a sense of safety so often was not true safety at all, but a psychic calm, Doreen Green sitting among her dear antiques from Ireland on the top floor of a London building saying, "This is nothing. You should have seen Dublin during the troubles. You could see the fires all the way from Balawly." She was remembering being 16, not the troubles.

I finally had found my own psychic safety, my own home away from home. I went like a pigeon to the cote to the top floor of a building in Soho, whose walls were a Twenties decor of small glass mirrors which would have shattered into a million shards if we had been hit. But I had found my pub, my local—the kind of place you go to unthinking, that becomes habit almost as soon as you see it.

No place else had done this until I had met another refugee in the corridors of the OWI. We made friends as quickly as children. He was the most ridiculous GI I have ever seen. Chinless, pop-eyed, hair cut by Trumpers, already and impressively a published poet in his early twenties, newly graduated from Harvard where he had been a protégé of Robert Hillyard, Dunstan Thompson made even the ill-fitting GI uniform of a private soldier look elegant. Someone had rescued him from the more useless service that he would have been given in the army, as I had been rescued. He already knew every "literary" name in London. When I told him I was a writer, he accepted me completely as what I thought I was. He was already used to people who wrote and published, rather than those who still only wanted to, or those who posed. I think that it was this, and his acerbic teaching kindness that came so naturally to him, that made me really begin to write, not as a caprice but as a dedication. He also made me realize how ignorant I was, and I began to read contemporary work and classics, filling a great hunger like somebody who had been starving and didn't know it.

We drank at the Gargoyle Club, and we ate our jugged hare, and there were evenings I remember when Dylan Thomas was sitting on somebody's knee, when Robert Newton broke things, the names, Cyril and Stephen and Guy, were called across the floor, boyfriends quarreled in the men's room, and somebody's mistress vomited in the ladies'. I was having lunch with two journalists from Belgium when a buzz bomb stopped overhead. No one else stopped eating. The Belgians, who were not fools, took one look at the glass walls and went under the table. I suspect that everyone else wanted to, but there was a kind of noblesse oblige about it. One feared more than anything else being embarrassed in front of the others.

## VI

Dunstan may have recognized me as a writer when I didn't deserve it, but Eric Hawkins, the editor of the *Paris Herald,* made me do some work, and I am always grateful to him for forcing me into a postgraduate course in journalism when I was hardly qualified for the first grade.

He gave me assignments and made me do them. He identified me from time to time. He looked around my door one day and said, "I know who your grandfather was—William Blake."

On another day, soon after I began to work for him, he stuck his head in the door and said, "Hey, kid, have you ever heard of the Grand Coulee Dam?" I stopped writing my wartime novel (long since lost) and said no. "Well, you better find out about it. I want five thousand words by next Wednesday." This article, for one of those OWI publications which seemed so tenuously connected with the war, scared me so that I still remember facts about the Grand Coulee Dam I would rather forget. I had never written anything five thousand words long.

He sent me to the British Museum, which had been bombed, and where the readers were relegated to a small back room. But it was my first visit to a place which would be a treasure house where later I would research and write three novels.

I had moved back to Carlos Place, and the news was pouring in day after day. There seemed to be some attempt, not at political censorship, but at not disturbing the American people more than they could take, like sitting upright when the buzz bombs halted over you so as not to disturb the others. When Belsen, the first of the concentration camps, was liberated, at first no one believed the evidence that was coming out. It was too much like the old "babies on bayonets" propaganda that too many people remembered from the First World War. A delegation of members of Parliament insisted on inspecting it to see if the news was true. One of them, a nice Conservative lady MP, Mrs. Smith, came back and put her head in the gas oven.

Then the first pictures came, and I was set to work as a kind of fuse. How much could people take? The pictures were shown me and if I retched, they were put to one side, to be censored. If I had no violent reaction they were passed for publication. Alas, I soon got inured to them, as one gets used to anything, and I was less successful at the job of protecting the public from the truth that was like a yawning hole in any hope. Gradually the findings began to be believed, and we had the sense then that we had been in more than a conventional war. We had been in an invasion of a hell run by efficient clerks.

On the beaches of Normandy the allied armies met such an international army of conscripts that they had to comb London for people who spoke obscure European languages and dialects in order to interrogate many of the prisoners, while Mark Blitzstein and I sat in an office and chose records from American composers to play on the loud speaker systems of trucks when they weren't calling in German, "Surrender."

The war was running down, and we knew that it was nearly over. There was some naïve hope—a lot of it—that things would be "better" than they had been before the war. The Beveridge Plan had been debated in Parliament in an all night session where Quentin Hogg had brought the members to their feet cheering at his words, "If you do not give the people social reform, they will give you social revolution!" When I asked another member about it, he said, "Oh, we always cheer when somebody uses two political clichés in the same sentence."

The Labor Party was getting its slate ready for the first postwar election, and when I asked Harold Laski who they were choosing, he answered, in his little pinched professorial voice, "One third workers with the hands, and two thirds workers with the mind." Labor, of course, won by a landslide when the British went to the polls in July 1945.

Lovely Kay Kendall sang, "I'm going to get lit up when the lights go on in London," and we all cried, and John Armstrong, the painter, asked me, as a "young person" he said, when I was as old that day as I will be until I die, "What do you young people believe?"

"I, for one, have no communal hope," I told him, "only a recognition that individuals must become just, as Keats said, before the world becomes just. That belief is all that is left to me."

"If I thought that I would commit suicide," he told me. He was an older, sweet, left-winger I was ashamed of hurting, with his hope retained as romantically as Doreen Green's "before the war" in Ireland.

On the eighth of September I was walking with a friend in Soho, when the ground under us heaved and then was still again. Six miles away the first V2 had landed in Chiswick. In some vague attempt to keep the hit from the Germans the news was released that a gas main had exploded in Chiswick. For a while the V2s were called Flying Gas Mains.

They were terrible, in all the classic sense of that misused word. There was no warning. If you heard the explosion you were safe. They killed hundreds more people than was ever admitted. Some of the shallower shelters became mass graves. It was a miracle that they weren't launched earlier. I believe that London could have panicked under too long a siege of them. It was an exhausted city by then, that deep brutal exhaustion that had seeped into our souls, our bodies, our relationships with each other, a kind of fatal disease of exhaustion that I believe had more to do with some older men killing themselves after the war, when the pressure ceased, and they realized how little was left, than any personal problem.

That crack-up at the release of pressure was common. I saw it happen to more men in New York after they had come back from war than I ever saw under the pressures of London. I had thought that I paid little attention after a while to the V1s and the V2s, but some weeks after I came back to New York I went to see *Meet Me in St. Louis.* The short was called *V One.* At the first sound of the familiar buzz bomb engine, I fainted and had to be carried out of the theatre. I remember that my last thought before I passed out was, "This is ridiculous. I'm in New York. I'm safe."

It was the targetless, unaimed V2s, even more than the atom bomb that was so far away, a tragedy read about, not suffered by us, that brought home the fact that war in the future was going to be nearly impossible, agonizing, and short. At least I thought so, but what humans can suffer and still survive in some kind of tatters in this bloody century has been seen over and over since.

Werner von Braun's V2s were the predecessors of those missiles that ever since have showered on the just and the unjust, without warning, without target, without hope, sold to whoever will pay for them.

In this brave new world, and this brave new kind of war, and still with the dim hope that something, at least, had changed after the terrible time, I came back to New York in the early spring of 1945. On the second day I was asked to dinner by Constantine Alajalov, the painter who painted so many prewar *New Yorker* covers. There were three other people at dinner, Alajalov, Tilly Losch, and an elegant Free French officer who had been sent in his beautifully cut uniform with his beautifully cut aristocratic face as a propaganda visitor. Recognizing that we Americans love a lord, it was his assignment to improve the image of the country that had been occupied since 1941, and obscure the truth that so many of its citizens had collaborated with Hitler or been passive under the Vichy regime.

He said at dinner, taking for granted in the company that it was an acceptable remark, "Well, at least Hitler did one thing for us. He got rid of the Jews in France."

I was too frozen with shock to move or speak. I felt drained of life. Despair can leave you too lost to resist seduction. The thing I had not known about what war can do I found out in that moment. You go along. I did not leave quickly enough. In short, I was polite.

But that, to them, casual moment has left me with something, when I think of it, like a darkness of soul, a cold recognition of the waste of the dead, the years of deprivation, of grayness, of dedicated uselessness. It has thrown the responsibility in any country straight onto a society that Turgenev called, "the rich, the happy, and unjust."

It has taken me a long time since that night to realize that the war years were not wasted. I have had to face the fact that social change does not change evil people. There is only this difference. Their seduction is no longer officially tolerated in democracies. Evil men and evil prejudices are with us still; "nice" people belong to anti-Semitic country clubs, and their imitators drive pick-up trucks with gun racks and hate "niggers." The only thing that saves us is that such beliefs have been unacceptable to decent people since 1945. I know that "unacceptable" is a small word for this enormity, but the world runs on shallowness for the most part. We are left, at least, with a residue of social shame as a weapon.

PATRICIA MEYER SPACKS

# The Necessity of Boredom

[ AUTUMN 1989 ]

> To ward off boredom at any cost is vulgar.
> —Nietzsche

> A certain power of enduring boredom is . . . essential to a happy life, and is one of the things that ought to be taught to the young.
> —Bertrand Russell

ABOUT nine o'clock most nights, when I'm reading, my cat leaps to the top of a small chest of drawers and begins with deliberation to knock the objects on it—perfume bottles, framed photographs—one by one to the floor. "He's bored," I say. "He wants attention."

"Fly the *Concorde* Around the World," an advertisement urges. "The future way to fly—NOW. Everything else is boring."

Such unlikely attributions of boredom, to an animal manifestly incapable of this particular form of psychic distress, implicitly to billions deprived of Concorde luxury, call attention to the concept's late-20th-century value as an all-purpose index of dissatisfaction. Advertisers could hardly do without it. A sexy woman lolls on a Directoire chaise. "I gave up chocolates," the copy reads. "I gave up espresso. I gave up the Count (that naughty man). And his little house in Cap Ferrat. The Waterman, however, is not negotiable. I must have something thrilling with which to record my boredom." Transgression and boredom: the only alternatives. The sphere of transgression enlarges: not just adultery and cocaine, but coffee and the sedentary life as well. So does that of boredom. We gaze at television to forestall boredom, and television generates more of it. The church socials and bingo games that contented previous generations strike contemporary intellectuals as ludicrously tedious. Watching football bores some people, baseball unaccountably bores others. A *National Review* ad during the election campaign read, "Is Mike Dukakis boring? Let's put it this way: if you loved Mondale, you'll like Dukakis." But the Reagan administration has also been declared boring, and so has George Bush. Cities, regions (Switzerland, the Middle West), occupations (tolltaker, file clerk): vast categories fall by assertion into limbo. On the other hand, when I tell someone that I plan to write a book on boredom, the immediate response—with what I can only call boring predictability—tends to be, "Oh, I'm never bored."

Never bored, finding a great deal boring, attributing boredom to others: what are we, collectively, up to?

One thing seems fairly clear: we *need* boredom, as concept and as experience. Boredom in other people serves the purposes of sociologists, philosophers, advertisers, psychologists, novelists, anthropologists. As cultural or personal sign or symptom, as metaphor, as window of opportunity (the bored person is almost by definition open to exploitation), boredom—object of observation or tool of manipulation—fuels various industries that use language as instrument. Boredom as a subjective experience possesses subtler kinds of value. Bertrand Russell recommended it; others have also discovered its charms. But in the self as in others, boredom acquires its positive valence by its function as a way station to something else: to wit or insight in its observer, to calm or wisdom, or at least a sense of superiority, in its sufferer.

The notion of boredom can serve diverse psychological and social purposes perhaps partly because its definition remains vague and inclusive. The word itself has only a modern history. It came out of nowhere, the *OED* suggests, with no traceable etymology, some time in the middle of the 18th century. Attempts to discover its linguistic origins have suggested a linkage with the reiterative action of the bore as drill or with the French *bourrée*, meaning stuffing. These associations appropriately call attention to the repetitiveness and the smothering effect we connect with boredom, but the dictionary endorses neither, although Eric Partridge accepts the tool as etymological source for the psychological condition.

In its nature, boredom opposes desire. More precisely than repulsion, the negative form of desire, it constitutes desire's antithesis, assuring its victim of the utter impossibility of wishing for anything at all. The sufferer from boredom finds it impossible to involve him or herself fully with any action, to believe any action worth the effort of involvement. "The thing that hath been, it is that which shall be; and that which is done is that which shall be done: and there is no new thing under the sun" (Eccl. 1: 9)—why bother? The hope of something new may dimly remain: one can always go round the world in the Concorde. But a sense of futility precedes and forestalls endeavor. As the protagonist of Maria Edgeworth's 1809 novel *Ennui* observes, "had I known how to enjoy the goods of life, I might have been happy". No bored person possesses that vital knowledge. A state of profound limitation, boredom appears—to put the point in the mildest terms—a condition to be avoided.

Pope saw boredom (in the guise of "dullness") as the potential destroyer of civilization. The yawn of the goddess Dullness concludes *The Dunciad* by bringing an end to culture. Conversely, the anthropologist Ralph

Linton has argued that all cultural advance derives from the human capacity for being bored. The victim of boredom acts in order to escape his condition—thus generating, in Linton's version of things, "cultural advance." More than one great writer has testified that his or her work originated in the experienced need to escape boredom. And if boredom entails literature as consequence, why not bicycles, electric lights, and laser printers?

## II

Boredom, then, if not responsible for *all* cultural advance, may yet provide a stimulus for creativity. It can also function as a rhetorical and psychological principle of meaning. *The Autobiography of Alice B. Toklas*, Gertrude Stein's crypto-autobiography published in 1933, and Edith Wharton's *A Backward Glance,* her 1934 autobiography, alike provide plots of self-invention in opposition to conventional expectations. Both use boredom as initiating pretext in narratives of literary careers. In effect Stein and Wharton apologize for their presumption as professional writers by insisting that they have participated, despite their unusual individual circumstances, in a psychological situation familiar to generations of women.

The theme of boredom explicitly emerges roughly a third of the way through *The Autobiography of Alice B. Toklas,* to inaugurate Stein's existence as someone whose life holds intense interest—for herself and presumably for any reader. The autobiographer explains that her first two years of medical school were all right because "She always liked knowing a lot of people and being mixed up in a lot of stories and she was not awfully interested but she was not too bored with what she was doing," but "The last two years at the medical school she was bored, frankly openly bored." Boredom thus becomes a figure for the impossibility of narrative. Only lots of people and lots of stories—the two sources of delight closely related to one another, as Eudora Welty for one has frequently pointed out—can avert it; as commitment to medicine begins to interfere with Stein's interest in both, it becomes intolerable.

Or so, at any rate, she says. "Gertrude Gertrude remember the cause of women," a friend pleads, and Stein reports herself as replying, "you don't know what it is to be bored." She gives up her proposed career and goes to Europe. She also, *The Autobiography* suggests, reinterprets her past. Retrospectively, she understands the pleasures of medical school as those of story. She thereupon dedicates her life to such pleasure.

Wharton's autobiography, too, thematizes boredom, although less explicitly than Stein's. In her prefatory remarks, Wharton observes that "habit," not time, produces old age. She defines habit as "the deathly process of doing the same thing in the same way at the same hour day after day." The story she goes on to tell indicates clearly (although politely) that the life expected of her gender and class depended upon habit in exactly this sense of the word. The deathly boredom she manifestly suffered in her own society declared her unlikeness to those around her. It forced her to discover, or to invent, a new way of life. That she could find such a life without blatantly violating social expectation testifies to the urgency of her need and the cleverness of her expedients.

In both autobiographies, then, boredom provides a form of retrospective interpretation. It also supplies a mode of self-justification. Boredom for Stein means the absence of available story; for Wharton, the impossibility of respectably telling stories. Her relatives ignored her writing, her cousins avoiding the subject "as though it were a kind of family disgrace, which might be condoned but could not be forgotten." The society of her heritage and of her marriage allowed no room for the storyteller. Asked what she wanted to be when she grew up, the child Edith responded, "The best-dressed woman in New York": her mother had filled the role before her. The stultification of an existence devoted to such aims justifies her choice of career.

Although both books employ boredom as a principle of causality, *The Autobiography of Alice B. Toklas* makes no attempt to render the imaginative dimensions of boredom as experience. It simply asserts the fact. Wharton, on the other hand, evokes the texture of tedium in upper-class life. But each autobiographer apparently takes for granted in the reader the sense of distaste aroused by even an allusion to boredom. Everyone understands the need to escape; Stein and Wharton, by choosing writing as their careers, demonstrate their capacity to find acceptable modes of evasion.

Boredom fulfills benign purposes in these autobiographies because of its immediate literary consequences in the story each writer makes of her life. The claimed experience promptly converts itself into protective compensatory activity. Looking back, two women who believe themselves to have suffered boredom declare their suffering the instrument of change. They function more distinctly as analysts than as victims of the condition. Analysts who separate themselves from the evil they diagnose, on the other hand, typically understand boredom as cause of more sinister effects, an index of moral and psychological danger. Constituting, from some points of view, sin as well as suffering, boredom may provide an inlet for evils worse than itself. Medieval commentators on the sin of *accidia* (or *acedia*), a complicated condition that eventually simplified itself into sloth but that in its origins implied specifically disaffection from the life of religious commitment, recognized boredom as a symptom of spiritual malaise. To the acute observer, its presence in a monk revealed a complex syndrome with dire potential consequences. The 5th-century commentator John Cassian describes a monk in an ominous state of weakness:

he looks about anxiously this way and that, and sighs that none of the brethren come to see him, and often goes in and out of his cell, and frequently gazes up at the sun, as if it was too slow in setting, and so a kind of unreasonable confusion of mind takes possession of him like some foul darkness, and makes him idle and useless for every spiritual work.

Surely we all recognize the condition, although we may not assume, as Cassian did, its necessary connection with sin.

From Cassian's point of view, the marked symptoms of boredom implied a necessary and sinister aftermath. Twentieth-century diagnosticians also understand boredom as rich in consequences, but its asserted effects cover a wider spectrum. Boredom fills our emergency rooms, a surgeon told me. People ride motorcycles, race cars, take drugs, shoot each other, as a result of being bored. [. . .] The results of boredom, in other words, depend on social and psychological context. One young man buys cocaine, another wrecks his motorcycle, another writes a poem: disparate actions demonstrating that boredom generates the need to elude it. Its dependable predictive value perhaps extends only so far. It can provide a cause for almost any effect.

But the meanings of boredom do not inhere only in its consequences. As a condition in itself, it may signal (though it also conceals) the simultaneous presence of depression and its antecedent, rage. Its utility thus manifests itself to members of the "helping professions." (Medieval commentators knew of these connections too. Cassian writes that "*Acedia* springs from sadness, which in its turn arises from wrath, and so forth.") If boredom disguises depression, the symptoms of depression may obscure the presence of boredom. The psychoanalyst Robert Seidenberg has suggested that women in particular often suffer misdiagnosis by professionals who fail to take seriously the psychological effects of social limitation. Reporting a case history of a housewife bored by her life's triviality, he observes that she endures real, external psychic dangers which "may not be apparent except to the observer who has thought about them". The distinction between depression and boredom, in other words, hinges on causality. At least in the 20th century, we typically attribute the causes of boredom to conditions outside ourselves: the tedious meetings we must attend, the dreary classrooms we inhabit.

Thus high school students, convinced of their oppression by an uncomprehending world of adults, respond with unyielding, often highly dramatized, boredom. "Schools prepare us for nine-to-five jobs," a student maintains. "They prepare us for boredom. They make our existences as restrictive and as boring as possible." Teachers may label such statements, and the state of mind underlying them, evidence of passive aggression, but labels do not make boredom go away. The students continue to believe in an adult conspiracy dooming them to tedium. [...]

From a middle-aged point of view, however, one may discern inner as well as outer causes for adolescent boredom. During eras when boredom was perceived as sin rather than sickness, there could have been no doubt about this point. The victim's insistence on external causes, typically unremovable causes, guarantees his or her continued suffering—and the continuing possibility of exploiting the state of victimization. The young display their symptomatic boredom as disturbing testimony of something wrong; but what is wrong may be their anger at the state of the world, not only the failings of secondary school curricula.

Sociologists as well as psychiatrists know the diagnostic power of boredom. What we proclaim boring reveals our values: what we consider it O.K. to reject and, implicitly, what we believe important or glamorous. Those who find oat bran boring announce their allegiance to other causes than good health. Or perhaps they only declare their superiority to undue anxiety. Despite the misery of true boredom, whether internally or externally caused (the Turkish phrase for the state of being bored translates literally, "My soul is squeezed"), self-presentation as bored implies a stance of superiority to a world unable to rise to one's demands. [...]

## III

An unknown woman approached me at a cocktail party. She wished to know what I was writing these days. When I told her, she exclaimed "Oh, I *love* to be bored!" Pressed to elaborate, she maintained that she always sought out boring movies, she looked for the most boring person at every party ("Thanks a lot," I said), she treasured boring books. Boredom, she insisted, was the best escape from anxiety. It filled the mind, it kept worse things away.

A Buddhist writes about the practice of meditation:

> It is a good feeling to be bored, constantly sitting and sitting. First gong, second gong, third gong, more gongs yet to come. Sit, sit, sit, sit. If we are to save ourselves from spiritual materialism . . . the introduction of boredom and repetitiousness is extremely important. Without it we have no hope. . . .

> Boredom has many aspects: there is the sense that nothing is happening, that something might happen, or even that what we would like to happen might replace what is not happening. Or, one might appreciate boredom as a delight. . . . It refreshes because we do not have to do anything or expect anything. But there must be some sense of

discipline if we are to get beyond the frivolity of trying to replace boredom.

Boredom here figures as a form of discipline and as the antithesis of "spiritual materialism"—whatever that is. Buddhists believe boredom a state to be actively sought, a stage on the road to Nirvana, not a condition to be resented and avoided. It brings hope rather than despair.

Walter Benjamin: "If sleep is the apogee of physical relaxation, boredom is the apogee of mental relaxation. Boredom is the dream bird that hatches the egg of experience. A rustling in the leaves drives him away."

Enthusiasts of boredom find the state desirable for the lack of desire it embodies. Opposed to anxiety, by the interpretations of Walter Benjamin and the Buddhist and my cocktail party acquaintance, it implies a kind of suspended attention comparable, perhaps, to that of a listening psychoanalyst. It "hatches the egg of experience" by allowing the semiconscious brooding that integrates and interprets past happenings. Avoiding distraction, it makes space for creativity. In Benjamin's view, it constitutes creativity's necessary precondition. [. . .]

We must posit two distinct versions of boredom: one marked by its tension (the midpoint between depression and rage, a psychoanalyst suggested to me), the other, for some at least, a form of serenity. Russell calls attention to a contrast between "fructifying" and "stultifying" boredom, the distinction dependent on whether the state derives from lack of excitement (this is the potentially fructifying kind) or "from the absence of vital activities." My division does not entirely correspond to his, but it implies the same point.

The kind of boredom conceivably valuable to its victim may feel every bit as irritating as the destructive variety. The child's familiar, maddening complaint, "I don't have anything to *do,*" epitomizes its form. Although empty time holds terrors for everyone, it contains the potential for discovery. It calls to mind Josef Pieper's definition of *leisure:* "an attitude of nonactivity, of inward calm, of silence; it means not being 'busy,' but letting things happen." Such is the emptiness that Walter Benjamin considers essential to the storyteller, that the Buddhist values as the path to meditation. However much we fear and deny the seduction of the lotus eaters, we may covertly long for the boredom that comes from lack of occupation, and we may profit from it: relief from the pressures of highly-constructed, overcommitted lives.

Unfortunately more familiar to 20th-century man and woman is the boredom with no redeeming social value: the kind that depends on excess rather than deficiency of stimulation. The tedium of required activity, of compulsory contact, of repetitive demand: these generate the tension we readily associate with boredom, leaving no room for creativity. This variety of boredom amounts to a tic of civilization. It figures important ways in which human beings impinge on one another in crowded, anxiety-ridden societies. The medieval monk suffered from solitude, from the temptation to invent distraction rather than abide by the routines of his faith. His late-20th-century secular counterpart more probably suffers from the need to listen to a tedious boss, a wife who fails to interest him, children who seem to say the same thing night after night.

Boredom of this kind possesses no manifest utility for its sufferer, only for its observer or analyst. Advertisers profit from it because those who endure it yearn for an alternative. Copywriters promise ways out for the woman who spends her time driving children from soccer practice to music lesson—ways in which she can imagine herself, if not her life, as interesting. Commercial messages of hope, rapidly converted into cultural clichés, sources of boredom themselves, give way to ever more extravagant promises.

## IV

Boredom's indispensability as a 20th-century novelistic subject reminds us as dramatically as advertisements do, as definitively as do the many enterprises dedicated to inventing distractions for those afflicted with life's tedium, that boredom has become, perhaps for new reasons, a paradigmatic ailment of our time. The ennui that afflicted characters in 19th-century fiction—Werther, Raskolnikov—or defined the pose of such poets as Byron and Baudelaire typically declared the sufferer's specialness, his or her awareness of society's intractable corruption and of alienation as its consequence for the sensitive spirit. Boredom possesses new forms of utility for the fiction-writers of our own era. Although the bored character still often makes at least formal gestures of superiority, he or she less frequently calls attention to the evils of "society" conceived as something outside the self. Instead, the bored man or woman in fiction may embody the conflicts of necessary involvement in a society so organized that its members grate on one another's nerves.

Two disparate examples come to mind: Evelyn Waugh's *A Handful of Dust*, first published in 1934, which concludes its narrative with an episode of purgatorial boredom, and Saul Bellow's 1975 novel, *Humboldt's Gift*, in which the subject of boredom preoccupies a protagonist only dimly aware of his own massive involvement in the problem about which he plans to write a definitive book. To glance at meanings assigned to boredom in these fictions may suggest how this psychic state has become essential to 20th-century imaginings of self and other.

One could say with equal plausibility that the term *boredom* has become for Waugh's upper-class English characters an empty social counter or that it defines the essence of their experience. They use it lightly, conventionally. When John Beaver, idle young-man-about-town, asks his mother about Brenda Last, his maternal mentor in her social wisdom responds, "I should say it was time she began to be bored. They've been married five or six years." Husbands and wives easily get bored with one another; both feel bored with the house guests they compulsively invite to stay with them and accordingly apologize for the likelihood that the guests themselves will find the visit boring; people readily dismiss one another as bores or boring. Out of boredom, Brenda embarks on a love affair with unattractive, unpopular Beaver, challenged by her initial belief that he feels "terribly puzzled, and rather bored in bits" with her, only to find herself victimized by her own unanticipated passionate feeling. The affair, in its unexpectedness, alleviates boredom for Brenda's social set. Her husband, Tony, bemused by her assertions that she must spend more time in London in order to study economics, decides that she must have been bored at home. Then, drunk, he confides that Brenda's new friends think him "a bore." Correspondingly, Brenda herself, plagued by at least vestigial guilt, decides that Tony must find it "pretty boring" on his estate without her and produces a young woman to entertain him.

The hypothesis of boredom, in other words, serves as satisfactory social explanation for every form and level of discomfort. Novelty, ever harder to find, is assumed to alleviate it. The reiterated, virtually automatic complaint of boredom betrays the limited imaginations of complainers who understand the social universe as monotonous in its principles of causality. Their paucity of analytic terms, as they dichotomize experience into "boring" and "amusing," condemns them to the tedium they hate and fear. But their inadequacy is more than verbal. Limitation of vocabulary reflects conceptual constriction, the impossibility, for Waugh's characters, of understanding what happens to them. They live desperately, failing to know their desperation, in a fog of unawareness, encased in social confidence that protects them from consciousness of realities larger than those of their privileged world.

The thematic of boredom in *A Handful of Dust* reiterates the pattern controlling the novel as a whole, whereby trivia reveal profundity. The threat of boredom adumbrates larger, vaguer threats. Men and women who know not what they fear declare their own and others' boredom and work to forestall it. They thus assert, among other things, their discomfort in relationship with their fellows. Although the Lasts posit one another's boredom as a function of lack of companionship, more typically the novel's characters understand boredom as resulting from the company of bores. Everyone at every minute risks relegation to that dread category.

To find the cause of boredom consistently in other people implies alienation that does not know itself as such. A friend once remarked to me that she considered it a sin to call someone a bore. Such dismissal denies the uniqueness—which implies the necessary interest—of every human being. Emily Post, in the 1945 version of her curiously mixed recommendations about manners and morals, makes the same point immediately after offering some harsh words about bores. "On the other hand," she concludes,

> to be bored is a bad habit, and one only too easy to fall into. As a matter of fact, it is impossible, almost, to meet anyone who has not *something* of interest to tell you if you are but clever enough yourself to find out what it is. Also you might remember that in every conversation with a "dull" person, half of the dullness is your own.

Waugh's characters, obviously, remember nothing of the sort. Assessing one another on the basis of entertainment value, they keep finding their companions inadequate. The novel's narrator does not take sides among them. If he suggests Brenda's moral inadequacy in her flight into adultery, he also uncovers in Tony a failure of discrimination and nerve that amounts to something almost comparable.

We last encounter Brenda in the novel burying her face in a pillow, "in an agony of resentment and self-pity," deprived alike of money and of what passes for love. Tony, also devoid of money and love, also suffering understandable resentment and self-pity, ends more luridly, condemned to spend the rest of his life reading Dickens aloud to an old white man he has encountered in the jungles of Brazil. Dickens, most immediately compelling of novelists, thus becomes the center of a parable of social boredom. Tony must endure, without intimacy, the endless intimate company of a man who does not interest—much less entertain—him. Doomed to Dickens (if he refuses to read, he does not eat), he discovers the tedium of repetition. His sadistically narcissistic companion, Mr. Todd, experiences no boredom in the situation. For him, Dickens remains endlessly interesting. Moreover, he possesses the power to control every aspect of his society. The natives, like Tony, do his will. The contrast between his condition and Tony's enables one to understand boredom as partly a function of powerlessness.

In the light of that understanding, the novel's earlier allusions to boredom take on new meaning. Characters' reiterated complaints about the tedium of their companions or their condition may reflect their painful experience of essential impotence, regardless of the amount of money or "love," most powerful of social counters, they possess. Boredom, then, is not a trivial complaint. On the contrary, it epitomizes the impossibility of effective action or knowledge in a world dedicated to the dulling of consciousness by meaningless activity, meaningless talk. At London parties, on their country estates, in bed, Waugh's personages find it impossible even briefly to change. They have no control over their real situations. Brenda may leap into implausible adultery, but only superficially does she alter her condition. Tony's jungle doom reiterates his earlier social fate. The complaint of boredom reflects the experience of futility at the center of a secular, frivolous society.

Waugh's narrator makes no direct claims of significance for the story he tells, and certainly none for boredom as literary subject or as personal emotion. Bellow's first-person narrator of *Humboldt's Gift,* Charlie Citrine, on the other hand, loudly asserts the importance of boredom as subject and as contemporary condition. He plans to write a book about it, about "the chronic war between sleep and consciousness that goes on in human nature." His subject, he says, is boredom. Before long, however, that subject has transmuted itself into "great bores of the world": a significant change.

The characters of *A Handful of Dust* inhabit a glittering social world and live mainly to entertain themselves. (Tony Last feels a serious interest in his estate, but circumstances—and his wife—soon conspire to deprive him of the opportunity to indulge it.) The world of *Humboldt's Gift* appears both more sordid (it contains crooked lawyers and incompetent ones, gangsters, women eager to sell themselves) and more serious, with higher stakes involved in most of its transactions. Charlie is in some sense an intellectual, not just a frivolous exemplar of self-indulgence. Yet his notion of boredom bears some relation to Brenda's. He, too, suffers resentment and self-pity; he, too, finally locates the causes of boredom in other people: the subject of boredom becomes for him the subject of bores. He generalizes, politicizes, distances his concern. [. . .] Such pronouncements alleviate Charlie's plight by providing the illusion of saving intellectual activity and by implying his superiority to the state he describes. He locates boredom elsewhere, condemns others as bores. If he has ever read Emily Post, he has not taken her seriously. Yet he himself suffers from the disease he purports to analyze. (It is even possible that he is himself a bore.) He worries a lot about "the boredom of the grave"; he experiences, inexorably, the boredom of the study, the courtroom, the couch, the car, the restaurant, the nightclub: the educated urban man's environment.

Like Waugh's characters, Charlie Citrine flees to sexual indulgence as escape. (In his world as in Brenda Last's, money and "love" constitute power.) He keeps a young, glamorous, sexy mistress whose presence at his side testifies to his vitality. She exploits him, and he knows it. He even knows that his need for such a mistress betrays his fear of the boring grave, of declining force, of his own intellectual and moral inadequacy. But knowledge brings no salvation. Like the Lasts, Charlie and his kind are doomed—to boredom and to what boredom means.

What it means, here too, is the failure of intimacy, the impossibility of power (in a society grown too complex and too dangerous to allow persons within it the sustained experience of power), the incapacity of individuals to take responsibility for themselves. Charlie is a more appealing character than even Tony Last, partly because the reader can know him more fully, more inwardly, partly because his environment bears a closer relation to ours, partly because he tries harder, tries constantly to understand and articulate his plight. Yet the effort at understanding and articulation only complicates that plight. Waugh's characters rely on a superficial and limited vocabulary to convey and to reflect their straitened experience; Charlie appears to possess endless verbal resources. But he, too, employs language as defense against the intolerable; he, too, finds change impossible. Tony Last reading Dickens novels aloud over and over, chapter after chapter; Charlie Citrine speculating repetitively about Humboldt—both supply figures of inescapable tedium.

If the story of Tony in his jungle captivity constitutes a parable of boredom, so does the novel that contains it. And so does *Humboldt's Gift*. In both works, the idea of boredom—through Charlie's exegeses and his experience, through the Lasts' life in and out of "society"—focuses an indictment of 20th-century failure. It calls attention to pervasive lassitude, to a malaise of futility. It summarizes something wrong with the response of contemporary men and women to their circumstances. The novelist, in short, locates boredom's utility in its very vagueness and inclusiveness as well as in the discomfort it embodies.

Those of us who are not novelists may likewise find the concept and the word indispensable for expressing levels of discontent too poorly defined, because too inclusive, for sharper articulation. For most people, boredom's utility as a state of mind resides not in its function as a means to serenity or creativity but in the signal it offers of disharmony between self and environment—a signal which, unfortunately, it also makes it difficult to respond to. The impossibilities of desire reflect themselves in the vocabulary of boredom that pervades our culture: a vocabulary that appears essential to advertisers, to novelists, to social scientists, and to the rest of us.

SCOTT DONALDSON

# The Jilting of Ernest Hemingway

[ AUTUMN 1989 ]

I

SEVENTY-ONE years ago Ernest Hemingway suffered the shock—or rather the *two* shocks—of his young life. He came to World War I at 18, fresh from a few months as a cub reporter in Kansas City and only a year out of Oak Park high school. His war didn't last long. He served as a Red Cross ambulance driver in Italy for only five weeks before he was badly wounded at Fossalta di Piave near midnight on July 8, 1918.

A great deal has been made of the effect of that wounding. Certainly the Austrian Minnenwerfer which threw the projectile across the river, to explode among the men Hemingway had just brought cigarettes and chocolate to, disabused him of any lingering belief in his own immortality. In Melville's memorable phrase from another war, *what like a bullet can undeceive*. Except that Hemingway was hit by more than a bullet: at the explosion hundreds of metal fragments ripped into his legs, and he thought he was dying. He tried to breathe and could not. He tried to move and could not. He felt his soul flutter up and away from his body like a weightless handkerchief. He survived that trauma, but did not soon outlive it. Time and again, in his fiction, he revisited the moment of his wounding and its aftermath. For years, he had difficulty sleeping without a light.

When the wounded Hemingway finally reached the Red Cross hospital in Milan, Agnes von Kurowsky was already there. It was she—this tall and vivacious American nurse with the Teutonic name—who was to administer the second wound, a blow that shaped the life and career of Ernest Hemingway every bit as much as the one he suffered on the Austrian front.

Even to begin with, it was an unequal romance. Hemingway, who turned 19 on July 21, was still a youth, and a youth without much experience in courtship. Though surrounded by women at home, he did not have a serious or steady girl friend in high school. He'd been an awkward lad and was only beginning to grow out of the gangling period into the extraordinary handsomeness and charismatic vitality of his young manhood.

Agnes, on the other hand, was 26, and knew something of the world. Before taking her training in nursing at Bellevue, she'd supported herself by working in a library and at other jobs. Attractive with her chestnut hair, sparkling grey eyes, and flirtatious manner, she'd had her share of beaux along the way, including a doctor in New York to whom she was officially engaged when she and Ernest met. Engaged or not, she was avid to see new places and meet new friends, and she could take care of herself.

Throughout her long life (and she outlived Hemingway by more than two decades), Agnes invariably maintained that she and Ernest had not been lovers. They saw a great deal of each other, she said, and she was very fond of him, but then again she was fond of a number of men, and matters had absolutely not proceeded beyond the petting stage. These disavowals, understandable from a married woman who was not eager to have her privacy trampled by a herd of biographers, do not entirely square with the love letters she wrote him in the fall of 1918. He saved her letters, of course, while it is one of American literature's minor disasters that she did not save his. The pattern was to be the same with F. Scott Fitzgerald and the rich and beautiful Ginevra King, the great love of his college years.

It took their romance a month or two to percolate in the hospital in Milan. A number of the patients and doctors paid Agnes suit, but Hemingway emerged as her favorite. They held hands more or less openly and wrote daily notes to each other during the hours they were apart. She worked nights so as to see more of him and carried his picture with her. Late in August, Hemingway wrote his mother that he was "in love again" but in no danger of getting married. Then as summer turned to fall, the relationship deepened in intensity.

In piecing out the story of this affair, a chronology will be useful, along with the introduction of one other character, a 36-year-old Red Cross captain from Philadelphia's Main Line named James Gamble. On October 15, Agnes was sent to Florence to nurse a flu victim. In late October Hemingway was dispatched to the Monte Grappa front, contracted jaundice almost immediately, and returned to Milan under the care of Jim Gamble. Sometime early in November Gamble offered Hemingway a year's stay in Italy, all-expenses-paid, as his secretary and companion. On November 11, Armistice Day, Agnes came back to Milan. On November 20, she and another nurse were assigned to Treviso. On December 9, Hemingway visited her there. Over the Christmas holiday, he stayed with Gamble in his villa at Taormina, Sicily. He had one more meeting with Agnes before he sailed for New York from Genoa on Jan. 6, 1919. It was then understood between them that they were to be married when she came back to the United States. Soon thereafter she was transferred to Torre di Mosto, where she met and fell in love with an Italian officer named Domenico

Caracciolo. On March 7 she mailed Hemingway his "Dear Ernest" letter.

While she was in Florence and Treviso, Hemingway wrote Agnes every day, and she replied nearly as often and with passion. She yearned for them to be together, she wrote from Florence, so that she could nestle in that hollow space he made for her face and then go to sleep with his arm around her. "I love you more and more and know what I'm going to bring you when I come home," she promised. Apparently to avert suspicion—nurses were not supposed to make love to their patients—she addressed some of the letters from Florence not to the Red Cross hospital but to the Anglo-American Officers Club in Milan. She did not want others to know of their relationship. "This is our war-sacrifice, bambino mio, to keep our secrets to ourselves—but, as long as you have no secrets from me, and I have none from you (at least, I can't think of anything you don't know already), why, we should worry about whether the older world knows. And, I'm afraid the world doesn't understand everything anyhow, and would make very harsh criticisms. But dopo la guerra—we should worry about criticisms, shouldn't we?"

The issue of age, not overtly discussed, runs like an undercurrent through these letters. He is her *bambino mio,* her *dear boy.* She called him "Kid" and herself "Mrs. Kid." She writes as to a younger person who needs flattery and approval. He mustn't think she's ashamed of him, she assures him. She's proud of him, she says, when he resolves to give up hard liquor. An ironic motif concerns her fear that he might abandon her as she had abandoned her doctor fiancé. "I never imagined anyone else could be so dear and necessary to me," she wrote. "Don't let me gain you only to lose you. I love you, Ernie."

During the November 11–20 period when both were in Milan, the two lovers solidified their marriage plans. Agnes maintained in retrospect that she'd consented to the engagement solely to keep Ernest away from Jim Gamble, a man she thought of as sexually interested in Hemingway's person. Ernest would never be "anything but a bum . . . if he started traveling around with someone else paying the expenses," she said. And in fact, they became engaged soon after Gamble proposed the year's holiday to Hemingway. In this connection, it is interesting that Agnes evidently knew nothing of Ernest's trip to see Gamble in Taormina during the Christmas holiday. Her December 20–21 letter from Treviso, one of the most loving she wrote, says nothing about this, instead confirming that she would not be able to be with him on Christmas day. "If this hits you about Xmas time, just make believe you're getting a gift from me (as you will someday). And let me tell you I love you and wish we could be together for our first Christmas . . . I miss you more and more, and it makes me shiver to think of your going home without me. What if our hearts should change? . . .

and we should lose this beautiful world of us." In the context of her letters, it seems clear that Agnes did indeed want Ernest to reject Gamble's offer and return to the United States, *both* to save him from his own worst instincts *and* to save him for herself. So he sailed on the *Verdi* early in January. She agreed to follow as soon as it could be arranged, but that was not soon enough for Ernest. At their last meeting in Italy, they quarreled because she refused to return immediately. That quarrel lay between them across the ocean.

## II

Agnes signed off her first letter to Oak Park cheerfully, though hardly passionately. "Well, good night, dear Kid," she concluded, "A rivederla, carissimo tenente, suo cattivo ragazza, Agnes." She was his naughty girl still, but even this lighthearted promise was withdrawn after she was transferred from Treviso to be placed in charge of the small Red Cross station at Torre di Mosto. She wrote him less often then, scaling down from twice a week to once every two weeks, and sounded less and less like his future wife. Reading these letters with the advantage of hindsight, it is obvious that she was preparing him for the final rejection.

Meanwhile, back in the United States, Hemingway continued to save money toward their marriage. As he wrote his friend Bill Smith, he had only 50 more years to live, and he wanted to spend every one of them with Agnes. By the first of March he had "$172 and a fifty buck Liberty Bond in the bank." Though he must have sensed the increasing chill in her correspondence—he was young but not stupid—he was not prepared to admit it to himself.

Feb. 3–5, 1919, Agnes van Kurowsky to Ernest Hemingway:

> My future is a puzzle to me, and I'm sure I don't know how to solve it. Whether to go home, or apply for more foreign service is the question just now. Of course, you understand this is all merely for the near future, as you will help me plan the next period, I guess. . . .

"I guess!" In any event, it looked as if she would not be returning soon. "I'm getting fonder, every day, of furrin' parts. . . . Goodnight old dear, Your weary but cheerful Aggie."

Feb. 15, 1919, Agnes to Ernest:

It was "hard work writing letters when you have none to answer," she wrote, implying that the Italian mails had not been delivering his letters. She'd had guests for dinner, including the "tenente medico [who was] the funniest and brightest one yet." Was this Domenico Caracciolo? "I have a choice of staying a year in Rome, but I'm thinking of going to the Balkans so I'm rather undecided as yet . . . work is going to be very dull at home after this life. . . . Ever Afftly—Agnes."

March 1, 1919, Agnes to Ernest:

Now there were too many letters from him. "I got a whole bushel of letters from you today, in fact haven't been able to read them all yet . . . I can't begin to keep up with you, leading the busy life I do," Agnes wrote. She was having the time of her life and never lacked for excitement. (With whom?) She had a star shell pistol and lots of cartridges to fire off on dark nights. (Alone?) She had learned to smoke and to play "a fascinating gambling game" called 7 1/2. (Who had taught her?) She certainly wasn't the perfect being he thought her. "I'm feeling very cattiva tonight, so goodnight, Kid, and don't do anything rash, but have a good time. Afft. Aggie." She was no longer *his* "cattiva ragazza," only feeling naughty 5,000 miles away.

Six days later, she broke off the engagement in a letter that has until now (unlike the ones quoted above) remained unavailable.

March 7, 1919, Agnes to Ernest:

Significantly, this "Dear John" letter did not begin "Dear Ernest" but instead "Ernie, dear *boy*." Even before he left Italy, Agnes admitted she had been trying to convince herself that theirs was "a real love-affair." She'd only given in (consented to the engagement) to keep him "from doing something desperate" (accepting Gamble's invitation?). After two months apart, she was still "very fond" of him, but "more as a brother than a sweetheart."

And not only a brother but a younger brother, for the real burden of her argument was that Ernest was simply too young for her. She had made him care for her, she knew, and regretted it "from the bottom of my heart. But I am now & always will be too old, and that's the truth, & I can't get away from the fact that you're just a boy—a Kid." (She was no longer "Mrs. Kid," however.) She thought she would be proud of him some day, but it was "wrong to hurry a career." It made no practical sense for an independent 26-year-old woman to marry a 19-year-old youth with no occupation or college education or apparent prospects. That was what she'd tried to tell him when they quarreled at their last meeting, but he'd acted "like a spoiled child" and so she stopped.

The last paragraph unveiled the rival hinted at in her letter:

> Then—& believe me when I say this is sudden for me, too—I expect to be married soon. And I hope & pray that after you have thought things out, you'll be able to forgive me & start a wonderful career, & show what a man you really are.

Or, at least, what a man he could become. The letter was signed "Ever admiringly & fondly, Your friend—Aggie."

## III

Literary history is full of jilted writers, suggesting that an early pang-at-the-heart may be salutary. Obviously, what matters is what one does with the hurt. Among the alternatives are sinking into the morass of sorrow, converting the pain to anger, adopting a stance of philosophical expertise, erecting barriers against future rejections, getting rid of the pain by writing about it, and above all proving the jilter wrong: *won't she be sorry, though?*

Hemingway went through all these reactions. He sank into a period of leaden despair after Agnes's letter arrived, and zombied around the house in Oak Park. Yet within days he was writing his friend Bill Horn about the rejection, appealing for sympathy and at the same time assuming the mantle of the expert on affairs of the heart. The letter began poignantly:

> She doesn't love me, Bill. She takes it all back. A "mistake." One of those little mistakes, you know. Oh, Bill, I can't kid about it, and I can't be bitter because I'm just smashed by it. . . . All I wanted was Ag. And happiness and now the bottom has dropped out of the whole world. And I'm writing this with a dry mouth and a lump in the old throat, and Bill I wish you were here to talk to. The dear Kid. I hope he's [Agnes's Italian lover] the best man in the world. Aw, Bill, I can't write about it because I do love her so damn much.

Then Ernest switched to the voice of authority. It never would have happened, he maintained, if he'd stayed in Italy.

> You, meaning the world in general, teach a girl—no, I won't put it that way—that is you make love to a girl and then you go away. She needs someone to make love to her. If the right person turns up, you're out of luck. That's the way it goes.

Looking at matters in this way reasserted Hemingway's authority. If only he, the 19-year-old tutor, had not taught Agnes, the 26-year-old tyro, the joys of lovemaking, she would not have succumbed to another. So, perhaps he was able to relieve some of the sense of frustration and powerlessness he must have felt.

Still, he longed to *do* something, to take some course of action that would enable him to ventilate his anger. So far as anyone has been able to ascertain, Hemingway did not rush out and contract a dose of gonorrhea from a girl who worked in a Chicago department store, though that is the course of foolish spite he described in his only fictional rendering of the jilting. He did, however, persuade himself that Agnes had cheated him out of a wonderful year in Italy. Her letter, he wrote Gamble, came as "a devil of a jolt because I'd given up everything for her, most especially Taormina."

In June Hemingway got a chance to take a measure of psychic revenge on Agnes. Her romance with Caracciolo was over, since his family regarded her as "an American adventuress" and he was—according to Hemingway, at least—the heir to a dukedom. This may or may not have been true, for in other accounts Ernest consistently inflated the status of his rival: he promoted him to a major in the crack Arditi, for example. Anyway, as he relayed the story to a friend, Agnes was "in a hell of a way mentally" after losing Caracciolo and had written to him asking for his sympathy. But he would do nothing for her now, Hemingway proclaimed: "I loved her once and then she gypped me." This purported letter from Agnes has not survived and may have been an invention. Hemingway may actually have got the news from Elsie MacDonald or another of their mutual friends from the Red Cross. It was Elsie to whom he wrote, on hearing that Agnes was coming back to the United States, to express his devout hope that she might trip on the gangplank and knock out her front teeth.

Satisfying as that bitter outburst may have been, it hardly succeeded in exorcising Agnes's ghost. Nor did it do anything to refute her assertion that he was still a boy, a kid, a spoiled child, and it was this accusation that rankled the most. As best he could, Hemingway set out to demonstrate that, though young in years, he was already a man.

He could not, however, grow up overnight. It took some time. Two years after the jilting, in the summer of 1921, he married Hadley Richardson, a woman almost eight years his senior and a year *older* than Agnes. He actually placed Agnes's name on a list of those to be invited to the wedding, but it is doubtful that she received an invitation. Eighteen months later, however, he had more news to tell her, and he wrote to her in November 1922. He had been traveling around Europe as a roving foreign correspondent for the *Toronto Star*. He was living in Paris, a city he knew she was enchanted by. He was married to Hadley. His first book—*Three Stories and Ten Poems*—was to be published soon. Did she begin to realize what she'd missed?

Again, this letter does not survive, but it is possible to reconstruct its contents from Agnes's reply and even to intuit that in making this overture three and a half years after his rejection Hemingway may have been contemplating a resumption of the affair. In fact he told Lincoln Steffens at about this time that he would leave Hadley if Agnes were to come back. In this context, her long letter of Dec. 22, 1922 must have been less than he hoped for.

She was awfully pleased to hear from him after so long, Agnes wrote, especially since "there has always been a little bitterness over the way our comradeship ended." After an account of her activities during the intervening years—she had wanted to break "somebody or something" when her Italian fiancé jilted her—she reverted to Ernest and their relationship. She was delighted to hear about his book. "How proud I will be, some day in the not-very-distant future to say 'Oh yes, Ernest Hemingway—Used to know him quite well during the war.' " But she went on to insist that events had proven her right in ending their "comradeship" and to reiterate the point about the differences in their ages, softening the blow this time by stressing her antiquity rather than his youth. (Apparently he did not tell her about Hadley's age.) "May I hope for an occasional line from you?" she inquired in closing. "Friends are such great things to have," and they'd been "good friends" once, hadn't they? Then she signed off with "best wishes to you & Hadley . . . Your old buddy Von (oh excuse me, it's Ag)."

There was not much to build on there. Hemingway must have felt that no matter what he did, he could not change Agnes's mind. She had thought him immature at 19, only a boy. She still thought him too young for her at 23, though he had married and moved to Paris and launched a promising career. Six months later, he vented his frustration in "A Very Short Story."

"A Very Short Story" is patently autobiographical. Patient and nurse fall in love, he returns to the States, she proves faithless and writes him a goodbye letter. In its earliest draft, the story remained sympathetic to the nurse as someone who succumbs to loneliness and muddy weather and the wiles of her Italian lover. But in the final draft, and it is certain that Hemingway wrote that draft after receiving Agnes's December 1922 letter, the tone becomes heavily sardonic at her expense. It is one of Hemingway's least effective short stories, because the dice are obviously loaded against Ag (or excuse me it's Luz, as Hemingway altered the name for publication), and in favor of the unnamed narrator-wounded patient who is too good, too noble, too unfairly wronged to be convincing.

The most interesting thing about the story, from a psychological standpoint, is that it drastically distorts the contents of the "Ernie, dear boy" letter. What the nurse writes, in the story, is that she regarded theirs as "only a boy and girl affair" and, again, as "only a boy and girl love." What Agnes actually insisted upon, of course, was that it was a boy and *woman* affair. This was an issue Hemingway chose not to confront, openly.

According to Hemingway's aesthetic canon, you could obliterate the memory of life's worst blows by writing about them. "You'll lose it if you talk about it," Jake Barnes warns in *The Sun Also Rises*, but some things were better lost. Some were also very hard to get down on paper. It took Hemingway four years to confront his jilting in a story, and when he did so he slurred over the principal reason for his rejection. By way of contrast, when he left Hadley in 1926, he put their breakup into a story—"A Canary for One"—within two months.

It is also important that only once did he present the jilting in fictional form. Some have thought that Agnes served as a model for Catherine in *A Farewell to Arms,* but the real nurse and the fictional one share almost no qualities whatever, and in any event Catherine does not jilt Frederic Henry. Here the difference between Hemingway and Fitzgerald could hardly be more pronounced. Both were badly hurt by their early rejections. But in Fitzgerald's case, when Ginevra King turned him down it provided him with the basic donnée of much of his fiction. Again and again he explored variations on the same situation in his stories and novels: the incredibly desirable rich girl and the worshipful poor boy who loves her beyond all reason.

Hemingway found it easier to write about his physical wounding in World War I than about his emotional one, and in fact the process of writing about what happened at Fossalta may have helped cure him of his trauma. Twenty years later, he behaved with conspicuous bravery during the Spanish Civil War. Twenty-six years later, he struck General Buck Lanham as the bravest man he had ever met, as together they suffered through the hell of the Hürtgenwald.

Agnes, unlike the Austrians, administered a hurt that not even time could make a healing of. Instead he internalized the lesson she taught him—that those who love can be betrayed—and made sure that he did not put himself at risk. Thus he had many friends and in almost every case broke off with them, sometimes viciously, before they could do so with him. In the mid-1920's he wrote and sold to *The New Yorker*—it was never printed—a humorous piece entitled "How I Broke with John Wilkes Booth," and "with Gertrude Stein, My Wife, Benchley, F. Scott Fitzgerald, Donald Ogden Stewart" and "with Dos Passos, Coolidge, Lincoln, Menken (sic) and Shakespeare." This attempt at comedy eerily predicted the future: Hemingway did break off relations with several of those listed, among them Stein, Fitzgerald, Stewart, Dos Passos, and not only his first wife but the next two as well.

Hemingway was married four times, and in each of the first three cases he was responsible for the divorce, and had a new wife waiting in the wings while the last scenes of the old marriage were being played out. He also behaved abominably to his fourth and last wife, and only the extraordinary determination of Mary Welsh Hemingway to stick it out kept that union from dissolving as well.

In looking back on that ill-starred love affair three score and 11 years ago, it now seems clear that his jilting by Agnes von Kurowsky may have been the most lasting of the many hurts that fate was to deal Ernest Hemingway. In his young manhood, it drove him toward achievement as he sought to belie her charge of immaturity. And throughout his life, he was reluctant to let anyone else get close enough to strike a blow to the heart. To ward off the danger, he severed any human ties that threatened to put him at risk. For Ernest Hemingway, even mortar shells seemed less dangerous.

FRANCES MAYES

## 10,000 Rules to Live By

[ AUTUMN 1989 ]

I COULDN'T wait to go to college. My grandfather walked in the dining room where I sat at the table reading catalogues. I wanted to go to Newcomb but knew nothing about it other than that it was in New Orleans. For years late at night, I'd listened to a black-cajun radio station that somehow made it across the air waves all the way to south Georgia. The music! I was pulled toward that raucous sound. The disc jockey advertised White Rose Petroleum jelly night after night. I knew about ruined plantation houses with oak *allées* and I kept a record album propped on my bedside table so I could see the cover photo of the golden crescent of the Mississippi at sunset.

I was a little interested in Vanderbilt because I heard that's where poets went. I ordered catalogues from Pembroke and Wellesley. Reading them, I had visions of myself in full wool skirt and starched white blouse editing the school news, a practical and serious person. The catalogue from Randolph-Macon came, too, sent by a very nice friend of my mother's who went there in the Dark Ages and told my mother it was the finest school for girls in the U.S.

Daddy Jack, who paid the bills at our house, thumbed through one and tossed it back on the table. I knew what he was going to say. "I went to the school of hard knocks myself," he rewarded me, "I didn't have any of this fancy education, and I've done pretty well if I do say so." And you do say so, I thought. "Well, you've got your head in the clouds, but I tell you one thing, sister, you can go anywhere you want as long as it's not north of Washington D.C. I'm not paying a dime for you to go off and marry some Yankee two by four much less mix with nigras not three generations removed from cannibalism." He puffed like a bullfrog.

My mother at the door, years past the middle of the 20th century, said, "And you can forget New Orleans—that's the white slavery capital of the world."

"*What* is white slavery?" I asked.

"White girls are kidnapped and sold to Arabs and other foreign sheiks and besides Tulane is for Jews. It's known as Jew-U."

I couldn't wait to go to college.

Given my strictures, I finally opted for Randolph-Macon. Virginia was within striking distance of places I wanted to know, whereas Tennessee was just as "hick" in my mind as where I sat, poets or no.

Randolph-Macon girls arrived with a lot in common. Most of us had similar reasons for being there: our parents had insisted. Randolph-Macon was thought to be better than the places we put first. We didn't know to ask, better for what? Louise wanted Radcliffe badly but her parents told her it was R-M or nothing. Anne longed to go to Stanford; her parents knew California was strange. I was determined to leave the state of Georgia and simply chose the farthest point north I could.

Academically the school was good—too good. When Eudora Welty made her first foray out of Mississippi back in '27, she chose Randolph-Macon. After a short time, she had to leave. The administration decided that her credits from Mississippi State College for Women weren't up to standard. Welty would have to repeat a year. She headed for Wisconsin, left "weeping across the James," and thereby escaped into literature. I had no goal other than to read, make friends, have fun. My purposes didn't fit the onerous requirements to master two languages, mathematics, economics, and a bag of other unintelligible subjects. I never saw the necessity to attend all those classes, so many days a week, or purchase unreadable texts when so much fiction and poetry waited in the bookstore. I was an ideal candidate for "alternative education," a concept unknown at the time. My grades tilted from one end of the A-F matrix to the other. Greek and Latin etymology fascinated me whereas whatever class happened at 8:10 a.m. sometimes escaped my notice. When I returned to graduate school as an adult, I could no longer remember why I'd had trouble in college courses. By then I'd caught on to the basic idea that one sometimes did one thing in order to be able to do another.

One rule at Randolph-Macon was the belt to breakfast rule. We could go downstairs in our robes when the bell rang, but we had to be belted, no sloppy free-hanging robes allowed. A student inspector, earning her scholarship, stood at the dining room door. Mine had no belt. It was a copy Miss Leila, our seamstress at home, made of a robe my mother saw in a magazine, a bubble line with narrow hem. A belt had nothing to do with it. But every morning I had to tie around me a string belt in order to eat. The dining rooms for each dorm were identical: round tables for eight with white cloths and the special R-M flowered Wedgwood. At lunch and dinner the rule was skirts or dresses. No one could leave the table until everyone had finished. The few Yankee girls hated this, and even the Southerners, who didn't know any other way of eating, hadn't counted on Becky Baltzer from Mississippi chewing every bite 27 times while the housemother drawled on about her youth and about good families of former students. We were served by scholarship girls. They went down early for dinner, then donned whites and served.

I was picky. So was Rena, a friend I'd spotted right away as a wild card in the deck. Across the street was a big house turned restaurant named the Columns. By the end of freshman year we were regulars. Even though Daddy Jack had to pay for my meals at school, I headed across the street several times a week, always when the odor of "train wreck," a tomato stew, or "mystery meat" drifted up the stairwell. Rena was always ready. We charged, blithely signing tabs which ran up into horrendous amounts by the end of the month. To this day I still make the Columns's brownie recipe, which we always finished lunch with, a rich chocolate pecan square topped with vanilla ice cream and fudge sauce. Then, hardly anyone in the South ate in restaurants at all except on state occasions. I told Daddy Jack The Columns was the name of the school store and I needed tights for modern dance, knee pads for hockey, a school blazer, a choir robe (choir robe!), endless pads and notebooks. He paid but was not amused. A couple of years later he got his revenge. At the reading of his will, with all the family assembled at the lawyer's, from my portion of the estate (picayune compared to his bombast about all his money) he deducted everything, down to telephone calls for $3.52 I made to fraternities from his house. I had to laugh. And his retort from the grave, never made in person, remains with me: you never know what someone silently stores up against you.

Yes, he really did this. The total was only a few hundred dollars. This person who went off to a woman's college ("we are not a girl's school, we are a woman's college") and sounds as remote as Emily Dickinson, was, to Daddy Jack, a wild girl who must be broken.

The school agreed. What might we do if we didn't have the 10,000 rules to live by? During the week, crossing the street was our only venture outside the red brick wall surrounding the campus. Sometimes we walked a couple of blocks to the ice cream shop on a long evening. Leaving the campus became a distinct sensation. R-M felt like an enclosed world, such a microcosm, a terrarium, that to leave began to seem odd. We became, some to a not mild degree, institutionalized. The only facts from the great world I remember from then are that Alaska became a state and that a handsome Latin in camouflage was acting up in Cuba and kicked out the sugar mills. Somewhere they were reading *On the Road,* but behind the red brick we weren't. We swooned over "The Lake Isle of Innisfree." Although Betty Friedan must have been putting the finishing touches on *The Feminine Mystique* then, not a word of that news had leaked to my part of the South.

Freshman year, we could not ride in a car during the day unless a senior accompanied us. We could have horses, not Jaguars. From this distance, our slowness seems impossible. I see myself trying to run underwater.

Recently I ran into Louise at an open house in Marin. She lasted only eight vivid weeks at R-M. Our time there was the late fifties, cusp of the sixties, just before girls were able to grab a little wheel of pills, that gesture that changed us forever. Louise reminded me of a talk in the gym. A nice girl got pregnant the year before, and her family was furious with R-M so now a gym teacher passed around a diaphragm and lectured. The woman spoke in such vague abstractions that no one had any clue what she was talking about until she concluded by holding up the diaphragm between thumb and forefinger and saying, "Now gulls, gulls, I have no idea what you'll do in your four years at Randolph-Macon Woman's College, no idea, but just remember if you're a good little actress on your wedding night, your husband never need know. There is no reason for him *ev-ah* to know."

Louise and I, retrospectively, decided that those old wise birds sniffed the winds of change and tightened the grip on freedom harder, one last time.

Dating R-M girls had built-in discouragements. Each dorm had date parlors. If you were dull enough to want your date to stick around the campus, you sat in there on linen or flowered chintz and kept the door open six regulation inches. The dorm mother paraded through, smiling and chatting about her courting days in Milledgeville (she had gone to the same school as my mother so always mentioned that). The boys rolled their eyes up as if on an elevator. They'd just driven the Blue Ridge Parkway or back mountain roads sometimes jammed six to a car from the University of Virginia or W & L in Lexington. They wanted to party, not see Miss Montgomery's sensible shoe and nose poked in the door. When a boy arrived, he filled out a date slip, stating his name, address, destination for the evening—everything but the occupation of his father. My luck was to have dates who listed their addresses as Mars or 10 Downing Street. This, the dorm mother said, implied disrespect toward me. Usually dates were blind dates, never seen before or after. Distance, the number of girls schools, the rules, everything stacked against getting to know someone normally.

We did have a unique advantage among W & L students for a while. Early in the fall, all of us had to line up at the gym for nude posture pictures. Why did we docilely line up? The women gym teachers in crisp, mannish shorts explained that posture was important to health. We had to strip, walk across the floor naked while they sized us up, photographed us in profile and straight on. We were later called in and a teacher would go over our body photos with us, giving us a grade and telling us to walk with our fannies tucked in, stomachs tight, shoulders back, chin up. To this day I can walk for blocks with a book on my head. Those with big busts were told they'd always have backaches and should wear dark colors. Those of us with small breasts were given an isometric exercise we could do in chapel or anywhere: grasp each forearm with the opposite hand and push, repeating rhythmically, "I must, I must, I must develop a bust."

Our rush in popularity happened when a drunk W & L boy climbed in the gym window and stole the photos, neatly labeled with our names. His fraternity passed them all over W & L. Somehow we didn't find this out for a long time; simply thought we were noticed at the Freshman mixer when boys were bused in, dumped, tagged, and brought to the gym to dance.

I loved the University of Virginia. The serene classicism of the architecture in the somewhat rough landscape appealed deeply to a sense of ideal education in an ideal setting. Those Thomas Jefferson "ranges," little rooms with fireplaces, each one opening to the walkway, seemed the epitome of romantic, intelligent design for students. I imagined Edgar Allen Poe scribbling madly in the firelight. But now the boys were hard drinkers by night. By day, dressed in suits and ties, they lounged about pretending they were at Oxford. Actually they were just hung-over. When we went to Charlottesville for parties, we were placed with a lady with spare bedrooms, usually a widow who attended R-M in the dim past. Three or four girls would be garrisoned with her. One of us was charged with the "yellow sheet" for signing everyone in and out over the weekend. It was an honor to be selected to monitor. Rules applied even though we were dreaming at Mrs. Blankenship's, miles away.

The most stringent rule was The Twenty Mile Rule. No drop of alcohol could be touched within that radius of the school. Even those who didn't drink began to plot ways to get 20.1 miles away every weekend. I had my first drink in Washington—a Cuba Libra, naturally. We elected Rena to go in the liquor store. She turned her ring around to look like a wedding ring and ordered a bottle of rum. What kind? "The best," she answered.

"Young lady, are you 21?"

Rena looks amazed, "I wish I'd see 21 again," she laughs. We're crazy with admiration for her. The four of us sharing a room at The Willard rush up and open the bottle. Anne's brother Paul is in town on leave from the Navy. He's older, a pilot, gorgeous, and engaged. He's not interested in us at all. What a pity. For hours we play bridge with him and sip rum out of hotel glasses, feeling we've succeeded in something but we don't quite know what. In Washington, we don't have hours, but we don't know anywhere to go after dark.

On weekends, I tried to go farther and farther, though there's a limit to how far you can get on trains and buses and still get back by 10:30 Sunday night. R-M made it difficult to go afield: they scheduled Saturday classes. I've never heard of another school in modern times with Saturday classes. Girls appeared at 8:30, raincoats wrapped over their nightgowns or pajamas, hair unrolled, barely combed, deeply demoralized, vacant eyes staring at Dr. Voorhis as he consulted his yellowed 3 × 5's. He harped on the Hapsburgs. World History. Invasion from without, decay from within. All wars begin in spring.

I cut. Made it to Annapolis or Princeton or Chapel Hill. Annapolis was one school more skewed than ours. Those constant salutes drove me crazy. And all the old crew cut officers always around. But one of the ladies who took in dates had a basement room that was a true pit. In the few minutes the midshipmen had to deliver the dates at curfew, something could happen, though not much took place on those cushions in the dark. For sure, everyone was stone sober after a dance with fruity fruit punch and crackers, the same snack served in Robert E. Lee kindergarten in Fitzgerald, Ga. The boy I dated there came from Des Moines, Iowa. West of the Mississippi, my imagination flattened out into an endless corn prairie. I simply could not imagine that anyone "cute" could come from such a place. Even so, he was. But he kissed fast and I was glad of the dark so I could wipe his saliva on my sleeve rather than swallow it. I felt stirred in chapel with all the midshipmen singing "Eternal Father" under the cold light from the highest windows. We went sailing in yawls on the Chesapeake Bay, held hands under the table in crowded tearooms crammed with uniforms and lovely girls who streamed in every weekend they were allowed. Princeton was even better. The dreaming spires of Scott Fitzgerald, the pink blooming trees along the lake, the big talk in the eating clubs, the town that looked like a model village for an HO scale train set. The football coach's wife gave us the run of her house. The coach had died, and one room was filled with his trophies and ribbons. My date called me "cara mia" and we took long walks across campus, past the Princeton Inn, to the grad school where the students went to dinner in robes. In 1968, my memories of the Princeton landscape and ambience, were strong enough that I talked my husband into going to graduate school there. It's too congested now, overrun and undifferentiated, but then it seemed an oasis, alone with U.Va., one of those permanent felicitous manifestations of architectural and therefore human grace. Late at night the living room was littered with couples making out in armchairs, on the floor, four to the sofa. Someone played "Misty" on the piano. We kissed until we were dizzy, breathing back and forth into each other's mouths until we almost expired from carbon dioxide. Heaven. That was heaven.

I get back at the last instant. All quiet on the western front. Slide my bag down the hallways then bump it up the stairs, looking up for waiting friends who want to know how it was, what did he say, did you meet anyone else, looking up at each scrubbed, creamed face, hair in rollers, book in hand. Probably I should have stayed here and studied for the anatomy quiz tomorrow. They'll do well and I'll be staring out my little dormer window at the smoky horizon of the Blue Ridge. [. . .]

Virginity seems quaint in these days of genital warts, herpes, AIDs, and other fallout of the sexual revolution. We had an old granite statue that was supposed to wink every time a virgin walked by. His eye must have been permanently closed, even though these were the last days of the virgin cult. Many of us didn't think for a minute sex was "wrong," but fear of pregnancy is a powerful deterrent to nice girls; that, compounded with the big word "reputation" kept us relatively chaste. Some did have developed senses of sin. Anne worried about the exact moment a kiss turned passionate and therefore sinful. She went to confession for such things. The priest defined passion as beginning after 15 seconds, no tongues included. So, while kissing, Anne had to count also. Many girls had never kissed anyone; they'd been sentenced even in high school to tidy girl's schools and never dated at all.

The town where I grew up is not the antebellum, heavy-duty South, with patriarchs reading Tacitus on the porch, but only the backwoods of Georgia, stratified as a midden but not hidebound like the Tidewater South. I'd stayed out late, kissed dozens of boys, fallen in love. I had steamy nights at drive-ins and summer cabins and swam naked down the river with my real high school love. But it was all natural, in the scheme of things. This corseting rubbed me wrong. I liked boys but never got to know any well while I was there. Wasn't I elected "Best Personality" in high school? Given even the smallness of the pond, wasn't I "Most Original?" "Prettiest Eyes"? I was popular. Now I began to feel less attractive. My natural instincts to be expressive physically started to snuff out. I couldn't think of anything to say to these Scotch drinking Virginia school dudes. Being "cool" never interested me. The endless loud party in a crummy fraternity house got old quickly, as did football games, especially since the U.Va. team had endured a three-year streak of solid loss and the tanked-up boys now cheered for what ever team theirs opposed. Every one I met had some Civil War name, Moseley, or Stuart, or Mead. Besides having to jump through hoops to date us, they faced the stigma that we were "smart." The Sweetbriar and Hollins students had better reputations as party girls and good riders. We were rule-ridden, and with a tight bit. [. . .]

The alma mater was in Latin. The composer, Miss Willie Weathers, was oblivious to the fact that in such a repressive atmosphere, the Latin words "quae ubi pinus exit" sung by a chapel of girls might have other reverberations than the context suggested. When we came to those lines we thundered "pinus" out. The deans all looked down; to mention it would be an acknowledgement that penises existed in the world and that did not happen. Poor Willie Weathers. I wonder if she ever noticed. [. . .]

At the end of sophomore year [there was] a performance of Euripides's "The Bacchae." Barefoot girls in fawn skins danced around the amphitheater in the moonlight in the service of Dionysus, god of wine and fertility.

Whoever chose the play had a diabolical streak. We were perfect for whipping up into a froth of fleshy, religious ecstasy. We could get into these parts as we could not get into "The Glass Menagerie." Racing around night after night whirling torches, wild with divinity, the Maenads sang:

> . . . crowned their hair with leaves
> ivy and oak and flowering bryony. One woman
> struck her thyrsus against a rock and a fountain
> of cool water came bubbling up. Another drove
> her fennel in the ground, and where it struck the
>     earth
> at the touch of god, a spring of wine poured out.
> Those who wanted milk scratched at the soil
> with bare fingers and the white milk came
>     welling up,
> Pure honey spurted, streaming, from their wands.

Power, mythic power. We felt in the blood. We sang in Greek. The words rang out:

> When shall I dance once more
> with bare feet the all-night dances,
> tossing my head for joy
> in the damp air, in the dew,
> as a running fawn might frisk
> for the green joy of the wide fields

The green joy felt cathartic. We wound back up the trail to the dorms, flashlights beaming the edges of the path, still singing like Maenads, in touch with all that fire the entire mechanism and history of the school sought to suppress, suppress, suppress.

Perhaps in the way someone cannot regret a bad marriage because it produced lovely children, I cannot regret going to R-M in the last throes of repression because of the friends I made there. I'm not the least regretful of following the president, Dr. Quillian, down Crush Path with my classmates singing "Gleam Little Lantern." We were supposed to be pure, coiffed, gracious, intelligent, unselfish, subtle, capable. We were. [. . .] Dozens of splendid young women, idealistic and nasty, intelligent and naïve, adventurous and unsophisticated. We began to forget we were supposed to please men. There weren't any. We were like the Spartan women during long wars. We were hell-raisers on sabbatical. We enjoyed each other thoroughly, since there was little else to enjoy, and so acquired the talent for friendship, one of the two or three chief pleasures of my life. [. . .]

To see the fall trees was a blessing. That golden raintree on front campus gave up all its fan-shaped leaves on the same day, a brilliant shower falling into a circle like the melted tigers in "Little Black Sambo." I loved kicking through the leaves of hundreds of scarlet and yellow maples, and that bright fall air touched with some stirring, unnameable scent. In spring, a sharp newness lasted weeks, then arrived the white and lavender lilacs, made to sing about, and the immense Japanese magnolia filling the library windows. The weeping cherry tree outside New Hall exists in my mind's eye as the paradigm even after for all trees. This tree was twisted and large, the limbs, trailing as weeping willows, effulgent with white blooms. I took pictures, wishing I had the Chinese landscape painter's delicate hand instead. To stand under those blossoms looking up at the intense spring sky was a pure pleasure that never will diminish. A friend and I typed Housman's "Loveliest of Trees" and tacked it to the trunk. I've heard that every spring since, someone repeats the gesture, that instinct for tradition at its best.

When I dream the anxiety dream, that I have not started the work and the exam is upon me and they've switched the subject anyway, the setting is Randolph-Macon. At least once a year I dream I'm back there for senior year and must make up all the requirements I skipped. I still wince at the memory of Mr. St. Vincent's remark in the margins of my creative writing notebook: "What is to become of you?" The Latin motto on our blazers meant "the life more abundant." But Anne's brother on a weekend visit said "I've been in Navy barracks all over the world and this is the most depressing place I've ever seen." Sandy tried to slit her wrists. Louise broke out as soon as she got the lay of the land, a woman before her time. I was balancing. I loved my friends and my sense of the place and the traveling. My own family was chaotic. Often I returned to R-M's structure with relief, a nun to the convent. There was just enough abundance to keep me attached, not enough for me to commit. No loneliness of any year has been as bad as staring out my fifth floor dormer window at bare trees, the river hidden, no clue where I'd been or was going.

For twelve years I've taught at a huge urban university. (Wouldn't Mr. St. Vincent be surprised?) If you walk through the student union you could be in the Miami airport there is such diversity. I've had wonderful people in classes. I've also had someone pull a gun and threaten to murder, several suicide threats in my office, students robbed and mugged. I've had male prostitutes, nurses, debutantes, normal students, waiters, 70-year-olds getting divorces, psychos in cross dress, you name it. One woman raped after class. I've had ominous calls at home. Notes from students saying "Want to have some fun with a younger man." But mostly serious people interested in writing poetry. Students hungry to know whatever I know. At worst, I sometimes come home feeling bare—as though picked clean by piranha. Young, or not so young, students fight to park or get the bus. Almost all work; indulgent parents are not deluging them with checks and words of caution. There is no coherent moral order. Every semester I examine myself as a teacher. Can I? How can I give them enough? They've not drifted into class, it was an upstream trip. I always considered the teacher as a being, entirely unapproachable as a person and therefore not really relevant to me. My students approach; they've paid their money. Also, I want to destroy hierarchy, that distancing I find inimitable to good learning. While I'm too reserved to be a pal, I've still heard the intimate lives of hundreds. Poetry is the most inner art. Words are closer to us than paint, marble, music. The good of teaching seems to be the full flowering. If I ever say "Whatever will become of you," I hope it's in wonder and anticipation.

Half the class transferred at the end of sophomore year. In spite of the contemplation, friendship, the seasons . . . enough was enough. The sense that an active world zoomed by the gates of the red brick wall became too strong. We went off to big universities, Texas, North Carolina, Florida. Rena and I got an apartment. Cruel, occasionally we'd call those who did stay and let them know we'd had five dates that week. We no longer had the rules to hamper us, but we also no longer had their protection. No handy excuse of curfew for tiresome dates or difficult situations. We had to face the real situations. We had long I.D. numbers, classes with hundreds. We got to know dozens of foreign students. We painted the rooms lavender with bunches of grapes on the corners of the ceiling. The rousing Russian army chorus and the Academic Festival overture we kept turned up loud. We put glasses to the wall and listened to the newlyweds next door squealing and bouncing. Daddy Jack up and died. I got his green 98 Oldsmobile and collected 47 parking tickets. We ate frozen vegetables. We roasted a turkey and didn't know to take the package of neck and gizzard out of the cavity. We were in paradise. We were living the life of exiles welcomed home. And like exiles we were charged and changed.

As soon as the pill hit, R-M as we knew it was lost. The truly revolutionary consequences of women having control over their own bodies kicked those date parlor doors closed, ripped up those destination slips, put those ladies in Charlottesville with their teapots and thin towels out of business forever. As preservers of The Way, how wise those women who ran the school proved; they invoked tradition, grace, protection, the concept of respect, culture, decorum, all those paternal gods of undamaged goods. We were imprinted with an intricate moral code of rules, from belted bathrobes to bedtime a hundred miles away.

Looking back, way back over the change and carnage and excitement of liberation, I see those deans and dorm mothers foresaw exactly, unleashed, how dangerous women would be.

PAUL BAROLSKY

## Joyce's Distant Music

[ WINTER 1989 ]

*In memory of George, Calliope,
and Arthur Drenios*

as with those musical airs which are for ever returning,
and cause you pain, you love them so much.
— Gustave Flaubert

WHEN John Huston's *The Dead* opened at the end of 1987, the film was acclaimed by many critics as a masterpiece. For the director who died in old age not long before its opening, the movie was surely a highly personal work—the meditation on death, which was imminent, a summing up, a giving form to this final summation.

Although the motion picture is a relatively new form of art, only a century old, Huston's final work belongs to a centuries' old tradition known as the *ars moriendi* or art of dying. In the Middle Ages and after, books were printed and widely diffused which offered instruction on how to die, religious tracts regarding the rituals immediately antecedent to death. Artists undertook, often for their own tombs, final works, appropriately devotional in character, which became a more specific form of the art of dying. Michelangelo's late Pietas, of which the Florentine version was originally planned for his tomb, were part of his *ars moriendi,* and his friend and biographer Vasari tells us how Michelangelo's thoughts at this time, when he worked on his sepulchral *Pietà,* were appropriately fixed upon death. Long after the explicit institutional and religious conditions which propagated such practices had vanished, the impulse to reflect deeply on mortality, on one's own finality, persisted naturally enough in art, which, by its very nature, has everything to do with mortality.

Joyce's book, *Dubliners,* from which Huston's film was made, is often regarded as a collection of short stories, although the word "collection" seems woefully inadequate to a work so richly orchestrated into a whole. If it is the chapters in the history of his city, as Joyce saw it, the book is a kind of cameo version of the magisterial novels of Balzac, in which Paris is the protagonist. Dublin, the subject of Joyce's novel, given form by its inhabitants, the Dubliners, is seen through the superintending, impersonal consciousness of the author—a consciousness which matures and expands throughout the book, reaching perfection, an all-encompassing depth and range, in the final chapter, "The Dead."

Like Flaubert, to whom he was so deeply indebted for the concision and resonance of his prose, for the sheer exactitude of his diction and imagery, Joyce created a work of formal perfection. He was the master of what, in a nearly archaic phrase, we might still speak of as prose style. "The Dead," a meditation on the living and the dead, draws together all that was contained in the previous chapters of Joyce's "novel." The two sisters at the story's center, the aunts Kate and Julia, carry the reader back through memory to the first chapter, to "The Sisters" of the Rev. James Flynn. Gabriel, at the end of the novel, meditates with a consciousness that, seeking to reconcile fancies of youth with thoughts of old age, expands backward in time as it confronts the last end, and his melancholy reflections represent a ripening of understanding far beyond those of the boy in the first chapter, who contemplates the initial mystery of the Rev. James Flynn's death. When, in "The Dead," conversation at table turns to the monks of Mount Melleray, we are drawn again to the first chapter, as well as toward the book's conclusion. Mr. Browne says that the monks, who get up at two in the morning, sleep in their coffins, and when he proposes that it would be better if they slept on comfortable spring beds, Mary Jane points out that the coffin is to remind them of their last end. Foretelling the novel's final image, the snow falling, like the descent of their last end, on all the living and the dead, the image also transports the reader, in remembrance, to the child's earlier contemplation of the Rev. James Flynn in his coffin.

Also like Flaubert, or the greatest creature of Flaubert's imagination, Joyce is still deeply romantic, and the unnamed boy in the first chapter enters into the world of romance when he dreams of Flynn's death. The grotesque memory of the dead priest, his nose stuffed with snuff, his teeth huge and discolored, his tongue hanging out—an image recorded with the nearly clinical realism of Flaubert—gives way to a Madame Bovary-like dream of the priest beneath long velvet curtains and a swinging lamp of antique fashion, in which the boy imagines that he would be "very far away, in some land where the customs were strange—in Persia." It is to a realm of "real adventure" that the boy in the second chapter, "An Encounter," aspires, a land, far away in space and distant in time, illuminated by Sir Walter Scott, a place called "Araby" in the third chapter. In his Flaubertian stories—suspended between realism and romance—episodes which introduce the dreams and delusions of childhood, youth, middle age, and old age, the world, as in Flaubert, is hostile to romance, until, finally, in "The Dead," Gabriel, capturing a glimpse of himself in a mirror, sees himself as a ludicrous figure, his life with Gretta, their former moments of ecstasy together, submerged beneath their dull existence. As in Flaubert, no word or sound is without significance, and when Joyce describes the snow falling softly, softly falling, falling faintly, faintly falling, these consonances, this music echoes still the wonder of the boy in the first chapter contemplating the Rev. James Flynn's death. Every night as he gazed up at old Flynn's window he heard the word "paralysis" in his inner ear. Said softly, it sounded strangely to him—as in a strain of music, suggesting a sentiment both subtle and vague. Becoming music, words in Joyce lift the reader beyond the range of conventional associations into a realm evocative of Persia and Araby and of places stranger still.

As a distinguished critic prior to Joyce justly observed, the English language in the second half of the last century increasingly assimilated the phraseology of pictorial art and, following this author, Joyce conceived of visionary images in perpetual motion, dissolving into music. In such music, individual pictures gradually fade into fugitive impressions, like the vague after-images of the earlier stories of *Dubliners* echoed in "The Dead"—fleeting, wandering spectres.

When we recall that Joyce once had a scheme for opening a motion picture theatre in Dublin, we cannot but wonder what he might have thought of Huston's transformation of part of his book into a moving picture with sound. Huston's movie presents images originally in the mind's eye of Joyce's reader, but such moving pictures of the film have certain affinities with those of the mind or consciousness. Whereas in a stage play the actors are living beings who play their parts in a real space, the motion picture projects flickering, spectral presences of lights and shades. The experience of a movie can be more nearly like a dream—a vision or even hallucination—than like a play, as if what we perceive upon the screen were the projection of our own inner experience, our own dream or reverie. It is such an effect that Joyce sometimes sought under the spell of Baudelaire, who aspired to dissolve all distinctions of art forms in aesthetic reverie filled with transient phantom images or spirits.

When in the final moments of "The Dead" Gabriel feels his own identity fading into an impalpable world, dissolving and dwindling, as he contemplates the wayward and flickering existence of the dead, he could almost be evoking the very medium into which Huston translates Joyce's work. As the inner mind's eye of the director's camera moves forward and backward into the distance, laterally and obliquely through a kind of "inscape," it conjures up a world of images suggestive of the vague shadows approached in the animated pictorial language of Joyce. Even in the first extensive scene of the movie, the camera's vision and hence our own, which becomes a dream, is one in which through the film of falling snow we sense—beyond the movement of arriving carriages and guests, within the home of the Morkans, illuminated by the ghostly street lamps, through the veiling curtains—spectral images of waltzing figures barely surmised beyond this filmy gauze. In their suggestiveness, such scenes, especially when accompanied by distant laughter or voices, are appropriate to moments of Joyce's

Symbolist aesthetic—the evocation of wayward presences beyond sight, touch, or full apprehension.

Huston's film is a translation of Joyce because it transfigures Joyce's words into a different language, the realm of animated visual images. Huston uses the camera to especially good effect during Aunt Julia's song, when he leaves her and her listeners and wanders to her now disembodied words, through vacant space, becoming a ghostly presence gazing upon Julia's empty but inspirited room, filled with objects and photographs pregnant with plaintive memories. The director or his eye is here the impersonal consciousness which dwells in memory on elusive moments in Julia's fading life. Some images follow one upon the other in the manner of collage, but in other instances they melt into one another, approaching in their visual effect of fading and reemergence, the quality of memory itself.

A film after a work of literature, necessarily, cannot achieve identity with the original, and it is for this reason that some critics will condemn such a work as not worthy of the original which it imitates. To this criticism there is in a sense no reply, except to suggest the possibility that it is perhaps too restrictive, for it does not allow the film to stand as a work on its own terms. Like any translation, a film after a literary work occupies an ambiguous position somewhere between the original and the medium and temperament of its translator. If for some no translation is possible, for others such a translation will be successful in varying degrees.

We might speak of Huston's interpretation or translation of Joyce's *Dubliners* as a performance of the original, in which we recognize the composer's music, notwithstanding the performer's interpretation, including even his modifications of the score, which are tactful, if not Joycean. The use of the word "performance" is especially appropriate to the description of Huston's film, since the work he performs constantly aspires to the condition of music. Flaubertian story becomes Baudelairean prose poem, with all of the suggestiveness of music in the story's last words, informed by what was once called "the power of music."

In Joyce's story music is a central theme, uniting all the characters at Aunt Kate's and Aunt Julia's for their annual Christmas dance, just as in a deeper sense music is expressive of Irish conviviality, thus unifying various motifs in the earlier stories of *Dubliners*. Gabriel calls the Misses Morkan the three Graces of the Dublin musical world—an image that evokes the Graces intertwined in dance, the appropriate symbol of the Christmas dance, which gives full expression to their very graciousness. Julia, who formerly sang in the choir, still is the leading soprano in Adam and Eve's; Kate had given music lessons, as does Mary Jane, who plays the organ at Haddington Road; their guests include former and current students and their friends. Music fills the story in the very allusions to dance, the "shuffling of souls," and the "skirts that sweep" through the evening's waltzes, embellished by the guests' peals of laughter in "musical echo." Music plays throughout, in fact and in memory: Mary Jane's piano performance; Aunt Julia's song *Arrayed for the Bridal;* the song sung in unison by all the guests in honor of the three hostesses; all the talk of singers current and old (of the great Trebelli Giuglini, Ravelli, Aramburo, names that roll from the lips in musical cadence); the faint memory of old Parkinson, who sang so long ago in a tenor voice pure and mellow; and, finally, the distant music of Bartell D'Arcy's song in the old Irish tonality, which echoes the even more distant song of the dead Michael Furey.

Bartell D'Arcy's song not only stirs the sad memory of Gretta's former passion but deepens Gabriel's gloomy consciousness, the sad reflections on himself, on Gretta, on the Misses Morkan. Reading *Dubliners* we experience a music filled with nostalgia, regret, and homesickness, a "thought-tormented music." For Joyce as for Flaubert language is like a cracked kettle upon which he beats out tunes for bears to dance to, while all the time he yearns to move the stars to pity. When Bartell D'Arcy's song evokes a distant music, it also liberates Joyce's prose, which becomes ever more lyrical. Describing Gabriel's soul swooning, approaching the region where dwell the vast hosts of the dead, where he is conscious of but cannot fully apprehend their wayward and fleeting existence, his identity dissolving, Joyce writes in language that achieves the status of pure song, the very sound of time passing. Singing of spirits and essences beyond words, themselves, of the deepest places in imagination, Joyce "scores" the snow falling in silver flakes:

> It was falling on every part of the dark central plain, on the treeless hills, falling softly upon the Bog of Allen and, farther westward, softly falling into the dark mutinous Shannon waves. It was falling, too, upon every part of the lonely churchyard on the hill where Michael Furey lay buried. It lay thickly drifted on the crooked crosses and headstones, on the spears of the little gate, on the barren thorns. His soul swooned slowly as he heard the snow falling faintly through the universe and faintly falling, like the descent of their last end, upon all the living and the dead.

Although Joyce wrote lyrical poems of no great distinction (for example, those in *Chamber Music*), the related lyricism of his story's final lines—a kind of prose-lyric—transcends that of the lyric poems, because they absorb into themselves and condense the music and attending emotion of the whole story. The soft, sweet music played on the invisible harp of Joyce's prose is transfigured into a song about all of the memories, thoughts, and experiences of Dublin and beyond. As he contemplates the secrets of the grave with heavy eyelids, he sees that all this has been to him as the sound of lyres. Performing Joyce's final words, Huston projects a series of accompanying phantom-pictures—the lonely churchyard, the crosses and headstones, the barren thorns—images which, as the camera moves slowly upward through the snow, falling softly, dissolve, finally, into darkness.

Joyce's biographer has told us much that is fascinating about how the author fabricated "The Dead" out of stories he heard, from characters he knew, from the wide range of his readings, including Homer and George Moore, and other scholars have elaborated on this account by further considering Joyce's uses of literary tradition. They have also recently dwelt on how Joyce's work self-consciously reflects his sense of place in the history of literature. And for all this we must be grateful. But it is to Huston's film that we must turn for the sensuous reenactment of Joyce's work, for the vivid performance of its emotional depth and fascination that no academic discourse can give us. Huston's film restores former readers to Joyce's story, just as it will attract new ones. Even if it transforms Joyce's work in detail, even if, necessarily, it does not rise, as a work of art in its own right, to the condition of the greatest art that Joyce's story reaches, it achieves what a fine performance does when it re-creates an original music. The music that Joyce aspired to in prose is filled with the force of that emotion we experience when, in rare moments of memory, we glimpse the mystery of our own existence, when we experience intimations of mortality not as mere idea but as something strange, mysterious, and fleeting, like consciousness and memory themselves, like falling snow in eerie twilight, descending in the delicate dance, between hopefulness and the sad, fading memory of a distant strain. For we are all like the flickering shades of Joyce's musical moving picture, to which the haunted Huston paid final, parting, and loving homage.

# The Nineteen Nineties

GEORGE WATSON

# Shakespeare and the Norman Conquest: English in the Elizabethan Theatre

[ AUTUMN 1990 ]

How much did Shakespeare know about language, or languages, in a deliberate sense: about language in general, about the languages of Europe in particular—and about English above all?

THAT QUESTION —or huddle of questions—is still unexplored. It is easy to accept that the great dramatist of England, and of Europe, is the master of his native tongue; but ever since his rival Ben Jonson made his famously slighting remark about "small Latin and less Greek," it has been doubted if he knew much else. Jonson may have been the better classicist, and there is a tradition supported by Milton, Voltaire, and Samuel Johnson that Shakespeare wrote more by nature than by art, "warbling his native woodnotes wild." I want now to propose another, and less familiar, Shakespeare: one who held general views about the nature of language, who was the conscious master of more than one European language: in short, a man learned in tongues. I believe that Shakespeare was a conscious linguist.

The difficulties that lie in the way of proving such a hypothesis are in the first instance practical. The truth is that, much as is known about Renaissance English, that knowledge as a whole is still largely unmarshaled. This is the biggest void there is in English studies. Renaissance English still lacks a dictionary, and it still lacks a grammar. There are both for Old English, or Anglo-Saxon; both for Middle English, or Chaucer's language; and for Modern English both, of course, and in abundance. Shakespeare's English is Early Modern, and in scholarship it has slipped through the cracks, so to speak, between Chaucer's English and what lexicographers since Dr. Johnson's day have successively recorded: it has been lost sight of, as a whole, through a sort of scholarly inadvertence. Though there is an old glossary of Shakespeare's vocabulary by C. T. Onions (1911), now revised (1986), there is none of 16th- and 17th-century English as a whole—though I have visited a workshop in a German university where a Renaissance dictionary once begun in the United States is still under way. It is a book badly needed. Until there is a dictionary of Renaissance English as a whole, we cannot easily judge Shakespeare's use of words: a Shakespeare concordance enables us to do no more than compare one usage in that author with another; and even a big historical dictionary of Modern English like the Oxford can offer only occasional clues. That is an odd way to treat the language of Sidney and Spenser, Marlowe and Shakespeare himself, Hooker and Bacon, Ben Jonson and Middleton, Burton and Sir Thomas Browne. No grammar, and no dictionary—at least, not yet. It is the widest gap in English studies that there is.

Shakespeare's standing as a linguist can be established most briskly by the claim that he is the only Elizabethan dramatist to write at length in a foreign language: a claim so nearly true, when one considers the brevity of Ben Jonson's Latin tags or of John Marston's snatches of Italian, as to be a demonstrable fact. The French scenes in Shakespeare's *Henry V* are surprising: not just that Shakespeare could write them, but that he should expect a London audience in 1599 to understand them. It is true that his French is boldly inaccurate, even allowing for the fact that some of it is meant to be spoken by ignorant Englishmen: "Suivez-vous le grand capitaine" is as unlikely in 16th-century French as it would be today. Shakespeare muddles "tu" and "vous" as no Frenchman then or since is likely to have done, and misplaces pronouns: "Je te prie, m'enseignez. . . .," the French princess says to her confidante (III.v), for "Je te prie, enseigne-moi . . ."; and he confuses "il est" and "c'est." But then I am arguing that Shakespeare was widely read and learned rather than scholarly. He was hugely read; his literary memory must have been one of the world's marvels; his mind could assimilate books greedily; and above all he could seize the spirit of an original, whether in French, or Latin, or perhaps even in Italian. Italian one imagines him reading, as many have done before and since, out of some half-remembered grasp of Latin acquired at school. That he was inaccurate is an effect of speed of mind, surely, rather than of lack of grasp. The public theatre was in any case no place to take trouble over linguistic accuracy. The French scenes in *Henry V,* essentially unique as they are, show that he could enter fully if inexactly into the spirit of a foreign tongue. As early as the 1590's, it is clear, French was an international language of elaborate courtesy—a courtesy linked in the Elizabethan mind to a notion of mannered, even decadent badinage. Henry V's proposal of marriage to Katherine in the last act of the play is a masterly summary of that style, moving confidently out of mannered French into bluff, blustering English and back again, as a conqueror's heart is enslaved by the conquered.

Shakespeare's sense of language, as a totality, is a humanist's sense, and it is one inherited from Aristotle, Rabelais, and Erasmus. Words are arbitrary signs, we are often told nowadays—and rightly. The notion has unfortunately been allowed to go about unchecked, at least among literary critics—modern linguists know better—that the Arbitrariness of the Sign is a 20th-century discovery. Shakespeare and his audience knew it as a truth already traditional and familiar. Words happen to be what they are ever since Adam, as told in the Book of Genesis, named the animals at Creation; exceptions apart, like onomatopoeia, they are arbitrary. "That which we call a rose / By any other word would smell as sweet," as Juliet remarks. Words are mere names: things, by contrast, are what God has made them. The point is familiar. Ferdinand de Saussure was not given to quoting Shakespeare, or indeed any literary source; but he is explicit in the *Cours de linguistique générale* (1916) that the Arbitrariness of the Sign is a traditional doctrine in linguistics: "The principle . . . is contested by nobody." He might have added that it was uncontested in the European Renaissance. In an early Shakespeare play, *2 Henry VI,* a charlatan claiming to have been born blind is whipped out of court for pretending to recover his sight by a miracle. Saunder Simpcox, as the rogue is called, answers questions about colors with suspicious ease: "What colour is this cloak of?," and he answers "Red"; and "What colour is my gown of?," and he answers "Black, forsooth, coal-black as jet"; and he is beaten for a liar. "If thou hadst been born blind," says Gloucester,

> Thou might'st as well have known all our names, as thus
> To name the several colours we do wear.
> Sight may distinguish colours; but suddenly
> To nominate them all, it is impossible. . . .
> (II.1.124–8)

I am not aware that Shakespeare has any reputation whatever as a theorist of language; and in this matter, as in others, he makes no claim to originality. But like Juliet's remark about "a rose by any other word," that scene from *Henry VI* shows his firm grasp of a humanistic doctrine of language as an arbitrary system that had been ancient and medieval before it was Tudor. It is in Aristotle and Aquinas. Languages only happen to be what they are; they could, after all, be otherwise. They are conventions and not necessary truths. That is surely something that anyone who has ever tried to learn a foreign language must know; and Shakespeare, it is certain, had more than once done exactly that. At one point, indeed, he invents a language (*All's Well IV. i*).

All that is shared knowledge, as between Shakespeare and his audiences. The story of Simpcox the charlatan, who tried to fool the court by pretending he could name colors at first sight, adds nothing to anyone's understanding of how language works, in a severely original sense, whether then or now. But it usefully disposes of the idea that Shakespeare's interest in linguistic questions was purely instinctive. Nobody could have composed that scene, or Juliet's remark, without having reflected about the nature of human speech—even if those reflections, at that simple level, are no more than traditional; and nobody could have written the French scenes in *Henry V* without a practical knowledge of how other languages differ from his own. I want now to suggest that Shakespeare's conscious interest in language goes far beyond familiar humanistic concerns of a lexical or rhetorical sort: that he is a conscious artist when he exploits, and almost for the first time in English, an aspect of the arbitrary principle unique to the language.

## II

English is the only great European language firmly and extensively based on a system of double derivation. Its derivation is at once Germanic and Romance. The Germanic aspect, which is fundamental, is by now more than a thousand years old, and derives from Anglo-Saxon. The Romance element, which had begun to appear even before the Norman Conquest, was powerfully amplified by that event and its consequences: above all by some three centuries of bilingual usage. For nearly three hundred years, from 1066 down to the 1340's, when Chaucer was an infant, England was ruled by a French-speaking ruling class; and by the time English reemerged as an official and literary language in the mid 14th century, it had been profoundly changed by its long immersion in a foreign idiom. That is what makes English fundamentally distinct from other Germanic languages, such as the Scandinavian, or modern German, or Dutch: English is that Germanic tongue that has absorbed most widely from the vocabulary of Mediterranean Europe—in most instances, from Latin by way of French. In a curious and (to the modern mind) paradoxical sense, English is an insular language: paradoxical, because for most of human history, it is easy to forget, it has been easier to travel by sea than by land. To be an island, then, was not to be cut off from Europe but to be fully exposed to it. It is in the remote, mountainous, landlocked corners of Switzerland that medieval German survives at its purest. It is in other remote corners of Switzerland that Latin—or something like it—best survives, in Romansch. English is the supreme instance there is of a fully European language. It is that language that has been most receptively open to the influences of all Europe; and since Shakespeare's time it has even become a world language, with a scattering of words from Asia, Africa, and the Americas.

Shakespeare inherited the double-derivation system that is the hallmark of English; and of all English poets he saw the profoundest possibilities in it, and saw it at its fullest extent. The revival of classical learning was threatening to choke English with long technicalities of Romance origin, as with

Holofernes the pedant in *Love's Labour's Lost*. Many such words proved unwieldy and have since been lost, so that the English of Shakespeare's time was probably the most Latinate there has ever been. Since his interest in linguistic theory was a conscious one, he was consciously interested in that, and Holofernes makes it plain. Indeed there is a moment in another of the *Henry V* plays where Shakespeare openly refers to the double derivation of English. When Sir William Lucy arrives too late to find Talbot alive, during the French wars, the Dauphin of France dares speak to him of surrender, or rather submission:

> On what submissive message art thou sent?

and he receives a defiant answer:

> Submission, Dauphin? 'Tis a mere French word;
> We English warriors wot not what it means
> (*1 Henry VI* IV.v.53–4).

Now of course "submission," or rather "soumission," *is* a French word—as Shakespeare, with his knowledge of French, could not fail to know. It had entered English some two centuries before him, so far as the documents show, or in the 14th century. Surprising if Shakespeare, after what may be presumed years of school Latin—and who knows how much subsequent reading of French and Italian too?—could not have thought of that for himself. English had no etymological dictionaries in Tudor times: but you hardly need a dictionary to know that some English words are Germanic and others Romance.

The last point needs some expansion. When the late Jürgen Schäfer of Augsburg University published his *Shakespeares Stil* in 1973, it was subtitled *germanisches und romanisches Vokabular*—Germanic and Romance vocabulary; and it attracted the criticism that he had exaggerated the extent to which a Tudor poet or audience could have retained any immediate sense of the double derivation of English. These doubts may be put to rest. The truth is that the British to this day retain an immediate and popular sense of the distinction between Germanic and Romance vocabulary, and not only linguists among them. I say British here, since the distinction of derivation is perhaps less strongly felt in American usage; and, what is more, the influence of American usage on British is tending to weaken the distinction. Let me illustrate what I mean by an instance or two.

I recently took a bus to a London suburb—a bus I had never taken before. Having been told by friends to stay on to the very end, I asked a schoolboy, when the bus showed no inclination to go any further: "Is this the terminus?" The boy looked blank, and I suddenly noticed that he was younger than I had supposed. So I altered my question to "Is this as far as it goes?," and he told me it was.

Translating ourselves is something we do in England every day; and we remark on it so little, as native speakers, because we are so used to it. The British filter their language, both in speaking and writing, using Germanic words for popular or childish conversation and admitting Romance words for learned and technical usage—or for ironic effect. If that amounts to a mild national difference between Britain and the United States, that is because Americans often have a fainter sense of the double derivation of English and are in consequence more polysyllabic. When I first lived in the United States, more than a quarter-century ago, I was struck by the way ordinary Americans would use the word "pregnant" in a domestic context, as in "My wife is pregnant"; whereas in England the word smacks of hospitals and law-courts, and to this day an Englishman would be more likely to say "My wife is having a baby": a remark that is Germanic through and through. (The phrase "with child" is by now archaic even in England, and I imagine it would strike an American, especially, as impossibly literary and Biblical in ordinary conversation.) No Englishman is likely to remark, as an explanation of why he isn't laughing, "I'm internalizing," as Mort Sahl once did in London; or to write about "Hamlet's sociological origins," as an American student once did when I was teaching in the Midwest. (He meant no more than that Hamlet was a prince.) American English can strike the British visitor as almost comically polysyllabic. But then the United States never suffered a Norman Conquest or three centuries of Anglo-French bilingualism.

Shakespeare's point about "submission," then, is something that the English still live by. It *is* a mere French word. It has no Germanic equivalent, as it happens—abstractions tend to be Romance in English—though there are phrases about "giving in." Alone among the great European languages, English has the odd facility of offering the chance to say most things in two ways. One may say "Is this the terminus?" or "Is this as far as it goes?" A woman can be pregnant, or she can be going to have a baby. One can teach or lecture. It is a subtly graded system, replete with ironic effects: but in the end it comes down to a set of alternatives, a duality. It is as if English were less one language than two.

## III

The matter has more than one aspect. Since Romance terms often reflect a higher rank, or education, or state of sophistication, they can boast a higher prestige than Germanic; though there are exceptions, and in the days of the U and non-U controversy it was diverting to be reminded that Germanic "napkin" is of higher standing than Romance "serviette." Another is a difference of length. There are rather few Romance monosyllables in

English; and exceptions like the verb "to pant" are somehow surprising to learn. (The word is ultimately related to Greek "phantasia.") Much of our Germanic vocabulary, by contrast, has been left as words of one syllable, as a consequence of the collapse of English terminal inflections in the later Middle Ages.

That leaves English poetry with a dimension unique in the Western world: the possibility of the monosyllabic line, the poetic equivalent of that remark I made on the bus: "Is this as far as it goes?" More than half a century ago the great Shakespearean A. C. Bradley was struck by the monosyllabism of Hamlet's dying speech to Horatio surrounded, as one great line there is, by lines of quite another order—

And in this harsh world draw thy breath in pain

—and he composed a classic essay on the rise, fall, and Victorian recovery of that strange species of utterance, essentially Germanic as it commonly is. Nowadays four-lettering means obscenity, and there are notoriously four-letter equivalents to police-report terms like "violation" and "fornication," startling as they would look, until recently, in any polite context. They are sometimes comically called "words of Anglo-Saxon origin." But such words are after all the heartbeat of some of the greatest lines of English verse, and not only Shakespeare's.

You do me wrong to take me out of the grave,

says Lear, at a moment of high intensity, and a polysyllabic version could only be weaker. It is one thing to do someone wrong, as Lear puts it; another, and a more technical thing, to commit an injustice. As "submission" is a mere French word, so is "injustice." So I suggest that what Shakespeare achieved with English was to see a new possibility in its Englishness, or rather its Anglo-Saxon-ness. He dared to make the traditionally less dignified of two derivations its supremely dignified form: he turned the less learned, momentarily, into the more. It is as if "sheep" and "mutton," or "veal" and "cow," were reversed: a sort of delayed revenge for the Norman Conquest. Perhaps this is what Coleridge meant when he remarked in August 1832, in his *Table Talk,* that Shakespeare was "particularly happy in his use of the Latin synonymes, and in distinguishing between them and the Saxon."

## IV

I want now to suggest that Shakespeare, being at once a good linguist and something of a conscious theorist of language, practices the translation-game of English in a deliberate sense and to serious purposes. Since it is possible in English to say most things in two ways, it is often possible to translate oneself—the only language, surely, where such an effect is common or even widely possible. In Shakespeare that game presumably reflects the social diversity of his audience. Not everyone in a Jacobean theatre would understand Macbeth's line about

> The multitudinous seas incarnadine

where the extremely rare verb "to incarnadine," meaning to dye red, and occurring nowhere else in Shakespeare, is paired off with the highly elaborate adjective "multitudinous" to keep it learned company. Such a line can only have made the vaguest sense for most of Shakespeare's first audience; but he promptly translates it into the simplest of terms, for the groundlings:

> Making the green one red,

so that a hard version is followed by an easy one.

From the beginning of his career, Shakespeare often prefers to play the translation-game in that oddly inverted order, from complex to simple. Consider Berowne's speech on love in that early play, *Love's Labour's Lost,* where Berowne is urging his three friends to abandon their vow of chastity.

> Love's feeling is more soft and sensible
> Than are the tender horns of cockled snails.
> Love's tongue proves dainty Bacchus gross in taste.
> For valour, is not Love a Hercules,
> Still climbing trees in the Hesperides?
> Subtle as Sphinx; as sweet and musical
> As bright Apollo's lute, strung with his hair.
> And when Love speaks, the voice of all the gods
> Makes Heaven drowsy with the harmony.
>     ... (IV.iii.334–42)

This is aureate, highly Elizabethan English, of a sort Shakespeare was soon to cease to write—a style straight out of the poetical worlds of his older contemporaries like Sir Philip Sidney and Spenser, though more vital and nervous in its movement than theirs. In its verbal derivations it is a system of compounds: Germanic and Romance, short and long, common and learned—"soft and sensible," "sweet and musical," "drowsy with the harmony." If you have two systems of derivation, after all, then (to speak broadly) you have three possibilities: to be one, or the other, or a compound of the two. What guarantees the ironic distance of Berowne's speech, where he is persuading young men who have no need to be persuaded of the charms of women, is their utterly deflating response:

> Now to plain dealing: lay these glozes by,

says Longaville, urging them on to "woo these girls of France." "And win them too," says the King bluntly. When it comes to the point, the point is usually monosyllabic. The movement is from the elaborate and the aureate to words of one syllable.

This seems an odd order to proceed in. Why does Shakespeare, whether in an early play like *Love's Labour's Lost* or a late one like *Macbeth,* make it hard before he makes it easy? Why does he play the translation-game inherent in the language backward, so to speak: first in Romance—or at least a mixture powerfully influenced by Romance—and then in Germanic? I am not aware that this question has ever been posed before, let alone answered. It strikes at the heart of his mastery of style, early and late in his career. And unlikely as the procedure looks, one cannot for a moment accept that he is getting it wrong, since it succeeds so well. In Henry V's proposal of marriage to Princess Katherine, in the same way, in the last act of *Henry V,* the scene begins mainly in French, which most of his audience presumably could not understand; and then moves into plain English, which even the most ignorant could grasp in a flash: "Your Majestee ave fausse French enough to deceive de most sage demoiselle dat is en France," says the Princess beguilingly; and Henry V bursts out in plain English:

> Now fie upon my false French! by mine honour, in true English, I love thee, Kate. . . . The elder I wax, the better I shall appear. . . . Thou hast me, if thou hast me, at the worst; and thou shalt wear me, if thou wear me, better and better. . . . Put off your maiden blushes, avouch the thoughts of your heart with the looks of an empress, take me by the hand, and say: "Harry of England, I am thine." (V.ii)

Shakespeare's confusion between "you" and "thou" here may help to explain and justify his cheerful confusion of "vous" and "tu" when he wrote French. The entire scene is shaped like Berowne's exchange with his friends, in stylistic terms, or like Macbeth's speech: from hard to easy. It is surprising that it should work at all; and yet it does work, and triumphantly.

Perhaps I can best attempt to explain what is happening here by a remote analogy. A Prime Minister of Singapore once remarked that he makes public speeches there in all the three official languages of Singapore: Chinese, Malay, and English. Much of his speech is in Chinese, which is the native language of most of his hearers; there is an obligatory paragraph on Malay culture, which has to be in Malay, even if few understand it; and there is a final passage in English, because it is in English that one announces what one is going to do. In other words, the speech moves from the least known to the best known, in political terms: from the circumlocutionary to the direct, from relative obscurity into the brightest of bright lights. Political speeches are dramatic events, among other things, and I hope the analogy will not be thought too remote here to be instructive. Dramatically speaking, there would be little point in moving from the clear to the obscure. That would be to deprive a dramatic language of much of its power to puzzle, to intrigue and to charm.

The principle can be illustrated by the most famous speech, perhaps, that Shakespeare ever wrote. An audience does not clearly understand what Hamlet means when he enters and says:

> To be or not to be—that is the question,

and it does not understand until he has uttered another three or four lines:

> Whether 'tis nobler in the mind to suffer
> The slings and arrows of outrageous fortune,
> Or to take arms against a sea of troubles,
> And by opposing, end them.

The question what is to be, then—or not to be—is whether he should kill the King or do nothing: to act by taking arms, or to "suffer" in the sense of staying passive. That shows the same pattern as the movement from hard to easy, where the riddling is unriddled, though the pattern is no longer dominated by the length or derivation of words. As a rhetorical device it comes close to the figure of suspension, whereby the unexplained is progressively explained. The genius of drama is to make you wait, and to make you want to wait. Rhetorical suspension makes for dramatic suspense; and the high tension of these plays—their unparalleled skill at awakening expectation, and holding it—is powerfully linked to that device of style. Shakespeare's is above all a purposeful world, where wills are formed in opposition to other wills, and where they clash and conflict, revealing oppositions only gradually and by degrees. What language more fitting, then, than one where a unique double derivation can be used to tease, baffle, and perplex all but the most learned and alert in an audience, until everything at last is made one-syllable and plain?

That plainness I take to be the greatest Shakespearean stroke of all. So much is said of the subtle complexity of Shakespearean language, and justly so, that it is easy to forget what a simple author he often is. The clearest test of all is to say that in Shakespeare it is always utterly clear, by the end of a scene, what has happened in it. He never, like Harold Pinter, deals in unclear situations; he is never knowingly mysterious. Shakespeare is a master of mystery only in the sense that he can portray the mystery and bafflement of his characters. But *we* are never deceived. Macbeth can be puzzled to know how to interpret the prophecies of the three witches; but we know, or easily guess, that Glamis will become Cawdor, and Cawdor King of Scotland. When Macbeth talks bitterly about the witches paltering with him "in a double sense," at the bitter end, we accept that it was natural for him to feel misled, but not that we ever were. In terms of dramatic situations, Shakespeare is as lucid a dramatist as ever was.

That clarity is perhaps Shakespeare's greatest debt to Marlowe, who has the same propensity for laying the dramatic facts on the line, and for explaining—often in a single line—what a total situation is. In that sense, though not in all others, Shakespeare is a Marlovian. When we are told at the start of *Romeo and Juliet* that

> A pair of star-crossed lovers take their life,

an outline of the total action of the play is presented before it is one minute old. Shakespeare forces one to understand.

## V

No mysteries, then, no obscurities, no silences. . . . Seeking exceptions to these rules makes one of the best question-games one can play, so here are some questions.

*Question 1:* Are there any scenes in Shakespeare where, by the end of the scene, we do not know what has happened in it? Surely none at all: in that sense Shakespeare never writes like Harold Pinter. He never forces one to wait to the end of a play, or even of a scene, before explaining what he means.

*Question 2:* Are there any single speeches in Shakespeare which we do not understand? Yes, a few, and mostly in the late plays: but usually because we suspect some textual corruption. The principle of clarity holds locally as well as for entire scenes.

*Question 3:* Are there any speeches which other characters signify they cannot understand? Yes, two, and both of them late in his career. In *Cymbeline,* when Iachimo is trying to seduce Imogen, he is so roundabout in his approach that she replies:

> I pray you, sir,
> Deliver with more openness your answers
> To my demands. Why do you pity me?
> (I.vi.87–9)

And in *Timon of Athens,* when the Poet indulges in some flowery talk, as poets will, the Painter replies 'How shall I understand you?' (1.i.51). Misunderstandings are of course something else. But these are perhaps the only two instances of failing to understand altogether, and admitting it—at least when both characters are speaking English.

*Question 4*: Are there any necessary silences in Shakespeare, where language runs out altogether into wordlessness? I mean silences on stage. Virgilia, to be sure, is silent when she touchingly greets her husband Coriolanus, and he teases her tenderly for it: "My gracious silence, hail!" (II.i.175); but that is not a silence on the stage which is necessary to the action, whatever actors may choose to do with it.

The answer is yes—two again: one in *1 Henry VI*, where the fiends who refuse to rescue Joan of Arc "walk and speak not" (V.iii); and another and far more moving instance in *Coriolanus*, where his mother Volumnia reproaches him for besieging Rome; and he replies, at first, in silence (V.iii.183).

But all that is only to say that, in all the 37 plays, Shakespeare is almost always clear, almost always ready with words, almost always self-explanatory—at least after due allowance has been made for the passage of nearly four centuries. Like Verdi, he was above all a popular artist. He wrote plays for the masses, though not only for them. Actors can speak his lines, audiences can receive and assimilate them. The poems, which often lack a similar transparency—especially the sonnets—suggest that clarity was a deliberate choice, and not the whole of his nature or of his talent. But when all is said, he is that dramatist of all Europe whose language seems most fully apt to delight at once the ignorant and the wise.

I am indebted to Jürgen Schäfer, *Shakespeares Stil* (Frankfurt, 1973); Emrys Jones, *The Origins of Shakespeare* (Oxford, 1977); and A. C. Bradley, "Monosyllabic lines and words" (1929), reprinted in my *Literary English since Shakespeare* (New York, 1970). My thanks are due to my colleagues E. E. Duncan-Jones and Professor Frank Kermode for general encouragement, and to Professor Peter Rickard for advice on 16th-century French.

LOUIS D. RUBIN JR.

# The Passionate Poet and the Use of Criticism

[ SUMMER 1992 ]

I

LIKE STYLES of interior decoration and ways of cutting the hair, poetic fashions change. What Thomas Stearns Eliot thought and wrote in the late 1940's and early 1950's, when as a young reader and would-be writer I was making his acquaintance, was considered almost canonical in its authority. Nowadays, as a critic he is out—way, way out. This is scarcely an occasion for surprise, because no author could maintain the kind of hegemony that Eliot did for very long; otherwise literature and literary taste would have to stand unchanged in their tracks.

Purely as poetry, nobody has succeeded in dropping "The Love Song of J. Alfred Prufrock," "The Waste Land," "Gerontion," etc., from the body of poetry in the English language that is to be read and absorbed. Harold Bloom can go on and on about the anxiety of influence, and claim that Eliot was overrated, that "the academy, or clerisy, needed him as their defense against their own anxieties of uselessness," and so on, but to any fair-minded observer it must be obvious that the imprint of Eliot's way of writing verse remains upon every serious practitioner of the art.

It is Eliot's critical personality, not his poetry or even his poetical personality, that is being repudiated. He was a poet who also wrote a great deal of criticism, which in its day was also highly influential, both for what it said and because of who was saying it. The criticism carried social, religious, and political ramifications, and not only the poetics but the politics of literature were involved.

More than any other critic Eliot was responsible for the intensified interest in the English Metaphysical poets during the 1910's, 1920's, and thereafter. He did not rediscover them; for one thing, they had never been completely lost, and during the 19th century good poets on both sides of the Atlantic read and valued them, even if popular anthologists, such as Francis Palgrave in his widely-read *Golden Treasury,* slighted them. It was Herbert

J. C. Grierson's edition of the Metaphysicals, published in 1912, that occasioned Eliot's essays. Yet it seems safe to say that had not Eliot championed Donne, Marvell, Herbert, Cowley and their contemporaries so powerfully, and tied in their poetics (and to a degree their politics) with the poetry of modernism that he and others were engaged in writing, so that a vote for Donne was a vote for modern poetry, so to speak, rather less would have been heard about the Metaphysicals during succeeding decades. As it was, to assert an interest in the Metaphysicals was to assert one's freedom from literary Victorianism.

The public face that Eliot showed in his criticism and—or so it seemed at the time—his poetry was that of the anti-romantic, the severe moralist who would suppress the brazen assertion of personality through immersion in the literary tradition. He introduced the term "dissociation of sensibility" to describe what he saw as a chasm between thought and emotion that has afflicted the Western world at least from the late 17th century onward. His own fondness for the 17th-century Metaphysical poets lay in what he considered their ability to fuse the material and the spiritual world within the tropes of an imagery that invested physical objects with emotional significance.

In retrospect, however, there seems to have been notably less suppression of personality on Eliot's part than everyone thought; what we took as reticence was more along the lines of impassioned self-mortification. Indeed, it is difficult to think of a poet of any era the rhythms of whose verses throb with more autobiographical passion than Eliot's, while his criticism, which once seemed so calm and magisterial, now appears to constitute a strenuous and even desperate insistence upon personal coherence in the face of near-chaotic emotions.

## II

The cultural and historical situation out of which Eliot emerged was similar to that of elders and contemporaries such as Henry Adams, James Russell Lowell, John Jay Chapman, Owen Wister, and other scions of the older, pre-Civil War American upper-middle class which felt itself in danger of being supplanted by newly-rich vulgarians. The Eliots were Boston and Cambridge all the way, even though the poet's grandfather, a distinguished Unitarian educator and theologian, had gone out to St. Louis, Missouri, in the 1830's and founded Washington University and the St. Louis Academy of Science.

It was axiomatic that Eliot, with his literary inclinations, would be educated at Harvard. What was not axiomatic, however, was that he would proceed to turn his back on the fashionable culture of Cambridge and Boston, and the high-minded, rational theology of New England Unitarianism, with its creed of moral uprightness and public service. For all that, however, he shared with his social peers a sense of being deprived of a privileged role by the leveling impact of industrialized urban democracy.

Eliot arrived in England in the summer of 1914 when the imminence of war caused him to cut short his doctoral study in Germany. His intention was to return to Harvard, defend his dissertation, and join the philosophy faculty there. Previously he had tried Paris, but found it tawdry and vulgar. England, however, was the proper place for him, and it did not take long for him to realize it. For Eliot was a *snob*—who was also a great poet. Among the qualities he liked about England was that its class distinctions were visible, open, and need not be blurred by egalitarian theory; subordination was built into its way of doing things.

He did not become an Anglican until the mid-1920's, but the spiritual crisis that led him to High Church orthodoxy dated from the early 1910's. The poems that placed him at the head of modernism were written not from a standpoint of belief, but the compulsive appetite for it, by a man who very much feared he might be damned to Hell (and who was also greatly drawn to the role of martyr). A considerable amount of arrogance is necessary, of course, to be able to view oneself in terms either of martyrdom or eternal damnation, but Eliot had no trouble managing it.

The technique he developed, mostly on his own, to write his verse was precisely what the poetry of his time required—intellectual rigor, concrete imagery, allusive reference, complexity in general. He and his generation were still very much in revolt against the high Victorians, whose example hung on. The Edwardians had proposed little more than a relaxation in the formal use of adjectives and nouns, whereas what was required was considerably more drastic—the overthrow of a pervasive cultural ideality that used high-sounding abstractions to minimize contradiction, and that avoided the historical duality of mind and matter through sentimental transcendence. Poetry, if it is to mean anything beyond inspirational utterance, must offer immanence; but the late Victorian, *fin de siècle* poetry could manage only a kind of wistful regret at the inability to escape the toils of mortality.

In the hands of the great Victorians, poetry in English had been able to address itself to a very large, educated audience, but the price paid for that kind of mass communication had turned out to be too high by far, because once the immediate excitement wore off the poets had begun to write not merely *to* but *for* that audience, and had developed a language convention and a set of ornamental emblems to facilitate the process. By adopting a specialized poetic diction, the poetry of waning Victorianism denied poets the right to document their own everyday experience. In subject matter, attitude, and vocabulary, the dominant verse of the late 19th century was tailored to what a cultural concensus of educated English and American middle-class taste and opinion was willing to approve, and as always happens, the absence of controversy soon produced a listless apathy.

What Eliot and his generation set about doing was to restore importance and intensity to poetic utterance by breaking up the cultural consensus. The modernists, as they came to be known, wanted no comfortable across-the-board agreement between poet and expectant audience, for the price of such agreement was intellectual platitude and emotional pablum. Eliot's enthusiasm for the English Metaphysicals was in part simply that, as Samuel Johnson had declared, they forced the reader of poetry to *think*. "We can only say that it appears likely that poets in our civilization, as it appears at present, must be *difficult*. . . ," Eliot wrote in 1921. "The poet must become more and more comprehensive, more allusive, more indirect, in order to force, to dislocate if necessary, language into his meaning."

The impact of the First World War had the effect of greatly reinforcing this attitude, because the chasm that opened up between the rhetoric of patriotic nationalism, on the one hand, and the horrendous, impersonal lethality of trench warfare on the Western Front, on the other, called into question the poetic abstractions and slogans through which the values of Western civilization had been articulated.

The footnotes that accompanied publication of Eliot's "The Waste Land" in 1922, in addition to commenting on the text of the poem, had a specific rhetorical function to perform. *This Poem Is Difficult*, they announced to an audience that was in effect being told to choose between intellectual complexity or blandness. *If you want to read the poem, you had better not be put off by the threat of having to use your intelligence, because this poem is not going to do your thinking for you in advance.*

Eliot in later years minimized the role of the footnotes, declaring them a spoof and saying that he wrote them to help fill out the pages of a too-thin volume. And doubtless the element of spoof was involved, but it was an insiders' joke, meant for the amusement of the initiated—which is to say, for the audience for modern poetry, which was a severely reduced audience by comparison with that of the poetry it had supplanted.

What Eliot did in his early poetry was to get down to the here and now. J. Alfred Prufrock himself may have been wistful and longed for transcendence; but the poem offered a flesh-and-blood character about whose physical immersion in the world there could be no doubt. Prufrock might say things fuzzily; the poem describing him as he did so was concrete. It was, moreover, psychologically complex: whenever Prufrock essayed a pose, he was quick to recognize and identify it *as* a pose. He was neither naïve nor vain; and he was *intelligent*. And because he was, intelligence was required to understand his situation.

## III

There was, however, considerably more to Eliot's aesthetic than the advocacy of verbal complexity, intellectual rigor, and linguistic precision in poetic utterance. His preference for the Metaphysical poets and the Elizabethan and Jacobean dramatists carried cultural ramifications. He was deliberately reaching back to a language convention that antedated John Milton as well as the Romantic and Victorian poets (of the 18th-century poets he had little to say, because it was no part of his aesthetic to find merit in a poetry based upon rhymed couplets and personification). In so doing he was rejecting a poetics that involved the open assertion of individual personality, in favor of a more stylized utterance. One doesn't find Elizabethan poets writing sonnets about their own blindness, or their career frustrations at the age of 22. In terms of their personal experience we scarcely know *who* the Elizabethan poets were. The key to Eliot's critical stance, I think, lies in just that: an abhorrence—one might even say a terror—of the unabashed declaration of personal identity on the part of a writer.

Significantly Eliot tended at all times to skirt the presence of Shakespeare, because even though the same kind of anonymity characterized Shakespeare's verse, the sheer richness and inimitability of the language was such that it called attention to itself and, by implication, the author composing it. Eliot's attack on *Hamlet* is famous; he based it upon what he considered was the assertion of the poet's personality in excess of the logic and plausibility of the protagonist's characterization, insisting that the secret of Hamlet's dilemma lay outside the play and in its author's personal consciousness. It was on this occasion that he coined (or reinvented) the term "objective correlative," declaring that the writer must find an objective—i.e., anonymous—image or symbol for his personal emotion, and that Shakespeare had failed to do so. This was nonsense, for a writer can—as Milton, Wordsworth, Keats and others did (including, as we shall see, Eliot himself)—assert his own personality in such strong and unmistakable terms that his emotion assumes palpable and believable form. The true sticking-point was that the distraught Prince of Denmark was in personality too close to a Romantic poet—i.e., to a person of acute sensibility, sicklied o'er with the pale cast of thought—for Eliot to feel comfortable in his presence.

Eliot disapproved of *all* the Romantics and Victorians, even Arnold, because not only did their aesthetic call for the outright assertion of personal sensibility, but also because the sensibilities being asserted were for the most part not to his liking. One might think, for example, that a poem such as Arnold's "The Buried Life" would have appealed powerfully to Eliot:

> But often, in the world's most crowded streets,
> But often, in the din of strife,
> There rises an unspeakable desire
> After the knowledge of our buried life;
> A thirst to spend our fire and restless force,
> In tracking out our true, original course. . . .

But even that was too public, too communal: "*our* buried life," "*our* true, original course"—and besides, the poem goes on to say that when "a belovéd hand is laid in ours" and "Our eyes can in another's eyes read clear," then "what we mean, we say, and what we would, we know. . . ." Prufrock, by contrast, realizes that "It is impossible to say just what I mean!" and that even if one could do so, there was every likelihood that it would be neither understood nor accepted. In short, Arnold's civilized melancholy would not do; what Eliot wanted expressed was civilized desperation.

*His* desperation. Yet one mustn't express one's own private desperation. *That* was the problem. What Eliot wanted to do, and he constructed a poetics that would enable him to do it, was to achieve a naked, unqualified expression of social, intellectual, religious, and sexual desperation—while appearing not to be personally involved at all! The truth is that Eliot was himself a dyed-in-the-wool romantic (how could he not have been, given his time and place?), but his own assertiveness took the form of an intensely self-conscious rejection of overtly public emotional assertion.

He called this "classicism," linked it to monarchism and Anglo-Catholicism, and announced it as his program. Yet however its outward form may have resembled classicism in the 1920's and 1930's, when it was in full flowering, it was in motivation and psychological stance at the furthest remove from any kind of classical severity, sobriety, and proportion. As we now realize from Eliot's published correspondence and Lyndall Gordon's two excellent biographical volumes, for Eliot his poetry was a way of asserting an intensely personal appetite for suffering, an agonizing fear of sexual appetite, and a shrinking from carnality, along with a desperate need for religious certainty and for civic and social coherence.

Here was no mere disgruntled Henry Adams, concerned over loss of supposed ancestral privilege and lamenting the erosion of government by the Best People; this was a man in full emotional recoil from democracy, the middle class, religious latitudinarianism, and the cramp of the flesh. His adopted English identity became a badge of virtue to signify his emancipation from vulgarity. Following his conversion, he used High Church Christianity as a weapon to defend himself against the excesses of political and social democracy, and also as an antidote to lustfulness.

Reading the edition of his letters from childhood through the year 1922, edited by Valerie Eliot, one is struck by the extent to which this man shared emotionally and intellectually in almost none of the political and social assumptions that we assume are characteristic of the ideological heirs of Thomas Jefferson and Abraham Lincoln. He used the word "European" to contrast with "American," and saw the latter as threatening the civilized integrity of the former (this was before the Second World War, of course). He was, all in all, a man thoroughly and desperately in flight from his country, his origins, his family, the academic career the family had expected of him, and from his own carnal appetite. And he shaped a series of antithetical responses into a poetics, an aesthetic, and, indeed, a theology and politics.

# IV

"Poetry is not a turning loose of emotion," Eliot wrote in a famous essay, "but an escape from emotion; it is not the expression of personality, but an escape from personality. But, of course, only those who have personality and emotions know what it means to want to escape from these things" ("Tradition and the Individual Talent.") My point is that T. S. Eliot was a powerful personality, and that personality *is* powerfully expressed, not escaped from, in his poetry and criticism. "The Waste-Land" and "Gerontion" may *look* like the "objective correlative" he insisted that the poet's emotions must assume and that Shakespeare supposedly failed to exhibit in *Hamlet,* but only because it is in the form of negation. That is, because especially in his earlier work (and, indeed, at least until *Four Quartets*) Eliot chose to depict his own contemporary society predominantly in terms of images drawn from his frustration, revulsion, disgust, and sense of loss, he identified what he portrayed as *not himself, not his own.* In that sense they are "objective"—but far from being "an escape from personality" they constitute, in their "not me," a passionate assertion *of* that personality.

In his old age, Eliot admitted as much, declaring that "The Waste-Land" was no more than the expression of a private peeve against the world. As it indeed was, but it was so powerfully expressed that it answered both the poetic and the emotional needs of a considerable audience. Otherwise it could never have had the vogue and influence it enjoyed.

He was greatly talented, and intensely ambitious. Poets who have programs and agendas cannot wait on their poetry to secure them a hearing and further their careers. They write criticism, make friends with editors. With calculated skill, Eliot set about the conquest of literary London. Consider the implications of the following, written to his mother in 1919 in the course of a letter explaining why he has turned down an editorial position offered him by the *Athenaeum:*

> There is a small and select public which regards me as the best living critic, as well as the best living poet, in England.... I really think that I have far more *influence* on English letters than any other American has ever had, unless it be Henry James. I know a great many people, but there are many more who would like to know me, and I can remain isolated and detached.
>
> All this sounds very conceited, but I am sure it is true, and as there is no outsider from whom you would hear it, and America really knows very little of what goes on in London, I must say it myself.

He is writing to his mother, and is concerned to justify his choice of a literary rather than an academic career, and moreover is aware that his parents in St. Louis probably believe he has squandered his talents and is wasting his life. Still, the terms in which he describes his success seem so thoroughly predicated upon reputation, and his satisfaction at his reputation thus far so obvious. The view he takes of what he has accomplished shows a highly realistic, even brazen acknowledgement of what it is that he has been seeking in literary London. It cannot be denied that he found it.

Eliot's literary criticism is filled with the articulation of his own emotional needs and assertions. He was a master at giving the appearance of disinterested objectivity, while in fact pursuing his own calculated goals. He used criticism, as he freely admitted in later life, to advance the kind of poetry he was writing, and he was none too gentle in how he went about denigrating whatever did not contribute toward that objective. His famous rejection of Milton's poetry in 1936 is an example. To watch him in action as he advanced toward his goal with, shall we say, waffled oars is to view a master at the art.

His opening sentence is a classic. "While it must be admitted that Milton is a very great poet indeed, it is something of a puzzle to decide in what his greatness consists." It *must* be admitted—an onerous chore, you understand, something that one doesn't wish to do or enjoy doing. Did his audience share the reluctance? It seems highly unlikely—but putting the matter as he does, Eliot averts his audience's anger, because, after all, he *is* saying that Milton is a great poet. Still, great in what way? The pretense is that justifying one's praise of the poetry of John Milton is going to be a difficult business.

Second sentence: "On analysis, the marks against him appear both more numerous and more significant than the marks to his credit." It *is* going to be hard to do, he concedes, but, so help him, somehow he is going to try to find a way to commend John Milton's poetry. "As a man, he is antipathetic. Either from the moralist's point of view, or from the theologian's point of view, or from the psychologist's point of view, or from that of the political philosopher, or judging by the ordinary standards of likeableness in human beings, Milton is unsatisfactory."

Unsatisfactory to whom? Why, to the speaker, of course; but since the speaker is obviously the very image and embodiment of Fair Play and reason, then maybe there *is* something wrong with a poet we had always thought of as being an ornament to English letters.

What is really unsatisfactory to the speaker, of course, is that Milton was a Puritan, and a regicide, and a supporter of Oliver Cromwell, and in favor of a republic rather than a monarchy, and above all the inventor and wielder of a style so formidable and expressive that the powerful personality of the poet infuses every line of his work. And all that *is* unsatisfactory and offensive *if* one is by contrast an Anglican and a believer in social subordination and a convert from the inherited political philosophy of Thomas Jefferson and Abraham Lincoln to the adopted political philosophy of Sir Robert Filmer and George III—and *also* the wielder of a formidable, inimitable personal style.

To resume the scrutiny of what John Hayward labeled as "Milton I," Eliot goes on to say that Milton subjected the English language to deterioration, and though a great literary artist was a bad literary influence. I cannot refrain from quoting in full one paragraph of quintessentially Eliotic demolition:

> There is a large class of persons, including some who appear in print as critics, who regard any censure upon a 'great' poet as a breach of the peace, as an act of wanton iconoclasm, or even hoodlumism. The kind of derogatory criticism that I have to make upon Milton is not intended for such persons, who cannot understand that it is more important, in some vital respects, to be a *good* poet than to be a *great* poet; and of what I have to say I consider that the only jury of judgement is that of the ablest poetical practitioners of my time. ("A Note on the Verse of John Milton")

As I read that paragraph, it first declares that anyone who will not let the author flail away at Milton without protesting is stupid. The first clause of sentence two then makes a distinction between "good" and "great" poets that appears to imply that routine competence is better than poetic genius, and that this is "important." Again, important to whom? The second clause of the sentence informs the audience that no one is permitted to have an opinion on the subject except other poets, and only the very best of these. Yeats? Pound? Auden? Who else, in 1936? Surely not Robert Frost!

Taken all in all, the paragraph is Eliot at his best, a classic of aggressive assertion, written on the theory that in literary skirmishing, offensiveness is the best possible defense. (James Joyce could have done no better.) He goes on to say that Milton had no visual imagination, that his language is ("if one may use the term without disparagement"!) "*artificial* and *conventional*," and that instead of a fusion there is a division between sense and sound in his poetry. He compares *Paradise Lost* to Joyce's *Finnegans Wake* (at the time still known as *Work in Progress*), sees both as blind alleys for the literature, and concludes that Milton has "done damage to the English language from which it has not wholly recovered."

This was not the end of it, of course. In "Milton II" (as Hayward calls it), a lecture to the British Academy in 1947, Eliot takes it all back, or rather, he says that he meant what he said at the time, but only *for* the time. The reason is that what his own generation of poets was engaged in doing back in the 1920's and 1930's was getting the language of poetry back into contact with everyday vernacular speech, extending the range of its subject matter to cover modern experience, and getting rid of the idea that poetry should be restricted only to certain kinds of material. To achieve this, "the study of Milton could be of no help; it was only a hindrance."

The revolution had now (1947) been accomplished, however. The language of poetry was sufficiently up-to-date, and it was time to go on to other things, such as seeing what kinds of variations and developments could be managed within the now-accepted language, and also keeping it from becoming *too* up-to-date, *too* addicted to the vernacular, and so on. Since Milton was, outside of the theatre (i.e., Shakespeare), "the greatest master in our language of freedom within form," it was all right to admire him again: "In short, it now seems to me that poets are sufficiently removed from Milton, and sufficiently liberated from his reputation, to approach the study of his work without danger, and with profit to their poetry and to the English language." *At last he rose, and twitched his mantle blue; / To-morrow to fresh woods and pastures new.*

Now in 1947, when Eliot announced that Milton was on the approved list again, he had published *Four Quartets* four years earlier, and he was more or less done with lyric poetry. (He was finished with some other things, too, including an insane wife who had made his life close to a hell on earth until he left her in 1933, and then had continued to harass and embarrass him until she was confined to an institution in 1938. In 1947 she died.) In the 1930's he had written two verse plays. Now he turned full time to the drama, producing three comedies which were highly successful on the commercial stage. For writing verse plays, Milton constituted nei-

## THE PASSIONATE POET AND THE USE OF CRITICISM

ther model nor menace; the language convention appropriate to drama was at opposite ends from that for lyric poetry. For, that is, *T. S. Eliot's* lyric poetry.

The plain truth is that in terms of the poetic personalities manifested through their verse, John Milton and T. S. Eliot have more in common, are more alike, than almost any other two major poets in the English language. Allowing for differences in historical idiom, as poets they think alike, they sound alike. There is the same moralizing sensibility, the same habit of delivering sonorous *ex cathedra* judgments. This is not usually realized. Listen, however, to their alternating voices, their personalities as makers of lines and words:

> The place of solitude where three dreams cross
> Between blue rocks
> But when the voices shaken from the yew-tree drift away
> Let the other yew be shaken and reply.
> As killing as the canker to the rose,
> Or taint-worm to the weanling flocks that graze
> Or frost to flow'rs, that their gay wardrobe wear
> . . . . . . . . . . . . . . . . .
>
> In vials of ivory and coloured glass
> Unstoppered, lurked her strange synthetic perfumes,
> Unquent, powdered, or liquid—troubled, confused
> And drowned the sense in odours. . . .
>
> With all her bravely on, and tackle trim,
> Sails filled, and streamers waving,
> Courted by all the winds that hold them play,
> An amber scene of odorous perfume
> Her harbinger, a damsel train behind?
> . . . . . . . . . . . . . . . . .
>
> O dark dark dark. They all go into the dark. . . .
>
> O dark, dark, dark, amid the blaze of noon. . . .
> . . . . . . . . . . . . . . . . .
>
> I said to my soul, be still, and wait without hope
> For hope would be hope for the wrong thing; wait without
>   hope
> For hope would be love of the wrong thing
>
> "Thoughts, whither have ye led me? with what sweet
> Compulsion thus transported to forget
> What hither brought us? hate, not love, nor hope

> Of Paradise for hell, hope here to taste
> Of pleasure, but all pleasure to destroy,
> Save what is in destroying: other joy
> To me is lost...."

These poetic personalities are not so much antithetical and contradictory voices, as they are *rival operators*. Who else, except perhaps William Wordsworth, could use the high style so satisfactorily, combine Latinate and Anglo-Saxon diction so variously and flexibly? *Who else could through cadenced and intensified language assert powerful personalities quite so unmistakably?* The fact that the one was a Puritan and the other a High Church Anglican is unimportant; both wished to place the muse of poetry in the service of theological truth, and clearly each was also privately seeking to convince himself that it was indeed *truth*.

The theological positions, as noted, made them competitors; the poetry they wrote, and their attitude toward it and toward the politics of poetry and poets, made them rivals, and Eliot responded to it without a moment's hesitation. In Milton's day one did not write critical prose to manipulate the audience and undercut the competition, or assuredly the author of "Lycidas" would have written it:

> Fame is the spur that the clear spirit doth raise
> (That last infirmity of noble mind)
> To scorn delights, and live laborious days....

In Eliot's day it was done, and he went about it with a masterful assiduity.

## V

As noted, there has been a powerful critical reaction against Eliot's position. He expected it, and would not have been surprised, though perhaps its vehemence might have dismayed him (*he* had been savage with his elders in his own day, but in his later years he grew quite benign). The revolt has been mainly along political rather than poetic grounds. His role has been attacked as snobbish (which it was), anti-democratic (which it also was), and cold-blooded and intellectual (which it decidedly was not). His way of voicing the assumptions of Anglo-Catholicism, so popular in the 1940's and 1950's, come across as terribly provincial and restricted in a world in which Christianity is very much a minority faith, and High Church Anglicans only a tiny, if socially elite, segment of that minority. It would be difficult for all but a small remnant of properly-sanctified readers to view the theological situation precisely as Eliot sketched it in 1931:

## THE PASSIONATE POET AND THE USE OF CRITICISM

> The World is trying the experiment of attempting to form a civilized but non-Christian mentality. The experiment will fail; but we must be very patient in awaiting its collapse; meanwhile redeeming the time; so that the Faith may be preserved alive through the dark ages before us; to renew and rebuild civilization, and save the World from suicide.

It is essential, however, to keep in mind that Eliot was doing the greater part of his writing about Christian societies and the like *before* the implications of that particular kind of cultural and social exclusivity were made manifest.

Eliot's hard-won High Church style has been used by some of his more superficial admirers to justify a kind of smug superiority to the common herd of middle-class citizens striving to cope with the necessities of earning a living and paying taxes. The desperate struggle for belief, the craving for order amid chaos, the hard-won accommodation of soul and body that characterized Eliot's own tortured religious experience—these can be neatly bypassed by a bloodless, self-centered, privileged sanctimoniousness that holds itself aloof from the modern world and chastizes godless materialism even while sipping Bloody Marys and driving Volvos.

On the political, as well as the social and theological front, Eliot's position *was* vulnerable, and remains so. And on the literary front, there seems little reason to go along with his contention that not only Milton but Blake, Wordsworth, Coleridge, Shelley, Byron, Keats, Tennyson, Arnold, Browning, as well as Whitman, Dickinson, etc., represent a falling off from the supposedly healthy, pre-dissociated literary sensibility of the 16th and early 17th centuries. This is a bit much, as they say.

Yet do his detractors come off any better? I must say that what the revolt against Eliot and what he stood for and advocated, as conducted by Harold Bloom, Geoffrey Hartman, and others of the so-called "Yale School" (now largely dispersed), would substitute in its place seems pretty shoddy stuff to me. As between the "dissociation of sensibility" on the one hand, and the use of the word "elitist" to stigmatize anyone who finds Shelley's "Indian Serenade" vacuous, it becomes a matter of "Go it, bear; go it, dame." The idea that the ultimate dramatic satisfaction lies in "a High Mass well performed" seems no more specious to me than (to quote Bloom) "The mind of Emerson is the mind of America, for worse and for glory...." If so, then God help us.

More importantly, almost all of that sort of thing is in Eliot's criticism, not his poetry. And when we look at the body of his literary criticism, what seems obvious is that not only was it usually placed in the service of his poetical ambitions, as he admitted, but also that most of it—including all the essays that attracted so much attention in the 1920's and 1930's—

remains of importance principally because it was written *by him*. We can read it with pleasure because we can watch him at work defending his turf and cutting down the competition. He was a master contestant, no doubt of that. An American in flight from his cultural and social situation, he set out to establish himself at the top of the British literary cosmos, and he succeeded. As Allen Tate wrote to Donald Davidson from London in 1928, "There is something very American about Eliot's whole procedure, and I like it. He came here unknown and without influence. In fifteen years he has become the acknowledged literary dictator of London. What I like is that he doesn't seem to feel the role." (Tate was wrong, however, about the last.)

But it is the *poetry* that matters, and that lasts. It survives the man, and it justifies him *as* a man because it testifies to and embodies the agony. "Poetry is not a turning loose of emotion, but an escape from emotion"—so asserted one of the most passionate, desperate men ever to write verse. His poetry is *not* an escape from passion; it is not *about* the passion. It *is* the passion, for it is the poet, the personality, who is speaking the lines and uttering the language. "The Love Song of J. Alfred Prufrock" is placed in the mind of a middle-aged gentleman who hears the mermaids singing but not to him; but what gives this early poem its power is the communicated sense of frustration, the struggle between decorum and libido, the contempt for mannered response juxtaposed with the dread of vulgarity. "The Waste-Land" is no diagnosis of contemporary society from outside and above; it is the articulated and agonized depiction of a participant sharing in the chaos, and the organization by juxtaposed montage is part of the condition of fragmentation. And so on.

These things are *in* the poetry, *are* the poetry. The notion that the cold-blooded poetic craftsman is drawing upon the man's human emotions to provide an "objective correlative" in language and symbol is not so much false as simply inaccurate, when expressed in such terms. The passion is present, for the poet and the reader alike, *in* the disciplining as well as the outpouring, and is communicated through and within the naming and versifying.

From the earliest lyrics through "Little Gidding," the poetry throbs with the communicated emotion of a powerful personality, who is not least in evidence when he affects to be unconcerned. We cannot read a stanza of Eliot's poetry without sensing at once that we are in the presence of a passionate man, who moves words, image clusters, and stanzas around with calculated bravado, and knows all the tricks of the trade:

> That was a way of putting it—not very satisfactory:
> A periphrastic study in a worn-out poetical fashion,
> Leaving one still with the intolerable wrestle
> With words and meanings. The poetry does not matter.

# THE PASSIONATE POET AND THE USE OF CRITICISM

It *does* matter; it matters so much that to save it from being undercut by irony he will pretend here that it doesn't—*in* a poem. Because if there is one thing that is more true of Thomas Stearns Eliot than of almost any other poet of his century, it is that neither in his verse nor in his life could he separate his personality into tidy, discrete segments. The voice is of a whole, a unified organism. But *not* one of harmony, balance, moderation—rather, a unique arena, a single sentient consciousness, made up of thought, emotion, desire, loathing, frustration, beauty, achievement.

How to account for his influence? In part for the reasons I noted earlier, about the condition of the art of poetry in the early decades of the 20th century. In part merely because, as he himself said, young men who think they know the answers and act upon that assurance attract attention (as for example a braggart like Robert Bly, who had *nothing* to say about the art of poetry but gained an audience for a time through sheer bravado and loud-mouthed assertiveness). But mainly Eliot was influential because he was not only a superb poet who got all of his personality into his poetry, but a poet whose verse strategies, whose *technique*, offered a model for shaping a response to the experience of his time and place. He showed his contemporaries *a way to express passion in language.*

In his public and his social life he could offer the illusion of having so compartmentalized his experience so that he could be now this, now that—poet, critic, publisher, Anglican layperson, humorist, philosopher, pornographer (or scatologist rather), ascetic, and so on. But the poetry gave the lie to the appearance. Walt Whitman's line, "I was the man, I suffered, I was there," is an apt epitaph for this poet who thought his American predecessor a vulgarian and poseur (and who baldly coopted Whitman's hermit thrush for his own use).

Eliot's complete poems, 1909–1950, are a virtuoso performance of monumental proportions. In their revelatory honesty and their ability to cast the most recalcitrant and refractory material into language and so convert it into art, they yield priority to no other verse of their time—not even Yeats'. To my mind they exhibit, through what they show of their author, so much of what makes poets the barbed, difficult creatures most of the good ones are (*Here we go round the prickly pear*).

In his life, his dealing with others, he wrote and did some wretched, lamentable things. For all his first wife's repellant qualities—and from all accounts, including her own in her letters, she must have been an absolute hell on wheels—it is clear that in marrying T. S. Eliot she had come up against an ego that could not unbend or forgive. There was no way that marriage could have worked, because neither party was then in a position to identify or accommodate the other's dimly-articulated needs. He was up against a virago; she was up against a male version of Charybdis. He could not help it; indeed, having contracted the engagement he assumed the burden manfully. Yet without "the awful daring of a moment's surrender" on his part there was no chance. And he could not manage it.

All this is in the poetry. The further away in time the historical figure recedes—if he were still alive he would be 103 as I write this—the more complete, and awesome, the poetry seems. Even today, during the full tide of the critical reaction against what he represented politically, socially, his verse cannot be ignored, and has not been. It is the day of the Harold Blooms: "Eliot is a poet whose poems, with some exceptions, tend to become weaker rather than stronger, the more provocatively they trope, defensively, against the burden of anteriority." (Come and trope it as you go, with a parricidal toe. Eliot asked for it, all right—and he got it. Bloom's whole protesting body of criticism is testimony to the *strength* of Eliot's influence.) But good poetry outlasts criticism and outlives fashion. We have no finer, more passionate poetry than Eliot's, and deserve no better.

SIMONE POIRIER-BURES

# Return

[ SPRING 1994 ]

OFTEN, now, I wake in the night to the distant whistle of a train, and for a moment it is the deep, mournful call of the foghorns off the coast of Nova Scotia. And the memory of those foggy days leaps at me whole, those days when downtown Halifax smelled of salt and fish, and it seemed as though the sea had swallowed the city, and we would be suspended forever in a limbo of sunless brine. Now the morning fog that hangs in the hollows of these Virginia hills, that rises through the trees in little, wispy fingers, that hovers eerily over the river, holds that memory taut—keeps it from slipping back to its old, hidden place.

I do not know why I am so haunted. Those were years of hardship, struggle, aching joy; Halifax a place I could hardly wait to leave. Perhaps it is the passing of my 40th birthday, the taking stock, the confusion of self that comes from a life now lived in equal parts there and away from there. I only know that I must return.

My mother, who has been pressing me for a long time to come, is elated. "I can hardly wait," she says, warbling into the phone. "Four years is much too long between visits."

Soon I am sorting through my drawers and closets: what to bring for walks, for picnics, for the visit to my old Convent School. I pack something for all kinds of weather, for I no longer remember what June is like there.

The trip is a long one, with hours between flights to wander through airports. Hours to tumble through memories from the first half of my life, memories that now cascade around me like rain. Though I leave my house at seven in the morning, it is ten at night before I reach the Halifax airport. As I walk through the terminal gates I see them: my mother and Sammy, her longtime friend; my brother, Pascal, and his wife, Vera; my sister, Jeannette, and her son, Louis. For a moment they are framed there, their faces, eager, expectant. They have come to claim me. Watching them, I feel a piercing sense of separateness: all these years, their lives have gone on without me.

Sammy is the first to spot me, waving a wiry arm, and suddenly there is a flurry of excited cries, of hugs and kisses, of how-wonderful-you-look. We smile and pat each other and balance on the balls of our feet, measuring the differences since we last met. Louis has grown a foot since I last saw him and now towers over my sister, who seems shorter than before, her face and body becoming more and more like my mother's. It is the old, shared memories that bind us—and the kinship—for in many ways our present selves are strangers.

"You talk like a Yankee now," my brother grouses.

"Down there they say I talk like a Canuck," I return, tweaking his beard, grown long and luxuriant since our last meeting. We go to the airport cafeteria where we drink mugs of hot tea and make rough plans for the days ahead: when and where to have our traditional lobster boil, which dinner I will eat at whose house, what I would like to do while I am there. Then the others return to their homes, and my mother and I return to hers.

Now begins a careful journey through each room of my childhood home. My mother follows me, touching my arm and hand: "See, those are the new drapes I got since you were here last. And I had that chair recovered. Do you like it?" "Yes," I say, "the house looks great." The living room is bright and attractive, not at all like the shabby room I remember from my girlhood. Thick carpets now cover the linoleum floors my mother used to scrub and wax on her hands and knees every Saturday.

Next comes my father's old bedroom, the one that sometimes haunts my dreams with its cluttered dresser and dusty piles of books, its smell of old age and the cheap cologne my father used to mask the smell of urine, after he became incontinent. But every trace of the old room and my father is gone. Now it is a cozy den, where my mother keeps the mementoes of her travels. The tiny bedroom next to the bathroom, where we four children once slept, is now my mother's dressing room. I stare at the two dressers and single bed that now fill the room. How did we all fit? Yet I was 11 before there was money enough to build an upstairs, with rooms for Jeannette and I, and my mother.

Except for a few new things, a few rearrangements, everything is much the same as it was the last time I visited, four years before. How is it, then, this is not what I remembered? Why do I feel vaguely disappointed?

We pause at the kitchen door. The old wringer-washer no longer dominates the kitchen; it has long ago been replaced by an automatic now in the basement. I flash on the many, many Saturday mornings my mother and Jeannette and I stood by the wringer, feeding load after load of sheets and long underwear through its hungry rollers.

"Do you remember the old washing machine, Mom? I'll never forget hanging the clothes on the line in winter. I thought my fingers would fall off from the cold!"

"Gosh, yes!" She shudders. "Sometimes the clothes were still frozen stiff when we brought them in at night. Too bad I didn't have these nice appliances when you children were little." She pauses for a moment, then adds, "Remember the old oil stove? We'd scrub it for hours with steel wool to get it clean."

"I sure do!"

But it is hard to picture now, with the sparkling, white electric stove that stands in its place. I try to recall the winter mornings, when my father got up at six to light the stove, so it would warm the kitchen before the rest of us arose. When he called from the bottom of the stairs, Jeannette and I would rush down from our frigid room, open the oven door, and hold out the bottoms of our heavy flannel nightgowns to let the warm air flow under them. None of that remains now. Not a trace in this bright, modern kitchen.

My mother stands beside me, hugging my arm, thinking her own thoughts, while I think mine.

"Oh, I have something special for you!" She draws me to the counter and opens a canister of home-made date squares and molasses cookies.

"These were your favorites when you were little," she says smiling. I grin, grab a handful of cookies, and give her a hug.

"It's nice to have you back," she says.

"It's nice to *be* back."

In my old bedroom upstairs, only the white wrought iron bed remains unchanged—the bed that came from my father's Cape Breton home, the bed that saw my transformation into womanhood. On the pillow I find a sheet of paper with a poem my mother has written to welcome me home. Though it is almost embarrassingly sentimental, it is heartfelt, and I am touched.

Later, while I am lying there remembering the old sufferings of this house, my mother comes in, in her nightgown, to kiss me good night. Always, I remember, it was this way. She would come up carrying a glass of water and pause at my room to open my window, tuck me in, and kiss me good night.

"Aren't you going to open my window too?" I ask as she begins to leave.

"Oh, do you want it opened?"

"No, but you always used to open it, whether I wanted it opened or not. Remember?"

She laughs, opens my window, and goes to her own room. It is very late by now, and I fall asleep instantly.

The next morning I awaken to sun streaming through the windows. For a moment I am jarred. I had expected fog, or overcast skies, for this is what I remember most. The air is cool and fresh, full of bird song.

Downstairs, my mother is preparing French toast and sausages. We take our plates outside and sit at the picnic table on the tiny patio, both new since I left home.

"The yard always looks so small now, when I come back," I remark. "And so lush." I remember scrubby weeds and patches of bare earth.

"Look how big your apple tree has grown," my mother says. "Remember when you planted that apple core? You were 11, and we all laughed at you, saying it would never grow. Now just look at it!"

I had forgotten the apple core soon after planting it, and the small seedling that miraculously sprouted went unnoticed for a long time. After I left home, my mother discovered it and quietly watched it grow. It bloomed for the first time well into my adult years; now, each spring, my mother reports on its progress. I am pleased that she cherishes the tree and the memory of that little girl, yet I do not recall the event itself, only her telling of it.

Since it is Friday, the rest of the family must work, so my mother and I drive around the city, hunting out the places I long to see. We stop at the Public Gardens and walk for a while. The peacock cages are gone. "They got rid of those years ago," my mother says, surprised that I am looking for them. "Of course," I say, "I remember now. They weren't here the last time I came either."

The Convent School across the street has also changed. The high, wrought iron fence has disappeared, as have the somber figures in long black habits who once paced the borders of their cloister clicking off prayers on trailing strings of rosary beads. A handful of women come and go through the main entrance, but nothing identifies them as nuns. Ten years ago they exchanged their habits for regular clothes; now they come and go as they please. I stand at the sidewalk, staring at the familiar red brick building, straining to recall the *feeling* of this place, how it was during my five years there—the hushed corridors, the spartan, disciplined life, the sense of journey. But the feeling will not come. In my study 1500 miles away, it came in great nostalgic waves.

"Halifax has really changed since you lived here," my mother says. "People are more prosperous. There are lots of things to do and see." This is true. I remember a stolid, gray city, muffled by blue laws. Now I find it charming, lively—a city I wouldn't mind living in. Why, then, do I feel this odd disappointment?

Over the weekend there is a good deal of visiting with my family, and I become absorbed in my sister's herb garden, the large workshed my brother is building, my mother's poetry group. I am a tourist in their lives now, admiring the views. The present has power: it is exciting, engrossing, immediate. But the old things, too, have power, and it is for them I find myself searching.

"Do you remember when you told me the facts of life?" I ask Jeannette. We are making pies in her kitchen and this quiet sharing reminds me of a summer afternoon long ago. "How innocent we were!"

"I didn't tell *you*," she says, "*You* told *me*."

"But that can't be right. I remember...."

"Listen, that's not something I'd forget. I was the older one, supposed to know everything. It was humiliating to have to find out such an important thing from my little sister." She grins, and I feel my mouth drop open. I watch her fingers flute the edges of the pie crust. Could I somehow have revised history?

"You're right about the innocent part, though," she adds. "Imagine anyone being 14 and 15 *now* and knowing as little as we did then."

On Monday morning I return to the Convent School to visit my old mentor, the one who took a special interest in the bright but unruly scholarship girl, who guided her transformation through several difficult years. The summer before my last year there, she was transferred to Vancouver, a loss I sorely felt. Now, I have learned, she is back in her old role of school principal.

Though I have prepared myself for the small shock of seeing her without the habit, I am still surprised by the tall woman dressed in a plain skirt and blouse who greets me. She is younger than I expected, only in her mid fifties.

"It's so good to see you again, Mother," I say.

"It's just 'Margaret' now," she smiles. "We don't go by 'Mother' anymore."

I want so much to tell her what I remember—her small encouragements, the subtle challenges to my spirit—for I have had more than 20 years to calculate her gifts to me. But it feels strange, relating such personal things to someone I barely recognize, and I find myself clothing her in an imaginary habit, focusing on her eyes, her familiar mouth.

"You gave me a little book once, one of those tiny pocket diaries with a half-page for each day. There was only enough room for a sentence or two in each space, so you suggested I write down something I learned each day. Do you remember?"

"No, I don't really. But it sounds like a grand idea."

"Then, when I'd come to see you—which was almost every day—you'd ask what I'd written, and we'd talk about it. That helped me through some really hard times."

Watching her, I sense that what I describe is simply her normal way with students. What she remembers most is her old affection for me.

After I have shared my treasure-hoard of memories and offered my gratitude, the present and the most recent past seem to nudge away those distant things. We talk of my life now, the great changes in her life, the school, the religious order. No longer do we speak as student and teacher. She becomes like someone I might meet on a train or at a professional meeting—a woman I find interesting and enjoy getting to know. The visit stretches on through lunch (I treat her to a lobster roll at the Lord Nelson Coffee Shop) and well into the afternoon. Intermittently I call her "Mother"; each time she corrects me gently. "It's 'Margaret' now."

"I just can't seem to say it," I admit finally, as I am preparing to leave.

"Practice it out loud a few times," she says goodnaturedly. "Mar-gar-et. Mar-gar-et." We both laugh.

"Perhaps I am afraid that in finding Margaret I will lose Mother Connolly," I say, suddenly seeing it.

"Oh you won't lose her. But that relationship can't go anywhere anymore. We have an opportunity for something new now."

The whole time I am in Halifax, the air is charged with this same odd tension: past and present fading into each other, old things shifting, rearranging themselves. My mother, too, seems to feel it. Together we make a short excursion to Louisburg in Cape Breton. I have never seen this rebuilt French fortress, though several of my American friends have, and my wish to see it now is part curiosity and part the need to claim it as my own. On the way we pass through areas which hold pieces of my mother's past— towns where she was a young, rural schoolteacher, many years ago. With some encouragement, she talks about those days: when it was nothing to walk ten miles, even in winter, to go to a dance; when people traveled by steamer; when rural schoolteachers boarded at the houses of their students. It is a world I know of only through her.

On the way back my mother suggests a detour through a small village she has not revisited in more than 30 years. "It's where I first met your father," she explains. There is very little to Pomquet Station: a cluster of houses along a dirt road, an old, boarded-up general store, some barren fields. "There used to be a railroad station, and there were more houses then," my mother says. We drive back and forth on the dusty road, looking for landmarks.

With the help of a local teenager, we find the site of the one-room school house where my mother once taught. Only the foundation remains, now overgrown with wild rose and raspberry bushes. We walk along the edges while my mother explains the layout, where the potbellied stove stood, where the children put their coats. I am struck again by the persistence of the past, its hold, its richness. It has been more than 40 years since my mother stood at the school house door ringing the bell, yet every detail is still alive in her.

"Your father was manager of that store." My mother points to a dilapidated, abandoned building. "It was a co-op then. I came down one day to buy a package of blue-lined envelopes and there he was. I was very impressed with him. He had traveled, he wrote poems and articles that were published in the paper. He wasn't like the local boys and farm hands who tried to court me."

We are both silent for a while. My mother's face is wistful, full of remembering. I stare at the old store with its boarded-up windows and doors, trying to picture that small event so long ago that changed my mother's life, and without which I would never have been.

For the remaining hours it takes us to drive back to Halifax, my mother talks about her years with my father: the courtship, the romance, the high expectations, the disillusionment, my father's illnesses, the four babies. I have never heard my mother talk of those years in quite this way before, with this joy of remembering that transcends the sorrows.

"Have you ever regretted marrying Dad?"

"Heavens no! I would never have had you children otherwise!"

"But weren't we an awful burden? If you had stayed single, you could have continued teaching, writing. You would have had a totally different life."

"That's the one thing I have never regretted; you children were and are the best part of my life!"

We cut across to the Eastern shore and drive through dozens of picturesque fishing villages. The sky and sea are a hard, bright blue. I remember now that there were many such days.

Soon it is time to return to Virginia. On my last full day in Halifax, I realize with a burst of panic that much I have come to do remains undone: I have not walked the mile-long path to Saint Agnes school, where I walked each day from third to sixth grade, nor found my old prom dresses and diaries, nor stood in fog, nor gazed at the sunset in dreamy longing from my old bedroom window—how is it I have forgotten these things? I rush upstairs to the window, but instead of the horizon, all I see is the leafy green of the trees in front of the house—trees once small and frail, whose great branches now crowd the sky. I open the closet door, but find only the things I brought with me, along with a few of my mother's winter clothes. There is a low cupboard in the room, a storage cubicle built into the front eave of the house, where I used to keep my treasures. Surely bits of the past still wait there, ready to disclose themselves.

I stoop before the door, but something in me hesitates. I recall the apple tree, the small book that changed my life, the shifting, slippery, selectiveness of memory. There is no retrieving the past. That fixed, solid whole does not exist; it is an invention. Invisible circuitries transform one thing into another and another; tracks grow over, cover themselves. I touch the small plywood door with the palm of my hand, and then I get up. Let whatever lies there keep its own secrets.

BOOTON HERNDON

## Corpses Thawing in Springtime: The Bulge Revisited

[ SPRING 1995 ]

I WISH that the teacher who assigned me to learn and recite Shelley's "O wind, if winter comes can spring be far behind," had been with me that day in early spring 50 years ago when I came up over a hill in the Ardennes region of Belgium in my army jeep and looked down on the lovely little town of Spa. It was dazzling in the bright warm sunlight following the last snowfall of the year. In the foreground two soldiers like me were pulling a sled toward the crest of the hill, and between them strode a beautiful young woman with shiny black hair, red lips, and white teeth, and a jacket open at the throat. Glorious as the scene was to look at, its meaning was even more rewarding. The girl's smile was completely uninhibited, brazenly revealing her happiness with the Amis without fear of German reprisal. And the two GIs were not wearing the ubiquitous steel helmets or carrying any kind of firearm. I automatically patted my .45 for my own reassurance, but I could still enjoy the rapture of the scene. Now, at last, I knew the Battle of the Bulge was over, the corpses were thawing in the Ardennes, and that gorgeous smile was the final reassurance that we had won, and the Germans weren't coming back.

It had been a long hard winter. One day in December I scrabbled down out of a box car at a railroad station in Belgium near the German border and blinked in the pale day light. "Everybody out! This is it!" somebody hollered. Up and down the line of funny little cars men were pouring out. It had been three or four days since I climbed into the waist-high opening in the center of the car, stenciled 40 HOMMES 8 CHEVAUX, somewhere northwest of Paris. Forty of us with backpacks and duffel bags jammed ourselves into the empty car. After several hours in a dark, smoke-filled box, most of us generally found somebody reasonably compatible to lean against, back to back. Even jammed up as we were, each of us was alone. We were replacements, unknown to each other, bound for unknown units, unknown locations, under unknown and unseen authority. Sometimes the train would stop, and we would clamber out to relieve ourselves in fields or woods or railroad yards.

So now, here we were out in the open, God knows where. The first thing you do with a group of soldiers anywhere anytime is line them up, so an officer hollered "Fall in!" Some of us questioned the goofy idea of lining a bunch of soldiers up in a war zone, but the word came down that this was a quiet sector.

And then came that sound that I'd first heard on the Normandy beachhead, a sound that I've heard in my nightmares for 50 years. An incoming .88, the German artillery shell. It screamed louder, then came the explosion, then the silence, then the cries of the wounded. I was on the ground, trying to dig a hole with my nose, almost before it hit. I looked up to see lines of open-mouthed, white-faced soldiers. Replacements, they didn't have enough sense to hit the ground. Another shell came in, and somebody, maybe me, hollered "Fall out! Scatter!" We all took off like bugs.

I didn't know or care what day it was—what difference did it make—but I know now that it was Dec. 16, 1944, the beginning of the most costly battle in American history, the Battle of the Bulge. It's hardly newsworthy that this military enormity came as a surprise to me, a Technician Fourth Grade in that most ignominious of all army units, a repple depple, but it does seem reasonable that some of our top generals—Supreme Commander Dwight D. Eisenhower, Commander of the 12th Army Group, Omar Bradley, Third Army Commander George S. Patton Jr., First Army Commander Courtney Hodges, and most of all that unabashed military genius, the commander of the British 21st Army Group, Field Marshal Sir Bernard L. Montgomery—should have had some inkling that 15 German divisions had gathered in the woods a few miles away and were ready to pounce.

The history of the Battle of the Bulge actually dated back to one precise instant exactly three months before when, at a meeting of his senior generals, Adolf Hitler announced that he had just made a "momentous decision." He would attack the allied forces in the Ardennes Forest in eastern Belgium and proceed westward to the major port of Antwerp. If any general present had the urge to remind Der Fuehrer that the German Army had suffered 3.8 million casualties on three fronts by late 1944 and was hardly in a position to hold what it had, he had good reason to suppress it. In July other high-ranking officers had unsuccessfully tried to assassinate Hitler and some had been hung alive on meat hooks.

Hitler's reasons for the offensive went beyond the military. Of the forces opposing him, he said, Communist Russia on the East and the capitalist nations on the West were unnatural allies who would break up at the first setback. By driving through Belgium, he would separate the forces of the United Kingdom in northern Belgium and Holland from those of their former colony, America, in the south. They would squabble and the U.S.

would go home. Then England would join with Germany under Hitler and crush the Communists.

Militarily and historically, the plan was not so far off the wall. The German Army had blitzkrieged through the Ardennes in 1914 and 1940; they'd gotten pretty good at it. The Ardennes, though absolutely lovely in peacetime with its picturesque little fir-covered mountains, narrow, winding roads and crossroad villages, is a region particularly difficult to fight in, especially in the zero temperatures of a European winter. Under tall firs and low clouds, munitions, tanks and food, and winter equipment could be assembled with stealth. By raiding other units of men and equipment, by hurriedly training boys as young as 15 and men in their 40's and 50's, the Germans put together three separate armies, complete with armor and artillery, as well as a special force of paratroopers and another of English-speaking terrorists wearing captured American uniforms and driving captured vehicles.

In that area the German border runs pretty much north and south from the town of Aachen (Aix-la-Chapelle in French, because Charlemagne said he was at his ease there) to the northern boundary of France. The distance is about the same as from Washington D.C. to Richmond. The first German objective was the Meuse river, about as far west as Charlottesville, and then Antwerp, another 40 miles, or into West Virginia.

Sprawled across the front were two American divisions, newly organized of raw recruits and stunned transfers plucked from non-combat units. On the morning of the 16th these troops received an enormous artillery barrage. Those who lived through it saw, advancing 12 abreast through the fog over snow-covered fields, the giant figures of Wehrmacht soldiers in their greatcoats and white camouflage coverings. They may have been 15-year-old boys under those grotesque wrappings, but nobody hung around for a closer examination. Whether in an orderly rearguard action or frightened flight, the Americans retreated along the entire front. For four days the Germans, men and tanks, sloshed through mud, but on the 21st came freezing temperatures and heavy snow. Tanks could advance smoothly over frozen ground without fear of being seen or attacked by Allied planes. Driving west, they formed a dagger between, roughly, two towns on roads leading to Liège, Malmédy on the north and Bastogne, 35 miles to the south.

In Malmédy, students of the war in Europe will remember, a group of about a hundred members of a field artillery observation battalion were captured. As they stood in a field, hands over their heads, a German non-com, passing by in a half-track, shot into the group. Other soldiers, apparently under orders, began systematically shooting the prisoners. A few feigned death successfully and, at nightfall, which comes early at that latitude, the same as Newfoundland, dragged themselves into the woods bordering the field. Eighty-six Americans were killed in the Malmédy massacre, and their frozen bodies lay stiff and snow-covered for days. Other prisoners and civilians were also killed during the advance.

On the south, elements of the 101st Airborne Division were rushed into Bastogne to hold it. A German army surrounded the town, and a delegation under a flag of truce approached the American commanding officer, General Anthony C. McAuliffe, with a formal demand for his surrender. McAuliffe, in the middle of a battle for survival, brushed the whole thing off with two words, "Aw, nuts." News of his answer was flashed around the world. Hitler, after some brave messenger translated *nuts* for him, ordered the complete destruction of Bastogne and everybody in it.

As the German armies drove west, commands from Supreme Headquarters American Expeditionary Forces on down through Army Groups, Armies, Corps and Divisions were scrounging up men to stop them. Cooks and clerks, anybody who could carry a rifle, and, of course, replacements were thrown into the front lines. Men were killed before they learned the names of their sergeants.

I still wonder why I wasn't one of them. My last duty had been with a medical supply depot in Paris, where I'd foolishly gone to a medical officer about the back I'd injured in the invasion. The medics flew me back to a hospital in England for an operation. Hah. One day I was lounging in a dayroom, the next I was heading back to France in a repple depple with the sorriest bunch of misfits I've ever seen. One fellow, who'd been sent back because he had fallen arches and couldn't walk, was given a pair of shoes with strips of leather tacked on the soles, told to stay off his feet, and returned to France for "limited service." From the embarkation point to the boat it was a two-mile hike, with full pack and duffel bag, and his strips fell off in the first hundred yards. As for me, I wound up in a six-man tent in a muddy field in northern France. My first night I put on my two wool uniforms, my overcoat, my shoes, and my raincoat, wrapped myself in my two blankets and my shelter half, and settled down for a good night's sleep. Next morning I was body-deep in the mud. I gave all the money I had, eight pounds, for a piece of 4 × 2 plywood. By assuming the fetal position on my wooden mattress, I could remain at ground level all night.

Looking for something to do, one morning I checked out sick call. One harassed medical officer and one equally harassed medical soldier were standing in a barn with 50 to a hundred GIs lined up outside in the rain. It was not as cold inside the barn as it was outside, and furthermore there was some hay in the loft. I immediately volunteered my services, not burdening the officer with the extraneous information that I'd been trained in medical supply, not first aid, and promptly went to work administering to the sick—and sleeping on the hay in the loft. I even sold my piece of plywood. Days went by. Medical officers came and went; some days I was the sole practitioner for 50 or more men. At least they got to be in the barn for a while, and their body heat and the activity kept me warm.

I received no mail, no money. Gradually it dawned on me that I was lost. One day a clerk stationed there came through sick call and I asked him about it. He looked around at my sheltered working space, at my dry hay loft, and questioned whether I really wanted him to look into it. "You could probably stay here for the rest of the war," he said.

It was a temptation. Winter was coming, and there was a war on. On the other hand, I'd volunteered for this mess. I was a little curious as to where I was supposed to be going, and maybe even a little patriotic.

"What the hell," I said, and gave him my number, 33638396. And that's how I found myself lying on my face at a railroad station somewhere between Liège and the German border when the Battle of the Bulge began. With inexperienced commanders on the front line, and many lines of communication destroyed, it took hours for the higher echelons to determine the attack was for real, and more to figure out what to do about it. In the meantime, here was a trainload of unarmed men under artillery fire. Someone, somewhere, made a decision to send us across the Meuse, west of Liège. I remember climbing out of a truck in the dark and following the man in front of me into a building that turned out to be a Catholic school. Inside was a young monk with a flashlight that shone only when he squeezed a lever on the handle. Tripping over his robes, making a buzzing sound and intermittent light with his hand, he directed us to individual classrooms. We dumped our packs and duffel bags in the rows between desks and slept on the floor.

Next day we choked down our emergency rations and went out in the school yard. It was Sunday, and the townspeople came by to gawk at us. I asked a well-dressed man where we were, in French, and the next thing I knew he was taking me home. I learned that he was a beet farmer, and that the town was Waremme, a good 25 miles east of Liège, and he learned that I had been in a boxcar for a week without hot food or drink or a chance to wash. After I washed some of the grime off, his wife led me to the kitchen table and put three eggs, already broken, in a skillet full of melted butter, then slid them, sunny side up, on a plate with a huge chunk of warm bread with lots more butter and filled a mug with fresh unseparated milk, heavy with cream.

In a couple of days we moved to a shoe factory in a town nearer Liège. I found space under an antiquated machine on the fifth floor. Hardly had I squirmed into position when here came what sounded like an old jalopy backfiring along on one cylinder. Then it stopped. Uh oh. Second of silence, then a heavy swooshing sound and one hell of an explosion. It was a buzz bomb, or V-1—the initial is from a German word meaning revenge—a robot with a huge explosive charge held up by stubby wings and powered with a simple motor. It was pointed toward a target and filled with just enough cheap gas to get it there. As long as you heard the motor you were okay. When it stopped, the bomb would fall. Sometimes it came straight down. Sometimes it circled around for seconds or even minutes. If you liked suspense, you'd love buzz bombs.

Next day I got into a conversation with a little busy-body of a man who said he had worked in the factory. He led me to a tenement building and up two flights to a dark little apartment. His wife gave me a cup of something delicious because it was hot, and a piece of bread with *crème à tartinier*—sandwich spread—on it. My first chocolate-flavored sandwich. They hesitantly offered a small settee in the living room to sleep on, and I unhesitatingly accepted. What a deal. I got out from under the shoe machine on the fifth floor, and he probably cadged drinks for the rest of his life on tales of the American sergeant in his living room. I don't remember how long I stayed with him, but I do remember giving him the ten pounds I'd gotten for my piece of plywood, and asking him to buy something for us on the black market. It may have been Christmas dinner.

By that time, the cloud cover had lifted, and Allied air planes were able to strafe and bomb the German advance. General Patton had turned his entire Third Army around and moved six divisions and 133,000 tanks and trucks to the southern flank of the Bulge and relieved the Battered Bastards of Bastogne. In the center the advance had slowed, but momentum was still pushing it on toward Namur and Liège. On the northern flank Montgomery was helping make Hitler's prediction come true. He told British correspondents that if he'd been in charge the whole thing would never have happened. London newspaper headlines screamed that he should take over the entire counter offensive. Bradley then told Eisenhower that if he placed Monty over him "you can send me home," and Patton said he'd go with him rather than serve under "that tired little fart." Good old Ike placated everybody by putting Montgomery in *temporary* command of only the northern shoulder of the bulge, appealing to Bradley, his West Point classmate, to be reasonable, and covering his rear with a full explanation to Roosevelt and Churchill.

To us grunts on the ground what one general said to another meant nothing even if we'd heard about it, which we didn't. (The Germans were jamming radio reception, and newspapers were hardly being dropped on our doorsteps.)

What mattered to us was that the Germans were coming. Germans in American uniforms had been dropped behind the lines and were killing people and generally disrupting things. The reaction was even worse. Sentries and roving bands of Military Police, nervous as rabbits but carrying cocked weapons, stopped troops and asked, Who's Babe Ruth? Who's Joe Louis? A general named Clark commanding a division on the front lines was thrown in a farmhouse cellar by his own MPs and kept there for five days because he said the Chicago Cubs were in the American League. A few Germans in American uniforms did indeed fail the tests and were shot on the spot.

The weather was another enemy. In the combat zone men lost toes, feet, legs and sometimes their lives to trench foot. They cut up blankets for foot muffs. Two wool shirts proved warmer than one, and a newspaper from home was great under your field jacket. But still, all across Belgium lay bodies of Americans and Germans, frozen stiff, some in the grotesque position in which they had fallen. A signal corps soldier, stretching a line, stumbled over a corpse who'd fallen forward with his hands over his head, stood it up, leaned it against a tree, and ran the line through its fingers.

About the time the Germans reached their deepest penetration, three miles from the Meuse near Namur, I was delivered to the headquarters of Advance Section (AdSec) Communications Zone in a huge facility built for the Belgian Army at Namur. I took a shower—cold, but you can't have everything—and shaved. Clean uniform, underwear, socks. Money, American money. I knew nobody, so I wandered alone through the living quarters looking through the open doors. Many men had received Christmas packages from home, and cakes, candies, and Christmas wrappings were all over the place. I had nothing, of course—my family still didn't know whether I was alive or dead, much less where to send a Christmas present—and the Germans may have been across the river, but nevertheless the spirit of Christmas came through to me, standing out in the hall. It was enough to make it a very merry Christmas.

I also had a unit. Long before, in Normandy, I had run across a Town Major team. Whatever they did, it sounded interesting. The Town Major section needed people who could speak French, type, and drive a truck. I'd studied French in prep school and college and spent a penurious fortnight in France as a student, so I could say I spoke French. I'd been a newspaper reporter in New Orleans for five years, so I could also say I could type. And I got the warrant officer in charge of the motor pool to say I could drive a truck. When I was shipped back to the hospital, I'd figured my request for a transfer had been cancelled. But now here I was, off on a new adventure. Driving trucks! Typing! Speaking French!

My new CO, a reserve lieutenant colonel named something like Ryan, explained my new assignment. Under international law it was understood that occupying armies would seize real estate—private homes, hotels, public buildings, anything—for their own use. Before I could be assigned to a team in the field, I must study the procedure with such diligence that I would know it backwards and forwards, in English and French, under the most perilous conditions. He would give me two days. He then reached into his brief case and dramatically pulled out a document.

It was one piece of paper, titled DEMANDE (REQUEST). It listed subheads for the names of the owner of the requisitioned property and the officer demanding it, and a description of the property, each followed by a lot of blank space. That was it.

In two days I had memorized the mostly blank piece of paper to the colonel's grudging satisfaction. As a reward, he sent me to:

Liège, buzz bomb capital of the universe.

The driver assigned to deliver me there was scared to death before we started. He wanted to know where my weapon was. Nobody had given me one, I said, and besides, I'd been a medical soldier and didn't know how to shoot one anyway. He groaned. The road to Liège runs on the east side of the Meuse, where the Germans were, and every few miles we pulled up at a roadblock and answered some trigger-happy sentry's stupid questions.

Ever try to find an address in a foreign city where the street signs have been taken down lest they guide the enemy, the streets are two feet deep in snow, the residents are cowering in their subcellars, it gets dark at four o'clock and there are no street lights, stormtroopers dressed like nuns are reported to be prowling the streets with knives and the jittery MPs shoot at anything that moves? We finally found a tiny sign, TOWN MAJOR, over what appeared to be a combination residence and professional office, and banged on the door until it was eventually opened by a white-faced major pointing a trembling .45 automatic. As I identified myself sirens suddenly began going. "Follow me," he croaked, and led us down three flights of narrow stairs to a small candlelit room, the bomb shelter. "When the air defenses pick up a buzz bomb coming in they sound the sirens," he said. Sure enough, in a couple of minutes here it came, *whap-whap-whap*. It stopped, and we hunched over. When it went off, blowing up somebody somewhere else, the major said, "One of those things is going to get me one day." He tried to smile but all his mouth did was twitch. I looked around the cellar. He'd brought a cot and a slop pail down. This was obviously the office of the Town Major.

If any American unit was foolish enough to move into Liège that month, it sure didn't track us down and tell us about it. I straightened up the office, running down to the shelter to join the major when the sirens sounded. One day a bomb landed in the block, and I went out to see if I could help. It had landed harmlessly in a little park. People from the neighborhood emerged, we started talking, somebody asked if I wanted a drink, and there I was in a friendly little cafe. I remember one drinking companion in particular. He had been arrested and tortured by the Germans to make him identify the other members of his undercover group, the local Rotary club. As a young reporter I had gotten many free meals covering Rotary Club luncheons. This was my first tale of torture by a Rotarian, interrupted by descents to the cellar when the sirens sounded.

One night, huddled in the shelter when a bomb went off nearby, the major asked, "Do you know what time it is, sergeant?" I didn't know what *year* it was, for he announced it was 0032, January 1, 1945. "Some Nazi bastard fired that at midnight on the dot...."

I thought at the time that the buzz bombs, by just splattering around the landscape, constituted an inefficient means of making war. Today we know that, from June '44 through March '45, they killed more than 5000 people in London and southern England, and injured another 40,000. They impeded the war effort there, but in Belgium, especially in Liège, which had long since been evacuated by any sensible military unit, there wasn't much effort to impede.

On into January those of us back in the support area began to feel the panic lessening. The German army had failed to reach Liège or any major objective. It became the Allies' turn to miss an opportunity. The American high command, schooled in the philosophy of attack, wanted to close the pincers between Malmédy and Bastogne and destroy what was left of several German divisions in the pocket. Montgomery wanted merely to hold pressure on the northern and southern flanks and "spank the monkey in the nose." Tens of thousands of Germans were able to withdraw, killing Americans as they went.

During the first month of the Bulge censorship was clamped down so heavily—correspondents were herded up in an enclave west of Liège—that few people realized what a huge operation was going on. By the time it was over 36 German divisions had been involved and they lost at least 100,000 men killed, wounded, and captured. Not one German division that fought in the Bulge was ever effective again. It took so many men from the Eastern Front that it helped Germany lose the war to the Russians as well.

As for us, the Americans committed 600,000 men in 29 divisions and other separate units, with casualties of 81,000—19,000 killed. In no other battle have we lost so many men. Of 55,000 British troops in two divisions and three brigades, casualties totalled 1,400, 200 killed.

As the Germans fell back from the Ardennes, a desperate need developed for someone with forms to fill in. Lord knows what happened to the major, but I was sent forward to Spa. Why, after months of contributing absolutely nothing to anything or anybody while others were fighting, freezing, and dying, I was rewarded with a tour of duty in paradise I do not know, but in war you take what you can get.

Spa, with its warm and bubbling springs, is located in a lovely little valley nestled in picturesque hills. There were luxurious hotels and bathhouses where you could lie in huge copper tubs while water warmed and carbonated by nature bubbled up around you. Springs around the world have been named in its honor. One of the mansions on the outskirts of the town belonged to a Monsieur Martin, the contractor who built the casino. He and his wife, in their seventies, were happy to move into the cozy servants' quarters with their groaning, drooling little dog, Teddy, and rent the house to the U.S. Town Major.

He was also willing to make another deal. Most evenings after dinner—First Army sent us supplies and we hired a cook and cleaning woman—Monsieur Martin and I would go down into his *caves*. There, with a candle illuminating the cobwebby bottles lying on their sides, we would stroll among them as he discussed the quality and vintage of each. They had been laid down for him over a half-century of prosperity—he had begun as an uneducated carpenter—by his wine merchant. He would make a selection, usually a Burgundy, then gently slide it off the rack into a *panier*. The bottom of the *panier* was worn out. "*C'est plus vieux que le vin*," he explained. We would go back up to the kitchen, where he and Madame Martin would sit in their worn comfortable chairs, and there he would gently open the bottle and lay it on top of the huge kitchen range. When it reached room temperature he would pour a taste for himself, a glass for me. I would then pass on to him two bottles of Coca Cola from the case delivered by the First Army quartermaster corps and the three of us, with Teddy groaning on Madame's lap, would happily pass a pleasant hour, each content with the exchange. It's not often you get to trade two Cokes for a bottle of '19 *Nuits St. George;* enjoy it while you can.

The Town Major himself was a cavalry captain, long overage in grade, who neither knew nor cared exactly what we were doing. I hired four nice Belgian girls who had studied English and typing in high school, and kept them busy filling in the blanks in the forms. The other American was a French Canadian from Maine who could actually speak the language. All this left me time for occasional visits to the neighborhood cafe and its always interesting habitues, and sometimes even a warm, bubbly bath.

Spring turned into summer, and I moved on to the east, to Mainz, and Fulda, where we ran a hotel, and Bamberg. Carrying on my duties as interpreter was no real problem in Germany; the Displaced Persons camps provided enterprising young Europeans as interpreters for the interpreter. Considering the comfort scale of the average GI, I was never discontent in the war again. When it ended, someone in personnel, reviewing my record and seeing where I had been but not knowing how little I had done there, rewarded me with five battle stars including one for the Bulge, and sent me home early.

But that was anticlimactic. It was after the Battle of the Bulge was over, 50 years ago in Spa in spring, that the world began to look bright again.

ALEXANDER BURNHAM

# Okinawa, Harry Truman, and the Atomic Bomb

[ SUMMER 1995 ]

## I

ON June 9, 1945, I was 19 years of age and a radio operator aboard a Navy ship that someone in Washington had given the improbable name of *USS Romulus*. On that day, sitting in the ship's radio shack, I composed a letter to my mother and father.

"I have no fear of the *Romulus*," I wrote in an attempt to ease parental worry at a time when the American Navy was suffering the greatest loss of men and ships in its history off the coast of Okinawa. "It was named after one of the builders of Rome, and Rome has lasted for centuries, and I have no doubt that my ship will last out the war." I added, in a burst of youthful pride and bravado, "It is really quite thrilling to think that I shall have a part to play, although small, in the invasion of Japan and victory," a remark that surely did not thrill my parents.

But luck was on the side of the *Romulus* crew and to countless other people—a million, perhaps two million, perhaps three million, perhaps 20 million, God knows exactly how many, who faced the specter of death and mutilation.

On June 18, nine days after I sent my letter, President Harry S. Truman met at the White House with the Joint Chiefs of Staff and the Secretaries of War and the Navy. He was told that they had agreed unanimously that the invasion of Japan should proceed on November 1. But Truman, an expert in the game of poker, had an ace to play. He decided to drop two atomic bombs—one fell on Hiroshima, the other on Nagasaki—in order to prevent "an Okinawa from one end of Japan to the other."

Like the Marine Corps and Army grunts on land and the Navy sailors at sea, Okinawa had scared the hell out of Truman, an old Army hand from the trenches of World War I. In the three-month period since becoming president following the death of Franklin Roosevelt on April 12, 1945, the Commander in Chief's land and sea forces in the Pacific had suffered almost half of all casualties inflicted on them by the Japanese in three years of warfare. Most of the casualties had occurred on atrocious, uncivilized islands during those jubilant months when war-weary Americans back home in the States were still enjoying the liberation of lovely, civilized Paris, thoughts of peace with Nazi Germany's collapse, and a return to the good life.

A substantial percentage of the Pacific casualties took place on the island of Iwo Jima, an odious volcanic nothing in the middle of nowhere. The battle there had cost the slaughter of three Marine Corps divisions, an engagement that some historians later dubbed an unnecessary waste of gallant young men and a U.S. military blunder. When the Japanese were eliminated, the shooting brought to a halt, and the American dead and wounded carried away, it was questionable whether the island served any useful purpose, even as a refueling station for B-29's returning to their bases in the Marianas after massive and decimating firebombings of Japan's cities.

Okinawa, in total casualties, was even worse. When the battle was over, more than 260,000 people would be dead.

## II

Four months before I wrote my letter to my parents, a young Okinawan student nurse named Miyagi Kikuko also related to *her* parents *her* pride and *her* bravado as she anticipated facing the enemy. Just before her mobilization in February 1945, she went home to say farewell. "I assured father and mother that I would win the Imperial Order of the Rising Sun, eighth class," she related to Haruko Taya and Theodore F. Cook for their book *Japan at War: An Oral History* (The New Press, 1992). "Father was a country schoolmaster. He said, 'I didn't bring you up to the age of 16 to die.' I thought he was a traitor to say such a thing. I went to the battlefield feeling proud of myself."

The invasion of Okinawa, a 60-mile long island 350 miles south of Japan, began on an Easter Sunday or on an April Fool's Day, take your pick. In either case, it started with a rare placidity for most of the invaders on April 1, 1945, as the U.S. Navy deposited the first wave of 180,000 Army soldiers and Marines on a "sweet and quiet beach," recalled Marine Corps Lieutenant David Brown, who would soon be dead, in a letter to a friend. "All around were furrowed fields of patches of ripe winter barley, and tiny field flowers were scattered over the light earth."

Also going ashore from one of 1,200 Navy ships assembled for the invasion was 23-year-old Marine Corps Sergeant William Manchester, now writer-in-residence at Wesleyan University in Connecticut. He was as surprised and as delighted as Fleet Admiral Chester W. Nimitz and other military bigwigs that the landings throughout the day were proceeding with only minimal opposition. There were "no roars of Jap coastal guns," Manchester wrote later in his book *Goodbye, Darkness: A Memoir of the Pacific War* (Little, Brown, 1979).

But if the ground forces were escaping the usual beach destruction, the Navy was getting a foretaste of the future. A tank landing ship that had participated in the assault of Iwo Jima, *LST 884*, with 300 Marines on board, was hit by a suicide plane on her port quarter. She immediately burst into flames and her ammunition exploded, resulting in the deaths of 24 sailors and Marines with 21 wounded. Other ships also were hit, including the minesweeper *Alpine* (16 dead, 27 wounded), the transport *Hinsdale* (16 dead, 19 wounded) and the battleship *West Virginia* (four dead, 23 wounded).

These aerial attacks had not been unexpected by the Navy. Although the formal date of invasion was April 1, the Battle of Okinawa really began for the sailors on March 18 when a carrier task force arrived 90 miles southwest of the southern coast of Japan. The objective was to destroy on various airfields as many Japanese aircraft as possible, including the suicide planes known as kamikazes, before the actual invasion took place. The Japanese waged a stiff counterassault. On the 18th the carriers *Enterprise*, *Intrepid*, and *Yorktown* were attacked with minimal casualties. But the following day heavy losses were sustained by the *Wasp* (101 killed, 269 wounded) and the *Franklin* (724 killed, 265 wounded).

The British Navy had also joined the fight. A task force that included the carriers *Indefatigable, Illustrious, Victorious,* and *Formidable,* with steel decks superior to those of the U.S. carriers and thereby better able to withstand the kamikazes, was given the job of blasting Japanese airfields in the Sakishima Islands east of Formosa as well as on Formosa itself. Thus the two task forces were able to crush a part of the Japanese air assault before the critical opening days of the invasion.

Unlike previous invasions, the Japanese plan on Okinawa was to allow the Americans to land their troops largely unopposed, then seal off any chance of escape by attacking and sinking the U.S. fleet with massive air attacks. In addition, an attack force of ships, led by the world's largest battleship, the *Yamato*, would sail down from Japan and fire away with its big guns at the Americans. While the sea destruction was underway, the plan envisioned, a force of 110,000 Japanese soldiers, snugly entrenched in hundreds of caves bristling with deadly firepower, would destroy the trapped Marines and soldiers on land.

It didn't work. In one appalling action after another—is appalling too soft a word for thousands of men slaughtering each other at close range?—

the Americans gradually annihilated more than 100,000 Japanese soldiers—an entire Japanese army.

At times the distance between the armies was less than 600 yards. During one engagement Sergeant Manchester was able to view from a hillock a complete battlefield. It reminded him of photographs of World War I battle scenes. Beyond, said Manchester, were two great armies, squatting in the mud and smoke, locked in unimaginable agony. Gone were Lieutenant Brown's peaceful fields of ripe winter barley with tiny bright field flowers. Artillery had denuded and scared everything in sight.

As casualties mounted, Manchester felt responsibility and guilt over his dead comrades, because he was alive, and frustrated, "because I was unable to purge my shock by loathing the enemy. I was ever a lover; that was what Christianity meant to me." But with "satanic madness" all about him, he and his fellow Marines who were still alive kept pushing ahead because "staying on the line was a matter of pride."

Years later Manchester remembered fallen comrades, "how they were hit and how they died." Lefty, Harvard '43. Swifty, Ohio State '44. Chet, Colgate '45. Wally, MIT '43. Knocko, Holy Cross '45. Shiloh, Williams '44; back in the States his mother had heard on the radio that his unit was fighting on Sugar Loaf Hill; she had spent the night on her knees praying for her son's life. And then there was Bubba, Ole 'Bama '45, a divinity student, crying "Vicksburg, Vicksburg" as he was carried from the battlefield bleeding from gunshot wounds. "I heard he was going to be written up for a Silver Star, but I doubt that he got it; witnesses of valor were being gunned down before they could report."

Early in June Sergeant Manchester was severely wounded. For hours his body was undisturbed, considered dead until a corpsman discovered a thread of life. He was evacuated to a tank landing ship that was serving as a clearing house for the wounded; the three hospital ships had departed; they couldn't handle any more casualties.

Miyagi Kikuko also survived. She had looked forward to the opportunity to express warmth and sympathy for brave soldiers, wrapping their gallant wounds with bandages while speaking with "tender voice." Instead, she had been petrified as young men were brought into the cave where she worked, some without limbs, some without faces, many mercifully dying quickly.

When the guns stopped firing, she and other nurses were rounded up by the Americans and taken to a camp. Japanese propagandists had told them that at the camp they would be stripped naked, raped, and run over by tanks. Rather, they were given food, something called "ra-shon." Finally, she was reunited with her parents. Her mother, barefoot, ran out of a tent and put her arms around her daughter.

"You lived," she said. "You lived."

## III

At sea the Navy death rate was greater than either the Marines or the Army on land. To understand why this is so one must grasp what it was like when ships were subjected to mass attacks by suicide planes.

The actual assaults occurred after days and weeks of tense, watchful waiting, sometimes to ships close to the shore providing fire power and logistical support to combat forces on land, frequently to vessels on patrol in what was known as picket duty along an outer ring around Okinawa called the ping line. The job of the pickets was to alert support vessels inside the ring as well as carrier and land based aircraft that could respond to the approaching kamikazes.

More often than not the picket ships became the prime targets of the Japanese intruders, the encounters developing usually at dawn or at dusk. Especially most fearsome were the attacks on moonlit, cloudless nights when ships were revealed like love boats on Caribbean cruises.

The tension aboard a ship as a suicide pilot aimed his plane at a target of two or three hundred Americans was extreme, with sailors with little sleep or rest sometimes near the breaking point. It was a condition that could lead to advice from a captain that was not authorized by Navy regulations.

"We have Jap planes en route heading directly for us," announced the skipper over one ship's loudspeaker system after the crew was called to general quarters. "If you characters ever want to sleep with a blonde again, you had better shoot down these bastards as soon as they come up."

And come up they did, sometimes two or three at a time, sometimes a dozen or so, sometimes more than 100 hitting at various points along the ping line and into the shelters of Okinawa.

An assault is like this: topside the sailors can see the enemy winging in from every different direction, first as small dots miles away, then within minutes as recognizable aircraft getting nearer and nearer. In an attempt to frustrate the kamikazes, the warship assumes flank speed and adopts evasive maneuverability as her gunners concentrate their efforts to kill the attackers. Many are shot down, but some are not, and when an aircraft smashes into a ship the impact is defiling. Death, fire, and destruction sweep over the vessel. The ship's power is often lost, its radar and radio communications destroyed, its ability to move seriously impaired.

Below decks, the crew works in claustrophobic fear as the battle rages unseen but vaguely heard as sailors almost hypnotically pass ammunition to the gun positions above or struggle to keep its engines alive. Sealed off in hot, watertight compartments, unaware of how the battle is going, hearing only the muffled sounds of the ship's guns, they are constantly mindful that death may strike them at any moment if the hull is penetrated by a suicide plane, allowing the sea to rush in to drown them all.

A ship attacked by only one kamikazi might consider itself lucky. Unlucky the ship that faces three or five or ten. Perhaps it can be likened to an attack by a swarm of wasps. One is coming in low over the water headed for the bridge, another high up but nose down aiming right for dead center, a third with its right wing torn to bits by the ship's guns but still on target, then a fourth, a fifth, a sixth, a seventh, an eighth, a ninth, a tenth. The first, second, third, fifth, seventh, and eighth are shot down, but not the fourth, sixth, ninth, and tenth.

The entire deck of the ship is smashed, fires rage from stem to stern, the engine room is flooded, the ship is not moving, but the guns are still firing. The dead, the wounded, the dismembered litter the wardroom, mess hall, sick bay, gun positions, fantail, passageways. Out in the water, around the ship, men blown over the side struggle to stay afloat and pray that nearby ships will pick them up before they're eaten by sharks.

In an hour or two the battle is over and the ship resembles "a floating junk pile." In time, if her luck holds out, she'll be towed to a safe Okinawan harbor. By then her dead will have been given their burial at sea and her wounded taken to somebody else's sick bay.

Now the scene of battle reverts to Homer's wine-dark sea. It will be unvisited by veterans from either side 50 years later because there will be no monuments, no crosses, nothing to view but an ocean forever anonymous.

The Battle of Okinawa came to its official end on June 21. Almost 5,000 sailors were killed and 5,000 wounded. More than 7,800 Japanese aircraft, kamikazi as well as conventional, were shot down and 36 U.S. warships were sunk and 368 damaged. On land, the Marines and the Army suffered a total of 7,000 killed while the wounded count soared to a devastating 32,000.

As for the Japanese army, the battle was a descent into oblivion. Its force of 110,000 men was almost totally annihilated. In addition, the Okinawan people—a peace-loving race before they were absorbed by the Japanese in 1879—became victims of violence. Close to 150,000 Okinawans died in the crossfire between the two armies.

## IV

Okinawa had shocked the American civilian and military leadership. The casualties over a three-month period in a confined land and sea area had been hideous and indicated what the armed forces and their families back home could anticipate in a massive invasion of the rugged, mountainous Japanese mainland. Against this background Harry Truman asked his advisers what they recommended as the next step. As a State Department paper put it, "He had hoped that there was a possibility of preventing an Okinawa from one end of Japan to the other."

An alternative to an invasion was a naval blockade and a conventional aerial bombardment even greater than that which had already ravaged Tokyo and other cities. This proposal was favored by the Navy hierarchy in Washington but opposed by Army leaders, including General Douglas MacArthur, who argued that a blockade could go on for years and that heavy bombardment had failed to bring down Germany.

So an invasion was recommended to the President, which he accepted, even though Admiral William D. Leahy, chairman of the Joint Chiefs of Staff, projected the Okinawan casualty rate of 35 percent to 268,000 Americans killed or wounded out of the 767,000 needed for the first invasion thrust against the southern Japanese land mass, Kyushu. The armed forces medical services were even more pessimistic. Almost certainly unknown to Truman, the medics estimated that there would be more than 390,000 casualties after four months of fighting.

And after the war, writing in the February 1947 issue of *Harper's Magazine,* Secretary of War Henry L. Stimson wrote that he had been informed—he did not say who did the informing—that the Kyushu invasion plus a second Honshu invasion striking in the heavily populated Tokyo area "might be expected to cost over a million casualties to American forces alone. Additional large losses might be expected among our allies, and, of course, if our campaigns were successful and if we could judge by previous experience, enemy casualties would be much larger than our own."

While Washington pondered, the Japanese were readying their forces for an all-out, death to the last man, woman, and child fight. The military was confident that its 10,000 planes, half of them kamikazes, would destroy upwards of 50 percent of the invasion fleet, and that those Americans who succeeded in getting onto the beaches would be met by two million defending soldiers and a civilian population that had been told to defend the motherland with any weapons they could devise, from hand-held explosives to wooden spikes.

But as the two military forces prepared for the ultimate battle, Truman and his associates were aware in June and July that *some* Japanese civilian leaders had decided that the war could not be won and were seeking a way to bring . . . [hostilities to an end]. But the conditions they proposed were absurd. They had the illogical idea that the Soviet Union could arrange a peace with the United States that would not require Tokyo to unconditionally surrender or accept an occupation of the Japanese mainland. Japan's envoy to Moscow, Ambassador Sato, rightly called his government's overtures ridiculous, and he urged Tokyo to accept the Allied demand to give up the fight without restrictions.

These exchanges between Tokyo and Moscow indicating that the government of Japan rejected unconditional surrender even if the house of the emperor was preserved "told the Americans two very important things," says Gerhard L. Weinberg, author of *A World at Arms: A Global History of World War II* (Cambridge 1994) and a professor of history at the University of North Carolina at Chapel Hill. "In the first place, these exchanges showed that the subject of surrender was actually under discussion in Tokyo, an entirely new feature. Secondly, they demonstrated that so far the advocates of continuing the war were winning out over those who were prepared to surrender, but they might not always be able to do so. Perhaps the blows of atomic bombs and of Soviet entrance into the war could swing the balance to the faction which urged surrender."

The Soviets imparted some of the Tokyo-Moscow exchanges to Washington, but the U.S. had independently confirmed the Japanese representations through radio interceptions and decoding. With this information, the United States leadership was eager to prod the Japanese to the peace table. But how should this be done? In May, while the Okinawa campaign was relentlessly underway, a peace feeler had been relayed to the Japanese, but there had been no response from Tokyo. So instead of sending a second feeler at this stage, Truman decided to await the critical new factor—the atomic bomb. A test was scheduled for July 16 in New Mexico, and the President wanted to see if this new weapon actually worked.

It did, and on July 26 a second call for unconditional surrender was issued to the Japanese from Potsdam, Germany, where Truman had been meeting with British Prime Minister Winston Churchill and Soviet dictator Joseph Stalin. The document, proclaimed by the governments of the United States, Britain, and China (but not the Soviet Union, since it was not yet at war with Japan), also implied that the Japanese could retain their emperor, a sensitive and most critical point, and indeed Tokyo got that message. But again the Japanese did not respond.

In an effort to encourage capitulation U.S. planes dropped Japanese translations of the Potsdam Declaration on Tokyo and elsewhere in the country. But Japanese newspapers immediately reported that the Japanese cabinet viewed the declaration "with silent contempt." When this news was received in Washington, Truman had no choice but to act. He ordered the first atomic bomb to be dropped. On August 6, 1945, at 8:15 A.M. the order was carried out when the bomb was released over Hiroshima from a B-29 called the *Enola Gay*.

Three days later the Soviet Union, which the Japanese had hoped would save them from surrendering unconditionally to a country they had attacked nearly four years earlier at Pearl Harbor, opportunistically declared war on Japan and invaded Manchuria. That same evening a second atomic bomb was dropped on Nagasaki. In all, 210,000 people are estimated to have died as a result of the two explosions, about 53,000 fewer than the number of people killed at Okinawa.

Now the fate of Japan was up to the emperor, whose continuance on the throne was assured by Truman's wise decision to accept a recommendation by some of his advisers to allow Hirohito to keep his position. (Secretary of War Stimson and Under-Secretary of State Joseph Grew were for retention; Secretary of State James Byrnes and Assistant Secretary of State Dean Acheson were against.)

In June the emperor had been told by two top military officers after inspection tours of the home islands and Manchuria that the nation's military situation was hopeless. With this information in mind plus the news of the two atomic bombs and the belated decision of the Soviets to enter the war, Hirohito had only one avenue available. He told his Imperial Council, which was evenly split between peace and continuing the war, that the terms of the Potsdam Declaration must be accepted.

Opponents of surrender were outraged and determined to stage a coup so that the war against the Americans could go on until the bitter end. But the plot failed when senior officers refused to join the uprising against the emperor. Among those declining to oppose the emperor was the Minister of War, Anami Korechika, an advocate of defending the motherland despite the atomic bombs, the Soviet declaration, and a succession of military defeats. He committed suicide rather than attempting to counter Hirohito. But the plot came near to success. "It was a close call," says Professor Weinberg.

On September 2, 1945, General MacArthur accepted the formal surrender of the Japanese aboard the battleship *Missouri* in Tokyo Bay. As a result, millions of people lived.

## V

Fifty years after the atomic bombs were dropped controversy continues in academic circles as to whether it was necessary for the United States to use these awesome weapons. History Professor William L. O'Neill of Rutgers University, author of *A Democracy at War: America's Fight at Home and Abroad in World War II* (The Free Press, 1993), points out that after the bloody Okinawa campaign, the Army's Chief of Staff, General George C. Marshall "concluded that if the bomb was not used, nothing short of invading it would force Japan to surrender." The shock value of the bomb, Marshall believed, "offered the hope of making a fundamental change in Japanese thought. With great reluctance, therefore, Marshall concluded that the atomic weapon had to be used."

After the war, Marshall said: "I was aware of the peace offerings Japan was making to the Russians in the summer of '45. But the Japanese Prime Minister was unable to control the Army. The Army was dominant in these matters, and they could only apparently be slugged into submission. And we slugged them. . . . The bomb stopped the war. Therefore, it was justifiable. I think it was very wise to use it."

O'Neill also notes that use of the second bomb on Nagasaki (together with the Soviet war declaration) was the goad that pushed the emperor to order surrender. He then adds:

"Terrible as they were, by forcing a quick and favorable outcome, the atomic weapons saved many more lives than they took. . . . During the Okinawa campaign one-third of the civilian population died . . . their suffering was indescribable. On the home islands, so much more strongly defended and with a vastly larger population, the agony and the deaths would have been beyond imagining. . . . Millions of Japanese civilians would have died, in addition to the fighting men on both sides. For this reason, the victims of Hiroshima and Nagasaki did not die in vain."

Ronald H. Spector, professor of history and international affairs at George Washington University's Elliott School of International Affairs and author of *Eagle Against the Sun: The American War with Japan* (The Free Press, 1985), writes that none of the critics of the atomic bomb decision "has been able to demonstrate how the Japanese high command might have been induced to surrender without the *combined* shock of Russia's entry into the war and the use of *two* atomic bombs."

Finally, there is the commentary of Churchill in his memoirs (*Triumph and Tragedy*, Vol. 6 of *The Second World War*, Houghton Mifflin, 1953). He wrote that up to the moment of the successful detonation of the atomic bomb in New Mexico an assault on Japan had been planned and that the Japanese had been expected to put up "desperate resistance," resulting in the deaths of a million Americans and 500,000 Britons.

"Now that nightmare picture had vanished," said Churchill. "In its place was the vision—fair and bright it seemed—of the end of the whole war in one or two violent shocks. I thought immediately myself of how the Japanese people, whose courage I had always admired, might find in the apparition of this almost supernatural weapon an excuse which would save their honor and release them from their obligation of being killed to the last fighting man."

One question that will forever remain unanswered is whether President Roosevelt would have authorized use of the atomic bomb. In her recent biography *No Ordinary Time: Franklin and Eleanor Roosevelt: The Home Front in World War II* (Simon & Schuster, 1994), Doris Kearns Goodwin is equivocal, although she notes that Eleanor Roosevelt "did not question the decision to use the bomb, believing that it would bring the war to a speedier end." But Professor Weinberg writes:

"The available evidence supports the conclusion that [Roosevelt] had expected any bombs built in time for use against Germany to be dropped on that country and any not ready in time to be dropped on Japan, in both cases in the hope of bringing the war to a quick end. . . . Nothing suggests that Roosevelt, had he lived, would have decided differently [than Truman]."

How many people would have died had the atomic bombs not been dropped and the Japanese had decided to continue the war for a year or two until the last garrison had been wiped out and the last female defender of the motherland had tossed her final homemade grenade?

On September 9, 1945, a month after the bomb fell on Nagasaki, the British had been scheduled to invade the Malay Peninsula and retake Singapore, an operation that would have cost the lives of tens of thousands. After the Okinawa campaign had concluded, an order went out from Japan to kill all 400,000 captives in Japanese prisoner of war camps when the British started their campaigns to regain lost possessions. In addition, the Japanese still had thousands of troops in China and Manchuria for the thrust from the Soviet Union, an invasion that would have caused countless deaths. Add these casualties to the total number of killings in Japan and the final figure is almost unimaginable. Author George Feifer, in his book *Tennozan: The Battle of Okinawa and the Atomic Bomb* (Ticknor & Fields, 1992), offers a minimum figure of 20 million people.

Years after he ordered the use of the atomic bomb to bring World War II to a close, Truman told an audience: "I could not worry about what history would say about my personal morality. I made the only decision I knew how to make. I did what I thought was right."

But perhaps George M. Elsey, a young naval intelligence officer assigned to the Truman White House, provided the best reply to revisionist historians and others who question the decision to drop the atomic bombs. Asked by David McCullough for his biography of the President (*Truman*, Simon & Schuster, 1992) about the decision, Elsey replied: "Truman made no decision because there was no decision to be made. He could no more have stopped it than a train moving down a track. It's all well and good to come along later and say the bomb was a horrible thing. The whole goddamn war was a horrible thing."

Author's note: Besides the nine books mentioned in the essay, I would like to cite four other exceptional works that were particularly helpful: *Victory in the Pacific 1945*, by Samuel Eliot Morison (Little, Brown, 1960); *Brave Ship Brave Men*, by Arnold S. Lott (Naval Institute Press, 1964); *Tin Can Sailor*, by C. Raymond Calhoun (Naval Institute Press, 1993); and *Little Ship, Big War*, by Edward P. Stafford (William Morrow, 1984).

# DAVID WYATT

## The Last Spring at Yale

[ SPRING 1997 ]

A BLUE postcard from New Haven has arrived. Postmark October 20, '95. "Outstanding!" the card reads. "Yale College Class of 1970. 25th Reunion Gift Total $2,980,575. 54% of You Participated." I did not attend the reunion, although I did make a small gift. Is 54 percent an impressive number, when it comes to reunions? I do a quick calculation and realize that if averaged across the entire class, each graduate gave close to $3,000. Revise that statement: I made a *tiny* gift.

A week ago I was asked by the department of drama at my home institution, the University of Maryland, to give a talk about the Sixties in conjunction with a production of *Hair*. I worked up some recollections under the title "The Draft: Fear and Loathing in New Haven." As I walked to the lectern, I realized that most of those in the audience had not been born at the time the last American ground troops were withdrawn from Vietnam, in March 1973. Few in the crowd possessed any memories that could challenge my version of events; for them, the defining moment—the one where we remember where we were when we heard the news—will not be the John F. Kennedy assassination, but the O. J. Simpson verdict.

In the middle of my talk a colleague wandered in, a member of the Yale Class of 1973. In closing, I spoke of the anti-war movement "dwindling" after the explosive spring of 1970. Afterward, the colleague raised his hand, praised the talk, and then reminded me that history reduced to autobiography could become, as I had admitted, "personal" indeed. "I arrived at Yale the year you were leaving," he said. "Just because you left doesn't mean that we didn't keep organizing and marching. I guess it's a matter of where you happened to be standing."

I had begun with a quote from Michael Herr, the last sentence from his brilliant *Dispatches*. "Vietnam Vietnam Vietnam," he writes, "we've all been there." Wherever we were standing—wherever we *are* standing, as the controversy over Bill Clinton's maneuverings on the draft reveals—we all were also *there*. The war that so many of the young men in my generation did not fight continues to work its secret ministry, cruising like an iceberg through our dreams, informing our ambitions and our divorces, creating minor or major disagreements between the partisans who remember, waiting for the day when it will fully surface in an account adequate to the experience of that great and terrible time.

In 1966, I boarded a plane in Los Angeles and flew to New York. I was headed for New Haven, Connecticut to begin my freshman year at Yale. At 17 I had ventured no further east than Dallas, Texas, for the 1964 International Key Club Convention. That had been a sober, even uncanny trip, since it had put me in a Hilton Hotel only a few blocks from the Texas State Book Depository, a year after Lee Harvey Oswald had climbed its stairs and taken up his fatal station. I had traveled to Dallas by riding in a car; now I was flying, for the first time in my life. Traveling with me was the other student from my hometown of San Bernardino, California, who had been admitted to the Yale Class of 1970.

"So this is the famous class of 1970!": with these words President Levin greeted the assembled class members who had managed to make it back a quarter of a century later. By "famous" he refers to the promise we once gave of exercising power in the world—and even of burning down the house. Yet in looking over the "biographies" in the *Twenty-fifth Reunion Class Book,* I am struck by how many of the contributors disdain public success or worldly power and seem to prize, instead, a kind of private happiness. The first entry, by an Abbott, begins as follows: "What has made me the happiest? First my family. . . ." Another classmate writes that "My greatest pleasure comes from my family." These sentiments form the volume's dominant refrain. My own entry begins with a memory of bodysurfing with my son at Nags Head and of the day of my second marriage, an event held on my college roommate's Virginia farm. For a wild bunch slated to shake things up, we appear to have lived out, with an almost literal devotion, the maxim that the personal is political. The last sentence in the *Class Book* thus nicely complements the first. It is from a Zuckerman: "I miss the passion of the time in which we came of age."

As who does not? They were awful, wonderful years, days of rage and summers of love. Those of us lucky enough to get into Yale were protected from their more extreme dangers by a largely benevolent institution, one that kept outflanking all but the most determined radicals among us. At the same time, as the old verities crumbled, we were initiated into the competitiveness and status-think that did and still does mark the lives of those who aspire to credentialing by the Ivy League. We saw the last of the old and the first of the new Yale.

By the fall of 1966, Yale stood on the cusp of the big change. My class of 1000 was the first admitted by the new Dean of Admissions, "Inky" Clark. Appointed in July 1965, he planned to open up Yale College through a carefully modulated profile of the desirable student. Legacies were to be granted fewer places at the table. Prep school applicants had to compete against a rising tide of high school graduates. Black students were at last heavily recruited; Kurt Schmoke, the future mayor of Baltimore, lived downstairs, and Skip Gates, author of *The Signifying Monkey* and *New Yorker* commentator on racial matters, was a class or two behind him. Our SAT scores were up: Verbal, 683; Mathematical, 687. But our weight was down: at an average of 154.9 lbs, we were the skinniest bunch since the class of 1951. At 5'9" and 125 lbs, I came in well under the averages; I was what we then called "wiry." With us, the ageless types of athlete, gentleman, and scholar began to collapse into a notion of "roundedness"; Clark looked for students whose strengths were also *extra*curricular. Old standards of decorum had not entirely died, however; anyone wanting a B.A. still had to pass a posture test, judged by nude photos, and swim one hundred yards.

I had picked Yale over Harvard because of its residential college system, and I had chosen what I needed. Harvard had "houses" four to five hundred students strong; Yale's 12 colleges were smaller, served better food—my particular college had been endowed with a fund for buying strawberries in the spring—and achieved, because of their courtyard designs, a greater spatial intimacy and coherence. Yale and Harvard had both offered me a full ride, along with a work study job. As a busboy in Berkeley College, I made $1.25 an hour; we struck on Prom weekend in the spring of 1967 and won a 15-cent an hour raise. As a Yale National Scholar, I was paid out of funds donated by the Arthur P. Sloan Foundation, so General Motors put me through school. The only obligation in return was to verify myself as a reliable product during an annual lunch at Mory's where, over the peach melba, I told the program officer that I was doing fine. In those days room, board, and tuition came to about $3000 a year, and, with the money I made during the term and the summers, I would graduate without a penny of debt.

The Yale I entered in 1966 required undergraduates to distribute course work between the humanities, the social, and the natural sciences. Yale College was still all-male. And the coat and tie rule still reigned at meals. The rule provoked the most dramatic protests of my freshman year; there were rumors of seniors coming to meals in a coat and tie—and nothing else. When I moved into Davenport College to begin my sophomore year, the rule was gone. As were the distributional requirements: it was suddenly clear that I could get through college without taking a single course in math and science. Raised on the permissive Dr. Spock, and soon to be trooping after him again, we were set adrift in a curricular sea of free choices.

About women, the issue seemed so apocalyptically distant as not to be a choice. Football half times reduced the much-touted Yale-Vassar merger into our Y marching slowing down into their V. Women were bused into

New Haven from all over New England for Friday mixers, and, during my first year, put up in proper hotels. The opposite sex equalled the weekend. Little did I know that as a senior College Aide I would design a plan for housing the first contingent of women—20 strong—in the maze of Davenport's entryways.

In those years all did not change utterly, nor was a terrible beauty born. We still cared, for instance, about traditional diversions like football. With Brian Dowling and Calvin Hill, the team was so good that Garry Trudeau, who lived across the Davenport courtyard, began drawing a comic strip about its exploits called "Bull Tales." Yale was and probably always will be a conservative place, in part because it believes in a certain kind of remembering. In even the most apocalyptic moments, with the National Guard in the streets and tear gas on the Green, I never believed that the university was the enemy, or that the revolution had come. Perhaps because of President Kingman Brewster, and his "loose bag" approach to campus dissent, perhaps because of Chaplain William Sloane Coffin, and his exemplary self-martyrdom, perhaps because we already felt so indulged, taken-seriously, and free, Yale never exploded like Harvard or Columbia. I, in any case, did not fight the university itself, perhaps because by my second year there I had discovered that I wanted the career and rewards that only universities can give.

Three human ties formed at school would survive the upheavals of those years: the roommate, the soulmate, the wife-to-be. The roommate was Barney O'Meara, with whom I shared a suite after moving to Davenport. An Irish Catholic from St. Louis, Barney majored in electrical engineering and became, by his senior year, battalion commander of Naval ROTC. To wear the uniform a day a week, as he was required to do, took more gumption than did most marches in the street. A born tinker, Barney loved to fiddle with machines and could fix anything. At one point, we owned six vacuums. He took the motor from an Electrolux and built a spin art machine. Behind the cinder block bookcase he installed a light organ, ten spots keyed into the stereo that converted Mahler into color on the ceiling. He also built a hideaway in the cupola that topped off our wing of the college. The cupola had eight sides, so he sawed off the corners of two mattresses and made an octagonal bed that flipped back on itself to allow entrance through a trap door below. Barney and I would later drive our boys from Charlottesville to Los Angeles, and, on a beautiful day in May, in 1991, I was married, a second time, on his Rappahannock County farm.

Dennis Evans was the soulmate, at least when we bonded over poetry. He opted for the Intensive English major and I took the standard one. A Mormon by birth, he had first met me on the long rides out to the chapel in North Haven when I flirted with the Latter-Day-Saints as way of reproducing my tiny religious community back in California while also breaking with it. Dennis had the credentials of a Big Man On Campus: an all-Oregon quarterback with the looks to match, a quick smile and an easy laugh, a Beatles collection, a cheerleader girlfriend back home. He married Cathy after his junior year and moved her to a drafty cottage by the shore. Weekday mornings, on her way to teaching school, Cathy dropped him at the York Street gate. I'd wake to find him in our rocking chair, dozing or reading, his bag lunch already eaten. Dennis was no longer paying for room and board, so I'd go downstairs for an early lunch and smuggle him out a hamburger or a piece of cake.

I met Libby Recknagel in January of 1969, when I returned from a road trip to Vassar to find her ironing a shirt by my roommate's bed. The roommate—he shared the suite of two bedrooms and a living room with Barney and myself—was a friend of her boyfriend. She had driven down to pay the boyfriend a surprise visit, but the next day's party given in his honor she spent dancing with me. Those who tried to cut in did not succeed; the boyfriend, holed up with my roommate, never tried.

A bond originating in a moment of competition persisted, in part, because I had to fight to keep her love. By early spring the boyfriend had been eliminated and she had consented to go to bed with me. I accompanied her on the trip to get her first prescription of birth control pills. We comforted each other with our mutual inexperience; she began to spend weekends in our room, a pattern that exiled Barney to the couch. We kept dancing; at the Yale Prom Wilson Pickett came on just before midnight and rallied the exhausted crowd with a show of energy that culminated in the spectacle of a woman in a full-leg cast frugging across the lip of the stage.

If I was possessive, she was receptive. Libby's ready smile accompanied a continual stream of exclamation. "Wowie-zowie" was a favorite locution. The enthusiasm attracted me because through it she expressed not only her feelings but mine. She also worked hard at her psychology courses and earned the grades that won her, in her last year at Mount Holyoke, a Phi Beta Kappa key.

The themes of my senior year at Yale, and especially of its bittersweet spring, were poetry and power. As an English major bent on graduate school, I polished off a senior project on Yeats while attending a seminar on his work taught by Harold Bloom. As a looming target of the draft, I watched the war news with apprehension and counted on the high number drawn for me in the draft lottery as protection against the attentions of my local board. "A golden age of poetry and power" was what Frost had forecast in the poem he wrote for Kennedy's inauguration in January 1961. Almost a decade later it had become well-nigh impossible to align the terms, to reconcile one's role as a student with one's duty as a citizen in the most powerful country in the world.

The story of my attempt to do so begins much further back than the space of this narrative will allow, so I might as well begin with the moment late in the fall of 1969 when, at Dennis's urging, I accompanied him to a seminar taught by the man who was and probably still is the most notorious genius ever to teach in the English department at Yale.

"The greatest poverty is not to live/In a physical world": those are the words I heard the professor read as I entered the room. I had never read the poem, or the poet, but they sounded like the lines for me. *Coup de foudre*, the French say. Blow to the heart. "The greatest poverty is not to live/In a physical world," the poem maintained, "to feel that one's desire/Is too difficult to tell from despair":

>            Perhaps,
> After death, the non-physical people in paradise,
> Itself non-physical, may, by chance, observe
> The green corn gleaming and experience
> The minor of what we feel.

It was the only moment in a career of sudden blows where the awareness of being affected was simultaneous with the moment it happened. Wallace Stevens and Harold Bloom are still inseparable in my mind, as I suppose they still are in Bloom's.

I had never seen a sadder face; the circles under his eyes were deep. Bloom's lower lip hung, or pouted, slightly out, as if drawing his features together were a vain effort. Eye-contact was fleeting; he was looking away. Bloom would enter class, put down his book, seat himself in his chair, and yank his sweater over his head. A plump, dishevelled body. Then he cupped both hands and pulled them slowly down over his face, as if trying to wake up, or repair a grief. The hair stirred up by all this stuck out in wisps around the heavy head. He rarely smiled, except as an irony; in our presence, he betrayed no lightness of being. His sense of rue could collapse into the lugubrious; a younger colleague reports standing next to Bloom at a urinal when the senior professor suddenly intoned: "You will wax and I will wane."

Dennis and I were quickly hooked on Stevens as well as Bloom. Stevens appealed to me because I was looking for a poetry of the earth and he seemed to promise it. "What spirit have I," he asked, "except it comes from the sun?" Life was coffee and oranges and the green freedom of a cockatoo on Sunday morning. Deer walk upon our mountains, and sweet berries ripen in the wilderness. Shall we not find in these comforts thoughts to be cherished like the thought of heaven?

Of course Stevens argued also for another vision of things, one we found attested to in the proofs of the book Bloom was reviewing and Dennis managed to borrow. Helen Vendler's *On Extended Wings* gave us Stevens as The Snow Man. Beneath his yes there was a no always being spoken. And, in reading the letters, the poet's life did look a little unlived. A bond lawyer and insurance company vice president. A house in the Hartford suburbs. One big vacation in his married life. A beautiful wife—she was the model for the Liberty Head dime—who in the photographs goes suddenly gray. Peter Brazeau interviewed a friend about Stevens and Elsie. "He treated her like ash," the friend said. Foucault would go on to claim that the author is the principle of thrift in the proliferation of meaning, and rule such evidence out of bounds. But Bloom not only believed in authors, he also believed in using whatever worked to enable a strong reading. His teaching method was to go through poems slowly, from the top down, three or four to a class hour. The margins of permissible commentary stopped nowhere. That spring, while unpacking Yeats's "The Second Coming," Bloom remarked that the poem had been written in 1919 by Yeats after his reading in the papers that the Czar and his family had been shot. Bloom told us that the poet was aggrieved at the act. So the "blood-dimmed tide" becomes the murderous Russian horde, slaughter in its eye, and the poem's revolutionary calling down of chaos becomes a dishevelment against which the reader is encouraged to react.

I had never sought out professors, outside of class; Bloom had befallen me, and I remained an auditor, unregistered and without a name, although from the day I entered the room I did not miss a single class. It was different with Leslie Brisman. In my last semester at Yale, the spring of 1970, I took his Milton course. He was the only teacher at Yale I actually got to know in a personal way, perhaps because he was lonely or because his first year was my last. Brisman was *applied* Bloom. He was thinner, younger, a little sad but less rueful, a Woody Allen compared to Bloom's Zero Mostel. Brisman loved quotations; his speech and writing were a tissue of them. They expressed his filial piety, the sense of the already-said. The critic and his disciple were seen often together, and a graduate student reported once greeting the two men on the street as the *eminence terrible* and the *enfant grise*.

In April Leslie invited Libby and me to dinner. The corner of the living room housed a clavichord he had built. The meal was also homemade, but in his cooking he did not quote. For each of us arrived a pineapple half, hollowed out and filled with itself and cubes of sweet and sour pork, this topped with a chicken breast baked in wine. He served it with a standing loaf of bread over which had been melted what looked like an entire pound of cheddar cheese. At one point, after I had seconded some comment of Libby's, his face spread into a huge grin and he said, "You must be very happy." As the weather warmed we'd drive out to Chatfield Hollow with him, cooling our bodies in the still, green pond. Then we'd repair to his generous picnics, one of which began with a dip composed of shrimp, peanut butter, and sour cream.

In the light of Brisman's attention I rapidly flowered, writing papers longer, more subtle, and assured. I was dazzled by Milton's counterplot, the argument of his similes. My applications for graduate school already in the mail, Leslie asked whether he could write a letter for me. I thought it too late, but he was willing to try. He wrote one letter, to Berkeley, and it was the only place that accepted me. Harvard and Yale turned me down; my grades had been solid but not exceptional. Leslie was also the go-between, the man who, after graduation, passed on my name to an inquiring Bloom.

Senior year brought the first class of women and the moratorium against the war, with Allard Lowenstein and 40,000 protestors on the Green. Some nights later we bent toward a radio in our room and heard the birth dates in the first draft lottery being read out; the initial 130 birthdays picked looked likely to be called up. Few of us went down to the TV Room to actually witness the spectacle. But the evening was one spent within shouting distance of one hundred Davenport seniors, and, as the first dates were read out, we learned to wait in silence for the screams echoing through the entryways. "They're bombing the courtyard," Barney muttered, as the second couch fell past our window. Small fires broke out; glass could be heard breaking; we huddled in our cell-like rooms and endured the mass sentencing.

It divided us, that evening; there was no forgetting the noises we had made. I pulled number 235, and was free to move on to graduate school. Barney didn't need to listen, although he had; he was headed for a mine sweeper in the Mekong Delta. A separated shoulder won him a discharge from the Navy in the spring, and a few months later he was working with Ralph Nader on auto safety in Washington, D.C.

Mayday came to Yale a month before the first of May. By the time the nation's universities boiled over in one last surge of rage at the Asian war we had nearly spent ourselves in another cause. Since 1968, I had worked against the war. A book called *Air War—Vietnam* by one Frank Harvey and read in my sophomore year convinced me that the war was less about heroism than the desire to take effect at a distance. I campaigned for [Eugene J.] McCarthy in California and walked the suburbs of New Haven for [Senator Abraham] Ribicoff, who had stood up to Mayor Daley in Chicago while his police cracked heads in the streets. The summer before my senior year I bought the blue *Handbook for Conscientious Objectors* and joined a study group taught by a Quaker under the Old Campus elms. I decided to apply for I-O status, which meant exemption from "both combatant and noncombatant training." The form consisted of four questions centered around my "religious training and belief." I began the application with these sentences:

> I object to warfare, and to my personal participation in it, because it involves a system of institutionalized killing in which one must surrender personal responsibility for his actions to the state. I also object to warfare because it destroys environment that sustains life and shatters my solidarity with all men.
>
> The first objection is a personal concern, the second a social one.

In proceeding to describe the connection between my childhood and my present beliefs, I fleshed out my case with quotations from Sartre, Camus, and Dostoevsky. On Sept. 15, 1969, Local Board No. 132 wrote back to say that "At the expiration of your present deferment, your complete file, including your SS Form 150, will be reviewed by the local board."

Soon thereafter the draft lottery rendered my application moot, and virtually no one I knew well then or later actually saw combat in Vietnam. No names from the Class of 1970 appear on Woolsey Hall's memorial to Yale's Vietnam dead. The two veterans with whom I did become acquainted had constructed for themselves a kind of ramshackle peace. After two years of withstanding continual fire on a PT boat in the Mekong, one had married and moved to Berkeley to write love songs. The other had become a Lutheran minister. He told stories about a German Shepherd trained to nose ahead in order to trip any mine wires strung across the trail. Back home, he had adopted the hobby of collecting airline booze. His living room was filled with thousands of tiny containers ranged neatly in glassed-in cabinets. I asked about drinking the contents. "You can't open them," he answered. "The bottles only have value if the seals stay intact."

But in April of that last college spring the war was not our first concern. A year earlier the body of a black man had been found in a nearby swamp. He had been a member of the New Haven branch of the Black Panther Party. Arrests had been made, informers located, and the charge of ordering the murder had been brought against the national chairman of the party, Bobby Seale. Seale had been arrested and extradited to New Haven; he was being held in a jail near the Green. By the spring of 1970 pre-trial motions had begun.

My morning's walk to class took me out of Davenport's front gate and left up York Street. It also meant running the gauntlet. The Panther Defense Committee had established a beachhead in front of the J. Press windows. Only a narrow strip of sidewalk remained between the rep ties and pink button-downs on one side and the oaths and waving papers on the other. Not a person I knew then thought or admitted to thinking that Seale was guilty, but the sense of a threat from some of his supporters also felt real. A rally had been proclaimed for the end of the month, and one voice spoke of "ending" the trial. Somewhere I saw a headline that read "Come to New Haven for a Burning on May Day."

The city had come to the citadel; built like a fortress with moats and battlements, the Yale I knew was not the Yale of that day, an embattled armed camp. I was a liberal; I had tutored an inner city black student named Mike. When he came to visit my room, we played chess, painted with watercolors, or listened to music. He was particularly fond of a song called "Your Love is Like a Seesaw." Racial justice was a cause I believed in and wanted to see embodied in specific, local acts. Yet I had never taken a course at Yale that had assigned a black author and, except for a day spent driving people to the polls, knew nothing about New Haven's black neighborhoods. I was a liberal, but did it matter what I called myself when there was talk of 50,000 hostile strangers streaming into town? When words like "burning" and "Yale" got coupled on the page, my gut response was defensive.

Conversation took on a doomsday tone. "Maybe we could stack couches in the front gate," someone ventured.

"What about the back—on Park Street?"

"They usually keep it locked. Besides, it would be a lot easier to attack from the front."

"There are women living in that entryway—what about them?"

Those I spoke to veered between gallantry and paranoia as the weather of the cruelest month wore on. Unlike the days before the moratorium against the war, which I had helped to organize, I found myself out of any planning loop. Kurt Schmoke, a leader in the Black Student Alliance, lived downstairs. While I carried on with my life, despite the rumors and tremors, it was pretty clear to me that people like Kurt were so embroiled in defending and confronting Yale that they had long since stopped going to class.

On April 13 a rally was held in Woolsey Hall. I did not attend, but the captain of the New Haven Black Panther Party was quoted as follows: "White folks are even going to have to kill pigs or defend themselves against black folks. We're going to turn Yale into a police state." A day later Black Panthers David Hilliard and Emory Douglas were sentenced by Judge Mulvey to six months in prison for contempt; while in court they had been passing or reading a note from Seale. French playwright Jean Genet, on hand for this episode of radical theater, later claimed to have scuffled with the police on behalf of his "black comrades."

A second meeting was held, in Harkness Hall. There was talk of getting guns, of cutting off New Haven's water supply. A moratorium somehow got proposed. The air was full of magnolias and dread.

In the days following, the undergraduate population worked its way round to a simple strategy: open the gates. The courtyards would become campgrounds. I found myself as much in favor of this response as I had been in favor of the opposite. The first weekend of May was then known as College Weekend and had been traditionally devoted to picnics, plays, and drinking contests. In Davenport we met and voted to abolish College Weekend. The money set aside for the festivities would be used to buy food for the out-of-towners. The fare would be cheap but hearty: granola, salads, and brown rice.

On Tuesday, April 21, Hilliard and Douglas apologized to the judge and were released. A rally was quickly arranged at Ingalls Rink. The headline in the *Yale Daily News* read: "Mass Meeting Called for Tonight: Student Strike Imminent." The rink had become the favored site for large gatherings; at the astonishing rally about the fate of ROTC, held a year before, more than 2000 undergraduates took part in a vote that, like the Harvard-Yale game of the previous fall, resulted in a *tie*.

Barney and I took the long walk up Prospect Street with the College Master and another faculty fellow and found seats in the crowded arena at the top of the bleachers.

Chaplain Coffin rose to speak against the violence; he had already urged that the charges against the Panthers be dropped. He spoke from a stage that rocked with tension: walking to the microphone, for the speakers that followed, was like walking the plank. There was a rustle in the crowd, and then Hilliard, surrounded by bodyguards, strode his way in. He took the mike and took back his apology to the judge. He began talking about someone charged with murdering a cop. The speech ended with the words "There ain't nothing wrong with taking the life of a motherfucking pig." I heard boos. The sound surprised me, but it did not come from me. It had come from the crowd of 4000, most of whom were white. I sat silent even as Hilliard, angered by the response, shot back his taunt—"I knew you motherfuckers were racist."

At the back of the stage something was happening. A man was trying to make his way to the mike. As the bodyguards began beating on him the crowd sickened and surged. Black students standing nearby stopped the beating and the man was let through. He mumbled words that could not be heard, stood for long pauses. Something was said about "A small step for mankind." The man tore up papers resting on the podium. At first I thought he had been dazed or hurt. Then it slowly became clear that he had nothing to say. We were living in a theater and he had wanted his 15 minutes of fame. He emptied his crazy mind until a professor managed to work him off the stage.

The rally broke up and we filed out sullenly. "What bullshit," the Master muttered as we walked back down the hill. I felt ashamed at having listened and yet still urged on by the cause. "All that you want to do," Hilliard had said near the end, "is to be entertained."

Two days later the Yale faculty met to discuss the "strike" that had finally been voted in by 11 of the 12 residential colleges. This was the meeting that generated one of Spiro Agnew's most carefully calculated putdowns: "I do not feel that students of Yale University can get a fair impression of their country under the tutelage of Kingman Brewster." At the meeting Brewster had made his now-famous statement that "I am skeptical of the ability of black revolutionaries to achieve a fair trial anywhere in the United States." Brewster angered some and galvanized many, but it was Kurt Schmoke who really moved the crowd. In a very short statement, he reminded the faculty that "You are older than we are, and more experienced. We want guidance from you, moral leadership. On behalf of my fellow students, I beg you to give it to us." The faculty responded by voting to "modify normal academic expectations." For an undergraduate this meant that for the remainder of the term he or she was free to decide when and whether to go to class.

I had kept going, although by late April the seminar on Yeats had winnowed down to Harold Bloom and me. We comforted each other, just by showing up, but the act could not have meant for him what it did for me.

"As I get older," he said one day, "I find that anger is a dominant emotion." Bloom had long since come to oppose the opposition to the war. In the fall of 1969, when I first began attending his seminar, Bloom was 39 and I was 21. He had spent the previous year at Cornell, and it had changed him. During that year a group of black students had taken over the Cornell student union. They had been unarmed, but, after some fraternity types broke in, they had found guns. The photograph of their leaving, rifles in hand, won that year's Pulitzer Prize. Bloom wrote a letter to the Cornell student newspaper about the incident. Whatever his politics had been before, when Bloom came back to Yale, they had been driven toward the right. We did not speak of such things, but they became clear as that fugitive spring wore on.

Word had it that after the faculty vote Bloom had called for the resignation of the dean. His commitment to poetry was so single-minded that he could not tolerate any act that directed attention away from it, even an act fully informed by that poetry. His was an inspired, a crazy devotion. But so was mine. I remember sitting alone with him in the classroom as he took the absent group through a poem by Yeats. I listened, managed to reply, there was a little give-and-take. We got through the time. Then the two of us went outside. He lingered for a moment, in front of Sheffield-Sterling-Strathcona Hall, as if there were something he wanted to say. He wanted to commiserate with me, I think, and tried to, while I held back from saying that if I came for him and the poetry it did not lessen my hatred for racism and the war. The line I walked was one that wavered. I thought then that the university was not the enemy, and that to strike against it, when it had nurtured the very possibility of resistance, made little sense. But I was stirred and buoyed up by the strike as well. In the words of an editorial I had written for the Davenport *Felon's Head,* about coeducation, I had "put my body where my beliefs were," but that meant straddling a good distance. There was more shaking of his head, and then Bloom walked away.

A rally on the Green had been planned for Mayday, and, after the faculty vote, the colleges got down to the work of preparing for the crowds to come. Davenport was to be converted into a child care center. The work went forward in an air of practical concern, while around us the greater world indulged in an orgy of projection. The *New York Times* represented Yale as a threat to the justice system of the United States. Reverend Coffin was so angered by an editorial entitled "Murdering Justice" that he called James Reston and said, "Frankly, you've got a horse's ass covering this thing up here." Hells Angels had arrived in New Haven and were camped in a nearby park. Rifles had been stolen from a truck in North Branford; a fire broke out in the Law School library. The governor announced that the Connecticut National Guard would spend the weekend of May 1st on the streets of New Haven.

On Wednesday, April 29th, I joined a group of seniors in the courtyard for a pick-up softball game. I hit a single the first time up; it felt like any other college spring. When we took the field, I played second base. A man got to first and was advanced toward second by the next batter. As the throw came to me, I swung my right arm around to make the tag and the runner came straight across it. I picked myself up, finished the inning, and then, my arm aching, left the game.

At the Yale infirmary an intern pronounced me perfectly whole. In bed that night my arm began to throb, so, the next day I walked to the Yale-New Haven hospital for an X-ray. The bone in the forearm was fractured, and I walked back to Davenport in a full arm cast.

It had been announced that President Nixon was to give a major address on the war that night. We gathered around the television in the Common Room, as we had when he had defeated Humphrey, 18 months before.

That was the night on which Nixon first used the phrase "pitiful helpless giant." He had been elected on the promise of a "secret plan" to end the war. Yet, once elected, he had begun declaring the war nearly over while still feeding it men. In mid-April of 1970 he had finally announced a withdrawal of 150,000 troops from Vietnam. That withdrawal now necessitated, he revealed in his television address, a further escalation of the conflict. The previous day he had ordered troops into the country that bordered Vietnam on the west. "This is not an invasion of Cambodia," he said. At the sound of those words, the room exploded. The rest of the speech was lost in a storm of abuse. It was just as well that we did not hear, as we boiled out onto the lawn, his closing claim that "Here in the United States, great universities are being systematically destroyed."

It was the speech that set fire to a hundred campuses and caught up our local fight into a bigger cause. With Nixon's words, the heat finally caught up with the light, and the explosion that had been happening all spring finally felt real. No one was shot or even badly hurt in the weekend's skirmishes on the Green; 37 people were arrested. Only one of these was a Yale student. As John Taft reports, in *Mayday at Yale,* the student "had been taken into custody for sitting in a car in which another passenger was brandishing a loaded water pistol." I sustained, I believe, the only broken bone. The hundreds of marshalls generated out of the student body and the black community kept the peace and washed the tear gas out of countless eyes. But in Ohio, and in Mississippi, the rifles were lowered and fired on students by young men who had joined a part of the army that was not supposed to have to fight. Thus an action "which started as an affair in support of the Black Panther defendants," Pierson Master John Hersey wrote in *Letter to the Alumni,* "ended up more or less a memorial to the white Kent State dead."

I missed all that; I had left town. On the morning of Mayday I was up early. Looking for a friend in the senior entryway, I stumbled on the college's makeshift nursery, seven babies in as many cardboard boxes, some crying, some sleeping, and none so puzzled as the attending sophomore about the strange winds of history that had blown them there. I maneuvered my cast outside, exited the courtyard gate, and walked straight into the National Guard. The young men stood along the far side of York Street in a tightly spaced row. They held their rifles at an angle across their chests; their khakis camouflaged them against the tan, pseudo-gothic stone. Behind me the courtyard teemed with frisbees and strangers, bedrolls dotting the intermittent grass. I stood on the curb and waited for my ride to come; Dennis and Cathy had arranged for me to spend the weekend with them at their house on the shore. The inconvenience of a broken arm had shaded my ambivalence into a posture of prudent retreat. As I watched for the blue Volkswagen, I felt that I did not want to leave and knew, as well, that I would not change my plans.

I was married the day after commencement and without the use of my right arm. My parents, two of my three sisters, and my grandmother had come east for the ceremonies. Libby had been embraced by the family at our Christmas visit. After deplaning at Los Angeles she had picked up her knitting while we waited for the family to arrive. "Oh, good," my mother said when she walked up, "she's not sophisticated." Mom insisted that an engagement ring be bought and went along to pick out and pay for the little diamond.

We held the wedding on the Mount Holyoke campus. My father scoured the woods around South Hadley and filled the chapel with hand-picked ivys and ferns. Dennis wrote and read a poem, Barney taped and played the music—Moussorgsky, Simon and Garfunkel, the Beatles—and my oldest friend, from San Bernardino, read something very short and then flew home for his own wedding in the shade of a California orange grove.

By two o'clock Libby had tired of the reception on the campus lawn and motioned to me that it was time to go. I took a gulp of punch and handed Dennis the empty silver cup. She was already moving fast, in the apricot dress that stopped above her knees. As I began to follow, the crowd came with us. When she broke into a run, I grabbed the elbow of my cast and pressed it hard against my chest. She reached the car and tried to start the engine until I crashed into the passenger side. "Get in!" she yelled, as I fumbled at the door. The rice fell around my head like angry hail. The engine wouldn't start; Barney had rigged the distributor. There was a lull, and then all the engines started at once. Another race began, up and down the hot, narrow, tree-lined country roads. Libby drove bent forward toward the wheel; I was along for the ride. The sweat stood out on her upper lip; her dress rode up around her hips. At the Springfield rotary she shook the last of those behind. We raced off into our wedding night, but not before a stop at the A & W for a cold root beer.

I saw Bloom one more time before leaving Yale. Libby and I had spent the summer in New Haven before moving west to graduate school. She worked at Sykes-Libby Jewelers and I gave campus tours. On our last day in town we were crossing the intersection of York and Chapel Streets, at an angle toward the Taft Hotel. My right arm was still encased in the cast. Crossing directly at us, along the same diagonal, was Harold Bloom. He stopped us in the intersection to say good-bye. A few words were exchanged; he reached out to shake my hand. Then he seemed to notice the cast. He faltered, and grabbed my left hand, the hand sinister. Suddenly I realized that I knew him, but that he did not know me. We had never been formally introduced; he had never read my written work. A sense of lovely anonymity descended on me, and I stood there still, as he moved on. In the middle of the street, in the shadow of the room where Wallace Stevens had 20 years before written "An Ordinary Evening In New Haven," I got the blessing and farewell from one of the fathers of my professional life, and he could not say my name.

# The Green Room

EDWIN A. ALDERMAN (1861–1931) was president of the University of Virginia from 1904 to 1931. He first suggested the *Virginia Quarterly Review* in 1915, and his essay on Edgar Allan Poe helped to launch the magazine in April 1925.

CARLOS BAKER (1909–1987) was one of America's leading literary biographers, including works on Hemingway and Emerson.

PAUL BAROLSKY (b. 1941) is Commonwealth Professor of Art at the University of Virginia and former chairman of the McIntire Department of Art. He is the author of *Walter Pater's Renaissance* (1987) and *Why Mona Lisa Smiles* (1991).

CLIFTON WALLER BARRETT (1901–1991) was a noted collector of books and manuscripts—more than 375,000 manuscripts and other items of 1,500 American writers that he collected are now in the Alderman Library at the University of Virginia.

STAIGE D. BLACKFORD (b. 1931) is the editor of the *Virginia Quarterly Review*. He showed his editorial courage early in his career when, as editor of the University of Virginia's student newspaper, he advocated integrated classes two years before the Supreme Court's landmark desegregation decision of 1954. This was followed by a Rhodes Scholarship to Queens College, Oxford. Mr. Blackford was employed by a diverse group of organizations, including the Central Intelligence Agency, the Norfolk *Virginian-Pilot,* Time Inc., and the Southern Regional Council, before returning to Charlottesville to assume the editorship of the *VQR.*

ALEXANDER BURNHAM (b. 1926), editor of this anthology, is a former staff writer of the *New York Times* and former managing editor of the New York publishing house of Dodd, Mead & Co.

MARCHETTE CHUTE, an authority on English literary history, was the author of *Shakespeare of London* (1949) and biographies of Ben Jonson and Geoffrey Chaucer.

KENNETH MACKENZIE CLARK (1903–1983) was director of the National Gallery in London from 1934 to 1945. A prolific author of such books as *Landscape into Art* (1949) (a study of Leonardo da Vinci) and *The Nude: A Study in Ideal Form* (1956), he received international recognition with his television series *Civilization,* which was also published in book form.

# THE GREEN ROOM

ARTHUR C. CLARKE (b. 1917) is a popular author of science fiction. His best known work is *2001: A Space Odyssey* (1968), which also was made into a successful motion picture.

CHRISTOPHER CLAUSEN (b. 1942) is a professor of English at Pennsylvania State University. He is the author of *The Place of Poetry* (1981), *The Moral Imagination* (1986), and *My Life with President Kennedy* (1994).

CLOVIS is the nom de plume of a distinguished scholar and author.

ROBERT P. TRISTRAM COFFIN (1892–1955), poet, novelist, and biographer, won the Pulitzer Prize for poetry in 1935.

ROBERT COLES (b. 1929), the author of sixty books, is an eminent child psychiatrist and a prominent professor throughout Harvard University's various schools. His love of literature was illustrated when he was asked to teach a course at the law school in 1981. Dr. Coles decided to combine literature and the law by examining the role of lawyers in the novels of Charles Dickens.

HENRY STEELE COMMAGER (1902–1998) was one of the twentieth century's most distinguished historians and teachers, author of such important books as *The American Mind* (1950) and co-author of *The Growth of the American Republic* (1940), a work which guided millions of American students into an understanding of their country's history.

VIRGINIUS DABNEY (1901–1995) was born at the University of Virginia, the son of a UVA history professor. After earning his master's degree, he soon entered the journalistic field and was appointed chief editorial writer of the *Richmond Times-Dispatch* in 1934. He won a Pulitzer Prize in 1948.

SCOTT DONALDSON (b. 1928), a former journalist and professor of English at the College of William and Mary, has written extensively on prominent American writers, including biographies of Hemingway, Fitzgerald, Cheever, and MacLeish. In 1996 he edited the *Cambridge Companion to Hemingway*, and his most recent book is *Hemingway vs. Fitzgerald*.

T. S. ELIOT (1888–1965), a major figure in English literature and a Nobel Prize winner, was the author of superior works of poetry and poetic drama, including *The Waste Land* (1922), *Murder in the Cathedral* (1935), and *The Cocktail Party* (1949). His essays were also remarkable, as exemplified by the essay in this book.

WENDY W. FAIREY (b. 1942) is a professor of English at Brooklyn College of the City University of New York, and she is the author of *One of the Family* (1992), a memoir.

ANDRÉ GIDE (1869–1951) was awarded the Nobel Prize in literature in 1947 for "his fearless love of truth and keen psychological insight."

ROBERT GRAVES (1895–1985) was one of England's outstanding poets, essayists, and novelists, but his most famous book is his autobiography, *Goodbye to All That* (1929), which among other things described the horrors he experienced in the trenches of World War I.

J. GLENN GRAY (1913–1977) was an authority on Georg Friedrich Hegel and edited selections of his work for American readers.

LOUIS J. HALLE (1910–1998) was an official at the State Department, a research professor of foreign affairs at the University of Virginia, and the author of fifteen books. In his last post he was a professor at the Graduate Institute of International Studies in Geneva.

WALTER HARDING (1917–1996) wrote and edited eighteen books about Henry David Thoreau and was secretary of the Thoreau Society.

BOOTON HERNDON (1915–1995) received five battle stars during his service with the U.S. Army in World War II. In civilian life he was a newspaper reporter and the author of numerous books and magazine articles.

ALDOUS HUXLEY (1894–1963) was one of England's most prolific writers during the 1920s and 1930s. He was the author of such notable novels as *Brave New World* (1932), *Point Counter Point* (1928), and *Antic Hay* (1923).

KONRAD KELLEN, a German-born writer who knew Einstein socially for three decades, was a biographer of Soviet Premier Nikita Khrushchev.

GEORGE F. KENNAN (b. 1904) served with great distinction with the U.S. Foreign Service from 1926 to 1953 and was the author of the famous U.S. policy of containment of the Soviet Union after World War II. He is a professor in the School of Historical Studies of the Institute for Advanced Study at Princeton University.

JOSEPH WOOD KRUTCH (1893–1970) taught English at Columbia University while writing numerous essays and books as a social and literary critic. He was also the drama critic for the *Nation* from 1924 to 1950.

D. H. LAWRENCE (1885–1930) struggled throughout his life for money and for acceptance of his work by authorities and by publications. The *VQR* from its inception welcomed Lawrence to its pages even as publishers in New York and London turned him down.

DUMAS MALONE (1892–1986) won the Pulitzer Prize in history in 1975 for his biography of Thomas Jefferson. He began his study in 1943 and completed the sixth and final volume in 1981. At his death he was a professor emeritus of History at the University of Virginia.

THOMAS MANN (1875–1955) won the Nobel Prize for literature in 1929 principally for his great novel *Buddenbrooks* (1901). He departed from Germany for the United States after the Nazis came to power, and he issued his *VQR* statement in 1941.

ANDRÉ MAUROIS (1885–1967) wrote a number of distinguished biographies, including works on Shelley, Proust, and George Sand.

FRANCES MAYES is the author of *Under the Tuscan Sun* (1996), a highly popular memoir, and five books of poetry, most recently *Ex Voto* (1995). Her latest book is entitled *Bella Tuscany: The Sweet Life in Italy* (1999).

MOLLY INGLE MICHIE (1932–1979) wrote her essay for anyone frightened by the prospect of dying, "particularly for those who will die without the comfort of a strong religious faith."

EDMUND S. MORGAN (b. 1916) is Sterling Professor of History Emeritus at Yale. He is an authority on colonial and revolutionary America.

SPENCE W. PERRY (b. 1942) served as assistant staff judge advocate for international law at Military Assistance Command, Vietnam, during the Vietnam War. His duties included prisoner-of-war exchanges.

SIMONE POIRIER-BURES (b. 1944) is a member of the English faculty at Virginia Polytechnic Institute. She is the author of *Candyman* (1994), a novel set in her native Nova Scotia, and *That Shining Place* (1995), a memoir of Crete.

ELEANOR ROOSEVELT (1884–1962), author, diplomat, and wife of President Franklin D. Roosevelt, was the indefatigable First Lady of the United States, champion of America's rank and file, and a leading exponent of the rights of ordinary people throughout the world.

LOUIS D. RUBIN JR. (b. 1923) is widely regarded as the dean of Southern literary criticism. A prolific author, he is Professor of English Emeritus at the University of North Carolina at Chapel Hill. In 1982 he founded Algonquin Books of Chapel Hill.

BERTRAND RUSSELL (1872–1970) wrote extensively on philosophy, logic, and other subjects, and he was awarded the Nobel Prize for literature in 1950. His major works include *The Principles of Mathematics* (1903) and *An Inquiry into Meaning and Truth* (1940).

JEAN-PAUL SARTRE (1905–1980), awarded the Nobel Prize for literature in 1964 (he declined), was a leading member of the French literary and political scene after World War II and a major exponent of existentialism.

JOHN H. SCHAAR is a professor at the University of California at Santa Cruz.

MARY LEE SETTLE (b. 1918), winner of the National Book Award for fiction in 1978, is the author of five novels and a memoir of World War II, all reissued by the University of South Carolina Press. Her latest work is *Addie: A Memoir* (1998).

EDGAR F. SHANNON JR. (1918–1997) was president of the University of Virginia from 1959 to 1974, and under his leadership the university began coeducation and racial integration. He was a Tennyson scholar, and during World War II he participated in ten battles while serving with the United States Navy.

PATRICIA MEYER SPACKS (b. 1929) is a scholar of eighteenth-century life and a professor at the University of Virginia. She was previously chair of the English Department at Yale.

NIKA STANDEN, a native of Italy, was a reporter in Europe and a researcher for *Fortune* magazine. After World War II she moved to Annapolis, Maryland, to assume the role of housewife.

MILDRED RAYNOLDS TRIVERS (b. 1912) is the wife of a retired American diplomat who served in Germany after World War II. She is the mother of seven children and the author of seven books of poetry.

GEORGE WATSON (b. 1927) is a fellow of St. John's College, Cambridge, and a former professor at New York University. He is the author of *Politics in Literature in Modern Britain* (1977).

EVELYN WAUGH (1903–1966) was in the forefront of English literature during the twentieth century for such exceptional novels as *Scoop* (1938), a brilliant satire on journalism; *Brideshead Revisited* (1945), which British television successfully dramatized; and *Sword of Honour* (1952–1962), his World War II trilogy.

THOMAS WOLFE (1900–1938), whose novels such as *Of Time and the River* (1935) and *Look Homeward, Angel* (1929) place him in the top rank of American writers, was a son of Asheville, North Carolina.

LOUIS B. WRIGHT (1899–1984), a Shakespearean scholar, was formerly director of the Folger Shakespeare Library in Washington, D.C.

DAVID WYATT (b. 1948) is a professor of English at the University of Maryland. He has also taught at the University of Virginia and at Princeton University. His most recent book is *Five Fires: Race, Catastrophe, and the Making of California* (1997).